Fodor's up CLOSE

GREAT BRITAIN

the complete guide, thoroughly up-to-date

SAVVY TRAVELING: WHERE TO SPEND, HOW TO SAVE

packed with details that will make your trip

CULTURAL TIPS: ESSENTIAL LOCAL DO'S AND TABOOS

must-see sights, on and off the beaten path

INSIDER SECRETS: WHAT'S HIP AND WHAT TO SKIP

the buzz on restaurants, the lowdown on lodgings

FIND YOUR WAY WITH CLEAR AND EASY-TO-USE MAPS

FODOR'S TRAVEL PUBLICATIONS
NEW YORK • TORONTO • LONDON • SYDNEY • AUCKLAND
www.fodors.com

Second Edition

ISBN 0–679–00379–7

ISSN 1098–6758

FODOR'S UPCLOSE GREAT BRITAIN

EDITORS: David Downing, Christina Knight

Editorial Contributors: Robert Andrews, Jacqueline Brown, Jules Brown, David Clee, Stephen Fraser, Lucy Hawking, Stewart Hennessey, Tim Perry, Sophie Mackenzie Smith, Roger Thomas

Editorial Production: Linda K. Schmidt

Maps: David Lindroth Inc., Eureka Cartography, *cartographers*; Robert Blake, *map editor*

Design: Fabrizio La Rocca, *creative director*; Allison Saltzman, *cover and text design*; Jolie Novak, *photo editor*

Production/Manufacturing: Mike Costa

Cover Art: Richard T. Nowitz

SPECIAL SALES

Fodor's upCLOSE Guides and all Fodor's Travel Publications are available at special discounts for bulk purchases for sales promotions or premiums. Special editions, including personalized covers, excerpts of existing guides, and corporate imprints, can be created in large quantities for special needs. For more information, contact your local bookseller or write to Special Markets, Fodor's Travel Publications, 201 East 50th Street, New York, NY 10022. Inquiries from Canada should be directed to your local Canadian bookseller or sent to Random House of Canada, Ltd., Marketing Department, 2775 Matheson Boulevard East, Mississauga, Ontario L4W 4P7. Inquiries from the United Kingdom should be sent to Fodor's Travel Publications, 20 Vauxhall Bridge Road, London SW1V 2SA, England.

CONTENTS

3. THE SOUTH 109

4. THE WEST COUNTRY 144

5. OXFORD AND THE HEART OF ENGLAND 174

6. EAST ANGLIA 198

7. CENTRAL ENGLAND 218

8. THE LAKE DISTRICT 256

9. YORKSHIRE 274

IO. NORTHUMBRIA 297

II. WALES 312

I2. SCOTLAND 344

INDEX 401

TRAVELING UPCLOSE

T ake a train through Wales. Stay in a bargain B&B (and get mothered with a full English breakfast). Shop for a picnic at the Queen's grocers. Prowl London's flea markets. Have lunch in Dickens's favorite pub. Go to a festival. Commune with Stonehenge. Memorize the symphony of Edinburgh's streets. In other words, if you want to experience the heart and soul of Great Britain, whatever you do, don't spend too much money.

A deep and rich experience of Great Britain is one of the things in life that money can't buy, and traveling lavishly is the surest way to turn yourself into a sideline traveler. Restaurants with white-glove service are great but they're usually not the best place to find the perfect ploughman's pie. Doormen at plush hotels have their place, but not when your lookalike room could be anywhere from Düsseldorf to Detroit. Better to stay in a more intimate place that truly gives you the atmosphere you traveled so far to experience. Don't just stand and watch—jump into the spirit of what's around you.

If you want to see Great Britain up close and savor the essences of the country and its people in all their charming glory, this book is for you. We'll show you the local culture, the offbeat sights, the bars and cafés where tourists rarely tread, and the B&Bs and other hostelries where you'll meet fellow travelers—places where the locals would send their friends. And because you'll probably want to see the famous places if you haven't already been there, we give you tips on losing the crowds, plus the quirky and obscure facts you want as well as the basics everyone needs.

OUR GANG

Who are we? We're artists and poets, slackers and straight arrows, and travel writers and journalists who in our less hedonistic moments report on local news and spin out an occasional opinion piece. What we share is a certain footloose spirit and a passion for England, Wales, and Scotland. We've revealed all of our favorite places and our deepest, darkest travel secrets, all so that you can learn from our past mistakes and experience the best part of Great Britain to the fullest.

Robert Andrews loves warm beer, hairy dogs, and soggy moors, but hates shopping malls, sheep poop, and the sort of weather when you're not sure if it's raining—all of which he found in abundance while covering the south and west of England for this book. British-born and based in Bristol, he drove, biked, and footslogged thousands of miles for the sake of authentic and up-to-date information, stopping only to refresh his spirits in dodgy pubs and blag his way into even dodgier clubs. He emerged a wiser, but wearier man, and has this word of advice to travelers in his native land: don't wear check trousers.

Jules Brown would rather be working on his house in the little North Yorkshire seaside town of Whitby, pottering down to the beach to look for fossils, or sizing up fish for dinner. But, oh no: You all want to go on vacation—and you want your guidebook to be accurate and informed—so, instead, he has to eat and drink in every county pub in the north of England, tramp the hills and valleys of the Lake District and Yorkshire Dales, and visit more castles and museums than you can shake a stick at. Give this exhausted Oxford University grad a break. Next time, go on holiday somewhere else.

David Clee is, it has to be admitted, a bit of a London nut. One of our three London updaters, he has spent almost the whole of his life living, working, and dreaming in London. A tub-thumping evangelist for the city, he writes about it as editor of independent e-zine LondonNet (www.londonnet.co.uk). Previously David was an editor for the London evening newspaper *Tonight*, and has also churned out some quite remarkable stuff for *The Times* and *The Independent*.

A native Scot, **Stephen Fraser** has worked on Scottish daily and Sunday newspapers for years and spends his days easing his battered car around the countryside in search of news and some decent fish-and-chips. His best experience when researching Scotland's northern climes for this book was a five-hour boat trip through the pastel pinks and somber reds of a Hebridean sunset on the way back from the island of Eigg. His worst? Upchucking copiously earlier that morning on the trip out to Eigg, as the boat pitched dizzyingly in the midst of a Force Five stormy gale.

Born and brought up in the university town of Cambridge, **Lucy Hawking** spent her formative years in and around East Anglia. Family holidays were taken on the Norfolk and Suffolk coasts, where she and her two brothers developed an admirable resistance to the cold waters of the North Sea. Now a trilingual Oxford graduate, Lucy Hawking lives in London and writes for several publications, including the *Times*, but given a chance would decamp to Norwich in a second.

Stewart Hennessey is a native Scot and former journalist whose work has appeared in *The Scotsman*, *Scotland on Sunday*, *The Observer*, *The Times*, *The Independent*, *GQ*, *Time Out* and sundry other much less dignified publications. With his English wife, Maisie, an ex-lawyer, he has just moved to a farmhouse—but it's got a pool—in southern France. They are both working on their first novels.

Since moving to London six years ago, music critic **Tim Perry** has become increasingly nocturnal as he covers the latest sounds and scenes for the *Independent* daily newspaper and other publications. He has also coauthored Fodor's *Rock & Roll Traveler: USA* and *Rock & Roll Traveler: Great Britain & Ireland*. A regular guide book and travel feature writer since the early 90s, he still manages to see the light of day in order to update the Exploring London section.

Oxford graduate and freelance writer **Sophie Mackenzie Smith** doesn't know how to turn on own her cooker because it's never occurred to her to eat at home. She may not know how to boil an egg, but she does knows how Dover Sole should be served, and not only which London restaurants are in, but which table numbers to ask for. She's also sternly ruled out any below par budget rooms, and has sussed out the best variety of affordable lodgings in London for you.

Roger Thomas, updater of the Wales chapter, spends most every minute tracking down the latest and the best of his native land. He has to: he's editor of *A View of Wales* magazine. In its pages, he has such noted contributors as Sir Anthony Hopkins and Sir Roy Strong uncover all the delights of "Britain's best-kept secret." A longtime writer and editor for Fodor's, he's known to make even a bus schedule sound positively Shakespearean. Roger has written many books on Wales.

A SEND-OFF

Always call ahead. We knock ourselves out to check all the facts, but everything changes all the time, in ways that none of us can ever fully anticipate. Whenever you're making a special trip to a special place, as opposed to merely wandering, always call ahead. Trust us on this.

And then, if something doesn't go quite right, as inevitably happens with even the best-laid plans, stay cool. Missed your train? Stuck in the airport? Use the time to study the people. Strike up a conversation with a stranger. Study the newsstands or flip through the local press. Take a walk. Find the silver lining in the clouds, whatever it is. And do send us a postcard to tell us what went wrong and what went right. You can E-mail us at: editors@fodors.com (specify the name of the book on the subject line) or write the Great Britain editor at Fodor's upCLOSE, 201 East 50th Street, New York, NY 10022. We'll put your ideas to good use and let other travelers benefit from your experiences. In the meantime, bon voyage!

INTRODUCTION

Nevermind whether or not you've been to Great Britain before—if you come from a land that the English once dabbled in, you'll recognize the wellspring of your country's cultural values. If there is a sense of tradition we share, vague and nostalgic or bitter and mocking, it was born in large part here. Romantic poetry, the King James Bible, Adam Smith's vision of capitalism, Charles Darwin's revolution, and that damned Puritan work ethic are all legacies of the Commonwealth, elements of the parent culture from which an empire sprang. Whether we come here with enthusiasm or misgivings, many of us come to Britain seeking our history.

There is a palpable sense of the past all over Britain. Stone circles off the main roads hint at prehistoric civilizations and ways of life we can only guess about. Westminster Abbey's worn stone floors have seen just about every kind of human footwear, from noble slippers to Doc Martens. Some pubs even have signs over their doors saying REBUILT 1618 and FOUNDED AD 1400. Yet if these places inspire an eerie sense of déjà vu, it's because we've seen them before, courtesy of William Shakespeare, Charles Dickens, Charlotte Brontë, Dylan Thomas, Robert Burns, James Joyce, Oscar Wilde, and a great host of others. Their stories and fairy tales have been handed down to us since we were tots, and here they are—or at least, here are their remains.

One of the benefits of the 20th century is that official histories of warring kings and clans, of manners and the manor-born, are no longer taken at face value. A new history is being told, the story of those who did not win: working-class Welsh, Irish bricklayers, and ex-colonials. Alongside museum displays of royal pomp and pageantry, there are now exhibits about coal miners and crofters. Even more telling, there's a vibrant culture thriving outside Britain's traditional centers. For years now, London's club scene has shared the spotlight with its counterparts in sooty industrial cities like Manchester and Glasgow, cities where the politics are unabashedly liberal, and the "wrong" accents are the ones that smack of southern snobbery. And despite the uncertain welcome extended to immigrants from India, Pakistan, the Caribbean, and Hong Kong, these groups have also done much to infuse new life into the country, pushing the stodgier elements of Britain into the periphery, like it or not.

Right now the future of Great Britain is being significantly altered by the devolution of Scotland and Wales. Their first steps towards independence are the creation of a Parliament of Scotland in Edinburgh and a Welsh National Assembly in Cardiff. This doesn't make Scotland and Wales independent countries, because although both will legislate their own commerce, law, and education systems, they do not have the power to raise taxes and remain subjects of the Queen of England. Given these developments, the average Englishman is somewhat peeved that the Westminster Government is still top-heavy with Scottish and Welsh members of Parliament. More feathers have been ruffled by the pending abolishment of the government's upper chamber, the House of Lords (Senate), although no details of a replacement have been announced. Likewise the decision over joining the European currency, the Euro, is being delayed. The whole island kingdom seems to be adrift in uncertainty.

But don't expect the keepers of Britain's cultural flame to roll over and play dead. When you come right down to it, the Brits are stubbornly passionate about their homeland and convinced of their innate superiority to the rest of the world. You only have to see the Brits abroad to realize that, despite their long experience of Empire (or perhaps because of it), they feel the British way is the right way. Even on holidays, they mope if they can't get beef burgers, chips, and a pint of bitter, and they get in a terrible snit if the locals don't speak English. Buy them a pint, in fact, and they'll tell you why your country's got it all wrong and how the Brits could do it a damn sight better.

Yet if you make the mistake of coming up with generalizations about how bland, uptight, and closed-minded the British are, you deserve to have a bland, uptight, closed-minded experience. Britain is as much about soot-faced coal miners as it is about Beefeaters—as much about burly sheep farmers as it is about the rasta man hawking Bob Marley and Eddie Grant bootlegs in a London street market.

Don't skip the classic sights: A peek at the spoils of empire housed within London's British Museum reveals more about imperialism than a stack of history books ever could. By the same token, a stroll around the grounds of Buckingham Palace or Edinburgh Castle gives a better sense of royal wealth, power, and influence than a thousand stories in the *Sun*. On the other hand, don't get sucked into the tour-package version of Britain—a Disneyesque montage of busbied sentries and kilted bagpipers. Don't be afraid to grab the latest copy of *New Music Express* and a Thermos full of strong Earl Grey, and plant yourself on Trafalgar Square in the wee hours of a Sunday morning. Or go and see what inspired Wordsworth in the Lake District, gawk at the grandeur of the West Country coast, head for the remote Scottish islands, attend a traditional music session in Galway, and eat Balti Indian food for the first time in Birmingham. The possibilities are truly endless, as peculiar and varied as the towns cluttering the map.

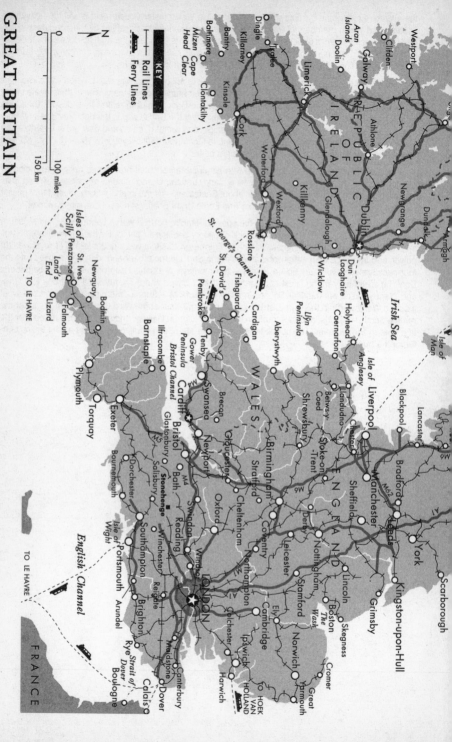

GREAT BRITAIN

GREAT BRITAIN

ATLANTIC OCEAN

OUTER HEBRIDES

INNER HEBRIDES

NORTHERN IRELAND

SCOTLAND

North Sea

Sligo
Donegal
Letterkenny
Omagh
Derry
Armagh
Portadown
M1
Belfast
Bangor
Portrush
Ballycastle
Giant's Causeway
Larne
Stranraer
Campbeltown
Isle of

Tiree
Coll
Iona
Islay
Jura
Tarbert
Inveraray
Oban
Arran
Ayr
Kilmarnock
Glasgow
Loch Lomond
Stirling
Callander
M8
Lanark
M90
Dumfries
Kirkcudbright
Keswick
Carlisle
Kendal
Windermere
M6
Peebles
Edinburgh
Jedburgh
Durham
Berwick-upon-Tweed
Newcastle-upon-Tyne
A696
Whitby
Scarborough

South Uist
North Uist
Barra
Harris
Lewis
Stornoway
Uig
Portree
Isle of Skye
Ullapool
Mallaig
Kyle of Lochalsh
Loch Ness
Fort William
Inverness
Aviemore
Braemar
Dornoch
Lairg
Thurso
John O'Groats
Wick
Banff
Fraserburgh
Peterhead
Aberdeen
Montrose
Dundee
Perth
St. Andrews
Firth of Tay
Firth of Forth

ORKNEY ISLANDS
TO SHETLAND ISLANDS

SHETLAND ISLANDS
Unst
Yell
Mainland
Lerwick

ORKNEY ISLANDS
Mainland
Hoy
Kirkwall

XI

BASICS

contacts and savvy tips to make your trip hassle-free

I f you've ever globe-trotted before, you know there are two types of travelers: the planners and the nonplanners. Travel can bring out the worst in both groups. Left to their own devices, the planners will have you goose-stepping from attraction to attraction on a cultural blitzkrieg, while the nonplanners will invariably miss the flight, the bus, and maybe even the point. This chapter—organized alphabetically by topic—offers you a middle ground; we hope it provides enough information to help you plan your trip to Great Britain without nailing you down. The first step in your vacation will, undoubtedly, be a visit or telephone call to the British Tourist Authority: You'll find the main branches listed below under **Visitor Information.** Your actual trip will begin once you step off your plane in London and wonder how to get from the airport to the city center. Don't panic: You'll find all the info in **Coming and Going** in the Basics section at the beginning of Chapter 2. When you purchase a bus or train ticket, note that "single" means one-way, and "return trip" is round-trip. Just remember: Be flexible and keep in mind that the most hair-pulling situations turn into the best travel stories back home!

AIR TRAVEL

For complete information on traveling to the main Great Britain airport hubs, *see* Coming and Going in the Basics sections of the following chapters: Chapter 2 for London's Heathrow and Gatwick, Chapter 7 for Manchester, Chapter 12 for Glasgow.

BOOKING YOUR FLIGHT

When you book **look for nonstop flights** and **remember that "direct" flights stop at least once.** Try to avoid connecting flights, which require a change of plane.

CARRIERS

MAJOR AIRLINES • Here is the basic list of leading international carriers that service Great Britain. **American Airlines** (tel. 800/433–7300, tel. 020/8572–5555 in London) to Heathrow, Gatwick. **British Airways** (tel. 800/247–9297, tel. 0345/222111 in London) to Heathrow, Gatwick. **Continental** (tel. 800/231–0856, tel. 0800/776–464 in London) to Gatwick. **Delta** (tel. 800/241–4141, tel. 0800/414–767 in London) to Heathrow, Gatwick. **Northwest Airlines** (tel. 800/447–4747, tel. 0990/561–000 in London) to Gatwick. **TWA** (tel. 800/892–4141, tel. 020/8814–0707 or 0345/333–333 in London) to Gatwick. **United** (tel. 800/241–6522, tel. 0845/844–4777 in London) to Heathrow. **Virgin Atlantic** (tel. 800/862–8621, tel. 01293/747747 in London) to Heathrow, Gatwick.

SMALLER AIRLINES • British Airways operates shuttle services between London Heathrow and Edinburgh, Glasgow, Belfast, and Manchester. Passengers can simply turn up and get a flight (usually hourly) without booking. There are also shuttle services from Gatwick. **British Midland** (tel.020/8745–7321) operates from Heathrow to Belfast, Dublin, Glasgow, Leeds Manchester, and Teesside. **Manx Airlines** (tel. 0345/256256) flies to the Isle of Man from Heathrow and London Luton.

CHECK-IN & BOARDING

Assuming that not everyone with a ticket will show up, airlines routinely overbook planes. When that happens, airlines ask for volunteers to give up their seats. In return these volunteers usually get a certificate for a free flight and are rebooked on the next flight out. If there are not enough volunteers, the airline must choose who will be denied boarding. The first to get bumped are passengers who checked in late and those flying on discounted tickets, so **get to the gate and check in as early as possible,** especially during peak periods.

Always **bring a government-issued photo I.D. to the airport.** You may be asked to show it before you are allowed to check in.

CUTTING COSTS

The least-expensive airfares to Great Britain must usually be purchased in advance and are nonrefundable. It's smart to **call a number of airlines, and when you are quoted a good price, book it on the spot**—the same fare may not be available the next day. Always **check different routings** and look into using different airports. Travel agents, especially low-fare specialists (*see* Discounts & Deals, *below*), are helpful.

Consolidators are another good source. They buy tickets for scheduled international flights at reduced rates from the airlines, then sell them at prices that beat the best fare available directly from the airlines, usually without restrictions. Sometimes you can even get your money back if you need to return the ticket. Carefully read the fine print detailing penalties for changes and cancellations, and **confirm your consolidator reservation with the airline.**

When you **fly as a courier** you trade your checked-luggage space for a ticket deeply subsidized by a courier service. There are restrictions on when you can book and how long you can stay.

CONSOLIDATORS • Cheap Tickets (tel. 800/377–1000). **Up & Away Travel** (tel. 212/889–2345). **Discount Airline Ticket Service** (tel. 800/576–1600). **Unitravel** (tel. 800/325–2222). **World Travel Network** (tel. 800/409–6753).

GO AS A COURIER

Courier flights are simple: You sign a contract with a courier service to baby-sit their packages (often without ever laying eyes on them, let alone hands), and the courier company pays half or more of your airfare. You then either pick up your ticket and package from the company using your service, or someone will meet you at the airport to hand you a ticket and customs form. After you land, you simply clear customs with the courier luggage, and deliver it to a waiting agent.

It's cheap and easy, but there are restrictions: Flights are usually booked only a week or two in advance—often only a few days in advance—and you are allowed carry-on luggage only, because the courier uses your checked luggage allowance to transport the shipment. You must return within one to four weeks, and times and destinations are limited. If you plan to travel with a companion, you'll probably have to travel a day apart. And you may be asked to pay a deposit, to be refunded after you have completed your assignment.

COURIER CONTACTS • Now Voyager (tel. 212/431–1616, fax 212/334–5243).

ENJOYING THE FLIGHT

For more legroom **request an emergency-aisle seat.** Don't sit in the row in front of the emergency aisle or in front of a bulkhead, where seats may not recline. If you have dietary concerns, **ask for special meals when booking.** These can be vegetarian, low-cholesterol, or kosher, for example. On long flights, try to maintain a normal routine, to help fight jet lag. At night **get some sleep.** By day **eat light meals, drink water** (not alcohol), and **move around the cabin** to stretch your legs.

FLYING TIMES

Flying time to London is 6½ hours from New York, 7½ hours from Chicago, and 10 hours from Los Angeles.

HOW TO COMPLAIN

If your baggage goes astray or your flight goes awry, complain right away. Most carriers require that you **file a claim immediately.**

AIRLINE COMPLAINTS • U.S. Department of Transportation **Aviation Consumer Protection Division** (C-75, Room 4107, Washington, DC 20590, tel. 202/366–2220). **Federal Aviation Administration Consumer Hotline** (tel. 800/322–7873).

AIRPORTS

The main airports in Great Britain are Heathrow and Gatwick. The leading gateway to northern England is Manchester. Scotland's main airport is in Glasgow.

AIRPORT INFORMATION • **Heathrow** (tel. 020/8759–4321). **Gatwick** (tel. 01293/535–353). **Manchester** (tel. 0161/489–3000). **Glasgow** (tel. 0141/887–1111).

DUTY-FREE SHOPPING

In 1999 the European Union countries put an end to duty-free shopping for those traveling from one EU country to another by boat, plane, or via the Channel Tunnel. Duty-free sales for travel outside the EU will be business as usual.

BIKE TRAVEL

Bikes are banned from motorways and most dual carriageways or main trunk roads, but you can be king of the shoulder on side roads and country lanes. The Ordnance Survey 1:50,000 maps are invaluable. Some parts of Britain have bicycle routes in towns and through parts of the countryside; for example, in the Peak District National Parks, bikes can be hired by the day for use on special traffic-free trails. Cyclists can legally use public bridleways—green, unsurfaced tracks reserved for horses, walkers, and cyclists. Build up your endurance for longer rides (this is no ride to the market), and outfit and equip yourself appropriately. This includes having the proper bike tools, a good repair book (try Tom Cuthbertson's *Anybody's Bike Book,* Ten Speed Press, $9.95), and a rear rack and some panniers (saddlebags). Also, British law requires that all bikes that are ridden at night have a full set of reflectors on the wheels and pedals, and lights at the back and front. You can rent bikes in most touristed towns for an hour (£3–£5), half day (£5–£10), or full day (£7–£20). In general, a deposit of £25–£50 will be required. Tourist offices throughout Great Britain have lists of local bike-rental shops.

BIKES IN FLIGHT

Most airlines accommodate bikes as luggage, provided they are dismantled and boxed. For bike boxes, often free at bike shops, you'll pay about $5 (at least $100 for bike bags) from airlines. International travelers can sometimes substitute a bike for a piece of checked luggage at no charge; otherwise, the cost is about $100. Domestic and Canadian airlines charge $25–$50.

BOAT & FERRY TRAVEL

The shortest and most frequent crossing to France is the 90-minute (45 minutes on a high speed catamaran) trip from **Dover** to Calais. The companies Hoverspeed, P&O Stena Line, and SeaFrance serve this route. Sea Cats also operate from **Folkestone** to Boulogne and sometimes to Calais. The standard return ferry fare is around £50 (£25 if you stay less than five days), but out of season it can be as low as £5–£15 and in the high season twice above the standard rate. With the channel tunnel opening, there have been fierce price wars to the travelers' benefit, so watch out for special offers. Otherwise you can reach Cherbourg from either **Portsmouth** or **Southampton** on P&O; Le Havre from **Portsmouth**; and Dieppe from **Newhaven.** In general there are about three to four sailings per day (less in winter), and the trip takes about four–six hours. From the East Anglia town of **Harwich** and the northern English town of **Newcastle,** ferries leave for Northern European destinations such as Hoek van Holland (The Netherlands), Hamburg (Germany), Esbjerg (Denmark), Göteborg (Sweden), and Bergen (Norway). On average, ferries leave two to three times per week, except for the Hoek van Holland route, which leaves Harwich about twice per day.

BOAT & FERRY INFORMATION • **Fjord Line** (tel. 0191/296–1313). **Hoverspeed** (tel. 0870/524–0241). **P&O** (tel. 0870/242–4999). **P&O Stena Line** (tel. 0870/600–0600). **Scandinavian Seaways** (tel. 01255/240240). **SeaFrance** (tel. 0870/571–1711). **Stena Line** (tel.0870/570–7070) has routes to Ireland and Holland. *Also see* the Coming and Going sections in the appropriate chapters.

BUS TRAVEL

Buses can take twice as long as trains, but tickets are often half the price, particularly on long-distance journeys. Although many regional, long-distance bus companies exist (we cover them in the appropriate chapters), the one with the most comprehensive coverage of towns and cities in England, Wales, and Scotland is **National Express.** Buses are like the Greyhound variety in the United States, and most have toilets and washroom facilities. The Rapide and Flightlink services even have stewardess service. If you plan to travel by bus during a busy travel time (summer) or in a direction many people are headed (to London), it's always best to reserve a seat in advance. There are 3,000 National Express agents across the country. In London, Victoria Coach Station is the central departure point for National Express.

For the most economical bus travel, consider **Stray Travel** (formerly the Slow Coach), a backpackers' bus that offers four passes. Three coaches a week run a clockwise all-Britain circuit from London. Stops include Windsor, Stonehenge, Bath, Crickhowell, Snodownia National Park, Llangollen (in North Wales), the Lake District, Edinburgh,York, Stratford-upon-Avon, and Oxford. Coaches stop at YHA and SYHA hostels in the above destinations, and you can board and get off any time you like. Best of all, their £129 All-Britain tickets are valid for four months and are completely transferable—any unused portion of your ticket can be given or sold to other travelers through the central office. Buy tickets from YHA and SYHA hostels en route, or in person from the **Youth Hostel** (38 Bolton Gardens, London SW5).

DISCOUNT PASSES

If you plan to travel frequently by bus in Britain, consider buying a bus pass or discount coach card. The **Tourist Trail Flexi-Pass** allows unlimited travel on National Express buses in England, Scotland, and Wales for specified periods of time. It will save you money if you're planning to travel mostly by bus. The Tourist Trail Flexi-Pass is *not* sold in Great Britain. It can only be purchased in the United States from **British Travel International.** Those ages 5–25 and over 50 are eligible for the discount fare; everyone else must pay the top rate. Passes are valid for three days out of five ($84, $63 discount); five ($146, $111 discount), eight ($211, $158 discount), and 15 ($306, $232 discount) days out of 30; and 15 days out of 60 ($317, $239 discount). Within Great Britain, National Express sells passes for *consecutive* days of travel, which is only useful if you plan on traveling between destinations every day. Passes are valid for five days of travel (£65, £50 discount), seven days (£95; £75 discount), 14 days (£135, £105 discount), and for 30 days (£185, £145 discount). These prices are slated to go up in 2000.

The **Young Persons Coach Card** from National Express is available to those 16–25 years old, costs £8, is valid for one year, and provides up to 30% discount on all fares (excluding the Tourist Trail Pass). Pretty much the same is the **Discount Coach Card.** It also costs £8 per year and offers a 20–30% discount on most standard fares to students and those under 25 or over 50 years old.

BUS AND PASS INFORMATION • **British Travel International** (Box 299, Elkton, VA 22827, tel. 540/298–1395). **National Express** (Eurolines/National Express Travel Shop, 52 Grosvenor Gardens, London SW1W 0AU, tel. 0990/808–080 or 0870/580–8080; to find the nearest agent, call tel. 0870/ 501–0104). **Scottish Citylink** (tel. 0870/550–5050). **Stray Travel** (171 Earls Court Rd., London SW5 9RF, tel. 020/7373–7737, www.straytravel.com). **Victoria Coach Station** (Buckingham Palace Rd., London, tel. 020/7730–3466 for automated switchboard).

BUSINESS HOURS

Standard business hours are Monday–Saturday 9–5:30.

BANKS & OFFICES

Most banks are open weekdays 9:30–3:30; some have extended hours on Thursday evening, and a few are open on Saturday morning.

SHOPS

Until recently, it was (thanks to the church) a no-no for stores to remain open on Sunday, but plenty of businesses now do. Outside big cities, most shops observe an early closing day once a week, often Wednesday or Thursday. In small villages, many also close for lunch. Pubs are usually open Monday–Saturday 11–11, and Sunday noon–10:30, though some may close Sunday between 3 and 7 PM.

CAMERAS & PHOTOGRAPHY

PHOTO HELP • **Kodak Information Center** (tel. 800/242–2424). *Kodak Guide to Shooting Great Travel Pictures,* available in bookstores or from Fodor's Travel Publications (tel. 800/533–6478; $18.00 plus $4 shipping).

EQUIPMENT PRECAUTIONS

If you do get a bright day, keep your film and tape out of the sun. Carry an extra supply of batteries, and **be prepared to turn on your camera or camcorder** to prove to security personnel that the device is real. Always **ask for hand inspection of film,** which becomes clouded after successive exposures to airport X-ray machines, and **keep videotapes away from metal detectors.**

VIDEOS

Most videos sold in the U.K. do not interface with American video players. Videos geared toward tourists often have versions made for the American market.

CAR RENTAL

You'll get the best deal by arranging your car rental in the U.S. before you depart, or by booking a fly-drive package. It's far more expensive to book after you've arrived in London, where rates are extremely high, and begin, on average, at $87 a day and $322 a week for a biscuit tin of a car (a Renault Clio or Fiat Corsa) with manual transmission and unlimited mileage. A slightly larger car (Vauxhall Astra) comes out at $99 per day, and $363 per week. Both of these types would generally have manual gears and no air-conditioning. For that, and automatic gears, you need to move up to the saloon (luxury) range, at $189 per day and $676 per week. Rates vary between companies, and can skyrocket during tourist season. There is also a vehicle license fee of £1.12 per day. The VAT tax (Value Added Tax) on car rentals is 17.5%.

MAJOR AGENCIES • **Alamo** (tel. 800/522–9696; 020/8759–6200 in the U.K.). **Avis** (tel. 800/331–1084; 800/879–2847 in Canada; 01344/70–70–70 in the U.K.; 02/9353–9000 in Australia; 09/525–1982 in New Zealand). **Budget** (tel. 800/527–0700; 0144/227–6266 in the U.K.). **Dollar** (tel. 800/800–6000; 020/8897–0811 in the U.K., where it is known as Eurodollar; 02/9223–1444 in Australia). **Hertz** (tel. 800/654–3001; 800/263–0600 in Canada; 0990/90–60–90 in the U.K.; 02/9669–2444 in Australia; 03/358–6777 in New Zealand). **National InterRent** (tel. 800/227–3876; 0345/222525 in the U.K., where it is known as Europcar InterRent).

CUTTING COSTS

To get the best deal **book through a travel agent who will shop around.** Also **price local car-rental companies,** although the service and maintenance may not be as good as those of a major player. Remember to ask about required deposits, cancellation penalties, and drop-off charges if you're planning to pick up the car in one city and leave it in another. If you're traveling during a holiday period, also make sure that a confirmed reservation guarantees you a car.

Do **look into wholesalers,** companies that don't own fleets but rent in bulk from those that do and often offer better rates than traditional car-rental operations. Payment must be made before you leave home.

WHOLESALERS • **Auto Europe** (tel. 207/842–2000 or 800/223–5555, fax 800/235–6321). **Europe by Car** (tel. 212/581–3040 or 800/223–1516, fax 212/246–1458). **DER Travel Services** (9501 W. Devon Ave., Rosemont, IL 60018, tel. 888/337–7350, fax 800/282–7474 for information; 800/860–9944 for brochures). **Kemwel Holiday Autos** (tel. 914/825–3000 or 800/678–0678, fax 914/381–8847).

INSURANCE

When driving a rented car you are generally responsible for any damage to or loss of the vehicle. Before you rent see what coverage your personal auto-insurance policy and credit cards already provide.

Collision policies that car-rental companies sell for European rentals usually do not include stolen-vehicle coverage. Before you buy it, check your existing policies—you may already be covered.

REQUIREMENTS & RESTRICTIONS

In Great Britain your own driver's license is acceptable, and there is no limit on the age of the driver. Getting an **International Driver's Permit (IDP)** before you leave home is a good idea though. To qualify for an IDP you must be 18 years old and hold a valid U.S. driver's license. The IDP is available from the

American Automobile Association (AAA). Some offices can issue an IDP in about 15 minutes, but be sure to call ahead; during the busy season IDPs can take a week or more.

SURCHARGES

Before you pick up a car in one city and leave it in another **ask about drop-off charges or one-way service fees,** which can be substantial. Note, too, that some rental agencies charge extra if you return the car before the time specified in your contract. To avoid a hefty refueling fee **fill the tank just before you turn in the car,** but be aware that gas stations near the rental outlet may overcharge.

AUTO CLUBS

IN AUSTRALIA • Australian Automobile Association (tel. 02/6247–7311).

IN CANADA • Canadian Automobile Association (CAA, tel. 613/247–0117).

IN NEW ZEALAND • New Zealand Automobile Association (tel. 09/377–4660).

IN THE U.K. • Automobile Association (AA, tel. 0990/500–600). **Royal Automobile Club** (RAC, tel. 0990/722–722 for membership; 0345/121–345 for insurance).

IN THE U.S. • American Automobile Association (tel. 800/564–6222).

EMERGENCIES

For aid if your car breaks down, contact the 24-hour rescue numbers of either the **Automobile Association** (tel. 0800/887766) or the **Royal Automobile Club** (tel. 0800/828282).

GASOLINE

Gasoline is commonly called "petrol" in the U.K. and is sold by the liter, with 4.2 liters to a gallon. Stations can be hard to find in rural areas, and most throughout the nation close on Sunday.

ROAD CONDITIONS

There's a very good network of superhighways (motorways) and divided highways (dual carriageways) throughout most of Britain, though in remoter parts, especially Wales and Scotland, where unclassified roads join village to village and are little more than glorified agricultural cart tracks, travel is noticeably slower. Motorways (with the prefix *M*), shown in blue on most maps and road signs, are mainly two or three lanes in each direction, without any right-hand turns. Other fast major roads are shown with the prefix *A*, shown on maps as green and red. Sections of fast dual carriageway have black-edged, thick outlines, have both traffic lights and traffic circles, and right turns are sometimes permitted. Turnoffs are often marked by highway numbers, rather than place names, so it's a good idea to always take note of connecting road numbers.

The vast network of lesser roads, for the most part old coach and turnpike roads, might make your trip take twice the time and show you twice as much. Minor roads drawn in yellow or white, the former prefixed by *B*, the latter unlettered and unnumbered, are the ancient lanes and byways, a superb way of discovering the real Britain. Some of these (the white roads, in the main) are potholed switchbacks, littered with blind corners and cowpats, and barely wide enough for one car, let alone for two to pass. Be prepared to reverse into a passing place if you meet an oncoming car or truck.

Service stations on motorways are located at regular intervals and are usually open 24 hours a day; elsewhere they usually close overnight, and by 6 PM and all day Sunday in remote country areas.

ROAD MAPS

Good planning maps are available from the **AA** and the **RAC** (*see above*).

RULES OF THE ROAD

Drive on the left! This takes a bit of getting used to, and it's much easier if you're driving a British car where the steering and mirrors are designed for U.K. conditions. You have to wear a seat belt in the front seat, and in the back, where seat belts exist. Traffic police can be hard on speeders, especially in urban areas. In those areas, the limit (shown on circular red signs) is generally 30 mph, but 40 mph on some main roads. In rural areas the limit is 60 mph on ordinary roads and 70 mph on motorways, circulation is clockwise, and entering motorists must yield to cars coming from their right.

THE CHANNEL TUNNEL

Short of flying, the "Chunnel" is the fastest way to cross the English Channel: 35 minutes from Folkestone to Calais, 60 minutes from motorway to motorway, or 3 hours from London's Waterloo International

Station to Paris's Gare du Nord. You can't drive through it, but you can put your car on the train known as **Le Shuttle.** (However, if you're taking a rental vehicle, remember about the drop-off charges.) Most visitors take the passenger trains operated by **Eurostar,** which allows them to depart its snazzy new terminal in London's Waterloo International Station and wind up in Paris's Gare du Nord or in Brussels. The Eurostar trip to Paris takes about three hours. Though standard seats run about £150 return (£99 for those with a EurailPass), you can get a ticket for as low as £69 as long as you meet certain restrictions. If you're a student or under 26, you can purchase a return ticket for £79 return (£59 for midweek travel), provided you don't change your dates of travel after the first day of travel is completed. Cars must begin their journey on Le Shuttle at Folkestone (near Dover) for the 35-minute journey to Calais. Le Shuttle trains depart daily every half hour during peak season, and tickets, including cars and all passengers, cost between £79 and £133 single, depending on time of travel. However, prices fluctuate depending on time of day, week, and year, so be sure to check prices before you make your plans.

CAR TRANSPORT • **Le Shuttle** (tel.0870/535–3535 in the U.K.).

PASSENGER SERVICE • In the U.K.: **Eurostar** (tel. 0870/518–6186), **InterCity Europe** (Victoria Station, London, tel. 0990/848–848 for credit-card bookings). In the U.S.: **BritRail Travel** (tel. 800/677–8585), **Rail Europe** (tel. 800/942–4866).

CONSUMER PROTECTION

Whenever shopping or buying travel services in Great Britain, **pay with a major credit card** so you can cancel payment or get reimbursed if there's a problem. If you're doing business with a particular company for the first time, **contact your local Better Business Bureau and the attorney general's offices** in your state and the company's home state, as well. Have any complaints been filed?

LOCAL BBBS • **Council of Better Business Bureaus** (4200 Wilson Blvd., Suite 800, Arlington, VA 22203, tel. 703/276–0100, fax 703/525–8277).

CUSTOMS & DUTIES

When shopping, **keep receipts** for all purchases. Upon reentering the country, **be ready to show customs officials what you've bought.** If you feel a duty is incorrect or object to the way your clearance was handled, note the inspector's badge number and ask to see a supervisor. If the problem isn't resolved, write to the appropriate authorities, beginning with the port director at your point of entry.

IN GREAT BRITAIN

Duty-free allowances were abolished in June 1999 within the European Union. For goods purchased outside the EU you may import duty-free: 200 cigarettes or 100 cigarillos or 50 cigars or 250 grams of tobacco; two liters of table wine and, in addition, (a) one liter of alcohol over 22% by volume (most spirits), (b) two liters of alcohol under 22% by volume (fortified or sparkling wine), or (c) two more liters of table wine; 60 milliliters of perfume; ¼ liter of toilet water; and other goods up to a value of £145, but not more than 50 liters of beer or 25 cigarette lighters.

If you are entering the United Kingdom from another EU country, you no longer need to pass through customs. If you plan to bring large quantities of alcohol or tobacco, check in advance on EU limits with Customs and Excise (tel. 020/8910–3600).

No animals or pets of any kind can be brought into the United Kingdom without a lengthy quarantine. The penalties are severe and strictly enforced. Similarly, fresh meats, plants and vegetables, illegal drugs, and firearms and ammunition may not be brought into Great Britain.

You will face no customs formalities if you enter Scotland or Wales from any other part of the United Kingdom.

IN AUSTRALIA

Australia residents who are 18 or older may bring home $A400 worth of souvenirs and gifts (including jewelry), 250 cigarettes or 250 grams of tobacco, and 1,125 ml of alcohol (including wine, beer, and spirits). Residents under 18 may bring back $A200 worth of goods. Prohibited items include meat products. Seeds, plants, and fruits need to be declared upon arrival.

INFORMATION • **Australian Customs Service** (Regional Director, Box 8, Sydney, NSW 2001, tel. 02/9213–2000, fax 02/9213–4000).

IN CANADA

Canadian residents who have been out of Canada for at least 7 days may bring home C$500 worth of goods duty-free. If you've been away less than 7 days but more than 48 hours, the duty-free allowance drops to C$200; if your trip lasts 24–48 hours, the allowance is C$50. You may not pool allowances with family members. Goods claimed under the C$500 exemption may follow you by mail; those claimed under the lesser exemptions must accompany you. Alcohol and tobacco products may be included in the 7-day and 48-hour exemptions but not in the 24-hour exemption. If you meet the age requirements of the province or territory through which you reenter Canada, you may bring in, duty-free, 1.14 liters (40 imperial ounces) of wine or liquor or 24 12-ounce cans or bottles of beer or ale. If you are 16 or older you may bring in, duty-free, 200 cigarettes and 50 cigars. Check ahead of time with Revenue Canada or the Department of Agriculture for policies regarding meat products, seeds, plants, and fruits.

You may send an unlimited number of gifts worth up to C$60 each duty-free to Canada. Label the package UNSOLICITED GIFT—VALUE UNDER $60. Alcohol and tobacco are excluded.

INFORMATION • **Revenue Canada** (2265 St. Laurent Blvd. S, Ottawa, Ontario K1G 4K3, tel. 613/993–0534; 800/461–9999 in Canada).

IN NEW ZEALAND

Homeward-bound residents 17 or older may bring back $700 worth of souvenirs and gifts. Your duty-free allowance also includes 4.5 liters of wine or beer; one 1,125-ml bottle of spirits; and either 200 cigarettes, 250 grams of tobacco, 50 cigars, or a combination of the three up to 250 grams. Prohibited items include meat products, seeds, plants, and fruits.

INFORMATION • **New Zealand Customs** (Custom House, 50 Anzac Ave., Box 29, Auckland, New Zealand, tel. 09/359–6655, fax 09/359–6732).

IN THE U.S.

U.S. residents who have been out of the country for at least 48 hours (and who have not used the $400 allowance or any part of it in the past 30 days) may bring home $400 worth of foreign goods duty-free.

U.S. residents 21 and older may bring back 1 liter of alcohol duty-free. In addition, regardless of your age, you are allowed 200 cigarettes and 100 non-Cuban cigars. Antiques, which the U.S. Customs Service defines as objects more than 100 years old, enter duty-free, as do original works of art done entirely by hand, including paintings, drawings, and sculptures.

You may also send packages home duty-free: up to $200 worth of goods for personal use, with a limit of one parcel per addressee per day (and no alcohol or tobacco products or perfume worth more than $5); label the package PERSONAL USE and attach a list of its contents and their retail value. Do not label the package UNSOLICITED GIFT or your duty-free exemption will drop to $100. Mailed items do not affect your duty-free allowance on your return.

INFORMATION • **U.S. Customs Service** (inquiries, 1300 Pennsylvania Ave. NW, Washington, DC 20229, tel. 202/927–6724; complaints, Office of Regulations and Rulings, 1300 Pennsylvania Ave. NW, Washington, DC 20229; registration of equipment, Resource Management, 1300 Pennsylvania Ave. NW, Washington, DC 20229, tel. 202/927–0540).

DINING

The joke used to be that Britain conquered half the world to get its hands on some decent food. Didn't Britons invade Rajasthan just for a good curry? In the '90s, London underwent a food revolution—its restaurant scene is Europe's hottest right now—and tasty recipes are trickling down to many British kitchens. Ethnic cuisines continue to make a large mark—Indian, of course, but also Chinese, Thai, and a myriad of other culinary delights—and even such old standards as bangers and mash, fish-and-chips, and meat and veggies have been given a new (in some fancy places, a newer-than-now-nouvelle) spin. Of course, there are always those Greek, Italian, and French restaurants that have reasonable prices and still give value-for-money and courteous service. But it's much more difficult to find a reasonably priced, friendly little restaurant in central London than it is in New York. Strike out to London's outlying "villages" such as Barnes, Clerkenwell, Camden, or Hampstead for a lively, less hyped experience with lower prices. In the countryside, smaller towns, and villages, the situation becomes a bit bleaker, unless you're armed with a food guide—many of the capital's Michelin-starred celebrity chefs started in well-established country hotels. There's always the good old standby of pub food, which is becoming far more adventurous, and the local Chinese takeout, which often doubles as a fish-and-chippie.

Whatever else ails British cuisine, the country deserves credit for the English breakfast. As Somerset Maugham once pointed out, "If you want to eat well in England, have breakfast three times a day." The morning meal can often be a masterpiece of bacon (usually with the rind still on), egg, grilled tomato, sausage, and fried bread. An English breakfast is often included in a B&B's rates. Pub lunches are another good way to cut down your eating bills, although the fare becomes rather tiring after a while. Staples are bangers and mash, cottage pie, steak-and-kidney pie, Cornish pasties (a type of savory pie), and fish-and-chips. A ploughman's lunch is probably the most appetizing of the lot, consisting of a hunk of fresh bread, English cheese, tomatoes, pickled onions, and Branston pickles or chutney. Some can be a real find though, and serve real ham, chicken or turkey fresh from the bone, smoked mackerel, lasagna, moussaka, with, yes, the ubiquitous optional chips. Portions are often generous.

PUBS

The Brits take their drink very seriously, and pubs (public houses) are where people go to chew over the drama of life and drink themselves into oblivion. Throughout Britain, even in villages that don't have banks or post offices, you'll find a handful of pubs with chatty locals enjoying a quiet pint of bitter. Almost every pub has a sign hanging outside, typically bearing a name like The Horse and Plough or The King George. Most pubs are affiliated with a particular brewer (Whitbread, Charringtons, Bass, whatever) and sell only that brewery's beer; others are "freehouses," which can sell independent brewers' beers and generally have a better selection of brews.

The restaurant price categories used in our city listings are loosely based on the assumption that you're going to chow down a main course and a drink. Antacids and dessert are extra.

The beer of choice among Britons is probably **bitter,** a lightly fermented beer with an amber color that gets its bitterness from the fermentation of hops. Names to try are Fuller's, Young's, Tetley's, Watney's Red Barrel, and Samuel Smith's. **Real ale,** served from wooden kegs, is another popular beer. It's flatter than regular bitters and is something else altogether.

Afficionados claim real ale has as many different characteristics as some vintage wines, and is comes with the most quirky names—Old Growler, Fuggies, and Umbel Magna. **Stouts** like Guinness and Murphy's are thick, pitch-black Irish brews that you'll either love or hate. They're as filling as a small meal. **Lagers** now come in an array of designer names and bottles, and make up half of Britain's beer consumption (try Harp, Carling, Tennent's, Whitbread, and Watney's). The light-colored and heavily carbonated beer is served cold, unlike bitters and ales, which are served only cool. **Cider,** made from apples, is an alcoholic drink in Britain. Most pubs feature at least one dry and one sweet variety; Bulmer's and Strongbow are the names to remember. For a real, rough country taste, without a hint of mass-produced flavor or fizz, try Scrumpy, the true cider of ciders. Blended drinks are another option, like **shandies,** a mix of lager and lemonade or orange soda; **black and tans,** a blend of lager and stout named for the distinctive uniforms worn by turn-of-the-century British troops. Be warned if you order a drink that would normally be served with ice in the United States—ice cubes are about as common in pubs as they are in Hades.

Unless otherwise noted, pubs are open Monday–Saturday 11–11 and Sunday noon–10:30. Exceptions to the rule are wine bars (which charge handsome prices to subsidize their costly after-hours liquor licenses) and small neighborhood pubs that just don't give a hoot. You'll know you've found one of the latter when, at 11 PM, the barman draws the curtains, locks the door, and asks people to leave at their leisure from a discreet side door. "Lock-ins" are an age-old tradition, and while they're definitely not legal, bobbies tend to overlook them.

DISABILITIES & ACCESSIBILITY

The good news is that many big tourist sights and entertainment venues in Great Britain are wheelchair accessible. Some museums and parks even have touch tours for the blind and interpreted events for the deaf. And currently, admission to all English Heritage properties is free for attendants (one) of persons with disabilities, but not for the persons themselves; contact **English Heritage Customer Services** (429 Oxford St., London W1, tel. 020/7973–3396) for details.

LOCAL RESOURCES • Royal Association for Disability and Rehabilitation (RADAR) (12 City Forum, 250 City Rd., EC1V 8AF, tel. 020/7250–3222) is command central for everything people with disabilities could need to know about living and traveling in the United Kingdom. It publishes both travel information and periodicals on political issues.

Tripscope (tel. 020/8994–9294; in the U.K., also Lo–call 08457/585641) runs an information line for travelers with disabilities. It even offers advice on how to get to and from your point of travel.

GETTING AROUND

Most major airlines are happy to help travelers with disabilities make flight arrangements, provided they're notified up to 48 hours in advance. **Main line national railways** also provide disabled passengers with additional services: Passengers can be met at stations by personnel, brought to a nearby taxi, etc. It's wise to call a day or two ahead of your journey to guarantee assistance getting on and off trains. **National Express** (tel. 0990/808–080 or 020/7730–3466 for Victoria Coach Station automated switchboard), Britain's largest bus company, will assist travelers with disabilities in getting on and off the coach, but none of their buses is equipped with wheelchair lifts. Give notice when booking if you will need extra help.

LODGING

When discussing accessibility with an operator or reservations agent **ask hard questions.** Are there any stairs, inside *or* out? Are there grab bars next to the toilet *and* in the shower/tub? How wide is the door-way to the room? To the bathroom? For the most extensive facilities meeting the latest legal specifica-tions **opt for newer accommodations.**

COMPLAINTS • **Disability Rights Section** (U.S. Department of Justice, Civil Rights Division, Box 66738, Washington, DC 20035-6738, tel. 202/514–0301; 800/514–0301; 202/514–0301 TTY; 800/514–0301 TTY, fax 202/307–1198) for general complaints. **Aviation Consumer Protection Division** (*see* Air Travel, *above*) for airline-related problems. **Civil Rights Office** (U.S. Department of Transporta-tion, Departmental Office of Civil Rights, S-30, 400 7th St. SW, Room 10215, Washington, DC 20590, tel. 202/366–4648, fax 202/366–9371) for problems with surface transportation.

TRAVEL AGENCIES

In the United States, although the Americans with Disabilities Act requires that travel firms serve the needs of all travelers, some agencies specialize in working with people with disabilities.

TRAVELERS WITH MOBILITY PROBLEMS • **Access Adventures** (206 Chestnut Ridge Rd., Rochester, NY 14624, tel. 716/889–9096), run by a former physical-rehabilitation counselor. **Accessi-ble Journeys** (35 W. Sellers Ave. Ridley Park, PA 19078, tel. 610/521–0339 or 800/846–4537, fax 610/521–6959). **Accessible Vans of the Rockies, Activity and Travel Agency** (2040 W. Hamilton Pl., Sheri-dan, CO 80110, tel. 303/806–5047 or 888/837–0065, fax 303/781–2329). **Accessible Vans of Hawaii, Activity and Travel Agency** (186 Mehani Circle, Kihei, HI 96753, tel. 808/879–5521 or 800/303–3750, fax 808/879–0649). **CareVacations** (5-5110 50th Ave., Leduc, Alberta T9E 6V4, tel. 780/986–6404 or 877/478–7827, fax 780/986–8332) has group tours and is especially helpful with cruise vacations. **Fly-ing Wheels Travel** (143 W. Bridge St., Box 382, Owatonna, MN 55060, tel. 507/451–5005 or 800/535–6790, fax 507/451–1685). **Hinsdale Travel Service** (201 E. Ogden Ave., Suite 100, Hinsdale, IL 60521, tel. 630/325–1335, fax 630/325–1342). **Tomorrow's Level of Care** (Box 470299, Brooklyn, NY 11247, tel. 718/756–0794 or 800/932–2012), for nursing services and medical equipment.

DISCOUNTS & DEALS

Be a smart shopper and **compare all your options** before making decisions. A plane ticket bought with a promotional coupon from travel clubs, coupon books, and direct-mail offers may not be cheaper than the least expensive fare from a discount ticket agency. Study the travel sections of major Sunday news-papers: You'll often find listings for good packages and incredibly cheap flights. Surfing on the Internet can also give you some good ideas. Travel agents are another obvious resource; the computer networks to which they have access show the lowest fares before they're even advertised. Agencies on or near col-lege campuses, accustomed to dealing with budget travelers, can be especially helpful. And remember, just because something is cheap does not mean it's a bargain.

DISCOUNT RESERVATIONS

To save money **look into discount-reservations services** with toll-free numbers, which use their buying power to get a better price on hotels, airline tickets, even car rentals. When booking a room, always **call the hotel's local toll-free number** (if one is available) rather than the central reservations number—you'll often get a better price. Always ask about special packages or corporate rates.

When shopping for the best deal on hotels and car rentals **look for guaranteed exchange rates,** which protect you against a falling dollar. With your rate locked in, you won't pay more, even if the price goes up in the local currency.

AIRLINE TICKETS • tel. **800/FLY–4–LESS**. tel. **800/FLY–ASAP**.

HOTEL ROOMS • **Hotel Reservations Network** (tel. 800/964–6835). **Steigenberger Reservation Service** (tel. 800/223–5652). **Travel Interlink** (tel. 800/888–5898).

PACKAGE DEALS

Don't confuse packages and guided tours. When you buy a package, you travel on your own, just as though you had planned the trip yourself. Fly/drive packages, which combine airfare and car rental, are often a good deal. If you **buy a rail/drive pass,** you may save on train tickets and car rentals. All Eurail- and Europass holders get a discount on Eurostar fares through the Channel Tunnel.

ELECTRICITY

Before tossing a blow dryer into your bag, consider that Great Britain's electrical outlets pump out 230 volts, 50 cycles, enough to fry American appliances. So you'll want a converter that matches the outlet's current and the wattage of your hair dryer (which still may blow). You'll also want an adapter to plug it in; wall outlets in Great Britain take plugs with three square-prongs, and for shaver outlets, two round oversize prongs.

You can get by with just the adapter if you bring a dual-voltage appliance, available from travel gear catalogs. Don't use 110-volt outlets, marked FOR SHAVERS ONLY, for high-wattage appliances (like your blow dryer). Most laptops need only an adapter.

Some feel the cruelest words in the English language are "Drink up, ladies and gents, time to go. Please lads, come now, drink up."

EMBASSIES

Australia (Australia House, Strand, WC2, tel.020/7379–4334). **Canada** (MacDonald House, 1 Grosvenor Sq., W1, tel. 020/7258–6600). **New Zealand** (New Zealand House, 80 Haymarket, SW1, tel. 020/7930–8422). **United States** (U.S. Embassy, 24 Grosvenor Sq., W1, tel. 020/7499–9000); for passports, go to the **U.S. Passport Unit** (55 Upper Brook St., W1, tel. 020/7499–9000).

GAY & LESBIAN TRAVEL

Although homosexuality is still a shadowy subject in some parts of Britain (in outlying regions, it can occasionally be met with hostility), there is a huge gay and lesbian subculture. Many towns have gay/lesbian pubs, bars, or clubs, and advertise this fact openly. However, gay bashing is a crime that is seldom punished in Britain, so watch yourself. London, Brighton, and Manchester are the best places to find bars, social events, and publications catering to gays and lesbians. Out in the hinterlands, precautions are always wise—just be tactful when you suggest to a B&B or hotel owner that you and your significant other would like to share a room.

GAY- AND LESBIAN-FRIENDLY TRAVEL AGENCIES • **Different Roads Travel** (8383 Wilshire Blvd., Suite 902, Beverly Hills, CA 90211, tel. 323/651–5557 or 800/429–8747, fax 323/651–3678). **Kennedy Travel** (314 Jericho Turnpike, Floral Park, NY 11001, tel. 516/352–4888 or 800/237–7433, fax 516/354–8849). **Now Voyager** (4406 18th St., San Francisco, CA 94114, tel. 415/626–1169 or 800/ 255–6951, fax 415/626–8626). **Skylink Travel and Tour** (1006 Mendocino Ave., Santa Rosa, CA 95401, tel. 707/546–9888 or 800/225–5759, fax 707/546–9891), serving lesbian travelers.

PUBLICATIONS • Your best bet is to pick up national or regional gay- and lesbian-oriented publications as soon as you arrive. Look for **Gay to Z,** published quarterly (£3), which provides listings of organizations, businesses, and services throughout Great Britain (call 020/7793–7450 for direct mailing). Gay Times, a monthly newspaper (£2.50), is on sale at most larger newsagents. **The Pink Paper** (free) is Britain's most well-established national paper of gay and lesbian news. It includes info on media, political events, clubs, and switchboard numbers and can be found in bookstores, cafés, and student unions throughout the country. **Pink,** and **Boys**—also freesheets available from similar sources—cover listings, information, and entertainment.

HOLIDAYS

In Great Britain, banks, shops, and most everything you depend upon close on the following national holidays: **New Year's Day** (January 1, and January 2 in Scotland); **Good Friday** (the Friday before

Easter); **Easter Sunday**; **Easter Monday** (Monday after Easter, except in Scotland); **Spring Bank Holiday** (first and last Monday in May); **Summer Bank Holiday** (the last Monday in August; in Scotland, it's the first Monday in August); **Christmas** (December 25); and **Boxing Day** (December 26). If Christmas or Boxing Day falls on a weekend, the following Monday is considered a holiday. Happily, since the new Sunday trading laws, more and more large supermarkets and village general stores are staying open on these major holidays. Sunday still can pose problems for travelers, especially in smaller towns: Not only do many shops and restaurants close, but bus and train service becomes less frequent or nonexistent.

INSURANCE

The most useful travel insurance plan is a comprehensive policy that includes coverage for trip cancellation and interruption, default, trip delay, and medical expenses (with a waiver for preexisting conditions).

Without insurance you will lose all or most of your money if you cancel your trip, regardless of the reason. Default insurance covers you if your tour operator or airline goes out of business. Study the fine print when comparing policies.

If you're traveling internationally, a key component of travel insurance is coverage for medical bills incurred if you get sick on the road. Such expenses are not generally covered by Medicare or private policies. U.K. residents can buy a travel-insurance policy valid for most vacations taken during the year in which it's purchased (but check pre-existing-condition coverage). Australian citizens need extra medical coverage when traveling abroad.

Always **buy travel policies directly from the insurance company**; if you buy it from an airline or tour operator that goes out of business, you probably will not be covered for the agency or operator's default, a major risk. Before you make any purchase **review your existing health and home-owner's policies** to find what they cover away from home.

TRAVEL INSURERS • In the U.S. **Access America** (6600 W. Broad St., Richmond, VA 23230, tel. 804/285–3300 or 800/284–8300), **Travel Guard International** (1145 Clark St., Stevens Point, WI 54481, tel. 715/345–0505 or 800/826–1300). In Canada **Voyager Insurance** (44 Peel Center Dr., Brampton, Ontario L6T 4M8, tel. 905/791–8700; 800/668–4342 in Canada).

INSURANCE INFORMATION • In the U.K. the **Association of British Insurers** (51–55 Gresham St., London EC2V 7HQ, tel. 020/7600–3333, fax 020/7696–8999). In Australia the **Insurance Council of Australia** (tel. 03/9614–1077, fax 03/9614–7924).

LODGING

This book lists the total price for a double room, including VAT, when outside the major cities. Within major cities, hotels and other accommodations are instead listed by price category. If not stated otherwise, all accommodations take credit cards. If they do not offer this service, we flag the fact by noting "No credit cards."

HOTELS AND BED-AND-BREAKFASTS

When hoping to stretch your pounds, your biggest concern will be choosing your accommodations. Options in Britain run the gamut from farmhouse bed-and-breakfasts whose owners treat their guest like long-lost children to chain hotels with dependable staff and predictable amenities. Hotels, of course, are the most expensive form of accommodation in England. Rates start around £25 per person and go as high as £200.

If you're sick of hostels and campgrounds but can't afford a hotel, bed-and-breakfasts (B&Bs) and guest houses—their slightly snootier cousins—are the perfect alternatives. There are far more B&Bs in Britain than any other type of accommodation. B&Bs, which cost £12–£15 per person at the low end, are usually private homes that owners open to the public. Some are grand old houses in the country and some are cramped flats in the suburbs. The quality of B&Bs varies widely—some owners go to great lengths to make their homes as comfortable as possible; others want your money and not a whole lot else. Be aware that some B&B owners discriminate blatantly, and you might be turned away based on your appearance.

Expect to share bathrooms with other guests, although many rooms have their own washbasin. Some B&Bs do offer rooms with private bath, but you'll pay an extra £5–£15 for the privilege. Breakfast is, as the name suggests, almost always included in the rates—and if you're lucky, the breakfast will be solid enough to keep you going for the rest of the day. For a small additional fee, many B&Bs also serve dinner upon advance notice. A great plus of staying in a B&B is getting grassroots information and a better feel of the town from the proprietors. Don't worry if the B&B is outside the center of town; there are almost always buses to ferry you around.

All tourist offices should have lists of local B&Bs, and the central tourist organizations produce national lists. One of the best guide books that highlights more of the best all rounders (with less of the UHT milk and sugar sachets) is *Special Places to Stay in Britain,* by Alastair Sawday (ASP, £10.95). The incisive *Which? Hotel Guide* (Which? Books, £14.99) gives the bottom line on modest hotels and B&Bs under £35 a night. Both are updated annually.

CAMPING

Camping makes sense out in the country, particularly in the national parks. Facilities at campgrounds vary dramatically: Primitive campsites may offer nothing but the ground itself, some hostels with backyards offer tent sites, while resort-style campgrounds offer showers, laundry facilities, bars, and amusement arcades. The latter tend to be overrun by caravanners, the British equivalent of the RV crowd. If you're planning to camp, keep the following in mind: (1) Even in summer, the wind on the northern moors can be bitingly cold and incredibly strong; (2) you're likely to get wet, no matter where you are; (3) campgrounds in rural areas are often poorly served by public transportation; and (4) many campgrounds close outside the summer months.

A Continental breakfast is tea or coffee, orange juice if you're lucky, rolls or toast, and jam and butter. An English breakfast includes the above as well as bacon, eggs, and cereal, perhaps even black pudding, fried toast, and soggy stewed tomatoes.

Nevertheless, Britain has more than 2,000 campsites, and camping is undoubtedly the best way to see the countryside if your interest lies in hiking and nature. Travelers who prefer a comfortable bed at night and a good pub down the road may want to go the B&B route. For more info, contact the British Tourist Authority (*see* Visitor Information, *below*) for its free pamphlet, "Self-Catering Holiday Homes." When camping, don't pitch your tent near those plants that look like a fuzzier version of garden weeds—called stinging nettles, they give you a nasty, burning sensation if your skin comes into contact with them.

HOSTELS

If you want to scrimp on lodging, **look into hostels.** In some 5,000 locations in more than 70 countries around the world, **Hostelling International (HI),** the umbrella group for a number of national youth hostel associations, offers single-sex, dorm-style beds, and, at many hostels, "couples" rooms and family accommodations. Membership in any HI national hostel association, open to travelers of all ages, allows you to stay in HI-affiliated hostels at member rates. Members also have priority if the hostel is full; they're eligible for discounts around the world, even on rail and bus travel in some countries.

Hostelling International is the umbrella organization beneath which the Youth Hostel Association of England and Wales (YHA) and the Scotland Youth Hostel Association (SYHA) operate. Purchase a Hostelling International membership card at any hostel for £11 (£5.50 under 18). Nonmembers must pay an extra £1.55 per night for a guest stamp; after accruing six stamps you're granted full membership. Students between the ages of 18 and 26 and in possession of an ISIC card (*see* Students, *below*) are given a £1 discount on hostel accommodations in England; be sure to ask.

To double-check your accommodation plans, we advise you **telephone the hostel in advance—certain hostels close during off-season months.** While we note if any hostel is closed during off-season (this can often occur in northern England and Scotland), it's best to inquire by phone as your arrival date approaches to **get the latest update.** Unlike England, Scottish hostels set their bed rates by nationwide grades; for complete info *see* Where to Sleep in Basics *in* Chapter 12.

Most HI hostels have sex-segregated dormitories. They usually have an 11 PM curfew (except in major cities), daytime bedroom lockouts (usually 10–4), check-in times between 8 AM–11 AM and 5 PM–9 PM, and check-out by 10:30 AM. Note that if a hostel keeps different hours, we note those hours separately in the review listing. Some hostels, usually at the lower end of the scale, may wish you to help with a simple chore. In many hostels, you must use a sleep sheet, which is sometimes included at no extra charge. All hostels have basic kitchen facilities and serve their own usually bland meals. If a hostel is full, the desk will have references to nearby places, or might let you sleep in the lounge. Hostels are not allowed to turn anyone away who can't get another place to stay, especially women traveling alone.

There are also a number of independent hostels sprouting up around Britain. These hostels cater to the international cheapo backpacker, with no curfew or lockout and 24-hour reception. Unfortunately, in some cases, the lack of rules often entails lack of cleanliness. Many independent hostels are part of the **Independent Holiday Hostels (IHH)** organization. The Independent Hostel Guide (£3.95, Backpackers Press, from most good bookstores, or contact 01629/580427) is a handy book listing their member hostels, though free lists are available at most tourist offices.

ORGANIZATIONS • **Australian Youth Hostel Association** (10 Mallett St., Camperdown, NSW 2050, tel. 02/9565–1699, fax 02/9565–1325). **Hostelling International—American Youth Hostels** (733 15th St. NW, Suite 840, Washington, DC 20005, tel. 202/783–6161, fax 202/783–6171). **Hostelling International—Canada** (400–205 Catherine St., Ottawa, Ontario K2P 1C3, tel. 613/237–7884, fax 613/237–7868). Scottish Youth Hostel Association (SYHA) (7 Glebe Crescent, Stirling FK8 2JA, Scotland, tel. 01786/891333, fax 01786/450198. Office open weekdays 9–12:30 and 1:30–5). **Youth Hostel Association of England and Wales** (Trevelyan House, 8 St. Stephen's Hill, St. Albans, Hertfordshire AL1 2DY, tel. 01727/855215 or 01727/845047, fax 01727/844126). **Youth Hostels Association of New Zealand** (Box 436, Christchurch, New Zealand, tel. 03/379–9970, fax 03/365–4476). Membership in the U.S. $25, in Canada C$26.75, in the U.K. £9.30, in Australia $44, in New Zealand $24.

UNIVERSITY HOUSING

During university holidays—usually around Christmas, Easter, and summer—colleges often rent out residence halls to foreign visitors. They're certainly no cheaper than B&Bs unless you pay weekly rates, and finding a room sometimes involves a lot of legwork if you just show up. Many British universities are actually collections of separate colleges; to find a room, you have to contact each individual college. On the plus side, you get your own single, you meet lots of other travelers, and the residence halls are usually within easy walking distance of cheap restaurants and pubs. If you're interested in planning university stays before you arrive, contact the **British Universities Accommodation Consortium** (Box 1735, University Park, Nottingham NG7 2RD, tel. 01159/504571). Before you walk in the door, be sure to **phone ahead to inquire if there are any minimum-stay requirements**—some university halls will not accept guests for just one or two nights. And certain university residence halls do not offer rooms to the general public, **inquire if they accommodate nonstudents.**

MAIL

The Royal Mail service, though fairly reliable, is very slow. Expect your letter to North America to take up to six days longer to arrive than it takes to receive one. Nearly every city, town, village, hamlet, or cluster of houses in the middle of nowhere has a post office—be it in a butcher shop, liquor store ("off-license"), or pharmacy ("chemist"). Keep your eyes peeled for signs bearing a red oval with yellow lettering (POST OFFICE). Most post offices are open weekdays 9–5:30 and Saturday 9–noon.

POSTAL RATES

Rates from the United Kingdom are from 44p (then more according to the weight) for an international airmail letter, 37p for an international aerogramme, and 38p for an international postcard. For countries within the European Union, the price is 30p. If you're sending a letter, do it by airmail (a week to 10 days), because surface mail can take up to nine weeks! Be sure to get the free PAR AVION/BY AIRMAIL stickers when you buy your stamps. Surface mail is really for sending home gifts or heavy items you don't want to carry around. You'll need to fill out a small green customs sticker that states the weight and contents (so much for surprise gifts).

RECEIVING MAIL

You can receive those precious letters from home via poste restante at any post office (or, if you have an AmEx card, at one of their offices). Here's what you do: Figure out where you'll be in 10 days, then tell the folks back home the address, town, and (most importantly) the postal code of the post (or AmEx) office to which they'll be sending the package. Tell them to write "Poste Restante" and "Hold for 30 days" in the upper left corner of the envelope. You will need to show ID (and/or your American Express card) to pick up this mail.

London's Main Post Office in Trafalgar Square (24–28 William IV Street, WC2N 4DL, tel. 020/7484–9307) is open weekdays 8–8, Saturday 9–8. You'll need your passport or another official form of identification for collection to pick mail up here. This service can be arranged over the phone (tel. 0345/740740), free, for any main or sub post office throughout the U.K.

MONEY MATTERS

For travelers with American dollars, prices in Britain are almost a third more what they are in the United States. After two weeks in England, you'll begin to feel that it's more than just a daunting exchange rate—the Brits themselves are fond of complaining they can hardly afford to live in the country. Even if you stay in hostels and eat only pub grub and cheap Indian food, you might wind up dropping $50 a day. If you're planning to stay in hotels and eat in restaurants, that daily bill could top $100 per person. Then, of course, the British government slaps a whopping 17.5% Value Added Tax (VAT) on almost everything. The VAT is usually included in prices, but not always—be sure to ask.

Lodging will probably be your greatest expense in Great Britain. In England expect to pay around £7–£20 for a bed in a hostel (the London prices are stacked the highest); prices are a bit cheaper in Scotland, about £5–£8 for basic hostel accommodations. Prices for bed-and-breakfasts (B&Bs) vary widely, but you can usually find something for £15–£30 per person. Hotels can be extremely expensive (£50 and up). You can camp for as little as £3, though fully equipped campgrounds may charge as much as £8 per site. Prices throughout this guide are given for adults. Substantially reduced fees are almost always available for children, students, and senior citizens. For information on taxes, *see* Taxes, *below.*

ATMS

Before leaving home, to increase your chances of happy encounters with cash machines in Great Britain, **make sure that your card has been programmed for ATM use there—ATMs in Great Britain accept PINs of four or fewer digits only**; if your PIN is longer, ask about changing it. If you know your PIN as a word, learn the numerical equivalent, since most Great Britain ATM keypads show numbers only, no letters. You should also have your credit card programmed for ATM use (note that Discover is accepted mostly in the United States). Local bank cards often do not work overseas or may access only your checking account; ask your bank about a MasterCard/Cirrus or Visa debit card, which works like a bank card but can be used at any ATM displaying a MasterCard/Cirrus or Visa logo. These cards, too, may tap only your checking account; check with your bank about their policy.

ATM LOCATIONS • Cirrus (tel. 800/424–7787). A list of Plus locations is available at your local bank.

COSTS

A local paper will cost you about 35p and a national daily 35p–50p (up to £1 on Sunday). A pint of beer is about £1.80, and a gin and tonic £2 (mixers are pricey in pubs, and remember that British measures for spirits are on the mean side). A cup of coffee will run from 60p to £2; a ham sandwich £1.75–£3.50; lunch in a pub, £5 and up (plus your drink).

A theater seat will cost from £8.50 to £35 or more in London, less elsewhere. Movie theater prices vary widely—from £3 in the daytime in the provinces (more in the evening) to up to £9.50 in central London.

Gasoline costs about £2.25 a U.S. gallon (67p a liter), and up to 10p a gallon higher in remote locations for unleaded petrol, and roughly £2.42 a gallon (70p a liter) for normal leaded gasoline (by the year 2000, however, 4-star leaded petrol will no longer be available, due to government law).

CURRENCY

£1 = $1.63 and $1 = 60p (at press time). The unit of currency in Great Britain is the pound (also known as the quid), broken into 100 pence. In Great Britain, colorful pound notes (nobody calls them "bills") come in denominations of £5, £10, £20, and £50. Coins are available in denominations of 1p, 2p, 5p, 10p, 20p, 50p, £1, and £2. Remember that coins, no matter how valuable, are not exchangeable outside the borders of the United Kingdom. Some Scottish and Northern Irish banks print their own version of the pound note, but throughout the U.K.–and in most E.U. countries–Scottish and Northern Irish currency notes are accepted as legal tender.

CURRENCY EXCHANGE

You'll get a better deal buying pounds in Great Britain than at home. Nonetheless, it's a good idea to exchange a bit of money into pounds before you arrive in England in case the exchange booth at the train station or airport at which you arrive is closed or has a long line. At other times, for the most favorable rates, **change money at banks.** Although fees charged for ATM transactions may be higher abroad than at home, Cirrus and Plus exchange rates are excellent because they are based on wholesale rates offered only by major banks. You won't do as well at exchange booths in airports or rail and bus stations, in hotels, in restaurants, or in stores, although you may find their hours more convenient.

EXCHANGE SERVICES • International Currency Express (tel. 888/842–0880 on East Coast; 888/278–6628 on West Coast). **Thomas Cook Currency Services** (tel. 800/287–7362). **Chequepoint** also has stores throughout London (548 Oxford St., W1, tel. 020/7723–1005).

TRAVELER'S CHECKS

Do you need traveler's checks? It depends on where you're headed. If you're going to rural areas and small towns, go with cash; traveler's checks are best used in cities. Lost or stolen checks can usually be replaced within 24 hours. To ensure a speedy refund, buy your own traveler's checks—don't let someone else pay for them: irregularities like this can cause delays. The person who bought the checks should make the call to request a refund.

OUTDOORS & SPORTS

BICYCLING

The national body promoting cycle touring is the **Cyclists' Touring Club** (Cotterell House, 69 Meadrow, Godalming, Surrey GU7 3HS, tel. 01483/417217). Membership is £25 a year, £15 for students and those under 18, £15 for those over 65, and £42 for a family of more than three; members get free advice and route information, a bed-and-breakfast handbook, and a magazine.

CAMPING

Contact the British Tourist Authority in the U.S., **Camping and Caravanning Club** (Greenfields House, Westwood Way, Coventry, West Midlands CV4 8JH, tel. 01203/694995), or the **YHA's Camping Barns Reservation Office** (16 Shawbridge St., Clitheroe, Lancs., BB7 1LY, tel. 01200/428366) for details on Britain's many and varied campsites.

WALKING

The Ramblers Association (1–5 Wandsworth Rd., London SW8 2XX, tel. 020/7339–8500), publishes a quarterly magazine and a yearbook full of resources, and a list of B&Bs within 2 miles of selected long-distance footpaths. Other organizations include the **Byways and Bridleways Trust** (The Granary, Charlcutt, Calne, Wiltshire SN11 9HL); **Long Distance Walkers Association** (The Secretary, 21 Upcroft, Windsor, Berkshire, SL4 39H, tel. 01753/866685); **Countryside Commission** (John Dower House, Crescent Place, Cheltenham, Gloucestershire GL50 3RA, tel. 01242/521381) and the **Farm Holiday Bureau** (National Agricultural Centre, Stoneleigh Park, Kenilworth, Warwickshire CV8 2LZ, tel. 01203/696909).

PACKING

In your carry-on luggage **bring an extra pair of eyeglasses or contact lenses** and **enough of any medication you take** to last the entire trip. In luggage to be checked, **never pack prescription drugs or valuables.** To avoid customs delays, carry medications in their original packaging. And don't forget to copy down and carry addresses of offices that handle refunds of lost traveler's checks.

Other stuff you might not think to take but will be darn glad to have: a miniature flashlight; a pocket knife for cutting fruit, spreading cheese, and opening wine bottles; a water bottle; sunglasses; several large zip-type plastic bags, useful for wet swimsuits, leaky bottles, and smelly socks; a travel alarm clock; a needle and thread; extra batteries; a good book; a day pack; and, if noise keeps you up, ear plugs.

CHECKING LUGGAGE

How many carry-on bags you can bring with you is up to the airline. Most allow two, but not always, so make sure that everything you carry aboard will fit under your seat, and get to the gate early.

Before departure **itemize your bags' contents** and their worth, and label the bags with your name, address, and phone number. (If you use your home address, cover it so that potential thieves can't see it readily.) Inside each bag **pack a copy of your itinerary.** At check-in **make sure that each bag is correctly tagged** with the destination airport's three-letter code. If your bags arrive damaged or fail to arrive at all, file a written report with the airline before leaving the airport.

PASSPORTS & VISAS

U.S. and Canadian citizens need only a valid passport to enter Great Britain for stays of up to 90 days. **Make two photocopies of the passport's data page** (one for someone at home and another for you, carried separately from your passport). If you lose your passport, promptly call the nearest embassy or consulate and the local police.

PASSPORT OFFICES

The best time to apply for a passport or to renew is during the fall and winter. Before any trip, check your passport's expiration date, and, if necessary, renew it as soon as possible.

AUSTRALIAN CITIZENS • Australian Passport Office (tel. 131–232).

CANADIAN CITIZENS • Passport Office (tel. 819/994–3500 or 800/567–6868).

NEW ZEALAND CITIZENS • New Zealand Passport Office (tel. 04/494–0700 for information on how to apply; 04/474–8000 or 0800/225–050 in New Zealand for information on applications already submitted).

U.S. CITIZENS • National Passport Information Center (tel. 900/225–5674; calls are 35 cents per minute for automated service, $1.05 per minute for operator service).

SAFETY

Money belts may be unfashionable and bulky, but it's better to be embarrassed than broke. You'd be wise to carry all cash, traveler's checks, credit cards, and your passport there or in some other inaccessible place: front or inner pocket, or a bag that fits underneath your clothes. Keep a copy of your passport somewhere else. Waist packs are safe if you keep the pack part in front of your body. Keep your bag attached to you if you plan on napping on the train. And never leave your belongings unguarded, even if you're only planning to be gone for a minute.

SENIOR-CITIZEN TRAVEL

To qualify for age-related discounts **mention your senior-citizen status up front.** When renting a car ask about promotional car-rental discounts, which can be cheaper than senior-citizen rates.

EDUCATIONAL PROGRAMS • Elderhostel (75 Federal St., 3rd floor, Boston, MA 02110, tel. 877/426–8056, fax 877/426–2166). **Interhostel** (University of New Hampshire, 6 Garrison Ave., Durham, NH 03824, tel. 603/862–1147 or 800/733–9753, fax 603/862–1113).

STUDENTS

To save money, **look into deals available through student-oriented travel agencies.** To qualify you'll need a bona fide student ID card. Members of international student groups are also eligible.

STUDENT IDS & TRAVEL SERVICES • Council on International Educational Exchange (CIEE, 205 E. 42nd St., 14th floor, New York, NY 10017, tel. 212/822–2600 or 888/268–6245, fax 212/822–2699) for mail orders only, in the U.S. **Travel Cuts** (187 College St., Toronto, Ontario M5T 1P7, tel. 416/979–2406 or 800/667–2887) in Canada.

TAXES

VALUE-ADDED TAX (V.A.T.)

Global Refund is a V.A.T. refund service that makes getting your money back hassle-free. In participating stores, **ask for a Global Refund Cheque when making a purchase**—this Cheque will clearly state the amount of your refund in local currency, with the service charge already incorporated (the service charge equals approximately 3%–4% of the purchase price of the item). Global Refund can also process other custom forms, though for a higher fee. When leaving the European Union, get your Global Refund Cheque and any customs forms stamped by the customs official. You can take them to the cash refund office at the airport, where your money will be refunded right there in cash, by check, or a refund to your credit card. Alternatively, you can mail your validated Cheque to Global Refund, and your credit card account will automatically be credited within three billing cycles. Global Refund has a fax-back service further clarifying the process.

VAT REFUNDS • Global Refund (707 Summer St., Stamford, CT 06901, tel. 800/566–9828).

TELEPHONES

COUNTRY & AREA CODES
The country code for Great Britain is 44. When dialing a British number from abroad, drop the initial 0 from the local area code. To give one example: Let's say you're calling Buckingham Palace—020/7839–1377—in London to inquire about tours and hours. First, dial 011 (the international access code), then 44 (Great Britain's country code) then 020 (London's area code), then the remainder of the telephone number. The former London area codes of 0171 and 0181 are being merged into one London area code—020—with a new prefix, 7 or 8 depending on the old area code, preceding the old phone number. The official changeover is April 22, 2000. Until that date London numbers can be accessed with parallel systems using *both* forms of area codes; this edition has gone with the 020/7 and 020/8 area coding. For example, 0171/222–3333 will become 020/7222-3333, with an increase up to eight digits for the telephone number proper.

DIRECTORY & OPERATOR INFORMATION
To reach an operator within the United Kingdom, dial 100. For directory inquiries, dial 192 for the whole of Britain—including Scotland and Wales.

LOCAL CALLS
Local calls cost 10p or one unit. Modern pay phones show you how fast your money is being gobbled up on an LCD display, but older phones make a few beeps as your money is about to run out. The public phones give you back any unused coins that you fed into the slot, but they don't make change, so think twice about using a £1 coin for a local call.

LONG-DISTANCE CALLS
For long-distance calls within Britain, dial the area code (which usually begins with a 01), followed by the number. Lo-call is the term for a number charged at a local rate, from wherever it is placed in the country.

To dial overseas direct from Great Britain, first dial 00, then dial the country code (1 for the United States and Canada, 61 for Australia, and 64 for New Zealand), then the area code and phone number. Calls to Northern Ireland from England, Scotland, or Wales can be dialed without the international code. Direct dialing is considerably more expensive from pay phones than from private ones, but now most residential phone bills are itemized, so you can reimburse your hosts. Have a phone card with lots of credit or a ton of change ready. To place an incredibly expensive collect call using BT, dial 155 to be connected with an operator. Thankfully, now you can buy phone cards that offer cheap access to international calls from newsagents and similar outlets. With a First National card, calls to the U.S. can be as little as 8p per minute, and can be made from any pay or residential phone. They're available in similar denominations as the regular phone cards, and work via an access code and a personal pin number.

LONG-DISTANCE SERVICES
AT&T, MCI, and Sprint access codes make calling long distance relatively convenient. If you're staying in a hotel, the local access number may be blocked. First ask the hotel operator to connect you. If the hotel operator balks ask for an international operator, or dial the international operator yourself. One way to improve your odds of getting connected to your long-distance carrier is to travel with more than one company's calling card (a hotel may block Sprint, for example, but not MCI). If all else fails call from a pay phone.

ACCESS CODES • AT&T USADirect (tel. 0800/890011 or 0500/890011). If you're in Great Britain and wish to dial a telephone number in the U.S, first dial 0800/013–0011. A USADirect operator will then log on to ask you for the U.S. area code and number plus your private telephone card number for billing. With Touch-Tone phones, this will be done automatically.

MCI Call USA (tel. 0800/890222). Calling from the U.K. to the U.S, dial 0800/890222. A World Phone operator will then come on the line, request your private telephone card number for billing, and will then access the number you wish to call in the U.S. With Touch-Tone phones, this will be done automatically.

Sprint Global One (tel. 0800/890877). From the U.K. to the U.S, dial 0800/890877. A Sprint Global One operator will then come on line to ask you for your card number and the U.S telephone number you wish to access. With Touch-Tone phones, this will be done automatically.

PHONE CARDS

Phone cards are available at newsagents, train and bus stations, tourist-information centers, and numerous other locations. Look for signs saying PHONECARDS SOLD HERE. Phone cards come with a fixed number of units (10, 20, 50, or 100), each valued at 10p.

PUBLIC PHONES

British Telecom (BT) is the major phone company operating in England, Scotland, and Wales, although it is fast been caught up by **Cable & Wireless.** BT pay phones are easy to find throughout the United Kingdom. The ones with a red stripe around them accept standard English coins, while phones with a green stripe require the use of a phone card.

TIME

England sets its clocks by Greenwich Mean Time, 5 hours ahead of the U.S. Eastern Standard Time. British summer time (GMT plus 1 hour) requires an additional adjustment from about the end of March to the end of October.

TIPPING

In the U.K., you only tip generously if the service is excellent. Standard practice is to tip 10%–15% in taxis and restaurants (unless service is included). Bartenders are almost never tipped.

TOURS & PACKAGES

On a prepackaged tour or independent vacation everything is prearranged so you'll spend less time planning—and often get it all at a good price.

BOOKING WITH AN AGENT

Travel agents are excellent resources. But it's a good idea to collect brochures from several agencies because some agents' suggestions may be influenced by relationships with tour and package firms that reward them for volume sales. If you have a special interest **find an agent with expertise in that area**; ASTA (*see* Travel Agencies, *below*) has a database of specialists worldwide.

Make sure your travel agent knows the accommodations and other services of the place they're recommending. Ask about the hotel's location, room size, beds, and whether it has room service if you care about these. Has your agent been there in person or sent others whom you can contact?

Do some homework on your own, too: Local tourism boards can provide information about lesser-known and small-niche operators, some of which may sell only direct.

BUYER BEWARE

Each year consumers are stranded or lose their money when tour operators—even large ones with excellent reputations—go out of business. So **check out the operator.** Ask several travel agents about its reputation, and try to **book with a company that has a consumer-protection program.** (Look for information in the company's brochure.) In the United States, members of the National Tour Association and United States Tour Operators Association are required to set aside funds to cover your payments and travel arrangements in case the company defaults. It's also a good idea to choose a company that participates in the American Society of Travel Agent's Tour Operator Program (TOP); ASTA will act as mediator in any disputes between you and your tour operator.

Remember that the more your package includes the better you can predict the ultimate cost of your vacation. Make sure you know exactly what is covered, and **beware of hidden costs.** Are taxes, tips, and transfers included? Entertainment and excursions? These can add up.

TOUR-OPERATOR RECOMMENDATIONS • American Society of Travel Agents (*see* Travel Agencies, *below*). **National Tour Association** (NTA, 546 E. Main St., Lexington, KY 40508, tel. 606/226–4444 or 800/682–8886). **United States Tour Operators Association** (USTOA, 342 Madison Ave., Suite 1522, New York, NY 10173, tel. 212/599–6599 or 800/468–7862, fax 212/599–6744).

PACKAGES

The companies listed below offer vacation packages in a broad price range.

AIR/HOTEL • American Airlines Fly AAway Vacations (tel. 800/321–2121). **British Airways Holidays** (tel. 800/AIRWAYS). **Celtic International Tours** (1860 Western Ave., Albany, NY 12203, tel. 518/463–5511 or 800/833–4373). **Continental Vacations** (tel. 800/634–5555). **Delta Dream Vacations** (tel. 800/872–7786). **DER Travel Services** (9501 West Devon Ave., Rosemont, IL 60018, tel. 888/337–7350). **United Vacations** (tel. 800/328–6877).

THEME TRIPS

Travel Contacts (Box 173, Camberley, England GU15 1YE, tel. 01276/677217, fax 01276/663477), which represents 150 tour operators, can satisfy just about any special interest in London. **Great British Vacations** (4800 S.W. Griffith Dr., No. 125, Beaverton, OR 97005, tel. 503/643–8080 or 800/452–8434).

ANTIQUES • Travel Keys Tours (Box 162266, Sacramento, CA 95816, tel. 916/452–5200).

BARGE TRAVEL HOTELS • H&H Narrowboat Hotels (7 Bramshill Gardens, London NW5 1JJ, tel. 020/7272–0033).

COOKING SCHOOLS • Le Cordon Bleu (404 Airport Executive Pk., Nanuet, NY 10954, tel. 800/457–2433 in U.S.).

EQUESTRIAN VACATIONS • Cross Country International Equestrian Vacations (Box 1170, Millbrook, NY 12545, tel. 800/828–8768, fax 914/677–6077).

HOMES AND GARDENS • Coopersmith's England (Box 900, Inverness, CA 94937, tel. 415/669–1914, fax 415/669–1942). **Expo Garden Tours** (70 Great Oak, Redding, CT 06896, tel. 203/938–0410 or 800/448–2685, fax 203/938–0427).

LITERARY AND HISTORICAL TOURS • Specialty World Travel (47 Elliot St., Natick, MA 01760, tel. 800/242–2346 or 508/650–3800, fax 508/650–4773).

PERFORMING ARTS • Dailey-Thorp Travel (330 W. 58th St., No. 610, New York, NY 10019-1817, tel. 212/307–1555 or 800/998–4677, fax 212/974–1420). **Keith Prowse Tours** (234 W. 44th St., No. 1000, New York, NY 10036, tel. 212/398–1430 or 800/669–8687, fax 212/302–4251).

TENNIS • Championship Tennis Tours (7350 E. Stetson Dr., No. 106, Scottsdale, AZ 85251, tel. 602/990–8760 or 800/468–3664, fax 602/990–8744). **Sportstours** (2301 Collins Ave., No. A1540, Miami Beach, FL 33139, tel. 800/879–8647, fax 305/535–0008). **Steve Furgal's International Tennis Tours** (11828 Rancho Bernardo Rd., No. 123-305, San Diego, CA 92128, tel. 858/675–3555 or 800/258–3664).

WALKING • The Wayfarers: Footloose Through the Countryside of Britain (Brayton, Aspatria, Cumbria CA5 3PT, tel. 0169/732–2383, fax 0169/732–2394).

TRAIN TRAVEL

Ever since "Iron Lady" Margaret Thatcher got hold of the reins on the "Iron Horse," the railway system (and industry in general) just hasn't been the same. The old BritRail was broken up and sold to private companies, which in turn sold shares to the public. (Simply put, the then government sold to the people what was theoretically theirs in the first place.) The official line was that if the railway was run by capitalist types, services would become more efficient. Things have not gotten much better, and in some cases customer complaints are at an all-time high. Yet there are newer trains on some lines. The Blair government is rapping the rail companies' wrists, compelling them to improve, but time will tell. The actual hardware, track, stations, and signaling equipment is run by Railtrack, while the trains and passenger services (which were guaranteed to remain running by the different purchasing companies) were made into 25 companies. In some cases, larger companies, such as National Express and Virgin, own more than one line, but each individual service is run as a separate company. The service is not radically different, but you may find some variance in the fare structure.

The traditional backbone of the national rail system hasn't moved, and high-speed trains still link Britain's major cities. The new services run by private companies simply added a regional name (i.e., InterCity East Coast, North London Railways). Train services to towns within London's commuter belt are extremely frequent and you probably won't have to wait more than an hour for a train. As you get farther into the countryside, however, service drops off dramatically and it's important to plan your itinerary carefully. This is particularly true on Sunday, and in remote areas of northern and western England, Scotland, and Wales. The O.A.G. Rail Guide (about £9.90), issued monthly, contains details of all rail services, as well as info on private, narrow-gauge, and steam lines; pick one up at any major train station or larger branches of WH Smith stationers.

If you plan to do a lot of traveling, it's probably worth investing in a rail pass (*see* Cutting Costs, *below*), since individual tickets can get very expensive (e.g., as much as £72 return from London to Durham, in northern England—though special deals can reduce the fare to £22). Remember that some rail passes cannot be purchased in the United Kingdom—you must get them before you leave home.

Finally, if you need answers while still in the U.S., the overseas number to call is tel. 011/44/1332–387601. In Britain, the new central information number is tel. 0845/748–4950.

CUTTING COSTS

Compare costs for rail passes and individual tickets. If you plan to cover a lot of ground in a short period, rail passes may be worth your while; they also spare you the time waiting in lines to buy tickets. To price individual tickets of the rail trips you plan, ask a travel agent or call **Rail Europe** (tel. 800/942–4866), **Railpass Express** (tel. 800/722-7151), or **DER Travel Services** (tel. 888/337–7350). It's cheaper to travel during off-hours. Many lines charge double the amount during the early morning and early evening rush hours, so it's best to travel before or after the frantic business commuter hours. For instance, a round-trip ticket to London from Bath can cost £62 per person at peak, but only £28 at other times. An APEX ticket bought seven days in advance can save even

Throughout the United Kingdom, "return" means round-trip and "single" means one-way.

more, and cost only around £14. If you're under 26 on your first day of travel, you're eligible for a youth pass, valid for second-class travel only (like Europass Youth, Eurail Youth Flexipass, or Eurail Youthpass). If you're older, you must buy one of the more expensive regular passes, valid for first-class travel, and it might cost you less to buy individual tickets, especially if your tastes and budget call for second-class travel. Be sure to **buy your rail pass before leaving the United States**; those available elsewhere cost more. Finally, don't assume that your rail pass guarantees you a seat on every train—seat reservations are required on some trains; see your travel agent.

BRITISH PASSES • If you plan on covering a lot of ground, it may be worth investing in a **BritRail Pass,** since full-price tickets (especially one-way) can be very expensive in the United Kingdom. Also remember that most BritRail passes cannot be purchased in the United Kingdom—you must **get them before you leave home.** A **BritRail Classic Pass** is good for consecutive days of travel and the best deals are the adult second class option and the youth (16–25 years old) rate. Costs are: for eight days ($265, $215 youth); for fifteen days, ($400, $280 youth); for 22 days ($505, $355 youth); and for one month ($600, $420). All BritRail passes entitle you to free travel on BritRail trains in England, Scotland, Wales, and Northern Ireland. The **BritRail Flexipass** allows a certain number of travel days within a two-month time period. Passes are valid for four days ($235, $185 youth), eight days ($340, $240 youth), fifteen days ($515, $360 youth).

Another option is the **Brit-Ireland Pass,** valid for travel on trains throughout the U.K. and Ireland and Sealink ferry service between the two, and available in the following increments: five out of 30 days ($408) and 10 out of 30 days ($570). All passes are available from most travel agents and from the **BritRail Travel Information Office** (1500 Broadway, New York, NY 10036, tel. 800/677–8585; 94 Cumberland St., Toronto, Ontario M5R 1A3, tel. 416/482–1777 in Canada).

About the only worthwhile pass available in Britain is the **Young Person's Railcard**; it costs £18 from any main line rail station and is good for ⅓ off most train tickets—an investment that will pay you back immediately. However, you must be under 26 to purchase one; also, you'll need two passport-size photos. Another option is a regional rail pass, which entitles you to free travel within a certain region (e.g., within Wales, Scotland, or Cornwall). These passes must be purchased in the U.K.; stop by any main line station for more info or call National Rail for details (tel. 0845/748–4950). Prices and schemes will vary according to the issuing rail company (there are now 25 in all).

REGIONAL RAIL PASSES • If you want to explore a specific part of Britain at length, unlimited travel tickets offer excellent value. For price structures and details go to a larger train station, such as Victoria, Paddington or King's Cross, which is the feeder for that main line out of London, or a national rail travel agent. Tickets are available for Scotland, Wales, and the many different regions of England. A more varied and separate series of tickets covers the Southeast and the London area.

TRAVEL AGENCIES

A good travel agent puts your needs first. Look for an agency that has been in business at least five years, emphasizes customer service, and has someone on staff who specializes in your destination. In addition **make sure the agency belongs to a professional trade organization.** The American Society of Travel Agents (ASTA), with 27,000 agents in some 170 countries, is the largest and most influential in the field. Operating under the motto "Integrity in Travel," it maintains and enforces a strict code of ethics and will step in to help mediate any agent-client disputes if necessary. ASTA also maintains a Web site that includes a directory of agents. (Note that if a travel agency is also acting as your tour operator, *see* Buyer Beware *in* Tours & Packages, *above*.)

LOCAL AGENT REFERRALS • American Society of Travel Agents (ASTA, tel. 800/965–2782 24-hr hot line, fax 703/684–8319, www.astanet.com). **Association of British Travel Agents** (68–271 Newman St., London W1P 4AH, tel. 020/7637–2444, fax 020/7637–0713). **Association of Canadian Travel Agents** (1729 Bank St., Suite 201, Ottawa, Ontario K1V 7Z5, tel. 613/521–0474, fax 613/521–0805). **Australian Federation of Travel Agents** (Level 3, 309 Pitt St., Sydney 2000, tel. 02/9264–3299, fax 02/9264–1085). **Travel Agents' Association of New Zealand** (Box 1888, Wellington 10033, tel. 04/499–0104, fax 04/499–0786).

VISITOR INFORMATION

TOURIST INFORMATION • British Tourist Authority (BTA). U.S.: (551 5th Ave., Suite 701, New York, NY 10176, tel. 212/986–2200 or 800/462–2748, fax 212/986–1188; open weekdays 9–6). Canada: (111 Avenue Rd., 4th floor, Toronto, Ontario M5R 3J8, tel. 416/925–6326). U.K.: Thames Tower, Black's Rd., London W6 9EL (mail queries only). The BTA also offers a 24-hour Fax Information Line at 310/820–4770. This service allows you to phone from a fax machine, listen to a menu, make a selection, then receive instant information by fax.

The London Tourist Board's **Visitorcall** phone guide (tel. 0839/123456) gives information about events, theater, museums, transport, shopping, restaurants, etc. A three-month events calendar (tel. 0839/123401) and a twelve-month version (tel. 0891/353715) are available by fax (set the machine to polling mode, or press start/receive after the tone). Visitorcall charges a rate of 50p per minute.

LOCAL OFFICES • In London, go in person to the **London Tourist Information Centre** at Victoria Station Forecourt for general information (Monday–Saturday 8–7, Sunday 8–5), or to the new **British Visitor Centre** (1 Piccadilly Circus, SW1Y 4PQ; weekdays 9–6:30, Saturday 10–4) for travel, hotel, and entertainment information. The **London Travel Service** (Bridge House, Ware, Hertfordshire SG12 9DE, tel. 01992/456187; weekdays, 9–5:30, Saturday 9–5) offers travel, hotel, and tour reservations.

U.S. GOVERNMENT ADVISORIES • U.S. Department of State (Overseas Citizens Services Office, Room 4811 N.S., 2201 C St. NW, Washington, DC 20520; tel. 202/647–5225 for interactive hot line; 301/946–4400 for computer bulletin board; fax 202/647–3000 for interactive hot line); enclose a self-addressed, stamped, business-size envelope.

WEB SITES

A wee bit of web surfing can help you get in the mood and get you up to date. You'll find everything from weather forecasts to virtual tours of famous cities. Fodor's Web site www.fodors.com, is a great place to start your online travels. Another excellent beginning is the Web site for the **British Tourist Authority:** www.visitbritain.com. Also log on to the **UK Directory** (www.ukdirectory.com), which provides pretty comprehensive listings of all Web sites in the country as well as hundreds of links. **Scotweb** (www.scotweb.co.uk/tp) provides a list of links to other Scottish pages, including **Scot-Highlands** (www.scot-highlands.com), which provides cultural information. You can compare travel options on **Rail Europe** (www.raileurope.com) and **DER Travel Services** (www.dertravel.com). The ultimate listings guide is *Time Out* (www.timeout.co.uk). Browse the online version of the *Sunday Times* (www.sunday-times.co.uk) for hard news.

WHEN TO GO

The main tourist season runs from mid-April to mid-October, but the hordes really descend in June, July, and August. During summer, prices predictably go up, and many accommodations—particularly inexpensive hotels and hostels—stop offering weekly rates. Even so, British high society hits its stride in June and July with events like Wimbledon and the Royal Ascot. Spring in Britain can also be pleasant— the spring flowers and hedgerows are in full bloom and the crowds of tourists are not yet overwhelming. For a very different view of Britain, go during autumn or early winter. With far fewer tourists around, you're more likely to get an honest— albeit a cold and wet—view of Britannia. The northern moors and Scottish highlands are at their most colorful in September and October. Unfortunately, during the off-season many campgrounds and youth hostels are closed, tourist offices and major attractions operate on limited schedules, and public transportation in many regions goes into semihibernation.

CLIMATE

Increasingly, Britain is blessed with warmer summers, almost as if to make up for those previous gloomy months of gray skies. Yet the weather can still be unpredictable. Though winter temperatures in southern England rarely fall below freezing, the air is quite damp, and the cold seems to go right to your bones. In the north, especially in Scotland, winters are much more severe: Hardly a winter goes by without a major, paralyzing snowfall. The weather in spring is incredibly schizophrenic; sun, rain, and hail can follow one another in rapid succession.

FORECASTS • Weather Channel Connection (tel. 900/ 932–8437), 95 cents per minute from a Touch-Tone phone.

FESTIVALS

The following list of major festivals only scratches the surface of the thousands of events staged in Britain. For information about smaller, local fairs, see the appropriate chapters.

Even in summer, rain is a threat and layering of clothing is de rigueur. Summer also means long, long days—sunrise by 6:30 and sunset around 10:30.

JAN. • Scotch whiskey is what's needed to warm the cockles of a chilly night, and celebrated Scots poet Robert (Rabbie) Burns is relished on January 25 with **Burns' Night** pub gatherings, poetry, and haggis suppers, up and down the country from north to south. Call the Scottish Tourist Board (tel. 020/7930–8661) for information.

FEB. • The **Jorvik Viking Festival** is a month-long celebration commemorating Northern England's Viking history. The festival is held in York and features parades of men in skins and horny helmets, and boat displays. Call 01904/643211 for tickets and schedules.

MAR. • On **St. Patrick's Day** (March 17), raise a celebratory pint of Guinness with the thousands of other Irish types in pubs throughout the British Isles. At the **Head of the River Boat Race,** held the penultimate weekend in March, you can watch 420 eight-men crews dip their 6,720 oars in the Thames as they race from Mortlake to Putney. The course is the same as the Oxford and Cambridge University Boat Race—since 1829 this battle of the boats has been known throughout the country as just **The Boat Race,** and the adversaries row it out on the last Saturday in March.

MAY • During the first week in May, join the surfers in Newquay for the English **National Surfing Championships.** To commemorate the rejuvenation of the Earth after a long winter, **Oxford's May Morning Songs** (May 1) are sung at sunrise from the tower of Magdalen College. Yes, the pagan traditions live on, and pubs open at 7 in the morning. The **Bath International Festival** (tel. 01225/463362), held late May–early June, features a variety of performances and raucous crowds.

JUNE • Trooping the Colour (usually held on the second or third Saturday in June) is Queen Elizabeth's big chance to show off nearly every horse and fancy uniform in the realm at the Parade Ground in London in honor of her own birthday (which is actually in April). Write for tickets at least four months in advance: The Brigade Major, H.Q. Household Division, Horse Guards, Whitehall, London SW1 2AX (tel. 020/7414–2479). The vibrant **City of London Festival** (tel. 020/7377–0540) fills the city with theater, poetry, classical music, and dance performed by a host of internationally known artists. The **Glastonbury Festival** (tel. 01749/890470), held June 24–25 in 2000, brings thousands of music fans and hundreds of bands to the town of Pilton, a few miles from Glastonbury.

JULY • On the first Saturday in July, London's huge **Gay Pride Festival** rallies, parties, and sashays around Clapham Common; check the local gay press for information or call the Pride Festival Helpline (tel. 0870/1210121). Brilliant jazz in Kew Gardens has become a regular feature of a week of concerts at the end of July. Details are available at the end of March (020/8332–5000).

AUG. • The **Edinburgh International Festival** (tel.0131/473–2001) is one of the world's largest arts festivals, featuring exhibits, plays, concerts, films, and more. It runs the last two weeks of August. Edinburgh's **Fringe Festival** (tel. 0131/226–5257) takes place concurrently with more alternative perfor-

THE HIGHS AND THE LOWS

Average daily high and low temperatures stack up as follows:

CITY	JANUARY: HIGH/LOW	JULY: HIGH/LOW
BELFAST	44°F/35°F	66°F/51°F
CARDIFF	45°F/35°F	67°F/50°F
DUBLIN	47°F/34°F	68°F/52°F
EDINBURGH	42°F/34°F	65°F/52°F
LONDON	43°F/39°F	71°F/56°F

mances. The **Notting Hill Carnival** (tel. 020/8964–0544), the biggest street fair in Europe, brings costumed bands, floats, food, crafts, and color galore to the London neighborhood on the last Sunday and Monday of the month.

NOV. • **Guy Fawkes Day** (November 5) tips a hat to mischievous Guy Fawkes, who in 1605 was caught with a huge cache of gunpowder in the cellar of the House of Lords. He and his merry band were later executed for their plot to blow up Parliament and James I. Since then, the anniversary of his attempt has been celebrated around Great Britain; bonfires topped with his effigy are burned under a sky lit by fireworks. If you want to see a pyrotechnical display, contact the London Tourist Board for details of the best shows (tel. 0839/123410). The **Lord Mayor's Procession and Show** (tel. 020/7606–3030), held on the second Sunday of November, is just a part of the inaugural festivities for the lord mayor of London; a huge procession sets off at Westminster and ends at the Law Courts.

DEC. • Rowdy crowds fill London's Trafalgar Square on **New Year's Eve** (December 31). Edinburgh's **Hogmanay** (December 27–January 1) takes the celebration a few steps further with ¼ million people flocking to the city to ring in the year with some authentic auld lang syne.

WORKING IN GREAT BRITAIN

Getting a job in Great Britain is no easy matter—prepare for piles of red tape, lengthy booklets of rules and tax regulations, and little respect from employers who just don't like American and Aussie accents. Unless you have a passport from another European Union country, your only real hope is under-the-table work at pubs and restaurants. These types of thankless positions pay £3–£5 per hour if you're lucky, and don't count on making much in tips. If you want to go the legal route, you should contact one of the following organizations long before arriving.

The Council on International Educational Exchange (a.k.a. "Council," *see* Students, *above*) publishes two excellent resource books with complete details on work/travel opportunities, including the valuable Work, Study, Travel Abroad: The Whole World Handbook and The High School Student's Guide to Study, Travel, and Adventure Abroad ($13.95 each, plus $3 first-class postage). The U.K.-based Vacation Work Press publishes the Directory of Overseas Summer Jobs ($14.95) and Susan Griffith's Work Your Way Around the World ($17.95). The first lists more than 45,000 jobs worldwide; the latter, though with fewer listings, makes a more interesting read.

The easiest way to arrange for work in Britain is through Council's **Work Abroad Department,** which enables U.S. citizens or permanent residents, 18 years or older, to work in Europe at a variety of jobs for three to six months; you must have been a full-time student for the semester preceding your stay overseas. **Travel CUTS** (*see* Students, *above*) has similar programs for Canadian students. And the Association for International Practical Training sponsors professional internships of 12 to 18 months in many foreign countries; you must be under 35 and seek a professional internship with a foreign company.

RESOURCES • The Directory of Summer Jobs in Britain (c/o Peterson's, 202 Carnegie Center, Princeton, NJ 05843, tel. 609/243–9111, www.petersons.com). **Association for International Practical Training** (10400 Little Patuxent Pkwy., Suite 250, Columbia, MD 21044-3510, tel. 410/997–2200, fax 410/992–3924, www.aipt.org).

LONDON

UPDATED BY DAVID CLEE, TIM PERRY, AND SOPHIE MACKENZIE SMITH

E n route to London for the first time, the American novelist Henry James was advised by a fellow train passenger to visit St. Paul's Cathedral. While running an errand in the city on his first morning, he happened to pass St. Paul's. Though the statue of Queen Anne in the forecourt struck him as "very small and dirty," he was much impressed by the scene: "All history appeared to live again, and the continuity of things to vibrate through my mind."

Your own musings may not be as eloquent as James's, but you'll undoubtedly be struck by the rich history of London, evident in the jumbled arrangements of its buildings. Low 12th-century fortifications are juxtaposed against soaring 20th-century office towers, and Victorian-era churches contrast with the remains of Roman city walls. Everywhere you look you'll see a confusion of ages, as well as a mix of countless images and symbols that have become ingrained in the global subconscious, whether by the likes of Defoe, Fielding, Dickens, and Woolf, or the Beatles, the Stones, Elvis Costello, and Oasis. Even people who have never set foot in London have vivid images of Big Ben, Tower Bridge, red double-decker buses, and ruddy rain coated people holding umbrellas aloft.

Yet, London is not merely a historical popup book; it is a living, thriving entity. As empire faded into commonwealth, large factions of former subjects relocated to the capital, bringing with them their traditions and beliefs. The presence of so many international influences is changing the very essence of what it is to be British. With a population of almost 7 million, London is both quintessentially English yet full of eccentric aberrations. For every pub lovingly serving hand-pulled ales to gentlemen in tweeds, there's one filled with throbbing techno music and clubbers getting liquored up on "designer booze" before a long night out. For every shop selling fish-and-chips, you'll find a Bengali or Vietnamese restaurant vying for your dining pounds. And, for every patriotic Londoner ranting about the importance of the monarchy, there are impassioned activists who press for its abolishment—after all, they point out, the mystique that once shrouded the royal family has been torn asunder, and revealed is a dysfunctional family that makes *The Simpsons* look good. London has become far more diverse and complex than Dickens could ever have imagined.

London has always inspired extreme reactions. James felt that people could be divided into London-lovers and London-haters, but in the past few years, the scales have been totally weighed to favor the former. Thanks to an ongoing, full-scale city renaissance, everybody's talking about swinging-again London. A booming economy has helped the city's art, style, fashion, and dining scenes to make headlines around the world. London's chefs have become superstars; its fashion designers have conquered Paris

(John Galliano, Alexander McQueen, and Stella McCartney have the reins at Dior, Givenchy, and Chloë); artists such as Damien Hirst and Rachel Whitehead have stormed the most august galleries and museums; the city's raging after-hours scene is packed with music mavens ready to catch the Next Big Thing; and *enfants terribles* are turning the National Theatre upside down with radical staging. Even Shakespeare is ready for the millennium: the Bard's own Globe—the most famous theater in the world—has been reconstructed on the banks of the Thames just 200 yards from where it stood in the 16th century.

The lure and kudos of the London Stage has been reconfirmed by Nicole Kidman's performance in the West End play "The Blue Room" and Kevin Spacey in "The Iceman Cometh". American stars just can't keep away from the British Film Industry, which is giving Hollywood a run for its money. Gwyneth Paltrow dusted off the 'Complete Works of Shakespeare' and Julia Roberts's smile and Hugh Grant's hair put trendy Notting Hill on the pop culture map.

The village scene has really taken off in London with more and more people spending time in colorful pockets of the city. Islington is now the hottest spot to hang out with young bohemian talent, songwriters, sculptors, and painters. Clapham is often affectionately referred to as South Chelsea because of the raging restaurant scene, and new clubs are springing up everywhere around town. To hear real Cockney rhyming slang get down to Spitalfields in the East End and hear the market traders sound off like Dick Van Dyck in *Mary Poppins*. Not far away in The City are The Bank of England, The Tower of London, and the famous square-mile skyline presided over by Lloyds of London, whose controversial building and reputation continue to cast a shadow over the most influential financial capital in the world. The sky at Greenwich has received the gift of the Millennium Dome and we ask if the toadstool will ever become to London what the Eiffel Tower is to Paris? Ignore the British sarcasm, it is surely the moment to visit London who like a bountiful goddess gives Time to the world and plenty of places to spend it within her many villages.

BASICS

AMERICAN EXPRESS

Amex has plenty of offices in London that offer the usual array of services, including commission-free currency exchange for cardholders. Only the main office in the Haymarket handles client mail. *6 Haymarket, SW1Y 4BS, tel. 0171/930–4411. Tube: Charing Cross or Piccadilly Circus. Open weekdays 9–5:30, Sat. 9–4 (until 6 for currency exchange), Sun. 10–6 (currency exchange only).*

Other full-service American Express locations in London include: **The City** (111 Cheapside, tel. 020/7600–5522; Tube: Bank or St. Paul's); **Knightsbridge** (78 Brompton Rd., tel. 020/7584–6182; Tube: Knightsbridge); **Mayfair** (89 Mount St., tel. 020/7499–4436; Tube: Bond Street); and **Victoria** (102–104 Victoria St., tel. 020/7828–7411; Tube: Victoria). There are also a dozen other Amex branches that only offer bureaux de change; look in the phone book for the location nearest you.

BUREAUX DE CHANGE

While bureaux de change are everywhere in London, using them is like flushing money down the toilet—their exchange rates are 10%–15% higher than what the banks offer. The only exceptions are **Thomas Cook,** which has travel offices all over town, and **American Express** (*see above*); both exchange their respective checks at bank rates. Otherwise, if you're desperate for cash after-hours, **Chequepoint** has six 24-hour branches with competitive rates: 37–38 Coventry Street (tel. 020/7839–3772); 222 Earl's Court Road (tel. 020/7373–9515); 71 Gloucester Road (tel. 020/7379–9682); 548 Oxford Street (tel. 020/7723–1005); 2 Queensway (tel. 020/7229–0093); and Victoria Station (tel. 020/7828–0014). Know that exchange rates go up and down daily, and even vary from branch to branch of a particular agency, so it pays to shop around.

DISCOUNT TRAVEL AGENCIES

If you're looking for discount flights or cheap train, ferry, and bus tickets, check the *Evening Standard* (35p), a daily newspaper, or *Time Out* (£1.80), a weekly magazine, both available at newsstands. The following bucket shops offer cheap tickets for flights, ferries, trains, and more: **Campus Travel** (52 Grosvenor St., SW1 and branches, tel. 020/7730–8111; Tube: Victoria); **Council Travel** (28A Poland St., W1, tel. 020/7437–7767; Tube: Oxford Circus); **STA Travel** (38 Store St., WC1 and branches, tel. 020/7361–6262; Tube: High St. Kensington); **Travel CUTS** (295A Regent St., W1, tel. 020/7255–1944;

Tube: Oxford Circus); and **Trailfinders** (42–50 Earl's Court Rd., W8, tel. 020/7938–3366 or 020/7937–5400; Tube: Earl's Court or High Street Kensington.

EMBASSIES

Australian High Commission. *Australia House, The Strand, WC2B 4LA, tel. 020/7379–4334. Tube: Temple. Open weekdays 9:30–3:30.*

Canadian High Commission, Consular Section. *McDonald House, 1 Grosvenor Sq., W1X 0AB, tel. 020/7258–6600. Tube: Bond Street. Open weekdays 9–4 (visas issued weekdays 9–11).*

New Zealand High Commission. *New Zealand House, 80 Haymarket, SW1Y 4TQ, tel. 020/7930–8422. Tube: Charing Cross or Piccadilly Circus. Open weekdays 8–5:30.*

United States Embassy. Passports are handled weekdays 8:30–11 (additional hours Monday, Wednesday, and Friday 2–4) around the corner at the Passport Office, 55 Upper Brook St. Visas are handled by appointment only. *Main Embassy Offices: 24 Grosvenor Sq., W1A 1AE, tel. 020/7499–9000. Tube: Bond Street or Marble Arch. Open weekdays 8:30–5:30.*

EMERGENCIES AND MEDICAL AID

The general emergency number for **ambulance, police,** and **fire** is 999, and you don't need to deposit money to call.

DENTISTS • Eastman Dental Hospital (256 Gray's Inn Rd., WC1, tel. 020/7837–3646; Tube: King's Cross) offers free walk-in emergency dental care on a first-come, first-served basis; word of advice—get there at the crack of dawn. **Guy's Hospital Dental School** (St. Thomas St., SE1, tel. 020/7955–5000; Tube: London Bridge) provides walk-in emergency dental care; for nonemergencies you must make an appointment.

DOCTORS • If you're a visitor from one of the EU or Commonwealth countries, be healed: You can receive free medical treatment while in London. Keep in mind that the ISIC card comes with hospitalization insurance; read its "Summary of Coverage" card for more info. For serious injuries, the following hospitals have 24-hour emergency wards: **Guy's Hospital** (St. Thomas St., SE1, tel. 020/7955–5000; Tube: London Bridge); **Royal Free** (Pond St., Hampstead, NW3, tel. 020/7794–0500; Tube: Belsize Park); **University College London Hospital** (Grafton Way, WC1, tel. 020/7387–9300; Tube: Euston Square or Warren Street).

PHARMACIES • Chemists (equivalent to American drugstores) are plentiful in London. Those with late hours include: **Bliss Chemists** (5 Marble Arch, W1, tel. 020/7723–6116; Tube: Marble Arch), open daily 9 AM–midnight, and **Boots** (75 Queensway, W2, tel. 020/7229–9266; Tube: Bayswater), open daily 9 AM until 10 PM.

LUGGAGE STORAGE

Heathrow, Gatwick, and London City airports all offer luggage storage, called "left luggage" (*see* Coming and Going by Plane, *below*). In town, the most convenient place to store luggage is the left luggage counter between Platforms 7 and 8 in **Victoria Station** (*see* Coming and Going by Train, *below*). Daily rates are £3–£3.50; lockers cost £2.50–£5. The nearby **Victoria Coach Station** (*see* Coming and Going by Bus, *below*) also has a left luggage counter at Gate 6 offering bargain daily rates of £2–£2.50. Both are mere steps from Victoria tube station. **Abbey Self-Storage** (tel. 0800/622244), with warehouses near Victoria, Earl's Court, and Euston, will store your stuff for approximately £35 per month and a locker can hold 5 suitcases.

MAIL

Besides the main offices, you'll find mini–post offices in general grocery stores and chemists. For locations near you, call **Customer Helpline** (tel. 0345/223344) or look for POST OFFICE signs bearing a red oval with yellow lettering. You can receive those dear letters from home via "Poste restante" at any post office—or, if you have an Amex card, at one of their offices (*see above*). A good post office address to give out at home before you leave is the **Post Office** (24–28 William IV St., WC2N 4DL, tel. 0345/223344). They hold mail for up to one month and are open Monday–Saturday 8–8.

PHONES

The former London area codes of 0171 (for inner London) and 0181 (for outer London) are being replaced with one code—020. A new prefix, 7 or 8 (depending on the number's former area code), is also being added before the first digit of phone numbers; the official changeover date is April 22, 2000. Until that date London numbers can be accessed using *both* forms of area codes. So for example, a telephone number of 0171/222–3333 will now become 020/7222-3333, with the telephone number proper now increased to eight digits. You don't have to dial 020 if you are calling inside London itself— just the eight-digit number.

Under the new system, 0800 numbers and national information numbers of 0345 will not change. Within England, there is a help line at 0808/224–2000; from the U.S., additional information and help can be received by dialing 0171/634–8700 (using the old system) or 020/7634–8700 (using the new system).

Local calls cost 10p (equivalent to one unit on phonecards). *See* Chapter 1 for long-distance calling information.

VISITOR INFORMATION

The main **London Tourist Information Centre** provides details on transportation, lodging, theater, concert, and tour bookings. It doesn't have a public info line—other than a reservations line (tel. 0990 887711) for overpriced lodgings at a hefty £5 booking fee—so go in person and pick up a fistful of brochures. Other information centers are located in **Harrods** (Brompton Rd.; Tube: Knightsbridge), **Selfridges** (Oxford St.; Tube: Bond Street or Marble Arch), **Liverpool Street Station, Waterloo International Terminal, Heathrow Airport** (Terminals 1, 2, and 3), and **Gatwick Airport** (International Arrivals Concourse). *Main office: Victoria Station, SW1, no phone. Tube: Victoria. Open daily 8–7 (shorter hrs in the off-season).*

British Travel Centre provides details about travel and entertainment for the whole of Britain and makes lodging reservations (£5 fee). They have no phone line for public inquiries, so you must visit in person. The center has different areas for different services, so make sure you're in the right queue. *12 Regent St., SW1, no phone. Tube: Piccadilly Circus. Open May–Sept., weekdays 9–7, Sat. 9–5, Sun. 10–4; Oct.–Apr., weekdays 9–6:30, weekends 10–4.*

COMING AND GOING

BY BUS

The most valuable number for information—020/7222–1234—connects you to London Transport, which has an overall grip of London transportation and will advise you on the best routes and modes. London's main terminal for all long-distance bus companies is **Victoria Coach Station** (Buckingham Palace Rd., tel. 020/7730–3466), just southwest of Victoria Station. Victoria Coach Station has a bureau de change and luggage storage. Travelers with disabilities, who need or will need disability assistance, should make this clear at the time of booking.

You can save lots of money by taking a bus instead of a train. **Economy Return** (round-trip) bus tickets, good for travel Sunday through Thursday, can be 30% to 50% cheaper than train tickets. Expect to pay about 20% more for **Standard Return** fares, which allow travel on Friday and Saturday. You can also buy cheap **APEX** tickets if you book seven days in advance and adhere to exact times and dates for departure and return. Book tickets on **National Express** (tel. 0990/808080) buses at Victoria Coach Station or at one of their branch offices at 52 Grosvenor Gardens or 13 Regent Street. For information on the various bus passes offered, *see* Bus Travel *in* Chapter 1.

BY PLANE

London has three major airports: Heathrow, Gatwick, and Stansted, all of which are regularly connected by bus with central London. Conveniently, Heathrow also has its own tube station as well as cheap bus connections to central London.

HEATHROW • Heathrow (tel. 020/8759–4321) handles the vast majority of international flights to the United Kingdom. Heathrow has four terminals: **Terminal 1** is mainly reserved for domestic and European flights with British airlines. **Terminals 2 , 3, and 4** are for international flights with terminal 2 handling European flights, terminal 3 inter-continental flights, and terminal 4 handling British Airways, KLM, and Air Malta international flights. It is vital that you check which terminal you will be using before arrival at the airport. **Tourist information counters,** bureaux de change, accommodations services, and luggage-storage facilities are in every terminal.

The cheapest and quickest way to get from Heathrow and to central London is by the Tube (Underground), on the **Piccadilly Line**: The 50- to 60-minute trip costs £3.20. There are two Underground stations at Heathrow: one serving Terminals 1–3 and one at Terminal 4. Hop aboard and you can ride directly to many of London's budget accommodation areas, like Earl's Court, South Kensington, and Russell Square. To reach other cheap lodging neighborhoods, such as around Notting Hill Gate or Victoria Station, change to the **District Line** at Earl's Court.

If you have a lot of heavy baggage, taking the tube can be a real hassle: It's crowded, and transfer points usually involve lots of walking and stair-climbing. In this case consider taking London Transport's shiny red **Airbuses** (tel. 020/8400–6656), which make 29 stops in central London. Airbuses run daily 6 AM to around 8 PM, at 15- to 30-minute intervals, and for this 60- to 90-minute voyage to the city center, you pay a reasonable £6. From Heathrow, Airbuses make pickups at all four terminals—just follow the AIR-BUS or BUSES TO LONDON signs. Heading to the airport, you can catch **Airbus A1** at Victoria Station, **Airbus A2** at King's Cross, or **Airbus Direct,** which stops at the doorstep of many central London hotels. For more information, call Airbus, or grab a brochure at a tourist office or at London Transport's Travel Information Centers (*see* Getting Around, *below*).

GATWICK • Gatwick Airport (tel. 01293/535353), 28 mi south of London, accommodates a steady stream of flights from the United States and the Continent. Gatwick has a left luggage counter (£3.50 for 24 hours; lower rates for long-term storage), accommodation services, and a bureau de change.

The train is your best bet for getting from Gatwick into central London. The **Gatwick Express train** (tel. 0990/301530) to Victoria Station departs Gatwick every 15 minutes daily 5 AM–11:45 PM and every half hour during the night. The 30-minute trip costs £9.50 single. The **Network SouthEast train** (tel. 0345/484950) goes to Victoria Station for £8.20 single; departure and travel times are similar to Gatwick Express (*see above*). **Flightline 777** (tel. 0990/747777) offers hourly bus service between Gatwick and Victoria Coach Station daily from 6:30 AM to around 5:30 PM. The 75-minute trip costs £7.50 single, £11 return.

STANSTED • Stansted (tel. 01279/680500) opened in 1991 to alleviate the overcrowding at Heathrow. It handles mainly European destinations, plus some charter flights. The airport has a **tourist desk** and a 24-hour bureau de change. To reach central London, catch the **Stansted SkyTrain** to Liverpool Street Station. Trains run every half hour, and the 40-minute trek costs £10 single.

LONDON CITY AIRPORT • The **London City Airport** (tel. 020/7646–0000), 9 mi southeast of central London in Silvertown, handles mostly European commuter flights. The main terminal has a **tourist info desk,** a left luggage service (£2 per item per day), and a bureau de change. To reach central London, take London Transport's **Bus 473** (80p), which shuttles between the airport and Stratford tube station. Buses depart every 12 minutes Monday–Saturday 5 AM–midnight and every 20 minutes Sunday 6 AM–midnight. Or catch an Airport Shuttle bus from the airport to Liverpool Street Station or to the Docklands Light Railway station at Canary Wharf (tel. 020/7918–4000 or 020/7222–1234 for more info).

BY TRAIN

London has eight major train stations (as well as a bunch of smaller ones). Each serves a specific part of the country (or the Continent), so be sure to figure out beforehand where your train leaves from. For nationwide 24-hour train information call 0345/484–950 (accessible from United Kingdom only). All eight stations have tourist and travel information booths, rip-off bureaux de change, and luggage storage (£2–£5 per day). They all also are served by the tube, so it's easy to get around after you arrive in London. The **British Travel Centre** (*see* Visitor Information, *above*) can provide you with train schedules, ticket prices, and other information. The *British Rail Passenger Timetable* (£7.50), issued every May and October, contains details of all BritRail services; pick one up at any major train station.

Charing Cross (Strand, WC2) serves southeast England, including Canterbury and Dover/Folkestone ferryports, and is on the Bakerloo, Jubilee, and Northern tube lines.

Euston (Euston Rd., NW1) serves the Midlands, north Wales, northwest England, and western Scotland, and is on the Northern and Victoria tube lines.

King's Cross (York Way, N1) marks the end of the Great Northern line, serving northeast England and Scotland. King's Cross is on the Circle, Hammersmith & City, Metropolitan, Northern, Piccadilly, and Victoria tube lines.

Liverpool Street (Liverpool St., EC2) serves East Anglia, including Cambridge and Norwich, and is on the Central, Circle, Hammersmith & City, and Metropolitan tube lines.

Paddington (Praed St., W2) mainly serves South Wales and the West Country, as well as Reading, Oxford, Worcester, and Bristol. Paddington is on the Bakerloo, Circle, District, and Hammersmith & City tube lines.

St. Pancras (Pancras Rd., NW1) serves Leicester, Nottingham, and Sheffield, and is on the Circle, Hammersmith & City, Metropolitan, Northern, Piccadilly, and Victoria tube lines.

Victoria (Terminus Pl., SW1) serves southern England, including Brighton, Dover/Folkestone, and the south coast. Victoria is on the Circle, District, and Victoria tube lines.

Waterloo (York Rd., SE1) serves southeastern destinations like Portsmouth, Southampton, and Exeter in the southwest. Waterloo is on the Bakerloo and Northern tube lines.

GETTING AROUND LONDON

London lends itself to walking. The heart of visitors' London is only about 3 mi across, and its streets, squares, and alleys are best seen at walking pace. That said, you're going to be sore, tired, and grumpy if you walk everywhere. Luckily, London's mass-transit system is tremendous, and it can get you almost everywhere you want to go, even if it is way overpriced.

London Transport (LT) (tel. 020/7222–1200 for recorded info; 020/7222–1234 for 24-hr help with routes, schedules, and fares). London Transport operates **Travel Information Centres** at all Heathrow terminals and in the following tube stations: Euston, King's Cross, Liverpool Street, Oxford Circus, Piccadilly Circus, St. James's Park, and Victoria. You'll want to get your hands on two of LT's free maps (available at all tube stations) when you get into town: the pocket-size **Tube Map** as well as **"Travelling in London,"** which shows Underground stops *and* bus lines for tourist attractions in central London. Additionally, travelers with disabilities should get the **"Access to the Underground"** (70p) brochure, which includes info on lifts and ramps, as well as Braille maps.

Don't ask Londoners where to catch the "subway." In Britain, a subway is an underground passage to allow pedestrians to cross under busy streets—ask for "the tube."

Fares for London buses, the Underground, Docklands Light Railway, and National Rail (*see below*), are based on **zones.** The Underground, Docklands Light Railway, and overground London services are divided into Zones 1–6. The bus network is divided into four zones: 1, 2, 3 and Bus Zone 4. (Bus Zone 4 covers approximately the same area as Zones 4, 5, and 6 for the Underground and railways.) The more zones you cross through on your trip, the more you pay. With few exceptions, everything you want to see will be within **Zone 1** (which includes Westminster, Soho, Trafalgar Square, Covent Garden, the City, Victoria, Earl's Court, Kensington, and more) and **Zone 2** (which includes Camden, Hampstead, the East End, Brixton, and Greenwich Park). The Jubilee line is being extended to provide convenient and direct access to the Millennium Dome at Greenwich (North Greenwich stop). The major stations along this new route will include Green Park, Westminster, Waterloo, London Bridge, Canary Wharf, and North Greenwich, where the station will be a wonder in itself.

The best way to get around London is with a **Travelcard** available at the "Tickets and Assistance" windows at most tube and train stations, from some vending machines in Underground ticket halls, from LT's Travel Information Centres, and from some newsstands and tobacconists. The most popular is the Travelcard for **Zones 1 and 2,** which costs £3.80 daily, £17.60 weekly, and £64.60 monthly. The **Weekend Travelcard** entitles you to discounted travel on weekends or public holidays; for Zones 1 and 2 the cost is £5.70. Your Travelcard gets you almost unlimited use of the Underground, London Transport buses (except Airbuses), Docklands Light Railway, and most National Rail services within greater London. If you're buying a Travelcard good for a week or more, you'll need a passport-type photo and a local address—a hostel or hotel address should work fine.

BY BOAT

A very pleasant way to get a feel for the city is a boat cruise on the Thames. Downriver trips to Greenwich from Westminster Pier are offered by **Thames Passenger Service Federation** (tel. 020/7930–4097) every 30 minutes and cost £7.30 return. **Westminster Passenger Service Association (WPSA) Upriver** (tel. 020/7930–2062) makes the trip from Westminster Pier to Kew (90 mins; £10 return) and Hampton Court Palace (3 hrs; £12 return) five times daily, Easter–October. A pricey option (£30) that includes admission to the Millenium Dome is a trip with **City Cruises** (tel. 020/7237–5134) that leaves from the South Bank.

BY BUS

Deciphering bus routes can be a bit more complicated than figuring out tube routes. For one thing, color-coded, comprehensive, bus-route maps are only posted at major bus stops; if you really want to master the system, pick up the free "Central London Bus Guide" at an LT Travel Information Centre or (*see above*). As with the tube, bus fares are based on zones: Inside Zone 1, the single fare is £1, or 70p for a "short hop" of less than ¾ mi; a single trip through Zones 1 and 2 is £1.20. But if you're doing a lot of sightseeing, you'll probably want to buy a Travelcard (*see above*).

Major bus stops are marked by plain white signs with a red LT symbol; buses stop at these points automatically. At some stops, known as **request stops** (marked by red signs with a white LT symbol and the word "request"), you'll need to flag the bus down—waving an arm once will do just fine. There are a few busy intersections in London where all buses seem to go, like Trafalgar Square, Victoria Station, and Piccadilly Circus; for these, you'll need to check a posted bus map to find out *exactly* where you should be standing for the bus to your destination.

On the newer buses, which you board at the front, pay the driver as you enter (exact change desired but not required). On older buses, in which the driver sits in a separate cab, just hop on, take a seat, and the conductor will swing by to check your Travelcard or sell you a ticket from a coffee grinder–like apparatus. In 1996 a blue-ribbon city panel discovered something Londoners have known for years: London buses rarely run on time. On most routes they're supposed to swing by every six minutes; in reality it can be a 15- or 30-minute wait. (For this, thank the hundreds of pushy BMW drivers who hog the city's bus lanes, rather than cursing the poor bus drivers.) Because of this tarnished service record, Londoners shun buses—and tourists like you shouldn't have any trouble getting a seat, even during rush hour (7–9:30 and 4–6:30). To get off a bus, pull the cord running the length of the bus above the windows, or press the button by the exit.

NIGHT BUSES • From 11 PM to 5 AM, some buses add the prefix "N" to their route numbers and are called **Night Buses.** They don't run as frequently and don't operate on quite as many routes as day buses, but at least they get you somewhere close to your destination. You'll probably have to transfer at one of the night bus nexuses like Victoria, Westminster, and especially either Piccadilly Circus or Trafalgar Square (the main transfer points for late-night buses). Note that weekly and monthly Travelcards are good for Night Buses, but One Day and Weekend Travelcards are not. Night single fares are also a bit more expensive than daytime ones. A final word of advice: Avoid sitting alone on the top deck of a Night Bus unless you would like to be mugged.

BY DOCKLANDS LIGHT RAILWAY

The Docklands, the massive area east of central London along the River Thames, is served by **Docklands Light Railway (DLR)** (tel. 020/7363–9700), which connects with the Underground at the following stations: Bank, Bow Road, Shadwell, Stratford, and Tower Hill. Dockland's Light Railway trains are overseen by London Transport and use the same system of passes, zones, and fares as the buses and Underground. Its two lines also show up on tube maps. Hours of operation are Monday–Saturday 5:30 AM–midnight and Sunday 7:30 AM–11:30 PM. The **London Travel Information** line (tel. 020/7918–4000) offers info 24 hours a day.

BY NATIONAL RAIL

The National Rail system is a network of aboveground train services that connect outlying districts and suburbs to central London. Recent privatization means its various routes are now handled by a variety of companies; one you're likely to encounter is the **North London** (tel. 0345/484950) line, running from Richmond to North Woolwich with stops at Kew Gardens, Holburn, Hampstead, Hackney, and Docklands. Prices for National Rail trains are comparable to prices for the Underground, and you can easily transfer between the Underground and National Rail at many tube stations (transfer points are marked on tube maps). You can sometimes even use your LT Travelcard instead of buying a separate ticket.

BY TAXI

Cabs are the most expensive form of transportation in London, but they can be reasonable if you're splitting the cost with a few other people. Traditional **black cabs,** which are not always black, are the most reliable. Drivers of these classy carriages have to pass a rigorous test of London streets, known as "The Knowledge," and are required to take passengers on the most direct route possible. That's not a guarantee that every cabby is 100% honest, which is why all cabs are equipped with a meter and fare table. Weekday fares start at £1.40 and go up 20p per unit of distance/time (every 257 yards or 56 seconds). There are surcharges for each additional person (40p), each piece of luggage (10p), and booking a cab by telephone (£1.20 minimum). If you're traveling on a weekday after 8 PM or on Saturday or Sunday, rates increase 40p–60p. It's customary to tip the driver 10% of your fare. If you wish to make a complaint, note the cab number and/or the number of the driver's badge, then contact the Metropolitan Police's **Public Carriage Office** (tel. 020/7230–1631 for complaints; 020/7833–0996 for lost property), open weekdays 9–4. London cabbies are a breed unto themselves and can spin out London tales that will make your hair stand on end. They'll always hear your problems and tell you theirs, but the weather is a favorite topic, too. A trip to London isn't complete without hearing, "Guess who I just had in the back of my cab . . ."

To hail a cab—fairly easy except on weekend nights and when it rains—first check that its yellow "For Hire" light is on, then flail away. You can also phone ahead, but most companies slap a hefty surcharge on "collections." **Radio Taxis** (tel. 020/7272–0272) is a 24-hour black-cab company that charges a maximum collection fee of £2.40.

An alternative to the black cabs are minicabs—their fares are usually cheaper, especially if you're traveling long distances or at night. They are run by private companies or individual drivers, and look just like regular cars. Although it's illegal for minicabs to pick up passengers on the street—you're supposed to call or walk into their office—you can usually find them lurking outside of clubs and on West End corners during the weekend wee hours. It's best to ask the bouncer to call a minicab or check if he knows whether a driver is officially with a company. Because minicabs aren't licensed or regulated like black cabs, bargaining is possible—but to avoid nasty surprises always confirm the price with the driver *before* you get in the car. You do hear some horror stories, so check that the radio is linked to headquarters before you get in, and if it seems dodgy, don't take the risk. Some of the reputable, insured minicab companies include: **Abbey Cars** (west London, tel. 020/7727–2637), **Greater London Hire** (north London, tel. 020/8340–2450), and **London Cabs Limited** (east London, tel. 020/8778–3000); **Town and Country Cars** (south London, tel. 020/7622–6222); **Churchill Cars** (Earl's Court, tel. 020/7373–2001); **Q Cars** (gay company in South London, tel. 020/7622–0011): or look in the Yellow Pages for a company near you.

If you're tired of being chatted up by creepy cabdrivers, Lady Cabs (tel. 020/7254–3314) has taxis for women who'd rather be driven by women.

BY UNDERGROUND

The Underground provides comprehensive service throughout central London and more sporadic service to the suburbs. Between 1999 and 2000 135 million pounds will have been spent on improving the system as part of a one-billion-pound scheme. Underground stations are marked by a large red circle overlaid by a blue banner that reads UNDERGROUND. London is served by a dozen Underground lines, each color-coded; it can seem extremely confusing until you get used to it, and you'll find yourself constantly referring to the Underground map.

If you don't plan to use public transport a lot, buy individual tickets for each journey—choose between single and return, the British equivalent of one-way and round-trip. Once again, ticket prices are based on **zones.** Zone 1, the cool zone, is a bit pricier than all the other zones: Scooting around inside it costs £1.40 single (£2.80 return). Get a **Carnet,** a book of 10 tickets, for zipping around zone 1 (£10), and you'll save money. Travel inside any one of the other zones is 90p single (£1.80 return), while a trip through all six zones costs £3.40 single. You can buy tickets at vending machines in most stations or at Tickets and Assistance windows. Remember to hold on to your ticket since you'll need it to get through the turnstiles at the exit. And beware: Roving inspectors issue an on-the-spot £10 penalty if you're caught without a ticket valid for the zones you're traveling in.

The Underground gets going around 5 AM and closes around 12:30 AM depending on which station you're in; you'll find the timetable for each station posted near the turnstiles. Generally the tube is pretty reliable, with trains every 10 minutes—but a multimillion-pound overhaul of the system has recently meant temporary station closures, route changes, and lengthy delays; listen for announcements in each station. You can roughly calculate how long a particular journey *should* take by adding three minutes for each station you'll pass through. Because the tube closes before the rest of London does, it pays to figure out London's Night Buses (*see above*) if you plan to party late. It's worth remembering that tube stops in central London can be very close together, so if you only intend to go one stop (£1.40), check if it isn't actually better, not to mention cheaper, to walk.

WHERE TO SLEEP

When it comes to London hotels, you have to make a decision. Do you want to pay a fair amount of money for a night's oblivion in chintz-adorned, antiques-bedecked surroundings, or would you rather spend your money while *conscious*. Every so often, of course, you need some pampering. A night or two in a classy hotel can make your bargain-hunting all the easier to bear. So we cover the entire range—from dirt cheap to top dollar (but not *too* top dollar: In London, you can pay an arm and a leg for a night's lodging if you don't watch out). In a city where it seems expensive is the rule, the good news is that there are some moderately priced hotels along the way (along with some guest houses masquerading under the name "hotel," but none the worse for that)—and we offer some top picks here. These offer lovely surroundings, excellent value, and a human-scale experience of London. As for bargains, needless to say, B&Bs and hostels will help salvage your budget. Bed-and-breakfasts in London are likely to fall significantly short of your aspirations of chintz, flowers, and plump matrons stuffing you with yummy food. On many occasions, you're more likely to find damp, dim, and dingy rooms and breakfasts of rolls and tea. Furthermore, finding a tolerable double room for less than £45 a night will be a coup; your best bet is to look around **Bloomsbury,** the streets around **Victoria** and **King's Cross** stations, the more attractive **Earl's Court,** and **Notting Hill Gate.** Even many of the hostels charge up to £20 for a dorm bed in a room crammed with nine other people. Winner of the "too good to be true—there must be a catch" category, **Tonbridge School Club** (120 Cromer St., WC1, tel. 020/7837–4406, fax 020/7278–7738), near King's Cross Station, provides safe, Spartan dormitory-style accommodation, along with showers, luggage storage, and use of a kitchen for a mere £5 per night. The catches: Your mattress is on the floor of the karate club gym. You're getting no more than what you pay for, but the atmosphere is kind and welcoming. Catch number two is that you must show a foreign passport, check in between 10 PM and midnight, abide by the midnight curfew, and check out by 9:30 AM. Understandably, the club's 50 beds are in high demand, especially during the summer months, so call ahead.

Your cheapest option is a dorm bed in a hostel or B&B for as little as £60–£100 per week. During summer, most places stop offering a weekly rate and charge a straight £15–£25 per night for a dorm bed. University residence halls (*see* Student Housing, *below*) also offer a cheap alternative but can be dodgy in standard. Reserve as far in advance as possible for all types of lodging from June through August—March is not too early. Reservations usually require a credit card number or a deposit for the first night. When making arrangements, be sure to inquire if the university residence hall has a minimum stay (many halls require at least a 3-night booking) and if they accept nonstudents (many do).

If you do arrive without reservations, the **Tourist Information Centre** on Victoria Station forecourt (look up and follow the signs) offers an accommodation booking service (tel. 020/7824–8844) and sells the handy *Where to Stay and What to Do in London* guide (£4.99), which lists hundreds of B&Bs and hotels throughout the city. They can book a bed in the £15–£25 range for a £5 fee and, rest assured, all accommodations are inspected—although we might want to put that between quote marks—before going into their books. They have other locations at Heathrow Airport and at the Liverpool Street station. There are also lodging hustlers in Victoria Station hoping to whisk you from the station to a local hotel via their free van service. Beware: It's generally best to avoid these vultures altogether.

HOTELS AND B&BS

AROUND VICTORIA STATION

The area around Victoria Station—including the neighborhoods of **Belgravia, Pimlico,** and **Westminster**—has a billion cheapish hotels, all of which make their living off this mammoth, sprawling terminal/bus depot/tube station. The farther from the station you go, the cheaper rooms become. B&B owners here compete fiercely for customers, so if you are willing to bargain, you could get cheaper rates, especially during the off-season and/or if you agree to stay more than a few nights. You might even try to walk down one of the main budget hotel drags, like **Belgrave Road, Ebury Road,** or **Warwick Way,** offer everybody £10 less than they're asking, and see who makes the best counteroffer.

UNDER £40 • Georgian House Hotel. You may be exhausted from a long journey and heavy luggage, but it's worth the final effort to climb to the top of this hotel. There are five bargain rooms on the fourth floor, a single at £23, double £36, triple £56, and quad at £62. Prices increase in the more accessible parts of the building: singles at £46, doubles £62, and triples £75, all with bath or shower rooms en suite and TVs. English breakfast is served in a pretty room opening onto a tiny garden. (Try asking about the hotel annex where you might get a basic room at a knockdown price). *35 St. George's Dr., SW1, tel. 020/ 7834–1438, fax 020/7976–6085. Tube: Victoria. Walk south on Buckingham Palace Rd., turn left on Elizabeth Bridge. (past Eccleston Square it becomes St. George's Dr.). 29 rooms, all with bath or shower rooms en suite.*

Limegrove Hotel. While this minuscule guest house can't offer much in the way of beauty or luxury, it handsomely compensates with friendly, caring management. Some rooms have been renovated, while others are a bit run down; all come with a TV. Singles are £28, doubles £38, triples £48—your double or triple can come with a shower room en suite if you add another £10 or £15 to the bill. English breakfast is served in your room. *101 Warwick Way, SW1, tel. 020/7828–0458. Tube: Victoria. Walk SE on Wilton Rd., turn right on Warwick Way. 18 rooms, 2 with shower rooms en suite. No credit cards.*

UNDER £50 • Cherry Court Hotel. If you have ever imagined an adorable family-run guest house where nothing is too much trouble for the proprietors, then look no further. Mr. and Mrs. Patel are proud to welcome you to their small, quiet, and albeit rather basic hotel. There's a walled garden at the back where you can sit out under parasols (if it's ever warm enough). Singles are £30–£40, doubles £45 with an en suite shower and one tiny triple goes for £65. A continental breakfast including fresh fruit is served in the rooms. *23 Hugh St., SW1, tel. 020/7828–2840, fax 020/7828–0393. Tube: Victoria. Walk south on Buckingham Palace Rd., turn left onto Elizabeth Bridge, turn first left on Hugh St. 11 rooms.*

Luna & Simone Hotel. The hotel has no particular character, but it is certainly modern, clean, and efficient thanks to an overhaul and restructure in 1999. All the rooms have TVs , phones, and hair dryers and the decor is attractive but unimaginative. The management has adopted the continental approach to pricing with three different seasonal rates. The prices quoted show the range—singles are £46–£55, doubles £55–£65 and triples £75–£90. English breakfast is included and there are smoking and no-smoking dining rooms. *47–49 Belgrave Rd., SW1, tel. 020/7834–5897, fax 020/7828–2474. Tube: Victoria. Walk SE on Wilton Rd., turn right on Bridge Pl., left on Belgrave Rd. 36 rooms, 28 with shower room en suite.*

Melita House Hotel. The place was overrun with builders and decorators in 1999, but since they were improving on an already comfortable little hotel, expect the results to be excellent. (With any luck they will have changed the lethargic reception staff as well!) The rooms are painted blue and have attractive curtains and bedspreads. Singles cost £45–£55, doubles £70–£85, triples £85–£90, quads £95–£110. English breakfast is included. *33–35 Charlwood St., SW1, tel. 020/7828–0471, fax 020/7932–0988. Tube: Victoria. Walk SE on Wilton Rd., turn right on Bridge Pl., left on Belgrave Rd., right on Charlwood St. 20 rooms, 16 with shower or shower/toilet cubicles.*

UNDER £60 • Collin House. There's no great feature of this hotel, but if you want a clean, plain, no-nonsense, comfortable hotel in a convenient location then this is ideal. Singles cost £48 with shower room en suite, doubles £62 and £73 with a shower room en suite. There is one triple, which costs £90; every room has a basin , a wood-framed bed and landscape photographs on the walls. English breakfast is included. *104 Ebury St., SW1, tel. and fax 020/7730–8031. Tube: Victoria. Walk south on Buckingham Palace Rd., turn right on Eccleston St., left on Ebury St. 13 rooms, 8 with shower room en suite. No credit cards.*

Lime Tree Hotel. You'll pay a little bit more than the other hotels on Ebury Street to stay here, but it is that bit different. The rooms are beautifully decorated and the bathrooms are done up with mirrors and marble. Breakfast is served among lime tree murals in a charming dining room that opens onto a rose garden. As a testament to the standard of the hotel, there are gifts from regular visitors dotted about the dining room. The building is listed Grade II of special architectural and/or historical interest. Singles are £70, doubles £95–£105, triples £130 and quads £150. All rooms have private bathrooms, TVs, phones, safe-boxes and tea/coffee-making facilities. *135-137 Ebury St., Belgravia. tel. 020/7730–8191, fax 020/ 7730–7865. Tube: Victoria. Walk south on Buckingham Palace Rd., turn right on Eccleston St., left on Ebury St. 25 rooms, all with bath.*

UNDER £75 • Lynton House Hotel. Don't be put off by the forbidding black door as it's always opened with a great welcome, and once inside you're in a cozy safe-haven a world away from bustling Victoria. Mary Batey charges £35–£55 for single rooms and £60–£75 for double rooms equipped with TVs and washbasins. There's a small common terrace and excellent security, and English breakfast is included. Do ask for deals on apartments for four people next door. *113 Ebury St., SW1, tel. 020/7730– 4032, fax 020/7730–9848. Tube: Victoria. Walk south on Buckingham Palace Rd., turn right on Eccleston St., left on Ebury St. 12 rooms, 2 with shower cubicles. No credit cards.*

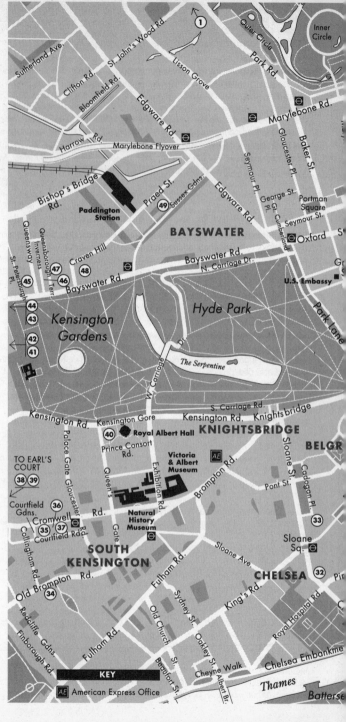

KEY

AE American Express Office

36

St. Athans
Hotel, **12**

St. Charles
Hotel, **47**

St. Margaret's
Hotel, **17**

Swiss House, **34**

Thanet, **18**

Tonbridge School
Club, **9**

Vicarage, **41**

Wilbraham
Hotel, **33**

Willet Hotel, **32**

Windermere
Hotel, **28**

Melbourne House Hotel. The service is efficient and cooperative, if somewhat charmless on occasions. The management make the kind gesture of holding your luggage if you go for a jaunt in the country or pop over to Paris. Rooms are clean and mostly no-smoking. Singles cost £30–£50, doubles are £70 and one triple is priced at £95. The two-room family suite for four is £110. The rooms generally have either shower rooms or bathrooms en suite, except for two single rooms that share a bathroom (£30). All rooms come equipped with TVs, tea/coffee-making facilities, and telephones. English breakfast is included. *79 Belgrave Rd., Victoria, SW1, tel. 020/7828–3516, fax 020/7828–7120. Tube: Victoria. Walk SE on Wilton Rd., turn right on Bridge Pl., left on Belgrave Rd. or Tube: Pimlico. Exit tube and turn right, look for mini roundabout and turn right onto Belgrave Rd. 17 rooms, 14 with shower rooms en suite, and 1 with bathroom en suite.*

UNDER £85 • Windermere Hotel. A two-minute walk from Victoria, this white stucco house is one of the smarter hotels in the area. There's a very professional attitude among the staff and the service is excellent. A great deal of effort has gone into the restaurant, which offers very good deals for hotel residents. The top-floor rooms have great views over the rooftops of London for £99. A basic single runs £64–£77 and doubles are £75–£93. Triples with en suite facilities are £125 and quads £135. English breakfast is included. *142–144 Warwick Way, SW1, tel. 020/7834–5163 or 020/7834–5480, fax 020/7630–8831. Tube: Victoria. Walk SE on Wilton Rd., turn right on Warwick Way. 23 rooms, 19 with bathrooms or shower rooms en suite.*

UNDER £95 • Wilbraham Hotel. There is a certain Agatha Christie quality about this stately galleon moored discreetly close to Sloane Square. The hotel is old fashioned and a bastion of British understatement. You'll be in the heart of smart London and close to superb restaurants and the financial dangers of shopping in Harrods Knightsbridge! At least half the rooms have been redecorated, but in keeping with the prevailing Victorian style. Doubles are £85–£98, triples £105 and quads £130. Note: overheard in the bar—"The Wilbraham has become just like home since we sold the house in Chelsea." *1–5 Wilbraham Place, Victoria, SW1, tel. 020/7730–8296, fax 020/7730–6815. Tube: Sloane Square. Cross the square to Sloane St., walk up to the second turn on the right. 53 rooms, 40 with bath en suite. 24-hr room service.*

Willett Hotel. An elegant Victorian town house hides the well-kept secret of the Willett Hotel. As you walk down the tree-lined street you wouldn't know it wasn't a private house. The hotel has all the facilities you would expect for the price including Sky TV, complimentary newspapers, and breakfast in bed. If you've been roughing it for a while, a night of luxury might just be deserved. Singles are £65, doubles £89–£99. *32 Sloane Gardens, SW1, tel. 020/7824–8415, fax 020/7730–4830. Tube: Sloane Square. Exit and turn right, take right-hand fork into Sloane Gardens. 19 rooms, all with bath.*

BAYSWATER, NOTTING HILL GATE, AND KENSINGTON

The selections here range from Bayswater—a budgeter's heaven—to Kensington, one of London's poshest neighborhoods. Bars and cheap eateries in Bayswater cater to the budget and middlebrow travelers who pack the neighborhood's innumerable hotels. Notting Hill is one of London's hottest neighborhoods, a fave for London's hip youth. **Queensway,** perpendicular to Notting Hill Gate and Bayswater, is a party-hearty tourist strip lined with pubs blaring "You Shook Me All Night Long" and other sing-along favorites. Luckily, the more sedate environments of Hyde Park and Kensington Gardens are just across Bayswater Road. Kensington is loaded with great shops, restaurants, pretty streets, and some nice splurge hotels.

UNDER £45 • Hyde Park House. The Hyde is one of the nicer hotels in the area, close to the Bayswater and Queensway tube stations and a short walk from leafy Hyde Park. It's on a side street, so noise is not a problem, and it is clean, with rooms of varying sizes. Prices have hardly changed for years, but all rooms were redone in a basic style in 1998. Singles cost £28, doubles £40. Continental breakfast is included. *48 St. Petersburgh Pl., W2, tel. 020/7229–9652 or 020/7229–1687. Tube: Queensway. Walk west on Bayswater Rd., turn right on St. Petersburgh Pl. 14 rooms, 1 with bath. No credit cards.*

UNDER £55 • St. Charles Hotel. The hotel has a peaceful and gentle atmosphere and is lovingly run by a quiet elderly lady who won't appreciate revelers, but offers instead an oasis of calm amid the storm of London life. The rooms are immaculate and you can watch TV in a paneled lounge on the ground floor. Singles are £35 and doubles are £49–£54. All rooms will have en suite bathrooms by the summer of 2000. *66 Queensborough Terr., W2 3SH, tel. 020/7221–0022. Tube: Queensway. Head west two blocks on Bayswater Rd, turn left at Queensborough Terr. 17 rooms with shower. No credit cards.*

UNDER £60 • Norfolk Court and St. David's Hotel and Border Hotel. It's hard to keep up with what's going on here because it's expanding and improving at the rate of knots. The manager (Baki) insists that the standard among the rooms is pretty much uniform, but in fact it varies. All three hotels are adjoining and under the same management. The location is good because Norfolk Square is a cul-de-sac so you can enjoy the quiet gardens in the day and sleep in peace at night. Prices are quoted with and without shower and toilet—singles £39–£49, doubles £59–£69, triples £70–£80, quads £80–£90. A famously good English breakfast is included. *16-20 Norfolk Sq., W2, tel. 020/7723–4963, fax 020/7402–9061. Tube: Paddington. Walk north on Praed St., turn right on Norfolk Pl., right on Norfolk Sq. 74 rooms, 30 with shower/bath.*

UNDER £70 • Commodore. This peaceful hotel of three converted Victorian houses is deep in the big leafy square known as Lancaster Gate. A great team of friendly staff will do all they can to help and advise you on making the best of your stay in London. The hotel has an ongoing refurbishment program so it always looks impeccable. Fodor's readers get special rates of a double for £70, triple for £90, quad for £110. When you see how grand the hotel is you'll realize what terrific value these rates are. *50 Lancaster Gate, W2, tel. 020/7402–5291, fax 020/7262–1088. Tube: Lancaster Gate. Exit and turn right, walk west along Bayswater Rd, turn right on Lancaster Gate. 90 rooms with bath.*

Abbey House Hotel. The fresh white paint and plants give the hotel a very clean and airy feel. Rooms are done in pastel colors and Laura Ashley florals. As the location and the building itself are rather salubrious, it comes as no surprise that past owners have included a Member of Parliament and even a Bishop. The staff are extremely helpful and make your stay really special as the thank-you letters they've kept prove. Sadly we are not the first to discover the quality and value here, so book well in advance. English breakfast is included. Singles are £43, doubles £68, a triple £85, and a quad £95. *11 Vicarage Gate, W8, tel. 020/7727–2594. Tube: Kensington High Street. See Vicarage Hotel, below, for directions. 13 rooms without shower.*

Some places may be prepared to drop their rates during the off-season, so try your luck at haggling. On multinight stays, you shouldn't be forced to pay the daily rate if you're staying somewhere for a week or more.

Vicarage. Run by the same family for nearly 30 years, the Vicarage feels like a real home. It's beautifully decorated in a Regency stripe with gilt mirrors. It's quiet and overlooks a garden square near Kensington's main shopping streets. There are some particularly beautiful shops on nearby Kensington Church Street. Expect to pay £43 for a single and £68 for a double. English breakfast is included. *10 Vicarage Gate, W8, tel. 020/7229–4030, fax 020/7792–5989. Tube: High Street Kensington. Walk right on Kensington High St., turn left on Kensington Church St., veer right at fork onto Vicarage Gate. 18 rooms, 2 with shower rooms and toilet en suite. No credit cards.*

UNDER £80 • Gate Hotel. It's the only hotel on Portobello Road and it's a gem! The landlady, a real Londoner if ever you'll meet one, says with pride, "it's my mini five star hotel." She and her husband will do everything to make sure you're comfortable in the tiny rooms and will chat about life over a cup of tea. Breakfast is served in the rooms as there is no space for a dining room; alternatively pop out to the trendy Notting Hill cafés and see if you can bump into Hugh Grant with a cappuccino. Singles cost £45–65, doubles £75–90, triples £84 (the third bed is a foldout). Laundry service is available and there are fridges in the rooms. *6 Portobello Rd., W11, tel. 020/7221–2403, fax 020/7221–9128. Tube: Notting Hill Gate. Walk north on Pembridge Rd., turn left on Portobello Rd. 6 rooms, 5 with bath.*

BLOOMSBURY AND KING'S CROSS

The former stomping ground of the Bloomsbury Group—the famed literary clique that included Virginia Woolf, E. M. Forster, Lytton Strachey, and John Maynard Keynes—is today the stomping ground of thousands of students from the nearby University of London and an equal number of tourists marching toward the British Museum. It is also prime lodging territory: Several student dorms, one great (and one not-so-great) hostel, and dozens of B&Bs line the streets all the way up to King's Cross Station. Try **Cartwright Gardens, Tavistock Place,** or **Gower Street,** if you're having trouble finding a bed for the night. The area around King's Cross Station is busier, noisier, and a touch seedier than Bloomsbury, though **Argyle Street** has some clean budget accommodations.

UNDER £45 • The Alhambra. This hotel is very clean and reliable because Mr. and Mrs. Valoti are in charge! They run the hotel beautifully and are now expanding into more properties across the road, which means they offer three different price ranges. Quoted here is the original Alhambra price list—singles £28–£55, doubles £38–£55, triples £55–£70 and one quad with en suite shower for £85. English breakfast is included. *17–19 Argyle St., WC1, tel. 020/7837–9575, fax 020/7916–2476. Tube: King's Cross. Head west on Euston Rd., turn left on Argyle St. 52 rooms, 15 with shower cubicles or shower rooms en suite.*

Hotel Cavendish. This is a clean, simple, family-run B&B with singles for £32–£36 and doubles for £44–£56, depending on the size of the room. English breakfast is included. The friendly owners will make a full vegetarian breakfast on request. *75 Gower St., WC1, tel. 020/7636–9079, fax 020/7580–3609. Tube: Goodge Street. Turn right on Tottenham Court Rd., quick left on Chenies St., left on Gower St. 22 rooms, none with bath or shower rooms en suite.*

Jesmond Dene Hotel. This is definitely a runaway winner. The whole charming Abela family are involved in making sure the hotel is special and the formula works. The rooms are decorated in daring black and white with pictures of the Hollywood Greats on the walls. The family is always making improvements and the latest is the new reception area. It's a pleasure to stay in a hotel that's so attractive and unusual (just like its owners). Singles cost £28, doubles £35–£55, triples £55–£66, and quads £85—add another £15 and any of these rooms can come with a small shower room en suite. English breakfast is included. Every room has a basin and TV. *27 Argyle St., WC1, tel. 020/7837–4654, fax 020/7833–1633. Tube: King's Cross. Head west on Euston Rd., turn left on Argyle St. 24 rooms, 7 with shower and toilet rooms en suite.*

UNDER £50 • Arosfa Hotel. Mr. and Mrs. Dorta run a perfectly straightforward friendly B&B. They'll give you a warm welcome to the simple rooms and a delicious breakfast. Single rooms are £33, doubles £46, triples £62, and one quad at £84. English breakfast is included. Every room is equipped with a TV and basin. *83 Gower St., WC1, tel. 020/7636–2115. Tube: Goodge Street. Turn left on Tottenham Court Rd., right on Torrington Pl., right on Gower St. 15 rooms, 2 with shower rooms en suite.*

Arran House Hotel. If you have ever made the mistake of thinking one guest house is much like another, then here is the proof of your folly. The bookcase in the lounge is stuffed with English classics, the walls are covered in faded photographs and memorabilia, old cartoons hang everywhere and the garden is a tangle of tumbling roses in the summer. Lovely rooms are very well priced and expect to add another £10 for a spotless en suite bathroom—singles £40, doubles £50, triples £68, quad £74. *77-79 Gower St., WC1, tel. 020/7636–2186, fax 020/7637–1140. Tube Goodge Street. See Arosfa Hotel, above, for directions. 30 rooms, 15 with bath.*

St. Athans Hotel. There are quite a few quirky touches to this hotel, the best of which, if you're on a budget, is that they encourage you to eat as much as you want at breakfast. Pets are welcome and you may end up risking a tenner on the hotel's racehorse St. Athan's Lad, whose pictures are in the hall. The atmosphere is super-relaxed and you wouldn't imagine there could be as many as 50 rooms. Singles are £38–£50, doubles £48–£60, triples £63 or £78, quads £80 or £92, and one room for five at £90. For another £10 or so your room will come with a shower room en suite. English breakfast is included. *20 Tavistock Pl., WC1, tel. 020/7837–9140, fax 020/7833–8352. Tube: Russell Square. Exit station to the left, turn right on Herbrand St., right on Tavistock Pl. 50 rooms, 8 with shower rooms en suite.*

UNDER £60 • Albany Hotel. It's not big and it's not smart, but it is like stumbling into a real home. The rooms are "pretty in pink" and the breakfast room is so warm and welcoming you could easily spend most of the morning there. The proprietor's wife runs a beauty salon at the back of the hotel. Singles are £42, doubles are £54, triple £75. *34 Tavistock Place, WC1, tel. 020/7837–9139, fax 020/7833–0459. Tube: Russell Square. Turn right on Bernard St., left on Marchmont St., right on Tavistock Pl. 11 rooms without bath.*

St. Margaret's Hotel. St. Margaret's may need a bit of a spruce-up, but any shabbiness can easily be overlooked when you meet the bustling Italian landlady who will charm you within minutes. The hotel feels warm and friendly if a little muddled at times, but it all adds to the charm. Another selling point is the size and height of the rooms. Singles cost £46, doubles £58–£74, triples £83–£96 and quads £96–£116; slightly less for multinight stays. English breakfast is included. *26 Bedford Pl., WC1, tel. 020/7636–4277, fax 020/7323–3066. Tube: Russell Square. Exit to left, turn left on Herbrand St., quick right on Guilford St., left on Southampton Row, right on Russell Sq., left on Bedford Pl. 64 rooms, 6 with bath or shower rooms/cubicles en suite. No credit cards.*

UNDER £85 • The Morgan. From the back of this stylish town house on an elegant Georgian street you can look onto the British Museum. The management has struck the perfect balance between professionalism and a relaxed attitude. The attractive rooms are small and functionally furnished and have phones and TVs. The five apartments farther down the street are particularly good deals: three times the size of normal rooms and complete with eat-in kitchens. (An apartment for two is £98 and £135 for three.) The tiny, paneled breakfast room (rates include the meal) seems straight out of a doll's house with cut glass and porcelain flowers displayed in cabinets. Singles are £52, doubles £78, and a triple is available for £115. *24 Bloomsbury St., WC1, tel. 020/7636–3735. Tube: Tottenham Court Rd. Walk east on New Oxford St., left on Bloomsbury St. 21 rooms with bath.*

Thanet Hotel. Even before you've gone inside, the cascading window boxes are a giveaway as to the effort and dedication of the owners, Richard and Lynwen Orchard, to ensuring the highest possible standards. They've gone to a great deal of trouble to preserve the original features of the interior because it's a Grade II listed building. The rooms all have a private shower and toilet, TV, hair dryer, phone, and tea/coffee-making facilities. Single rooms are £62, doubles £80, triples £96, and quads £105. English breakfast is included. *8 Bedford Place, WC1, tel. 020/7636–2869, fax 020/7323–6676. Tube: Russell Square. Exit and turn left on Bernard St., left on Southampton Row (and cross the road), right on Russell St. and right again on Bedford Pl. 16 rooms, all with shower and toilet.*

EARL'S COURT

The area around Earl's Court and Gloucester Road tube stations has the highest concentration of inexpensive lodging in London. Unfortunately, some of the rooms are also the skankiest, though we've picked some real winners for you. If you want to troll the neighborhood for bargains, try **Hogarth Road, Earl's Court Gardens, Penywern Road,** and **Eardley Crescent**; all are chock-full with budget sleeping options. Earl's Court didn't rate too high with Londoners a while ago, but it's definitely on the up in popularity, with a lot of globetrotting Aussies and New Zealanders overnighting in the area. Culturally speaking it is convenient to a number of London's best museums, including the great Victoria and Albert, the Natural History Museum, and the Science Museum.

UNDER £45 • Curzon House Hotel. Courtfield Gardens is a lovely leafy square with an old church in the center, so try to get a room with a view. The exterior may be rather chic, but don't expect the interior to match up by any stretch of the imagination. This place is ideal for the hail and hearty who don't mind sharing their space. Singles cost £33, doubles £40, triples £18 per person, dorms for 4 and 5 cost £16 per person, and there's a few studio apartments. The cheapest rooms have bunk beds and none of the singles or doubles offer en suite facilities. Weekly rates for shared rooms start at £80 and every week after that is £70. There's a kitchen for guests' use and Sky TV and Internet access (for a small fee) in the lounge. The atmosphere is laid back and friendly and almost everyone, including the staff, is young. Look out for Muffin, the hotel cat, who receives mail from all over the world from past guests. Continental breakfast is included. *58 Courtfield Gardens, SW5, tel. 020/7581–2116, fax 020/7835–1319. Tube: Earl's Court. Walk south 2 blocks on Earl's Court Rd., turn left on Barkston Gardens (which becomes Courtfield Gardens). Tube: Gloucester Road. Exit and turn right into Courtfield Rd., second right is Courtfield Gardens. 19 rooms, 10 with shower or bathroom en suite.*

UNDER £55 • Abcone Hotel. It's plain and practical, but extremely clean and feels very spacious. It's the perfect place for a night in London when you need to be organized, perhaps before an early flight or on arrival, because it offers laundry and dry cleaning, secretarial services, can arrange airport transport, etc. What's more it is right by Gloucester Road tube. The high ceiling rooms all have TVs, video and satellite movies, phones, and hair dryers. A single is £45, and a double for £55 seems very reasonable. Continental breakfast is included, but there is a £2.95 supplement for a full English breakfast. *10 Ashburn Gardens, SW7, tel. 020/7460–3400, fax 020/7460–3444. Tube: Gloucester Road. Exit and turn right onto Courtfield Rd., first right again is Ashburn Gardens. 37 rooms, 30 with bath or shower.*

Albert Hotel. The "hotel" is on the impressive avenue of Queens Gate, which runs from Kensington to South Kensington (Gloucester Road is the best tube). A few nights here is the closest you'll get to an English boarding school experience. It's a fabulously fine building with carved staircases and beautiful moldings, but there's linoleum on the floor and the scruffy dorms have a hint of disinfectant about them. The atmosphere is very relaxed and happy-go-lucky; everyone mucks in and has a good time making friends. Rooms come in many shapes and sizes: singles £35, doubles £50, four- to six-person rooms are £16 per person and dorm rooms for 8, 12, and 14 are £13 per person. Beds are given on a first-come, first-served basis. Continental breakfast is included. *191 Queen's Gate, SW7, tel. 020/7584–3019, fax 020/7581–5209. Tube: Gloucester Road. Walk east 1 block on Cromwell Rd., turn left on Queen's Gate. 30 rooms, 22 with shower rooms en suite; 39 dorm beds.*

UNDER £65 • Philbeach Hotel. This friendly and eccentric hotel has been building up a reputation over the last 20 years and is now firmly established as London's most celebrated gay hotel. It's part of a sweeping crescent of white houses and has a pretty walled garden where you can join in the summer cocktail parties. Both Jimmy's bar and the French-style restaurant called 'Wilde about Oscar' are independently successful and characterful. The rooms are beautifully decorated in deep Victorian colors and singles are £45–£55, doubles £60–£80. Continental breakfast is included. *30–31 Philbeach Gar-*

dens, SW5, tel. 020/7373–1244 or 020/7373–4544, fax 020/7244–0149. Tube: Earl's Court. Use Warwick Rd. Exit and turn right, cross the road and first turn left onto Philbeach Gardens. 35 rooms, 18 with shower room or bath en suite.

UNDER £75 • Swiss House. Trailing ivy and hanging baskets on the portico of this Victorian town house lend it a charm all its own. The staff is delightfully kind and you're sure to like the attractive rooms. Pine furnishings and the breakfast room's dresser of blue and white china and dried flowers make the hotel seem like a misplaced country cottage. It's a very special little place so do book well in advance. All rooms have TV and phone. Singles are £37 with shower, doubles start at £66 and are £73 with shower and toilet, triples are £83, and a quad is £93. Continental breakfast is included, or pay a £5 supplement for an English breakfast. *171 Old Brompton Rd., SW5, tel. 020/7373–2769 or 020/7370–6364, fax 020/7373–4983. Tube: South Kensington. Follow the Old Brompton Rd., south 500 yards on the left. 15 rooms with bath.*

UNDER £90 • Mayflower Hotel. The granite and marble reception area may be a bit harsh, but the pride of this hotel is its friendly and efficient staff. The rooms are individually decorated and equipped with everything you might need, but without frills. A single room is £69 and a double is £89. If this is beyond your budget, ask about the Court apartments, which if shared by four people can work out as a great deal. They have immaculate Bosch kitchens with washing machines and dryers, ironing boards, etc. A one-bedroom apartment, with a double sofa bed in the sitting room, can easily be shared by four and is £109 (£150 for the luxury version). A standard two-bedroom apartment is £139. *26-28 Trebovir Rd., SW5, tel. 020/7370–0991, fax 020/7370–0994. Tube: Earl's Court. Exit at the Earl's Court Rd. exit and turn left, first left is Trebovir Rd. 48 rooms, 46 with shower/bath. 35 apartments.*

UNDER £170 • Forum Hotel. The price is steep, but you might be grateful in a pinch; with this impersonal hotel's 900 rooms, you shouldn't have a problem getting a room. Singles are £145 and doubles are £165. *97 Cromwell Rd., SW7, tel. 020/7370–5757, fax 020/7370–1448. Tube: Gloucester Road. The hotel is literally behind the tube station, so exit and turn right and right again.*

NORTH LONDON

For a taste of bohemian suburbia (i.e., nice neighborhoods with cool cafés) and a less-touristy atmosphere than Earl's Court or Bayswater, try the neighborhoods north of central London, which roughly encompass the massive expanse of trees, ponds, and rolling hills known as the Heath. You may have to sit on the tube an few extra stops or even catch a bus to central London, but that's the price you pay for a quieter, more residential quarter for your London home-away-from-home. Hotel rates are about the same in north London as in most other areas, but you're more likely to get what you pay for here.

If you want a taste of English country–style living, contact the **Primrose Hill Agency** (14 Edis St., NW1 8LG, tel. 020/7722–6869, fax 020/7916–2240), a small B&B association that believes that "travel shouldn't be a rip-off." To prove it, they book guests into beautiful family homes in or around leafy Primrose Hill and Hampstead at reasonable rates—approximately £35 per person, with a minimum three-night stay. Expect cozy rooms, your own latchkey, and scrumptious breakfasts. Speak with Gail O'Farrell, who will adroitly find just the right place given your needs and preferences.

UNDER £35 • Five Kings Guest House. Although the neighborhood is quintessentially residential, you're only 15 minutes by foot from both Camden and The Heath. The friendly proprietors run a tight ship and offer nothing fancy. Singles are £20, doubles £32, with another £8 getting you a shower/toilet en suite. English breakfast is included. *59 Anson Rd., Kentish Town, N7, tel. 020/7607–3996 or 020/7607–6466. Tube: Tufnell Park. Turn left on Brecknock Rd., left on Anson Rd. 16 rooms, 7 with shower/toilet en suite.*

UNDER £50 • Kandara Guest House. The main reason to stay here is location—just a short bus ride from the heart of lively Islington, which has become super trendy. Loads of great eateries have opened and there is a vibe on the street. The guest house is small, tidy, no-smoking and on a quiet road. Singles are £35, doubles £47. English breakfast is included. *68 Ockendon Rd., Islington, N1, tel. 020/7226–5721 or 020/7226–3379. Tube: Angel. From station, take Bus 38, 56, 73, or 171A northeast on Essex Rd. to Ockendon Rd. 10 rooms, without bath.*

Oxford Arms. This traditional pub and inn is the place to stay if you want a neighborhood atmosphere and easy access to local brew. (The landlady can sound a bit sharp, but the bark is worst than the bite.) The double rooms (£45) are equipped with showers and toilets. All rooms have TVs and tea/coffee-making equipment. There's no cooked breakfast but there's always self-service cold cereal. *21 Halliford St., Islington, N1, tel. 020/7226–6629, fax 020/7226–5302. Tube: Angel. From station, take Bus 38, 56, 73, or 171A NE up Essex Rd. to Halliford St. 5 rooms.*

HOSTELS

England's **Youth Hostel Association (YHA)** (tel. 020/7248–6547 or fax 020/7236–7681 for reservations) operates seven hostels in central London (some are more central than others). These Formica-and-linoleum wonders tend to be clean to the point of sterility: Even if the outside looks cool, it's a safe bet that the rooms are basic and bland and packed to the rafters with space-age bunk beds. None of the three YHA hostels listed below has a lockout, and the reception desks are usually open daily 7 AM–11 PM, though some provide 24-hour access. Purchase a YHA membership card at any hostel for £9.50, or pay an extra £1.55 per night for a guest stamp; after accruing six stamps you're granted full membership. **Astor Hostels** (tel. 020/7229–7866, fax 020/7727–8106), a private hostel firm, runs four places in London that cater to international budget travelers. Astor also provides free Continental breakfasts of cereal, rolls, and tea or coffee. Wherever you stay, reservations are *imperative* June through August, particularly if you want a single or double room in one of the few hostels that offer such things (many are booked solid for summer by the end of May). Unless otherwise noted, the non-YHA hostels listed below do not have curfews or lockouts and are open 24 hours for check-in.

Some London B&Bs also offer dorm-style accommodations in addition to their more expensive private rooms. B&Bs can be a welcome respite from snoring bunk mates, noisy school groups, and 8 AM wake-up calls.

City of London Hostel (YHA). Formerly the home of the St. Paul's boys choir, this hostel has a great location in the middle of town. Unfortunately, it has zip for character. Even so, it's a popular option for the middle-aged hostel set. Dorm beds cost £19.70 per person in a dorm for 10–15 people, £22.15 with 5–8 beds, £23.30 with 3–4 beds, £25.40 for a double and £36 for a single room. English breakfast is included. *36–38 Carter La., EC4, tel. 020/7236–4965, fax 020/7236–7681. Tube: Blackfriars or St. Paul's. From Blackfriars, walk east on Queen Victoria St., turn left on St. Andrew's Hill, right on Carter La. From St. Paul's, follow signs to cathedral, cross in front of cathedral entrance to Dean's Ct., turn right on Carter La. 191 beds. Laundry.*

The Generator. This hostel is easily the grooviest in town, with a friendly, funky vibe, lots of young people, and vibrant decor—blue neon and brushed-steel decor downstairs and upstairs dorm rooms painted in bright blue and orange. The corridors can be described as "space age" or "prisonlike" (after all it is an ex–police station). The Generator Bar (open 6 PM–2 AM) has cheap drinks, and the Fuel Stop cafeteria provides inexpensive meals. Rooms are simple but clean; singles £38, twins £26 per person, dorm beds £20.50–£22, depending on the number of beds in the room. Note that if you are traveling alone you have to take a single room; dorm beds are for groups who know each other already. Prices drop by a few pounds October–March. The luggage storage is open 24 hours a day with video surveillance inside. Continental breakfast is included. *MacNaghten House, Compton Pl., WC1, tel. 020/7388–7666, fax 020/7388–7644. Tube: Russell Square. Turn right on Bernard St., left on Marchmont St., right on Tavistock Pl., left on Compton Pl., which looks like a tiny alley. 900 beds.*

Holland House Youth Hostel (YHA). This hostel is one of the most famous in the world: It incorporates part of a fabled Jacobean mansion, and it's set right in the middle of woodsy Holland Park. Unfortunately, it's also a hike from the nearest tube station. For £19.45 per person you can take a spot in the 12–20-bed dorm rooms. English breakfast is included. *Holland Walk, Kensington, W8, tel. 020/7937–0748, fax 020/7376–0667. Tube: High Street Kensington or Holland Park. From High Street Kensington, walk west on Kensington High St., turn right on Holland Walk; or take Bus 9, 9A, 10, 27, 28, or 49 west to Commonwealth Institute, then walk north on Holland Walk. From Holland Park, walk east on Holland Park Ave., turn right on Holland Walk. 201 beds. Kitchen, laundry.*

Oxford Street (YHA). The big draw at this hostel is its location: smack in the center of hip Soho. It's so convenient (imagine staggering home from the pubs instead of dealing with the tube), you won't mind the cramped rooms. You'll also battle hordes of other backpackers who want to stay here, so make reservations. Beds go for £19.50, except the doubles, which go for £21 per person, regardless of age. All rooms are doubles, triples, or quads. On site are a bureau de change and a TV lounge. *14 Noel St., W1, tel. 020/7734–1618, fax 020/7734–1657. Tube: Oxford Circus. Walk east on Oxford St., turn right on Poland St., left on Noel St. 76 beds. Kitchen.*

Palace Hotel. There's nothing palatial about this setup; in fact it's about as scruffy as they come, but the atmosphere is friendly and everyone gets along really well. You can share the messy kitchen, watch TV in the shabby chairs, and sleep in sagging bunks, and definitely have a bundle of laughs with a fun bunch of fellow travelers. The tacky but convenient Queensway is nearby and you can easily escape into

Kensington Gardens for peace and quiet. Beds in the six- to eight-bed dorms are £12. If there is space, they may offer a weekly rate of £65, however this goes up in the summer depending on bookings. Continental breakfast is included. Reservations are strongly recommended, especially June–August. The building is open 24 hours a day. (Note: do not confuse this hotel with the seedy Palace Court Hotel.) *50 Inverness Terrace, W2, tel. 020/7221–5628. Tube: Queensway. Walk east on Bayswater Rd., turn second left onto Inverness Terrace. 120 beds.*

STUDENT HOUSING

Many university residence halls earn some extra pounds by throwing their doors open to backpackers and other travelers during school vacations. Life in college dorms will introduce you to young expatriates, but the most significant advantage is location: Student housing is often in northwest Bloomsbury, an easy 10-minute walk from London's West End. Though the dorms can be Spartan, they're usually much cleaner than cheap hotels, and you get access to such amenities as tennis courts, laundry rooms, kitchens, gyms, and cheap eats at the university pubs and cafeterias. These places fill up fast in summer, and reservations are a must.

As noted above, when making reservations, be sure to inquire if the university residence hall has a required minimum stay and if they accept nonstudents. If you're having trouble finding space in one of the following student dorms, contact the **Vacation Bureau at King's College** (127 Stamford St., SE1, tel. 020/7928–3777). It offers bed and breakfast in six halls around central London, during April and June–September. Rates are £17–£23. There's no minimum stay, and a 10% discount by the week. Unless otherwise specified, the following dorms rent available space year-round.

Campbell House. Students love to complain, so the reports are that the rooms are terrible, but in fact they aren't too bad. Some are large and have fireplaces (not for use), and those in the back overlook a private terrace and garden. Kitchen facilities make this somewhere you could settle in for a while. Singles cost £16.25 nightly, £99 weekly; doubles are £29 nightly, £190 weekly. *5–10 Taviton St., WC1, tel. 020/7391–1479, fax 020/7388–0060. Tube: Euston Square. Walk east on Euston Rd., turn right on Gordon St., left on Endsleigh Gardens, right on Taviton St. 100 rooms, none with bath or shower rooms en suite. Kitchen, laundry. No credit cards.*

College Hall. This hall in the center of London's student ghetto gives you easy access to university pubs and facilities—it's across the street from the student union and just down the block from Dillon's bookstore. Rates are £20 with breakfast, £25 with breakfast and dinner. There's a library and TV room. Smoking is not allowed. You'll be lucky to get a place here as groups often book months in advance. *Malet St., WC1, tel. 020/7580–9131, fax 020/7636–6591. Tube: Goodge Street or Russell Square. From Goodge St., turn left on Tottenham Court Rd., right on Torrington Pl., right on Malet St. From Russell Square, walk SW across square to Montague Pl., turn right on Malet St. 200 rooms, none with bath or shower rooms en suite. Laundry. No credit cards.*

International Student House. This fun, monstrously huge establishment sits at the southeast corner of Regent's Park, right across from Great Portland Street tube station.Despite its size, this place fills up fast with international students, and reservations are almost obligatory . A dorm bed in a clean three- or four-bunk room costs £17.50; a bed in an "economy" dorm with six or more beds is £9.99. Singles with facilities are £30, and twins are £21 per person. The best deal, is for stays of three months or longer: If you pay in advance for an entire month, a dorm bed costs a mere £42 a week without breakfast. A single will be £98 a week for the first 4 weeks and from then on £83.30. Continental breakfast is included. On site are a fitness center, bar, cyber-café and restaurant. *229 Great Portland St., W1, tel. 020/7631–8300, fax 020/7631–8315. Tube: Great Portland Street. 800 short-term beds. Laundry.*

FOOD

Once upon a time, eating in London was an experience to be endured rather than enjoyed. Not anymore. Today, the city has the most talked-about dining scene in Europe and the newer-than-now-*nouvelle*-spin of Modern British Cuisine is trickling way down the scale: Pub grub is even getting a full-blown renaissance, thanks to some hot new "gastro-pubs." Pennypackers can always find yummy fish-and-chips, or bangers and mash (sausages and mashed potatoes), or any other of the other indigenous options in British budgetland, but now there's numerous exotic options as well. Diets are changing, as health consciousness replaces the Church of England—by now good sandwich bars are more ubiquitous in central London than the old greasy spoons! Quite a few former greasy spoons have taken to opening evenings, wearing tablecloths, and serving, say, the owners' native Thai food.

Indeed, a Londoner with *nouse* (British for savvy), when starving and not rich, always heads to the city's fabulous ethnic eateries—there's an endless array, one of the benefits of London's having been an imperial capital with far-flung dominions. Italian, Continental, and Middle Eastern restaurants are ubiquitous; other regional feathers flock together in particular parts of London. Wander along **Gerrard Street** (Tube: Leicester Square), in Soho, and enter a Hong Kong street scene with crates of fresh produce, skinned ducks hanging in shop windows, and the omnipresent aroma of yesterday's fish. Bustling later into the night than other eateries are the Middle Eastern places along **Edgware Road** (Tube: Edgware Rd.).You'll find Bengali on the East End's **Brick Lane** (Tube: Aldgate East), Indian on Bloomsbury's **Drummond Street** (Tube: Euston Square), and Vietnamese on **Lisle Street** (Tube: Piccadilly Circus).

In all, there are more than 8,000 restaurants in London, many serving so-called British cuisine. Though the phrase "traditional English food" can mean a stale shepherd's pie, greasy sausages, and soggy peas, it can also mean a delicate seafood dinner that even a gourmet would approve of. Saving your pennies by living on bread and butter should entitle you to a little caviar every so often—so we list several jacket-and-tie splurge places to treat yourself with.

Overall, London *is* expensive. The cheapest sit-down meals cost at least £4, more likely £6–£9, and if you want any sort of ambience, you'll pay £8–£14. Usually the 17.5% VAT (Value Added Tax) is already included in the prices, but you may want to check the menu just to be sure. Some restaurants also include a mandatory service charge; inspect the bill to avoid paying twice. Otherwise, the standard tip is 10%. In the end, any lengthy stay in London requires a strategy for eating on the cheap—like making lunch the biggest meal of the day to take advantage of discounted lunch specials. The city's pubs typically serve soups and sandwiches for less than £5, and fish-and-chips or steak and peas for £4–£7. If you can't afford to eat out all the time, acquaint yourself with ubiquitous department store **Marks & Spencer** (*see* Clothing *in* Shopping, *below*), which sells surprisingly yummy and diverse prepared meals at decent prices. A good and relatively inexpensive grocery chain is **Tesco**, with convenient locations at 21 Bedford Street in Covent Garden and 224 Portobello Road in Notting Hill. You'll also find chains like **Safeway** and **Sainsbury's** all over town. Most of London's neighborhoods also have regular fruit and vegetable markets with great deals on fresh produce (*see* Street Markets *in* Shopping, *below*).

BAYSWATER AND NOTTING HILL GATE
Bayswater is crowded with kebab joints, fish-and-chip shops (chippies), and delis. Good restaurants are a bit thin on the ground here, and those in the know join British trendsetters in Notting Hill Gate, which is a cut above Bayswater when it comes to food.

UNDER £10 • Calzone. This is the original branch, but because it's so good three more have sprung up in the blink of an eye. (The latest one is at 335 Fulham Road, tel. 020/7352–9797.) Sporting crisp modern decor and great views out onto busy Kensington Park Road, Calzone is a great place to people-watch over yummy pizzas or calzones. The selections come with a great combination of toppings and the salads are good, too. Tables are cramped so it's best to dine in twos or fours. Most pies cost around £6. *2A Kensington Park Rd, W11, tel. 020/7243–2003. Tube: Notting Hill Gate. Walk west on Notting Hill Gate and turn right onto Pembridge Rd.*

Churchill Thai Kitchen. Unlikely as it sounds, this excellent Thai restaurant is hidden in an enclosed patio of tangled greenery at the rear of a traditional British pub. Faves include spicy *khao rad na ga prao* (rice with a choice of chicken, prawn, or meat sauce) or *kwaitiew pad thai* (Thai noodles with prawns). The more prawns, the pricier. *Churchill Arms, 119 Kensington Church St., W8, tel. 020/7727–1246. Tube: Notting Hill Gate. Walk east on Notting Hill Gate, turn right on Kensington Church St.*

Geales. The purveyor of the best fish and chips in London is a hotly contested title and everyone will have their favorite in the race. Geales has been in the business for over 50 years and is a firm believer in cooking fish in beef dripping—guaranteed you'll be surprised how good it is. The homemade fish soup makes an excellent appetizer; follow it with a small fillet of haddock, plaice, or cod. A main course is not cheap at around £9. *2 Farmer's St., W8, tel. 020/7727–7969. Tube: Notting Hill Gate. Walk west on Notting Hill Gate, turn left on Farmer St. Closed Sun.–Mon.*

Magic Wok. Sure, you can eat sweet and sour chicken here, but why bother when you can experiment? This unassuming place is known for some of the most authentic pan-Chinese food in the city, allowing you to try such specialties as deep-fried crispy hog intestines, hog's trotters, ox tripe, jellyfish and—will you live to tell?—deep-fried fox leg with chili and garlic. Proving the city is full of nutters, this place is usually packed so do book ahead. *100 Queensway, W2, tel. 020/7792–9767. Tube: Bayswater or Queensway.*

Manzara. This place doubles as a pâtisserie in the early hours, but come noon, the kitchen kicks into high gear and starts serving good-size portions of tasty Turkish food like grilled lamb with pine nuts on hummus and grilled chicken skewers with rice. The set lunch costs £6.85. After 7 PM, indulge in their buffet, where you can help yourself from a traditional Turkish hotplate. Manzara serves food until midnight, which is ideal if you've been to a movie at Whiteleys. *24 Pembridge Rd., W11, tel. 020/7727–3062. Tube: Notting Hill Gate. Walk north on Pembridge Rd.*

Norman's. This neighborhood spot serves up simple café food in a friendly environment—the kind of place where diners at different tables strike up conversations with one another. Enjoy full English breakfasts and staples like omelets with chips, sandwiches, or spaghetti bolognese. *7 Porchester Gardens, W2, tel. 020/7727–0278. Tube: Bayswater. Walk north on Queensway, turn left on Porchester Gardens.*

Paradise by Way of Kensal Green. A converted Victorian pub, this spot is a bit off the main drag but is worth hunting out—it's got superb-value Modern Brit dishes and a lively clientele of music-industry mavens, to boot. Roast cod with green salsa and saffron mash or rack of organic lamb with an herb and garlic crust are two top choices *and* everything comes in generous portions. Vegetarian dishes are also highly rated. *19 Kilburn La., W10, tel. 020/8969–0098. Tube: Notting Hill Gate. Then take Bus 52 and get off at the stop after Sainsbury's supermarket.*

UNDER £25 • The Cow. Sir Terrence Conran's son, Tom, owns this tiny and chic gastro-pub that consistently attracts hordes of the local fabulous people. A faux-Dublin backroom bar serves up oysters, crab salad, and pasta with wine; upstairs, a serious chef whips up Tuscan/British specialties—skate poached in minestrone is one temptation. It's low-key until you get the bill and then you know it's a lot more gastro than pub. *89 Westbourne Park Rd., W2, tel. 020/7221–0021. Tube: Notting Hill Gate or Westbourne Park. From Westbourne Park station, turn right, walk down Great Western Rd., turn left at Westbourne Park Rd., and head for right-hand side. Open Mon.–Sat. 7 PM–midnight, Sun. 12:30–5.*

Halepi. It's probably best to come here for dinner because the wooden interior is dark and cozy. Greek specialties like moussaka and dolmades go for around £7. The fish is always cooked to perfection and is brought in daily, depending on the weather. The restaurant will celebrate 40 years of success in 2002, and is the favorite of a certain British balloonist. *18 Leinster Terrace, W2. tel. 020/7262–1070. Tube: Queensway. Walk east on Bayswater Rd and take third left into Leinster Terrace.*

Prince Bonaparte. This is one of the gastro-pubs drawing the crowds (and why not—food is great but prices are gentle, since there's no restaurant-scale overhead). Forget bangers and mash: here you'll get blackened salmon with refried beans, a toffee pudding, and a wide range of beers. Singles take over during the week, young families move in on the weekends. As the night wears on, the place—accented with large windows, church pews, and farmhouse tables—becomes a lively pre-club stop (complete with thumping music on weekends). *80 Chepstow Rd., W2, tel. 020/7229–5912. Tube: Notting Hill Gate or Westbourne Park. From the latter, turn right out of station, head down Great Western Rd, then left on Chepstow Rd. Open Mon., Wed.–Sun. noon–11, Tues. 5–11. No credit cards.*

BLOOMSBURY

Once London's literary slum, Bloomsbury is now better known for its thriving Asian and Indian communities. **Drummond Street,** in particular, is lined with east Indian curry houses and southern Indian vegetarian restaurants. Bloomsbury is also home to the original **Wagamama** (*see* Soho and Mayfair, *below*), if you need your ramen fix.

UNDER £5 • Anwars. Super-low prices make this simple canteen especially popular with students from nearby colleges. Though the interior has seen better days (the 1970s, by the looks of things), the prices are right: You can get a bowl of chicken or meat curry or a yummy mutton biryani for around £3. *64 Grafton Way, W1, tel. 020/7387–6664. Tube: Warren Street. Walk south on Tottenham Court Rd., turn right on Grafton Way.*

Coffee Gallery. What a perfect spot to rest your weary limbs after a day of coursing through the glorious British Museum. The café is perhaps known for its lovely teatime goodies like chocolate cake or plum tart. However, don't overlook the Italian lunchtime specials and the huge sandwiches with imaginative fillings are £3. The interior is homey and cheerful. *23 Museum St., WC1, tel. 020/7436–0455. Holborn Tube. Walk north on Southampton Row, turn left onto Vernon Pl., which becomes Bloomsbury Way, and turn right on Museum St. Closed Sun.*

Diwana Bhel Poori House. They serve up fresh southern Indian (read: vegetarian) cuisine on big plates at Diwana. Try the *thali*, a set meal with rice, dal, vegetables, chapatis, and pooris, or come between noon and 2:30 daily for their all-you-can-eat buffet (£4). BYOB. There are also some vegan dishes. *121–123 Drummond St., NW1, tel. 020/7387–5556. Tube: Euston. Walk right on Melton St., turn left on Drummond St.*

Greenhouse. This subterranean veggie heaven is beneath the Drill Hall, a gay and lesbian theater and cultural center, and gets quite crowded just before performances. Main courses like lentil stew with rice or pasta with veggies change daily. Greenhouse is "womyn only" on Monday nights, and always no-smoking. (Don't confuse this with the Greenhouse in Hay's Mews where it's almost obligatory to arrive by limo.) *16 Chenies St., WC1, tel. 020/7637–8038. Tube: Goodge Street. Walk south on Tottenham Court Rd., quick left on Chenies St.*

The Lamb. Conduit Street is peppered with bars and cafés, but The Lamb is the best of the bunch. Bask in the sun (if applicable) at an outdoor table with the relaxed crowd of locals and students. *Lamb's Conduit St., WC1, near Guilford St., tel. 020/7405–0713. Tube: Russell Square. Walk east on Guildford St., turn right onto Lamb's Conduit St.*

Museum Tavern. If you think you deserve more than a cup of weak tea after the British Museum, pop directly across the street to this big, ornate Victorian pub, agleam with mirrors. Karl Marx refreshed his thirst here while writing *Das Kapital*, and today it hosts a mix of scholars, tourists, and locals. *49 Great Russell St., WC1, tel. 020/7242–8987. Tube: Tottenham Court Road. Walk east on New Oxford St., turn left onto Bloomsbury and right onto Great Russell St.*

No chippie worth its salt is open on Monday; with most fishermen sitting at home on Sunday, Monday's fish would be more than a day old.

UNDER £10 • Chutney's. It's on everybody's short list for London's best vegetarian Indian restaurant. The £5 buffet is one of the city's few culinary steals. If you come for dinner, start with the vegetable kebab and continue with spicy mixed vegetable curry of potatoes, cauliflower, and courgettes (that's zucchini to Americans), or *muttar panir* (tofu and peas in a hot sauce) over a plate of rice. Add a glass of passion fruit, mango, or pineapple juice, or the cool yogurt lassi drink that's available either with salt or sugar. *124 Drummond St., NW1, tel. 020/7388–0604. Tube: Euston. Walk right on Melton St., turn left on Drummond St.*

La Bardigiana. It's simple, it's small, and the staff is sometimes curt, but the price is right—especially if you can't face another Indian biryani. There's a wide selection of yummy pizzas and pastas. *77 Marchmont St., tel. 020/7837–5983. Tube: Russell Square. Turn right on Bernard St., left on Marchmont St. Closed Sun.*

CAMDEN TOWN

There's no shortage of food in Camden, with dozens of stalls in the markets serving up all kinds of cheap feeds. **Camden High Street,** surprise, is the main drag, interspersed with stands selling kebabs, pizza, and sausage, and the odd café. **Inverness Street, Parkway,** and **Bayham Street** have eateries that are slightly less clogged with Camden shoppers.

UNDER £5 • Bagel Bar. This is the perfect place to grab a filling, cheap breakfast before hitting the markets. Full English breakfasts are a mere £2–£3, and freshly made sandwiches are a bargain at 90p–£2. Hot salt-beef (that's "corned beef" to you) bagels make a mighty good snack. *12 Inverness St., NW1, tel. 020/7284–0974. Tube: Camden Town. Walk north on Camden High St., turn left on Inverness St.*

Cactus. Halfway between Camden Town and Hampstead this funkily decorated basement restaurant serves up the best value all-you-can-eat deal in the city. For just £4.88 there's a massive spread of 15 freshly cooked hot dishes, plus a bevy of salads and dips. Load up on a good chili, mussels, burritos, and other Tex-Mex foods and enjoy the upbeat atmosphere of this joint. Due to the place's popularity, reservations are essential. *83 Haverstock Hill, NW3, tel. 020/7722–4112. Tube: Chalk Farm or Belsize Park. From Chalk Farm, walk up Haverstock Hill; from Belsize Park, walk downhill.*

UNDER £10 • Daphne's. Daphne's has fast, friendly service and excellent appetizers—try the grilled sausages or deep-fried calamari—and main dishes like moussaka, *tavvas* (cubes of lamb baked with herbs), and *ortikia* (quail with lemon and oregano). If the weather is even remotely pleasant, sit in the rooftop garden. Set lunch menu is £5.75. *83 Bayham St., NW1, tel. 020/7267–7322. Tube: Camden Town. Walk SE on Camden High St., turn left on Greenland St., right on Bayham St. Closed Sun.*

BEYOND MICKEY D'S

If the thought of dining in a chain restaurant makes you break out in a rash, relax—we're not suggesting McDonald's. The places listed below all have great food, decent prices, attractive decor, and, hey, they just happen to have more than one location. Maybe there's one near you.

Aroma. This bright, vibrant string of cafés was voted best in a *Time Out* reader poll. Its specialty coffee is a hit, perhaps because it's served with a little piece of chocolate. 273 Regent St., W1, tel. 020/7495–4911; 120 Charing Cross Rd., WC2, tel. 020/7240–4030; 1B Dean St., W1, tel. 020/7287–1633; 381 Oxford St., W1, tel. 020/7495–6945; 168 Piccadilly, W1, tel. 020/7495–6995; 36A St. Martin's La., WC2, tel. 020/7836–5110.

Café Rouge. The interiors are always welcoming and familiar—all 34 branches have the oh-so-popular French bistro look, but you can't fault it because it is tastefully and attentively carried out. The food is good and the set menu of soup, pepper steak and chips, followed by warm tart tatin and ice-cream can't be beaten.

Dôme. One of the best deals in town is the £5 three-course meal available all day long at this string of hip French bistros. The selection changes daily, with possibilities like ginger-carrot soup, onion tart, liver pâté, roast chicken, and many delicious desserts. 32 Long Acre, Covent Garden, WC2, tel. 020/7379–8650; 35A Kensington High St., W8, tel. 020/7937–6655; 289–291 Regent St., W1, tel. 020/7636–7006; 354 King's Rd., SW3, tel. 020/7352–2828; 57–59 Charterhouse St., EC1, tel. 020/7336–6484.

Pizza Express. For a pizza chain, this place ain't bad: Pies arrive at your table hot and tasty, and the prices are pretty cheap. Some of the branches even host live jazz. Approximately 25 locations throughout London.

Pret A Manger. For quick sandwiches, salads, and even sushi, Pret A Manger cannot be beat. Everything is prepared hourly on the premises, with the emphasis on fresh, natural ingredients (no grease, no preservatives). Approximately 40 locations throughout London.

The Stockpot. Count on these old-time café/diners for inexpensive English and Continental fare like soups, omelets, and casseroles. 6 Basil St., SW3, tel. 020/7589–8627; 273 King's Rd., SW3, tel. 020/7823–3175; 40 Panton St., SW1, tel. 020/7839–5142; 18 Old Compton St., W1, tel. 020/7287–1066; 50 James St., W1, tel. 020/7486–1086.

The Engineer. Serving some of the best food that you can find in a pub, the Engineer makes a wonderful place to hang out after a walk along the canal. The cosmopolitan (leaning towards Italian) menu changes biweekly, but you can expect inventive salads—such as rocket (arugula), pecan, and poached pear. Staples include eggs Benedict or eggs Florentine and salmon fish cakes. The steaks are organic. Reserve ahead if you're coming for dinner; try for an outside table if the weather's warm. *65 Gloucester Ave., NW1, tel. 020/7722–0950. Tube: Camden Town or Chalk Farm (recommended after dark). From Camden Town, walk north on Camden High St., at bridge turn left on the Canal and watch for signs. From Chalk Farm, walk south across Adelaide Rd., veer left on Gloucester Ave.*

Jazz Café. Food is very much secondary to music, but the balcony restaurant allows you to combine the two in a perfect harmony. The music covers the whole spectrum, not just jazz, and the food is just as eclectic. Call to find out what's on. *5 Parkway, NW1, tel. 020/7916–6060. Tube: Camden Town. Walk south on Camden High St. to corner of Parkway.*

The New Culture Revolution. Quite simply, it's cheap and lively. You can get Asian noodles prepared any way with pretty much anything you want for a fiver. Is anyone complaining? *43 Parkway, NW1, tel. 020/7267–2700. Tube: Camden Town. Walk south on Camden High St. and right on Parkway.*

Thanh Binh. Just north of Camden Lock, Thanh Binh is deservedly a longtime *Fodor's* favorite. Sit down and enjoy the delicate Vietnamese prawns or finger-licking-good Mongolian lamb, or order a chicken with lemongrass and rice lunch box to take away and eat by the lock. On weekends, they sell takeout boxes with curried chicken or beef and rice or noodles from the front of their restaurant all day. *14 Chalk Farm Rd., NW1, tel. 020/7267–9820. Tube: Chalk Farm. Walk SE on Chalk Farm Rd.*

CHELSEA AND BELGRAVIA

Trendy Chelsea is loaded with good places to graze, but many of the restaurants price entrées like they're major investments. If you're looking to dine on a budget, stick to the restaurants at the top of **King's Road,** or try **Fulham Road** where the pace is less frenetic and the prices more reasonable. Café life on the King's Road is alive and well. People park their bikes and cars, sit out and watch others admiring them! Check out Blushes, Guys n' Dolls, and Café Picasso.

UNDER £5 • Boisdale. The famous whisky bar and the odd flash of tartan in the claret-colored interior is more Scottish than the food is. Think beyond haggis as the chef is truly brilliant and mainly French-inspired, but uses Scottish ingredients like lobster, salmon, and game. The prices can be as steep as the Highlands, but after a fabulous dinner and a fat Havana it will be worth every penny of your extravagance. *15 Eccleston St., SW1, tel. 020/7730–6922. Tube: Victoria. Walk south on Buckingham Palace Rd. and take third right into Eccleston St.*

Café Internet. The best net joint in the city, this is a spacious, friendly place by Victoria Station and on the outskirts of Belgravia, serving up freshly made food including a big daily special for around £4, savory pie and a generous portion of salad (a bargain £1.80), as well as coffees and cakes. It also has a full bar. Internet access is £3 per 30-minute session. *22 Buckingham Palace Rd, SW1, tel. 020/7233–5786. Tube: Victoria. Exit and turn right onto Buckingham Palace Rd.*

Chelsea Bun Diner. The oddly named "Bun Diner" is always jam-packed with locals, and here's why: damn good breakfasts. They serve breakfast the whole day long, but if you show up before 10:30 AM, you can get the "Early Bird Breakfast" for £2.30. P.S.: Lunch and dinner are terrific here, too. BYOB. *9A Limerston St., SW10, tel. 020/7352–3635. Tube: Earl's Court or Sloane Square. From either tube station, take Bus 11, 19, 22, or 31.*

Vingt Quatre. Tiara-clad Audrey Hepburn ate a croissant for breakfast outside Tiffany's and here Lucinda Benson-Hedges eats eggs Benedict in her pearls after dancing all night. The delicious and familiar food is served 24 hours a day so it's a perch for the lark or the nightingale. Burgers, fishcakes, pasta, and all kinds of breakfast combinations are served, and during traditional waking hours, the food is a little more sophisticated. *325 Fulham Rd., SW10, tel. 020/7376–7224. Tube: Fulham Broadway. Take any bus going east along Fulham Rd. and alight just past Chelsea and Westminster Hospital.*

UNDER £10 • Buona Sera at The Jam. The Jam is a classy little '70s-era restaurant with a surprise: There appear to be only six tables, but then the host will direct you to climb above those already seated into a little cubby that makes a romantic, cozy setting for sampling the special pastas and new-British dishes. The effect is like dining in a double-decker bus, and, best of all, you can do it until 1 AM. *289A King's Rd., SW3, tel. 020/7352–8827. Tube: Sloane Square. Walk SW on King's Rd.*

My Old Dutch. There is a touch of tulips and clogs as you can guess from the name, but the main point are the enormous and the most delicious pancakes. They're 12 inches across and are topped with all sorts of combinations. Particularly recommended are salmon and crème fraiche and the Dutch beef. *221 King's Rd., SW3, tel. 020/7352–6900. Tube: Sloane Square. Cross the square and walk down the left-hand side of King's Rd.*

Market Place. On warm days, it's worth wandering into the über-touristy Chelsea Farmer's Market for a decent breakfast or lunch at one of this café's peaceful, outdoor tables. During summer evenings it's home to a popular à la carte BBQ feast-o-rama. *215 Sydney St., SW3, tel. 020/7352–5600. Tube: South Kensington. Walk south on Onslow Sq., turn right on Fulham Rd., left on Sydney St.*

THE CITY AND ISLINGTON

Restaurants in the city mainly cater to suited office folk; after all, this is the financial heart of London. Predictably, the area is busiest on weekdays from dawn until early evening, and it slows to a crawl on weekends. There's no lack of sandwich shops, delis, pubs, and restaurants, but if you're not desperately hungry as you explore the city, consider a short tube ride to nearby Islington. Once the center for '70s dropouts, Islington is now a community on the rise, with a surfeit of happening places to dine, especially along **Islington High Street.**

UNDER £5 • Alfredo's. Virtually unchanged since the 1920s, Alfredo's is more than your average neighborhood café. Join the crowd of regulars for hearty English breakfasts, sandwiches, and home-made pies with two veggies, served in a homey interior. *4–6 Essex Rd., N1, tel. 020/7226–3496. Tube: Angel. Walk north on Islington High St., veer right on Essex Rd. No credit cards.*

Compton Arms. On a quiet alley, the Compton feels like a country pub, yet it's a two-minute walk from all the traffic chaos around the Highbury & Islington tube stop. It carries a range of well-kept beers, cheap homemade food (sausages and mash, pie and fries) for just a few pounds, and has a very mixed bunch of regulars. All in all, a good spot to escape the madding crowd. *4 Compton Ave., N1, tel. 020/7359–2645. Tube: Highbury & Islington. Walk south on Upper St., turn left on Cannonbury La. and left on Compton Ave. No credit cards.*

Ravi Shankar. Filling, cheap Indian food is served in this airy space with pale yellow walls. If you're especially hungry, order *Mysore thali*, with dal, *bhaji* (deep-fried veggies), rice, and chapati. Partake in the 22-item all-you-can-eat lunch buffet for £4, served noon–2:30 (Sunday until 5), or grab take-away packs with veggie curry, rice, *samosa* (a stuffed deep-fried savory pastry), and salad for £2. *422 St. John St., EC1, tel. 020/7833–5849. Tube: Angel. Walk south on St. John St.*

UNDER £10 • Arkansas Café. For barbecue, this stall with tables in Spitalfields Market is the *only* place to come. Try a pork rib plate with salad or veg, a USDA Texas beef brisket platter, or probably the best half-pound handmade burger in the capital. Pecan and other pies are on the menu. The beer prices are reasonable, and with an American owner who insists on being called Bubba, it's a fun place to eat. More importantly, it's totally authentic. *Unit 12, Old Spitalfields Market, E1, tel. 020/7377–6999. Tube: Liverpool St. Walk north on Bishopsgate, right onto Brushfield Rd. and left onto Steward St.; enter the covered market and the café is right at the back. Closed Sat. No credit cards.*

The Eagle. Originator of the "good food in a pub" genre, The Eagle has the requisite open kitchen, young city folk, and changing menu of Mediterranean edibles. Spanish ham, bruschetta, and tomato salad and home-salted cod with mash are both good bets. They also stir up a tasty homemade soup du jour, almost a meal in itself. *159 Farringdon Rd., EC1, tel. 020/7837–1353. Tube: Farringdon. Walk right on Cowcross St., turn right on Farringdon Rd. Closed Sun. No credit cards.*

The Place Below. It takes some gumption to bill yourself as "London's best vegetarian restaurant," but The Place Below—set in the crypt beneath St. Mary-le-Bow church—may be justified. The changing menu features large portions of salads, and hot dishes like ratatouille and quiche with salad. For a light meal consider a bowl of soup with bread. *St. Mary-le-Bow, Cheapside, EC2, tel. 020/7329–0789. Tube: Mansion House. Walk north on Bow La., left on Cheapside. Closed weekends.*

COVENT GARDEN

The lively open-air market that once captivated visitors (and fed Londoners) is long gone, and in its place are pricey shops and a boggling array of yuppie bistros. They're fun, but you can also get your food from produce- and snack-sellers on **Endell Street** or **Neal Street,** then picnic on the Covent Garden plaza or try the tiny **Neal's Yard** (just north of Shorts Gardens), which is packed with juice bars, natural-foods shops, and idyllic outdoor tables.

UNDER £5 • Food for Thought. Food for Thought serves large portions of fresh, inventive vegetarian and vegan food like roast pepper and almond soup and pasta with mushrooms and sage. Everything on the menu is under £3.50—which explains why this snug basement café is never empty. BYOB. There's no charge for corkage, and it's a no-smoking joint. *31 Neal St., WC2, tel. 020/7836–9072. Tube: Covent Garden. Walk right on Long Acre, turn left on Neal St.*

Rock & Sole Plaice. This family-run diner—a cross between your basic fish-and-chips bar and a pretheater bistro—has no aspirations to be anything other than traditionally British, with options like cod and chips and chicken mushroom pie. Expect small crowds after the pubs close. *47 Endell St., WC2, tel. 020/7836–3785. Tube: Covent Garden. Walk right on Long Acre, turn left on Endell St.*

UNDER £10 • Belgo Centraal. Step onto the industrial elevator and descend into deep, deep trendiness. The Belgian restaurant has exposed brick arches, brushed copper walls, and stylish furniture—and waiters dressed like Trappist monks. Belgo's specialty is mussels, prepared in a variety of ways on platters or in pots. At lunchtime try their wild-boar sausage with mash and a beer. Weekdays, come early for dinner and play Beat the Clock: Order one of three set meals (chicken, sausages, or mussels and a beer) and pay a price corresponding to the time you order—if it's 6:10 PM, you pay £6.10. Wash it down with a selection of the 101 Belgian beers. *50 Earlham St., WC2, tel. 020/7813–2233. Tube: Covent Garden. Cross Long Acre to Neal St., turn left on Earlham St.*

Calabash. Re-creating Kenya in a London basement isn't easy, but this excellent African restaurant does the job with bright woven tablecloths, colorful paintings, and lots of leafy plants. Go for *yassa* (onion stew with pepper and lemon juice), veggie or lamb couscous, or hearty groundnut (peanut) stew. *38 King St., Africa Centre, WC2, tel. 020/7836–1976. Tube: Covent Garden. Walk south on James St., turn right on King St. Closed Sun.*

Cranks. The Covent Garden outpost of this no-meat-allowed chain trumpets itself as "the largest vegetarian restaurant in Europe." The menu changes weekly and usually includes a vegan soup and enterprising but occasionally disappointing entrées. Never less than heavenly are the desserts. If you're looking to conserve cash, get your grub from the self-service counter upstairs. *1 The Market, WC2, tel. 020/7379–6508. Tube: Covent Garden. Walk down James St. and into the covered market.*

Mars. Mars is definitely on a planet of its own: It's got funky blue and orange walls, broken-china mosaics, and strangely named, vaguely French food. The ever-changing menu features specialty soups and an entrée list that always has some interesting veggie options as well as meat and fish. *59 Endell St., WC2, tel. 020/7240–8077. Tube: Covent Garden. Walk right on Long Acre, turn left on Endell St. Closed Sun.*

Neal's Yard Dining Room. Let the drifting sounds of mellow worldbeat music lead you upstairs from Neal's Yard to this "world food" café. On the changing menu you'll find a choice of light meals (soup, mixed salad, Indian thali, oat pancake) and larger plates such as groundnut stew, Turkish *meze*, more thali, and a Mexican platter. After 3 PM, buy an afternoon special of tea and a cake. BYOB. No smoking. *14 Neal's Yard, WC2, tel. 020/7379–0298. Tube: Covent Garden. Walk right on Long Acre, turn left on Neal St., left on Shorts Gardens, right on Neal's Yard, and look for stairway on right. Closed Sun.*

Texas Embassy Cantina. You won't find much Tex-Mex food in the city, but this big Texan-owned eating house will answer your craving for a burrito. The best bets are the combo plates—filling enough to forgo the starters. The honky-tonk style bar upstairs can also be a good laugh at times. *1 Cockspur St., SW1, tel. 020/7925–0077. Tube: Leicester Square. Walk south down Charing Cross Rd., turn right onto Trafalgar Square and walk past the National Gallery.*

UNDER £40 • Rules. Come, escape from the 20th century. Almost 200 years old, this gorgeous London institution has welcomed everyone from Dickens to Charlie Chaplin to the Prince of Wales. The menu is historic and good, even if some food critics feel it's "theme-park-y"; try the noted steak, kidney, and mushroom pudding. The decor is even more delicious: With plush red banquettes and lacquered Regency-yellow walls (which are festively adorned with 19th-century oil paintings and dozens of framed engravings), the ground-floor salon is probably the most beautiful dining room in London (note there are three floors). If you love period decor and want to have one truly grand London splurge, do it here. Of course, reservations are essential and this is jacket-and-tie territory. *35 Maiden La., WC2, tel. 020/7836–5314. Tube: Covent Garden or Charing Cross. Walk east on Strand, turn left on Bedford St. and right onto Maiden La.*

EARL'S COURT AND SOUTH KENSINGTON

Earl's Court has loads of cut-rate kebab shops, greasy chippies, and generic sandwich shops—perhaps that's why some folk refer to this neighborhood as a culinary black hole. Your choices are better in neighboring South Kensington, particularly in the blocks surrounding the museums and along **Pelham Street** and **Brompton Road.**

UNDER £5 • Admiral Cordington. You'll find an upscale crowd chatting on the outdoor patio of this handsome Victorian relic; note the gas lamps and antique mirrors. Come for a satisfying pub-grub lunch. *17 Mossop St., off Draycott Ave., SW3, tel. 020/7581–0005. Tube: South Kensington. Walk east on Pelham St., cross Fulham Rd./Brompton Rd. and veer left onto Draycott Ave., turn left onto Mossop St. No credit cards.*

Spago. You know you're in a good Italian restaurant when everyone else in there is Italian. The menu consists of straightforward pasta dishes and salads. Pasta Spago is penne served with aubergine (eggplant), plum tomato, parsley, and mozzarella sauce. The atmosphere is very informal and the prices are low despite its South Kensington location. *6 Glendower Pl., SW7, tel. 020/7225–2407. Tube. South Kensington. Walk down Brompton Rd. and turn first right down Glendower Pl.*

UNDER £10 • Al Rawshi. Quick and greasy satisfaction is guaranteed from the chicken or lamb schwarma and falafel at this tiny Lebanese snack bar. Wash it all down with a variety of fresh fruit juices. *3 Kenway Rd., SW5, no phone. Tube: Earl's Court. Walk north on Earl's Court Rd., turn right on Kenway Rd. No credit cards.*

Benjys. The deal at divey Benjys is breakfast: It's big, it's cheap, and it's served all day. If you're ravenous, order the Builder's Breakfast for £3.40, a freight load of baked beans, two sausages, two pieces of toast, a heap of fries, bacon, one egg, and as much tea and coffee as you can put down. Would you like extra sausage with that? *157 Earl's Court Rd., SW5, tel. 020/7373–0245. Tube: Earl's Court. Turn left and Benjys is opposite the 7-Eleven. No credit cards.*

Kramps Creperie. This unfortunately named restaurant serves up dozens of delicious crepes, both sweet and savory. The selection ranges from chicken Creole down to sugar and lemon. Be on the lookout for their occasional special offer coupons that allow you to get two crepes for the price of one on your next visit. *6 Kenway Rd., SW5, tel. 020/7244–8759. Tube: Earl's Court. Walk north on Earl's Court Rd., turn right on Kenway Rd. No credit cards.*

Thai Taste. Thai Taste is an elegant oasis in a wasteland of fluorescent-lit chip shops. On the menu you'll find expertly prepared traditional dishes like pad thai, red curry chicken, and beef with black beans, ginger, and mushrooms. Note: The entrance is easy to miss, so keep a sharp eye out. *130 Cromwell Rd., SW7, tel. 020/7373–1647. Tube: Gloucester Road. Walk north on Gloucester Rd., turn left on Cromwell Rd.*

UNDER £30 • Bibendum. When it opened a decade ago, this reconverted Michelin showroom, adorned with art deco decorations and brilliant stained-glass and tile work, became one of London's dining showplaces and scene-arenas. You can come here for the Conran Shop or Oyster Bar, but most arrive to enjoy the kitchen's offerings, superlatively created for the most part. Nighttime is very pricey but the £27 set-price menu at lunchtime is money very well spent. However, sticking to the Oyster Bar can be just as good and a very sexy date. *Michelin House, 81 Fulham Rd., SW3, tel. 020/7581–5817. Tube: South Kensington. Walk east on Pelham St. and turn right onto Fulham Rd. Reservations essential. Closed Sun.*

HAMPSTEAD AND HIGHGATE

The wealthy, genteel surroundings ensure that this neighborhood is peppered with trendy bistros and cafés. Don't restrict yourself to **Hampstead High Street**; explore the side streets for tearooms and a smattering of mellow cafés. Highgate is much of the same, with little beyond the usual faux French or Italian chain cafés on Highgate High Street. If **Café Vert** (*see below*) doesn't appeal to you or is full, catch a bus to Hampstead, or even Camden Town.

UNDER £5 • Café Vert. Tucked away in a community center inside a converted church, Café Vert serves up delicious vegetarian food. Try a huge portion of spinach and mushroom lasagna served with a tasty salad, quiche and salad, or a big veggie breakfast. There's live jazz on Sunday. *Jacksons Lane Centre, 269A Archway Rd., N6, tel. 020/8348–7666. Tube: Highgate. Directly opposite the station in the church next to Jackson's La. No credit cards.*

UNDER £10 • Zamoyski's. Start off your meal by sampling some of the 30 different vodkas—those with a sweet tooth should try the honey vodka. Then get to work on the Polish *mezze,* nine dishes for a bargain £5.50, or the amazing *pieczeń po husarsku* (marinated lamb roasted with wild mushroom sauce). Portions lean toward the small side, but the food is rich and perfectly seasoned. This is a very popular spot, so phone ahead on weekend nights or expect a long wait. *85 Fleet Rd., NW3, tel. 020/*

7794–4792. Tube: Hampstead. Walk south on Hampstead High St., turn left on Pond St., veer right on Fleet Rd.

KENSINGTON AND KNIGHTSBRIDGE

Kensington and Knightsbridge are posh neighborhoods, full of lavish boutiques and "my god, you're joking"–priced restaurants. Best bets for cheap noshes in Knightsbridge are the pubs and sandwich shops on **Beauchamp Place** (off Brompton Road), and in Kensington, the fast-food joints scattered along **Kensington High Street.**

UNDER £5 • La Barraca. The menu at this mellow, attractive place features tons of tapas like calamari with white beans, garlic chicken, and steamed mussels. Weekends, young Londoners use La Barraca as a late-night watering hole (kitchen closes at midnight). *215 Kensington Church St., W8, tel. 020/7229–9359. Tube: Notting Hill Gate. Walk east on Notting Hill Gate, turn right on Kensington Church St. No credit cards.*

UNDER £10 • Curry Inn. In a city packed with Indian restaurants vying for the title of "best," it's easy to overlook this tiny, tastefully decorated contender. The dishes here, like biryani and curries, are generous and expertly prepared, and the staff will cheerfully make suggestions or explain ingredients. *41 Earl's Court Rd., W8, tel. 020/7937–2985. Tube: High Street Kensington. Walk west on Kensington High St., turn left on Earl's Court Rd.*

Maroush. Practically opposite the legendary San Lorenzo's so frequented by stars, you wouldn't expect to find this tasty little takeout Lebanese restaurant—not to mention the affordable prices. The sticky baklava made of light pastry, pistachio nuts, and honey is too wonderful. *38 Beauchamp Pl., SW3, tel. 020/7581–5434. Tube: Knightsbridge. Walk west along Brompton Rd. and take fourth left past Harrods into Beauchamp Pl.*

Palms. This is a lovely café-style restaurant just off Kensington High Street where you can meet friends for coffee after shopping or eat a proper meal. The salads are particularly good, but the pasta dishes are what Palms is known for. The homemade ravioli with three cheeses and cream and tomato sauce is not to be missed. The interior is full of—surprise, surprise—palms. *3-5 Campden Hill Rd., W8, tel. 020/7938–1830. Tube: Kensington High Street. Exit and turn left, cross the road at crossing and walk straight into Campden Hill Rd.*

Scandies. You may want to kneel and kiss the ground before entering this tidy eatery, because if you're hungry and you're in Knightsbridge, it's gonna save your derrière. The fairly standard pan-European menu changes daily, but regular items include salad, salmon fishcakes, and bangers and mash. *4 Kynance Pl., SW7, tel. 020/7589–3659. Tube: Gloucester Road. Walk north on Gloucester Rd., turn left on Kynance Pl.*

SOHO AND MAYFAIR

Soho is a happy hunting ground when it comes to restaurants, cafés, trattorias, and food stands—in fact, it's tops for just about every type of eatery imaginable. In London's small Chinatown, on **Lisle Street** (pronounced Lyle) and **Gerrard Street** between Leicester Square and Shaftesbury Avenue, you'll find the city's best Asian restaurants, as well as plenty of stores selling bulk herbs, produce, fresh fish, meats, Asian teas, and miracle cures. **Wardour Street** has an amazing array of international cuisine: Asian, American, French, Italian, you name it. **Old Compton Street** is *the* place to go for a traditional (though often expensive) Italian meal. Mayfair, on the other hand, is mainly a ritzy residential neighborhood, with a sprinkling of sandwich shops along **Piccadilly** and around the **Marble Arch** tube station, and fast-food stands of all types along **Oxford Street.**

UNDER £5 • Bunjie's Folk Cellar. Opened in 1954 this is the only remaining coffee bar from London's folk-music scene, and the little basement joint still has that old-time atmosphere. More importantly, this period treasure is a great alternative to bustling Soho cafés and you can linger over an espresso and vegetarian food (mega slices of pizza) or cakes for as long as you like. Their beer prices are refreshingly good for the West End; in the evening acoustic music and spoken-word sessions take place. A blast from the past, and a real find. *27 Litchfield St., WC2, tel. 020/7240–1796. Tube: Leicester Square. Walk north on Charing Cross Rd. and turn right onto Litchfield St.*

Cafe Sofra. If you're looking to escape the fast-food frenzy of Piccadilly, duck down windy, historic Shepherd Street and start hunting for this cozy café. On the menu are Middle Eastern–type snacks and light meals, like mixed mezze or lentil casserole, plus standard sandwiches and desserts. *10 Shepherd St., W1, tel. 020/7495–3434. Tube: Green Park. Walk SW on Piccadilly, turn right on White Horse St., left on Shepherd St. No credit cards.*

Govinda's. There's no proselytizing at this friendly Hare Krishna restaurant, just tasty vegetarian grub at rock-bottom prices. On the regular menu are basics like baked potato with cheese, spinach lasagna with salad, and a small vegetable curry. A full meal of rice, soup, two veggies, salad, and bread goes for £6. Every night from 7:30, it's all-you-can-eat for £4, and if that isn't good enough, on Sunday at around 4 PM or 5 PM the Krishnas serve a free—yes, *free*—feast. (On Sunday it's only open at free food time.) No alcohol is allowed. *9–10 Soho St., W1, tel. 020/7437–4928. Tube: Tottenham Court Road. Walk west on Oxford St., turn left on Soho St. No credit cards.*

Living Room. There's no better place to chill for a few hours in Soho than this café, which offers comfy chairs, sofas, and stacks of old books for your lounging pleasure. Cappuccino and tasty sandwiches (there are some wonderfully weird ones, including a great PBJ-and-marshmallow-fluff number) are popular. *3 Bateman St., W1, tel. 020/7437–4827. Tube: Leicester Square. Walk north on Charing Cross Rd., turn left on Old Compton St., right on Greek St., left on Bateman St.*

Mildred's. This eatery offers above-average, 100% organic veggie food, a genial staff, and a Soho hipster clientele. The menu changes daily, but always includes entrées like stir-fried vegetables, frittatas, or a chili bean burrito. For dessert, spoon into a bowl of yogurt, honey, and nuts. *58 Greek St., W1, tel. 020/7494–1634. Tube: Leicester Square. Walk north on Charing Cross Rd., turn left on Shaftesbury Ave., right on Greek St. No credit cards.*

New World. It's a world unto itself at this huge Chinese dim-sum-o-rama with paper tablecloths, schlocky Chinese lanterns, and tacky Muzak. A variety of dumplings, noodles, steamed buns, and even chickens' feet are offered. It's a great bargain and you can get stuffed to the gills for £5. *1 Gerrard Pl., W1, tel. 020/7734–0677. Tube: Leicester Square. Walk north on Charing Cross Rd., turn left on Little Newport St., and continue 1 block to alley.*

Pâtisserie Valerie. This cool, dark Soho café has been around since 1926. Most recently it's become a hangout for artsy types, and it's packed day and night. For snacking, there are sandwiches; luscious desserts like éclairs, berry tarts, and white-chocolate truffle cake; and a stellar selection of handmade chocolates. *44 Old Compton St., W1, tel. 020/7437–3466. Tube: Leicester Square. Walk north on Charing Cross Rd., turn left on Old Compton St. Other locations: 215 Brompton Rd., SW3, tel. 020/7589–4993; 66 Portland St., W1, tel. 020/7631–0467.*

Pollo. The original budget restaurant of London is this Soho institution, where you can pick from an extensive menu of cheap pastas. The atmosphere is jovial, noisy, and crowded—you may have to share a table. *20 Old Compton St., W1, tel. 020/7734–5917. Tube: Leicester Square. Walk north on Charing Cross Rd., turn left on Moor St. (which becomes Old Compton St.). No credit cards.*

Poons. Once a hole-in-the-wall, now a smart restaurant, Poons offers more than just stir-fry. Try the special "wind-dried" duck with rice or hotpot (soup with stuffed bean curd), or deep-fried oysters. The staff is friendly, and they'd like you to be so, too—when the place gets busy, waiters don't ask before seating people at your table. *27 Lisle St., WC2, tel. 020/7437–4549. Tube: Leicester Square. Walk north on Charing Cross Rd., turn left on Newport St., left on Newport Pl., right on Lisle St. No credit cards.*

UNDER £10 • Hamine. Patrons of this slick noodle shop run the gamut from homesick Japanese businessmen to local cognoscenti. Most are here for one thing: huge, steaming bowls of ramen with meat or vegetables, guaranteed to fill. Note to the uninitiated: Place your order and pay at the counter first, then take a seat. *84 Brewer St., W1, tel. 020/7287–1318. Tube: Piccadilly Circus. Walk north on Sherwood St., turn left on Brewer St. No credit cards.*

Wagamama. A Japanese word meaning "selfishness," Wagamama is the home of positive eating and the first of the trendy noodle houses in the capital. Don't let the long lines put you off; rest assured that the turnover rate of customers is high at this ramen bar. The menu features a staggering variety of noodles, including *yaki soba* (pan-fried noodles with chicken and prawns flavored with peppers, ginger, and sesame) and the spicy chili chicken ramen. The menu is nearly as entertaining as the staff, who are clad in Paul Smith gear or the logo T-shirt of the latest designer. Slurping is encouraged; apparently the extra oxygen helps the flavor. *10A Lexington St., W1, tel. 020/7292–0990. Tube: Oxford Circus. Walk south on Regent St., turn left on Beak St., right on Lexington St. Other location: 4 Streatham St., WC1, tel. 020/7323–9223.*

UNDER £25 • Mezzo. The 700-seat Mezzo isn't only London's biggest glamour restaurant; it's the most gigantic eatery in all of Europe. Downstairs the restaurant proper (dinners here can top £45) has a huge glass-walled kitchen. Upstairs, the bar overlooks a canteen-style operation called Mezzonine. Finally, a late-night café/patisserie/newsstand has a separate entrance next door. The prices in the canteen and café are reasonable, with meals going for £10 to £30. The place was a London landmark from day one, with a see-and-be-seen bustle, despite its low celebrity count. Wear your spiffiest threads. *100 Wardour St., W1, tel. 020/7314–4000. Tube: Tottenham Court Rd. Walk west on Oxford St., left onto Wardour St., then 100 yards down on the left-hand side. Mezzo closed Sat. lunch, Mezzonine closed Sun.*

SOUTH OF THE RIVER

For a bit of river culture, grab a sandwich in Gabriel's Wharf and chill out in South Bank, London's answer to Paris's Left Bank. A number of expensive restaurants have sprung up along the river, but for better value you'll need to wander farther afield into the urban sprawl of Waterloo. **Lower Marsh,** behind Waterloo Station, is dotted with anonymous little cafés. A couple of miles south, **Brixton** has a couple of great budget options.

UNDER £5 • M. Manze. Eels aren't for everyone, especially not the squeamish, but M. Manze has been serving steaming plates of them to happy/daring customers since 1892—making it the oldest remaining eel, pie, and mash shop in the world. A traditional meat pie and mash, eels and mash, and (ulp!) jellied eels are all served with a ladle full of "liquor," a spring green, parsley-based sauce. *87 Tower Bridge Rd., SE1, tel. 020/7407–2985. Tube: London Bridge. Walk SE on St. Thomas St., turn right on Bermondsey St. (which joins Tower Bridge Rd. just before M. Manze). Closed Sun.*

Pizzeria Franco. "London's most famous pizzeria"—that's how this place touts itself—is high on atmosphere and good on garlic-intensive pizza, from the margarita (tomato and mozzarella) to the *quattro stagioni* (ham, mushrooms, artichokes, olives, and anchovies). You'll find this tiny trattoria tucked away in one of Brixton Market's colorful covered arcades. *4 Market Row, SW9, tel. 020/7738–3021. Tube: Brixton. Walk south on Brixton Rd., turn left on Electric Ave., right on Electric La., and look for Market Row arcade entrance on left. Closed Sun. and Wed.*

UNDER £10 • Bah Humbug. Though it won't break the bank, this is a cozy restaurant in a church crypt that not only has a cool ambience but high-quality food. The menu is exclusively vegetarian and fish. Starters includes baked goat's cheese; entrées, a terrific teriyaki tuna. Reservations are highly advisable. Linger in the adjacent Bug Bar to make a night of it. *The Crypt, St. Matthew's Peace Garden, Brixton Hill, SW2, tel. 020/7738–3184. Tube: Brixton. Walk south on Brixton Rd. and it's in the big building where the road forks.*

Côte à Côte. If it's rich French food you're craving, look no further. The restaurant is a bit dark, but the food is guaranteed to satisfy the requirements of both wallet and palate. Generous starters are a steal at £1.85; try the mussels in wine and garlic or the avocado, mozzarella, tomato, and basil salad. Delicious entrées like chicken marinated in chili and coconut milk served over pasta, or baked eggplant stuffed with tofu and vegetables cost a mere £4.45. *74–76 Battersea Bridge Rd., SW11, tel. 020/7738–0198. Tube: Sloane Square. From station, take Bus 19 or 249 to Battersea Bridge Rd.*

Waterloo Fire Station. This huge establishment occupies a converted fire station: The old tiles and metal supports remain, but the red engines have been replaced by a huge bar, an open kitchen, and rows of wooden tables. The menu changes daily but expect goodies along the lines of grilled pigeon breast, swordfish with green coconut sauce, or a calves liver salad, served up by a friendly staff. The Irish rock oysters with shallots are available when there is a letter "R" in the month. *150 Waterloo Rd., SE1, tel. 020/7620–2226. Tube: Waterloo. Exit the station at exit 2, walk south on Waterloo Rd.*

UNDER £30 • OXO Tower Restaurant Bar and Brasserie. How delightful it is for London finally to get a room with a view, *such* a view. On the eighth floor of the beautifully revived OXO Tower Wharf building near the South Bank Centre is this elegant space, run by the same people who put the chic Fifth Floor at Harvey Nichols on the map. The menu features Euro food with trendy ingredients (roast leg of milk-fed Pyrnean lamb with braised lettuce and button onions, or a suckling pig with black pudding and fennel jus: the mushroom of the moment is wild cepes). The ceiling slats turn and change from white to midnight blue, but who on earth notices, with St. Paul's dazzling you across the water? Book at the Brasserie for this price range; the restaurant proper is more pricey, but both share great vistas. *Bankside, SE1, tel. 020/7803–3888. Tube: Waterloo or Blackfriars. From Blackfriars, head over Blackfriars Bridge to the Southwark side, walk to Stamford St., and aim for the tower.*

EXPLORING LONDON

No matter how long you stay, you won't get bored wandering through London's distinctly flavored streets. Londoners tend to be very neighborhood-oriented, spending a lot of time in their particular residential pockets, many of which function as self-contained communities. Indeed, until the industrial revolution of the 19th century, a hodgepodge of villages—today we would call them suburban satellites—made up the *original* City of London. This ancient core has evolved into what locals call "the City," the financial heart of London that sprawls along the banks of the River Thames.

Many of London's sights are in a relatively compact area in the West End, and the most famous attractions—including Parliament, Westminster Abbey, and many of the palaces—are within walking distance of one another. Apart from a few sights located on the outskirts, you're better off checking out London on foot. In the central area, tube stations are abundant and fairly close together, but if you always hop on the tube to travel between sights, you won't get a complete picture of the city. Going afoot, you may end up hopelessly lost within minutes, so pick up a copy of the *London A to Z* street atlas (Brits pronounce it "A to Zed") sold at newsstands and W. H. Smith newsagents all over town. Buy the mini-London (£3.75) edition—it's just the right size for your pocket. Locals, including cab drivers, swear by it.

Walking tours are truly a perfect way to meet fellow travelers and lead you to some of London's most historic (and often overlooked) byways and roads without getting you lost first. The best and biggest conductor of walking tours is the **Original London Walks** (tel. 020/7624–3978), whose witty, knowledgeable guides offer a wide selection of routes, including tours devoted to the London haunts of Oscar Wilde, Jack the Ripper, and the Beatles, as well as innumerable other theme tours and a bunch of jolly pub crawls. If you're planning to go on several walks, ask your guide for a discount walkabout card. All tours are listed in the "Around Town" section of *Time Out* (£1.80), average £4.50 per person, and last about two hours. A more flexible (and cost-effective) way to structure your wanderings is to purchase one of the many DIY (or do it yourself, as the native lingo has it) walking tour booklets or cassettes, available at most tourist offices for a few pounds. The Theatreland Walk includes many of the historic buildings of central London's theater district as well as some more distant. If you would prefer to remain seated while someone else points out the sights, a huge mass of companies are just begging for your tourist dollars. The **Original London Sightseeing Tour** (tel. 020/8877–1722), the **Big Bus Company** (tel. 020/8944–7810), and **London Pride Sightseeing Company** (tel. 01708/631122) all have open-top, double-deck buses that frequently circumnavigate the major sights of Central London; charge £12 for a 24-hour ticket; and allow you to hop on and off the company's buses at will throughout the day. **London Bicycle Tour Company** (tel. 020/7928–6838) conducts bike tours of various London neighborhoods for £12; call for schedules and to make reservations.

MAJOR ATTRACTIONS

When choosing which of London's major sights to visit, listen closely to your internal tour guide. Although the best and most famous museums are free, many other attractions aren't cheap—though an ISIC card may get you a slight discount. As for the madding crowd, arrive early in the day or, even better during the off-season, to avoid brushing up against the 5 million other tourists who charge through London every year. But the best advice of all is to admit when you've reached your limit and head for the pub when your feet decide to call a sit-down strike. It shows a measure of respect for the great metropolis, which has more to offer than you could possibly take advantage of in a day, a week, or even a year.

BRITISH LIBRARY

By royal decree, the gigantic British Library is entitled to one copy of everything that is published in the United Kingdom. The library's entire holdings were removed at enormous cost from the residence it shared with the British Museum to its new home in St. Pancras. Many think the harsh structure lacks the historical gravitas peculiar to its predecessor. But this much more visitor-friendly place grants everyone who enters access to artifacts like the Magna Carta (1215), one of Britain's founding constitutional documents; hand-written prose by Milton, Joyce, Woolf, and the Brontës; sheet music by Haydn, Bach, and Schubert; letters written by Henry VIII, Elizabeth I, and a host of other monarchs; as well as more recent manuscripts (like records of the Beatles' endeavors). Regular lectures and exhibitions cover popular subjects, such as the Poems on the Underground, which adorn many a tube carriage. For £3 (£2 students) you can take a tour (Mon., Wed., Fri., Sat., and Sun. at 3; Sat. also at 10:30) of the library; call 020/7412-7332 to book ahead. St. Pancras Station next door is also well worth a look. The facade (built in 1872) is one of the most extreme examples of Victorian High Gothic, a breathtaking sight made all the more intriguing given that it fronts up a huge 100-ft-high glass-and-iron train shed. *The British Library at St. Pancras, 96 Euston Rd., NW1, tel. 020/7412-7000. Tube: King's Cross. Turn right out of King's Cross station, walk past St. Pancras Station; the library is next door. Admission free. Open weekdays 9:30-6 (Tues. until 8), Sat. 9:30-5, Sun. 11-5.*

BRITISH MUSEUM

Anybody who's trying to write about the British Museum better have a large pail of superlatives close at hand—most, biggest, earliest, finest. This is the golden hoard of 2½ centuries of Empire, and the sheer magnitude overwhelms. Even those suspicious of the museum's role in rationalizing colonialism can't fail to admit that it's an amazing collection, full of goodies of world historical importance. The Rosetta Stone, the Elgin Marbles, the Black Obelisk, the Dead Sea Scrolls, the Lindow Bog Man—heck, that only begins the list. If you really catch the British Museum bug, you'll be back four or five times. On the other hand, like millions of Londoners who have never even visited this place, there are those who will feel rather underwhelmed with what is, in essence, Mankind's Attic.

Parliament was inspired to found London's first public museum in 1753, after acquiring the extensive natural history and antiquities collection of Sir Hans Sloane, as well as several smaller collections of books and manuscripts. Soon, it seemed everyone had something to donate—George II gave the Royal Library, Sir William Hamilton (husband of Nelson's mistress, Emma) gave antique vases, Charles Townley gave sculptures, the Bank of England gave coins—and the museum's holdings quickly outgrew their original space in Montague House. After the addition of such major pieces as the Rosetta Stone and other Egyptian antiquities (spoils of the Napoleonic War), and the incomparable Parthenon sculptures (brought from Greece via an Odyssean voyage by Lord Elgin in 1816), Robert Smirke was commissioned to build an appropriately large and monumental building on the same site—though, due to lack of funds, the construction work was dragged out over 20 years by several architects.

If the sheer magnitude of the collection (and sometimes the crowd) get to you, a good strategy for exploring is to take the free "Eye-Opener" tour or the 90-minute tour (£7; ask at the info desk for times), and come back later to whatever intrigued you the most. Another is to buy a £1 souvenir map and follow one of its recommended routes. In many ways the **ground floor** is the most impressive in the museum, featuring big-name treasures from Greece, Rome, and western Asia. The **basement floor** features more antiquities from Greece and Rome, including huge Ionic capitals from the temple of Artemis, the poorly restored Discus Thrower, and a single, very large foot, spoils from a colossal statue of Alexander the Great. The **upper floors** house treasures from all over the world, including exhibits from prehistoric and Roman Britain, the medieval, Renaissance, and modern collections, and the greater part of the Egyptian collection, where you'll find the mummies. Note that a number of galleries may be closed, and some objects relocated, due to the ongoing Great Court Project refurbishment scheme.

The **British Library** (*see above*) used to be housed here but has now been shifted lock, stock, and barrel to its new site at St. Pancras, leaving behind the magnificent domed **Reading Room** (tel. 020/7412-7677)—where George Bernard Shaw and Karl Marx (to name only two) warmed their seats while cogitating. This architectural delight will become an information center as part of the museum's "Great Court" scheme and will also house a swanky restaurant. *Great Russell St., WC1, tel. 020/7412-7111. Tube: Tottenham Court Road. Walk north on Tottenham Court Rd., turn right on Great Russell St. Admission free; small charge for special exhibits. Open Mon.-Sat. 10-5, Sun. 2:30-6.*

BUCKINGHAM PALACE

One of the most famous buildings in the world, this is Her Majesty's London home (a flag bearing the Royal Standard flies above the palace whenever the Queen is in residence, usually on weekdays). Never intended as a royal palace, it was originally built in the 18th century for the J. Paul Getty of his day, the Duke of Buckingham. George III—the tea-taxing king that the American colonists revolted against—bought the place in 1762. When George IV ascended to the throne in 1820, he decided that the man-

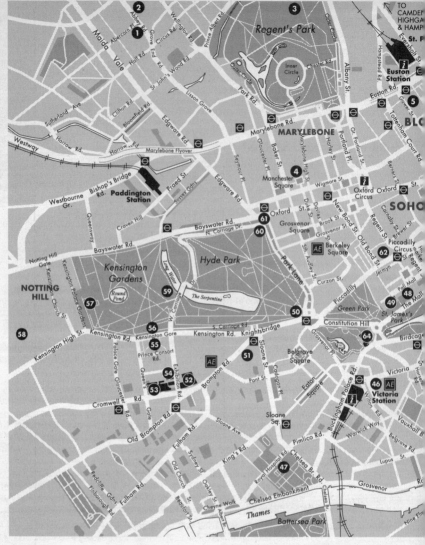

10 Downing Street, **41**

Abbey Road Studios, **1**

Albert Memorial, **56**

Apsley House, **50**

Banqueting House, **38**

Barbican Centre, **15**

Big Ben, **42**

British Airways London Eye, **29**

British Library, **6**

British Museum, **7**

Buckingham Palace, **64**

Cabinet War Rooms, **40**

Chelsea Physic Garden, **47**

Covent Garden, **35**

Design Museum, **21**

Dickens House, **8**

FA Premier League Hall of Fame, **28**

HMS *Belfast*, **22**

Harrods, **51**

Horse Guards and Parade Ground, **39**

Houses of Parliament, **43**

Imperial War Museum, **25**

Inns Of Court, **10**

Institute of Contemporary Arts (ICA), **48**

Kensington Palace, **57**

Leighton House, **58**

Lloyd's Building, **17**

London Aquarium, **27**

London Transport Museum, **34**

London Zoo, **3**

Marble Arch, **61**

Monument, **16**

Museum of Garden History, **26**

Museum of London, **14**

Museum of the Moving Image, **30**

National Gallery, **63**

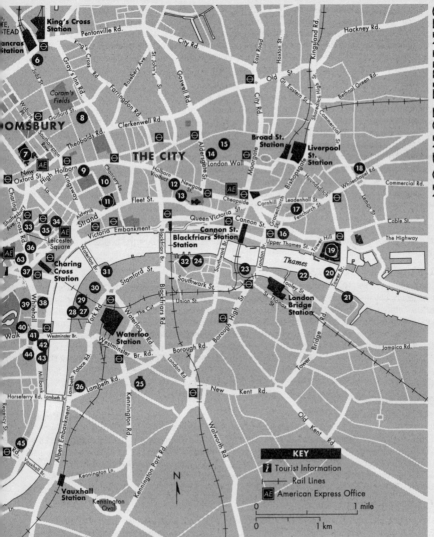

King's Cross Station

Pentonville Rd.

ancras Station

6

Gray's Inn Rd.

King's Cross Rd.

City Rd.

Pentonville Rd.

Hackney Rd.

Kingsland Rd.

Coram's Fields

8

Guilford St.

Clerkenwell Rd.

OMSBURY

Theobalds Rd.

THE CITY

7

AE

New Oxford St.

High Holborn

9

Kingsway

Chancery La.

10

Holborn Viaduct

14

15

London Wall

Broad St. Station

Liverpool St. Station

18

Whitechapel Rd.

Commercial Rd.

11

Fleet St.

12

Newgate St.

13

Cheapside

AE

Cornhill

Leadenhall St.

17

Fenchurch St.

Cable St.

The Highway

34

33

35

AE

Strand

Victoria Embankment

Queen Victoria St.

Cannon St.

Blackfriars Station

Cannon St. Station

16

Upper Thames St.

19

Lower Thames St.

36

Leicester Square

63

37

Charing Cross Station

31

Stamford St.

32

24

Southwark St.

23

Thames

22

20

Tower Bridge

30

The Cut

Union St.

London Bridge

London Bridge Station

21

39

38

29

27

28

York Rd.

Waterloo Rd.

Blackfriars Rd.

St. Thomas St.

Tooley St.

40

41

Whitehall

Waterloo Station

Borough High St.

Walk

42

44

43

Westminster Br. Rd.

Borough Rd.

London Rd.

Tower Bridge Rd.

Jamaica Rd.

Millbank

Lambeth Rd.

26

Lambeth Rd.

25

New Kent Rd.

Horseferry Rd.

Kennington Rd.

Walworth Rd.

Old Kent Rd.

45

Albert Embankment

Kennington Park Rd.

N

Vauxhall Station

Kennington Oval

Kennington Ln.

KEY

i Tourist Information

Rail Lines

AE American Express Office

0 ——————— 1 mile

0 ——————— 1 km

sion looked far too middle class, and enlisted the help of architect John Nash to remodel with a vengeance. For the past two centuries, the palace's great gray bulk has summed up the imperious splendor of so much of London: stately, magnificent, and ponderous. The palace contains some 600 rooms, including the State Ballroom and, of course, the Throne Room, but Elizabeth II occupies only a dozen rooms on the first floor of the north wing overlooking Green Park. When more pressing matters aren't on her mind, she probably likes nothing more than to curl up in front of the telly with her corgis watching *Coronation Street.*

Several years ago, the Queen opened the palace to the public—for a fee, mind you—to pay for the restorations to Windsor Castle (*see* Windsor, *below*) after the fire in 1992. During summer months, various rooms are open to view—but forget about poking into medicine cabinets: only 17 of the sumptuous (and rather cold) **State Rooms** are on the tour. Here you'll find pomp and circumstance, but little else: These salons are where much of the business of royalty is played out—investitures, state banquets, receptions, lunch parties for the famous, and so on. Needless to say, these palatial rooms are chock-full of treasures—the entire spectacle will either leave you queasy about humankind's acquisitive nature, or drooling with envy. With the high cost of castle restorations these days, it's likely the palace will remain open for years to come—in any event, it has become one of London's most popular sights. The palace opens its doors each August and September. *Queen's Gardens, SW1, tel. 020/7839–1377. Tube: Green Park or St. James's Park. From Green Park, walk ½ mile south on Queen's Walk. From St. James's Park, walk north on Queen Anne's Gate, turn left on Birdcage Walk. Admission £10. Open Aug.–beginning Oct. daily 9:30–4:15. Note that you can prebook your admission ticket over the phone by using credit cards.*

QUEEN'S GALLERY

A short distance down Buckingham Gate, the Queen's Gallery houses rotating exhibits of pieces from her majesty's private art collection. Gainsborough, Rembrandt, Reynolds, and Rubens are among the regulars featured, but the museum is cluttered and only worth the price if an interesting temporary exhibition is occurring; check *Time Out* for details. It's due to close for renovations that will make room for the many pieces that have been kept in storage. The new gallery is scheduled to throw open its doors in wild celebration of the Queen's Golden Jubilee in 2002. That's also the year some Royal watchers expect HM to abdicate the throne in favor of Charles, but that's by the by. For further info, call the Visitor Office, tel. 020/7839–1377. *Buckingham Palace Rd., SW1, tel. 020/7930–4832, ext. 3351. Tube: St. James's Park or Victoria. Admission £4. Open daily 9:30–4:30 (last admission 4).*

ROYAL MEWS

One of the oldest and finest operating stables in the world, the Royal Mews houses the monarch's magnificent state carriages (including the Gold State Coach—better known as the Coronation Coach—built in 1762), together with their horses and state liveries. If you visit when both the Queen's Gallery and the Royal Mews are open, you can cop a slightly cheaper combined ticket for £6. Otherwise, some may feel it's a lot to pay to look at horses. *Buckingham Palace Rd., SW1, tel. 020/7930–4832, ext. 3351. Tube: St. James's Park or Victoria. Admission £4. Open Apr.–July, Tues.–Thurs. noon–4; Aug.–Sept., Mon.–Thurs. 10:30–4; Oct.–Mar., Wed. noon–3:30.*

GUARDS MUSEUM

This museum occupies a set of underground rooms in Wellington Barracks, the regimental headquarters of the palace's Guards Division. Exhibits trace the history of the five Foot Guards regiments—Grenadier, Coldstream, Scots, Irish, and Welsh—from the 1660s through to the Gulf War. The massive toy soldier shop is definitely worth a look, even if you're not into that kind of thing. *Wellington Barracks, Birdcage Walk, SW1, tel. 020/7930–4466, ext. 3430. Tube: St. James's Park. Admission £2. Open daily 10–4 (last admission 3:30).*

CHANGING OF THE GUARD

One of the biggest crowd-pleasers in town is the Changing of the Guard, when the soldiers guarding the queen hand over their duties to the next watch. Marching to live music, the relieved Queen's guard proceeds up the Mall from St. James's Palace to Buckingham Palace; the new guard approaches from Wellington Barracks via Birdcage Walk. When the two columns meet, they continue marching for 30 minutes, after which the old guard symbolically hands over the keys to the palace. The ceremony takes place daily at 11:30 AM, April–July; on alternating days, August–March. Note that the ceremony is often canceled due to bad weather; check the signs posted in the forecourt to find out when and if it will take place. Unless you arrive by 10:30 AM, forget about a decent frontal view of all the pomp and circumstance. Early birds should grab a section of the gate facing the palace, since most of the hoopla takes place inside the fence. If you arrive late, try standing along Constitution Hill, the thoroughfare leading to Hyde Park Corner. For more information, call 0891/505452.

HOUSES OF PARLIAMENT

The Empire may be dead, but it's still fascinating to explore the site from which Britain once ruled with imperial impunity. The Houses of Parliament is actually one large building, home to the chambers of the House of Commons and the House of Lords, which meet on opposite sides of the octagonal Central Lobby. The complex is officially known as the **Palace of Westminster,** indicative of the strong influence the monarchy held over Parliament for centuries. Parliamentarians rebelled against Charles I during the English Civil War (1642–1648), but before then, they were very much at the beck and call of the monarch. In fact, many kings summoned Parliament only when they needed money (it was Parliament's responsibility to levy taxes).

A major fire in 1834 destroyed almost all of the original Palace of Westminster except for the massive **Westminster Hall,** built in 1097–1099 by William II and rebuilt by Richard II in 1394–1399. The only other remnants of the old parliamentary building are the **Crypt of St. Stephen's Chapel,** where the House of Commons met for 300 years, and the medieval **Jewel Tower** (*see below*). After the blaze, a competition was held for the design of a new Parliament building, and the winners were Charles Barry, a classical architect, and his assistant Augustus Welby Pugin, a Gothicist. While Barry was responsible for the building's practical plan, the elaborate details are the work of Pugin, a converted Catholic who believed that the Gothic style was the only "true" Christian architecture. Not surprisingly, sparks flew between the two men over the new design, but the result was pretty magnificent.

As an overseas visitor, you can request a special "line of route" tour of the Houses of Parliament by writing to the Public Information Office (House of Commons, Westminster, SW1A 2PW) at least a month in advance. The tour takes you through the Queen's Robing Room, Royal Gallery, House of Lords, Central Hall (where MPs meet their constituents), House of Commons, and out into the spectacular Westminster Hall. If you don't arrange for the tour, you can still visit the **Strangers' Galleries** of the House of Commons or the House of Lords while the houses are in session. You can listen in from the galleries as long as debate rages on the floor—sometimes it lasts through the night. Getting into either gallery is tough, however, so try to get tickets in advance from your embassy, or be prepared to wait in line for several hours (lines are shortest after 5:30 PM). *Parliament Square, SW1, tel. 020/7219–4272. Tube: Westminster. For Strangers' Galleries, line up at St. Stephen's Hall Entrance (to the left for the Commons, to the right for the Lords). Admission free. House of Commons open Mon., Tues. 2:30–late, Wed. 9:30–2, 2:30–late, Thurs. 11:30–7:30, Fri. 9:30–3. House of Lords open Mon.–Wed. 2:30–late, Thurs. 3–late, Fri. 11 AM–late.*

HOUSE OF COMMONS

The House of Commons, comprised of 659 elected members from around the country, is where the real power lies. Although destroyed by incendiary bombs in 1941, a sympathetic reconstruction by Sir Giles Gilbert Scott, completed in 1950, modernized the chamber—albeit on strictly utilitarian, green benches—while restoring some of the traditional touches. A pair of red lines running the length of the floor date back to more turbulent times when impassioned debate really raged; the lines are placed exactly two sword lengths apart, and members must still remain behind them.

Nowadays, the level of verbal sparring can produce a parliamentary session more exciting than many a "drama" playing in the West End. The ultimate spectacle is quick and cutting repartee during the prime minister's **Question Time,** held Wednesday between 3 and 3:30 PM. This is when the PM defends himself against the slings and arrows aimed at him by his "right honorable friends." Foreigners are required to secure tickets from their respective embassies, and Brits from their MPs. The next-best time to visit is either chamber's regular Question Time, held Monday–Thursday between 2:30 and 3:30 PM. You're more likely to get into the Commons during an evening session, starting around 5:30 PM. To discern if Parliament is still sitting, look to see if the light at the top of Big Ben is illuminated.

HOUSE OF LORDS

The more prestigious but less powerful of Parliament's two houses is composed of both the **lords spiritual**—archbishops and senior bishops of the Church of England—and the **lords temporal**—British peers and peeresses who inherited their titles, were elevated to their ranks by the queen, or are so-called "lords of appeal" who assist with judicial duties. As a nonelected body, the Lords wield little parliamentary power: They may amend or delay bills, but it is what the House of Commons rules that becomes law. The Lords do interpret the law, however: As the final court of appeal for civil cases in Britain and criminal cases in England, Northern Ireland, and Wales, the Lords hear about 80 cases a year.

The Lords' chamber, masterfully designed by Pugin, is a sumptuous affair, with lots of carved wood paneling, gilt, and leather. It must have been quite a letdown for the members of Commons to return to their own plain chamber after meeting here while theirs was being rebuilt. The Royal Gallery, adjacent to the Lords' chamber, is decorated with frescoes by Daniel Maclise, depicting scenes from British history. The queue is always shorter for the House of Lords, but if you're looking for drama, forget it. The Lords may appear to be snoring the day away, but they are actually leaning their heads close to speakers embedded in the back of the benches—or so they claim. Slumped over like that, it's difficult to picture them as, to use one of their own terms, "not content."

BIG BEN AND VICTORIA TOWER

The clock tower on the north end of the Palace of Westminster, perhaps the most enduring symbol of both London and Britain, has come to be known as **Big Ben.** Actually, it's only the 13½-ton bell on top that's named Big Ben, though few people are aware of the distinction. Details aside, for the millions of colonials worldwide who hear the Westminster chimes nightly on the BBC World Service, the 16 tones evoke a wide range of emotions: home, security, patriotism, and a sense of belonging. Especially when lit up at night, Big Ben's stature seems to dwarf the other buildings in the Parliament complex, even though it's not the tallest. That distinction belongs to the 323-ft-high **Victoria Tower,** reputedly the largest square tower in the world——and it needs to be, as it holds the 5-million-document parliamentary archives. A Union Jack waves from the top of Victoria Tower whenever Parliament is in session.

JEWEL TOWER

Across the street from Victoria Tower, the stumpy Jewel Tower was built in 1365 to house Edward III's precious gems. It survived the fire of 1834, was severely damaged in the Blitz, and was restored in the 1950s. It is now a very worthwhile museum. On display is the "History of Parliament: Past and Present" exhibit. Don't miss the 1,200-year-old Westminster Sword, found on the riverbank alongside Victoria Gardens, or the elaborately embroidered Speakers' Robes. *Abingdon St. (also called Old Palace Yard), just south of Parliament Sq., SW1, tel. 020/7222–2219. Tube: Westminster. Admission £1.50. Open Nov.–Mar., daily 10–4; Apr.–Oct., daily 10–6.*

ST. PAUL'S CATHEDRAL

Right in the center of the City, St. Paul's is instantly recognizable by its huge dome, towering 365 ft (to the top of the ball and cross) above street level. St. Paul's is also the symbolic heart of the city; unlike Westminster Abbey, which is perceived as a royal and national church, St. Paul's is viewed as a church for Londoners. The present structure, the fourth in a series of cathedrals erected on the site, was designed by Christopher Wren and built between 1675 and 1710, shortly after the Great Fire of 1666 ravaged London. Miraculously, the cathedral escaped major damage during World War II, when much of the city was reduced to blazing rubble. The interior of the inner dome's base is encircled by the **Whispering Gallery;** once you've caught your breath from the 259-step climb, whisper into the wall and you'll be heard 100 ft away on the other side of the gallery. Continue upward another 116 steps to the **Golden Gallery** at the top of the dome, and you'll be rewarded with amazing views of London.

Many people will already be familiar with the interior of the cathedral from watching the television broadcast of the wedding of Prince Charles and Lady Diana, but take some time to study the fine points. The placement of **Samuel Johnson's monument,** by the north choir aisle, is as distant from the truth as from his remains: Dr. Johnson is actually buried in Westminster Abbey, and this idealized monument, in the view of present-day pundits, transforms the obese 18th-century lexicographer into a stately Roman dignitary. The **choir** is the most highly decorated part of the cathedral, with 1890s mosaic ceilings, stalls carved by Dutch artist Grinling Gibbons, and iron screens wrought by the French master Jean Tijou. Far below, the **crypt** contains a display on the cathedral's architecture, as well as a small treasury and dozens of tombs of famous people. The tomb of the great builder himself, Christopher Wren, is adorned by his son's famous epitaph: LECTOR, SI MONUMENTUM REQUIRIS, CIRCUMSPICE (Reader, if you seek a monument, look around you). Wren's **Great Model,** an 18-ft-long, exquisitely detailed model of the way things might have been had Wren been allowed to build St. Paul's on a Greek cross design, is in the **Trophy Room** (at triforium level). Wren's classical plan was deemed far too modern and opposed to the clergymen's demand for a traditional long nave. Ironically, plans for rebuilding the cathedral's neighboring structures have been criticized for being too modern because they aren't classical. Attending services is the only way you'll be able to visit on Sunday. As you leave the front steps of St. Paul's, give a thought to the pigeon lady from Mary Poppins. *St. Paul's Churchyard, EC4, tel. 020/7236–4128. Tube: Mansion House or St. Paul's. From Mansion House, walk west on Cannon St., turn right on New Change. From St. Paul's, follow signs. Admission to the cathedral and crypt £4; admission to the galleries £3.50; combined ticket for £6. Open Mon.–Sat. 8:30–4; crypt and treasury open Mon.–Sat. 8:45–4; galleries open Mon.–Sat. 9:30–4.*

TATE BRITAIN

The year 2000 marks the Tate Gallery's name change to Tate Britain and the opening in May of the **Tate Modern** (*see* The South Bank, *below*) across the river in the Bankside Power Station. The large new space will hold most of the Tate's famous 20th-century collection (excluding most British works, but you will find Francis Bacon on both sides of the Thames, for example). The works of contemporary artists will also be located there. The Tate is one of England's principal museums—more contemporary and controversial, but no less impressive, than the National Gallery. The Tate annually rearranges its permanent collection into brilliant and thought-provoking exhibits, often quirkily juxtaposing movements and time periods in rooms dedicated to literature and fantasy, and nudes, to name a few. A major highlight of the collection is the **Clore Gallery,** dedicated to J. M. W. Turner, hailed as Britain's greatest artist. As with the rest of the museum, Clore Gallery exhibits are rotated annually, with selections culled from the Tate's holdings of more than 300 of Turner's paintings, 300 of his personal sketchbooks, and over 19,000 rough drawings and watercolors. Another 19th-century star attraction is the work of artist/poet/proto-hippie **William Blake,** who died in poverty—but is now regularly lauded as "the greatest of England's geniuses." Tate curators like to liven things up a bit by hanging works by artists whom Blake inspired next to art by

The Houses of Parliament's daily schedule, posted at St. Stephen's Gate, can be eye-opening. Debate on the European Union might be allotted, say, an hour, while the issue of "dog fouling" in London streets gets an entire afternoon's thrashing-out.

the great man himself. By no means should you miss the Tate's most unforgettable British image: Sir John Everett Millais's breathtaking Pre-Raphaelite oil painting of Ophelia.

On Saturday at 3 PM, the staff will guide you through a condensation of highlights of the entire Tate collection. "Touch tours" of sculptures are also available for visually impaired visitors; call 020/7887–8725 for bookings. Free lectures, films, and video screenings take place almost daily in the auditorium. *Millbank, SW1, tel. 020/7887–8000 or 020/7887–8008 for recorded info. Tube: Pimlico. Walk north 1 block, turn right on Vauxhall Bridge Rd. (which becomes Bessboro Gardens), left on Millbank. Admission free; £1–£6 for special exhibits. Open daily 10–5:50.*

TOWER OF LONDON

A genuine spine-chiller, the Tower of London is one of the city's leading sights—and it deserves all the attention it gets. With its winding staircases, tunnels, bridges, and narrow passages, the Tower is a great place to get lost in history. It's far more than one tower, though. Some 20 towers comprise the fortress (the largest in medieval Europe), which spreads over 18 acres on the bank of the Thames. Besides serving as the residence of every British sovereign from William the Conqueror (he built the original fortress in 1078) to Henry VIII in the 16th century, the Tower has performed a wide variety of other roles as armory, jewel safe, garrison, and zoo—yes, it's home to Cedric, Gwylum, Hughie II, Munin II, Odint and Thor, the famed Tower ravens (legend has it that if they were to desert the Tower, the kingdom would fall, but the Yeoman Ravenmaster takes no chances—the ravens' wings are clipped). The Tower is most famous, however, for its role as a prison and historic place of execution. Some of England's most notable figures met their deaths here, including Robert Devereux—the Earl of Essex—when he somersaulted from favor with Elizabeth I, and three queens of England: Lady Jane Grey (crowned in 1553 but deposed and executed after only nine days), Anne Boleyn, and Catherine Howard (Henry VIII's second and fifth wives, respectively). The chapel of **St. Peter ad Vincula,** adjacent to the Tower Green execution site, houses their headless skeletons.

A good way to get a sense of the layout of the Tower grounds is to take the free, hour-long tour led by the witty Yeoman Warders—better known as "Beefeaters"—dressed to the gills in Tudor-style costume.

Tours leave from just inside the main entrance every half hour until 3:30 (2:30 in winter), except in bad weather. If you fancy yourself as a dashing figure in that costume, you'll have a long wait—Warders must have 22 years of honorable service in the Army, Royal Marines, or Royal Air Force before they can even apply for the job.

The most impressive and oldest of the towers is the **White Tower.** It was one of a number of fortified structures erected in London by the justifiably nervous William the Conqueror. The White Tower is currently being refurbished with new displays from the Royal Armouries collection that will unfold the story of this medieval building along with a floor-after-floor dazzling display of the Tower's immaculately polished and beautifully crafted arms and armor collection. Must-see: the four suits of Henry VIII's armor marking his transmogrification from a "very fair" and "admirably proportioned" young king to the bloated, middle-aged tyrant he became. The tranquil **Chapel of St. John,** on the tower's first floor, is a serene haven amid all the military paraphernalia. The oldest church in town, the structure's curved Norman-period arches are stunning in their simplicity and grace. In jarring contrast, a small collection of **torture instruments** lurks in the basement below.

The Crown Jewels, now housed in the **Jewel House** just north of the White Tower, are the star attraction. The Sovereign Sceptre wields the largest cut diamond in the world, a 530-carat monster from the Cullinan diamond. The Imperial State Crown, made for the coronation of George VI in 1937 and altered for Her Majesty Queen Elizabeth II in 1953, is studded with 3,000 precious stones, including the second-largest diamond in the world. Though the design of the new Jewel House speeds things up a bit, shiny objects tend to stall the huge crowds. It's best to visit immediately after the Tower opens or just before it closes. The wait could last for hours at midday, especially on weekends.

Other points of interest include **Beauchamp Tower**—which has more than 400 eerie notes and doodles carved over centuries into the stone by prisoners—and **Lanthorn Tower,** which contains small but excellent exhibits on life in Medieval England. **Bloody Tower** is one of the possible locations where the so-called Little Princes, Edward V and his brother, were murdered in the 15th century, probably by henchmen of either Richard III or Henry VII. It is also where Sir Walter Raleigh spent 13 years of imprisonment, during which he wrote his immodestly titled History of the World. Not too shabby, really. The **Medieval Palace** is the site of Edward's Magna Camera (Great Chamber), used as the seat of rule on the rare occasions he was in residence, and **Wakefield Tower** has an impressive Throne Room with 13th-century replicas showing the opulence of Edward's court. The **Wall Walk,** linking the Wakefield and Lanthorn towers, offers great views of Tower Bridge. You'll notice the so-called moat around the Tower is in fact a dry old ditch. It was drained in 1840 but could once again host the wet stuff if plans for a refill come through. After a day in the tourist crush you might wearily wonder why they need to attract yet more visitors. *Tower Hill, EC3, tel. 020/7709–0765. Tube: Tower Hill. Walk south following signs. Admission £10.50. Open Mar.–Oct., Mon.–Sat. 9–5, Sun. 10–5; Nov.–Feb., Tues.–Sat. 9–4, Sun. and Mon. 10–4 (last admission 1 hr before closing; last entry to exhibits 30 mins before closing).*

TOWER BRIDGE

A three-minute walk along the Thames from the Tower of London brings you to Tower Bridge, a Gothic fancy built in 1894. Inside the twin towers, you'll find The Tower Bridge Experience, a multimedia attraction recounting over 100 years of the bridge's fascinating history. Highlights include storytelling animatronic characters, interactive computers and other hands-on activities, the original Victorian steam rooms, and of course, the magnificent views of London from the 140-ft-high walkways above the Thames. The bridge itself still opens approximately 500 times a year; if you're lucky you'll catch the spectacle (call 020/7378–7700 for a current schedule). *Tel. 020/7403–3761. Tube: Tower Hill. Admission £5.95. Open Apr.–Oct., daily 10–6:30 (last admission 5:15); Nov.–Mar., daily 9:30–6 (last admission 4:45).*

TRAFALGAR SQUARE

To you, Trafalgar Square might seem no more than a huge traffic circle or a place to spend an afternoon poking through some pretty cool museums. Many Londoners, however, consider it the heart of their town, and its notable landmark, Nelson's Column, probably makes it the city's most famous square. In 1829, Trafalgar Square was transformed from royal stables to public square in honor of nationally revered naval honcho Lord Horatio Nelson, who died in battle after decimating the French and Spanish fleets at Cape Trafalgar (on the southwest coast of Spain) in 1805. In 1840, architect E. H. Baily began work on the 185-ft-tall column, Trafalgar Square's most obvious landmark (and a heroic overstatement, considering wee "Baron Nelson of the Nile" measured only 5 ft 4 inches in life). Four gigantic bronze lions were added by sculptor Sir Edward Landseer in 1858.

The square is great for people-watching as it attracts quite an odd assortment of characters. Long after sunset, its role as the main stopping point for late-night buses makes it one of the trippiest, coolest places in London. Packs of clubbers and tourists mill around boozily, making nocturnal hot-dog vendors rich and happy. On New Year's Eve, you can multiply the nightlife factor at Trafalgar Square by about 100: It's the most popular place in the city to ring in the new year. This might have something to do with the large clocks around the square; most being perpetually out of sync, loopy crowds end up celebrating the coming of midnight two or three times in a row.

NATIONAL GALLERY

After Great Britain got rich in the 19th century, it felt compelled to hoard a little accredited culture to prove it wasn't arriviste. It began to amass a huge haul of Renaissance Italian paintings, as well as masterworks by Dutch, Flemish, German, English, and French masters. To accommodate the growing collection, Parliament bought a plot of land on the edge of Trafalgar Square in 1828 and began to build the National Gallery, a bland classical structure best known for its tall, sandy-brown columns. Today, if you can get past the legions of pigeons guarding the front doors, you'll find one of the world's most impressive collections of Western European art, ranked right up there with Paris's Louvre and Florence's Uffizi.

A very small Whitman's Sampler of masterpieces: Jan van Eyck's *Arnolfini Marriage,* Leonardo's *Madonna of the Rocks* and *Burlington Virgin and Child,* Uccello's *Battle of San Romano,* Giovanni Bellini's *The Doge Leonardo Loredan,* Caravaggio's *Supper at Emmaus,* Velázquez's *"Rokeby Venus,"* and that icon of golden-age rural England, Constable's *Hay Wain.* There are plenty of other treasures by Tintoretto, della Francesca, Michelangelo, Monet, Titian, Rubens, Van Dyck, Goya, Rembrandt, Turner, Gainsborough, Seurat, et cetera, et

For its 150th birthday, the statue atop Nelson's Column received a present: a good scrubbing and a coat of pigeon-proof gel.

cetera. Ready yourself for a staggering variety of Virgins and Sons. Thanks to government patronage and public lottery monies, the salons here gleam with expensive brocades and silks, and the collection continues to be enriched year by year with legendary works of art.

The National Gallery's collection is displayed chronologically in the building's four wings. The **Sainsbury Wing** (paid for by the Sainsbury supermarket family) displays medieval and early Renaissance works (1260–1510). The **West Wing** is devoted to the High Renaissance (1510–1600), the **North Wing** to the Dutch masters (1600–1700), and the **East Wing** to English portraiture and some of the better-known Impressionists, spanning the centuries from 1700 to 1900. Free, one-hour guided tours begin in the Sainsbury Wing weekdays at 11:30 AM and 2:30 PM, and on Saturday at 2 PM and 3:30 PM. Brave souls who decide to go it alone should pick up a floor plan at the entrance, or stop by the museum's free, technophobe-friendly **Micro Gallery,** where you can use a computer to look at your favorite paintings and then print out your own personalized "grand tour." Also available for use is the Gallery Guide Soundtrack, which allows you to select the pictures you want to hear about in any order. Free lectures on a variety of topics take place weekdays (1 PM) and Saturday (noon); check at an information desk for details. Since admission is free here and the collection is that rich, plan on coming back for several visits. *Trafalgar Sq., WC2, tel. 020/7747–2885. Tube: Charing Cross or Leicester Square. Admission free. Open Mon.–Sat. 10–6, Wed. until 6:30 PM, Sun. noon–6.*

NATIONAL PORTRAIT GALLERY

Painted faces, sculpted faces, drawn faces, photographed faces—the National Portrait Gallery is as much about the act and the art of portraiture as it is about the men and women (mostly men) who made Britannia great. The portraits of aristocrats, military men, thespians, and politicians are arranged chronologically from the top floor to the bottom; take the elevator to the top and wind your way down through the ages. The final leg of the exhibit brings you right up to the present, and walking out onto the streets of London afterward provides a fitting sense of closure, and for many, a sense of relief. *St. Martin's Pl., WC2, tel. 020/7 306–0055. Tube: Charing Cross or Leicester Square. Admission free; small fee for some special exhibitions. Open Mon.–Sat. 10–6, Sun. noon–6.*

ST. MARTIN-IN-THE-FIELDS

In the northeast corner of Trafalgar Square stands the plain, white-marble church of St. Martin-in-the-Fields. This is where the prestigious Academy of St. Martin-in-the-Fields was founded in 1958 (its orchestra was made famous by the soundtrack of Amadeus). Handel played on the church's first organ, and Mozart is reputed to have given a concert here on one of his megaworld tours. These days, free music recitals take place Monday, Tuesday, and Friday at 1:05 PM—and are probably the best way to take in the church's grim memorials to the British war dead. Evening concerts (£6–£16), performed by candlelight, usually feature big-name ensembles. Like most churches, St. Martin's possesses a crypt, but this isn't your typical musty repository of old bones. Instead, the **Cafe-in-the-Crypt** (tel. 020/7839–4342) is one of the coolest, most atmospheric places for latte in all of London. With rough-hewn stone pillars, low, vaulted ceilings, and floors tiled with worn grave markers, it's the perfect place to pen moody, intense postcards to the folks back home. Additionally, the crypt houses a modest art gallery and bookstore, and the **London Brass Rubbing Center** (tel. 020/7930–9306), where for £2.50–£15 (depending on size) you can make rubbings from historic brasses using gold, bronze, or silver wax. *East side of Trafalgar Sq., WC2, tel. 020/7930–0089 or 020/7839–8362 for box office. Open Mon.–Sat. 10–8, Sun. noon–8.*

WESTMINSTER ABBEY

Westminster Abbey has become so popular a tourist attraction—blaring announcements from nave loudspeakers even request moments of silence from the milling throngs—that it's easy to forget its enormous religious and cultural importance. Founded in 1065 by Edward the Confessor, who was both king and saint, it reflects the close relationship of church and state in Britain. The country's monarchs have been crowned and buried here since William the Conqueror assumed the English throne on Christmas Day, AD 1066. Burial in Westminster is one of the highest honors the country can bestow, and accordingly, a walk through this vast, ornate abbey is like perusing a *Who's Who* of British history. Among the deceased sovereigns buried here are Elizabeth I, Mary Queen of Scots, Richard II, and Henry VII. Though you can enter the Abbey's nave for free, it costs a sizable investment—£4—to see Poets' Corner and the Royal Chapels—the most memorable parts of the Abbey. There is a reduced admission charge to the Royal Chapels on Wednesday from 6 to 7:45 PM, which is also the only time photography is allowed in any part of the Abbey.

Behind the altar, the **Chapel of St. Edward the Confessor** is home to the Coronation Chair, still used for the coronation of Britain's kings and queens. In recent years, hooligans have managed to etch graffiti all over the wooden chair; when or if Prince Charles is crowned, his royal derriere will rest on incisive comments like "C loves S forever" and "smoke dope." The chair was built in 1300 to enclose the Stone of Scone (pronounced Skoon), which Edward I swiped from Scotland in 1296. The Stone of Destiny, as it is also known, is a symbol of Scottish independence and its location contributed to the friction between the two countries. Scottish nationalists stole back the stone in 1950, but Scotland Yard (a misnomer) recovered it six months later. In an attempt to appease the Scottish nationalists, John Major had the stone returned to Edinburgh Castle in 1996—the 700th-year anniversary of its removal. It will, however, be brought back to London for the coronation of future monarchs. Farther back you'll find **Henry VII's Chapel,** one of Britain's most beautiful examples of the rich Gothic style. The tomb of Henry VII and his wife, Elizabeth, was created by Italian artist Torrigiano, better known for popping Michelangelo on the nose during an argument.

Nearly all the deceased greats of English literature are featured in Westminster's **Poets' Corner,** in the south transept. Geoffrey Chaucer was the first to be buried here, in 1400. Memorial plaques pay homage to other luminaries, such as Shakespeare, T. S. Eliot, Byron, Tennyson, Dylan Thomas, and, more recently, Oscar Wilde. Ye olde monks once pontificated and wandered through the **Cloisters** on the south side of the nave. Open to the air, the cloisters retain a tranquillity that the main portion of the Abbey loses after the early morning hours. At the end of a passage leading from the Cloisters is the octagonal, spacious **Chapter House,** once a meeting place of England's Parliament. *Dean's Yard, SW1, tel. 020/7222–5152. Tube: Westminster. Cross Parliament Sq., follow Broad Sanctuary. Admission £5. Royal Chapels open weekdays 9–4:45 (last admission 3:45), Sat. 9–2:45 (last admission 2) and 3:45–5:45 (last admission 2:45). Closed Sun.*

LONDON NEIGHBORHOODS

London is best approached as a series of its highly distinct, diverse neighborhoods, many of which were once towns or villages in their own right. Regardless of who you are or what you're after, London has a neighborhood to fulfill your every whim. If it's government buildings and famous monuments, Whitehall has more than enough for the hardiest tourist. If you prefer a little boho culture, head for the likes of **Brixton, Camden, Notting Hill, Hampstead,** or **Hoxton.** For a vicarious taste of the good (or at least expensive) life, sashay over to ritzy **Mayfair, St. James,** or **Chelsea.** If you're interested in London's legal and financial institutions, make your way to **Holborn** and **the City,** respectively. There's great people-watching at **Covent Garden,** as well as in the various central squares. And for a taste of authentic, workaday London (and an earful of Cockney accents), check out the **East End.** The following section explores these exciting neighborhoods, moving westward from Chelsea over to the City district, which borders on the East End. Within each neighborhood, sights are discussed in the sequence of a pleasant walk.

CHELSEA

Chelsea, just south of Knightsbridge, is mostly quiet and residential—except for its famous King's Road (*see below*), which is a swell place for a stroll if you like to shop. South of **King's Road,** running along the Thames between Battersea and Albert bridges, is a short strip called **Cheyne Walk** (pronounced Chainy), where George Eliot (No. 4), Dante Gabriel Rosetti (No. 16), and Mick Jagger (No. 48) once lived. Certainly no artists or literary masters roam the streets now; all you'll find are privileged Chelseans walking their pampered Labradors along the manicured streets. You can, however, get a glimpse into the life of one long-gone literary giant. **Thomas Carlyle's House** (24 Cheyne Row, SW3, tel. 020/7352-7087) is just as the Carlyles left it more than 150 years ago—Thomas's hat is still where he put it before he died, and all the furniture, books, and possessions remain intact. It's open April–October, Wednesday–Sunday 11–5, and admission is £3.30. The romantic **Ranelagh Gardens,** off the Chelsea Embankment (that's what they call Cheyne Walk east of Albert Bridge), is a fine place to visit, especially on warm summer nights. Mozart gave a concert here in 1764 at the age of eight, and it's easy to imagine the London elite of past centuries putting on airs while meandering along the footpaths. The famed Chelsea Flower show is held here in May.

CHELSEA PHYSIC GARDEN

Established in 1676 by the Society of Apothecaries, this garden was used for the teaching of the medicinal properties of herbs and other plants. The high walls surrounding the garden create an almost Mediterranean ambience, encouraging flowers to bloom out of season. Afternoon tea is served between 2:30 and 4:45—it's a double treat to munch cakes while surrounded by riotously blooming exotics. *66 Royal Hospital Road (entrance on Swan Walk), SW3, tel. 020/7352–5646. Tube: Sloane Square. Walk south on Lower Sloane St., turn right on Royal Hospital Rd. Admission £4. Open Apr.–Oct., Wed. noon–5, Sun. 2–6.*

KING'S ROAD

King's Road has gone yuppie in the last decade or so, but this was where rebel chicks bought the world's first miniskirts (invented by designer Mary Quant, who had a boutique on King's Road) in the '60s, and where punk rock was born in the 1970s. Legend goes that the whole punk thing started when the Sex Pistols popped into fashion designer Vivienne Westwood's little King's Road boutique, named Sex, for a few pairs of bondage trousers. Voilà! Within a few years the whole boulevard was crammed with counterculture clothing shops, record stores, and members of the disaffected youth generation. The aggressively weird still assemble on weekends at the northeast end of King's Road, around **Sloane Square.** *Tube: Sloane Square.*

KENSINGTON AND KNIGHTSBRIDGE

Kensington is museum central: In one large block you'll find three major museums—the Victoria and Albert Museum, the Natural History Museum, and the Science Museum. The neighborhoods of **South Kensington** and **Earl's Court** are riddled with budget lodgings and hordes of travelers—Londoners themselves can be a bit thin on the ground around here. As you move northeast toward Knightsbridge, however, the streetscape gets more ritzy and prices go through the roof—only Mayfair and St. James's carry more snob value. Just north of Knightsbridge lie two of London's best parks, **Hyde Park** and **Kensington Gardens** (*see below*).

HOLLAND PARK

Beautiful Holland Park inhabits a sizable chunk of posh Kensington, just north of the intersection of Kensington High Street and Earl's Court Road. To the north you'll find stunning gardens and woodlands where wild peacocks roam. At the park's center is the formal **Dutch Garden** (first planted by Lady Holland in the 1790s) and a glass-walled art gallery, the **Orangery.** At the south side of the park stands the **Commonwealth Institute** (230 Kensington High St., W8, tel. 020/7603–4535), whose small museum is dedicated to the 50 member-nations of the former British Empire. It's open daily 10–5 (last admission 4:30). *Tube: High Street Kensington or Holland Park.*

LEIGHTON HOUSE

The former home and studio of Lord Frederic Leighton (1830–1896), a classical painter and avid collector of Islamic art and other Asian treasures, is now a beautifully decorated museum. The **Arab Hall,** constructed with intricately detailed tiles and mosaic friezes, is breathtaking. Leighton and pals were not bad painters either, as evidenced by the wonderful Victorian oils in the other rooms. *12 Holland Park Rd., W14, tel. 020/7602–3316. Tube: High Street Kensington. Walk west on Kensington High St., turn right on Melbury Rd., left on Holland Park Rd. Admission free. Open Mon.–Sat. 11–5:30.*

NATURAL HISTORY MUSEUM

A thorough collection of plants and animals is housed in the impressive Earth and Life galleries of this fun museum. There are fossils, dinosaur skeletons, a Creepy Crawlies Gallery, stuffed animals (in the literal, taxidermic sense) from every corner of the earth, and amazing interactive exhibits such as a simulated earthquake—the whole shebang. Perhaps more impressive than the contents is the building itself. Designed by Alfred Waterhouse in 1862, the museum was built as a cathedral to science, decorated throughout with images of living and extinct animals and fossils. Stop in during the free hours just to take a peek. *Cromwell Rd., SW7, tel. 020/7938–9123. Tube: South Kensington. Walk north on Exhibition Rd., turn left on Cromwell Rd. Admission £6; free weekdays after 4:30, weekends after 5. Open Mon.–Sat. 10–5:50, Sun. 11–5:50.*

SCIENCE MUSEUM

The Science Museum's six floors are chock-full of neato, user-friendly exhibits about science, technology, industry, and medicine. In all, they've got 15,000 objects and 2,000 interactive exhibits. *Exhibition Rd., SW7, tel. 0207/938–8111 recorded info; 0207/938–8000 info desk. Tube: South Kensington. Walk north on Exhibition Rd. Admission £6.50; free daily after 4:30. Open daily 10–6.*

VICTORIA AND ALBERT MUSEUM

The best way to take in the enormous collection of this stellar and chic museum, affectionately called the V&A, is to allow yourself a whole day to get lost in its 7 mi of gallery space, then try to find your way out. The place is packed with a vast and eclectic collection of fine and decorative arts, crossing all disciplines, all periods, all nationalities, and all tastes. The V&A was founded in 1852 as a Museum of Manufacturers, to motivate and educate British manufacturers and designers by building on the fantastic success of the Great Exhibition of the previous year. In 1899, it was renamed the Victoria and Albert Museum in honor of the widowed Queen Victoria. Now, nearly a century later, the V&A has stirred up enormous controversy with announcements of a £42 million extension. Called the **Boilerhouse Project,** it will house a state-of-the-art multimedia section full of computers and virtual reality gizmos and galleries for contemporary exhibits.

Inside the main museum, you'll pass treasures weird and wonderful, like the snuff box believed to have been a gift to Nell Gwyn from Charles II, the great Mughal emperor Shah Jahan's jade cup, and the 12-ft-square, solid-oak, four-poster **Great Bed of Ware,** immortalized by Shakespeare in Twelfth Night. The **Art and Design Galleries** exhibit everything from Indian art to Italian Renaissance sculpture. Absolutely fabulous is the **Dress Collection** (Room 40), with clothing from 1600 to the present day. The **Raphael Gallery** displays seven priceless tapestry cartoons by the great Renaissance master, and the **Frank Lloyd Wright Gallery** houses the only re-created Wright interior in Europe. And that's just a fraction of what this unique museum has to offer. Two varieties of free guided tours are offered daily; check at the info desk for topics and times. During two-thirds of the year the V&A stays open 6:30–9:30 PM on Wednesday evenings for what is called "Late View," when there's live music, a garden wine bar, free gallery talks, and lectures. Invariably, these events manage to draw some of the most decorative people in London. *Cromwell Rd., SW7, tel. 020/7938–8500; 020/7938–8349 recorded info. Tube: South Kensington. Walk north on Exhibition Rd., turn right on Cromwell Rd. Admission £5; free entry between 4:30–5:50. Open daily 10–5:45.*

HARRODS

This is the granddaddy of all London department stores, and a magnet for every tourist on the planet. Don't come here to shop—it's incredibly expensive—but rather to browse. Many of the upper floors are just like any other department store, so you're much better off moseying down to the lavish **food halls** where an amazing array of food is available, including exotic fruits and vegetables, delectable cakes, and over 300 cheeses. If you don't mind carnage, visit the meat hall where skilled butchers and fishmongers in crisp aprons bustle under ceiling tiles illustrating *The Hunt,* painted by W. J. Neatby in 1902. Throughout the store, however, are other sights, such as the Egyptian-themed central escalators. If you're here around Christmas, ogle the decorations and displays—they really do it up in style. *87–135 Brompton Rd., SW1, tel. 020/7730–1234. Tube: Knightsbridge. Walk south on Brompton Rd. Open Mon.–Tues. and Sat. 10–6, Wed.–Fri. 10–7.*

ROYAL ALBERT HALL

This prestigious venue (named after Queen Victoria's hubby) is currently undergoing a major renovation program costing £40 million-plus, funded in part by the National Lottery and not due to finish until 2003. Home to the acclaimed **Royal Philharmonic Orchestra** and the enormously popular **Promenade Concerts** (*see* After Dark, *below*), the interior—a huge amphitheater done up in wine-red and gold—is the height of Victorian imperial architecture and is graced with the largest pipe organ in Great Britain. Unfortunately, tours of such splendors are not available to the public while the renovation work is being done. To see it you'll have to buy a concert ticket. Barring that, pop by for a look at the exterior, if only because the concert hall is mentioned in the Beatles song "A Day in the Life." *Kensington Gore, near Exhibition Rd., W8, tel. 020/7589–3203; 020/7589–8212 box office. Tube: Knightsbridge. Walk west on Knightsbridge (which becomes Kensington Rd. and Kensington Gore).*

HYDE PARK AND KENSINGTON GARDENS

Hyde Park and Kensington Gardens blend together to form one large 634-acre park, the largest in London. Though these days it's difficult to tell where one ends and the other begins, each has a unique origin: Hyde Park began as the hunting grounds of Henry VIII (who swiped the land from the monks at Westminster), while Kensington Gardens was first laid out as the grounds for William and Mary's Kensington Palace (*see below*). In summer, this is a great place to lounge in one of hundreds of conveniently placed deck chairs, available for hire (80p). Small boats cruise on the **Serpentine**, a long, thin lake that arcs through the middle of the two parks. You can rent a rowboat or a pedal boat at the boathouse for £7 an hour. Not far away, overlooking the Long Water, is one of the most beloved spots in London, the **statue of Peter Pan,** designed in 1912 by George Frampton to honor E. M. Barrie's fabled creation—the boy who never grew up.

Famous faces in the National Portrait Gallery include Chaucer, Shakespeare, and the Brontës (minus their brother—look for the smudge). However, the ones that draw the largest crowds are the portraits of Diana and Charles.

You're also duty-bound not to miss **Speakers' Corner** on the northeast edge of Hyde Park (Tube: Marble Arch). Since 1873, this has been hallowed ground for amateur orators burning to make a point—in the early days, speakers used soapboxes; now they climb aboard aluminum stepladders. The oratorical fireworks hit full swing by about 2 or 3 PM on weekends, as spielers spiel, hecklers heckle, and free speech dovetails into street theater. In 1996 Speakers' Corner became a sparring ground for Islamic extremists and Christian evangelists, who still make appearances on a regular basis. The park also makes a great place to crash after haggling at the splendid **Portobello Road Market** (*see* Street Markets *in* Shopping, *below*).

APSLEY HOUSE • At the southeast corner of Hyde Park stands Apsley House, also known as the Wellington Museum. This was once considered the best address in town—No. 1 London—and was home to the august Duke of Wellington. Inside you'll find the "Iron Duke's" collection of paintings, silver, porcelain, furniture, and sculpture, including Canova's massive, nude-but-for-a-fig-leaf statue of his archenemy, Napoléon Bonaparte. The highlight is the Waterloo Gallery—one of the most sumptuously spectacular rooms in England. *149 Piccadilly, tel. 020/7499–5676. Tube: Hyde Park Corner. Admission £4. Open Tues.–Sun. 11–5.*

KENSINGTON PALACE • Kensington Palace has seen a lot of history since it was converted by Christopher Wren in 1689 from plain old mansion to royal homestead. Once the London residence of Prince Charles and Princess Diana, it was the venue for Diana's suicide bid down a sweeping staircase. Visitors can do the once-over of the **Cupola Room,** where Queen Victoria was baptized; the **King's Gallery,** filled with fine 17th-century paintings; and the **State Apartments,** where the once newly crowned Queen Mary II and William III first lived the connubial life. Part of the complex and just a few steps from the palace is the Orangery—a delightful place for an expensive cuppa. *Kensington Gardens, W8, tel. 020/7937–9561. Tube: High Street Kensington or Queensway. Admission £5.50. The palace is open May–Sept., daily 10–4:45.*

ALBERT MEMORIAL • Across from the Royal Albert Hall is the grandiose Albert Memorial, commissioned by Queen Victoria as an expression of her obsessive reverence for her dead husband. Here a 25-

ft-tall, gold-plated Albert sits under an ornate canopy, clutching a catalog of the Great International Exhibition of 1851 (his brainchild). The base is decorated with 169 life-size figures of poets, composers, architects, and sculptors. The Albert Memorial recently underwent a £14 million restoration; its almost garish new appearance caused a small sensation. *Kensington Gardens, SW7. Tube: High Street Kensington or Knightsbridge.*

MAYFAIR

Mayfair is an ultraritzy residential neighborhood lined with beautiful 18th-century apartment towers faced with deep red brick. Many national embassies, and some of London's wealthiest citizens, call Mayfair home. But, unless you have a ton of money, window shopping could be your only option. The sheer number of Rolls-Royces, Bentleys, and Jaguars rolling around Mayfair is staggering; even the delivery vans seem to bear a royal coat of arms, proclaiming them to be purveyors of fine goodies for as long as anyone can remember. The one exception is noisy, rollicking **Oxford Street** (*see below*). To reach Mayfair, take the tube to Baker or Bond streets.

WALLACE COLLECTION

Hertford House makes a suitably impressive gallery for this incredible art collection, including 18th- and 19th-century French paintings and furniture; Dutch, Italian, English, and Spanish paintings; Medieval, Renaissance, and Baroque works of art; and even arms and armor. Titian, Rembrandt, and Poussin are among the bigger names here, but the collection is very strong on Greuze's doe-eyed, soft-focused maidens, and Franz Hals's *The Laughing Dutchman* hangs in an upstairs gallery. The Wallace Collection is a perfect place to contemplate the art, since the place is relatively quiet and not crammed with tourists. *Hertford House, Manchester Square, W1, tel. 020/7935–0687. Tube: Bond Street. Walk west on Oxford St., turn right on James St., left on Manchester Square. Admission free. Open Mon.–Sat. 10–5, Sun. noon–5.*

BERKELEY SQUARE

Shaded by tall trees and populated by cheeky squirrels, Berkeley Square (pronounced Barkley) is a great place to get the feel of Mayfair. The park is ringed with a high iron fence, and on one side you'll find a Rolls-Royce dealership that stays open late during the annual Berkeley Square Ball—in the hope that wealthy revelers will spring for a new £60,000 roadster. Though the square suffered from a poor redevelopment plan in the 1930s, a line of fine Georgian houses (circa 1737) remains on the west side. No. 44, built in 1740 for one Lady Isabella Finch, has been called London's finest terraced house. Clive of India overdosed on laudanum next door at No. 45 in 1774. Just west of Berkeley Square, **Mount Street Gardens** (also called St. George's Gardens) is a fine place for a picnic. *Tube: Green Park. Walk NW 1 block on Piccadilly, turn left on Berkeley St.*

SHEPHERD'S MARKET

The May Fair, the market famed for its ribald entertainment that gave its name to the neighborhood, moved here in 1686 from the Haymarket. Today, Shepherd's Market is a charming nest of pedestrian-only alleys loaded to the gills with cafés and wine bars. It's tony, quiet, and an exceedingly pleasant place to while away an hour over a cappuccino. *Tube: Green Park. Walk west on Piccadilly, turn right on Half Moon St., left on Curzon St.*

OXFORD STREET

Oxford Street—which runs from Marble Arch to Tottenham Court Road—is busy, noisy, packed with wild-eyed shoppers, and often quite tacky. Cramming both sides of the street are some 300 clothing stores, plus lots of steak houses, a few mammoth department stores, scads of souvenir shops, and four major music and video stores. A worthwhile detour from such Sturm und Drang is South Molton Street, a pedestrian arcade at the corner of Oxford and Davies streets. If you ferret around in the little alleys and passageways, you'll find some nice sandwich shops and pubs. *Tube: Bond Street, Marble Arch, Oxford Circus, or Tottenham Court Road.*

BOND STREET

Perpendicular to Oxford Street, Bond Street may be the most exclusive shopping street in London. It's divided into **New Bond** and **Old Bond,** and is just chock-full of the kind of people who coo over £10,000 dresses and £60 silk cravats. As far as shops go, jewelers, antiques dealers, and sellers of original art predominate, and many of them won't give you a second look unless you're trailed by a liveried chauffeur. Maybe you find that shtick sick, but even the impoverished will get a kick out of attending an auc-

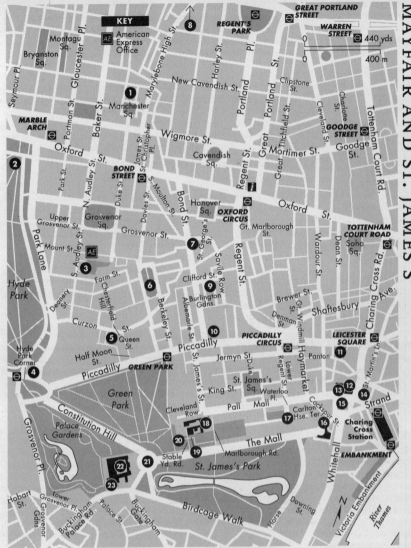

KEY

AE American Express Office

440 yds
400 m

Admiralty Arch, **16**

Apsley House, **4**

Berkeley Square, **6**

Buckingham Palace, **22**

Clarence House, **19**

Cork Street, **9**

Institute of Contemporary Arts (ICA), **17**

Lancaster House, **20**

Leicester Square, **11**

Madame Tussaud's/London Planetarium, **8**

Mount Street Gardens, **3**

National Gallery, **13**

National Portrait Gallery, **12**

Queen Victoria Memorial, **21**

Queen's Gallery and Royal Mews, **23**

Royal Academy of Arts, **10**

Shepherd's Market, **5**

Sotheby's, **7**

Speakers' Corner, **2**

St. James's Palace, **18**

St. Martin-in-the-Fields, **14**

Trafalgar Square, **15**

Wallace Collection, **1**

tion at **Sotheby's** (34 New Bond St., W1, tel. 020/7493–8080). Dress nicely, and see who you can fool. They usually have morning lots at least three days a week between 10 and 11, and sometimes an afternoon run at 2:30. East of Bond Street is **Savile Row,** famous for its many accomplished tailors and the site of the Beatles' last public appearance: an impromptu performance on the roof of the Apple Records building (No. 3—today, private offices) in 1969. *Tube: Bond Street, Green Park, or Piccadilly Circus.*

CORK STREET

Parallel to Bond Street is Cork Street, the center of the established commercial art scene in London, with more than a dozen private galleries between **Burlington Gardens** and **Clifford Street.** They're close together, so it's easy to hit them all within a few hours—and though they sometimes look intimidating, all are open to the public free of charge. *Tube: Green Park or Piccadilly Circus. From Green Park, walk east on Piccadilly, turn left on Old Bond St., right on Burlington Gardens. From Piccadilly Circus, walk NW 1 long block on Regent St., turn left on Vigo St. (which becomes Burlington Gardens).*

SOHO

Soho began its tenure as one of the leading bohemian neighborhoods of London during the 1950s, when it emerged as a beatnik stomping ground and the heart of the London jazz scene. In the 1960s, rock took over and the area became home to a new counterculture, with clubs featuring headliners like the Rolling Stones, the Who, and the Kinks, in their respective heydays. With the coming of punk and seminal bands like the Sex Pistols, Generation X, the Clash, and X-Ray Specs, Chelsea's King's Road replaced Soho as the home of London's pop culture, leading to a resurgence of jazz sounds in Soho, which continue to this day. Soho's streets are lined with an odd amalgam of fashionable clothing stores, gourmet restaurants, high-power hair salons, trendy cafés, theaters, and nightclubs, plus a smattering of XXX-rated sex shops (remnants of the 'hood's long-ago incarnation as the red-light district of London). Still, this remains one of London's most human-scale and delightful neighborhoods. No wonder Sir Paul McCartney still has offices overlooking Soho Square.

Soho has an international flavor that many of central London's neighborhoods lack; generally, you'd have to go to the city outskirts to find such a polyglot community. French Huguenots arriving in the 1680s were the first foreigners to settle the area en masse, followed by Germans, Russians, Poles, and Greeks—though Soho today has more Chinese and Italian influences. The Chinese community is clustered around **Gerrard Street** (*see* Chinatown, *below*). If you're looking for traditional Italian restaurants and cafés, head **for Old Compton Street,** which is also a major center for gay life in the city. Tourists and locals alike browse **Berwick Street**'s market. If you catch the tube to Leicester Square, Oxford Circus, Piccadilly Circus, or Tottenham Court Road, you'll find yourself right on the edge of Soho.

LEICESTER SQUARE

Leicester Square is often compared to New York's Times Square, but it isn't as big or bright. Like any major entertainment district, Leicester (pronounced Lester) has some shady characters and an off-and-on drug scene. Huge movie houses, many converted from grand old theaters, surround the square, tacky tourist attractions line some of the side streets, and weird street theater is often staged on the pedestrian mall at the western edge of the square. On the west side is the **Society of West End Theatres** ticket kiosk (*see* Theater *in* After Dark, *below*), where you can buy half-price, same-day tickets for many shows. Just off Leicester Square on Leicester Place stands the oasis-like **Notre Dame de France,** a modern French Catholic church worth visiting if only to see an impressive Jean Cocteau mural in a chapel dedicated to the Virgin.

PICCADILLY CIRCUS

Only the most gullible of tourists still believe Ringling Brothers tigers and acrobats perform at Piccadilly Circus. Rather, the weird name comes out of the dark days of the 17th century, when men wore *picadils* (ruffled collars) and one smart young tailor grew rich enough on the proceeds to build a fine house. Snobs sneeringly labeled it "Piccadilly Hall," and when the mansion was later ripped down to build a circular junction for five major roads, the name morphed into "Piccadilly Circus." Despite the lack of rainbow-haired clowns, the circle offers plenty of fine people-watching, especially on the steps of the famous **Eros** statue (which earned this nickname from its reputation as a meeting place for lovers) or on the wall of the fountain beneath the bronze **Horse of Helios** sculpture. While electric signs make Piccadilly Circus one of London's bids to look like Tokyo, many of the buildings here are Edwardian marble extravaganzas and are nobly beautiful in their own right. Note to kitsch-seekers: Piccadilly Circus is also home to treasures like an animatronic Janis Joplin, a 100% wax Artist-Formerly-Known-As-Prince, a

SOHO AND COVENT GARDEN

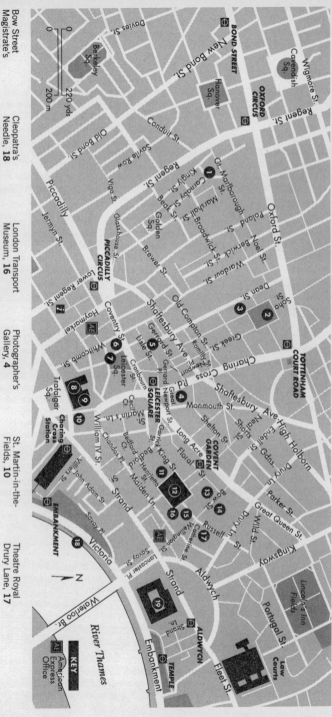

wondrous "Wall of Hands," lots of laser lights, and plenty of taped guitar solos. All are at Madame Tussaud's Rock Circus (1 Piccadilly Circus, tel. 020/7734–7203). They call it the "No. 1 Rock Attraction in Britain," but you'd have to overdose on post-modern irony to get any genuine enjoyment from these singing stiffs, although a recent refurbishment has improved matters somewhat. Admission is £8.25. *Tube: Piccadilly Circus.*

CHINATOWN

Known as **Tong Yan Kai** (Chinese Streets) by residents, Chinatown has some purely Disney-like trappings—telephone booths topped by pagodas, for example. But before you work yourself into a tizzy thinking you've rediscovered Shanghai in Greenwich Mean Time, understand that London's Chinatown is very small. In fact, it's really only two short streets, **Gerrard** and **Lisle,** that run between Leicester Square and Shaftesbury Avenue. Even so, it's home to many of London's 50,000 Chinese residents—most came to Britain from Hong Kong in the '50s and '60s, and quite a few more have arrived with Britain's recent handover of Hong Kong to China. It's fascinating to poke around in the tiny stores that sell Chinese herbs and oddly shaped vegetables, or feast on a meal of dim sum in one of the many restaurants. *Tube: Leicester Square. Walk north on Charing Cross Rd., turn left on Lisle St.*

SHAFTESBURY AVENUE

Cutting through the center of Soho, Shaftesbury Avenue is one of London's three principal theater streets (along with the Haymarket and Coventry Street). Built side by side in the early 1900s, many of the theaters survived the war and retain the grand look espoused by Edwardian theater. Sir Noël Coward, Sir John Gielgud, and Sir Laurence Olivier all made it big in Shaftesbury Avenue theaters like the Apollo, the Lyric, the Globe, and the Queen's. Today, you're likely to find these theaters hosting the works of such playwrights as Tom Stoppard and Peter Shaffer. *Tube: Leicester Square or Piccadilly Circus.*

CARNABY STREET

During the '60s and '70s, this pedestrian area was a groovy place to hang out, buy flowery fashions, and pick up the latest tunes. Although times have changed, Carnaby Street and the surrounding area still deserve a look. You can find everything from classic shoes to original '70s wigs, hot new makeup to ultra-cool designer jewelry. Come early or late in the afternoon to miss the worst of the crowds, but don't spend much time on Carnaby Street itself—despite its recent improvement, it's still mostly soccer-scarf merchants and cheap pocketbook stores. Instead explore the small alleys and streets to the east, which have some hip clothing stores and tiny crafts shops; try **Marshall** and **Broadwick** streets. *Tube: Oxford Circus. Walk south on Regent St., turn left on Great Marlborough St., right on Carnaby St.*

SOHO SQUARE

Built in the 1670s to honor Charles II, Soho Square is one of the oldest public squares in London. Nowadays this pleasant village green is a welcome open space in the middle of hectic Soho. It's shared in perfect harmony by businesspeople on lunch break, pram-pushing nannies, tourists, elderly folks, and homeless people—all under the watchful gaze of a dilapidated 19th-century statue of King Charles himself. At the center of this sylvan stretch of green is a storybook timber-and-thatch cottage—a dreamy sight when enjoying a takeout munch in the park during summer. *Tube: Tottenham Court Road. Walk west on Oxford St., turn left into Soho Sq.*

ST. JAMES'S

After Henry VIII's lovely **Whitehall Palace** burned down in 1698, all of London turned its attention to St. James's Palace (*see below*), the new royal residence. In the 18th and 19th centuries, the area around the palace became the fashionable place to live, and many of the estates surrounding the palace disappeared in a building frenzy, as mansions were built, streets laid out, and expensive shops established. Today, St. James's—along with Mayfair and Belgravia—remains London's most elegant and fashionable address. For a detail of the area, *see* the Mayfair and St. James's map, *above.*

REGENT STREET

It's not surprising to learn that a stream once splashed where this grand thoroughfare stands today—the street unfolds in hypnotically graceful curves. John Nash designed Regent Street in the 1820s as a compliment to the Prince Regent (later George IV). It was to have been a processional route linking Carlton House, where the Prince resided, to the palace he was planning to build in Regent's Park (never built).

Located in the heart of Central London, Regent Street is now a continuous stream of traffic and pedestrians, drawn by some of the best shopping in town. Stores include Liberty (legendary for its prints and paisleys); famed clothing emporiums such as Austin Reed, Burberrys, Dickins & Jones, and Jaeger; and London's answer to F.A.O. Schwarz, the vast Hamleys Toy Shop. Newcomers to the street include the flagship stores of the Disney Store, Warner Bros., Reiss Menswear, and Levi's.

PALL MALL

Pall Mall (pronounced pal mal) is a haven of quiet and refinement that has managed to survive from more regal days. The street gets its name from *paille maille*, a French version of croquet that was popular during the reigns of Charles I and II. A number of gentlemen's clubs, those quintessentially elitist English institutions, line Pall Mall, including the Athenaeum, United Oxford and Cambridge University Club, Travellers' Club, and the Reform Club (where Jules Verne's Phineas Fogg accepted that around-the-world-in-80-days bet). **Christie's** (8 King St., SW1, tel. 020/7839–9060), that extremely debonair auction firm, is north of Pall Mall. The auctions are open to the public and are free, but loitering is discouraged—unless, of course, you look like you're pocketing a platinum card. Pall Mall runs almost parallel to the Mall from Trafalgar Sq. and dead-ends at St. James's Palace. *Tube: Charing Cross, Green Park, or Piccadilly Circus.*

ST. JAMES'S PALACE

This elegant redbrick palace lies at the end of Pall Mall, on the former site of a hospital for women lepers. The ever-so-sensitive Henry VIII bought the hospital in 1532 and erected a royal manor in its stead. Only the **Chapel Royal** and four-story **Gatehouse** remain of Henry's original manor—most of the palace was rebuilt after a fire in 1809. For much of its existence, the palace has played second fiddle to the now-gone Whitehall Palace and to Buckingham Palace, though all foreign ambassadors to Britain are still officially accredited to "The Court of St. James." The palace is not open to the public, as it currently serves as the London residence of Prince Charles. *Pall Mall, at St. James's St., SW1. Tube: Green Park. Walk east on Piccadilly and turn right on St. James's St.*

London's 1851 census lists a "Charles Mark, Doctor (Philosophical Author)" living at 28 Dean Street, southwest of Soho Square. Today, a blue plaque commemorates this site as Karl Marx's residence from 1851 to 1856.

THE MALL

The red-tarmac Mall cuts a wide swath from Trafalgar Square all the way to Buckingham Palace. It was laid out in 1904, largely to provide the British monarchy with a processional route in keeping with its imperial status. After all, the French had their Champs-Elysées and they didn't even have a sovereign anymore. The 115-ft-wide Mall is no Champs-Elysées, however; without a royal procession dressing it up, the Mall seems soulless. **Admiralty Arch,** a triumphal arch bordering Trafalgar Square, marks the start of the Mall. Built in 1911, the central gate is now opened only for royal processions. From here, the Mall sweeps past St. James's Park and **Carlton House Terrace,** a stately 1,000-ft-long facade of white stucco arches that is home of the ICA (*see* Museums and Galleries, *below*), a first-rate contemporary gallery. Farther down on the right is **Clarence House,** home of the Queen Mother. The Mall ends in front of Buckingham Palace at the **Queen Victoria Memorial,** an irritatingly didactic (say some) monument to the glory of Victorian ideals. The broad avenue of the Mall displaced a much smaller, gravel boulevard that now lies a little to the north. Together with St. James's Park, the Mall was the place to see and be seen in 17th- and 18th-century London. Nowadays, the best time to explore the Mall is Sunday, when it is closed to traffic.

ST. JAMES'S PARK

Sitting amid London's grandest monuments, this 93-acre park is remarkably peaceful—it enjoys an almost librarylike hush. It is a stroller's park, a place to wander among the flowers, feed the ducks, or sit and read. The focal point is an ornamental lake, added by Charles II and redesigned by George IV, crisscrossed with geese, a few wandering pelicans (really) and surrounded by weeping willows. For the better part of the 17th and 18th centuries, the park was the playground for England's elite, who would gather here to stare down their noses at one another, before heading off to be idle elsewhere. At night—when the fountains, Westminster Abbey, and the Houses of Parliament are illuminated—the scene is honestly breathtaking. *Tube: Charing Cross, St. James's Park, or Westminster.*

WHITEHALL AND WESTMINSTER

Whitehall is both the name of a street and a vast, faceless bureaucracy. Whitehall the street runs from Trafalgar Square to Parliament Square through the heart of official London—which means it's a major tourist stomping ground. Whitehall the bureaucracy can't be so easily demarcated. Essentially, the term applies to the central British government, whose ministries fill many of the buildings off Whitehall and around Richmond Terrace. Adjacent Westminster is a small section of London most noted for its abbey, bridge, and palace, each named Westminster—though the palace is more commonly known as the **Houses of Parliament** (*see* Major Attractions, *above*). Southern Westminster is a sleepy residential area with charming old homes—worth wandering through if you're on your way to the splendid **Tate Britain** (*see* Major Attractions, *above*).

HORSE GUARDS AND PARADE GROUND

As you walk down Whitehall toward Parliament Square, you will pass Horse Guards on the right. This stone building was constructed between 1745 and 1755, and was once the headquarters of the British Army. It's the traditional entrance to St. James's Palace, which is why mounted troopers of the Household Cavalry Regiment can be seen during daylight hours in the sentry boxes facing across Whitehall. Each day at 11 AM (10 AM Sunday), you can witness the change of the Queen's Life Guard on Horse Guards Parade, the open area behind Horse Guards (adjacent to St. James's Park). On occasions such as the State Opening of Parliament or a State Visit, the whole thing is usually postponed until the afternoon. The new guard on horseback makes his way from Hyde Park Barracks, past Buckingham Palace and along the Mall to Horse Guards Parade, where the old Guard is waiting to meet him. Once the site of a jousting arena in Henry VIII's time, the area in front of the building is still known as the Tilt Yard. During the year the parade ground comes alive with some of London's most important State occasions, including the Queen's Birthday Parade (Trooping the Colour), Beating Retreat (both in June), and the royal receptions for state visits.

BANQUETING HOUSE

Designed by Inigo Jones and built between 1619 and 1622, Banqueting House is one of the earliest examples of Renaissance architecture in England. It's also the only surviving building from the original Whitehall Palace, the onetime home of Henry VIII that burned down in 1698. The House's main room was originally used as a venue for the court entertainments of Charles I. In 1649 it became the backdrop for his beheading. These days, it's a popular spot for state banquets. The chief attractions are Rubens's ceiling paintings, commissioned by Charles I, which portray him and his father James I in a favorable, even divine, light. *Whitehall, across from Horse Guards Arch, SW1, tel. 020/7930–4179. Tube: Charing Cross or Westminster. Admission £3.25. Open Mon.–Sat. 10–5.*

DOWNING STREET

If it weren't for the massive security measures and the ogling tourists, you would never suspect the importance of the rather ordinary homes on this street. The mammoth iron gate gives a first gentle hint, but the guys checking every car for bombs are a dead giveaway. Until now, Britain's prime minister has lived at 10 Downing Street, guarded by a black door and more than one policeman. However, Tony Blair—the youngest British prime minister this century—has moved, family in tow, into the larger No. 11. Wife Cherie raised a few eyebrows when she insisted on having the house done in accordance with Feng Shui principles.

CABINET WAR ROOMS

Winston Churchill, the Cabinet, and the Chiefs of Staff coordinated Britain's war effort from this fortified basement in a civil-service building—definitely worth a few hours' exploration. A free audio tour guides you through rooms that have been reconstructed to look as they did at the close of World War II. Especially interesting is a map covered with pushpins representing the paths of advancing Allied armies in the final weeks of the war. Old American vets and young German tourists roaming the war rooms together make for their own curious spectacle. *Clive Steps, at end of King Charles St., SW1, tel. 020/ 7930–6961. Tube: Westminster. Walk west on Bridge St., turn right on Parliament St., left on King Charles St. Admission £4.80. Open daily 9:15–6 (Oct.–Mar., 10–6); last admission 5:15.*

WESTMINSTER CATHEDRAL

The center for Roman Catholicism in England was designed by J. F. Bentley in an architectural style that wouldn't out-Gothic the ultra-Gothic Westminster Abbey. The result: a rather over-the-top "London Byzantine." Look for the remarkable Eric Gill sculptures of the stations of the cross. *Victoria St., SW1,*

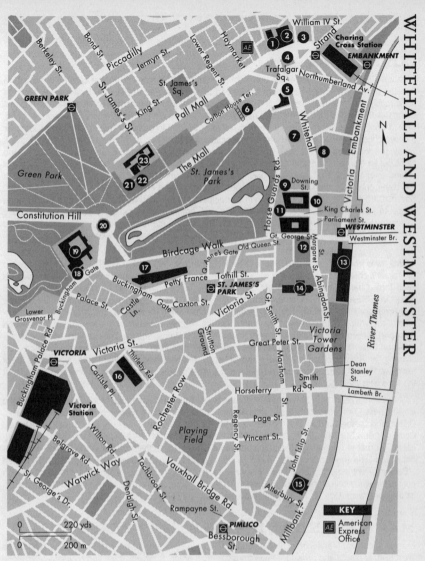

KEY

 American Express Office

10 Downing Street, **9**

Admiralty Arch, **5**

Banqueting House, **8**

Buckingham Palace, **19**

Cabinet War Rooms, **11**

Centotaph, **10**

Clarence House, **22**

Guard's Museum (Wellington Barracks), **17**

Horse Guards and Parade Ground, **7**

Houses of Parliament, **13**

Institute of Contemporary Arts (ICA), **6**

Lancaster House, **21**

National Gallery, **1**

National Portrait Gallery, **2**

Nelson's Column, **4**

Parliament Square, **12**

Queen Victoria Memorial, **20**

Queen's Gallery and Royal Mews, **18**

St. James's Palace, **23**

St. Martin-in-the-Fields, **3**

Tate Britain, **15**

Westminster Abbey, **14**

Westminster Cathedral, **16**

tel. 020/7798–9055. Tube: Victoria. Walk west on Victoria St., look for cathedral plaza on right. Admission free. Open daily 7–7.

COVENT GARDEN

"Wouldn't It Be Loverly?" Under the portico of St. Paul's Church, you can almost imagine hearing Eliza Doolittle warble her famed song from Lerner and Loewe's *My Fair Lady*——that is, if it weren't for the noisy musicians, buskers, jugglers, and comics all busy performing in the adjacent streets and squares of the Covent Garden district. A nest of narrow streets, arcades, and pedestrian malls just east of Soho, Covent Garden has become one of the best places in London to come for free entertainment: Look for a daily schedule of events posted in the **management office** (41 The Market, Covent Garden, WC2). Today, the renovated area is packed with snazzy dress shops, vast eateries, and floods of tourists and teens out for a smashing evening. Back when, however, the original Covent Garden was just that—a plot of land used to grow fruit and vegetables for the 13th-century Abbey of St. Peter at Westminster. With the 16th-century dissolution of the monasteries, the land passed into the hands of the Earls of Bedford. Covent Garden then evolved into London's principal produce market, a bustling maze of stalls and shops. In 1830 the **Central Market Building** was built, but increasing traffic congestion forced produce sellers to relocate south of the Thames in 1974. The original market building is completely renovated and filled with boutiques and health-food stores. For a detail of the area, *see* Soho and Covent Garden map, *above.*

Facing away from the market, **St. Paul's Church** (Bedford St., WC2, tel. 020/7836–5221) is often called the "actor's church" because of the walls lined with memorials to well-known British thespians such as Ellen Terry, Charlie Chaplin, and Noël Coward. The rest of the church, built by Inigo Jones in 1631 and rebuilt in 1795 after a fire, is rather stark. The rear portico, site of the opening scene with Eliza Doolittle and Professor Higgins in *My Fair Lady,* serves as a great stage for the daily program of free entertainment—everything from mimes to fire-eaters. On the southeast corner of the square are the **London Transport Museum,** housed in the former flower market building, and the **Theatre Museum** (*see* Museums and Galleries, *below*). **Neal Street** pedestrian mall, just north of the market across Long Acre, has a young, laid-back, bohemian crowd, plenty of happy shoppers, and tiny **Neal's Yard,** a courtyard full of funky world- and natural-food cafés. Have a pint in front of one of the many pubs and take a gander at the folks who walk by.

East of the market is Bow Street, famous for the **Royal Opera House,** home to the Royal Ballet and the Royal Opera Company—but closed until at least 2000 for massive renovations (*see* Classical Music, Opera, and Dance *in* After Dark, *below*). Opposite the opera house stands the **Bow Street Magistrates' Court** (28 Bow St., WC2, tel. 020/7379–4713), established in 1749 by Henry Fielding, who was a magistrate, journalist, and author. Fielding employed a group of detectives known as the "Bow Street Runners" and paid them out of fines levied by the court. Eighty years later, Home Secretary Sir Robert ("Bobby") Peel used the Bow Street Runners as the basis for his newly formed battalion of London police, familiarly called "bobbies" or "peelers" after his name. Attend a session in London's oldest magistrate court weekdays 10:30–1 and 2–4:30, Saturday 10:30–noon.

MARYLEBONE AND REGENT'S PARK

Frankly speaking, Marylebone (pronounced MARE-ra-le-bun), one of the main city zones outside the West End, is boring and crowded. Away from the main drags, however, you'll find pleasant cafés along **Marylebone High Street,** takeout stands north of Marylebone Road, and some absolutely smashing Regency-era terrace houses around **Regent's Park.** For reasons unknown—to each his own?—people have been flocking to **Madame Tussaud's Wax Museum** (Marylebone Rd., tel. 020/7935–6861) for eons. Madame Tussaud's is full of dummies: both the waxy sort and the sort willing to pay the £10 admission. Don't say you weren't warned. The **London Planetarium** in the same building as Tussaud's is less hokey, and the virtual-reality effects of space and motion are quite good, but did you really come to London to see a simulation of the night sky? In case you did, shows start every 40 minutes, and tickets are £6.50 (£13 for combined ticket with wax museum).

REGENT'S PARK

Yet another one of Henry VIII's hunting grounds, Regent's Park was developed in the early 19th century by architect John Nash for his pal the Prince Regent as an elite residential development for "the wealthy and the good." Today it is one of central London's biggest parks, with a small lake and an even tinier pond, both of which can be traversed by rented rowboats, pedal boats, and canoes. The **Inner Circle,** a perfectly round lane, encloses the beautiful **Queen Mary Gardens.** Architecture and art lovers will want to take in a stroll along the streets bordering the park to see some of John Nash's most spectacular Regency-era white-stucco terraced mansions. The highlight is Cumberland Terrace, adorned with snow-white statuary and a central block of Ionic columns surmounted by a triangular Wedgwood-blue pediment that is like a giant cameo—certainly one of London's most suave and ritziest edifices. The nearby Lord's Cricket Grounds is the most prestigious cricket venue in the world. Tickets to a match start at about £7. *Tube: Baker Street, Great Portland Street, or Regent's Park.*

LONDON ZOO

The northern end of Regent's Park is the site of the London Zoo, opened in 1828 as the world's first institution dedicated to the display *and* study of animals. The zoo's focus is wildlife conservation and breeding programs. Recent successes include two cubs birthed by their red panda mama in 1999 while the tiny kowari (otherwise known as Byrne's pouched mouse) have also increased their numbers. These nocturnal marsupials are on show in the Moonlight World exhibit in the Small Mammal House. The Elephant and Rhino Pavilion, the Snowdon Aviary, and the daily 2:30 feeding at the Penguin Pool are other attractions. The abstract building by Bernard Lubetkin makes an interesting backdrop for the playful birds. The reptile house is extensive, as is the aquarium. New exhibits simulating a desert, rainforest, and cave are under construction. The most direct way to get here is Bus 274, heading west from the Camden Town tube station (get off the bus at Ormonde Terrace). *Regent's Park, NW1, tel. 020/7722–3333. Tube: Baker Street or Camden Town. Admission £9. Open daily 10–5:30.*

BBC EXPERIENCE

The British Broadcasting Corporation, the world's best-known television and radio company, celebrated its 75th anniversary by opening its first permanent exhibition center in October 1997. Spanning three floors of the corporation's administrative and radio headquarters, the "Beeb's" center focuses more on radio than TV. The first display incorporates an audiovisual show and memorabilia that traces the BBC's history from the earliest days of radio to the present day. Following this is the interactive section where you can try your hand at commenting on a sports game, presenting a weather forecast, or making your own director's cut of a segment of *Eastenders,* their most popular soap program. There's also a chance to learn some sound mixing and DJ skills. The final part of the visit (well, the penultimate one really, as there is a massive gift shop between here and the exit) is a look at the future of broadcasting. Tours leave on the half-hour. *Broadcasting House, Portland Place, W1, tel. 0870/603–0304, 01222/57771 outside U.K. Tube: Oxford Circus. Walk north on Regent St., which becomes Portland Place; the center is on the right. Admission £6.50. Open Mon. 1–4:30; Tues–Sun. 10–4:30*

ABBEY ROAD

Here, outside the legendary Abbey Road Studios, is the most famous crosswalk in the world. Immortalized on the Beatles's *Abbey Road* album of 1969, this zebra-striped footpath is a spot beloved to countless Beatlemaniacs and baby boomers, many of whom venture here to leave their signature on the white stucco fence that fronts the adjacent studio facility at No. 3 Abbey Road. "Strawberry Beatles Forever," "Imagine—John coming back!", and "Why don't you do it in the road?" are a few of the sentimental flourishes left; these are whitewashed out every three months, by agreement with the neighborhood community, to make room for new graffiti. Studio 2 is where the Beatles recorded their entire output, from "Love Me Do" onwards, including, most momentously, *Sgt. Pepper's Lonely Hearts Club Band* (early 1967). It was on August 8, 1969, that John, Paul, George, and Ringo posed for photographer Iain Macmillan (walking symbolically *away* from the recording facility, incidentally) for the famous album shot. Today, fans like to follow in the Beatles' footsteps, but be careful: Rushing cars make Abbey Road a dangerous intersection. There are few places in London that commemorate the mop tops, so the best way Beatle-lovers can enjoy the history of the group is to take one of the in-depth walking tours offered by the Original London Walks, including "The Beatles In-My-Life Walk" (11 AM at the Baker St. Underground on Saturday and Tuesday) and "The Beatles Magical Mystery Tour" (11 AM outside Tottenham Court Rd. tube station at the Dominio Theatre exit, on Sunday and Thursday and at 2 PM on Wednesday; tel. 020/7624–3978). The studio itself is not a skipping record of the 1960s; groups and artists like Oasis, Red Hot Chili Peppers, Massive Attack, and Kate Bush record here today. Abbey Road is in the elegant, residential neighborhood of St. John's Wood, a 10-minute ride on the tube from central London. Take the Jubilee subway line to the St. John's Wood tube stop, head southwest three blocks down Grove End Road—and be prepared for a heart-stopping vista right out of Memory Lane.

CAMDEN TOWN

One of the most bohemian and diverse neighborhoods in London, Camden Town developed around Regent's Canal during the industrial revolution. Once a working-class neighborhood, successive waves of immigrants helped shape Camden's cosmopolitan atmosphere—though it's becoming increasingly gentrified. It becomes a serious mob scene on weekends, when tens of thousands of people shop the Camden markets, particularly **Camden Lock** (*see* Street Markets *in* Shopping, *below*). The crowds don't thin much at night, either, since Camden has some great bars and clubs.

The Camden Town tube station is on **Camden High Street,** which runs north–south through the heart of the district. Take a right from the station to reach Camden Lock. If being jostled by hip, acquisitive shoppers give you claustrophobia, visit during the week when you can snooze on the banks of Regent's Canal or enjoy the village's many cool cafés, restaurants, and pubs in relative peace; the spectacle of the masses is absent, as are many of the vendors, but it's a great place to spend a sunny day in London.

PRIMROSE HILL

Like Regent's Park, Primrose Hill was once part of Henry VIII's hunting grounds. A tall hill commands a fine view of central London—check out the plaque identifying the buildings on the skyline. A young, cool crowd, many from nearby Camden Town, hangs out here, as do plenty of dogs. Every November 5th, the park is the focus of huge Guy Fawkes Night celebrations complete with fireworks and a huge bonfire. *Tube: Chalk Farm. Walk south on Regent's Rd.*

BLOOMSBURY AND LEGAL LONDON

The **British Museum** (*see* Major Attractions, *above*) and the **University of London** (*see below*) impart something of an intellectual atmosphere to the residential neighborhood of Bloomsbury. Yet apart from some blue plaques on **Gordon Square,** you're far more likely to find a schmaltzy B&B than any reminders of Virginia Woolf, Vanessa Bell, Lytton Strachey, J. M. Keynes, E. M. Forster, and G. E. Moore—the so-called "Bloomsbury Group" that would assemble on Thursday nights in the 1920s and 1930s to drink and discuss the Victorian era's resistance to sexual, religious, and artistic enlightenment. Few traces remain of the personalities that brought Bloomsbury renown as the cradle of British philosophical and aesthetic modernism, yet Bloomsbury still has an active café and pub scene, fortified by the students who liven up the area after classes. The intimate **Sir John Soane's Museum** makes a nice, eclectic visit, and hard-core fans will enjoy poking about the **Dickens House** (*see* Museums and Galleries, *below*). If you're wandering around Euston Street, near King's Cross Station, definitely check out the fairy-tale exterior of the edifice (once a famed hotel) atop the St. Pancras train station—a Victorian extravaganza that is Sir George Gilbert Scott's most stunning feat of architecture. Russell Square tube station puts you right in the belly of the beast; otherwise, it's just a short walk north from the Tottenham Court Road or Holborn tube stations to Russell Square.

When you hear the word "lawyer," the immediate tendency is to yawn, grimace, or check your wallet. It's surprising, then, just how pleasant it can be to wander around the **Inns of Court** in Holborn, the heart of legal London. In the 15th and 16th centuries, the Inns of Court were exactly what they sound like—crash pads for lawyers who had business at the city's courts. Eventually, the lawyers took over the hotels and added offices and dining halls. Over time, the various inns were consolidated into just four—Lincoln's, Gray's, Middle Temple, and Inner Temple—and became the focal point of legal work in the city. London barristers (trial lawyers) are still required to maintain an association with one of the inns, such as keeping an office there or eating a certain number of meals in the dining hall each year. Law students must take their examinations at an inn and dine in one of the halls 24 times before they are admitted to the bar. Similar in style to the courtyards of Cambridge and Oxford, the inns retain a dignified academic air. Hang out on **Chancery Lane** and watch all the bewigged and gowned lawyers heading for court. The legal attire is just one indicator of how differently British and Americans approach the question of law: It's tough to imagine these guys coming on TV and saying, "Have you or a loved one been injured lately?"

SIR JOHN SOANE'S MUSEUM

This fascinating abode of one of Britain's greatest architects is full of antiquities, gargoyle heads, pediments, and a plethora of other chunks of buildings. Soane had so much stuff that special walls—which open on hinges to reveal other walls—were constructed so that he could hang three times as many paintings in his small Picture Room. Fortunately, Soane liked Hogarth's *The Rake's Progress* enough to put it on the outside. The Sepulchral Chamber holds the alabaster sarcophagus of Seti I; Soane was so pleased with his purchase that he held a three-day party to celebrate its installation in 1825. As you walk around the homey museum, make sure you peep out the windows and over the railings—Soane left bits and pieces everywhere. The museum stays open until 9 PM on the first Tuesday of every month. *13 Lincoln's Inn Fields, WC2, tel. 020/7405–2107. Tube: Holborn. Walk south on Kingsway, turn left on Remnant St. Admission free. Open Tues.–Sat. 10–5.*

UNIVERSITY OF LONDON

University College, the oldest of several colleges and schools that make up the University of London, was once accused of being that "godless college in Gower Street." It was founded in 1827 by educators who objected to the fact that Oxford and Cambridge would accept only students indoctrinated by the Church of England. With a curriculum modeled after German universities, University College was the first English school to accept Jews, Catholics, and Quakers. Women were the next group to make it onto the roster in 1878. Today, students at the college and the university have access to probably the best nightlife in the nation—pubs, cafés, and cheap restaurants dot the residential streets around the university, and the lively clubs and action of Soho are nearby.

One of several art collections administered by the university, the **Percival David Foundation of Chinese Art** (53 Gordon Sq., WC1, tel. 020/7387–3909), open weekdays 10:30–5, has a magnificent collection of 10th- to 18th-century Chinese ceramics. The top floor features some jewel-like colored pottery—sort of like 17th- and 18th-century Fiestaware. Inside the D. M. S. Watson Library, the small **Petrie Museum of Egyptian Archaeology** houses a deservedly famous collection of Roman-era mummy portraits and an amazing array of objects relating to Egyptian everyday life. The museum is a real hidden treasure and is free. *Malet Pl., off Torrington Pl., WC1E, tel. 020/7504–2884. Tube: Euston Square. Walk south on Gower St. Open Tues–Fri. 1–5; Sat. 10–1.*

LINCOLN'S INN

Beautiful gardens and immaculate lawns surround Lincoln's Inn, the only inn untouched by World War II bombings. The impressive architectural features of Lincoln's Inn range from the 15th-century Old Hall to New Square, the only surviving 17th-century square in London. Don't miss the chapel, redesigned by Inigo Jones between 1619 and 1623. *Chancery La. at Lincoln's Inn Fields, WC2, tel. 020/7405–1393. Tube: Chancery Lane or Holborn. Admission free. Chapel open weekdays noon–2:30; grounds open weekdays 9–7.*

GRAY'S INN

Gray's Inn, on the other side of High Holborn from Lincoln's Inn, was heavily damaged during the Blitz, and much of it had to be rebuilt in the 1950s. Before he was caught taking bribes and imprisoned in the Tower of London, Francis Bacon (1561–1626), whose statue is on the grounds, kept chambers here and is thought to have designed the impressive gardens. Charles Dickens, a former clerk at the inn, looked "upon Gray's Inn generally as one of the most depressing institutions of brick and mortar, known to the children of men." *8 South Sq., Gray's Inn Rd., WC1, tel. 020/7458–7800. Tube: Chancery Lane or Holborn. Grounds open weekdays early morning–midnight.*

THE TEMPLE

South of Fleet Street and technically in the City, the Middle and Inner Temples (collectively known as the Temple) got their name from the Knights Templar, an 11th-century chivalric order that owned the land here. Sadly, the only part of the complex that is open to the public are the gardens of the Middle Temple. If you can sneak a peek inside the Middle Temple Hall, look for the 29-ft-long Bench Table, donated by Elizabeth I. Though little of the original church survives, nearby **Temple Church,** built by the Knights Templar in the 12th century, is one of only three round churches in England and one of Britain's finest examples of early English Gothic. *The Temple, EC4, tel. 020/7797–8250. Tube: Temple. Grounds open Mon.–Sat. 10–4, Sun. 1–4.*

ROYAL COURTS OF JUSTICE

G. E. Street's impressive Law Courts lie on the Strand, a block away from the Temple. To watch the proceedings, walk (quietly) into a public gallery at the rear of any of the 58 courts. Don't come expecting to be regaled with tales of horror and gore, however: The murder trials you read about in the tabloids are held at the Old Bailey (*see* The City, *below*), while the Law Courts deal with more mundane cases involving fraud and swindle. It's still fun to wander around the cavernous, neo-Gothic building with all the judges and lawyers in their wigs and gowns, carrying papers bound with the traditional red ribbon. *The Strand, WC2, tel. 020/7936–6000. Admission free. Open weekdays 9:30–4:30. Closed Aug.–Sept.*

HAMPSTEAD AND HIGHGATE

Four miles north of central London, Hampstead is a posh, stylish area popular with writers, musicians, and artists. Cool cafés, chic restaurants, trendy boutiques, and a growing number of chain stores line the two main drags, **Hampstead High Street** and **Heath Street,** both right by the Hampstead tube station. Hampstead is well known for its grand houses, winding streets, country lanes, and the beautiful **Hampstead Heath** (*see below*). On **Church Row,** just off the bottom end of Heath Street, you'll find some of the finest 18th-century houses in London. Hampstead also has some historic, friendly little pubs, including the **Holly Bush** (22 Holly Mount, tel. 020/7435–2892), north of Hampstead High Street off Holly Hill; and **Spaniard's Inn** (Spaniard's Rd., tel. 020/7455–3276), where Keats, Shelley, and Byron tipped pints, as did highwayman Dick Turpin. Northeast of Hampstead across the Heath, **Highgate** is another tony residential area. **Highgate High Street** is lined with boutiques and a few cafés that give it a bohemian flair. If you want to avoid paying the extra 80p, it costs to get off at Highgate station (it's in Zone 3), get off at Archway and hike up Highgate Hill past Waterlow Park.

FREUD MUSEUM

The pad of the father of psychoanalysis still feels eerily lived in. Freud spent the last year of his life here, having fled Vienna in 1938 to escape Nazi persecution. After he died, his daughter Anna—a pioneer in the field of child psychology—maintained the house as a shrine to him, and after her death it was turned into a museum. Take a peek into Freud's life and try to analyze *his* psyche by inspecting the strange toys, art, and curious knickknacks. You can also check out his library and study—complete with the (in)famous couch—where he spent his final year doing some of his most important theorizing. On the landing there is a remarkable drawing of Freud by Dalí, who sketched Freud secretly and later completed this portrait. *20 Maresfield Gardens, NW3, tel. 020/7435–2002. Tube: Finchley Road. Walk south on Finchley Rd., turn left on Trinity Walk, left on Maresfield Gardens. Admission £4. Open Wed.–Sun. noon–5.*

KEATS HOUSE

The great romantic poet John Keats (1795–1821) wrote many of his masterpieces during his two-year stay at this Hampstead home. It was also here that he met and fell in love with the girl next door, Fanny Brawne, for whom he pined for years. Though they became engaged in 1819, Keats's declining health prevented the marriage from taking place. He sailed to Italy in 1820, hoping to recuperate but instead his condition worsened and he died in Rome at the ripe young age of 25. Their two houses have since been combined to form an all-encompassing Keats museum, furnished just as it was during the poet's lifetime. Be sure to check out the full-scale plaster "lifemask" of Keats's head, created by a painter friend, and other personals like the engagement ring Keats gave to Fanny, his letters, and first editions of *Poems* (1817) and *Endymion* (1819). The adjacent **Keats Memorial Library** (tel. 020/7794–6829), open by appointment only, contains all the poet's compositions, as well as scholarly studies dedicated to him. *Keats Grove, NW3, tel. 020/7435–2062. Tube: Hampstead. Walk SE on Hampstead High St., turn left on Downshire Hill, veer right on Keats Grove. Or take BritRail to Hampstead Heath, walk north on South End Rd., turn left on Keats Grove. Admission free. Open Apr.–Oct., weekdays 10–1 and 2–6, Sat. 10–1 and 2–5, Sun. 2–5; Nov.–Mar., weekdays 1–5, Sat. 10–1 and 2–5, Sun. 2–5.*

HAMPSTEAD HEATH

If you dig traipsing over hill and dale, following narrow paths to nowhere, and crashing through bushes, the 800-acre Hampstead Heath is the place for you. For a big-city park, Hampstead Heath is surprisingly rural—even despite the omnipresent litter. There are views of central London from Parliament Hill, but beware the deadly stunt kites flown by well-meaning novices. Swimming, tennis, cricket, and even the occasional softball game are some of the sports you can watch or participate in. Otherwise, the principal sight is **Kenwood House** (Hampstead La., tel. 020/8348–1286), a 17th-century mansion designed by Robert Adam with landscaped gardens. There are only one or two period rooms, but the real reason to visit the house—and what a reason—is to enjoy the **Iveagh Bequest,** a spectacular collection of paintings, including works by Gainsborough, Van Dyck, Rembrandt, and Turner. The high point is *Lady Playing a Lute*—London's most beautiful Vermeer. The house is open daily 10–6 (October until 5; November–March until 4), and admission is free. *Tube: Hampstead. Walk ½ mi north on Heath Street. Or take BritRail to Hampstead Heath or Gospel Oak.*

HIGHGATE CEMETERY

A light drizzle (not unlikely in London) creates a wonderful gloom in Highgate Cemetery, where a maze of narrow footpaths cuts through a forest of vine-covered Victorian tombstones. The cemetery is divided into two parts: The **Eastern Cemetery** is still in use and contains the somber tombs of George Eliot (a.k.a. Mary Ann Evans) and Karl Marx. Coincidence makes strange bedfellows: Just a few feet away, across the gravel path, lies Marx's dialectical opposite (and one of George Eliot's lovers), social Darwinist Herbert Spencer, who once wrote that "socialism is slavery." The **Western Cemetery**, open only for tours (£3), has a spectacular Egyptian Avenue, incredible landscaping, and eerie catacombs. Buried here are Radclyffe Hall, author of *The Well of Loneliness,* the poet Christina Rossetti, pre-Raphaelite model and Dante Gabriel Rossetti's wife Elizabeth Siddal, and bare-knuckle prizefighter Tom Sayers, whose tomb is guarded by a sculpture of Lion, his devoted dog. **Waterlow Park,** at the northern border of the cemetery, is one of the only parks in London where you'll encounter some formidable hills, which run down to rush-bordered ponds inhabited by waterfowl. *Swains La., N6, tel. 020/8340–1834. Tube: Archway. Walk north on Highgate Rd., turn left on Bisham Gardens, left on Swains La. Admission to East Cemetery £1. Open weekdays 10–5, (Oct.–Mar. until 4). Tours of West Cemetery offered weekends, hourly 11–4 (also Mar.–Nov., weekdays at noon, 2, and 4).*

STRAND AND EMBANKMENT

In a moment of grief, Dante Gabriel Rossetti buried some love poems in his wife Elizabeth Siddal's coffin. A few years later, Rossetti had a change of heart and had poor Lizzie's corpse exhumed to recover the manuscript so the poems could be published.

Strand, which turns into Fleet Street about ½ mi from Charing Cross, is smelly, noisy, and dirty. And not in an interesting way either—just a lot of cars in a boring concrete canyon that's bordered by mediocre restaurants. Tea totalers may be interested in the oldest tea shop in London, **Twinings** (216 Strand, tel. 020/7353–3511), but unless you're a very methodical sightseer or really into carbon monoxide, you could forgo this particular area with no adverse effect. The Embankment, on the other hand, is a bit more intriguing. Constructed between 1868 and 1874 by Sir Joseph Bazalgette (the same man who designed London's sewers), the Embankment, which runs all the way from Westminster to the city, was designed to protect the city from flooding (a job now handled by the Thames Barrier). For a detail of the area, *see* Soho and Covent Garden map, *above.*

SOMERSET HOUSE

Constructed between 1776 and 1786 by William Chambers, Somerset House replaced a Renaissance palace used by members of the royal family. Until 1973, Somerset House was the home of the Registrar General of Births, Deaths, and Marriages, as well as a number of other government offices. Today, the building houses Inland Revenue (the British equivalent of the IRS) and the **Courtauld Institute Galleries,** affiliated with the University of London. The gallery has a collection of oils from the 15th through 20th centuries, of which the Impressionist and Post-Impressionist movements are the best represented. The Cézanne collection is considered the finest in London, as is the collection of Manet's works, including *A Bar at the Folies-Bergère* (you know, the one with the bored-looking waitress). Modigliani's wonderful *Female Nude* coyly looks away from poor van Gogh's *Self-Portrait with Bandaged Ear,* while Degas's dancers stand en pointe. Classical works by such artists as Lely, Giovanni Bellini, and Rubens are also exhibited. The renovated gallery will reopen in early 2000, at which time the entire building will be open to the public for the very first time. It will include a new £75 million gallery to house the storied **Gilbert Collection** of silver, gold and mosaics. The whole thing is a gift from Cali real estate dealer Arthur Gilbert and there will be a separate entrance fee to the collection. *Strand, WC2, tel. 020/7873–2526. Tube: Temple. Walk west on Temple Pl., turn right on Surrey St., left on Strand. Admission £4; free on Mon. 10–2. Open Mon.–Sat. 10–6, Sun. 2–6.*

THE CITY

The City is to London what Wall Street is to New York. It smells of money and deals. And like all good capitalist animals, the city answers to the markets and nothing else, not even the rest of London—it's an administrative and legal entity in itself. Taking up just over a square mile in east London, the City is home to the stock exchange, the Bank of England, Lloyd's, and a host of large banking and trading firms. The traditional view of the City has always been that of upper- and upper-middle-class gentlemen in bowler

THE CITY

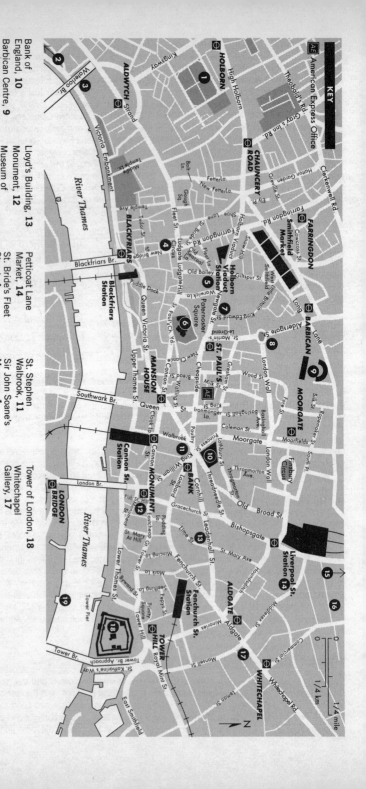

AE American Express Office

Bank of
England, **10**
Barbican Centre, **9**
Cleopatra's
Needle, **2**
Geffrye Museum, **15**
HMS *Belfast*, **19**

Lloyd's Building, **13**
Monument, **12**
Museum of
London, **8**
National Postal
Museum, **7**
Old Bailey, **5**

Petticoat Lane
Market, **14**
St. Bride's Fleet
Street, **4**
St. Paul's
Cathedral, **6**

St. Stephen
Walbrook, **11**
Sir John Soane's
Museum, **1**
Somerset House, **3**
Spitalfields
Market, **16**

Tower of London, **18**
Whitechapel
Gallery, **17**

84

hats carrying brollies and briefcases. That all changed in the headlong rush for money during the Thatcher '80s, when once-staid companies began hiring employees who could produce the goods, even though they may not have attended the right schools. Of course, the Old-Boy network hasn't dried up and blown away—the snobbery has just grown a little more subtle. In fact, the City's newly made millionaires are still referred to by their upper-class brethren as "barrow boys." On weekdays, you'll find the sidewalks positively vibrating with tension, cellular phones, and power ties, making for some interesting people-watching and eavesdropping.

Although the City lies to the east of central London, it actually rests on the original Celtic settlement that the Romans conquered and built up into Londinium. Vestiges of this ancient heritage pop up all over the city, even though the Great Fire of London, which started in a baker's shop in Pudding Lane in September 1666, destroyed almost every building in the area. In the years that followed, architect Christopher Wren redesigned the entire district, building 51 new churches, including **St. Paul's Cathedral** (*see* Major Attractions, *above*), which stood as the focal point of a new city of spires. German bombers wrecked most of Wren's work, however (fewer than half remain), and postwar London architects managed to brutalize much of the rest. Unfortunately, the once-dramatic views of St. Paul's have slowly disappeared behind modern concrete behemoths.

ST. BRIDE'S FLEET STREET

Known as the printers' church and where many journalists are buried, St. Bride's is surrounded by now predominantly empty offices that once made up the Fleet Street newspaper empire. The first St. Bride's was destroyed in the Great Fire. Rebuilt by Wren, St. Bride's' spire is the highest he ever built; its distinctive shape is said to have been the inspiration for the first tiered wedding cake. Though gutted in the Blitz, with only the steeple and outer walls surviving, the church has been nicely restored and provides a welcome haven from the anxiety of

Quirky Victorians buried a time capsule beneath the Cleopatra's Needle on the Embankment, including such oddities as a railway guide, a portrait of Queen Victoria, and a baby's bonnet.

City life. The **crypt** contains an excellent exhibition about the history of the church, revealing its Roman and medieval foundations, and a history of Fleet Street itself. Free lunchtime recitals are held Tuesday, Wednesday, and Friday at 1:15 PM, and evensong is held on Sunday at 6:30. *Fleet St. at Bride La., EC4, tel. 020/7583-0239. Tube: Blackfriars. Walk north on New Bridge St., turn left on Fleet St. Open weekdays 8–5; Sat. 9–4:30.*

MONUMENT

The Monument, designed by Christopher Wren, is now rather dwarfed by the City's office buildings, though it used to loom majestically as one of the world's tallest columns. Completed in 1677 to commemorate the Great Fire, the column is 202 ft high—the exact distance westward from the fire's Pudding Lane origin. For amazing views of the city, climb the spiraling 311 steps to the platform at the top. The platform was enclosed in 1847, following several suicides. *Monument St., EC3, tel. 020/7626–2717. Tube: Monument. Admission £1.50. Open daily 10–6 (last admission 20 mins before closing).*

OLD BAILEY

If you can't afford theater tickets or you're a fan of *Rumpole of the Bailey,* go and watch a trial at the Old Bailey, officially known as the Central Criminal Court. You can't beat the drama (it's all for real) or the price (it's free). Just line up outside and scan the offering of trials—they're posted on a sort of legal menu du jour at the Newgate Street entrance; it only lists the cases by name of defendant so you'll have to ask a regular voyeur exactly where the accusations of murder and mayhem are going down. Generally, the juiciest trials are held in Courts 1–3, the old courts. In the modern Courts 4–19, it's difficult to see unless you're in the front row (or actually on trial yourself). No bags or cameras are allowed in the building, and there's nowhere to safely store them nearby, so come empty-handed. While you're waiting for the show to begin, check out Pomeroy's famous bronze statue of Justice atop the building, overlooking the spot where prisoners of notorious Newgate Prison were once executed. Rough justice indeed. *Old Bailey, at Newgate St., EC4, tel. 020/7248–3277. Tube: St. Paul's. Walk NW on Newgate St. Public Gallery open weekdays 10–1 and 2–4.*

BARBICAN CENTRE

This large complex of residential towers and cultural venues was built between 1959 and 1981 in an attempt to resurrect central London as a living city instead of merely a place of work. Though the complex's modern concrete blocks are inordinately ugly and look more like something you would find in

Eastern Europe than London, the added grand entrance portal softens the blow a little. The seemingly ill-fated Barbican Centre has managed to evolve into one of the city's principal cultural institutions. Varied musical performances are held in **Barbican Hall** (*see* Classical Music, Opera, and Dance *in* After Dark, *below*), **Barbican Theatre** is the London home of the Royal Shakespeare Company, which also stages smaller performances in **The Pit** (*see* Theater *in* After Dark, *below*), and the **Barbican Cinema** shows mostly mainstream films. There are also some impressive visual-arts displays at the **Barbican Art Gallery.** Free music and art exhibitions are usually mounted in one of the many foyers. *Silk St., EC2, tel. 020/7638–4141; 020/7638–8891 for box office. Tube: Barbican or Moorgate. Admission to Barbican Art Gallery (tel. 020/7382–7105) £5 (£3 weekdays after 5). Gallery open Mon.–Sat. 10–6:45 (Tues. until 5:45, Wed. until 7:45), Sun. noon–6:45.*

LLOYD'S BUILDING

Like it or not, the Lloyd's steel-and-glass medium-rise is the most aggressively "modern" building in the city and certainly one of the most architecturally important structures built in the '80s. The duo that put it up, celebrity-architect Richard Rogers and structural engineer Peter Rice (engineer of the Sydney Opera House), also worked together on the equally revolutionary Centre Georges Pompidou in Paris. The institution that trades in insurances hit hard times in the early '90s, resulting in a number of its investors, the so-called Names, going bankrupt. There used to be an observation deck that was open to the public, but for security reasons, it's now closed. *1 Lime St., EC3, tel. 020/7623–7100. Tube: Monument. Walk north on Gracechurch St., turn right on Fenchurch St., right on Lime St.*

ST. STEPHEN WALBROOK

Considered by many to be Wren's most perfect church, St. Stephen Walbrook has a high-domed ceiling supported by 16 Corinthian columns. The dark wood of the organ and pulpit contrasts wildly with the church's most controversial feature: a gray, marshmallowy, marble altar sculpted by Henry Moore from Roman travertine marble and dedicated in 1987. The Samaritans organization was founded here in 1953; the original helpline telephone sits on a pedestal in the southwest corner of the church. Eucharist is sung on Thursday at 12:45 PM with a full choir while the organ recitals on Friday at 12:30 PM bring in some of the top players in the world. *Walbrook, EC4, tel. 020/7283–4444. Tube: Bank. Open Mon.– Thurs. 10–4, Fri. 10–3.*

SOUTH OF THE THAMES

THE SOUTH BANK

The Thames weaves and winds a watery curtain that divides the city in half. North Londoners often claim they never venture south across the river and, until recently, the area was rarely troubled by tourists unless they were departing from Waterloo Station or going to a performance at the **South Bank Centre** (*see* Chapter 6). Much of the area was bombed flat during the war, so no one was likely to bandy about clichés like "quaint" to describe it. During the '80s, the area was known as "Cardboard City," where hundreds of homeless people slept in cardboard boxes abutting subways and railroad arches to keep warm. Redevelopment cleaned up the area and brought a new IMAX cinema, but poverty and panhandling are still evident. Throughout the late '90s, the South Bank has been exploding with life— all sorts of headline-making attractions are opening, like the spectacular reconstruction of **Shakespeare's Globe Theatre,** just 200 yards from where the first "wooden O"—the most famous theater in the world—originally stood.

Right next to Westminster, the bulky colossus of County Hall is being converted into various ventures including the **London Aquarium** (*see below*), the **FA Premier League Hall of Fame** (*see* Museums and Galleries, *below*), a couple of hotels, apartments, and various chichi restaurants. The adjacent Jubilee Gardens have been torn up, and by 2000 the space will feature a 450-ft-high **British Airways London Eye** (*see below*), the largest Ferris wheel in the world. The stunning **Eurostar Terminal** at Waterloo Station is located between here and the South Bank Centre. The terminal and its intricate roof of huge, overlapping glass panels was designed by Nicholas Grimshaw. Walking farther east, just beyond the South Bank Centre, the **Gabriel's Wharf** area is full of fancy places to eat, none more so than the swank top-floor restaurant at **OXO Tower,** a glitzy, neon-bedecked Art Deco showpiece that's now apartments and malls.

On the east side of Blackfriars Bridge looms the forbidding brick **Bankside Power Station,** soon to be home of the **Tate Modern** (due to open in May 2000). The Globe Theatre and HMS *Belfast* (detailed below) follow before the tourist magnet of **Tower Bridge** (*see* Main Attractions, *above*) appears. Next to the bridge is **Butler's Wharf,** a gaggle of tumbledown warehouses that have been spruced up and interspersed with ultramodern architecture that houses trendy bistros, delicatessens, and offices, along with the excellent **Design Museum** (*see* Museums and Galleries, *below*).

THE BRITISH AIRWAYS LONDON EYE

London's millennium fever broke out a new lookout point for the city's skyline. The South Bank's 450-ft-high observation wheel will begin rotating in time for the year 2000. It takes a full half-hour to rotate, taking a maximum load of 770 passengers in 32 fully enclosed capsules. There will be river access via the new Waterloo Millenium Pier. *Jubilee Gardens, SE1, Tube: Waterloo. Admission £6.95. Open Apr.–Oct., daily 10–9; Nov.–Mar., daily 10–6.*

LONDON AQUARIUM

London's only attraction of its kind stands just across the river from the Houses of Parliament. The 40-plus display tanks—including two massive ones containing sharks and stingrays—are arranged along darkened corridors that try to conjure up a *Jaws* vibe but, in the end, just seem claustrophobic and dimly lit. It's no bargain, but kids will probably love it. *County Hall, Riverside Building, Westminster Bridge Rd., SE1, tel. 020/7967–8000. Tube: Westminster or Waterloo. Admission £7. Open June–Aug., daily 9:30–7:30; Sept.–May, daily 10–6.*

In the Middle Ages, Southwark was London's equivalent of Las Vegas, where everybody would go to drink, pick up ladies, and party.

SOUTH BANK CENTRE

This sprawling, multitier monument to modernist poured concrete is home to the **Royal National Theatre,** the **National Film Theatre,** and the **Royal Festival Hall** (*see* Chapter 6)— the only structure that remains from the 1951 Festival of Britain that kickstarted this area into being, as well as the **Hayward Gallery** and the **Museum of the Moving Image** (*see* Museums and Galleries, *below*). This progressive institution hosts a number of free foyer events; pick up a thick monthly brochure listing these and other attractions at the various buildings of the complex. Having grown in a piecemeal fashion, the complex is awkward and fragmented, and to label it a centre is a slight misnomer. In the late '90s the famed British architect Richard Rogers was commissioned to unify the site by throwing a wavy blue-tinted glass roof over the area, turning it into something between a cultural shopping mall and Disneyland. However that fell through and the government's arts ministry has now turned back to the drawing board to try to make this prestigious gaggle of institutions a little more aesthetically pleasing. It's likely that some buildings will be expanded, new ones erected, and others—perhaps the ugly Queen Elizabeth Hall—demolished, but nothing much is likely to happen before 2004. *South Bank, Belvedere Rd., SE1, tel. 020/7960–4242. Tube: Embankment or Waterloo.*

SOUTHWARK

It 's difficult to tell that Southwark (pronounced *suth*-uk), directly opposite the Tower of London, is London's oldest suburb, dating back to Roman times. Most of the buildings today are post–World War II, with a few notable exceptions. The site of London's entertainment district in Tudor times, Southwark is again set to become a popular area through projects like the rebuilt **Globe Theatre** (*see below*), and the **Tate Modern** (*see below*) the **Bankside Power Station** (past Blackfriars Bridge). Clink Street, east of Southwark Bridge, was the site of the notorious prison that gave its name—the Clink—to jails everywhere. Inmates were those who ran afoul of the Bishops of Winchester, who controlled this part of Southwark and licensed prostitutes ("Winchester Geese") and brothels, among other entertainments—taxing the profits heavily. **The Clink** exhibition (1 Clink St., SE1, tel. 020/7403–6515) tells the story of the prison and its inmates but is a bit run down for the £4.50 admission. If you like your gore a little more graphic, don't miss **The London Dungeon** (28–34 Tooley St., tel. 020/7403–7221, open daily 10:30–5). It's a total hoot of a place—tacky, expensive (£9.50), and packed with waxwork tortures, executions, and disembowelments—the place is like a lower-brow Madame Tussaud's with more blood. An enormous hit with kiddies *and* medievalists, it's "a perfectly horrible experience" (as the posters proudly proclaim).

SHAKESPEARE'S GLOBE • That long-missing Exhibit A of Elizabethan-era England—the **Globe Theatre**—has finally (re)appeared thanks to this grand reconstruction of the arena where Shakespeare premiered many of his peerless dramas. The Bard of Bards staged many of his plays in Southwark at the old Globe Playhouse, which burned down in 1613 when a spark from a cannon used in *Henry IV* ignited the thatched roof. Though the theater was rebuilt immediately after the fire, the brimstone of the Puritans proved too much and the Globe was closed in 1642. In those days, people didn't pay £20 a ticket for a theater seat, and they didn't look for neo-Marxist-feminist symbolism in Shakespeare's works. Going to the theater, it seems, was more like going to a baseball game, with people in the cheap seats acting oafish. Instead of peanuts, the playgoers cracked filberts (hazelnuts), whose hulls now scatter the floor again. Mark Rylance, an actor and the artistic director of the Globe, is "delighted" when audience members shout during performances or even throw fruit, as they did in Shakespeare's time—so come prepared to hiss Iago.

A performance at the new Globe is not at all like your usual after-dinner theater. Most performances begin in the afternoon and, while flood lighting will be used to illuminate the theater at dusk, there are no spotlights to focus the action on stage. The audience, on view at all times, becomes as much a part of the theatrical proceedings as the actors onstage. There's also no scenery per se—rather, the magnificent twin-gabled stage canopy, framed by *trompe l'oeil* marble columns and a "lords' gallery" is the one-fits-all setting—but, to quote Master Will, "the play's the thing." Then again, the entire theater is one amazing stage set: A soaring 45-ft-high arena picturesquely encircled by three half-timber galleries. In the center of it all is the "pit," or orchestra level, with room for 500 standees. If you're planning to be one of these "groundlings"—at £5, the ultimate London theater bargain—be sure to bring an umbie if the London skies look threatening.

The reconstruction of the Globe Theatre is the work of the late American filmmaker Sam Wanamaker, who slaved for two decades to raise funds for the project, which even uses the same construction materials and techniques as 16th-century craftsmen did. A second indoor theater, the **Inigo Jones Theatre,** based on the venerable architect's 17th-century designs, is also planned. Both theaters will be used for performances of old and new plays in 16th- or 17th-century style. Note that the Globe will be open May through September only; performances are Tuesday–Saturday at 2 and 7:30, and Sunday at either 1, 4, or 6:30. Tickets run from £5 to £25. Happily, the theater can be seen all year long if you purchase a ticket to the accompanying **Shakespeare's Globe Exhibition,** a fascinating look at the archaeological research and quest to re-create the theater, the Soho of Elizabethan London, and a behind-the-scenes tour of the theater itself. *Bear Gardens, SE1, tel. 020/7401–9919 (box office), 020/7902–1500 (exhibition). Tube: London Bridge. Walk south on Borough High St., quick right on Southwark St., right on Southwark Bridge Rd. Exhibition admission £6. Exhibition open May–Sept., daily 9–noon; times vary according to performances so phone ahead; Oct.–Apr., daily 10–5.*

OLD OPERATING THEATRE MUSEUM • Don't come to this museum if you're facing surgery anytime soon. The display of a 19th-century operating room, complete with sawdust to soak up the blood, is enough to convert anyone to Christian Science. The operating room, glimpsed in the film *The Madness of King George III,* is all that remains of the original St. Thomas's Hospital, which occupied the site from the 13th to the mid-19th century, before moving to Lambeth. It's been restored to its original, gruesome, and doubtlessly unsterile state. *9A St. Thomas St., SE1, tel. 020/7955–4791. Tube: London Bridge. Follow signs from station. Admission £2.50. Open Tues.–Sun. 10–4 (and most Mon.).*

HMS *BELFAST* • Part of the Imperial War Museum, HMS *Belfast* was the pride of the Royal Navy during the mid-20th century. It remains the largest cruiser ever built for the British and is the only warship of the British fleet still afloat. It helped shell the Normandy beaches on D-day and later served in the Far East. Roam around the decks, which feature dioramas of life on the ship; climb in the "A" turret near the fo'c'sle (the ship's front to you, landlubber) and aim the big, empty gun; or sit in the Captain's Chair and bark orders at wax dummies or other tourists. A nice way to arrive (or leave) is to ferry across from Tower Pier (75p each way). Ferries leave daily, April–October, every 15 minutes from 11 to 5. *Morgan's La., off Tooley St., SE1, tel. 020/7407—6434. Admission £4.90. Open daily 10–6 (Nov.–Feb. until 5); last admission 45 mins before closing.*

TATE MODERN • Beginning in May 2000, most of the Tate's renowned collection of 20th-century art will be shown off here. Works by van Gogh, Matisse, Picasso, Dalí, Rothko, Leger, Duchamp, and Ernst will be exhibited alongside contemporary artists' creations. Sculpture, paintings, photographs, and other works are arranged by theme, rather than by chronology or discipline. Tate Britain will hold most of the British art of the 20th- and 21st centuries, though there will be cross-over between the two museums. The Modern's home in a renovated, huge brick power station with a lofty central chimney dominates this reach of the Thames. It was designed just after World War II by Sir Giles Gilbert Scott who also planned the beautiful Battersea Power Station just east of Chelsea Bridge, as well as those cute red telephone boxes. The station ceased generating in 1980 and a Swiss team of architects gave it a £134 million facelift and refit. They spent a lot of that money creating a roof-top glass structure to provide natural lighting for the artwork and great views of the capital's skyline. *25 Sumner St., tel. 020/7887–8000.*

Tube: Blackfriars, then walk across Blackfriars Bridge. Admission free; £1–£6 for special exhibits. Open daily 10–5:50

BRIXTON

Brixton, in south central London at the end of the Victoria line, looks pretty funky and is rarely visited by tourists. Another of the city's multiethnic areas, Brixton is where many young Londoners venture for raves and to dance to world-beat sounds in the district's innumerable clubs. Another draw is the excellent **Brixton Market** (*see below*), an open-air affair that runs from Monday through Saturday on Electric Avenue (that's right, the one in the Eddy Grant song), right around the corner from the tube station. Brixton's population is mostly of West Indian and African descent, and primarily working class, but a joint private and public sector plan—the Brixton Challenge—seems intent on yuppifying the place. Although some of the new bars and restaurants are popular, the neighborhood's gritty yet likable character is at stake. The free **Black Cultural Archives** (378 Coldharbour La., SW9, tel. 020/7738–4591), open Monday–Saturday 10–6, has a small collection of photographs, letters, storyboards, and artwork chronicling the plight and achievements of black immigrants from Roman times until today. To get to the Archives, take the tube to Brixton, make a left onto Brixton Road and turn left onto Coldharbour Lane. A half-mile south, uphill on Effra Road, is the reasonably pleasant **Brockwell Park** (open daily 8 AM–dusk), most notable for its fine lido.

RICHMOND

The wealthy borough of Richmond-upon-Thames, southwest of central London, is full of startlingly lavish mansions, including some that you can tour for a price. Some have belonged to the families of various countesses and earls for generations; the rest house a sprinkling of rock stars and TV celebrities. After poking around the antique shops, climb up **Richmond Hill** for sweeping views over the river. From Richmond Hill it's an easy walk to **Richmond Park,** one of the largest parks in Europe, with about 2,500 acres of heathland still roamed by herds of wild deer. *Tube or BritRail: Richmond.*

KEW GARDENS

Founded in 1759 by Princess Augusta (wife of Frederick, Prince of Wales), the amazing 300-acre Kew Gardens (also known as the Royal Botanic Gardens) is the mother of all botanical gardens. Wild thickets, manicured flower beds, lakes, ponds, and paths abound. Seven glass greenhouses—many huge and architecturally magnificent—house some of Kew's 60,000 species of plants, from arctic to tropical vegetation, and from huge trees to humble ground cover. Although it's hard to choose favorites, the **Princess of Wales's Conservatory** is especially charming. Here in a modernist structure, a tropical jungle is re-created in lush detail: Mist blows out of pipes every 45 seconds, birdcalls resound from hidden speakers, and the atmosphere is hot and sultry. *Kew Rd. at Lichfield Rd., tel. 020/8332–5000; 020/8940–1171 for recorded info. Tube: Kew Gardens. Follow the signs to Victoria Gate on Kew Rd. Admission £5. Open daily 9:30–7 (Oct.–Mar. until 6); greenhouses close 75 mins before the gardens.*

HAMPTON COURT PALACE

Up the Thames west from Richmond is Hampton Court Palace, party house of English royalty since the early 16th century. The palace was built in 1514 for Cardinal Wolsey, Henry VIII's primary advisor. The jealous king compelled Wolsey to give him the palace, and added the great hall in 1532. Henry is said to have rushed construction of the hall by having laborers toil 24 hours a day in shifts, working by candlelight at night. Centuries later, William III and Mary II toyed with tearing the whole thing down and building an imitation British Versailles, but contented themselves instead with adding the graceful South Wing, designed by Wren. The amazing extravagance of the palace is evident in its size, but the ornate interior and exterior decoration puts its value far beyond comprehension. Within the grounds are the world's first indoor tennis court, massive state bedrooms, kitchens capable of feeding a thousand a day, plus gardens, canals, and a 220-year-old grapevine. For some, the top draw is the centuries-old, giant maze of hedges— a good deal better than the one in *The Shining.* Most people can negotiate their way to the center in under half an hour but often gardeners have to dive in and rescue lost souls. *Hampton Court Bridge, tel. 020/8781–9500. Take London Transport Bus R68 from central Richmond, BritRail to Hampton Court, or the ferry from Westminster Pier. Admission £10; Maze only, £2.50; Gardens £2.50. Open Mon. 10:15–6, Tues.–Sun. 9:30–6 (Oct.–Mar. until 4:30). The gardens are open until dusk or 9 PM—whichever is earlier.*

NEAR LONDON

GREENWICH

The village of Greenwich (pronounced *gren*-itch) is only a few miles east down the Thames from the city, but it feels worlds apart. It's no inconsequential backwater though—the world keeps its time by Greenwich Mean Time, set by the Old Royal Observatory since 1884. Given its important job, Greenwich and its cobblestone streets will receive a huge pat on the back in 2000 with the United Kingdom's main millennium celebrations. The enormous theme park–like Millennium Dome will entertain for one year beginning January 1, 2000, on a 300-acre site at Greenwich Peninsula, northeast of the town center.

Urban planners have fallen all over themselves to give transportation options to suit every Greenwich time-traveler's whim. The scenic trip takes just over ½-hour via boats leaving from Westminster Pier, Tower of London, and the British Airways London Eye on the South Bank river (*see* Getting Around London, *in* Basics, *above*). The Underground's Jubilee Line (the gray one), extended to both Greenwich and Greenwich Peninsula (North Greenwich), will get you to the Dome's shuttle service (the peninsula area is car-free) in about 12 minutes. From Bank, Tower Hill, or Canary Wharf station in London, Docklands Light Railway (DLR) takes 25 minutes to arrive at the Island Gardens station, on the Isle of Dogs; the next stop is Greenwich Railway station. From the Charlton railway station, the Millenium Transit Link shuttles to and from the dome.

If you arrive via the DLR, check out the view from the Island Gardens before crossing the Thames, and then head for the squat, circular brick building with a glass roof—this marks the entrance to the Greenwich Foot Tunnel, a passage with tiled curved walls and magnificent echoes that is the final leg of your journey. You'll emerge at Greenwich Pier, very near where the **Cutty Sark** (tel. 020/8858–3445) sits in dry dock. Now more familiar as the symbol of a brand of rum, this 19th-century, tea-trading clipper was once the fastest ship in the world: In 1871 it completed the journey from China to London in only 107 days. You can climb aboard the decks, ogle the world's largest collection of figureheads, or grab hold of the wheel and play captain. It's open daily 10–5 and costs £3.50. For landlubbers, there's **Greenwich Royal Park** (tel. 020/8858–2608), the oldest of London's Royal parks, containing incredible flower gardens, a Victorian tea pavilion, a boating lake, the Royal Greenwich Observatory (*see below*), and a stunning view of London from Greenwich Hill.

Greenwich's markets command reasonable popularity, though the trail of quaint tea shops in the area can sometimes feel like tourism industry overload. The small, covered **Bosun's Yard Market** (59 Greenwich Church St., tel.020/8293–4804) is packed with stalls selling arts and crafts, books, and other small items; it's open daily in summer (weekends only in winter). **Greenwich Market** (College Approach, Stockwell St., High Rd., and surrounding alleys) is held weekends 9–6 and features a wide range of antiques, old books and records, and odd bits of bric-a-brac. Fewer tourists means better deals; still, you should bargain hard. For information on guided walks and the like, stop by the **Greenwich Tourist Office** (46 Greenwich Church St., tel. 020/8858–6376); it's open daily 10:15–4:45 (shorter hours in winter).

Meanwhile, closer to the town center at Greenwich Reach there are plans to build a cruise liner terminal and spin-off facilities such as hotels, restaurants, and other tourist essentials. It won't be long before this trendy little 19th-century neighborhood is much more accessible—and a lot more crowded.

MILLENNIUM DOME

Prior to its opening on January 1, 2000, plenty of Brits were struggling to imagine what sort of futuristic theme park could be brilliant enough to require £758 million in funding. Almost three-quarters of a mile in circumference, the tentlike structure covered by a translucent roof can hold two Wembley Stadiums or the Eiffel Tower on its side. Fourteen interactive exhibition zones enclose a central theater, which hosts several daily Millennium Shows with visual effects and 200 performers competing for your attention. Surrounding the arena are exhibitions celebrating British ideas and technology. Themes range from the earnest, school-trip-like Work and Learn, to the more enticing temptations to your inner child—Dreamscape, Serious Play, and Body Zone. Passageways through a monumental-size human body model in Body Zone will give you the inside scoop on the way things work. All of these displays will last for exactly one year. At press time, the government was inviting bids for taking over its operation, so its usage from January 1, 2001, is unknown.

NATIONAL MARITIME MUSEUM

When King Charles II ordered Christopher Wren to build "a small observatory within our part of Greenwich" in 1675, few realized the impact this unassuming building would have on the future of world navigation. Although the **Royal Greenwich Observatory** is no longer used for astronomical observations (London's bright lights obscure the view), this is the place the BBC is talking about when it announces **"Greenwich Mean Time (GMT)"**; it's also the point from which sailors around the globe determine their bearings, using Greenwich as the prime meridian (0° longitude). The building holds a remarkable collection of beautiful antique timepieces and several antique telescopes. The observatory is now part of the nearby **National Maritime Museum,** which holds the world's largest collection of maritime artifacts, including paintings, medallions, the uniform Lord Nelson was killed in, and reclaimed wreckage from England's mighty days of thalassocracy. Fourteen new galleries increase the museum's scope significantly. The £9.50 admission gets you into the observatory, the museum, and the Queen's House (*see below*). The cover for the museum only is £7.50, the observatory £5. *Romney Rd., SE10, tel. 020/8858–4422. Open daily 10–5 (last admission at 4:30).*

QUEEN'S HOUSE

Completed by Inigo Jones in 1635 and inherited by Charles I's wife Henrietta Maria, the Queen's House was Britain's first classical building. The royal apartments have been restored to their 1660 state and feature a surprisingly vibrant color scheme. The Tulip Stair spirals without a central support to the **Great Hall,** a perfect cube, 40 ft in all three directions, decorated with paintings of the Muses, the Virtues, and the Liberal Arts. For admission prices, *see* National Maritime Museum, *above. Romney Rd., SE10, tel. 020/8858–4422. Open daily 10–5 (last admission at 4:30).*

The brass line over the cobblestone courtyard in Greenwich's Old Royal Observatory humbly divides the world into the Eastern and Western hemispheres.

ROYAL NAVAL COLLEGE

Founded by William III as the naval equivalent to Chelsea Royal Hospital (*see* Chelsea, *above*), these Wren buildings were converted into a college for aspiring sailors in 1873. The symmetrical blocks preserve the view from the Queen's House to the river, and wandering around the grounds and the two buildings open to the public makes a nice diversion. Students dine in the **Painted Hall,** decorated with Baroque murals (1707–17) of William and Mary by Sir James Thornhill, who also painted the interior of the dome of St. Paul's. The **College Chapel** was rebuilt after a fire in 1779 in a neo-Grecian style. Nelson's body lay in state here after his death at the battle of Trafalgar in 1805. *West gate, King William Walk, tel. 020/8858–2154. Admission free. Open daily 2:30–4:45.*

WINDSOR

Windsor, some twenty miles west of central London along the Thames, is the sort of place where rowboats roll gently upriver, where swans along the riverbank noisily lap up crumbs, and where families stroll eating ice cream. Of all the day trips you could make from London, this is one of the nicest; Windsor Castle and the royal pomp are simply bonuses. That said, the royal presence draws throngs of foreign and English visitors, packing the narrow, cobbled streets of what would otherwise be a charming village. Trains make the trip from London's Waterloo to **Windsor and Eton Riverside Station** (Datchet Rd., tel. 0345/484950) and from London's Paddington to **Windsor and Eton Central Station** (Thames St., tel. 0345/484950). Both trips leave about every half hour, last 35–50 minutes, and cost £6 return. The **Tourist Information Centre** (24 High St., tel. 01753/743900) is just around the corner from the castle. Across from the tourist office is Christopher Wren's **Guildhall,** begun in 1687. Look carefully at the pillars in the center of the forecourt—Wren added them later when townsfolk expressed their concern that the slender outer pillars weren't strong enough to support the upper story. Note that they don't rise all the way to the ceiling, proving Wren's design to be sound. Running the length of the Market Cross House you'll find **Queen Charlotte Street,** recognized as the shortest street in Britain at 51 ft, 10 inches long.

WINDSOR CASTLE

What William the Conqueror originally built out of dirt and wood (and what Henry II rebuilt in stone) has survived countless alterations over the centuries to become today's Windsor Castle. The process of restoration continues: A 1992 fire heavily damaged several rooms in the State Apartments, most of which were for the private use of the queen, who spends most of her weekends here (the castle remains open even when she's in residence). Whenever the queen is at Windsor, the Union Jack that usually flies from the Round Tower is replaced with the royal coat of arms.

The castle is divided into the Lower, Middle, and Upper Wards. Many of England's kings and queens are buried in the 15th-century **St. George's Chapel,** the principal structure of the Lower Ward. The tomb of Henry VIII is located in the choir—a simple slab in the floor that he shares with Charles I, and a remarkably meager monument to such a megalomaniac. The Gothic chapel is the shrine of the Order of the Garter, a chivalric order founded in 1438 by Edward III. The **State Apartments** are in the Upper Ward and feature an amazing collection of royal portraiture and other paintings, including works by Dürer, Rubens, and Van Dyck. Check out the Gobelin tapestries, too, and the Louis XVI bed. The **Gallery** hosts changing exhibitions taken from the Royal Collection, one of the finest art collections in the world. For an additional £1 fee you can visit **Queen Mary's Dolls' House,** a masterpiece by the architect Edwin Lutyens. The Dolls' House, measuring 8 ft by 5 ft, is a fully functional marvel of miniature engineering with electric lights, running faucets, and elevators. Prominent authors and artists of the day contributed miniature paintings and handwritten books to the house's library, and seamstresses invested some 1,500 hours stitching monograms on the tiny little linens. Be aware that the State Apartments are sometimes closed when the queen is in residence; call ahead before making the trek, to avoid disappointment. The Gallery is closed January–May; St. George's Chapel and the Albert Memorial Chapel are closed every Sunday. The **Changing of the Guard** takes place Monday–Saturday at 11 AM from April through June. During the rest of the year it occurs only on odd-numbered days of the month except Sunday. *Castle Hill, tel. 01753/831118. Admission £10; £8.50 when State Apartments are closed. Open Mar.–Oct., daily 10–5:30 (last admission 4), Nov.–Feb., daily 10–4 (last admission 3).*

MUSEUMS AND GALLERIES

In addition to the museums reviewed below, the following museums are discussed above: **Apsley House** (*see* Kensington and Knightsbridge); **Barbican Art Gallery** (*see* The City); **BBC Visitor Centre** (*see* Marylebone and Regent's Park); **British Museum** (*see* Major Attractions); **Cabinet War Rooms** (*see* Whitehall and Westminster); **Courtauld Institute Galleries** (*see* The Strand and Embankment); **Freud's Museum** (*see* Hampstead and Highgate); **Guards Museum** (*see* Buckingham Palace, *in* Major Attractions); **HMS *Belfast*** (*see* The South Bank); **Jewel Tower** (*see* Houses of Parliament *in* Major Attractions); **Keats House** (*see* Hampstead and Highgate); **Kensington Palace** (*see* Hyde Park and Kensington Gardens *in* Kensington and Knightsbridge); **Leighton House** (*see* Kensington and Knightsbridge); **London Aquarium** (*see* The South Bank); **London Dungeon** (*see* The South Bank); **Madame Tussaud's Wax Museum** (*see* Marylebone and Regent's Park); **National Gallery** (*see* Trafalgar Square *in* Major Attractions); **Natural History Museum** (*see* Kensington and Knightsbridge); **National Portrait Gallery** (*see* Trafalgar Square *in* Major Attractions); **Percival David Foundation of Chinese Art** (*see* University of London *in* Bloomsbury and Legal London); **Queen's Gallery** (*see* Buckingham Palace *in* Major Attractions); **Science Museum** (*see* Kensington and Knightsbridge); **Shakespeare's Globe Exhibition** (*see* The South Bank); **Sir John Soane's Museum** (*see* Bloomsbury and Legal London); **Tate Britain** (*see* Major Attractions); **Thomas Carlyle's House** (*see* Chelsea); **University of London** (*see* Bloomsbury and Legal London); **Victoria and Albert Museum** (*see* Kensington and Knightsbridge); **Wallace Collection** (*see* Mayfair).

Bank of England Museum. Housed in the Bank of England Building, this multimedia museum has some cool historical artifacts, early photographs, collections of old coins and banknotes, original artwork from Britain's currency, and interactive videos about the history of banknotes. *Bartholomew La., EC2, tel. 020/7601–5545. Tube: Bank. Walk east on Threadneedle St., turn left on Bartholomew La. Admission free. Open weekdays 10–5.*

Camden Arts Centre. This is one of the best places in London to see contemporary international art. *Arkwright Rd., NW3, tel. 020/7435–2643 or 020/7435–5224. Tube: Finchley Road. Walk north (uphill) on Finchley Rd., turn right on Arkwright Rd. Admission free. Open Tues.–Thurs. 11–7, Fri.–Sun. 11–5:30.*

Design Museum. This elegantly laid-out museum houses two floors of 20th-century international design, with an emphasis on mass-produced consumer goods. The hypermodern **Review gallery** displays a constantly changing survey of contemporary design, while the **Collection gallery** has a more historical emphasis. *Butler's Wharf, 28 Shad Thames, SE1, tel. 020/7403–6933; 020/7378–6055 for* *recorded info. Tube: Tower Hill. Cross Tower Bridge and head east along the Thames. Admission £5.50. Open daily 11:30–6.*

Dickens House. During the three years (1837–1839) he lived at 48 Doughty Street, Charles Dickens churned out *Oliver Twist* and *Nicholas Nickleby* and finished up *Pickwick Papers.* The house is now an interesting museum and library, containing a large collection of Dickens's household goods, his desk, and the ubiquitous lock of hair. *48 Doughty St., WC1, tel. 020/7405–2127. Tube: Russell Square. Walk east on Bernard St., turn right at Coram's Fields, left on Guilford St., right on Doughty St. Admission £4. Open Mon.–Sat. 10–5.*

Dulwich Picture Gallery. Britain's oldest public art gallery (opened in 1817) is from a grand design by the neoclassic architect Sir John Soane. Housed within is a breathtaking display of old masters, such as Rembrandt, Rubens, Canaletto, and Van Dyck, still hung as tightly together as they would have been in the 19th century. It will be closed for rehangings until May 2000. *College Rd., SE21, tel. 020/8693–5254. BritRail: West Dulwich. Or take Bus 3 from Oxford Circus, Trafalgar Square, or Westminster. Admission £3. Open Tues.–Fri. 10–5, weekends 11–5.*

FA Premier League Hall of Fame. Opened in spring 1999, this is the country's main soccer museum spread over two floors and tracing the "beautiful game" from medieval times right up to the present. A flashy collection, in vogue with the game's current status and high profile, it celebrates the superstars of today as well as educational and interactive exhibits on the heroes of yesteryear. A particularly interesting section is the Hall of Fans that looks at what drives celebrities and ordinary Joe's to be so passionate about their favorite clubs. *County Hall, Westminster Bridge Rd., SE1, tel. 020/7928–1800. Tube: Westminster or Waterloo. Admission £9.95. Open daily 10–6.*

Geffrye Museum. This wonderful museum features 11 excellent complete period rooms, dating from the 16th century to the 1950s. Sir Robert Geffrye, a merchant and once Mayor of London, left part of his fortune to the Ironmongers' Company to build almshouses for the elderly poor. This place is a must for lovers of the decorative arts. There's also a wonderful herb garden. *Kingsland Rd., E2, tel. 020/7739–9893. Tube: Liverpool Street. From station, walk east to Bishopsgate and take Bus 242 or 149. Admission free. Open Tues.–Sat. 10–5, Sun. noon–5.*

Hayward Gallery. The forte of this art gallery in the South Bank Centre is assembling retrospectives of modern artists such as Magritte, Jasper Johns, Dalí, and Toulouse-Lautrec. *South Bank, Belvedere Rd., SE1, tel. 020/7960–4242. Tube: Embankment or Waterloo. Admission £6 or £12 for a multivisit ticket. Open daily 10–6 (Tues.–Wed. until 8).*

Imperial War Museum. Housed in the former home of the Bethlehem Royal Hospital for the Care of the Insane, or "Bedlam," this museum outlines the history of Britain's 20th-century wars using weaponry, mementos, and reconstructions. Don't think the lunatics have taken over the asylum—despite a bristling array of planes, field guns, and other war toys in the entrance hall, the museum's exhibits focus on the *horror,* rather than the "glory" of war. Two galleries upstairs house large collections of art from the two world wars. Downstairs you can visit "The Trench Experience," re-created from the Great War, and "The Blitz Experience," an excellent eight-minute trip through London's Blitz. The "Secret War" exhibit details the world of espionage, especially the work of MI5 and MI6, Britain's intelligence forces. *Geraldine Mary Harnsworth Park, Lambeth Rd., SE1, tel. 020/7416–5000. Tube: Lambeth North. Walk south on Kennington Rd. and turn left onto Lambeth Rd. Admission £5.20; free after 4:30. Open daily 10–6.*

Institute of Contemporary Arts (ICA). Lectures, avant-garde films, and rotating exhibits of photography, painting, sculpture, and architectural drawings by international and homegrown talent make ICA the headquarters for lusty cultural upheaval. Its café and bar are hangouts for black-clad hip intellectuals, who love to smoke, drink, and discuss German Expressionist films or vernacular architecture. *Nash House, The Mall, SW1, tel. 020/7930–6393 for recorded info; 020/7930–3647 for box office. Tube: Charing Cross or Piccadilly Circus. From Charing Cross, walk SW on The Mall. From Piccadilly Circus, walk south on Regent St., turn right on The Mall. Admission for exhibits £1.50 weekdays, £2.50 weekends. Gallery open daily noon–7:30 (Fri. until 9); café open Mon.–Sat. noon–3 and 5:30–9; bar open Mon. noon–11, Tues.–Sat. noon–1 AM, Sun. noon–10:30.*

London Canal Museum. In a former ice storage house, this museum illustrates the growth and decline of London's canal network. These waterways were once important venues for trade and transportation, and a distinct way of life evolved for the "canal people" who lived and worked on them. Make sure to look at the trippy narrow boats of modern canal dwellers on nearby Regent's Canal. *12–13 New Wharf Rd., N1, tel. 020/7713–0836. Tube: King's Cross. Walk north on York Way, turn right on Wharfdale Rd., left on New Wharf Rd. Admission £2.50. Open Tues.–Sun. 10–4:30 (last entry 3:45).*

London Transport Museum. Dozens of buses, trams, and trains from the early 1800s to the present day (including an improbable-looking double-decker tram once pulled by a single, overworked horse) make up this museum's fascinating collection. The accompanying info tells the story of mass transportation's impact on both the growth of London and the class stratification within it. If that sounds dry, you can gambol with costumed actors, watch multilingual videos, or "test-drive" your own bus or tube train. *39 Wellington St. (entrance on The Piazza), WC2, tel. 020/7836–8557. Tube: Covent Garden. Admission £4.95. Open daily 10–6 (Fri. from 11).*

Museum of Garden History. This peaceful little spot of green housed in the former St. Mary-at-Lambeth Church is hidden away from the smoggy, concrete world. The churchyard contains a replica of a 17th-century garden, built to honor Charles I's royal gardeners, the Tradescants, who are buried here—as is William Bligh, captain of the *Bounty. Lambeth Palace Rd., SE1, tel. 020/7261–1891. Tube: Lambeth North. Walk SW on Hercules Rd., turn right on Lambeth Rd. Admission free. Open Mar.–Dec., weekdays 10:30–4, Sun. 10:30–5.*

Museum of London. Come here for an extremely thorough look at the history of the city, starting from the Stone Age. A lot of the older material on display was found in the Thames or at modern building sites. Be sure to see the sculptures from the Temple of Mithras, god of heavenly light. Worshipers of Mithras buried the sculptures so they wouldn't be destroyed by their rival cult, the Christians. Other "don't miss" items include the amazing Cheapside Hoard of jewelry, a beautiful art deco elevator from Selfridge's, and the glitzy Lord Mayor's Coach. Admission is good for an entire year from the date of purchase, so you can visit over and over. *150 London Wall, EC2, tel. 020/7600–3699. Tube: Barbican or St. Paul's. From Barbican, walk south on Aldersgate St. From St. Paul's, walk north on St. Martin's-Le-Grand. Admission £5; free after 4:30. Open Tues.–Sat. 10–5:50, Sun. noon–5:50.*

Museum of the Moving Image (MOMI). This impressive television and film showcase traces the history of man's manipulation of light and shadow. Tons of interactive exhibits—plus snippets from groundbreaking flicks—make this a definitively cool museum. The museum also has a wide collection of movie memorabilia, like the goldfish models from *The Meaning of Life* and Charlie Chaplin's costume from *Modern Times.* Mildly embarrassing actors employed by the museum float around, trying to add period flavor—*some* of them succeed. *South Bank, Belvedere Rd., SE1, tel. 020/7401–2636. Tube: Embankment or Waterloo. Admission £6.25. Open daily 10–6 (last admission 5 PM).*

Photographer's Gallery. This is the leading locale in London for contemporary British and international photography. *5 Great Newport St., WC2, tel. 020/7831–1772. Tube: Leicester Square. Walk north on Charing Cross Rd., turn right on Great Newport St. Admission free. Open Mon.–Sat. 11–6.*

Royal Academy of Arts. The venerable Royal Academy, an art school founded in 1768, is the oldest institution in London devoted to the fine arts. It houses a permanent collection of works by Royal Academicians and stages impressive special exhibitions throughout the year. In 1999 it had its most successful exhibit ever with a major collection of Monet's works. The new millenium kicks off with "The Year 1900: Art At The Crossroad", a retrospective of the 20th century though 250 paintings and sculptures curated in conjunction with the Guggenheim Museum in New York. The Academy's annual Summer Exhibition of contemporary art is a noted event that usually takes place between early June and mid-August—anyone can submit work, though only 1,200 are chosen from an average of 12,000 applicants. The Academy's postgraduate students show off their final exam projects to the public every June and July. *Burlington House, Piccadilly, W1, tel. 020/7439–7438. Tube: Green Park or Piccadilly Circus. From Green Park, walk NE on Piccadilly. From Piccadilly Circus, walk west on Piccadilly. Admission varies; average £7. Open daily 10–6. Last admission at 5:30.*

Saatchi Gallery. The megabucks of adman Charles Saatchi fuel this huge gallery, one of the most coveted venues in the land. As one of the most influential private collectors, Saatchi has made the careers of a number of artists, and spent the '90s focusing on British artists like Damien Hirst (the dead-animals-in-formaldehyde guy) and Rachel Whiteread (the plaster-casts-of-rooms-and-buildings woman). Exhibits change frequently; the annual Young British Artists show is always thought-provoking. *98A Boundary Rd., NW8, tel. 020/7624–8299. Tube: Swiss Cottage. Walk ⅓ mi south on Finchley Rd., turn right on Boundary Rd. Admission £4; free Thurs. Open Thurs.–Sun. noon–6.*

Serpentine Gallery. Search for this tea-pavilion-turned-art gallery just north of the Albert Memorial in Kensington Gardens. Consult *Time Out* to see what's new here (usually some sort of modern multimedia work) because the gallery closes sporadically throughout the year. Free "gallery talks" are offered Sunday at 3 PM during exhibitions. *Kensington Gardens, W2, tel. 020/7402–6075. Tube: Lancaster Gate or South Kensington. Admission free. Open daily 10–6; closed occasionally for 2–3-wk periods.*

Theatre Museum. The Theatre Museum illustrates life on the British stage from Shakespeare's time through the present with theatrical memorabilia galore, including prints and paintings of the earliest London theaters, early scripts, costumes, and props. It's not all highbrow drama stuff either—the galleries include art and artifacts of the circus, modern musicals, and puppetry. For the price of admission you can also join guided tours and attend stage-makeup demos and costume workshops. *1E Tavistock St. (entrance on Russell St.), WC2, tel. 020/7836–7891. Tube: Covent Garden. Admission £4. Open Tues.–Sun. 11–7.*

Whitechapel Art Gallery. This large, well-designed venue with lots of natural light was built in the 1890s to bring culture to the East End; these days cheap studio spaces have attracted more than 7,000 artists to the area. Besides the gallery's regular exhibits, they have a great lineup of art talks and other special events; call them or see *Time Out* for details. *80 Whitechapel High St., E1, tel. 020/7522–7888; 020/7522–7878 for recorded info. Tube: Aldgate East. Follow signs to museum. Admission free; small charge for some exhibits. Open Tues.–Sun. 11–5 (Wed. until 8).*

SHOPPING

Name your poison, because London rivals any place in the known universe when it comes to shopping. Join the connoisseurs of funky at roaring weekend street markets, the most discriminating ears at music shops, and the rich or "just-looking" escapists at swank department stores. London may not trumpet its fashion sensibility the way other European capitals do, but there's no disputing that fashion slaves worldwide look to this city for the latest trends. Be warned: Competition doesn't do much to keep prices low. You can easily empty your wallet before blinking. *Time Out* magazine lists bargains regularly in their "Sell Out" section, and many of London's stores have huge, gala sales in January and July. Otherwise, street markets are your best bet. The vibe is better, and they offer plenty of items at bargain prices.

CLOTHING

London has the best of both high and low fashion, but the best deals are generally hidden in the nooks and crannies of dusty shops or crammed in between the junk sold at London's street markets. If you insist on browsing the high-priced selection at **Harrods** (*see* Kensington and Knightsbridge, *above*), get an early start—crowds can be maddening by midday. Some other upscale department stores include **Selfridges** (400 Oxford St., tel. 020/7629–1234), **Liberty & Co.** (210–220 Regent St., tel. 020/7734–1234), and **Harvey Nichols** (109 Knightsbridge, SW1, tel. 020/7235–5000)—HN was, of course, the home-away-from-home of *Absolutely Fabulous*'s Patsy and Edina. Prices at these stores can be absurd, except during one of their holiday sales. Better yet, **Marks & Spencer** (458 Oxford St., tel. 020/7935–7954) is less highbrow, offering some great bargains on new clothes; look for other branches on Baker Street, Kensington High Street, King's Road, and Queensway.

NEW CLOTHES • Clothing boutiques of all shapes and sizes crowd the "Golden Mile" of **Oxford Street,** stretching east and west of the Oxford Circus tube station. You'll also find happy hunting around Covent Garden, Kensington High Street, King's Road in Chelsea, and South Molton Street in Mayfair. **Petticoat Lane Market** (*see* Street Markets, *below*) is home to a number of cutting-edge fashion designers.

Alchemy Sale Basement. Alchemy's label is synonymous with funky clubwear. Its basement sale space carries samples, end-of-lines, and experimental pieces as well as clothes by other young clubwear designers. Discounts range from 20%–60%. *1 Short's Gardens, WC2, tel. 020/7240–7600. Tube: Covent Garden. Open Mon.–Sat. 11:30–7.*

Hype DF. This is one of the biggest stores for designer collections in London. It's a purpose-built miniature department store featuring the hottest, trendiest designers and targeted at the 18–40 age group. Look around and you'll find some cool bargains. *48–52 Kensington High St., W8, tel. 020/7938–4343. Tube: High Street Kensington. Open Mon.–Sat. 10–6 (Thurs. until 8), Sun. noon–6.*

Jigsaw. One of the best of the chain stores, Jigsaw is more on the pulse than closest rival Next and less deliberately in-yer-face than French Connection. Launched initially as a women's shop, its men's fashions knock the spots off most of its rivals. Branches are all over London, but the concrete and frosted glass of the flagship Bond Street store takes top prize. *126–127 New Bond St., W1, tel. 020/7491–4484. Tube: Bond Street. Open Mon.–Sat. 10–6:30 (Thurs. until 7). Also located all over London.*

Kensington Market. The indoor stalls here ply everything from silk scarves to studs to records to hair dye. Goths and grebos (motorcycle types) come here for denim and leather; club kids come for outrageous PVC and rubber gear. You'll find quite a few booths offering vintage clothing, shoes, and accessories from the '20s, '50s, and '70s, too. *49–53 Kensington High St., W8, tel. 020/7938–4343. Tube: High Street Kensington. Open Mon.–Sat. 10–6.*

Next. This British equivalent of The Gap offers a much wider range of styles, and the shops themselves are pretty classy, too. Men's and women's clothes are reasonably priced and fashionable. There are Next stores all over London, found in all the major shopping districts. *327–329 Oxford St., W1, tel. 020/7409–2746. Tube: Bond Street. Open Mon.–Wed. 10:30–7, Thurs. 10–8, Fri.–Sat. 10–7, Sun. noon–6.*

Paul Smith. Adored by anglophiles around the world for his clever takes on traditional English wear, Smith has achieved almost the status of a national institution. Now even kids can prance around in his well-tailored cuts and subdued colors, as long as their mummies and daddies don't mind splashing out a bit extra for a touch of latter day class. *40-44 Floral St., WC2, tel. 020/7379-7133. Tube: Covent Garden. Open Mon.–Sat. 10–6:30 (Thurs. until 7).*

Red or Dead. This cool seller of threads and shoes began as a stall in Camden Market. Now, people flock to the four stores for the reasonably priced stock of dresses, jeans, jackets, and accessories. Their line of big clunky shoes is a major draw. *33 Neal St., WC2, tel. 020/7379–7571. Tube: Covent Garden. Open Mon.–Sat. 10:30–7, Sun. 12:30–5:30. 38 Kensington High St., W8, tel. 020/7937–1649.*

Vivienne Westwood. The Godmother of the whole Cool Britannia fashion generation continues to baffle and delight her (mostly) adoring public. Her Pompadour-punk smoking jackets and stunning Lady Hamilton frock coats can be yours for £2,000 a pop. With a new store opened in New York and new house south of the Thames, Westwood is definitely not finished yet. *6 Davies St., W1, tel. 020/7629-3757. Tube: Bond Street. Open Mon.–Sat. 10–6 (Thurs. until 7). Other locations: 44 Conduit St., W1, tel. 020/7439–1109, 430 King's Rd., SW3, tel. 020/7352-6551.*

SECONDHAND AND THRIFT CLOTHING • One of the best places to get used clothes in London is Oxfam, which runs 94 charity shops citywide. Each one offers the usual thrift-store finds: sturdy duds, household items, used books, and the like. Hipsters favor the shop near Oxford Circus, called Oxfam Originals (*see below*). Otherwise, try the Oxfam branches at 89 Camden High Street, NW1 (tel. 020/7387–4354), 23 Drury Lane, WC2 (tel. 020/7240–3769), and 202B Kensington High Street, W8 (tel. 020/7937–6683).

Blackout II. Attention, kitsch shoppers: Blackout stocks glam fashions from the 1920s to the 1970s, plus a wide selection of secondhand handbags and shoes. Look in the basement for real bargains (stuff that's out of season or needs repair). *51 Endell St., WC2, tel. 020/7240–5006. Tube: Covent Garden. Open weekdays 11–7, Sat. 11:30–6:30.*

Oxfam Originals. Of all the Oxfam shops in London, this is the best for funky castoffs. New stock arrives almost daily: As the sign proclaims, HUBBA HUBBA—WE'VE GOT SOME LOVELY NEW CLOTHES. *26 Ganton St., W1, tel. 020/7437–7338. Tube: Oxford Circus. Open Mon.–Sat. 11–6.*

Salvation Army Charity Shop/Cloud 9. Skip quickly past the ground-floor offerings (sportswear, kid's clothes, old books, etc.) and head upstairs to Cloud 9, where you'll find retro and groovy threads. *9 Princes St., W1, tel. 020/7495–3958. Tube: Oxford Circus. Open weekdays 10:30–6, Sat. 11:30–5:30.*

Yesterday's Bread. Take a step back in time and outfit yourself in "retro" gear. Yesterday's Bread specializes in never-before-worn garments from the '60s and '70s. *29–31 Foubert's Pl., W1. tel. 020/7287-1929. Tube: Oxford Circus. Open weekdays 11:30–6:30, Sat. 11–6.*

BOOKSTORES

Generations of great authors have scribbled their lives away in London, from Henry Fielding, Charles Dickens, Oscar Wilde, and Virginia Woolf, to current champs like Martin Amis, Kazuo Ishiguro, Doris Lessing, and Jeanette Winterson. And London has a plethora of bookstores to deal with its massive literary output. It is indeed quite possible to get lost amid the secondhand bookstores on **Tottenham Court Road, Charing Cross Road,** and the adjacent **Cecil Court.**

NEW BOOKS • As far as chains go, one of the best is **Waterstone's,** whose main branch is at 121–129 Charing Cross Road (tel. 020/7434–4291). Nearby is **Books Etc.** (120–122 Charing Cross Rd., WC2, tel. 020/7379–6838), another major chain with a friendly and helpful staff and a basement full of bargains. The award for largest and most chaotic bookstore goes to **Foyles** (119 Charing Cross Rd.,

WC2, tel. 020/7437–5660); if it's in print, they probably have it. The flagship store of the Dillons chain (*see below*) is considered by many to be the best bookstore in town.

Compendium. With its potpourri of political tracts, New Age manifestos, and radical poetry, this alternative bookstore draws a devoted crowd. The store hosts frequent readings, and employees are extremely helpful and knowledgeable. *234 Camden High St., NW1, tel. 020/7485–8944. Tube: Camden Town. Open Mon.–Sat. 10–6, Sun. noon–6.*

Dillons. This chain has about a dozen stores in London, but the best one to visit is the colossal, five-story bookstore in Bloomsbury. At any given time it stocks 250,000–300,000 titles. Browsing at length is encouraged and there's even a "Cyber.St@tion" for net surfing. *82 Gower St., WC1, tel. 020/7636–1577. Tube: Goodge Street. Open weekdays 9–7 (Tues. 9:30–7), Sat. 9:30–6.*

Dillons Art Bookshop. This first-rate bookshop, part of the Dillons chain (*see above*), tempts academics, art students, and poets with a wide range of works on film, theater, fashion, art, and architecture. *8 Long Acre, WC2, tel. 020/7836–1359. Tube: Covent Garden or Leicester Square. Open Mon.–Sat. 9:30 AM–10 PM (Tues. from 10), Sun. noon–6.*

Gay's the Word. The name says it all. This Bloomsbury shop carries London's finest selection of gay and lesbian books (new and used), magazines, and videos. *66 Marchmont St., WC1, tel. 020/7278–7654. Tube: Russell Square. Open Mon.–Sat. 10–6:30, Sun. 2–6.*

Silver Moon Women's Bookshop. This friendly, feminist bookshop is London's sisterhood central for literature by and about women. *64–68 Charing Cross Rd., WC2, tel. 020/7836–7906. Tube: Leicester Square. Open Mon.–Sat. 10–6:30 (Thurs. until 8), Sun. noon–6.*

USED BOOKS • Henry Pordes Books. The musty smell here cues visitors to the great selection of old books—some of the antiquarian variety and some just plain old. Fiction is one of the strongest sections. Prices for paperbacks start at £1.50. *58–60 Charing Cross Rd., WC2, tel. 020/7836–9031. Tube: Leicester Square. Open Mon.–Sat. 10–7.*

Skoob. This is one of the best and most popular used bookstores in town, and the slightly higher prices reflect it. Most impressive are the humanities, foreign literature, and political science sections. Next door, Skoob Two focuses on a more eclectic assortment of books about the occult, religion, anthropology, and so on. *15–17 Sicilian Ave., WC1, tel. 020/7404–3063. Tube: Holborn. Open Mon.–Sat. 10:30–6:30.*

GIFT IDEAS

Like any tourist Mecca, London is stuffed full of tacky gift shops and souvenir stalls. Nothing wrong with that, of course; the capital would be a poorer place without fake police helmets, plastic Carnaby Street signs and big-eared Prince Charles masks. But, if you want to go that extra mile, impress the folks back home, then get your hands on a more lasting memento from a specialist shop.

Beatles for Sale. Okay, Liverpool might be the Fab Four's birthplace, but London was where they recorded the most memorable music of the pop age. You can back up your own Beatle memories with an incredibly wide range of souvenirs and bric-a-brac here. *8 Kingley St., W1, tel. 020/7434–0464. Tube: Oxford Circus. Open Mon.–Sun. 10–7.*

Crafts Council. Jewelry, glassware, and fine textiles by the best of contemporary craftsmen and women, mostly from the U.K., are sold here . *44A Pentonville Rd., N1, tel. 020/7806–2559. Tube: Angel. Open Tues.–Sat. 11–5:45, Sun. 2–5:45. Other location: Victoria & Albert Museum, Cromwell Rd., SW7, tel. 020/7589–5070.*

Past Times. If you're determined to take a piece of old England home with you, you could do a lot worse than visit Past Times, where nostalgia is king. Juicy morsels for sale include bath salts from medieval times and enough Celtic accessories to invite another Roman invasion. The price range is very wide, so you don't have to blow that last traveler's check on a cute little tea pot. *146 Brompton Rd., SW3, tel. 020/7581–7616. Tube: Knightsbridge. Open Mon.–Sat. 9:30–6 (Wed. until 7), Sun. 11–5.*

R. Twining & Co. If tea is the English champagne, Twinings is the Moët. This fascinating shop has a museum as well as a broad collection of superb teas, including fine versions of the all-time classics English Breakfast and Earl Grey. *216 Strand, WC2, tel. 020/7353–3511. Tube: Charing Cross. Open weekdays 9:30–4:30.*

MUSIC

From post-punk and rockabilly to hip-hop and rave, London's music scene is first-rate. Multinational chains like **HMV** (150 Oxford St., W1, tel. 020/7631–3423), **Tower Records** (1 Piccadilly Circus, W1, tel.

020/7439–2500), and **Virgin** (14–16 Oxford St., W1, tel. 020/7631–1234) have megastores the size of small villages. And, there are tons of tiny, funky, independent shops specializing in rare vinyl, bootleg recordings, dance 12-inchers, you name it. If you're in no hurry, you can spend an entire day cruising the music shops: Try **Berwick Street** in Soho, **Camden High Street**, and **Hill Gate** at Ladbroke Grove. Wherever you go, expect to pay £7–£12 for vinyl, £9–£16 for CDs. Though prices aren't cheap, that same record or CD sells for at least $20 as an import when it hits the shelves in the United States.

Black Market. Twelve-inch import singles take up most of the ground floor, sharing some space with Euro music and listening turntables. Follow the booming music downstairs to the basement, which houses all varieties of techno, rap, and hip-hop. *25 D'Arblay St., W1, tel. 020/7437–0478. Tube: Oxford Circus. Open Mon.–Sat. 11–7.*

Music & Video Exchange. Those in the know give this London minichain top marks for prices (low), selection (enormous), and staff (friendly and helpful; never snarling, abrupt, or rude). The shop has expanded fourfold in recent years. The used CDs are tucked away in glass cases, and you have to crane your neck to read the titles, but the substantial markdowns are worth the trouble. *34–65 Notting Hill Gate, W11, tel. 020/7243–8573. Tube: Notting Hill Gate. Open daily 10–8. Other locations: 95 Berwick St., W1, tel. 020/7434–2939; 229 Camden High St., NW1, tel. 020/7267–1898; 480 Fulham Rd., SW6, tel. 020/7385–5350; 28 Pembridge Rd, W11, tel. 020/7221–1444.*

Reckless Records. Nothing but bargains in these aisles: secondhand 12-inch dance singles, classical, reggae, rock, soul, jazz, and even country music. The Islington branch (79 Upper St., N1, tel. 020/7359–0501) has a good collection of rare titles at rare prices. *30 Berwick St., W1, tel. 020/7437–4271. Tube: Oxford Circus. Open daily 10–7.*

Rough Trade. The fine selection of indie music, grunge, and U.S. imports draws lots of young skinheads to this store in the basement of a skateboard shop. Then again, it could also be Rough Trade's fairly impromptu (and free) performances by visiting bands. The original shop (130 Talbot Rd., W11, tel. 020/7229–8541) has a lot more punk junk on the walls, but the selection is the same. *16 Neal's Yard, WC2, tel. 020/7240–0105. Tube: Covent Garden or Tottenham Court Road. Open Mon.–Sat. 10–6:30.*

STREET MARKETS

You'd be hard pressed to find a better way to shop than in London's street markets, where one person's junk routinely morphs into another person's treasure. The biggest and best markets are in **Camden** and on **Portobello Road** (*see below*), and draw correspondingly huge crowds. Other, smaller markets are where Londoners have been going for centuries to stock the fridge (even before there was such a thing).

BERWICK STREET • Soho's once-thriving produce mart has downsized, but it's still a great place to buy a cheap lunch of fruit, bread, and cheese. Stop by around 5 PM—when the merchants are desperate to get rid of their produce—and you'll walk away with incredible deals. Cheapie clothes, used records, and assorted trinketry can be found on Rupert Street. *Berwick and Rupert Sts., W1. Tube: Leicester Square or Piccadilly Circus. Open Mon.–Sat. 8–6.*

BRICK LANE • You can find anything your heart desires at this East End institution, although it's primarily about tacky new clothes and cheap fruit. Best of all, it's rarely glutted with tourists. Listen and learn as the Cockney vegetable sellers twist the English language to hawk their wares. *Brick La. and surrounding streets, E1 and E2. Tube: Aldgate East and Shoreditch. Open Sun. 8 AM–1 PM.*

BRIXTON MARKET • Rock down to vibrant Electric Avenue for this sprawling, Latin and Afro-Caribbean-flavored market. You'll find a scattering of used clothing, exotic produce, good deals on reggae tapes and records, and mounds of more mundane wares like soap, batteries, and shampoo. *Electric Ave., SW9, tel. 020/7926–2530. Tube: Brixton. Open Mon.–Sat. 8–6 (Wed. until 3).*

CAMDEN MARKETS • Wait a few moments after stepping off the tube to orient yourself in the crushing mob; after all, Camden's markets are the best and busiest in London, unparalleled in atmosphere and selection. The sprawl actually includes five markets, of which **Camden Lock** (Camden Lock Pl., tel. 020/7284–2084) is indisputably the best. Get your used clothes, bootlegs, incense, crystals, knickknacks, smart drinks, and bongs here. Other markets include: **Camden Canal Market** (Chalk Farm Rd.), featuring everything from clothes to old toys; **Camden Market** (Camden High St., near Buck St., tel. 020/738–4343), with stalls selling new clothes, transformed clothes (like knit hats made from former sweaters), and unique accessories; the indoor **Electric Ballroom** (Camden High St., near Dewsbury Terr., tel. 020/7485–9006), best for clubbing garb and used clothes; and the **Stables** (Chalk Farm Rd., tel. 020/7485–5511), which has organic produce, some antiques, and lots of junk. *NW1. Tube: Cam-*

den Town. *Camden Lock open weekends 10–6 (indoor stalls open Tues.–Sun. 10–6); Camden Canal Market open weekends 10–6; Camden Market open Thurs.–Sun. 9–6; Electric Ballroom open Sun. 9–5:30; Stables open weekends 9–6.*

PETTICOAT LANE • Though not as hip as the Camden Markets, Petticoat Lane is almost as mammoth, swallowing Middlesex Street and a host of side streets. Goods for sale include cheap fashions, old watches, new and used shoes, luggage, household goods, and miscellaneous bric-a-brac. *Middlesex St., E1. Tube: Aldgate, Aldgate East, or Liverpool Street. Open Sun. 9–2.*

PORTOBELLO ROAD • The Portobello Road Market is second only to the Camden Markets for liveliness and funkiness. The southern end is the most touristy and has tons of Portobello's trademark item: antiques. At the northern end, locals shop for fruit, vegetables, flowers, and secondhand clothes. The whole affair lines Portobello Road for over a mile and can take the entire day to conquer, but the best time to go is Saturday morning. *Portobello Rd., W10 and W11, tel. 020/7727–7684 or 020/7341–5277. Tube: Ladbroke Grove or Notting Hill Gate. Open Sat. 6–4; some clothing and produce stalls also open Mon.–Wed. 9–5, Thurs. 9–1, Fri. 7–6.*

SPITALFIELDS MARKET • Spitalfields Market is held inside a huge barnlike warehouse, with stalls selling antiques, crafts, and snacks. It's also one of few markets selling organic meat, cheese, and produce (Friday and Sunday only). Performances of various sorts are held periodically on its small stage. *Commercial St., at Brushfield St., E1, tel. 020/7247–6590. Tube: Liverpool Street. Open weekdays and Sun. 9–6.*

AFTER DARK

London has a raging after-hours scene that's been setting global trends for decades. Rock music, jazz, raves, trip-hop, you name it, London probably did it first and often still does it best. The cost, however, can be stiff: A pint will cost you £2.50, movie tickets are £4–£9, and clubs usually charge covers of £6 and up-up-up. Jazz joints, dance clubs, big-name theaters, and first-run movie complexes are concentrated around Soho and Covent Garden, but you'll find hip, alternative clubs and theaters all over town. A number of publications give detailed rundowns of what's on and where. The best of the lot by far is the weekly *Time Out* (£1.80), invaluable to travelers and Londoners for its listings and reviews of the ever-evolving night scene. Useful descriptions will help you wade through the barrage of options. *What's On* (£1.30) is a cheaper and slightly less comprehensive version of the same thing. The *Evening Standard* (35p) also has all-purpose entertainment info, especially in the free Thursday supplement, "Hot Tickets." Whatever place you choose to check out, peruse the weekly listings first: Today's cool spot is often tomorrow's forgotten or closed venue.

PUBS

The English take their drink seriously, and pubs are where Londoners hang out, to see and be seen, act out the drama of life, and sometimes even drink themselves into varying degrees of oblivion. Unless otherwise noted, all pubs listed below—as well as most pubs throughout London—are open Monday–Saturday 11–11 and Sunday noon–10:30. For late-night drinking, try the new breed of club-bars where DJs spin, wine bars (which charge handsome prices to subsidize their after-hours liquor licenses), pubs that feature theater or music, or hope to find a small neighborhood pub that just doesn't give a damn. There's also a growing distinction between traditional pubs and more stylish designer-bars that often offer food and/or entertainment; the listings below divide drinking dens into these two categories.

Once you decide where to drink, the big decision is what to drink. Most English pubs are affiliated with particular breweries and are beholden to sell only beers produced by that brewery. In contrast, "free houses," (in effect chain pubs such Weatherspoons) can serve whatever they wish and tend to offer a more extensive selection. Besides cask-conditioned real ales (made without chilling, filtering, or pasteurization) and more commercial beers, there are a number of new bottled drinks on the market, including alcoholic lemonades and seltzers, and bottled mixed drinks. Finally, remember that even though you pay a handsome price for bottled beers, they are rarely served cold enough; this city needs bigger fridges.

Black Friar. This pub is one of London's most amazing—it's an Art Nouveau/Arts & Crafts spectacular of mosaic work, burnished wood, and gilt trim. Let the wealthy brokers from the nearby City hang out on the large outdoor terrace—you have to check out the back stone-walled room whose barrel-vaulted ceiling is decorated with maxims like "Industry is all" and "Wisdom is rare." The pub closes at 5 on Saturday and isn't open on Sunday. *174 Queen Victoria St., EC4, tel. 020/7236–5650. Tube: Blackfriars. Open weekdays noon–11. Sat. noon–5.*

Coach & Horses. Bright orange lights and lots of Naugahyde make up the decor, but the crowds aren't here for that. It's a historic hard-drinking place—local character Jeffrey Barnard (a British Bukowski) spent the 1950s tanked at this bar, his mission to observe Soho's "Low Life" for *Spectator* magazine. *29 Greek St., off Shaftesbury Ave., W1, tel. 020/7437–5920. Tube: Leicester Square.*

Crown & Goose. This is one of several clean modern pubs in the area that serves up good food. Fill up on excellent, inventive pastas and salads for around a fiver in a relaxed, cosmopolitan atmosphere. *100 Arlington Rd., off Parkway, NW1, tel. 020/7485–8008. Tube: Camden Town.*

French House. The unofficial Resistance headquarters during World War II, this pub still maintains a distinctly French aura. Predictably, there's an excellent wine selection. *49 Dean St., at Shaftesbury Ave., W1, tel. 020/7437–2799. Tube: Leicester Square.*

Front Page. This classy, intimate pub is currently the in spot for Chelsea's in crowd. By day, it's more mellow, and perfect for lingering. The menu features delicious "new British"–style dishes (£3–£9). *35 Old Church St., just south of King's Rd., SW3, tel. 020/7352–2908. Tube: Sloane Square.*

Gordon's. Inside and out, Gordon's looks like it's still in Dickensian times. This shabby, time-warp of a cellar attracts suits and streetlife who endure the smoky interior for a range of reasonably priced wines, ports, and sherries (they don't serve beer). It's a rare and an undersung institution. Hours are short on Saturday (5–11) and doors shut on Sunday. *47 Villiers St., WC2, tel. 020/7930–1408. Tube: Embankment or Charing Cross.*

Hollybush. Up a steep hill from the tube station in a hard-to-find cul-de-sac, this delightful pub is truly a real find. With tiny rooms, wooden boards and furniture, gas lamps, and all-round coziness, this is as close as you can get to a Dickens setting. Hollybush keeps normal hours other than closing between 2:30 and 5:30 weekdays. *22 Holly Mount, NW3, tel. 020/7435–2892. Tube: Hampstead.*

Lamb & Flag. "The oldest tavern in Covent Garden" sits in an alley just off Floral Street. With the cobblestone courtyard and wee fluffy lamb on the sign outside, you'd never guess people once boxed bare-knuckle upstairs, prompting the pub's nickname, "Bucket of Blood." *33 Rose St., between Long Acre and Flora St., WC2, tel. 020/7497–9504. Tube: Covent Garden.*

Old King Lud. A young, friendly crowd gathers in this woodsy pub on the east end of Fleet Street. Along with frequently changing guest kegs, 20 cask-conditioned real ales are served. The pub closes on weekends. *78 Ludgate Circus, EC4, tel. 020/7329–8517. Tube: Blackfriars. Walk north on New Bridge St.*

Orange Brewery. Many champion the solid, clubby, Victorian-era Orange as the "best pub in London." It makes its own brews: Try SW1 (a bitter) or Pimlico Porter (a dark ale) for £1.85–£2.10 per pint. Brewery tours are £2. *37 Pimlico Rd., off Lower Sloane St., SW1, tel. 020/7730–5984. Tube: Sloane Square.*

Prince Bonaparte. A lively pre-club stop with thumping music on weekends, the Bonaparte is a minimalist place with wooden tables, big windows, and a range of interesting beers. *80 Chepstow Rd., W2, tel. 020/7229–5912. Tube: Notting Hill Gate or Westbourne Park.*

Princess Louise. This fine, popular pub has an over-the-top Victorian interior—glazed terra-cotta, stained and frosted glass, and a glorious painted ceiling. It's not all show, either; the food is a cut above normal pub grub (especially the Thai dishes) and there's a good selection of real ales. *208 High Holborn, WC1, tel. 020/7405–8816. Tube: Holborn.*

Trafalgar Tavern. This huge, elegant pub regularly picks up awards from the capital's media. It's a busy joint but don't let that put you off. It's rich in atmosphere, promotes jazz sessions, and has excellent food. *Park Row, SE10, tel. 020/8858–2437. Rail: Greenwich.*

Ye Olde Cheshire Cheese. One of the oldest pubs in London (*rebuilt* after the Great Fire of 1666), YOCC has long been a famous haunt of Fleet Street journalists. Charles Dickens and lexicographer Samuel Johnson both drank here. Though it's an institution, you're still more likely to see suits than tourists. *Wine Office Court, 145 Fleet St., EC4, tel. 020/7353–6170. Tube: Blackfriars.*

BARS

291. A magnificent restoration of an old church now holds east London's one true drinking destination. The nave is now a video art gallery and the smaller bar has DJs spinning tunes every evening. A good but pricey restaurant serves modern takes on British food. *291 Hackney Rd., E2, tel. 020/7613–5676. Tube: Bethnal Green or Old Street. Open Tues.–Thurs. noon–midnight, Fri. and Sat. noon–2 AM.*

A.K.A. The main room at this big, new club-bar serves as a pre-clubbing meeting point, but many take one look at the huge lines for The End (a superb dance club) next door and stay here all night. What they get is some rather big-name DJ's spinning house and techno on the weekends, as well as costly cocktails, which become increasingly sloppily mixed as the night progresses. It's always free and plans are to open on Sunday soon. *18 West Central St., WC1, tel. 020/7836–0110. Tube: Tottenham Court Rd. or Holborn. Open Mon. 6 PM–1 AM, Tues.–Thurs. noon–4 and 6 PM–3 AM, Fri. noon–3 AM, Sat. 6 PM–3 AM.*

Cantaloupe. A friendly and trendy bar just a short walk from—and a big contrast to—the stuffy City. DJs spin background sounds for a hip but unpretentious clientele of pre-clubbers and residents of the increasingly young and upscale Hoxton Square neighborhood. *35 Charlotte Rd., EC2, tel. 020/7613–4411. Tube: Old St. Open weekdays 11 AM–midnight, Sat. 6 PM–midnight.*

Dog House. The Dog House has the hippest divey scene in Soho. It's below ground, with weird little rooms, funky furniture, and bright spacey murals on the walls. The music kicks, it's smoky, and it's loud. *187 Wardour St., W1, tel. 020/7434–2118. Tube: Tottenham Court Road. Open weekdays 5:30 PM–11 PM, Sat. 6 PM–11 PM.*

> Bartenders don't get tipped in pubs. If you want to show appreciation for exceptional service, buy the bartender a drink; after placing your order, add "and one for yourself."

Filthy McNasty's. Don't think Filthy's is another Irish theme bar. It preceded the flood of fake bars and has a genuine arty/bohemian/heavy-drinking feel. Big plates of country-style food cost between £4 and £7, and two evenings a week there's the Vox 'n' Roll nights with spoken word interspersed with musical interludes. They also manage to cram some indie and Irish bands into the smoky back room on weekends. Cover charges are very rare. *68 Amwell St., EC1, tel. 020/7837–6067. Tube: Angel. Open weekdays and Sat. 11 AM–11 PM, Sun noon–10:30 PM.*

The Market Bar. Weird, drippy candles and heavy velvet curtains give this very crowded Notting Hill locale an almost clubby feel. A mix of urban trendies, rastas, trustafarians, and punks haunt the bar, which has a selection of cocktails in addition to your basic beer. *240A Portobello Rd., at Lancaster Rd., W11, tel. 020/7229–6472. Tube: Ladbroke Grove. Open Mon.–Thurs. 11–11, Fri.–Sat. 11 AM–midnight, Sun. noon–10:30.*

Point 101. This new, snazzy club-bar near Soho plays loud funk, soul, and jazz mixes to a clubby, well-dressed crowd. Given its huge full-length windows close to the busy Oxford Street and Tottenham Court Road intersection, it's an equally good day hangout as you can watch the world go by over a plate or two of designer nibbles. *101 New Oxford St., WC1, tel. 020/7379–3112. Tube: Tottenham Court Road. Open Mon.–Thurs. 11 AM–1 PM, Fri. and Sat. 11 AM–2 AM, Sun. 2 PM–11:30 PM.*

WKD. Camden's trendiest club-bar, WKD has a wide range of clientele and music. Truly brave souls may want to try "Cool Runnin's" (£4), a vicious, opaque mix of rum, blue curaçao, and fruit juices—tasty, but deadly! During happy hour (weekdays 4–8) jugs of cocktails are £7.50; beers, £1.50. After 9, there's live music and a £3–£7 cover; check *Time Out* for live music listings. *18 Kentish Town Rd., NW1, tel. 020/7267–1869. Tube: Camden Town. Open Mon.–Tues. noon–2 AM, Wed.–Fri. noon–2.30 AM, Sat. noon–3 AM, Sun. noon–1 AM.*

GAY AND LESBIAN PUBS

London has a great gay scene, but pubs are a bit hard to find, especially if you're looking for something that caters exclusively to lesbians. A wander around London's **Gay Village** in Soho (the area around Old Compton Street) will lead you to any number of gay-owned or gay-friendly nightspots, where you'll also find many free magazines covering details of pubs and clubs. *Time Out* also lists some pubs in its "Gay" section.

Candy Bar. Spread over three swish Soho floors, this is the country's first every-night-of-the-week lesbian club-bar. Super-friendly, men are welcome as long as they come as "guests" of women friends. *4*

Carlisle St., W1, tel. 020/7494–4041. Tube: Tottenham Court Road. Open Mon.–Thurs. 5 PM–midnight, Fri. 5 PM–2 AM, Sat. noon–2 AM, Sun. 5 PM–11 PM.

Freedom. During the day the predominantly gay Freedom is a relaxed designer café with a huge choice of cutesy sandwiches and flavored coffees. In the evenings the music gets pumped up and it's a popular hangout for both gay men and women with club nights downstairs (usually with a small cover charge around £3). *60–66 Wardour st., off Oxford st., W1, tel. 020/7734–0071. Tube: Oxford Circus or Tottenham Court Road. Open Mon.–Sat. 11 AM–3 AM, Sun. noon–midnight.*

King William IV. One of the oldest gay pubs in Britain, the popular, noisy King William is patronized by a mixed group—all ages, both sexes. You can drink in the leafy courtyard out back or squeeze into the upstairs lounge. *77 Hampstead High St., NW3, tel. 020/7435–5747. Tube: Hampstead.*

The Yard. Thanks to its courtyard at the end of a short alley, this gorgeous, almost idyllic mixed gay bar and restaurant seems miles from the noise of Soho. There are all the fancy import beers and alcoholic sodas that you could care to try, and the food is also excellent. A club sandwich is deliciously overstuffed, and keep an eye out for the daily two-course special that includes coffee. *57 Rupert St., off Shaftesbury Ave., W1, tel. 020/7437–2652. Tube: Piccadilly Circus. Open Mon.–Sat. noon–11.*

CLUBBING

If you're a clubber, you'll be in seventh heaven in London. Every night of the week, scores of clubs spin contemporary dance music (jungle, drum & bass, *every* variety of house and techno, old R&B hits, '70s funk and disco, and the occasional indie platter. One-nighters (nomadic "theme" nights that take place at particular clubs on the same night every week, or move around from club to club) are very popular, but tend to confuse matters with erratic opening and closing times—always check the daily listings in *Time Out* for current info. Pete Tong, Danny Ramping, Paul Oakenfeld, Judge Jules, and Tall Paul are just some of the DJs to look out for. The dress code at most of London's clubs is casual; jeans are almost always okay, though some places will specify "no trainers" (athletic shoes). Throughout London, clubs typically open by 10 PM and close around 3 AM, though many are now open until 6 AM and some afterhours clubs *open* at 3 AM and run until sunrise. Midweek cover charges usually cost £5–£7—though you may get a break by arriving early—and can run up to £15 on weekends.

Bagley's Studio. Possibly the largest club in town, Bagley's is notable for getting in the big DJs for onenight blitzes. It doesn't come cheap though. *King's Cross Freight Depot, off York Way, N1, tel. 020/7278–2777. Tube: King's Cross. Walk north on York Way, turn left on Goods Way. Cover: £10–£15.*

Bar Rumba. A variety of wildly crowd-pleasing one-nighters take place at this underground hotspot every night of the week. Check out the well-established but still immensely popular and pioneering "Movement" (Thursday) for edge drum 'n' bass, "Bubblin Over" (Sunday) for R&B, "Space" (Wednesday) and the "Disco Spectrum" (Friday) for eclectic house. Saturdays are regularly packed to the rafters, so come early or prepare to queue. There's good hip-hop on Monday and a lively salsa night on Tuesday. Despite the joint's name, the club's drinks are well beyond standard bar prices. *36 Shaftesbury Ave., W1, tel. 020/7287–2715. Tube: Piccadilly Circus. Cover: £3–£10.*

Camden Palace. A wide mix of nights draws large crowds of dancers throughout the week. Tuesday's "Feet First" features a fun mix of indie, guitar, and rock music, along with a live band that might just be the next big thing. The lively "Peach," featuring garage and house music, rears its oh-so-pretty head on Friday until 6 AM. Look for flyers near the Camden Town tube station for discounted admission. *1A Camden High St., NW1, tel. 020/7387–0428. Tube: Camden Town. Walk south on Camden High St. Cover: £5–£12. Wheelchair access.*

The Complex. Owned by the Mean Fiddler organization, this big post-industrial club gets in all the top names from Detroit, Chicago, and every other music hotspot that you would expect with such connections. The big night is "Camouflage" (Saturday) with techno, hard-driven house, and eclectic sounds spread over the three floors. *1–5 Parkfield St., N1, tel. 020/7428–1986 or 020/7428–9797. Tube: Angel. Cross street to Liverpool Rd. then take sharp right on Parkfield St. Cover: £10–£15.*

The Cross. Inside a set of converted railway arches that also offer a patio space, the Cross draws an upfor-it crowd for mad house and garage. Beautiful people reign, so dress *way* up or stay home. *Goods Way Depot, off York Way, N1, tel. 020/7837–0828. Tube: Kings Cross. Walk north on York Way, turn left on Goods Way. Cover: £5–£15.*

Dog Star. Basically the first of London's club-bars to make it big, the Dog is a large, restyled pub, but all week it's packed with dancers who appreciate the very eclectic DJ samplings. The weekends are so popular it commands a £5 cover and sizable lines outside, though Sunday has an odd, cheesy disco feel to it. It costs no extra to get to the more exclusive rooms upstairs but you'll have to get an invite flyer or look like you belong. Drink prices are good compared to the West End. *389 Coldharbour La., SW9, tel. 020/7733–7515. Tube: Brixton. Turn left out of station and left onto Coldharbour La. Cover: free–£5.*

The End. The Shamen's Mr. C set up The End to be a club for clubbers run by clubbers. And he's done a pretty good job—air-conditioning means you won't sweat to death without really trying. Mr. C takes over the decks himself a couple of nights a week along with big-name U.S. techno DJs and the best homegrown drum 'n' bass names. Wednesday is a good night to sample this stylish club; there are often promotions by the best underground breakbeat labels and admission is as low as £3. The first Friday of each month is the Skint records night where Fatboy Slim has played on several occasions. *16A West Central St., WC1, tel. 020/7419–9199. Tube: Tottenham Court Road. Walk west on New Oxford St., turn right on West Central St. Cover: £3–£15.*

The Fridge. Brixton's major dance venue is like a three-ring circus, often with multimedia displays, live performances, and go-go dancers. Friday nights see monthly clubs such as "Escape To Samsara" plying psychedelic trance and hippie visuals to a Day-Glo-painted crowd. Saturday is much more of a gay male night but is still fairly mixed. The adjacent Fridge Bar usually charges no cover and the small downstairs room gets overly sweaty at weekends for some top rootsy DJs. *Town Hall Parade, Brixton Hill, SW2, tel. 020/7326–5100. Tube: Brixton. Walk south on Brixton Rd. Cover: £7–£15.*

Heaven. This massive club turns into London's largest lesbian and gay party spot several nights a week. The partied-up "Fruit Machine" (Thursday) night has been going for over six years, while the big blast of "Heaven" (Saturday) brings in a throbbing gay crowd. Monday night's "Popcorn" session brings a nice relaxed start to the week. Heaven's maze of rooms is great for getting lost. *Under The Arches, Villiers St., WC2, tel. 020/7930–2020. Tube: Charing Cross or Embankment. From Charing Cross, walk NW on the Strand, turn left on Villiers St. From Embankment, walk NW on Villiers St. Cover: £3–£12.*

Smithfields. Now incorporating the Jazz Bistro venue, this dark warren presents cutting edge underground sounds to rival anywhere else in the city. Friday sees big one-off events while the wide-ranging but up-to-the-second "Happiness Stan's" (Saturday) mixes soul, psychedelia, and jazz. There's no dress code (imposed either by management or style fascists) but remember it gets real sweaty. *334–338 Farringdon St., EC1, tel. 020/7236–8112. Tube: Farringdon. Cover: £5–£8.*

Subterrania. Dance all night long at this small but outrageous and funkily decorated club, which showcases live rap, hip-hop, funk, and R&B acts during the week. On Friday, "Rotation" whoops up a party atmosphere for funky hip-hop grooves, and "SoulSonic" on Saturday explores every corner of the house. Both nights get big-name DJs and the balcony makes a great chill zone. Wednesday brings a reggae vibe to the joint. *12 Acklam Rd., W10, tel. 020/8960–4590. Tube: Ladbroke Grove. Walk north on Ladbroke Grove, turn right on Cambridge Gardens, right on Acklam Rd. Cover: £8–£10.*

Turnmills. Though the legendary "Heavenly Jukebox" night has now shut down, Turnmills still thrills with all sorts of one-nighters, including Saturday's "Headstart" with big-name guest DJs and a diverse policy that takes in breakbeat, hip-hop and ambient. It's followed by the hugely popular gay rave "Trade" from 4 AM until 1 PM. Friday's long-running "The Gallery" plays a tough brand of house to a smartly dressed crowd. *63B Clerkenwell Rd., EC1, tel. 020/7250–3409. Tube: Farringdon. Walk north on Farringdon Rd., turn right on Clerkenwell Rd. Cover: £6–£10.*

Velvet Room. This intimate venue with velvet couches and bubble pillars regularly goes through changes, but it's the current home of the ever-popular funky techno "Ultimate BASE" night (Thursday). Also good are "Swerve", serving up massive breakbeats on Wednesday, and the pumping house of "Whoop It Up" on Friday. *143 Charing Cross Rd., WC2, tel. 020/7439–4655. Tube: Tottenham Court Road. Cover: £4–£10.*

LIVE MUSIC

On any given night, London hosts a stupefying number of shows, but nothing comes cheap: Covers and tickets cost anywhere from £3 to £20, with most falling in the £5–£8 range. On the upside, you generally get what you pay for: London's jazz clubs are first-rate, as are its rock and indie venues. There's also a flourishing international music scene, with Caribbean, African, and Latin bands playing to enthusiastic crowds. Britpop still has a presence, but a new, more innovative breed of crossover dance music bands (i.e., Chemical Brothers, Asian Dub Foundation, A3) are the highlight of many of the small venues these days.

Acts like the Rolling Stones and U2 are usually booked at **Wembley Stadium** or the **Wembley Arena** (Empire Way, Wembley, tel. 020/8900–1234), both an easy walk from the Wembley Park tube station. Some of pop music's royalty also grace the stage of the **Royal Albert Hall** (*see* Classical Music, Opera, and Dance, *below*). Smaller (and often free) gigs are also held at colleges around town, at pubs, and at local record stores like HMV and Virgin Megastore; check bulletin boards or *Time Out* for the latest.

MAJOR VENUES

The Astoria/LA2. All sorts of good bands play at this 2,000-capacity venue—lots of rock, some indie, a splash of reggae and crossover dance acts. Come early and snag a seat in the upstairs bar; it overlooks the stage. Under the same roof is its half-size sibling LA2 (London Astoria 2). It also hosts bands and one-night clubs, so make sure you're in the proper queue. Arrive on time as the bands are made to stick firmly to schedule so that the venue can turn over to club nights. *157 Charing Cross Rd., WC2, tel. 020/ 7434–0403. Tube: Tottenham Court Road.*

Brixton Academy. This Brixton institution is one of the bigger venues for hip indie and established acts. Despite a capacity of 4,000 people, the Academy's atmosphere seems more clublike than crowded, with interesting decor, plenty of bars, and upstairs seating. *211 Stockwell Rd., SW9, tel. 020/7924– 9999. Tube: Brixton. Walk north on Brixton Rd., turn left on Stockwell Rd.*

Forum. This popular venue is similar though smaller than Brixton Academy, so everyone has a great view. In addition to top bands through the week, they host clubs on the weekend. "House of Fun" on Saturday sees new wave and club classics, plus circus acts and trendies galore. *9–17 Highgate Rd., NW5, tel. 020/7284–2200. Tube: Kentish Town. Walk north on Kentish Town Rd., veer left on Highgate Rd.*

Shepherds Bush Empire. This award-winning venue in a former BBC TV theater lines up an interesting roster of hot new bands and old favorites. The downstairs area has three bars to quench your thirst; don't sit on the upper two tiers if you have vertigo. *Shepherds Bush Green, W12, tel. 020/8740–7474. Tube: Shepherds Bush.*

ROCK

Barfly Club. Right here is the finest and most eclectic small club in the capital. The trouble is that sometimes the little square back room gets crammed with people eager to see the next flash-in-the-pantheon. There are three bands seven nights a week with events regularly sponsored by the *NME, Melody Maker,* and *Kerrang!* publications. *The Falcon pub, 234 Royal College St., NW1, tel. 020/7482–4884. Tube: Camden Town. Cover: £4–£5.*

Borderline. When record companies want to try out new bands, they send 'em to this subterranean, Tex-Mex-themed Soho establishment. Who knows, maybe you'll see the next big thing—or, better yet, *the* big thing playing under an assumed name. After the bands, there are indie and alternative-rock club nights with a small cover of £3–£5. *Orange Yard, off Manette St., W1, tel. 020/7734–2095. Tube: Tottenham Court Road. Walk south on Charing Cross Rd., turn right on Manette St. Cover: £5–£10.*

Dingwalls. After spending several years as an exclusively comedy venue, Dingwalls is now back to what it was meant to do—hosting a variety of established and breaking rock acts several nights a week. It's in the cutesy Camden Lock warehouses. *Middle Yard, Camden Lock, off Camden High St., NW1, tel. 020/ 7267–1577. Tube: Camden Town. Cover: £6–£12.*

Garage. Clear views of the stage and a killer sound system make this a good place to see live rock and indie acts. It has earned a reputation for presenting the U.K. debuts of soon-to-be-mega U.S. bands. The appropriately named Upstairs at the Garage shares the building and telephone but hosts different acts—mostly lo-fi, acoustic, and spoken word—for a separate cover every night. Both places get pretty busy no matter what's offered. Be sure to join the correct line. *20–22 Highbury Corner, N5, tel. 020/ 7607–1818. Tube: Highbury & Islington. Cover: £4–£9.*

Mean Fiddler. The original piece of the ever-growing Mean Fiddler empire, this Irish-flavored club features a diverse mix of roots, rock, reggae, heroes of days gone by, and a few big surprises. The adjacent Acoustic Room hosts—you guessed it—acoustic acts. This homestead is in an out-of-reach part of the city, and a long walk from the station. *22–28A High St. Harlesden, NW10, tel. 020/8961–5490. Tube/Rail: Willesden Junction. Turn right out of station, then right onto Tubbs Rd. and left onto High St. Harlesden. The venue is on the left. Cover: £3–£12.*

Water Rats. The small stage in the cozy old back room hosts gigs most nights of the week. The usual fare is the tipped new bands (plus generally unknown support acts) mentioned in *Melody Maker* and *NME*. The music tends to be a little more rootsy and less in yer face than in the small Camden venues. *328 Gray's Inn Rd., WC1, tel. 020/7837–7269. Tube: King's Cross. Walk NE on Euston Rd., turn right on Gray's Inn Rd. Cover: £5–£6.*

R&B, FUNK, AND WORLDBEAT

Africa Centre. Visiting musicians from Africa and the Caribbean often play here. On other nights, DJs mix it up for a fairly diverse group of dancers. *38 King St., WC2, tel. 020/7836–1973. Tube: Covent Garden. Turn right on James St., right on King St. Cover: £5–£9.*

Ain't Nothing But Blues Bar. The name says it all. Come in and chill out to the nightly live blues in a crowded atmosphere. Most nights there's no cover. *20 Kingly St., W1, tel. 020/7287–0514. Tube: Oxford Circus. Walk south on Regent St., turn left on Great Marlborough St., right on Kingly St. Cover: free–£8.*

Station Tavern. This West London pub is known for excellent blues bands and mellow followers that pack the place every night of the week. And you can't beat the price—it's free. *41 Bramley Rd., W10, tel. 020/7727–4053. Tube: Latimer Road. No cover.*

12 Bar Club. A smattering of rock, a sprinkle of folk, and a heavy dollop of blues are served up at this tiny venue. Pity there aren't really 12 bars here; the queue for drinks can be long. *Denmark Pl., Denmark St., WC2, tel. 020/7916–6989. Tube: Tottenham Court Road. Walk south on Tottenham Court Rd., turn left on Denmark Pl. Cover: £4–£8.*

JAZZ

Bull's Head Barnes. One of the best jazz pubs in town, even if it is far away in Hammersmith. The pleasant scene—right on the Thames—and big names who jam here regularly make it well worth the trip. Shows start nightly at 8:30. *Barnes Bridge, SW13, tel. 020/8876–5241. Tube: Hammersmith. From station, take Bus 9 to Barnes Bridge. Cover: £3–£10.*

Jazz Café. Lines can be long, and empty seats few and far between, but the JC is a great relaxed place to see big-name talents (e.g., Gil Scott-Heron, Abdullah Ibrahim) as well as some of the best new sounds from the club world. Admission and drink prices do lean toward the high end. *5 Parkway, NW1, tel. 020/7916–6060. Tube: Camden Town. Cover: £6–£20.*

Ronnie Scott's. This legendary Soho club, opened in the early '60s, is the leading venue for jazz in London—if they're the best, they'll play here. Its status is, unfortunately, reflected in the prices. Book in advance or get in line early. *47 Frith St., W1, tel. 020/7439–0747. Tube: Tottenham Court Road. Walk west on Oxford St., turn left on Soho St., cross Soho Sq. to Frith St. Cover: £12–£29. Closed Sun.*

CLASSICAL MUSIC, OPERA, AND DANCE

The arts scene in London is rich and varied. A bounty of internationally respected orchestras, opera companies, and ballet troupes make their homes here, including the **London Symphony Orchestra,** the **London Philharmonic Orchestra,** and the world-famous **Royal Ballet.** Tickets for classical concerts, ballet, and opera range anywhere from £2.50 to over £100 for special performances. Many churches offer free (or low-cost) **lunchtime concerts** throughout the year.

In summer your arts options expand exponentially, as gala festivals fill theaters, concert halls, and even the air, in parks and squares. Probably the biggest—and most affordable—spectacle for lovers of classical music are the **Proms,** more formally known as the BBC Henry Wood Promenade Concerts, held at the gorgeous Royal Albert Hall (*see below*). The series runs for eight weeks from mid-July to mid-September and features a smorgasbord of well-known pieces, as well as a smattering of new works. Tickets are £5–£30; call 020/7589–8212 for more info. The **City of London Festival,** held the first three weeks in July, features classical performances in venues and squares throughout the city; many are free. The **South Bank Centre** (*see below*) hosts the summertime dance festival **Ballroom Blitz,** and **Meltdown,** a showcase for contemporary music. During summer you can also enjoy al fresco opera and ballet performances at **Holland Park Theatre** (Kensington High St., W8, tel. 020/7602–7856) and classical concerts at **Kenwood House** (Hampstead La., NW3, tel. 020/7973–3427).

Barbican Centre. The music hall at this giant arts center is home to the famous **London Symphony Orchestra** and the **English Chamber Orchestra.** Frequent guests include the Royal Philharmonic, City of London Symphonia, and the Philharmonia Orchestra. And if that's not music to your ears, perhaps its eclectic menu of everything from brass bands to smoky jazz acts will have something for you. *Silk St., EC2, tel. 020/7638–8891. Tube: Barbican or Moorgate. Signposted from the tube stations. Admission £5–£45.*

London Coliseum. For opera and ballet, the Coliseum is a good bet. In 1997 it became the permanent home of the **English National Ballet** troupe, formerly in residence at the South Bank Centre. It also attracts talented dance companies from around the world. Sharing the stage, so to speak, is the **English National Opera (ENO) Company.** It's well known for English-language operas and offers lower prices (and less stodgy renditions) than the Royal Opera Company. One drawback: The Coliseum is *huge.* The cheapest upper balcony seats are known jokingly as "the gods"—consider renting a pair of opera glasses (20p) unless you like your art served up with severe eyestrain. One hundred balcony seats go on sale the day of the performance at 10 AM for £5. *St. Martin's La., WC2, tel. 020/7632–8300. Tube: Leicester Square. Walk NE on Long Acre, quick right on St. Martin's La. Admission £5–£50.*

Royal Albert Hall. This beautiful major-league concert venue really comes into its own during the summer when it hosts the **Proms** (*see above*). Otherwise, it's home to the acclaimed **Royal Philharmonic Orchestra.** Looming in the near future for Royal Albert Hall is a £40-million-plus refurbishment. *Kensington Gore, SW7, tel. 020/7589–8212 or 020/7589–3203. Tube: Knightsbridge. Walk west on Kensington Rd. Admission £5–£40.*

Royal Opera House. This fabled theater—the classiest and most expensive in Britain, home to both the world-renowned Royal Ballet and the Royal Opera—closed its doors between summer 1997 and November 1999 for a grand-scale renovation. During this time, they also rethought their admission and pricing policies in the face of rabid accusations of elitism from the media and the public. In the past most shows sold out because corporate bodies gulped up all the hideously high-priced tickets. Now, as well as most seat prices being reduced, the ROH promises that around twenty percent of all tickets will be sold to the public. In general the ROH will be much more accessible. It's now open for milling around in during the day and the new Studio Theatre and the Studio Upstairs will offer recitals, workshops, and small-scale performances.

Anticipated **Royal Opera** productions planned for early in 2000 include Otello and Romeo and Juliet, while the **Royal Ballet** also has star-studded presentations of new works by Matthew Bourne and Siobhan Davies. *Bow St., Covent Garden, WC2, tel. 020/7304–4000. Tube: Covent Garden. Turn right onto Long Acre and right onto Bow St. Admission £6–£150.*

Sadler's Wells. The city's primary venue for dance was almost completely rebuilt over two years and is now a state-of-the-art space for productions of both traditional and innovative dance from around the world. *Rosebery Ave., EC1, tel. 020/7713–6060. Tube: Angel. Walk south down St. John St. and right onto Rosebery Ave. Admission £5–£35.*

St. John's Smith Square. This beautiful Baroque church, blessed with excellent acoustics, has rapidly become one of London's leading venues for classical music. Programs vary widely but renowned chamber orchestras and soloists are frequently featured. The BBC hosts lunchtime concerts (£6) Monday at 1 PM. *Smith Sq., SW1, tel. 020/7222–1061. Tube: Westminster. Walk south on St. Margaret St. (which becomes Old Palace Yard, Abingdon St., and Millbank), turn right on Dean Stanley St. Admission £5–£20.*

South Bank Centre. This mammoth arts complex is a haven for fans of music, opera, and dance, with three venues to choose from: The largest is the **Royal Festival Hall,** which reigns as one of the finest concert halls in Europe. It's home to the **London Philharmonic Orchestra** and the **Philharmonia Orchestra.** A bit smaller in size is **Queen Elizabeth Hall,** which features visiting dance companies, chamber orchestras, and performances of lesser-known symphonies by the Philharmonic. The tiny **Purcell Room** hosts performances by up-and-coming chamber groups and soloists, plus the occasional visiting tap-dancing troupe. The South Bank Centre is also home to two major annual festivals: **Ballroom Blitz,** with free performances and classes in everything from belly dancing to the waltz, and **Meltdown,** featuring contemporary music. *South Bank, Belvedere Rd., SE1, tel. 020/7960–4242. Tube: Waterloo. Admission £5–£30.*

Wigmore Hall. The Wigmore's Sunday "Coffee Concerts" (11:30 AM), held year-round, are enormously popular with musically inclined Londoners; tickets are £8, including program and a coffee, sherry, or juice, while breakfast is available from the Wigmore Hall café. Otherwise, chamber music, period music, and all sorts of other soothing melodies fill the air of this pleasant, acoustically stellar forum most evenings. *36 Wigmore St., W1, tel. 020/7935–2141. Tube: Bond Street. Walk north on James St., turn right on Wigmore St. Admission £4–£35.*

THEATER

London is the theater capital of a country that truly loves the stuff, training would-be actors as if they were actual professionals, to be taken as seriously as bankers and academics. The theater sections in *Time Out* and *What's On* run for pages and pages, with everything from Shakespeare to Mike Leigh to Brecht. Theater in London falls into two basic categories: West End and Fringe. The **West End** is London's equivalent of Broadway, featuring big-budget productions and musicals like *Cats, Les Misérables,* and *Sunset Boulevard*. It's a dubious distinction, but London has even overtaken New York as the launching ground for new Andrew Lloyd Webber-ish "vehicles." **Fringe** theaters present everything from small productions by prominent playwrights—folks like Samuel Beckett, Harold Pinter, Caryl Churchill, David Mamet, and Tom Stoppard—to experimental offerings by young local talent. Fringe performances are sometimes pretentious or obscure, but rarely boring. These days, top billing in the everything-old-is-new-again department is the spectacular reconstruction of **Shakespeare's Globe** (*see* The South Bank, *above*).

MAJOR VENUES

The Barbican and the National Theatre are major-league houses, but the productions they stage are often "fringe" in style—partly because they're state subsidized and housed within larger arts centers.

Barbican Centre. This giant arts complex has two venues for drama: Its **Barbican Theatre** is home to the Royal Shakespeare Company, which stages productions of the Bard's great works on a regular basis, while its smaller, more intimate theater, **The Pit,** is the place for avant-garde and whimsical stuff. *Silk St., EC2, tel. 020/7638–8891. Tube: Barbican. Barbican Theatre tickets: £7–£25; The Pit tickets: £6–£17.*

National Theatre. The National Theatre (home of the Royal National Theatre Company) offers three performance venues: the **Olivier Theatre,** the **Lyttleton Theatre,** and the **Cottesloe Theatre.** The Cottesloe is the smallest and usually puts on new works by up-and-coming playwrights. The range at the other two spans everything from cutting-edge stuff to imaginative interpretations of old standbys. *South Bank, Belvedere Rd., SE1, tel. 020/7928–2252 box office; 020/7633–0880 for recorded info. Tube: Waterloo. Tickets: £10–£24.*

WEST END THEATERS

The principal West End theaters are centered around Shaftesbury Avenue in Soho, the Haymarket in St. James's, and around Covent Garden. Half-price, same-day tickets are available from the **Society of West End Theatres** kiosk on Leicester Square. It sells these tickets (which are usually the top-priced seats) for a £2 service charge Monday–Saturday noon–30 minutes before curtain for matinees, and 2:30–6:30 for evening shows. You'll have to turn up and get in line because the kiosk has no phone.

Some prominent West End theaters include: **Her Majesty's Theatre** (Haymarket, SW1, tel. 020/7494–5400), home indefinitely to *The Phantom of the Opera*; **Dominion Theatre** (Tottenham Court Rd. at New Oxford St., W1, tel. 020/7656–1857), hosting Disney's *Beauty and the Beast* until at least mid-2000; **New London Theatre** (Drury La., WC2, tel. 020/7405–0072), now and apparently forever, London's keeper of *Cats*; **Old Vic** (Waterloo Rd., SE1, tel. 020/7928–7616), with its old standards and new works; **St Martin's Theatre** (West St., W2, tel. 020/7836–1443), holding Agatha Christie's *The Mousetrap* for five decades and counting; and **Theatre Royal, Drury Lane** (Catherine St., WC2, tel. 020/7494–5062), host indefinitely to *Miss Saigon*.

FRINGE THEATERS

For the price of one West End splurge you can afford to see three fringe plays—shoestring affairs staged in basements, pubs, or anywhere else they can squeeze in a small stage and an audience. Tickets are usually in the £4–£10 range. Fringe theaters generally sell standing-room tickets just before show time.

The Almeida. This old, successful theater maintains high standards for its contemporary and classical offerings. *Almeida St., N1, tel. 020/7359–4404. Tube: Highbury & Islington.*

Donmar Warehouse. Boasting a cutting-edge program and circular stage, the Donmar—which recently made an international name for itself by getting Nicole Kidman to play here before Broadway—is a bit more pricey than other small theaters. *Thomas Neal's Yard, Earlham St., WC2, tel. 020/7369–1732. Tube: Covent Garden.*

Drill Hall Arts Centre. All sorts of cool plays are here for the watching; its forte is excellent gay and lesbian productions. *16 Chenies St., WC1, tel. 020/7637–8270. Tube: Goodge Street.*

Hampstead Theatre. A discerning clientele attend this prestigious local theater—and its good bar. It's often used as a sounding board to see if plays will make it in the West End. They lured Ewan McGregor here for just £250 a week for *Little Malcolm and His Struggle Against the Eunuchs. Swiss Cottage Centre, Avenue Rd., NW3, tel. 020/7722–9301. Tube: Swiss Cottage.*

Lyric Studio. Mainly contemporary works, with plenty of literary adaptations that will appeal to bookworms, get put on here. *Lyric Theatre, Kings St., W6, tel. 020/8741–2311. Tube: Hammersmith.*

New End Theatre. This intimate theater in Hampstead is known for presenting flavorsome period works rarely staged in London's bigger venues. The New End also tackles modern politics, both left- and right-wing. *27 New End, NW3, tel. 020/7794–0022. Tube: Hampstead.*

The Young Vic. The nominal offspring of the nearby Old Vic (that still puts on the best quality programs of the major theaters), this venue showcases cutting-edge productions and actors. *66 The Cut, SE1, tel. 020/7928–6363. Tube: Waterloo.*

FILM

London is home to many small repertory cinemas that specialize in seminal, epochal, and downright funky flicks. These repertories are much more interesting than the multiscreen complexes around Leicester Square—which screen big-budget-small-plot Hollywood flicks—and they're cheaper to boot. Most every London newspaper lists movie schedules in the entertainment section, though the detailed reviews in *Time Out* are most useful.

Everyman Cinema. Billing itself as "London's oldest repertory," this cozy venue shows an excellent selection of classic, foreign, avant-garde, and almost-new Hollywood titles. Many shows are double (even triple) features at no extra cost: Tickets are £4.50–£5, and membership costs 60p a year. *Hollybush Vale, NW3, tel. 020/7435–1525. Tube: Hampstead. Walk south on Heath St., turn right on Hollybush Vale.*

ICA Cinema. Housed within the Institute of Contemporary Arts, this cinema shows practically anything arty and/or esoteric. Tickets for the main screen cost £6.50, but £5 on Monday. A £1.50 day membership includes admission to exhibits. The frequently changing films at the small **ICA Cinematheque** make the selection on the big screen look downright mainstream. Tickets cost £5, including day membership. *Nash House, The Mall, SW1, tel. 020/7930–3647. Tube: Charing Cross Road or Piccadilly Circus. From Charing Cross, walk SW on The Mall. From Piccadilly Circus station, walk south on Regent St., turn right on The Mall.*

Minema. This small venue is a film freak's dream. It seats 68 lucky people in broad, comfy chairs with plenty of legroom, and prides itself on showing "only the best" international cinema. There's even a chic little café attached. Tickets are £7.50, £5.50 for students. *45 Knightsbridge, SW1, tel. 020/7369–1723. Tube: Hyde Park Corner.*

National Film Theatre. The NFT is one of London's best repertory cinemas. Its three cinemas screen more than 2,000 titles each year, including foreign films, documentaries, Hollywood features, and animation. Tickets are £6 or £4.50 for students. *South Bank Centre, SE1, tel. 020/7928–3232. Tube: Waterloo.*

Prince Charles. Come for reasonably recent flicks, as well as artier and cult ones, at rock-bottom prices. Tickets are a real bargain for the West End: £2.50, £2 for weekday matinees. *7 Leicester Pl., WC2, tel. 020/7437–8181. Tube: Leicester Square. Walk west on Cranbourn St., turn right on Leicester Pl.*

THE SOUTH 3

UPDATED BY ROBERT ANDREWS

T he South of England is like London's plump, rich, self-satisfied old mother-in-law. It is the wealthiest, most resented region in all of England, as well as the most conservative. Of course, even here, change is in the wind: The Tories lost a significant number of seats in the last general election—and most inhabitants of the area aren't dismissing this liberal shift as just a phase. For the most part the area's stuffiness as a traveler, apart from the occasional snobbish attitudes of bed-and-breakfast proprietors who discourage backpackers from staying in their homes. Moreover, the general wealth of the region—coupled with its proximity to London—does ensure that any changes in the air will soon make their way down to the (sometimes) sunny South.

The proximity of the South to the Continent has generally defined the region's history, from the earliest Roman settlements to the modern engineering marvel known as the Eurotunnel. The coastline still bears witness to past invasions: More than any other region in England, the South features castles, defensive battlements, and various other Roman and Norman ruins, not to mention pillboxes and gun pivots left over from World War II. During Britain's seafaring heyday, the region was essential to both commercial and military/imperial concerns, with Portsmouth (which was later the launching point for the Allied invasion of Normandy) leading the way. In fact, you'll find it difficult to tour the South coast without happening upon some monument of Britain's former seafaring glory.

The biggest mistake you could make would be to visit only the towns featured below and nowhere else. Yes, **Canterbury, Brighton,** and **Winchester** all have fascinating sights. But sometimes you may just wish to use these cities as bases from which to explore the surrounding stately houses—including such jewels as **Hever Castle, Chartwell, Ightham Mote, Knole, Leeds Castle, Penhurst Place,** and **Sissinghurst Castle**—and those lovely backwater villages, often tiny affairs with a pub, a butcher, and a few stoic homes. What's really special about these small villages is their peaceful rural atmosphere, and in this sense many are remarkably similar. Most have little to offer in the way of tourist attractions; if anything, their appeal lies in their *lack* of such things, and in finding them for yourself rather than in a tourist-board brochure. On a warm summer day, rent a bike (preferably one of those black "bone-rattlers" that look so at home in English towns) and just follow any narrow country lane between the hedgerows. Sooner or later, you'll stumble upon a village, doubtless with its own pub and, perhaps, a cricket game on the village green. This, if anything, will let you experience what summer in southern England is meant to be.

English Channel

TO
DIEPPE

SURREY

WEST SUSSEX

EAST SUSSEX

SOUTH DOWNS

NORTH DOWNS

THE WEALD

KENT

LONDON

Windsor
TO OXFORD
Richmond
Staines
Merton
Bromley
Beckenham
Chichester
Midhurst
Bignor Roman Villa
Petworth House
Farnham
Hog's Back
Goddalming
Guildford
Dorking
Crawley
Horsham
Arundel
Amberley
Littlehampton
Storrington
Burgess Hill
Haywards Heath
East Grinstead
Westerham
Kemsing
Sevenoaks
Penshurst Place
Chartwell
Knole
Ightham Mote
Hever Castle
Medway
Royal Tunbridge Wells
Sissinghurst Castle
Kits Coty
Rochester
Chatham
Herne Bay
Whitstable
The Swale
Margate
Broadstairs
Brighton
Telscombe
Newhaven
TO LE HAVRE
Lewes
Alfriston
Jevington
Pevensey
Pevensey Bay
Eastbourne Bay
Battle
Bodiam Castle
Leeds Castle
Hastings
Rye
Winchelsea
Rye Bay
Romney Marsh
New Romney
Lydd
Hythe
Folkestone
Dover
Deal
Sandwich
Ramsgate
St. Margaret's Bay
Capel-le-Ferne
Ashford
Great Stour
Wye
Chilham
Canterbury
Thames
Way
Rother
Medway
Ouse
Arun

Strait of Dover

TO CALAIS, BOULOGNE

EUROTUNNEL

Ferry Lines
Rail Lines

N

0
0
10 miles
15 km

A287 A31 A3 A286 A283 A285 A284 A272 A259 A24 A264 A22 A23 A27 A259 A26 A275 A265 A21 A229 A262 A268 A2100 A2069 A259 A258 A256 A257 A28 A251 A252 A290 A2 A299 A20 A259 A225 A21 A224 B2163 B2176 B2169 B2068 B2065 M3 M25 M23 M20 M26 M2

BASICS

VISITOR INFORMATION

The **South East England Tourist Board** is in Royal Tunbridge Wells, on the rail line between London and Hastings. It's out of the way, but you can write or call and ask them to send you pamphlets on the Home Counties (*see box*). They don't, however, book rooms. *The Old Brew House, 1 Warwick Park, Royal Tunbridge Wells, Kent TN2 5TU, tel. 01892/540766. Open Mon.–Thurs. 9–5:30, Fri. 9–5.*

The **Southern Tourist Board,** just north of Southampton, offers the same information as the South East board (*see above*), but also covers Hampshire, the Isle of Wight, Berkshire, Dorset, and Wiltshire. *40 Chamberlayne Rd., Eastleigh, Hampshire SO50 5JH, tel. 02380/620006. Open Mon.–Thurs. 8:30–5, Fri. 8:30–4:30.*

COMING AND GOING

Travelers in southern England will generally find it very easy to move around. **National Express** (tel. 0990/808080), England's largest long-distance bus company, serves just about every town in the region from London's Victoria Coach Station. A number of passes and discount cards are available (*see* Bus Travel *in* Chapter 1). The Southeast also has the most extensive rail network in the entire country. Despite the recent breakup of British Rail's **Network Southeast,** the grid of interconnected rail lines that converge on London remains intact since a number of smaller operators took over the old lines. If you plan on taking the train around the Southeast, pick up the free "Rail Services Around London and the South East" map in a train station, which lists all stations, phone numbers, and London connections; or call 0345/484950 for 24-hour travel information.

> *Though the South controls as much as 65% of the nation's private businesses, it has actually suffered, proportionally, the worst from the recession. Just note the numerous FOR SALE signs in windows of homes and shops.*

Connex South Eastern trains run east from Victoria, Waterloo, and Charing Cross stations in London toward Canterbury, Dover, and Hastings. **Connex South Central** lines run south from Victoria and then follow the coastline from Hastings all the way to Bournemouth. The **ThamesLink** runs from Brighton through Gatwick Airport and London to the King's Cross ThamesLink station, and then north to Luton Airport and Bedford. South West Trains run from Waterloo to Weymouth, Bournemouth, Southampton, Exeter, Salisbury, Portsmouth, and Guildford. The Isle of Wight has the **Island Line,** serviced by refurbished London Underground cars, though it doesn't cover much ground. The rail companies offer a number of rail passes (*see* Train Travel *in* Chapter 1), which is the only bargain you'll get because the Southeast is unfortunately not covered by its own Rail Rover Pass, though, the Network Railcard, at a cost of £20, entitles you to savings of one-third on most rail fares and is valid for one year. The only "deals" are the Network Away Break (five-day return) and Stay Away (one-month return) tickets, which usually cost just a few pounds more than a standard day return. Even these, however, are not offered on all routes.

GETTING AROUND

In the wake of the deregulation of bus services, travel by bus has undergone considerable upheaval in recent times, with a proliferation of small local companies. Apart from **National Express,** which runs services from London to larger towns in the region, **Stagecoach** has become the major provider of both long-distance and local services throughout Kent, East Sussex, and parts of West Sussex. You can contact the main bus operators directly on the following numbers: for Kent, **Stagecoach East Kent** (tel. 01227/472028) and **Arriva Kent** and **Sussex** (tel. 01634/281100); in East Sussex, **South Coast Buses** (tel. 01273/474747), and in West Sussex, **Coastline Buses** (tel. 01903/237661), both operated by Stagecoach; for the area between Bournemouth and Salisbury, **Wilts & Dorset** (tel. 01202/673555), and, around Salisbury and Winchester, **Solent Blue** (tel. 02380/226235). In addition, **Brighton and Hove** (tel. 01273/886200) run buses in and around the Brighton area. The **Explorer** ticket will get you one day of unlimited travel for £5, and a **Master Rider** will get you one week of unlimited travel for £18, both of which are accepted on all services. For information about travel by bus and train throughout the Southeast, your best bets are the following transport coordinators: **Kent Public Transport Helpline** (tel. 0345/696996); **East Sussex County Busline** (tel. 01273/474747 or 01797/223053); **West Sussex Traveline** (tel. 0345/959099), and **Surrey Travel Line** (tel. 01737/223000).

DOWN HOME IN ENGLAND'S DEEP SOUTH

Kent, Surrey, East and West Sussex, Hampshire, Berkshire, and Essex compose the so-called Home Counties, which act as a sort of commuter belt for London. If you take the train out to villages such as Virginia Water or Ascot, you'll see the England of retired brigadiers, civil servants, and upper-middle-class families who read the "Daily Telegraph" and quietly yearn for the old days of the Empire. Sir John Betjeman, Britain's late poet laureate, captured exactly the mood of the Home Counties in his poems, which are peopled with strapping gents and ladies who play a mean game of squash and then adjourn for a gin and tonic and the evening news.

At the same time, the Home Counties' wealth has its price—many small-town High Streets have sacrificed their character and charm to national chain stores, and towns such as Staines, Slough, and Reading have expanded willy-nilly, scarred by that hideous architectural disease that afflicted England from 1960 to 1980. It's tough to imagine what remedy Betjeman would have for these blighted towns today; as far back as World War II, he wrote a poem that started "Come, friendly bombs, and fall on Slough."

OUTDOOR ACTIVITIES

The famous North and South Downs are huge expanses of softly rolling hills, nibbled smooth by years of sheep and cattle grazing. Instead of gazing longingly at the Downs, tramp over them on either the **North** or **South Downs Way,** easily accessed from many places in the South. Each Way refers to a main path, but there are hundreds of little trails that branch off to all sorts of fields, woods, towns, and villages. The paths are well marked with the National Trail symbol (an acorn), but it's still essential to pick up a handy Ordnance Survey map of the portion(s) you'll be covering. The network of trails is suitable for everything from loop day hikes to weeklong rambles across the southern countryside. For those on longer treks, many farmhouses, B&Bs, and hostels are viable lodging options near the paths. Helpful maps and pamphlets detailing the routes are available from tourist offices in southern England, or contact the **Ramblers Association** (tel. 0171/5826878) for itineraries and advice.

NORTH DOWNS WAY • This 140-mi path runs across Surrey and Kent, from Dover in the east to Farnham in the west. The southern route runs along the coast between Dover and Folkestone before turning inland; a northern route, part of which is called the Pilgrim's Way, runs through Canterbury, then rejoins the other just west of Wye. **Kit's Coty,** 2 mi south of Rochester, is an impressive neolithic burial site, consisting of a massive capstone balanced on top of three upright stones. Nearby **Blue Bell Hill** is a good vista point. The entire Way would take two weeks to walk; the relevant Ordnance Survey maps are numbers 178, 179, 186, 187, 188, and 189. But if you want to limit your exploration to a specific part, pick up the handy "North Downs Way Practical Users' Guide" (£2.95), available at most area tourist offices or direct from Kent County Council. It details villages and lodging along the route, including the following YHA hostels: **Canterbury** (*see below*), **Dover** (*see* Charlton House, *below*), **Hindhead** (Devil's Punchbowl, Thursley, near Godalming, tel. 01428/604285), **Holmbury St. Mary** (Radnor La.,

Holmbury St. Mary, Dorking, tel. 01306/730777), **Kemsing** (Church La., Kemsing, tel. 01732/761341), and **Tanners Hatch** (Polesden Lacey, Dorking, tel. 01372/452528).

Cyclists are legally entitled to 76 mi of the route, by means of bridle paths along certain sections. Unfortunately, these do not follow any particular logic or order, and there is no specific map beyond the Ordnance Survey's detailing exactly where the bridle paths lie. The general consensus among serious cyclists is that if you exercise safe cycling, as well as consideration and deference toward walkers, you may in practice use the footpaths in the remaining sections without fear of prosecution. Contact the **Cyclist's Touring Club** (tel. 01483/417217) in the North Downs for information and advice. **Kent County Council Countryside Department** provides a wide range of guides for walkers and cyclists using the area; call 01622/696185 and ask for the North Downs Manager.

SOUTH DOWNS WAY • This 80-mi footpath leads all the way from Eastbourne (in the east) to Winchester (in the west), and is very popular due to its stupendous views of the sea and of the river valleys of Sussex and Hampshire, as well as for the walkable distances between towns and sleeping spots. The Way itself is thought to have been a major trade route back in the Bronze Age. Recently, a bridle path was added for horses, cyclists, and even wheelchairs. It normally takes about 10 days to walk the whole thing, but certain ambitious hikers have done it in three. One particularly picturesque portion starts right after Eastbourne and leads to **Beachy Head,** a magnificent high cliff (and notorious suicide spot). Another is the 5½-mi stretch between **Alfriston** and **Jevington,** where you'll pass a huge anthropomorphic figure—nicknamed the Long Man—carved into the chalk hills. For a full guide to the path, pick up a copy of *The South Downs Way* (£10.99) by park ranger Paul Millmore, one of a series of National Trail Guides published by Ordnance Survey (tel. 0345/330011) and available from most local bookshops and tourist offices. You can also write or call the **Sussex Downs Conservation Board** (Chanctonbury House, Churl St., Storrington, West Sussex RH20 4LT, tel. 01903/741234), or the **South Downs Way Officer,** based at the Queen Elizabeth Country Park, near Petersfield, Hants., (tel. 02392/595040). The Ordnance Survey maps numbered 185, 197, 198, and 199 cover the area. For information on an easy way to access the South Downs Way, *see* Brighton, Outdoor Activities, *below.*

Camping is an option worth considering; you can pick up a leaflet listing camping and caravan sites in Sussex and Surrey available through Tourist Offices, or contact the **Caravan Club** (tel. 01342/327490). Most hikers stay at one of the YHA hostels en route: in **Alfriston** (Frog Firle, tel. 01323/870423), **Arundel** (*see below*), **Brighton** (*see below*), **Eastbourne** (E. Dean Rd., tel. 01323/721081), **Telscombe** (Bank Cottages, tel. 01273/301357), **Truleigh Hill** (Tottington Barn, tel. 01903/813419), and **Winchester** (*see below*).

CANTERBURY

While Chaucer's *Canterbury Tales,* the ultimate chronicle of church hypocrisy and gender politics in medieval England, tells us more than enough about pilgrims on their way to visit Canterbury Cathedral, it says nothing about the city itself (Chaucer died before his characters could get there). In his day, horse-borne hundreds made their way from London across harsh terrain in bad English weather to visit the shrine of martyr St. Thomas à Becket, who was killed by knights of Henry II in 1170. The stupendous cathedral in which the deed was done—and the surrounding town, with its curving streets and tightly packed Tudor-style buildings—keeps the tourists flooding in by the busload. While Canterbury is encircled by a Roman wall, it's the city's medieval aspect that prevails—which is quite a feat considering that Canterbury was heavily damaged in the Blitz of 1941.

Modern Canterbury pilgrims are more concerned with moderately priced lodgings and picture-perfect moments than with spiritual enlightenment. On the plus side, B&Bs are generally of high quality and competitively priced, and the presence of local University of Kent students prevents the city from becoming a complete Disneyland. Every April, Chaucer fans follow in the footsteps of his characters on a pilgrimage from London's Southwark Cathedral to Canterbury, sending the city into the throes of a large and raucous medieval fair. The **Chaucer Festival** runs from spring to autumn with events coordinated by the **Chaucer Heritage Trust** (tel. 01227/470379). In October a calmer air falls on the city for the duration of the **Canterbury Festival** (tel. 01227/452853), a renowned arts festival lasting two weeks.

KEY

AE American Express Office

i Tourist Information

Sights ●
Canterbury
Cathedral, **9**
Canterbury Heritage
Museum, **7**
Canterbury Tales
Exhibition, **8**
Dane John
Monument, **12**
St. Augustine's
Abbey, **10**
WestGate
Museum, **5**

Lodging ○
Canterbury YHA, **13**
Clare Ellen Guest
House, **11**
Courteney Guest
House, **2**
Dar-Anne, **3**
Hampton House, **14**
Kingsbridge Villa, **6**
Pointers, **4**
St. Stephen's Guest
House, **1**

BASICS

BUREAUX DE CHANGE

Avoid changing money at the hostel, the tourist office, or the post office, if you can help it: They all have bad rates and even worse commissions. Banks—where you get a vastly better rate if you change traveler's checks rather than cash—are scattered along High Street and all its aliases. Thomas Cook has a counter at **Midland Bank** (9 High St., tel. 01227/597800), as good a place as any in town to change traveler's checks.

LAUNDRY

The launderette at 20 Dover Street, on the corner of Vernon Place behind the movie theater, charges £1.40 per wash and about £1.50 to dry. Your wash is done for you at the environmentally friendly launderette at 36 St. Peter's Street, a few yards from West Gate. Small loads cost £3.20, large loads £4.

MAIL

Canterbury's largest **post office** (29 High St., CT1 2BA, tel. 01227/454972) is often distressingly crowded. If you're in a hurry, try the one at the corner of Church and Lower Bridge streets. Both are open weekdays 9–5:30, Saturday 9–12:30.

VISITOR INFORMATION

The **Tourist Information Centre** offers free lodging guides and a Book-a-Bed-Ahead service. Wherever you stay, there is a fee of £2.50 for booking one person (£4 for phone bookings), and a 10% deposit is charged toward your bill. The office also sells a number of good hiking and biking maps and stocks "What, Where, When," a free fortnightly guide to current events. *34 St. Margaret's St., tel. 01227/766567. From Canterbury East, turn right and follow city wall, turn left on Watling St., right on St. Margaret's St. Open Mon.–Sat 9:30–5:30, Sun. 10–4 (closes at 5 in winter, and closed Sun. in Jan. and Feb.).*

COMING AND GOING

BY BUS

The main bus station's entrance is on the corner of St. George's Lane and St. George's Place, near the shopping district on High Street. **National Express** coaches (tel. 0990/808080) leave hourly throughout the day for London's Victoria Coach Station (£6 single) and Dover (£2.50 single). You'd be well advised to make your reservation in advance, especially on weekends and public holidays for journeys to the Channel ports. **Stagecoach East Kent** (tel. 01227/766151 or 01227/472082) also run an hourly service between Canterbury and Dover.

BY TRAIN

The **Canterbury East** station is a major stop between London and the ferry/hovercraft port in Dover. Trains leave London Victoria for Dover twice an hour Monday–Saturday, with an hourly service on Sunday. The trip takes 1½ hours and ticket prices start at £17.50 single, £20.60 for a five-day return. From Canterbury, the journey to Dover takes under 30 minutes and costs £4.40 day return. *Station Rd. E, off Castle St. Ticket window open Mon.–Sat. 6:10 AM–8:20 PM, Sun. 6:40 AM–9:20 PM.*

The **Canterbury West** station serves coastal resort towns such as Margate and Broadstairs (tickets cost £3 for a day return to either place), as well as London's Charing Cross Station. The South Eastern lines pass through some of the best scenery in Kent. *Station Rd. W, off St. Dunstan's St. Ticket window open Mon.–Sat., 6:15 AM–8 PM; Sun. 9:15–4:40.*

GETTING AROUND

Canterbury is encircled by a medieval city wall and is so small that you can walk almost anywhere in less than 20 minutes. The main road that bisects the city center changes names several times: It's St. Peter's Street in the west, High Street in the center, St. George's Street in the east, and New Dover Road even *farther* east. Walk northwest on this main road for 2½ mi or take Bus 604, 605, or 608 to reach the University of Kent. **Stagecoach East Kent** and **Arriva Kent and Sussex** run buses in and around Canterbury (fares from 60p). Contact them directly or the **Kent Public Transport Helpline** for further travel information (*see* Basics at the start of the chapter for phone numbers).

WHERE TO SLEEP

Abundant B&Bs line New Dover, London, and Whitstable roads. During the summer, Canterbury is a popular destination and most B&Bs are tiny, so try to reserve ahead. The majority of Canterbury's B&Bs observe a strict no-smoking policy, so smokers should always inquire ahead. Top of the line B&Bs include **St. Stephen's Guest House** (100 St. Stephen's Rd., tel. 01227/767644), which charges £24–£35 per head, while **Clare Ellen Guest House** (9 Victoria Rd., tel. 01227/760205) charges around £25 per head. Both have rooms with private bath and are about a 10-minute walk from town.

Courtney Guest House. This immaculate house has large, bright rooms and a sunny conservatory where you can catch up on your Chaucer. Doubles with bath cost £40 (the double without bath is £32), and singles go for £20–£30 per person. *4 London Rd., CT2 8LR, tel. 01227/769668. From Canterbury West, turn right on St. Dunstan's St., left on London Rd. 5 rooms, 4 with bath.*

Dar-Anne. Theresa Morey loves students, and her place is always filled with young people. She is a vegan, so herbivores don't get that sidelong look when they pass up sausages at breakfast. Sadly, she is thinking about moving on, but it's possible the guest house will continue with a new owner—in any case, you'd be well advised to phone first. The facilities are excellent (both rooms have TVs), and the house is only a short walk from the city center. Singles run £16, doubles £28. *65 London Rd., CT2 8JZ, tel. 01227/760907. Follow directions to Courtney Guest House (see above). 2 rooms without bath. Cash only.*

Hampton House. The decor of this Victorian house is floral and romantic, and the beautiful garden features a pond. Double-glazed windows offer peace and quiet, while Frank and Coral, the owners, lend the place added character. Singles are £20, doubles £40, slightly less in winter. *40 New Dover Rd., CT1 3DT, tel. 01227/464912. From bus station, turn right on St. George's Pl. and continue straight for ¾ mi. 4 rooms with bath. Cash only.*

Kingsbridge Villa. With single rooms starting at only £20 per person, this large B&B with a very central location offers great value for money. You can practically touch the Cathedral from most of its south-fac-

HEADS UP!

Chaucer isn't the only literary ghost haunting Canterbury; Joseph Conrad is buried in Canterbury Cemetery, while the head of Sir Thomas More (author of "Utopia") lies in St. Dunstan's church, on Dunstan Road. After his execution, More's body was buried within the Tower of London while his head was displayed on Tower Bridge. The head was recovered by his daughter, who had a friend knock it down from its spike while she waited below in a boat to catch it and steal it away to Canterbury.

ing rooms. As a bonus, the downstairs breakfast room becomes a popular Italian restaurant by night. Unlike most Canterbury B&Bs, this one is a haven for smokers. *15 Best La., CT1 2JB, tel. 01227/ 766415. From tourist office, turn left on High St., right on Best La. 10 rooms, 9 with bath. Cash only.*

Pointers. This friendly hotel in a Georgian building is within easy walking distance of the cathedral and city center (straight out beyond Westgate). There's an on-site restaurant and bar. Prices range from £45 for a single room to £67 for a double. *1 London Rd., CT2 8LR, tel. 01227/456846. From Canterbury West, turn right on St. Dunstan's St., left on London Rd. 12 rooms with bath or shower. Closed Dec. 20– mid-Jan.*

HOSTELS

Canterbury YHA. This place is often full, so try to book a week or two in advance. However, if you do arrive without reservations, don't despair: The proprietors will always refer you to another cheap bed. Dorm beds cost £10.15. *54 New Dover Rd., Kent CT1 3DT, tel. 01227/462911, fax 01227/470752. From bus station, turn right on St. George's Pl. and continue straight for 1 mi. From Canterbury East, turn right on Station Rd. E, veer right on Rhodaus Town (which becomes Upper Bridge St.), then right on St. George's Pl. 85 beds. Curfew 11 PM, lockout 10–1. Laundry.*

CAMPING

The Caravan and Camping Club Site. A huge number of sites guarantees little privacy. Of course, if you want to meet people, that should be no problem—a lot of characters hang out at the shop. The campground is in a rural area 1½ mi out of town and just ¼ mi from a main road. There's a laundry on site. Tent spaces cost £4.20, with an additional charge of £5.20 per person per night. *Bekesbourne La., tel. 01227/463216. From Canterbury East, turn right on Rhodaus Town, right on Church St., right on Long-port (which becomes St. Martin's Hill), continue for 1½ mi, then right on Bekesbourne La. 210 sites. Showers.*

FOOD

One good method for finding a decent, affordable meal in Canterbury is to look for places filled with students. The cheaper restaurants are found mostly along the smaller lanes and alleys off High Street. Self-caterers can find a variety of ethnic and vegetarian foods near the North Gate at **Canterbury Wholefoods** (10 The Borough, tel. 01227/464623), which also sells scrumptious filled rolls.

UNDER £5 • August Moon. With its enormous menu and low prices, August Moon packs in the university crowd. For an even cheaper meal, request self service from the take-out counter, then bring your food to the seating area across from the bar. Dim sum, Kung Po Chili Chicken, or the Vegetarian Feast for two are just a few of the tantalizing options. *49A St. Peter's St., tel. 01227/786268. Cash only.*

Green Court Cafe. Slip into this side-street café for cheap sandwiches, jacket potatoes, and three-course lunches available for an amazing £4.30. It's low on atmosphere, but you can grab a window seat and watch the world go by. *17–18 The Borough, at Palace St., tel. 01227/458368. Closes around 6:30.*

UNDER £10 • Beaus Creperie. This bright creperie serves a variety of sweet and savory crepes, and interesting starters such as prawns with peaches and rye. Choices range from the basic cheese to those loaded with goodies, costing from £2.15 to £7.25. Treat yourself to the specialty selections such as Crepe Indonesia (chicken curry). *59 Palace St., tel. 01227/464285.*

Il Vaticano. Pilgrims with a yen for pasta should try out this cheerful, modern pasta parlor. It's easy to find (on the same street as the tourist office), and has an attractive walled garden. Freshly made sauces include grilled prawns and mushrooms in garlicky cheese. Italian ice creams round off the calorific feast. Pastas start at about £6.50. *35 St. Margaret's St., tel. 01227/765333.*

UNDER £20 • Alberry's Wine Bar. A stone's throw from Il Vaticano (*see above*), this popular bistro makes a good place to sit and recharge your batteries. There's a wide, daily selection of inexpensive and hearty soups, salads, and pies: sample the venison casserole, if it's offered, or the turkey and ham pie. *38 St. Margaret St., tel. 01227/452378. Closed Sun.*

WORTH SEEING

Canterbury's small size and high density make it easy to see everything in one day. To avoid the crowds, get an early start, and remember that most attractions are less crowded an hour or so before closing time. For a fine view of Canterbury, climb up Pin Hill to **Dane John Mound,** a short walk from Canterbury East station. For a good overview of the city, consider the walking tours (£3.50) arranged by the **Canterbury Guild of Guides** (tel. 01227/ 459779); they kick off from the tourist office March–October daily at 2 PM, also at 11:30 AM in July and August.

Canterbury's Norman Castle (Castle and Gas Sts.), built for William the Conqueror in 1175, is now a crumbling mass of gray bricks neighbored by a parking lot.

CANTERBURY CATHEDRAL

As you come through the main entrance, built to commemorate Henry V's 1415 victory at Agincourt, the view across and up the cathedral is dizzying, with row upon row of towering pointed arches. Christ Church Cathedral— to use its official name—is a living textbook of medieval architecture and for centuries housed one of the most extravagant shrines in Christendom—Thomas à Becket's tomb. The oldest part of the church is the Norman crypt, built by Archbishop Lanfranc between 1070 and 1077 over the ruins of St. Augustine's church, destroyed by fire in 1067. This construction was hasty and resulted in a structure that was too small, so it was replaced by a larger building in 1130. Immediately after Thomas à Becket's canonization in 1173, a new Gothic-style choir was installed. Archbishops have traditionally been enthroned at **Trinity Chapel,** east of the choir area, on St. Augustine's chair behind the altar. Inside the chapel are the tombs of Henry IV and his wife, Joan of Navarre, and an effigy of Edward the Black Prince, the warrior son of Edward II. Beneath the chapel is the crypt where Thomas à Becket was first buried and where Henry II completed his penance for the murder. Becket's tomb was later destroyed during Henry VIII's smash-and-grab attempts to weaken the church while securing some of its treasures for himself.

The northwest transept is the site of Becket's murder. Becket, a dissident priest who disagreed with King Henry II's meddling in the church's business, was murdered in 1170 by four of Henry's more literal-minded knights seeking to gain the king's favor; it had been said they had overheard him exclaim, "Who will rid me of this troublesome priest?" Becket's assassins probably entered by the door from the cloisters, which contain amazing vaults decorated with the paintings of almost 1,000 heraldic shields. A marker indicates where Becket fell more than 800 years ago. Don't miss the 13th-century stained-glass windows that illustrate Becket's miracles. By 1172, Becket had been canonized St. Thomas of Canterbury, which did little to appease the French king (who took the murder of Becket, formerly under his protection, as a personal affront). It was only a matter of time before the pressure on Henry II, who felt enormous remorse at the death of his old friend, became too great, and he relinquished a great deal of power to the church. Subsequently, Canterbury Cathedral was made the hub of English Catholicism and is now the center of the Anglican Church. If the cathedral seems too daunting to explore alone, free guided tours leave from the pulpit weekdays at 10:30, noon, and 2 (also 2:30 in summer), and Saturday at 10:30, noon, and 1:30. *Sun St., at St. Margaret's St., tel. 01227/762862. Admission £3; free Sun. Open Mon.–Sat. 8:45–6 (Oct.–Easter until 5), Sun. 12:30–2:30 and 4:30–5:30 (open all day Sun. for worship). Precincts open daily 7–9 (free). Access may be restricted on Sat. afternoons when evensong is performed.*

CANTERBURY HERITAGE MUSEUM

Medieval Canterbury was filled with impoverished clergymen, many of whom fell ill as a result of poor living conditions. To cope with this growing problem, the lord mayor ordered a poor priests' hospital built specifically for the purpose of treating sick clergymen, although being confined in this drafty building usually worsened their condition. This onetime hospital is now the site of the popular Canterbury Heritage Museum, which exhibits a collection of artifacts left by pilgrims at Canterbury. *Stour St., tel. 01227/ 452747. From tourist office, turn right down Hawks La. Admission £2.30. Open Mon.–Sat. 10:30–5 (June–Oct., also Sun. 1:30–5). Last admission 4 PM.*

THE CANTERBURY TALES

Canterbury's attempt to re-create a historically accurate, multisensory version of Chaucer's stories has resulted in "The Canterbury Tales"—perfect for children, but insulting to anyone of a more mature intellect. Multilingual radio-controlled headphones guide you from room to room, where excerpts from Chaucer's *Canterbury Tales* are illustrated by moving plywood cutouts. The stories are funny, but it's less expensive (and more fulfilling) to read the book. *St. Margaret's St., tel. 01227/454888. Admission £5.25. Open Mar.–Oct., daily 9–5:30; Nov.–Feb., Sun.–Fri. 10–4:30, Sat. 9:30–5:30.*

ST. AUGUSTINE'S ABBEY

In 589, Pope Gregory I bought Augustine the Monk a one-way ticket from Rome to England in an attempt to convert the Saxons. Ethelbert, king of Kent, allowed Augustine and his 40 followers to build a church outside the city walls. Ethelbert's wife, Bertha, was the daughter of a Frankish king and already a Christian, so she went to the new church daily through the **Queningate.** Eventually Ethelbert converted, and Augustine established Canterbury Cathedral. Enough stones and walls remain in the grassy ruins to evoke the former whole—a cloister, church, and refectory. *Corner of lower Chantry La. and Longport Rd., tel. 01227/767345. Admission £2.50. Open daily Apr.–Sept., 10–6; Oct. 10–5; Nov.– Mar., 10–4.*

WESTGATE MUSEUM

The only surviving city gatehouse now houses a collection of medieval bric-a-brac and armaments used by the city guard, as well as more contemporary weaponry. There are exhibits on Canterbury's historical defenses, Roman walls, and examples of the chains and manacles used on the prisoners who were once detained here. Climb to the roof to catch a panoramic view of the city spires before walking along the landscaped riverside gardens. *At one end of St. Peter's St. (an extension of High St.), tel. 01227/ 452747. Admission £1. Open Mon.–Sat. 11–12:30 and 1:30–3:30.*

AFTER DARK

According to the Church of England, gluttony is a deadly sin but beer drinking is not. To take full advantage of this lucrative loophole, many pub owners have set up shop in the shadows of the cathedral. When you go pub crawling, try to avoid lingering on the streets after 11 PM; the sometimes less-than-tolerant Canterbury police seem to enjoy getting a little harassment in before the end of their shift. Most pubs in Canterbury are open Monday–Saturday 11–11, Sunday noon–10:30.

PUBS

Flying Horse. This updated, 16th-century pub may be one of the friendliest places in town. Amazingly, it attracts the young university crowd as well as old-timers who may bend your ear about the glory days of big bands and dance halls. *1 Dover St., at Upper Bridge St., tel. 01227/463803.*

Simple Simon's. Housed in a 14th-century building, this pub faithfully maintains the atmosphere of a medieval hall—including an open fire. If you're looking for a bite to eat, they specialize in homemade pies; try the vegetable one, a pie without peer! *St. Radigund Hall, 3 Church La., off The Borough, tel. 01227/762355.*

CLUBS

Penny Theatre. This lively spot, a 15th-century theatre, is highly regarded by hipsters as both a venue for live music and an after-hours club with an eclectic range of theme nights. *30–31 Northgate, tel. 01227/470512. Cover £2–£6. Open daily noon–midnight.*

THEATER AND FILM

The **Marlowe Theatre** (The Friars, off St. Peter's St., tel. 01227/787787) stages first-rate London shows as well as punky pop bands and cheesy British slapstick plays. Before spending £4–£24 on a ticket, pick up a copy of their seasonal brochure to gauge what's on. Amateur drama, performance art, and live music get top billing at the University of Kent's **Gulbenkian Theatre** (University Rd., tel. 01227/

769075), where tickets cost £4–£15. **Cinema 3,** which shares the same box office as the Gulbenkian, shows avant-garde oldies and some independent flicks for £4.

OUTDOOR ACTIVITIES

If you're interested in mountain biking, pick up an Ordnance Survey map of the area from the tourist office; it shows altitude contours in the **North Downs.** The **Canterbury Cycle Mart** (19 Lower Bridge St., tel. 01227/761488) rents mountain bikes for £7 per half day, £12 per day, and £40 per week. A credit-card number or £50 cash deposit is required.

About 3 mi northwest of Canterbury, the little-used **Forest of Blean** is the remnant of a much larger ancient forest of the same name. The hiking trails are quiet, and the forest is renowned for its bird life. The Ordnance Survey Map available at the tourist office gives details of various hikes. Many trails start at Rough Common, which can be reached by Bus 602 from Canterbury. Alternatively, you can walk a portion of the **North Downs Way** (*see* Outdoor Activities, *in* Basics, *above*). From Canterbury, you could walk these public footpaths southeast to Dover, or even over 100 mi westward into Surrey.

NEAR CANTERBURY

For maximum enjoyment, travel from east to west on your hikes. The scenery keeps getting better in that direction.

BROADSTAIRS

Broadstairs is a small, seaside town that was Charles Dickens's favorite summer retreat, as well as the childhood home of Queen Victoria. There's little to do in this clean resort other than enjoy the rays, swim, and check out a few museums. A plus in summer are the free concerts held at the bandstand by the water every Sunday at 2:30 PM. The 30-minute train ride from Canterbury to Broadstairs (£3 off-peak return) will take you into a colder climate, so dress warmly. Trains leave from Canterbury West station hourly (more frequently on weekends) until just after 11 PM and connect with other lines at Ramsgate.

While here be sure to visit the **Dickens House Museum,** in the middle of the promenade. Sideline collections include, among its assorted Victoriana, an assemblage of racist "Uncle Mack" cartoons and a gallery of 19th-century costume. *Victoria Parade, near beach, tel. 01843/862853. Admission £1. Open Apr.–mid-Oct., daily 2–5.*

If you still haven't had your fill of Dickensian heritage, visit **Bleak House.** Located on the cliffs above the beach, the justly named fortress was where Charles Dickens completed *David Copperfield* and began the novel that eventually gave its name to the house. In addition to Dickens's personal possessions there is a collection of relics dating from Victorian times and earlier, all found by divers in the ocean near Broadstairs. The cellar also houses an exhibit entitled "The Golden Age of Smuggling: 1780–1830." *Fort Rd., tel. 01843/862224. Follow High St. as it turns into Albion St., then turn right on Church Rd. Admission £3. Open Mar.–mid-Dec., daily 10–6 (mid-July–Aug. until 9 PM).*

WHERE TO SLEEP • Broadstairs's lone hostel is the excellent **Broadstairs YHA,** which is very close to the station and even has laundry facilities. Dorm beds are £9.15. *Thistle Lodge, 3 Osborne Rd., Broadstairs, Kent CT10 2AE, tel. and fax 01843/604121. From station, turn left on Broadway, left on Osborne Rd. 33 beds. Laundry, kitchen. Closed mid-Nov.–mid-Mar.*

THE SOUTH COAST: KENT AND SUSSEX

The coast of Kent and Sussex is an odd place. On one hand, there's no denying the beauty of the coastline itself: The cliffs of Dover, for example, are far more spectacular in reality than they appear on postcards and tourist brochures. The region also has its share of ruined castles and forts, not to mention rural walking trails that meander from field to beach to cliff. But the towns—oh, the towns. The Kent and Sussex coast is the holiday destination for thousands of Britons each year. And, sadly, Brits at the sea-

THE UNDERWATER UNION

Since the early 1800s, visionaries have thought of building a tunnel between England and the European continent, but endless obstacles stood in the way. The least problematic was the channel itself; the chalk on the seafloor is actually quite firm and amenable to tunneling. The English psyche, however, has proven far more formidable. Real and imagined fears of disease and unfettered Frenchness invading England have sent shivers through the island for centuries. To this day, the Brits have yet to build a high-speed rail link from London to Folkestone, which everyone agrees is necessary to goad people into using the tunnel.

From either side of the channel, the Eurotunnel is an amazing piece of technology—and one that far surpasses a previous Anglo-French project, the money-losing Concord. The tunnel, built with a combination of public and private funds, consists of two main train tracks. The first train to actually commence service was the freight- and car-carrying "Le Shuttle," the second was the passenger train christened the "Eurostar." Now instead of schlepping from airport to airport, you can hop on the Eurostar at its snazzy new terminal in Waterloo Station and wind up three hours later in Paris's Gare du Nord.

side like their fun tacky. Prepare yourself for a scad of amusement parks, snow cones, burgers, and pier attractions.

Towns like **Margate** and **Ramsgate** are the schlockiest, and **Brighton** has its gaudy side, though its vibrant student scene, gay population, and café society help to redeem it and give it a genuine buzz. Dover, on the other hand, has served as the welcome mat to Britain for decades, and looks it. You're much better off using these towns as bases for exploring the small towns and villages along the coast, and as starting points for dramatic cliffside walks. You can find a few sandy strands, but if you want to bake on a beach, you can do a lot better on the Continent.

Inland, of course, lie some of Britain's most fabulous treasure houses, from **Petworth** to **Knole,** with fabled castles—**Sissinghurst, Leeds,** and **Hever**—among them.

DOVER

Due to its geographical position, Dover has played a unique role in English history for the last 2,000 years. From a time when all government business was transacted in French, it was one of the original "Cinque Ports"—a defensive league of seaports set up in the 13th century—and more recently survived heavy bombardment in World War II. As the closest town to the Continent, it is visited mainly by people passing through when crossing to and from Europe by ferry. However, the port of Dover and its ferries now face stiff competition from the Channel Tunnel and the shuttle operating from **Folkestone,** 10 mi south (see Coming and Going, below). Despite some early setbacks, the trains have been steadily increasing their share of the cross-channel traffic and ferry companies have been feeling the squeeze.

Dover's future remains uncertain, particularly when you consider that the town's dull nightspots and many of its sights aren't worth visiting unless you're on the way to or from France. But despite some serious dirt under its fingernails, it has a handful of attractions that should be checked out, mostly neglected by the hasty hordes trampling through each day. Dover also makes a convenient base for exploring the nearby **White Cliffs**—Dover's famous chalky sea cliffs, a source of inspiration for lovers, lyricists, travelers, and, at one time, for soldiers sailing off to war. If the weather is even slightly fair, rent a bike, pack a picnic, and head for the cliffs on any of a dozen peaceful rural roads. You will be rewarded with a grand panorama of the Straits of Dover—the world's busiest shipping lanes—and a bird's-eye view of the harbour and the surrounding cliffs. On a clear day you might even see France.

BASICS

Dover's **tourist office** (Townwall St., tel. 01304/205108), across from the water, has lodging info and—when not too busy—will book you a bed for a 10% deposit. The major banks that change money are all in **Market Square;** you'll get fair rates at the **Dover Eurochange** (Townwall St., tel. 01304/210949), next to the tourist office, open daily 8–6 (July and August until 8). To reach Market Square and the tourist office from Priory Station, turn left on Folkestone Road and continue over the roundabout to High Street, which becomes Biggin Street and Cannon Street, leading to the square and Townwall Street. **The post office** (68–72 Pencester Rd., CT16 1BW, tel. 01304/241747) is opposite the bus station and is open Monday–Saturday 8:30–5:30.

COMING AND GOING

Despite a shaky start—with some spectacular breakdowns that left passengers stranded for several hours—**Eurostar** has now become the stylish choice for travel to the Continent. Trains leave London's Waterloo new state-of-the-art international terminal, a sweeping high-tech glass and steel structure designed by Sir Norman Foster. Although a high-speed link between London and the tunnel is still some years away, journey time is still just 3 hours (plus 20 mins for check-in) to Paris, making it more accessible than many parts of the UK. At press time, the lowest, highly restricted Eurostar fares were £99 return from London or Ashford (in Kent) to Paris, or £79 to Brussels. The highest second-class fare was £249 return to Paris or Brussels for a completely flexible, refundable ticket. You can buy much cheaper tickets on weekends (£89 with advance booking, £99 without). For reservations, contact **Eurostar** (tel. 0990/186186). For more information on the Eurotunnel and Eurostar *see* The Channel Tunnel *in* Chapter 1 *and* By Car, *below.*

BY BUS • **National Express** coaches arrive and depart from the station on Pencester Road, which has an hourly service to and from London (£9 single). **Stagecoach East Kent** (Pencester Rd., tel. 01304/240024) run to and from neighboring towns. The trip to Folkestone costs £2. Pick up a schedule at the office, open weekdays 8:30–5:30, Saturday 8:30–noon.

BY CAR • **Eurotunnel**—which previously operated as Le Shuttle—is a train shuttle service that will transport you and your car through the tunnel from Folkestone to Calais. The service operates 24 hours a day with up to four departures an hour during peak times. The original idea was to be able to drive through customs and onto a train and arrive in France a mere 35 minutes later, although travelers have reported occasional customs delays of up to two hours on either side of the tunnel. Remember you will need to add another half hour to check in. The cheapest fare currently available is a Mini Break five-day return, which costs £99 per car, including all passengers, if you book in advance. Open return fares per vehicle range from £159 to £279 depending upon the time of travel, flexibility of ticket, advance purchase and so on. For more information, contact **Eurotunnel** (Cheriton Parc, Cheriton High Street, Folkestone CT19 4QS, tel. 0990/353535).

BY FERRY • The opening of the Channel Tunnel has led to a complete shake-up of the ferry industry. P&O and Stena have merged to form **P&O Stena Lines** (tel. 0870/6000600), the largest carrier with six ships and at least 30 crossings a day between Dover and Calais. A standard return fare for foot passengers is £48. An open return fare for a car plus two passengers during the summer will cost £189 (larger vehicles pay extra). The journey takes 75–90 minutes, with sailings every half hour at peak times. Bikes are transported free (but their riders still have to pay). **SeaFrance** (tel. 0990/711711), with only two ferries and 15 sailings a day, usually works out a bit cheaper. The standard return fare to Calais for foot passengers is £30 year-round. For a car plus two passengers during the summer, prices start at £175. Both companies offer a range of different fares, so plan ahead to get the best fare. Call the tourist office (*see* Basics, *above*) for current schedules.

BY HOVERCRAFT AND CATAMARAN • **Hoverspeed** (tel. 0870/5240241) will whisk you to France by hovercraft in only 35 minutes, weather permitting (there's no service when the Channel is stormy). The trip is noisy and bumpy, but quick **SeaCats**—which skim over the water—have a longer crossing time of 55 minutes. Both leave for Calais from Dover's Western Docks hourly from 7:30 AM to 6:30 PM during the summer months of June through September, and every two hours the rest of the year. The SeaCat service also operates between Folkestone and Boulogne, with four departures daily in summer. A ticket for either crossing will cost you £25 for a five-day return (without a car). Those interested in a brief French stint should inquire about early bird same-day returns to France (£5), where you depart at an ungodly 7 AM, buy lots of good, cheap French wine and cigarettes, and return to England later that day. It is especially important on these day trips to bring your passport and remember the one-hour time difference for the return journey. Hoverspeed also runs a service to Ostend in Belgium.

BY TRAIN • Frequent trains (at least one per hour) travel directly to **Dover Priory station** (tel. 0345/484950) from London's Victoria and Charing Cross stations (£17.50 single, £20.60 five-day return). If you are continuing across the Channel, ferry companies operate courtesy shuttles to and from their respective docks. Hourly trains from Canterbury East (£4.40 day return) take about 25 minutes to reach Dover Priory.

WHERE TO SLEEP

Since so many people come to Dover for just one night, it sometimes feels like you're stuck in a grimy shantytown of hopeful immigrants waiting to make a daring dash across the border. In general, the quality of Dover's B&Bs is low, though some are definitely lower than others: Be sure to see the room before money changes hands. Most B&Bs are along Folkestone Road, near Priory Station.

Clare House. You'll find reasonable prices and extra-soft mattresses—so much for your back—in this well-kept B&B, now under new ownership, A single room costs £22 with doubles from £26 per person. Luggage storage is available. *167 Folkestone Rd., CT17 9LL, tel. 01304/204553. From Priory Station, turn right and walk straight about 1 mi. 6 rooms without bath. Check-in after 6 PM. Cash only.*

Number One. This corner terrace guest house—centrally located in one of Dover's more pleasant neighborhoods—is a great bargain, with cozy doubles between £42–£46. Built at the beginning of the last century, it's now decorated with mural wallpapers and porcelain collections, and the walled garden offers a view of the castle. The owners are happy to give advice on local sightseeing, and there's garage parking. *1 Castle St., CT16 1QH, tel. 01304/202007, fax 01304/214078. From Priory Station, go left to roundabout, cross onto Pencester Rd., turn right on Maison Dieu Rd. as far as Castle St. on right. 4 rooms with bath or shower. Off-street parking. Cash only.*

St. Alban's. The decor at St. Alban's is only slightly less tacky than the Dover norm, but at least it's right across from the train station and near the water. The clean rooms all have TVs, a double with breakfast costing £50. *71 Folkestone Rd., CT17 9RZ, tel. 01304/206308. 6 rooms, 3 en suite.*

HOSTELS • **Dover YHA.** The facilities are ugly but there are some colorful characters on the staff, and it's still the best deal in town. If the hostel is full, you'll be directed to the 64-bed overflow hostel on Godwyne Road. Dorm beds cost £10.15, doubles £25, quads £42. *306 London Rd., Kent CT17 0SY, tel. 01304/201314, fax 01304/202236. From Priory Station, go left to roundabout, turn left on Priory Rd. (which becomes London Rd.), and continue straight for 1 mi. 68 beds. Reception opens at 1 PM. Curfew 11 PM, lockout 10–1. Kitchen.*

For the low price of £6, you can sleep on a mattress in a gymnasium at the **YMCA** (4 Leyburne Rd., CT16 1SN, tel. 01304/206138); you also get a shower in clean facilities and a light breakfast. From High Street, go east on Ladywell Road (which becomes Godwyne Road), then turn right on Leyburne Road. Bedding is provided, but the management prefers that you BYOSB (Bring Your Own Sleeping Bag). At press time, a move to more upmarket premises (with correspondingly higher prices) was scheduled for late 1999, to Prince of Wales House (Princes St., CT17 9AZ, tel. 01304/225500). Phone first for confirmation.

CAMPING • The nearest campground is **Little Satmar Holiday Park** (Wine House La., CT18 7JA, tel. 01303/251188), in the village of Capel-le-Ferne near Folkestone. The campsite is closed November–February. Most of the space is allotted to motor homes and cars, with a section for hikers and cyclists. Tent sites cost £8.50 for two people during low season, £11 at peak times, cash only. A taxi from Dover Priory train station will set you back about £8, or take any bus (£2) heading toward Folkestone and ask the driver to drop you off near the campground.

FOOD

Though it's hard to find a clean restaurant in Dover that serves anything appetizing, you can still find a few tolerable places. For bulk supplies, do your shopping at **Iceland's** on High Street or the **Late Stop Convenience Mart** (49–50 London St.), which is open nightly until 10 PM. **Curry Garden** (24 High St., tel. 01304/206357) serves spicy curries that will leave you begging for water. Lace tablecloths give **Riv-**

iera Coffee House (9–11 Worthington St., between York and Biggin Sts., tel. 01304/201303) a kind of fancy feel, but don't be scared away: Sandwiches are cheap, and a cup of tea plus "scones and things" costs less than £2.

WORTH SEEING

Dover is small and extremely walkable. High Street is Dover's main north–south road. Heading north, it turns into London Road; at the south end it forks into pedestrians-only Biggin Street, which runs into Market Square. Because of Dover's one-night-stand nature, most people don't make it to the sights, even though some historical attractions (emphasis on *some*) are truly worthwhile. Dover has a long, rich history and was once much more than a revolving door to the Continent.

DOVER CASTLE • Dover has been a symbol of England's imperial strength from way back when, partly because its natural surroundings—notably Shakespeare Cliff (referred to in *King Lear*), the Eastern Heights, and the frigid waters of the Channel—make it an opportune place for a fortress. Dover Castle resisted attacks during the 17th-century Civil War and also survived relentless attacks by the German Luftwaffe, which during World War II pounded the area with an average of 1,000 bombs per week over a 1,500-day period (that's four years of continuous bombing). The awesome view of Dover Castle from Castle Hill Road gives visitors a sense of its fortitude and impregnability. The castle's keep has historical graffiti by prisoners (covered with Plexiglas to distinguish it from the newer stuff) and a bottomless pit of a well. On the castle grounds check out the **Pharos,** the world's only existing Roman lighthouse, built in the early 1st century AD.

During the late 18th century, the British constructed the labyrinthine **Hellfire Corner** within the cliffs under Dover Castle to defend themselves against an attack by Napoléon. In World War II, a communications center installed within these tunnels served as headquarters for the Allied evacuation from Dunkirk. Guided tours through a small portion of the miles-long catacombs offer a unique peek into a truly underground lifestyle. They last approximately 45 minutes and take you through the reconstructed command post. Be prepared for a long walk. *Castle Hill Rd., tel. 01304/201628. Castle and Hellfire admission £6.50. Open Apr.–Sept., daily 10–6; Oct. 10–5 or dusk if earlier; Nov.–Mar., daily 10–4.*

THE GRAND SHAFT • Though one tourism official described it as "just a big hole in the ground," the Grand Shaft is actually a triple circular staircase built in Napoleonic times. Like the poles firefighters slide down, the shaft was designed to get soldiers from their barracks on the Western Heights down to the beach in a jiffy to meet the enemy. Basically, though, you pay to climb down and up a long flight of stairs—perfect if you're feeling StairMaster-deprived. *Snargate St., tel. 01304/201200. From tourist office, head west on Snargate St. Admission £1.25. Open July–Aug., Tues.–Sun. 2–5.*

OLD TOWN GAOL • Creepy, real-looking wax figures of jailers and prisoners illustrate what life was like in this Victorian prison. Children, lunatics, and vagrants were locked up here for the pettiest of crimes, such as stealing bread. Vivid images of torture, confinement, and lunacy make this a wild place; it's probably the best exhibit of its kind (definitely better than the London Dungeon). *Dover Town Hall, Biggin St., tel. 01304/202723. From Priory Station, walk toward town on Folkestone Rd., turn left at Priory Rd. Admission £3.50. Open June–Sept., Tues.–Sat. 10–4:30, Sun. 2–4:30; Oct.–May, Wed.–Sat. 10–4:30, Sun. 2–4:30.*

THE WHITE CLIFFS EXPERIENCE • The White Cliffs Experience houses the Historium and Dover Museum. In the Historium, you can view a truly uninspired, 15-minute performance recapping Dover history; witness dull Celtic mannequins with tattoos fighting stiff Roman mannequins; and stand in a re-creation of a bombed-out Dover street in the 1940s. The Museum features archaeological finds and a more scientific history of Dover. *Market Sq., tel. 01304/210101. Admission £5.50. Open Apr.–Oct., daily 10–5; Nov.–Mar., daily 10–3.*

OUTDOOR ACTIVITIES

Probably the best thing to do in Dover is to take a walk. The tourist office has a free pamphlet called "White Cliffs Trails" that outlines many good walks near Dover, both inland and coastal. For casual viewers, a good panorama of the cliffs flanking Dover can be had from the Prince of Wales pier. Striking out for a closer look, though, is certainly more rewarding. To reach **Shakespeare Cliff**—named after famous scene in King Lear (Act 4, scene 6) in which Lear raves on a clifftop, thought to be near Dover—take Bus D2A from Worthington Street towards Aycliff, ask the driver to let you off across from the cliff, then go through the underpass and turn right.

Cycling along the starkly bleached cliffside can be a (literally) chilling experience—but one you should not miss. Rent bikes at **Andy's Shop** (156 London Rd., tel. 01304/204401) for £8 per day or £50 per week (ID. required). A steep, 2½-mi ride to Shakespeare Cliff begins on North Military Road, off York Street, and takes you by the Western Heights, a series of defensive battlements built into the cliff in the 19th century. For more White Cliffs, the walk from Langdon Cliffs, above the Eastern Docks, towards St. Margarets Bay and the **South Foreland Lighthouse** (about 2 mi) is exhilarating. The lighthouse (tel. 01304/852063)—where Marconi conducted his first ship-to-shore radio experiments in 1898—is worth a visit (£1.50) in its own right. Recently acquired by the National Trust, it's only open April–October on weekends and Bank Holidays (12:30–5:30), but daily in August, 12:30–5:30. Further inland, you can follow the **Vineyard Trail** and sample some of the local vino. The 7-mi trail loops around the towns of Woodnesborough, Ash, and Staple, about 10 mi north of Dover, and can be reached by bus via Sandwich. Stop by the **Staple Vineyard,** in Staple, where for £1.80 you get a tour and free wine tastings, so you can judge for yourself how close to France you really are.

RYE

The sleepy, hillside village of Rye is a welcome relief from other tourist-laden towns of the South. Though it *is* packed with tourists in the high season, Rye is still refreshingly slow and genteel, with its reddened rooftops and numerous boats lining the Strand Quay. While the village was a corrupt smuggling center for over 400 years, it's now a quiet, provincial town—the kind of place wealthy English families drive into for weekends of strolling around in search of antiques. The best time of year to visit is during the **Rye Festival,** which begins around the second week in September and lasts a fortnight (that's two weeks in Yankspeak), when the town overflows with music and art exhibits.

BASICS

The **tourist office** inside the Heritage Centre (Strand Quay, tel. 01797/226696) features a handmade model of Rye in its smuggling heyday (downstairs) and some cool exhibits about the town's history (upstairs). They also book rooms for a 10% deposit. The center is open 9–5:30 daily from Easter through October, shorter hours in winter. **Lloyd's Bank** (High Street), open weekdays 9:30–5, gives good rates for traveler's checks. Apart from the odd red phone box here and there, most of the pay phones in town line the street in front of the train station.

COMING AND GOING

Connex South Eastern trains (tel. 0345/484950) run from Ashford to Hastings, stopping at every one-horse town along the way before connecting to other lines. Train service to and from Rye ends around 9:45 PM on Sunday, so plan ahead. A single ticket to Brighton costs £11.30 and to Dover £9.70. The fare to London is £16.90 and you'll have to change trains in Ashford or Hastings. **South Coast Buses** (tel. 01424/433711) run the 711 service between Dover and Brighton stopping in Rye and Hastings, and **Arriva Kent and Sussex** (tel. 01634/281100) will take you north to Maidstone. Buses leave from the area directly in front of the train station. For general information on local routes, call the **East Sussex County Busline** (tel. 01797/223053) between 9 AM and 4 PM. The tourist office distributes "Fixtures," a guide detailing bus lines and schedules, but be forewarned: On-time buses are the exception, not the rule. Note that National Express buses do not service Rye.

Even though Rye is small (it takes 10 minutes to walk across town), it's disturbingly easy to **get lost.** From the train station, head straight up to reach the center of town, and keep climbing to reach the church and castle.

WHERE TO SLEEP

The tourist office publishes a brochure that lists B&Bs with rooms from £15 per person—but you better not mind staying 3 mi out of town in a cottage or farmhouse. Many B&Bs also line Military Road, Winchelsea Road, and Ferry Road, which turns into Udimore Road (a.k.a. B2089) as you head toward Battle. Prices jump at least £2.50 during summer. For a splurge, check into the ever-popular **Mermaid** (*see* Food, *below*), whose restaurant is also one of the finest in the area.

Half House. Not only do you get to stay in an old house with loads of character, you also get a healthful breakfast and beautiful rooms, all with views of the River Rother and the surrounding marsh. Doubles cost £17.50–£20 per person. *Military Rd., TN31 7NY, ¾ mi NE of train station, tel. 01797/223404. Walk straight ahead from station, turn left on Cinque Ports St., left on Landgate, right on Military Rd. 3 rooms, 1 with shower.*

Old Vicarage. If it's time for a bit of a splurge, try this place. There are cozy little pluses, including the fact that the kitchen serves up that rare English brew, fresh-ground coffee. Comfy doubles with private bathrooms cost £59 and the lone double without bath costs £44; there's a 15% discount for three nights or more from November through March, or 10% for a week or more throughout the rest of the year. *66 Church Sq., TN31 7HF, tel. 01797/222119. Through Landgate Arch to High St., take third left into West St., bear to left along footpath. 5 rooms with bath. Cash only.*

Owlet. Mrs. Ball runs a tight ship, and she cooks a fine breakfast, although you do have to trudge through the family's living quarters every time you want to use the bathroom. Doubles are £18 per person. *37 New Rd., TN31 7LS, tel. 01797/222544. Walk straight ahead from station, turn left on Cinque Ports St., left on Landgate, right on Fishmarket Rd., left on New Rd. (¾ mi total). 2 rooms with shower (shared bath). Cash only.*

CAMPING • Rye Bay Caravan Park (Pett Level Rd., TN36 4NE, tel. 01797/226340), closed November–February, has 70 sites mainly used by caravans and motor homes, but they'll take carless folk for £11 per tent (cash only). To reach the site, take Bus 44, 344, or 345 to Winchelsea Beach (about 4 mi down A259) and ask the driver to let you off at the entrance. Buses leave Rye hourly throughout the day. If you're in a bind, take a cab or Bus 711 to Winchelsea and walk the short distance to the campground. The nearest YHA is 8 mi away in Guestling, just outside Hastings, where you can pitch your own tent from £4.57 per person. *Hastings YHA, Guestling Hall, Rye Rd., Guestling, Hastings, East Sussex, TN35 4LP.*

The Rye Shakespeare Company occasionally performs snippets of Shakespeare right in the streets of town. Don't be surprised if you suddenly find yourself in the middle of a "Tempest" on Mermaid Street.

FOOD

As an upscale town, Rye is a place to consider treating yourself to a fine meal. Although definitely a bistro, with all its liveliness and bustle, the **Landgate Bistro** (5–6 Landgate, tel. 01797/222829) is serious about its food. Try the scallops and monkfish in an orange and vermouth sauce—all the local fish is excellent—or the Williams pears sorbet. In an old, small building, in keeping with Rye's atmosphere, the restaurant attracts a steady local clientele. A fixed-price menu is available Tuesday through Thursday; it's closed Sunday and Monday. A town landmark—and one of the most famous hostelries in England—is **The Mermaid** (Mermaid St., tel. 01797/223065). A crooked black-and-white half-timber building, this classic inn looks as though it's come straight off a movie set. But its place in history is assured: It was once the headquarters of one of the notorious smuggling gangs that ruled Romney Marsh. It's true that the management trades shamelessly on the hotel's olde worlde character, claiming ghosts and secret passageways, but it's all quite genuine: Those creaking floors, twisting passages, and huge brick fireplaces have been here for the best part of 300 years. If you want a blow-out evening, splurge on those guest rooms with four-poster beds (doubles with bathrooms start at £66 if you're going to spend the night)—but seekers of atmosphere will be happy enough just enjoying the pricey restaurant (Mediterranean prawns are £11, steaks are £16.50) or a drink by the hearth. Be warned, however: The Mermaid is *very* popular with tourists.

Eating inexpensively is no easy task in Rye. Apart from a few chippies and **Anatolian's Kebabs** (16A Landgate, tel. 01797/226868), there's hardly a budget place in sight. Shopping at **Budgen's Supermarket,** across from the rail station, will save you those few precious pounds. Another exception is the **Bell Inn** (33 The Mint, tel. 01797/223323), a pub whose owners don't seem to realize they're smack in the middle of tourist territory—there's no other way to explain the cheap, good food. **Toasties** (grilled ham and cheese sandwiches) go for less than £2, and best of all, honest-to-goodness locals actually drink here. The sweets in the window may tempt you inside **Simon the Pieman** (Lion St., tel. 01797/222207), a traditional tearoom specializing in flavored fudges. They also serve quiches, pies, and jacket potatoes. **The Peacock** (8 Lion St., tel. 01797/226702), a café/restaurant with a large open hearth and heavy oak beams, has a tempting display of cakes and gateaux in the window, if you're looking for afternoon tea. They also serve three-course meals in the afternoons and evenings, including a variety of vegetarian platters.

WORTH SEEING

The Old English word for "small passageways" is "twittens" and Rye is full of them. One interesting passage is near the corner of East and Market streets. At the corner of Tower and Hilder's streets is **Land Gate,** which guarded the only entrance into town by land when Rye was a peninsula. The gate was installed in 1329 and remains an impressive piece of architecture. **Saint Mary's Church,** on Church

Square, has a calm, unadorned interior and one of the oldest clocks in England. The clock was restored to commemorate the marriage of Charles and Diana in 1981. The church's best feature is the surrounding churchyard, where tall, skinny tombstones tilt with age. Find a seat here and relax, far from the crowds. Elsewhere in town, the **Rye Art Gallery** (107 High St.) exhibits innovative art, from decorative woodcarving to paintings by contemporary British artists.

LAMB HOUSE • Henry James lived in Lamb House from 1898 until his death in 1916, though the garden cottage where he actually did his writing was destroyed by German bombs in World War II. The house contains various trinkets belonging to James, and will only appeal to die-hard fans of the prolific wordsmith. *Top of West St., tel. 01892/890651. From station, walk 1 block past High St. along West St. Admission £2.50. Open Apr.–Oct., Wed. and Sat. 2–6; last admission 5:30.*

YPRES TOWER AND RYE CASTLE MUSEUM • The ancient Ypres Tower (4 Church Sq.) was built to withstand naval invasion, though the French repeatedly sacked Rye in the 14th century anyway; it now contains several small cannon replicas and other exhibits chronicling its history as the town gaol. The nearby Gun Garden—installed to protect this section of coast when the Spanish Armada threatened in 1588 (anti-aircraft guns were later placed here during World War II)—makes a fine picnic spot, with sweeping views of the Flatlands and ocean to the south. Ypres Tower is a part of the **Rye Castle Museum,** now installed in a separate building nearby, which has a number of relics, including an 18th-century fire engine and the pottery for which Rye is famous. *3 East St., tel. 01797/226728. From station, walk up the hill to the High, turn left and East St. is 50 m up on the right. Admission £3 (including Ypres Tower). Open Apr.–Oct., daily 10:30–5:30; Nov.–Mar., weekends 10:30–4. Last admission 45 min before closing.*

BRIGHTON

The back-to-back palatial hotels along Brighton's waterfront attest to its status as England's premier 19th-century beach resort. And despite the thin layer of seaside grit covering the entire town, Brighton remains England's premier beach resort, even if the modern clientele is far removed from the ritzy trendsetters who once frequented these shores. While **The Lanes,** where lords and ladies once browsed for finery, still retains some prestige, the old shopping quarter has since been largely supplanted by the younger, more colorful **North Laine,** a veritable potpourri of cafés, shops, street musicians, and honest-to-goodness atmosphere. Of course, if you're majoring in art history or the decorative arts back home, Brighton will have to be a must: That Xanadu of Regency England is here—the Royal Pavilion, a gorgeous and fantastic palace built for the Prince of Wales in the 19th century.

If the Royal Pavilion tops Brighton's short list of worthwhile monuments and sights, it's the town's absorbing and distinct youth culture that makes it so popular. It's the liberal hole in the conservative belt of the South, and home to Britain's largest, most vibrant gay community outside London. With two universities and countless English-language schools, Brighton manages to sustain the feel of a large international city.

Most Americans don't respond well to the magnetic draw Brighton exerts on British and other Euro-youth, perhaps due to the town's reputation as a sleazy entertainment mecca. It certainly has its share of problems, among them polluted water and a rising petty crime rate. However, the town has recently agreed to participate in an expensive, long-term water-improvement project, and you'd be hard-pressed to find a rumble between mods and rockers these days. If you can somehow avoid Brighton's usual seaside tourist trappings, you'll find that it's a fine place to blow off steam before heading off to your next quaint, medieval town.

BASICS

The **Tourist Information Centre,** across the street from the town hall, is swamped during peak months. They don't answer the phone at all if too many people are waiting to be helped, so you're better off just coming in for accommodations bookings (£1 fee), maps, and pamphlets. *10 Bartholomew Sq., tel. 01273/323755. From train station, take Brighton Bus Lines Bus 27, get off at North St., and follow the TOWN HALL signs. Open July–Aug., daily 9–6; June and Sept., weekdays 9–5, Sat. 10–6, Sun. 10–5; Oct.–May, weekdays 9–5, weekends 10–4.*

For information on gay events and resources, contact the **Gay Switchboard** (tel. 01273/204050) or the **University of Sussex's Lesbian, Gay, and Bisexual Society** (LGB), which meets currently Tuesday at 6:30 PM in the LGB room on the campus (write first c/o Room 232, Falmer House, Brighton BN1 9QF).

American Express (82 North St., tel. 01273/321242) provides the usual services for cardholders. The money-changing offices in the train station are a rip-off, so head to one of the banks along North Street; Lloyd's Bank (171 North St., tel. 01273/324971) has good rates for traveler's checks. The post office (51 Ship St., BN1 1BA, tel. 01273/573209) is open Monday–Saturday 9–5:30.

COMING AND GOING

Trains leave Brighton's main **rail station** (top of Queen's Rd., tel. 0345/484950) about three times an hour for London (£13.30 day return). The rail station is a 15-minute walk up Queen's Road from the clock tower. **National Express** (tel. 0990/808080) operate an express Shuttle service to London (£6; up to 17 times a day) from the Pool Valley Coach Station near the waterfront on the southern edge of Old Steine. **Brighton and Hove Buses** (tel. 01273/886200) serve the surrounding area, or **South Coast Buses** (tel. 01424/433711) for short hops to places such as Rye. General information on public transport in the Brighton area can be had by calling the West Sussex Traveline (tel. 01273/474747).

GETTING AROUND

Brighton's four main roads—Queen's Road, North Street, West Street, and Western Road—converge at the clock tower, and roughly divide the city center into four quadrants. The southwest quadrant is dominated by Churchill Square, a central bus depot for local routes. The southeast quadrant, bounded by Palace Pier and the waterfront, is considered to be the heart of old Brighton and is where you will find The Lanes and the Royal Pavilion. North of North Street is the area known as North Laine. Brighton is large and hilly, so walking may be a little draining. The main bus company, **Brighton and Hove** (see Coming and Going, above) serves the area frequently and efficiently. Free maps detailing bus routes are available at the tourist office (see Basics, above). Local fares are 70p.

WHERE TO SLEEP

Brighton has a wide range of accommodations, running from elegant Regency-era town-house hotels to more moderately priced options on Madeira Place, Charlotte Street, and Upper Rock Gardens (which are—nice surprise—just a short walk east of the fabled Royal Pavilion). If you're booking into the latter options, as usual, ask to see your room before paying for it. The tourist office has a free list of approved lodgings. In May, hotels fill up for conventions, and reservations are a fine idea.

Alvia Hotel. Here you get a full breakfast with your lovely, sunny room. Some of the rooms have dark-wood, four-poster beds, and most have showers. This hotel is far better than the others nearby, yet not more expensive. Singles are £18, doubles from £36 (or £42 en suite). *36 Upper Rock Gardens, BN2 1QF, tel. 01273/682939, fax 01273/607711. From Palace Pier, walk east on Marine Parade, turn left on Upper Rock Gardens. 10 rooms, 7 with bath.*

Chester Court. This small, immaculate hotel is near the seafront and nicer than most of the other hotels on Charlotte Street. Singles cost £22–£25, doubles £46–£50. *7 Charlotte St., BN2 1AG, tel. 01273/ 621750. From Palace Pier, walk east on Marine Parade, turn left on Charlotte St. 11 rooms, 6 with shower. Cash only.*

The Dove. This recently refurbished, converted Regency house has one luxuriously large room with a balcony for £89 a night, but for budget purposes, be sure to ask for the less expensive quarters, some with a sideways sea view from their bow windows. Double rooms start at £49, and there is a 10% discount if you stay for a week or more. There is no restaurant. *18 Regency Sq., BN1 2FG, tel. 01273/ 779222. From Palace Pier, walk west on King's Rd., turn right on Regency Sq. 10 rooms with bath.*

Marina House Hotel. Ten minutes walk from Palace Pier, this family-run hotel is tucked away just off the seafront. With flexible breakfast times and the sea in your face at the end of the road, what more do you need in Brighton? Double rooms start at £39, or pay a bit extra for a four-poster. *8 Charlotte St., Marine Parade, BN2 1AG, tel. 01273/605349. From Palace Pier, walk east on Marine Parade, turn left into Charlotte St. 10 rooms with bath. Restaurant. Cash only.*

Topps. A pricier alternative to The Dove, next door, this delightful hotel consists of two connected Regency houses. Well-equipped double rooms, all with lush bathrooms, cost between £79 and £129. The atmosphere is relaxed and friendly, and the owners are always ready with useful advice. *17 Regency Sq., BN1 2FG, tel. 01273/729334. From Palace Pier, walk west on King's Rd., turn right on Regency Square. 15 rooms with bath.*

HOSTELS • Brighton Backpackers. This fun, funky independent hostel is a great place to hang out and meet adventurers from around the world. It's also right next to The Lanes and a half block from the waterfront. Dorm beds cost £9 per night or £50 per week. Around the corner is its other complex with

ALL HAIL THE REGENT

The distinctive (verging on the absurd) architecture of the Royal Pavilion is a prime example of the Regency style, popularized by architect John Nash in the early part of the 19th century. This style is characterized by a diversity of influences: French, Greek, Italian, Persian, Japanese, Chinese, Roman, Indian, you name it. It's almost as if Nash had some sort of eerie postmodern premonition.

The term "Regency" itself comes from the last 10 years of the reign of George III, a period during which he was deemed unfit to rule due to advancing insanity (more recently found to have a medical base). As a result, real power was placed in the hands of the Prince of Wales, also known as the Prince Regent, who became King George IV in 1820. Throughout his regency, George IV spent grand sums indulging his flamboyant tastes in architecture, art, and interior decorating (and concurrently proving to be an utter failure in matters of diplomacy and affairs of state). Nash was King George IV's favorite architect, beloved for his interest in Indian and Asian designs and for his use of simple neoclassic designs, as evidenced in his plans for Regent's Park in London.

12 large rooms, some containing a double bed, bunk bed, and bath. These rooms cost £25 for two people, plus £10 for each additional person per night. The reception desk in the hostel, which issues sheet sleeping bags, handles booking for both complexes. Some handy facilities include a bar, key deposit, luggage storage, and TV room. *75–76 Middle St., BN1 1AL, tel. 01273/777717. From Brighton station, walk straight down Queen's Rd. to seafront, turn left, then left again on Middle St. 85 beds. Kitchen, laundry. Cash only.*

Friese-Greene. Although similar in price (beds £10 per night, £45 per week), quality, and clientele to the Backpackers Hostel just down the road, this house is more spacious. Film fanatics may want to stay here for the sheer fact that it was in this very house that Mr. William Friese-Greene invented the art of cinematography. The owner also runs overnight excursions around the Isle of Wight in his 40-ft sailboat for about £30. There is a key deposit, TV room, poolroom, and basement cinema. *20 Middle St., BN1 1AL, tel. and fax 01273/747551. Follow directions to Brighton Backpackers Hostel. 50 beds. Kitchen. Cash only.*

FOOD

Brighton has a host of terrific restaurants and cafés, though stay away from overpriced restaurants near clusters of hotels and B&Bs. Reasonable semi-upscale restaurants can be found along The Lanes, off North Street. Head to North Laine for cheaper cafés and a funkier atmosphere. If you really want to save money, stock up at **Sainsbury's** (1 London Road) or **Safeway** (9 St. James's Street), just up the street from the Pavilion. The best traditional cream tea is served in The Lanes at the **Mock Turtle** (4 Pool Valley, no phone).

English's Oyster Bar. Buried in the Lanes, this 150-year-old restaurant is one of the few old-fashioned seafood havens left in England. You can either eat succulent oysters and other seafood dishes at the counter or have a table in the restaurant section, where there's a two-course set-price menu. *29–31 East St., tel. 01273/327980. From clock tower, walk down North St., turn right on East St.*

Food for Friends. This well-established whole-food restaurant just off The Lanes is convenient for quick and tasty organic and international dishes. The rotating menu features chimichangas, falafel, Chinese stir-fry, and Sussex shepherdess pie. *17A–18 Prince Albert St., tel. 01273/202310. From the clock tower, walk down North St., turn right on Ship St., veer left on Prince Albert St.*

Gardner's Café. Amid a bargain-shopper's fantasyland, this tiny, bustling North Laine vegetarian café promotes a health-conscious diet; there's a choice of vegan dishes and 95% of the menu is organic and guaranteed genetically unmodified! Try a plate of "Cheese melts"—assorted sautéed vegetables topped with melted cheese in a pita—or one of the various bakes and fresh soups. Work by local artists is splattered on the walls, as are flyers advertising various goings-on in Brighton and Hove. *50 Gardner St., tel. 01273/670743. From clock tower, walk down North St., turn left on Bond St. (which becomes Gardner St.). Cash only.*

Piccolo. A hungry traveler's dream—the hefty portions of pasta are fresh and flavorful and the pizzas are cheap. *56 Ship St., in The Lanes, tel. 01273/203701. From clock tower, walk down North St., turn right on Ship St.*

WORTH SEEING

Every year, usually from the first weekend of May and throughout the month, Brighton breaks out with a huge festival celebrating every imaginable artistic form and the whole town buzzes with excitement. At other times of the year, the least expensive escape from the beachfront jungle is an afternoon in one of the town's many parks. From downtown, hike uphill to Queen's Park, or stroll westward into Hove, the town that borders Brighton, through the grassy area along the coastal road Kingsway.

BRIGHTON MUSEUM AND ART GALLERY • This free museum is housed in a wing of Brighton's main library. Contained within its various galleries are exhibits of armor, art deco glass, archaeological finds, fashion, and costume. Check out Salvador Dalí's outrageous red "Lips Sofa" from the 1930s, inspired by the face and glamour of Mae West. There's also a fun Balcony Café inside the gallery if you need a breather. *Church St., at Marlborough Pl., tel. 01273/290900. Around corner from Pavilion. Admission free. Open Mon., Tues., Thurs.–Sat. 10–5, Sun. 2–5.*

THE LANES • This narrow maze of lanes or "twittens" was originally the quarter where the local fishermen lived. The houses were eventually masked with Georgian and Victorian facades, transforming The Lanes into *the* shopping area for the well-heeled. Today, a healthy wallet is still useful to bring along on your visit, as The Lanes are cluttered with jewelry, antiques, and collectibles. Even if you're not in a buying mood, take a walk down claustrophobia-inducing Meeting House Lane. **North Laine** can't compare in quaintness or age, but draws the young and hip with a multitude of friendly cafés and trendy stores selling records, art, and clothing. Both The Lanes and North Laine are best accessed from North Street.

PALACE AND WEST PIERS • The West Pier, once a marvel of high Victorian architecture, is currently undergoing complete restoration after storm damage, with funding from the National Lottery and private sponsors, and is not due to open until 2002. However, guided tours of the pier under reconstruction are available all year, organized by the Brighton West Pier Trust (tel. 01273/207610; £10). Palace Pier, with the requisite amusement rides, arcade, and slot machines, was featured in a number of films, notably *Mona Lisa* and *Quadrophenia*. At night, the pier sparkles like an airport runway; a seedier crowd emerges then, but it's still reasonably safe. *Old Steine, at Grand Junction Rd., tel. 01273/609361. From station, head south on Queen's Rd. (which becomes West St.), turn left at the ocean. Open daily 9 AM–midnight.*

PRESTON MANOR • This Edwardian manor is the former home of the Prestons, once Brighton's leading aristocratic family, who had fabulous taste (despite a weakness for dog portraits). Check out the Flemish leather wall covering in the small salon behind the living room, and definitely have a look at the kitchen, the oldest part of the house. Also look for evidence of the upstairs/downstairs relationship between the masters of the house and their servants. *Preston Dr., off Preston Rd., tel. 01273/292770. From Marlborough Pl. (behind the Pavilion), take Bus 5 or 5A to Preston Manor. Admission £3. Open Mon. 1–5, Tues.–Sat. 10–5, Sun. 2–5.*

ROYAL PAVILION • No, you are not imagining it. There, presiding over the eastern section of Brighton—not somewhere east of Shangri-la—sits a magical palace out of the *Tales from the Thousand and One Nights*. One blink, and you half expect this Scheherazadian extravaganza to vanish. But this is not any abode built for Kubla Khan. In fact, the Royal Pavilion is a dazzler of the Regency era, built in the early 19th century for the Prince Regent. Ever since then, it has never failed to shock and delight in equal measure: Queen Victoria wanted to pull it down, while art historians now regard it as a monument of Regency-era design. In 1786, the Prince Regent (later King George IV) commissioned architect Henry Holland to build a simple seaside villa for his mistress, Mrs. Fitzherbert (whom he was later forbidden to see by his mother). Shortly afterwards, another architect, John Nash, was given license to rebuild the villa into something a bit more grandiose. By the time Nash was through with it in 1822, Brighton found itself with a palace that looks less like a seaside retreat and more like the Taj Mahal—note the extravagant Persian/Indian architecture and Chinese interior decor. For a real dose of decadence, check out the **Banqueting Room,** with its 1-ton bronze dragon and glass orb chandelier, or the ornately furnished **Music Room.** All this and more was completed at no small expense—the royal family nearly went bankrupt over construction costs. During the summer, deck chairs are spread out on the lawn for musical performances. *Corner North St. and Old Steine, tel. 01273/290900. From station, walk down Queen's Rd., turn left on Church St., and look for the domes. Admission £4.50. Open June–Sept., daily 10–6; Oct.–May, daily 10–5.*

ST. BARTHOLOMEW'S CHURCH • Supposedly built to the exact dimensions of Noah's Ark (upside down?) as described in the Bible, St. Bart's was initially laughed at for being too tall and lacking certain churchly attributes, like aisles or chancels. It was called a "barn," a "cheese warehouse," and a "monster excrescence," but its height and kaleidoscopic rose window are what make a visit here an experience. Don't miss the glittering, almost Byzantine, altar. *Ann St., tel. 01273/620941. From Brighton Station, take underpass down Trafalgar St., turn left on York Pl. (which becomes London Rd.), left on Ann St. Admission free. Open Tues.–Sun. 11:30–3:30.*

AFTER DARK

The backbone of Brighton's famed nightlife is, unquestionably, the clubs; even Londoners come to Brighton for the experience. What the clubs lack in inventiveness is made up for by good DJs spinning some of the latest tunes, and throbbing crowds of people of all sexual orientations out for a good time. For the best information on Brighton's nocturnal diversions, peruse the posters and flyers in the windows of stores in North Laine, or pick up *Impact* (50p), *The Latest* (30p), or *New Insight* (45p) at newsstands or the tourist office. Expect to pay £5–£10 to get into the larger, trendier clubs. Smaller clubs charge £3–£5.

PUBS • The **Smuggler's Pub** (Ship Street) is a popular student pub with an upstairs dance club, **Enigma,** and a downstairs jazz club, the **Jazz Place** (tel. 01273/328439 for both). The **Leek and Winkle** (39 Ditchling Rd., tel. 01273/624434) plays good music and has a beer garden that's popular with students. **Squid and Starfish** (78 Middle St., tel. 01273/727114) is a hip pre-club watering hole across from Casablanca (*see below*).

CLUBS • Beachfront **Zap** (King's Rd. Arches, tel. 01273/821588) and **Event II** (West St., tel. 01273/732627) are Brighton's largest and most mainstream clubs, drawing kids from all over Britain with the latest dance music and most expensive speakers. **Revenge** (32–34 Old Steine, tel. 01273/606064) is the best gay club, while **The Lift** (Queen's Rd., tel. 01273/730515) hosts a regular lesbian night. **The Escape Club** (10 Marine Parade, tel. 01273/606906) is in a cool building with an outdoor terrace and draws a trendy university crowd. **Casablanca** (Middle St., tel. 01273/321817) is a velvety subterranean den featuring live acid jazz and Latin funk. **The Beachcomber** (214 Kings Rd. Arches, tel. 01273/202807) draws a funkier crowd for its weekly Soul Kitchen.

OUTDOOR ACTIVITIES

The **South Downs Way,** an 80-mi National Trail running from Eastbourne to Winchester, can be easily accessed from Brighton. Simply take the train 4 mi to Falmer Station (£2 day return), walk straight through the University of Sussex, cut across a couple of cow fields (this is legal, as long as you don't mess with the cows and watch your step), and you'll soon hit a trail. The Brighton Tourist Office has a pamphlet entitled "Dawdle on The Downs" (20p), which details three circular walks in the area. Highlights along the walks include the Clewton Windmills, Heathy Brow, and Ditchling Beacon, the second highest point on the South Downs. For more information on the South Downs Way, *see* Basics, *above.*

NEAR BRIGHTON

SEVEN SISTERS

The spectacular chalk cliffs around Beachy Head, where the South Downs reach the sea, is one of the most romantic places on Britain's coastline, and definitely worth a visit. The 2-mi stretch between the **Belle-Tout Lighthouse,** built in 1832 and dramatically moved back from the edge of a crumbling cliff-face in 1999, and the **Beachy Head Lighthouse,** itself built on rocks in 1902 to make such a move easier, is known as the South Downs. This dramatic, rolling landscape ends abruptly in the magnificent set of seven contiguous cliffs known as the Seven Sisters, now part of the Seven Sisters Country Park. The snow-white cliffs, topped by rolling green hills and bounded by the sea, make for a worthwhile day trip away from the hordes of Brighton. To reach the cliffs, take hourly South Coast Bus 711 to Exceat, the entrance to the Seven Sisters National Park, and follow the obvious trail to the sea. A 2½-mi walk along the cliffs brings you to **Birling Gap,** which provides stupendous views. If you continue north another mile to East Dean, you can catch a bus back to Brighton, or a 3-mi walk farther east along the coast will bring you to Eastbourne.

ARUNDEL

Arundel is a very small town with a few disproportionately large sights; it's a strange combination of local wealth and rural countryside. The castle's towering turrets look down on swans floating along the River Arun, while cows stop chewing their cud to give a loud snort as another BMW speeds on its way into a "Neighborhood Watch Zone," reminding you that you're still within commuter radius of London. In fact, there's direct service from London's Victoria Station to Arundel (£18 five-day return), as well as frequent connections to Brighton and Portsmouth. To reach town from Arundel's station, go left on A27 and walk five minutes into town. Arundel's **Tourist Information Office** (High St., tel. 01903/882268) is open weekdays 9–5, weekends 10–5 (Sept.–May until 3). They stock fat accommodations handbooks and can point you toward the town's cheaper beds. The **post office** is off High Street on Mill Road (tel. 01903/882113).

WHERE TO SLEEP

Unlike most "jewel of the past" towns, you don't have to trudge miles from the center to find a good, affordable place to stay in Arundel. The **Castle View B&B** (63 High St., tel. and fax 01903/883029) has three pretty doubles (£40) and a nice restaurant with reasonable prices. They don't call it Castle View for nothing—you're literally eye-to-eye with the battlements, just across the road. **Arundel House** (11 High St., tel. 01903/882136) has double rooms with cool timber-beamed ceilings from £20 to £25 per person.

HOSTELS • Arundel YHA. This large Georgian building lies a mile or so from town, but on the plus side, beds are only £9.15, and the manager knows a shortcut along the river into town. *Warningcamp, West Sussex BN18 9QY, tel. 01903/882204, fax 01903/882776. 60 beds. Curfew 11 PM, lockout 10–5.*

FOOD

High Street has plenty of cafés and tearooms. For a substantial meal, try the **Tudor Rose Restaurant** (49 High St., tel. 01903/883813), open lunchtimes and afternoons only, which serves piping-hot scones with its cream teas, an excellent prelude to roasted chicken with potatoes and veggies. Castle Tandoori Indian Restaurant (3 Mill La., off High St., tel. 01903/882140) cooks a mean chicken tikka, as well as appetizers such as *sag aloo* (potatoes and spinach).

WORTH SEEING

If you want info on the town's "glorious" past, grab an armload of historical pamphlets at the **Arundel Museum and Heritage Center** (61 High St., tel. 01903/882344). If you're fond of feathered things, the **Wildfowl and Wetlands Centre** (tel. 01903/883355), a mile north of Arundel's town center, is aflap with ducks, geese, and swans from all over the world. Admission is £4.75 and it's open daily 9–5:30.

ARUNDEL CASTLE • Arundel's hulking castle was built at the end of the 11th century by Roger de Montgomery, the earl of Arundel. Later, it was home to the dukes of Norfolk, including heroic Lord Howard, the earl of Surrey. You can wander around the giant corridors and admire paintings by big names like Van Dyck, Gainsborough, and Reynolds, and visit **Fitzalan Chapel,** site of the tombs of the Norfolk family. *Mill St., off High St., tel. 01903/883136. Admission £6.70. Open Apr.–last Fri. in Oct., Sun.–Fri. noon–5. Last admission at 4.*

CATHEDRAL OF OUR LADY AND ST. PHILIP HOWARD • Saint Philip Howard isn't quite a household name as far as saints go (he was only canonized in 1979), but he has a bulky hilltop cathedral named after him. Philip, the 13th Earl of Arundel, had a profligate youth but became a serious Catholic and ended up going against the Anglican Church of England in a big way. He was imprisoned by Queen Elizabeth I in the Tower of London, where he died of malnutrition (or poison, according to some). He was a martyr before he became an official Catholic saint, and in 1868 the Duke of Norfolk commissioned this cathedral in his honor. Saint Philip's remains are kept in a shrine in the north transept. The first week in June is the **Corpus Christi Festival** (tel. 01903/882297), a celebration that culminates in a carpet of flowers some 90 ft long being laid along the central aisle of the cathedral, followed by a procession to the castle. *King's St., at London Rd., tel. 01903/882297. Admission free. Open daily 9–6 or dusk if earlier.*

OUTDOOR ACTIVITIES

The main outdoor attraction is the **South Downs,** with relatively smooth walking paths that meander through peaceful rural countryside. The longest and most famous path is the **South Downs Way** (*see* Chapter Basics, *above*). Other good options are the four walks, ranging from 4 to 9½ mi, outlined in the pamphlet "Four Walks From Arundel Youth Hostel," available at the hostel (*see* Where to Sleep, *above*). One of the best is the 9½-mi trek along the river to **Bignor Roman Villa** (tel. 01798/869259), an ancient ruin. Admission to the villa, with its 82-ft mosaic, is £3.35. It's open June–September, daily 10–6, March–May and October, Tuesday–Sunday 10–5. If a 19-mi hike seems a bit long for a day's walk, you can take the train to Amberley, 4 mi north of Arundel, and walk from there.

NEAR ARUNDEL

THE BODY SHOP TOUR

You've heard the hype, you've smelled the mango-placenta foot lotion, you've been to the mall, now visit the factory. The tour lasts about 1 hour and 20 minutes and takes you through the entire process, from the selection of ingredients to how the unguents and ointments are prepared and packaged. Is it PC or just PR? You decide; call to reserve a space. Take the train to the nearby town of Littlehampton, then call The Body Shop Tour Taxi (tel. 01903/715117) for a ride to the factory (50p). *The Body Shop, Watesmead, Littlehampton, tel. 01903/844044. Admission £3.95. Open Mon.–Sat. 10–3:40. Guided tours every 20 mins.*

THE SOUTH'S STATELIEST HOMES

Pity those poor English aristocrats! On the one hand, they are expected to live a conspicuously regal life, appropriate to the enormous houses—stuffed to the gills with Gainsborough daubs and Louis XV furniture—that they live in. On the other hand, their ability to support this lifestyle is compromised by the day-to-day costs of keeping the shine on such abodes, which can take the form of a 4,000-acre estate with a mansion of 365 rooms. What to do? Some aristos decided to sell their gilded holdings—lock, stock, and Adam fireplaces—at auction and move to a nice manageable little apartment in London. Many others, however, decided to open the doors to you and me—and bless them for it. Today, thousands of travelers surge onto the Stately House Trail every year, and many discover there's nothing like an idyllic afternoon spent at a great English treasure house. Happily, Kent and Sussex possess one of the greatest concentrations of ancestral houses in Great Britain, and here we explore the best. So get ready to enjoy the Lifestyles of the Rich and Titled. Just remember: don't go leaping over any velvet ropes.

PETWORTH

Twelve mi northwest of Arundel, Petworth House, one of the National Trust's greatest treasures, stands in a particularly picturesque stretch of Sussex. Art lovers adore this place, as its sumptuous interiors were immortalized in some of the most beautiful watercolors of J. M .W. Turner, the noted proponent of romanticism. Inside, ancestors peer down at you from portraits painted by Gainsborough, Reynolds, and Van Dyck. Outside are a dreamy 700-acre deer park, designed by the famous Capability Brown; a near-perfect village, Wisborough Green; and the town of Petworth itself, a jewel studded with old, narrow streets and timbered houses. *Tel. 01798/342207. Admission £5.50; gardens only £1. House open Apr.–Oct., Sat.–Wed. 1–5:30; last admission 4:30. Gardens open Apr.–June and Sept.–Oct., Sat.–Wed. noon–6; July and Aug., Sat.–Wed. 11–6. Park open daily 8–dusk.*

PENSHURST PLACE

At the center of the hamlet of Penshurst (from Tunbridge Wells follow A26 and B2176), one of England's finest medieval manor houses, Penshurst Place, lies hidden behind a walled garden. While retaining its Baron's Hall dating back to the 14th century, the house is mainly Elizabethan, having been in the Sidney family for centuries. It still is. The most famous Sidney is the Elizabethan poet, Sir Philip, author of

Arcadia. The Baron's Hall, topped in 1341 with a timber roof, is truly eye-knocking—you'll need a chin wrap when studying its soaring ceiling. While the little hamlet of Penshurst is basically just an appendage of the "Great House," it is a delightful destination in its own right, centered as it is around pretty-as-a-picture Leicester Square. *Tel. 01892/870307. Admission: House and grounds £5.70; grounds only £4.20. House open Mar. weekends noon–5:30, Apr.–Oct., daily noon–5:30; grounds open daily 11–6; last admission 30 min before closing.*

HEVER CASTLE

For some, 13th-century Hever—located just 3 mi west of Penshurst Place—fits the stereotype of what a castle should look like, all turrets and battlements, the whole encircled by a water lily moat. Hever's main attraction is that it was the home of ill-fated Anne Boleyn, second wife of Henry VIII and mother of Queen Elizabeth. It was here that she was courted by Henry, who later gave Hever to his fourth wife, Anne of Cleves. The place was acquired in 1903 by American millionaire William Waldorf Astor, who built an entire Tudor village to house his staff and had the gardens laid out in Italianate style, with a large topiary maze. *Near Edenbridge, tel. 01732/865224. Admission: Castle and grounds £7.30; grounds only £5.80. Castle open Apr.–Oct., daily noon–5; Mar. and Nov., daily 11–4; grounds open daily Apr.–Oct., 11–6; last admission 30 mins before closing.*

CHARTWELL

Chartwell was Sir Winston Churchill's home from 1922 until his death in 1965. Standing 9 mi north of Hever Castle, the Victorian house was acquired by the National Trust and has been decorated to appear as it did in Churchill's lifetime—even down to a half-smoked cigar in an ashtray. To arrive here from Hever, take the minor roads B2027 and B2026 north. *Near Westerham, tel. 01732/866368. Admission: House and garden £5.50; garden and studio only £2.75. Open Apr.–June and Sept.–Oct., Wed.–Sun. 11–5; July–Aug., Tues.–Sun. 11–5; last admission 4:15.*

KNOLE

From a distance, Knole—home to the Sackville family since 1603—looks like a small town. It's that large, comprised of countless rooms, courtyards, and portals. It was begun in the 15th century and grew almost exponentially. Today, you'll need most of an afternoon to explore its collection of tapestries, embroidered furnishings, and other delights—including an amazing Stuart-era staircase and the most famous set of 17th-century silver furniture to survive. The noted writer Vita Sackville-West grew up at Knole and set her novel *The Edwardians* here. Set in a 1,000-acre deer park, the house lies in the center of Sevenoaks, opposite St. Nicholas Church; to get there from Chartwell, drive north to Westerham, then pick up A25 and head east for 8 mi. *Tel. 01732/450608. Admission: £5; gardens £1; grounds free. House open Apr.–Oct., Wed.–Sat. noon–4, Sun. 11–5; gardens open May–Sept., 1st Wed. of each month 11–4 (last admission one hr before close); grounds always open.*

IGHTHAM MOTE

If you've ever dreamed of a house that could have been the childhood home of King Arthur, this is it. Like a vision out of the Middle Ages, Ightham Mote is a particularly classic example of a 14th-century manor house. Well, there are no turrets or Rapunzel windows—this is not a castle—but the storybook, medieval aura is so tangible you can taste it. There's a little stone bridge over a moat, and interiors that will please any antiquarian. Finding Ightham Mote requires careful navigation—it's 7 mi east of Sevenoaks—but it is worth the effort. An extensive restoration program of the house is ongoing; be sure to call for opening times. To reach the house from Sevenoaks, take A25 east to A227 (8 mi) and follow the signs. *Ivy Hatch, Sevenoaks, tel. 01732/810378. Admission £5. Open Apr.–Oct., Sun., Mon., and Wed.–Fri. 11–5:30.*

LEEDS CASTLE

The bubbling River Medway runs right through Maidstone, Kent's county seat, with its backdrop of chalky downs. Only 5 mi east on A20 stands Leeds Castle, a fairy-tale stronghold commanding two small islands on a peaceful lake. Leeds is among the most beautiful of Britain's great medieval fortresses, though today its incomparable setting makes it anything but warlike. This was a favorite home of many English queens, and Henry VIII liked the place so much he had it converted from a fortress into a grand palace. Inside the house is over-restored but has a fine collection of paintings and furniture. The castle is 18 mi east of Sevenoaks, 19 mi northwest of Tunbridge Wells, 12 mi east of Ightham. To get to Maidstone from Ightham, go east along A20 and then A25. *Tel. 01622/765400. Admission: Castle and grounds £9.30, grounds only £7.30. Open Mar.–Oct., daily 10–5; Nov.–Feb., daily 10–3. Castle closed Sat. on last weekend in June and first weekend in July.*

SISSINGHURST CASTLE

One of the most famous gardens in the world, Sissinghurst is nestled deep in the Kentish countryside, around the remains of a moated Tudor castle. Unpretentiously beautiful, quintessentially English, they were laid out in the 1930s by the writer Vita Sackville-West (one of the Sackvilles of Knole) and her husband, the diplomat Harold Nicolson. The grounds are at their best in June and July, when the roses are in bloom. From Leeds Castle, make your way south on B2163 and A274 through Headcorn, then follow signs. Admission is often restricted since space is limited: the best times to come are outside the summer months of June–August, and Wed.–Fri. after 4. *Cranbrook, tel. 01580/715330. Admission £6. Open Apr.–mid-Oct., Tues.–Fri. 1–6:30, weekends £10–5:30.*

HISTORIC HAMPSHIRE

Beyond Portsmouth and Southampton—two modern metropolises that have seen better days—lies one of the most delightful vacation destinations in Britain: the **Isle of Wight,** made world famous by Queen Vicky, who moved into grand Osborne House, designed by her very own Prince Albert. Cowes, with its great regattas, also remains a lure. But most Londoners who head down this way for the weekend are not interested in grand Renaissance-style palaces or millionaire yachting parties. They, and other pale Britons, are just out desperately trying to tan on cloudy summer days. Before you take in the sun and surf, why not first opt, however, for some more cultured diversions in **Winchester?**

WINCHESTER

History, history, and more history. That's all anyone hears about when they walk into an English tourist office. But Winchester, the "ancient capital of England," does take the historical cake. The first king of England, Egbert, was crowned here in AD 827, and Winchester's Great Hall was the seat of government until the Norman invasion of 1066. (It was also allegedly the home base of King Arthur and his Knights of the Round Table, but, then again, so were Tintagel in Cornwall and a few other places.) William the Conqueror had himself crowned in London first, but thought it prudent to repeat the ceremony here. He also brought a fair amount of prestige to the city by commissioning the local monastery to produce the *Domesday Book,* a record of the general census taken in England in 1085. If that isn't enough, Winchester Cathedral was also the center of religion in England until Canterbury rose to power in the 13th century.

Not surprisingly, Winchester has some incredible old buildings. Besides the fantastic cathedral, Winchester College and several original Tudor Houses (which look like they were built without a straight-edge) remain standing in feats of sheer stubbornness. While Winchester goes out of its way to preserve its past, it also embraces the future in the form of fast-food chains and retail clothing outlets along otherwise photogenic High Street. Happily, the city's blend of medieval and mall culture is fairly fluid and inoffensive.

BASICS

Winchester's **tourist office** (The Guildhall, Broadway, tel. 01962/840500) is one of the nicest, neatest, and best-stocked around; it's also open year-round. **Lloyd's Bank** (High Street) and **Barclays Bank** (Jewry Street) have poor rates for cash but good rates for checks (both charge a 1% commission with a £3 minimum). The main **post office** (Middle Brook St., SO23 8WA, tel. 0345/223344) is open Monday–Saturday 9–5:30. **Winnall Launderette** (27 Garbbett Rd., tel. 01962/840658), the only one in town, charges about £2 to wash and £1 to dry a load, £5.50 for a service wash. It's about a 15-minute walk from the tourist office: Follow the road north over the river, bear left onto Magdalen Road, turn right on Alresford Road, left on Winnall Manor Road, and left on Garbbett Road.

COMING AND GOING • Winchester is on a direct British Rail line from London's Waterloo (2–3 hourly, 1 hr, £16.50 single) that continues on to Portsmouth and Southampton. Buy tickets at the kiosk on Station Road (tel. 0345/484950). Buses leave from the **Winchester Bus Station,** across the street from the tourist office, as well as from signposted stops on Broadway. **National Express** (tel. 0990/

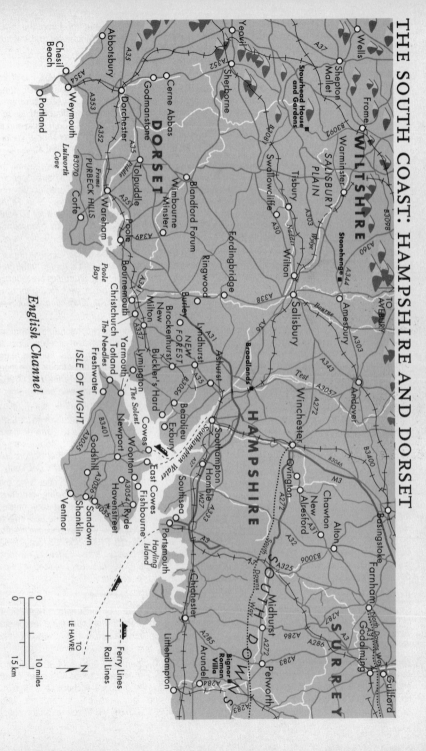

WILTSHIRE

HAMPSHIRE

DORSET

SURREY

SOUTH DOWNS

ISLE OF WIGHT

English Channel

Chesil Beach
Portland
Weymouth
Abbotsbury
Lulworth Cove
Corfe
Wareham
Dorchester
Godmanstone
Cerne Abbas
Sherborne
Yeovil
Wells
Shepton Mallet
Frome
Warminster
Stourhead House and Gardens
Tisbury
Swallowcliffe
Wilton
Nadder
Wylye
Stonehenge
SALISBURY PLAIN
Amesbury
TO AVEBURY
Andover
Salisbury
Fordingbridge
Ringwood
Blandford Forum
Wimborne Minster
Tolpuddle
Piddle
Frome
PURBECK HILLS
Poole
Poole Bay
Bournemouth
Christchurch
Milton
New Milton
Burley
Brockenhurst
NEW FOREST
Lyndhurst
Ashurst
Broadlands
Winchester
Ovington
New Alresford
Chawton
Alton
Basingstoke
Farnham
Godalming
Guildford
North Downs Way
Test
Bourne
Avon
The Needles
Freshwater
Totland
Yarmouth
The Solent
Lymington
Buckler's Hard
Beaulieu
Cowes
Exbury
Southampton
Southampton Water
Hamble
Newport
Godshill
Ventnor
Shanklin
Sandown
Ryde
East Cowes
Wootton
Havenstreet
Fishbourne
Hayling Island
Southsea
Portsmouth
Chichester
Littlehampton
Arundel
Bignor Roman Villa
Midhurst
Petworth
P'worth

English Channel

Ferry Lines
Rail Lines
TO LE HAVRE
N

0   10 miles
0   15 km

808080) runs buses to London (2 hrs, £9–£11 single) every two hours; buy your ticket from the driver. **Stagecoach Hampshire** (tel. 01256/464501) is the main company serving Winchester and the surrounding area, or call the council's information line for the bus services throughout Hampshire (tel. 01962/846924).

WHERE TO SLEEP • If you're feeling decadent and have the funds to support your habit, the **Wykeham Arms** (75 Kingsgate St., tel. 01962/853834, fax 01962/854411) is a luxurious place to eat, drink, be merry, and pass out. You can be housed and fed dinner, accompanied by some very tasty beverages, for £69–£99 for a single (though one small single goes for just £45), £10 more for a double. If you're a little less flush, several B&Bs lie southwest of the cathedral, especially along Christchurch Road and its intersecting streets. Many B&Bs don't have signs, so look for listings in the *Winchester Official Visitor's Guide* available from the tourist office. It also features great maps and tons of useful information.

Brymer House. In a quiet corner of Winchester, this double-fronted Victorian building provides all the home comforts. You can swing a couple of cats in the two palatial rooms (£45–£50 for a double), or curl up in the separate TV room, a cozy nook with an open fire. Owners Guy and Fizzy Warren occupy one half of the house, so there's a separate entrance for guests. No smoking in the bedrooms. *29 St. Faith's Rd., St. Cross., SO23 9QD, tel. 01962/867428, fax 01962/868624. From bus station, walk for 10 mins, or take Bus 47 to Romans Rd., walk down this, turning right on Kingsgate Rd. (which becomes St. Faith's Rd). 2 rooms with bath. Cash only.*

Mrs. P. Patton. With a grandfather clock, a large dog, and a cat, this B&B has a homey feel. The immaculate condition of the house is indicative of owner Mrs. Patton's vigilance. Breakfast is served in the conservatory. Singles are £22–£25, doubles £30–£35. If you stay more than one night, doubles are reduced slightly. *12 Christchurch Rd., SO23 9SR, tel. 01962/854272. From bus station, walk for 10 mins, or take Bus 47 to Romans Rd., cross St. Cross Rd., and go to end of Beaufort Rd., Christchurch Rd. is on left. 2 rooms without bath. Cash only.*

Royal. At this classy hotel, you'll find an attractive walled garden and some very comfortable bedrooms. It's within easy reach of the cathedral, but lies on a quiet side street. You can have an excellent lunch in the bar, or a fuller meal in the moderately priced restaurant. This is a Best Western hotel, and one of the swankier links in the chain. Some of the rooms are in a recent extension, but the older rooms have more atmosphere. Doubles run about £100 to £110. *St. Peter St., SO23 8BS, tel. 01962/840840, fax 01962/841582. From bus station, turn right down High St., right at St. Peter St. 75 rooms with bath.*

Shawlands. Even if you show up looking schlumpy, Bill and Kathy Pollock will treat you like royalty—which is some compensation for the 2-mi trek to the suburbs. The very comfortable doubles go for £38–£44, singles for £27–£30, with discounts for multinight stays. Mrs. Pollock makes her own delicious bread and brews coffee in a press pot, so breakfast here is a joy. Smoking not allowed. *46 Kilham La., SO22 5QD, tel. and fax 01962/861166. Take any bus heading up Romsey Rd., get off at Battery Hill, walk to the next stoplight (Kilham La.), turn right, and walk 2 blocks. 4 rooms, 1 with bath. Cash only.*

HOSTELS • **City Mill YHA.** During the day it's a National Trust tourist attraction. But after 5 PM, this 18th-century mill on an island in the middle of the River Itchen becomes the most amazing youth hostel in the South. Views of the river from the garden are top-notch. The sound of rushing water outside the window soothes the nerves and helps to drown out the sounds of other sleepers. The best time to stay is during the summer, since the common room isn't heated, but book way ahead because it's also fairly small. Beds cost £9.15. *1 Water La., Hampshire SO23 OEJ, tel. 01962/853723, fax 01962/855524. From tourist office, turn right on Broadway and cross the bridge. 31 beds. Curfew 11 PM, lockout 10–5. Open mid-Feb.–June, Mon.–Sat; July–Aug., daily; Sept.–Oct., Tues.–Sat.; Nov.–Dec., Fri.–Sat. Closed Dec. 21–mid-Feb.*

FOOD

Simple basics may be obtained from markets such as **Sainsbury's** (Middlebrook Street, off High Street) or **Gateway** (High Street). Ethnic restaurants are strangely absent in the town center, but a few cluster near the train station. Pubs, many located on Broadway, offer cheap alternatives to the town's few decent restaurants.

The **Cathedral Refectory** (Cathedral Yard, tel. 01962/853224), open daily 9:30–5 (4:30 in winter), serves snacks and cooked meals such as soups, tomato, pesto, and sheep's cheese with green salad, and Welsh rarebit with watercress salad. Inside the landmark God Begot House, **Richoux** (101 High St., tel. 01962/841790) cooks a mean vegetable stir-fry and serves up fancy sandwiches in carpeted, cushioned, Tudor luxury. The **Spinning Wheel** (42 High St., tel. 01962/865709) will fill you up on the cheap side with giant sandwiches and quiche. If you're staying at the hostel, grab some good Chinese takeout from **Wonderful** (6 Bridge St., tel. 01962/862268), just around the corner. One of the best options in town is **Nine the Square** (9 Great Minster St., The Square, tel. 01962/864004). This restaurant and wine bar (closed on Sun.) makes the most of its prime position opposite the cathedral. The menu, which the downstairs wine bar shares with the more sedate dining area upstairs, changes regularly, but may feature Royal Gressingham Duck and, in season, game, while a selection of homemade pastas is always available. Vegetarians will also find something to please.

WORTH SEEING

Once upon a time, Winchester was the nation's capital, until it was so rudely supplanted by London. Although the town's glory days are over, it's still full of majestic sights—the majority of which are clustered near the cathedral. Winchester's center is laid out in typical Roman fashion—the streets are at right angles to one another and the town center is rectangular. To the north of the tourist office (and running parallel to Broadway and High Street) are the North Walls—really just fragments of Winchester's medieval fortifications—and to the south is Winchester College. The River Itchen serves as the eastern border of the city center, and the youth hostel is built directly over the river. If you're not already staying at the hostel (see Where to Sleep, above), you can (and should) check out the grounds, especially the mill. For nonguests, it costs £1 to tour the grounds, which are open April–October, Wednesday–Sunday 11–4:45, as well as on weekends in March (same hours).

For a nice stroll, follow the winding **Water Meadows** walk south along the River Itchen to the 12th-century St. Cross Hospital. The tourist office has several guidebooks (£1–£3) that identify sights along the way. The walk takes about 1½ hours round-trip. For an excellent view of the town, hike up **St. Giles's Hill**, visible from behind King Alfred's statue. Numerous roads and paths lead up the hill, including a signposted route near the beginning of the Water Meadows walk.

The longer you spend in Winchester, the less you'll want to leave. Its YHA hostel is one of the finest in England, near dozens of walking and hiking trails that cut through local fields. Streams flow through town, and centuries-old bells stir the air on Sunday.

THE GREAT HALL • This hall has been the site of crucial historical events for centuries: Parliament held its first meeting here in 1246; Sir Walter Raleigh was tried for treason here *twice*; and the infamous Judge Jeffreys sentenced Dame Alice Lisle to be burned at the stake for sheltering a fugitive after Monmouth's Rebellion in 1685. These days, most visitors come to check out the Great Hall because of an event that didn't happen here. To the right, just past the entrance, hangs a painted wooden disc about 18 ft in diameter. This is claimed to be the Round Table of King Arthur fame, but don't you believe it. The hall was built early in the 13th century, and a blank table hung on the wall for the first 150 years. In a fit of megalomania, Henry VIII commissioned the table to be painted with an Arthurian figure made after his own likeness. *Upper High St., at Castle Hill, tel. 01962/846476. From train station, walk down Station Rd. (stay to the left at fork) and follow signs. Admission free. Open daily 10–5 (closes at 4 winter weekends).*

MILITARY MUSEUMS • Winchester's rich military heritage stems from the long, affable relationship between the city's army barracks and Winchester College, which supplied well-bred officer material over the years. If you walk through the garden at the Great Hall and up the stairs, you'll see several cannons and tanks parked outside a rather plain building. These are the Peninsula Barracks, home to many of Winchester's military museums. The **Gurkha Museum** (admission £1.50) tells the story of the mercenary regiment recruited by the British from among the Gurkhas, who live in Nepal and northern Bengal. Founded in the early 19th century, the Gurkhas were among the most feared and revered military units ever, and saw action in the Falkland Islands and the Gulf War. Learn about the symbolic kukri swords, traditionally worn in battle, then buy one in the gift shop (that's right, short swords that U.S. customs officials probably won't like). Some great hats are on display in the **Royal Hussars Museum** (admission free), in the same building. The highlight is the actual armoire wherein a trooper hid for three years (!?) after getting lost behind enemy lines during World War I. *Peninsula Barracks, Romsey Rd. Gurkha Museum: tel. 01962/828536. Open Mon.–Sat. 10–5. Royal Hussars Museum: tel. 01962/828541. Open Tues.–Fri. 10–12:45 and 1:15–4, weekends noon–4.*

The **Royal Green Jackets Museum,** across the courtyard, has guns, medals, swastikas, and a book labeled EX LIBRIS ADOLF HITLER. Fascists would go wild over this place. The **Light Infantry Museum,** in the same building, has spoils from more recent conflicts: the civil war in Northern Ireland and the Gulf War.

Peninsula Barracks, Romsey Rd. Royal Green Jackets Museum: tel. 01962/863846. Open Mon.–Sat. 10–1 and 2–5, Sun. noon–4. Admission £2. Light Infantry Museum: tel. 01962/828550. Admission free. Open Mon.–Sat. 10–5, Sun. noon–4. Last admissions to both museums 1 hr before closing.

WINCHESTER CATHEDRAL • Westminster Abbey may have more royalty buried within its walls, but Winchester Cathedral is still a strong contender for the Most Prestigious Dead People Award, with the remains of Saxon kings, the Viking conqueror King Canute, his wife Queen Emma, and even Jane Austen. Aside from its celebrity corpses, this cathedral also has the distinction of being one of the longest medieval churches in Europe. Building began in 1079, and the Norman architecture (low, rounded arches) remains in the transepts and the crypt. The nave was remodeled in the 14th century by William of Wykeham in the Gothic style. With magnificent stained-glass windows filling the pointed arches, Winchester Cathedral is one of the most remarkable and massive edifices in the Christian world.

The church's **library** houses an illuminated 12th-century copy of the Winchester Bible, as well as a copy of Bede's 8th-century *Historia Ecclesiastica.* The Vulgate (Latin) Bible, printed on the skins of more than 250 calves and elaborately decorated with gold leaf and cobalt-blue lapis lazuli, is embellished with painstaking detail (check out the patterns on the subjects' stockings). The Bible was never completed, but the sketches for the unfinished sections are on display. Also on display is a 17th-century American Bible (made in Massachusetts) translated into the language of the Algonquin tribe; a Ptolemaic map of the world (circa AD 150); a pair of 17th-century globes; and the massive library of the late bishop of Winchester, George Morley.

The **Triforium Gallery** holds, among other less interesting trinkets, the Shaftesbury Bowl, a glass bowl from the 10th century that is believed to have held the heart of King Canute, who died in Shaftesbury in 1035. Occasionally, a jarring announcement breaks out over the loudspeakers, reciting the Lord's Prayer and asking you to join in. Amazingly, the church's majesty is so penetrating that even this techno-spirituality is moving. *5 The Close, tel. 01962/857200. Cathedral admission free (£2.50 donation requested). Open daily 7:15–6:30 (though East End closes at 5, and many areas are closed during Sun. services and evensong at 5:30 or 3:30 on Sun.). Library and gallery admission £1.50. Call for hours.*

WINCHESTER COLLEGE • Bishop William of Wykeham, who has his own chapel in Winchester Cathedral, founded Winchester College in 1382. From April through September, take a guided tour of this 600-year-old landmark for £2.50, or wander around the grounds unattended, affronted only occasionally by signs reading PRIVATE, KEEP OUT. At some point make your way through the courtyards and through the giant, space-age glass doors into the college **chapel** for an up-close look at the stained-glass windows and the delicately vaulted ceiling designed by Wykeham's master carpenter, Hugh Herland. On your way in or out of the college, look for the inconspicuous yellow house next door where Jane Austen finished her novel *Persuasion,* and died at the age of 42. *College St., tel. 01962/621209 or 01962/ 621227. Admission £2.50. Open Mon.–Sat. 10–1 and 2–5, Sun. 2–5. Call to arrange a guided tour (for groups of ten or more), or turn up at 11, 2, or 3:15 for unbooked tours (Apr.–Sept.).*

WOLVESEY CASTLE • No, you can't go into that fantastic manor house next door—the current Bishop of Winchester lives there. But you can check out the ruins of Wolvesey Castle, which was once home to Winchester's medieval bishops, as well as the site of Mary Tudor and Philip II of Spain's wedding party. At the time it was built, Wolvesey was the largest private dwelling in England. So much for the clergy's vow of humility. *College St., tel. 01962/854766. Admission £1.80. Open Apr.–Sept., daily 10–6; Oct., daily 10–5.*

AFTER DARK

Winchester, although well-suited to day-tripping tourists, is fairly dull at night. The entire nightlife scene consists of a handful of pubs and the **Theatre Royal** (Jewry Street), which features small productions of bedroom farces and an occasional Shakespeare play between screenings of second-run films. Despite the pubs being the only source of entertainment for most people, the price of beer ranges from reasonable to extortionate.

Although the patrons at **India Arms** (High St., tel. 01962/852985) sometimes fight, the pub has a good jukebox and usually packs 'em in. If it's centuries-old beer stains you're after, try the pints at the **Royal Oak** (Royal Oak Pass, tel. 01962/861136), which has the distinction of being the oldest verifiable pub in Britain (over 900 years!). If you just want a quiet beer, drop into the **Old Vine** (8 Great Minster St., tel. 01962/854616). The closest you'll come to a club scene is the **Guildhall Tavern** (High St., tel. 01962/ 856301), a trendy pub in an old building with club sounds, or **The Porthouse** (Upper Brook St., tel. 01962/869397), whose three stories escalate from quiet (basement) to a rollicking dance venue at the top, with different theme nights. Try also the smaller **Charles House** (22 Sussex St., tel. 01962/863848).

NEAR WINCHESTER

JANE AUSTEN'S HOUSE

The former home of the woman responsible for such works as *Emma* and *Pride and Prejudice* is so low-key you may mistakenly start toward one of the exotic-looking, thatched-roof houses nearby before noticing the small OPEN sign in front of this simple, 17th-century brick structure. Austen lived here from 1809 to 1817, the years in which she wrote her six major novels. Around the house, handwritten letters hang behind glass, and her jewelry and a lock of blondish hair are on display. Snooping around, you'll see the "creaking door," which alerted her if someone was coming (and enabled her to put away her manuscript), as well as mannequins dressed as the main characters from her books. When it comes right down to it, though, this house is mainly a thrill for fans who simply want to *be* where she lived and worked, and not for its exhibits. *Chawton Village, tel. 01420/83262. From Winchester's bus station, take Bus 64 or X64 to Alton, alight at Chawton, walk back across roundabout, and follow signs. Admission £2.50. Open Mar.–Dec., daily 11–4:30; Jan.–Feb., weekends 11–4:30.*

ISLE OF WIGHT

When southern Brits rave about the Isle of Wight (pronounced white), they're actually giving themselves a boomerang compliment, because the Isle of Wight is a microcosm of the South. Who would have thought this small island could contain the best kind of English landscape?" Paul Theroux asked, in his *Kingdom by the Sea*. Green hills and fields cover the center, while towns on the coast alternate between tacky and tranquil. **Ryde** in the east and **Newport** in the center are the island's main towns, but you'll find some real gems only a brief way off the beaten track—**Ventnor**, on the south coast, and tiny hamlets on the western end such as **Totland** and **Freshwater**. Inland, untrammeled villages such as **Godshill** and fabled houses with royal connections (specifically **Carisbrooke Castle** and **Osborne House**) definitely warrant the boat ride over.

> Winchester still maintains a number of almshouses that provide food and shelter for the elderly, as they have for hundreds of years. On your wanderings, look for the alms recipients dressed in traditional black gowns.

The southeast coast of Wight was once a popular destination for young families, old folks, and people on tight budgets with a desire to trade in the big island for a smaller, more sedate one, if just for a weekend. Nowadays, most can't afford to spend their hard-earned pounds on both the ferry ride and the island's B&Bs (which aren't so cheap anymore). It's generally more affordable to stay on the mainland, explaining why former island boomtowns such as **Sandown** and **Shanklin** have degenerated into crass resorts with grimy piers and tacky cafés.

Although the Isle of Wight was pummeled by Axis bombs during World War II, the residents rebuilt their homes with great attention to detail. Thanks to their persistence, many island towns retain a tranquillity and beauty that even the tourist trade can't completely destroy. In the end, it's the island's natural beauty that makes a visit truly rewarding. The web of footpaths that covers the entire island continues to attract backpackers and others who don't mind having to walk to find something good. The west coast, in particular, has been developed primarily for people with walking shoes, good taste, and (sadly) a lot of money. But you can still find some relatively affordable places to situate yourself and see the beautiful coastline and demure Victorian architecture that neither Nazi bombs nor commercialization could destroy.

BASICS

The Isle of Wight has an unnatural number of tourist centers, all of which—except where indicated below—are open Monday–Saturday 9–5. Most are open daily until 7 in the holiday season, and until 9 in the main centers during July and August. For general information on the isle, call 01983/813818, fax 01983/823032, or go to the centers at **Cowes** (The Arcade, Fountain Quay, tel. 01983/291914), **Newport** (South St., in bus station parking lot, tel. 01.983/525450), or **Ryde** (Western Esplanade, tel. 01983/562905). Other offices include: **Sandown** (8 High St., tel. 01983/403886), **Shanklin** (67 High St., tel. 01983/862942), **Ventnor** (34 High St., tel. 01983/853625), closed October–April, and **Yarmouth** (The Quay, tel. 01983/760015), closed October–April. The **Thomas Cook** (47 High St., tel. 01983/273400) in Newport is a decent place to change money; or try changing at banks in Cowes or Ryde.

SOME PLACE THERE IS THAT DOESN'T LOVE A BRIDGE

Some people believe that island locals refuse to build a bridge between Portsmouth and Ryde because they want to keep out tourists, and they're only half wrong. This island depends entirely on tourism and would like nothing better than more tourist dollars year-round. But a bridge or tunnel doesn't mean more tourists coming to stay in hotels and to eat in restaurants—it means more day-tripping coaches full of big-eyed lazies who get home by nightfall and don't spend a penny. The bottom line for islanders is simple: Building a bridge would mean no big spenders.

COMING AND GOING

The only way on or off the island is by water or private plane. No ferry reservations are required for foot or bicycle passengers. **Wightlink** (tel. 0990/827744) runs car and passenger ferries from Lymington in Dorset to Yarmouth on the island's west side (twice hourly, or hourly on winter weekends, 30 mins, £8.20 standard return or £6.60 day return); and from Portsmouth to Ryde (same frequency as above, 15 mins, £10.50 for standard return or £7 same-day return) and Fishbourne, a few miles west of Ryde (hourly or twice-hourly, 40 mins, £8.20 return). **Hovertravel** (tel. 01983/811000) has hovercrafts from Southsea to Ryde (10 mins, £10.20 return, £8.40 same-day return), but they don't transport cars. **Red Funnel** (tel. 02380/334010) runs ferries from Southampton to East Cowes (hourly, 1hr, £7.80 return), and pedestrian-only catamarans from Southampton to West Cowes (twice hourly, 25 mins, £11.80 return). Bikes go free on ferries, but you can't take them on catamarans.

Note that British Rail heads to **Portsmouth and Southsea Station** (Commercial Rd., tel. 0345/484950) frequently from London's Waterloo. If you're headed to the Isle of Wight, continue on to **Portsmouth Harbour Station** (The Hard, tel. 0345/484950), ¾ mi to the west. Tickets from London to either station cost £21.70 return. **National Express** (tel. 0990/808080) buses depart for London's Victoria Coach Station (2½ hrs, £9 single, £14.50–£17.50 return) eight times daily from the Isle of Wight terminal at Portsmouth Harbour. **Stagecoach** (tel. 02392/498894) operates many of the routes in the Portsmouth area.

GETTING AROUND

Newport, the island's main city, is right in the center of things. Ryde, Sandown, Shanklin, and Ventnor line the commercialized eastern shore from top to bottom, diminishing in size as they descend. Yarmouth and Freshwater are the major towns—major *villages* is closer to the mark—on the quieter west side. Cowes and (fairly unpleasant) East Cowes are central hubs on the north coast, facing the Solent (the stretch of water between the Isle of Wight and Southampton). All the roads on the island were designed for horse-drawn carriages, so they always seem crammed with traffic. Car-rental agencies on the southeast coast, such as **Wilton Car Hire** (72 Wilton Park Rd., Shanklin, tel. 01983/864414) and **South Wight Rentals** (10 Osborne Rd., Shanklin, tel. 01983/864263), tend to charge less than those agencies closer to the entry ports, but you should still expect to pay about £25 a day or £140 per week. At most agencies you must be 25 to rent.

BY BIKE • Bikes are an enjoyable (and convenient) way to get around the island: Ask for the free leaflet and/or a trail guide (90p) from a tourist office, which will also point you toward local rental shops. One of the best deals on the island is Sandown's **Island Cycle Hire** (17 Beachfield Rd., tel. 01983/407030), which charges £5 for four hours, £8.50 for eight, plus a £25 cash deposit and ID. They also offer a full repair service and sell loads of parts and accessories.

BY BUS • From Ryde, you can catch buses almost everywhere; from Cowes or Yarmouth you'll have to switch in Newport to cross the island. **Southern Vectis** (tel. 01983/827005) goes almost everywhere on the island, but its buses are infrequent and expensive. Pick up comprehensive schedules (50p) at the tourist office or at any of the four Southern Vectis offices, in **Cowes** (32 High St., tel. 01983/292082), **Newport** (bus station, tel. 01983/523831), **Ryde** (bus station, tel. 01983/562264), and **Shanklin** (49 Regent St., tel. 01983/862224). If you're crossing the island, you can save some cash by investing in a day pass (£5.20 in winter, £6.25 in summer).

BY TRAIN • Stagecoach's **Island Line** (tel. 01983/812591) bumps and squeaks along the eastern edge of the island, from Ryde Pier to Shanklin. At Smallbrook Junction, you can transfer to Victorian and Edwardian antique steam trains that chug along the **Steam Railway** (tel. 01983/882204) from the end of March through October, taking in Ashey, Havenstreet, and Wootton (£5.65 return). A day pass encompassing travel on the Island Line and Steam Railway services is available for £8. Call 01983/884343 for the "talking timetable."

WHERE TO SLEEP

The Isle of Wight used to attract many of its visitors with the promise of a cheap vacation. Now, you can hardly find a place for under £15 a head. If you want to be on the east side, Ventnor is the least spoiled town because it's off the train line; the surrounding steep hills also act as a tourist barrier. Ryde, Sandown, and Shanklin have a B&B on almost every block, but they're so devoid of island character you might as well have stayed in Eastbourne or Hastings on the mainland. Staying on the vastly superior west side costs more, but it's worth it. Wherever you stay, reserve in advance during the Cowes Week Yachting Festival (held in July or August).

One of the finest walks on the island is from Freshwater Bay along a raised grass mound known as Tennyson Downs, which, after about 3 mi, leads to the Needles, a natural rock formation vaguely shaped like the eye of a needle.

Brookside Forge Hotel. David and Jacqui Reynolds are a down-to-earth couple who run this quiet hotel with a mixture of tactful reserve and scrupulous attention to the whims of their guests. It's in a leafy road in Freshwater's center, just behind School Green Road and close to tennis courts, a swimming pool, and a basketball court. If the thought of all that exercise is a little daunting, then just veg out in the patio bar by the large terraced garden. Rooms are a steal at £20 per person. Phone ahead for a pick-up from the ferry at Yarmouth. *Brookside Rd,. Freshwater, PO40 9ER, tel. 01983/754644. 7 rooms with bath.*

Chalet Hotel. This old, seaside house has great character and is perched, like a castle, on a cliff that slowly cascades to the ocean. A pleasant terrace, gardens, and in-house bar are added bonuses, though the deciding factor might be the authentic Thai cuisine (not included in room price), offered between May and October, whose spicy aromas waft incongruously out of the kitchen all morning. The rooms are a good deal at £16.50 a head, rising to £18.50 in summer, slightly more for en suite. The hotel may close in winter. *The Esplanade, Ventnor, PO38 1TA, tel. 01983/852285. 13 rooms, 5 with bath.*

Farringford Hotel. Once the splendid home of the Victorian poet laureate Alfred, Lord Tennyson, this is now an unpretentious hotel, set next to Alum Bay, 19 mi northwest of Ventnor. The 18th-century house is set on 33 acres of grounds; outbuildings contain 24 self-catering suites and cottages, as well as standard bedrooms. You'll need to save some pennies to book here: Doubles range from £52 to £98, but the facilities are great. There's a restaurant, outdoor pool, croquet lawn, nine-hole golf course, tennis court, and lots of that fabulous Isle of Wight air, which, to quote the poet, is "worth six pence a pint." *Bedbury La., Freshwater PO40 9PE, near Alum Bay, tel. 01983/752500, fax 01983/756515. 68 rooms with bath.*

Island Charters. Jovial John Gallop runs one of the coolest sleeps on the island: cabins inside two ships moored in the Wootton estuary (between Cowes and Ryde). Hang out on deck sipping a pint, sleep in double beds or bunks, and have breakfast in the galley. Conditions may be lean, but you're at sea, matey! At £16 per person the price is good, so book ahead and ask for Cabin 5 on the M.V. Seawasp— a great double with its own bathroom and afterdeck (£17). *Barge La., Wootton Creek, PO33 4LB, tel. and fax 01983/882315. Take Bus 1 or 8 from Newport or Ryde to Wootton. 15 cabins, 1 with bath. Closed Nov.–Feb. Cash only.*

Sandford Lodge. The immaculate, nicely decorated rooms in this beautiful house go for £20–£25 per person. The friendly young couple that owns the place (which is no-smoking) makes you feel at ease. *61 The Avenue, Totland, PO30 0DN, tel. 01983/753478. 6 rooms, 5 with bath. Closed Dec.*

Sandpipers. If you've come to Wight to get away from it all and to have some serious outdoor fun, this is the right place. The large house lies off of desolately beautiful Freshwater Bay, close to the isle's best hiking and biking. The owners rent mountain bikes (£10 per day) and offer introductory parasailing lessons. Rooms are sparse and simple, but £18–£25 a head is not a bad deal for great surroundings; there is also a self-catering cottage available for a weekly rent of about £285. No reservations accepted. *Coastguard La., Freshwater Bay, PO40 9QX, tel. 01983/753634. Take Bus 7 or 7A from Newport to Freshwater Bay. 13 rooms, 10 with bath.*

Sea House. Owner Sonia Price has been running a B&B for years and will give you a warm welcome and lots of good advice about the isle. The clean rooms are £15 per person, a couple of pounds more in summer, but given that the doors don't lock, it feels more like you've been invited to stay at a friend's house. Two rooms have great ocean views. *Main Rd., Yarmouth, PO41 OUR, tel. 01983/760527, fax 01983/754364. About 1 mi east of town on the road to Newport just before the view point. 3 rooms, without bath.*

Spyglass Inn. This jolly pub at one end of Ventnor's Esplanade has three self-catering apartments to rent, all overlooking the sea. They're on either side of the pub, so that you don't get the late-night hullabaloo full blast, though still close enough to catch the alluring whiffs of locally caught crab and lobster from the pub's kitchen. Each is fully equipped and sports a small balcony. Expect to pay around £45 per night for two people, with discounts for longer stays. Reserve well ahead, as they're snapped up quickly. *The Esplanade, Ventnor, PO38 1JX, tel./fax 01983/855338. 3 apartments.*

HOSTELS • Totland Bay YHA. This hostel—by far the best budget base on the island—sits near cliffs and beautiful walks on the west side of the island. Most rooms are cozy and have large wooden dressers. Beds cost £10.15. *Hurst Hill, Totland, Isle of Wight PO39 OHD, tel. 01983/752165, fax 01983/756443. From Totland War Memorial, take road to left, go straight, turn left at Hurst Hill. 72 beds. Curfew 11 PM, lockout 10–5. Closed Nov.–mid-Feb. and Sun. Sept.–Oct., mid-Feb.–June.*

CAMPING • There are 21 campsites scattered around Wight, though more than half lie on the island's eastern side. The "Isle of Wight Camping and Touring Guide," a free pamphlet available from tourist offices, lists all campsites, prices, and facilities. Most campgrounds only open in summer, and rightly so; in winter you'd probably get blown away by gale-force winds.

The western side of the Isle of Wight has the most tranquil campsites. **Compton Farm** (Brook, 1 ½ mi east of Freshwater Bay on A3055 coast road, tel. 01983/740215) is one of the best rural sites surrounded by chalk downlands and within walking distance of the beach. Pitches cost £4 per night, and there are caravans available for a weekly rent (£130–£240), but book early. On the eastern side of the island, try the **Camping and Caravanning Club at Cheverton Farm** (tel. 01983/866414), in a countryside setting near the tiny village of Apse Heath, 2 mi from downtown Sandown off the A3056 Newport road. There are showers and kitchen on site; tent sites cost £3.65–£5.20 per person plus a flat pitch fee of £4.20 per site for use of the facilities (add £1.70 if you want electricity). A bit south of here is **Landguard Camping Park** (Landguard Manor Rd., tel. 01983/867028), which has good facilities, including laundry, free showers, and a pool, for £3.50–£5.50 per person, with a two-person minimum in summer. All the island's sites are generally closed October–April.

FOOD

If you thought food was a problem in southern England, wait until you reach the Isle of Wight. Owing to the lack of restaurants, B&Bs typically offer an evening meal for £6–£10. The **Gateway** supermarket chain has branches in most towns on the island. There's also a **Tesco** market in Ryde (Brading Road), and a **Safeway Superstore** (South Street) in Newport.

The **Royal Standard Pub** (School Green Rd., Freshwater, tel. 01983/753227) serves homemade English fare such as roasts and pies for around £4.50. Just off Yarmouth's pier, **Gossips Café** (The Square, tel. 01983/760646) has good sandwiches among its fast-food fare. Nearby, the **Wheatsheaf Inn** (Bridge Rd., Yarmouth, tel. 01983/760456) serves homemade dishes such as mushroom stroganoff, or fish or meat. In Cowes, **Tonino's** (8 Shooters Hill, tel. 01983/298464) has pizzas and chicken cacciatore. Newport's **Galley Coffee Shop** (Chapel Street, at Upper St. James Street) is above a former church that now hosts a crafts market and a place to head for pita sandwiches and quiche. In Ventnor, try the **Country House** (11 High St., tel. 01983/855500) for simple hearty meals.

WORTH SEEING

Queen Victoria's favorite vacation spot was the ostentatiously decorated **Osborne House** (1 mi SE of Cowes, tel. 01983/200022), where she died in 1901. The exterior—designed by Prince Albert himself—

is an homage to Italian Renaissance architecture, while the interior remains an unabashed tribute to one of the gaudiest periods of decor ever. All in all, an amazing place to peek at the domestic side of royalty. Admission is a high £6.90—though the house does contain some unique Victoriana. It's open Apr.–Sept., daily 10–6; Oct., daily 10–5. Catch Bus 4 from Ryde or Bus 5 from Newport, or either from East Cowes.

In 1647 Charles I was imprisoned in the Norman **Carisbrooke Castle** (tel. 01983/522107), 1¼ mi southwest of Newport. While the castle is run-of-the-mill, it makes a nice walk from East Cowes or Newport, but you need to walk ¼ mi anyway from where the bus lets you off (Bus 6, 7A, 11, or 12 from Newport, Yarmouth, or Ventnor). Castle admission is £4.50, open Apr.–Sept., daily 10–6; Oct., daily 10–5; Nov.–Mar. daily 10–4. The very last castle built by Henry VIII, from bricks of wrecked churches, was **Yarmouth Castle** (Yarmouth Harbor, tel. 01983/760678). You can see bits of churches sticking out of the walls and floor. Upstairs, don't miss the carved hand protruding from the floorboards, clutching a cross. Admission is £2.10, and it's open daily April–September, 10–6, October until 5.

THE WEST COUNTRY

UPDATED BY ROBERT ANDREWS

The southwestern peninsula known as the West Country is one of the most magical and enchanted places in England. Outside of the numerous historic cathedral towns, glorified maritime ports, and tourist-laden fishing villages, the region can resemble an ancient ghost town. Scattered throughout the countryside are eroded castles and enigmatic prehistoric stone structures that continue to evoke mythic voices, legends, and speculation. To many, the mystery of the West Country is embodied by the legend of King Arthur, who is thought to have been born in Tintagel, to have battled with Mordred at Bodmin Moor, and to be buried in Glastonbury. While the tourist dollar may have guaranteed the existence of an Arthurian-themed pub in many a town, it's still tempting to let the marvelous sense of place unleash your imagination.

Whatever your take on the spiritual history of the land, no one can deny that the beauty of the West Country is any less magical today. The charming landscape and engaging towns of Lyme Regis, St. Ives, and Newlyn have attracted artists and writers for generations. The weather can be surprisingly amenable, and you may have to remind yourself that you're in England as you gaze at the palm trees, white beaches, and turquoise waters of Cornwall. Although busloads of travelers do arrive in summer, it's still a treat to explore the scenic coastal towns and bays—if you stray far enough, you'll find stretches of countryside where the sense of isolation can be both alarming and exciting.

When it comes down to fabled must-sees, this region is the peak of the pick. As if by a flick of a Wellsian time machine, you can amble from prehistoric **Stonehenge** to Victorian-era **Salisbury** in just a few days (or a long weekend). Along the way, you can walk through literary landscapes, turning, metaphorically speaking, the pages of the landscape with your feet. In **Bath**—that relentlessly elegant 18th-century town—you can follow in the footsteps of Jane Austen's heroes and heroines. Is that the tinkle of Captain Wentworth's teacup? In **Dorchester,** the center of "Thomas Hardy Country," you'll feel like you've stepped into the very pages of *The Mayor of Casterbridge.*

BASICS

For general info about the region, contact the **Southern Tourist Board** (40 Chamberlayne Rd., Eastleigh, Hants SO50 5JH, tel. 01703/620006, fax 01703/620010), the **West Country Tourist Board** (60 St. David's Hill, Exeter, Devon EX4 4SY, tel. 01392/276351, fax 01392/420891) and **Cornwall Tourist Board** (Pydar House, Pydar St., Truro, Cornwall TR1 1EA, tel. 01872/274057, fax 01872/240423). The most useful Web site for the region is the official site of the West Country Tourist Board; visit them at www.wctb.co.uk.

COMING AND GOING

If heading west on the train, prepare yourself for a cauldron of confusion. To help speed privatization, rail lines within the West Country have been divided among three separate carriers, each with its own fare structure. **Great Western Railways** handles the main line between London's Paddington and Penzance and has four types of return fares: APEX, Saver, Super Saver, and Open. In general you won't need to purchase an unrestricted Open return, which is twice the single price. Saver and Super Saver are most common and basically the same in terms of restrictions—travel is allowed only during off-peak periods (usually 9 AM–4 PM and after 7 PM), though the conditions vary for each journey and should always be checked. Usually, Super Saver does not allow travel on Friday and some Saturdays in July and August, bank holidays, and two weeks around Christmas. APEX tickets are the best deal, but they have numerous restrictions and require a seven-day advance purchase (a Super Advance round-trip also gives a discount of around 10% when purchased by 2 PM the previous day). **South West Trains**—the line from London's Waterloo to Exeter as well as tracks to Dorchester—and **Regional Railways,** which runs branch lines to places like Falmouth, Newquay, St. Ives, and Barnstaple, have fares that only vary according to time of travel (peak or off-peak).

The system is still run as one big network, however, and one ticket is good on all routes to your destination. Fares are determined by the departure point and primary carrier for your journey. In this chapter we quote the Saver fare, unless otherwise noted. If you're going to be traveling extensively, consider a Rail Rover pass good on all trains in a given area. The **Freedom of the South West** pass (£61–£71.50 according to season) is good for unlimited travel throughout the region on any eight days out of 15. Other regional passes good for three out of seven days, or eight out of 15 days of unlimited travel, include **Cornish Rail Rover** (£25.50 or £40.50) and **Devon Rail Rover** (£30 or £46.50), but those fares drop by 20% or more between October and May. **National Express** (tel. 08705/808080) buses from London serve all major towns in the area. **Western National** (tel. 01209/719988) is the main carrier in the far west, and offers one-, three-, and seven-day Explorer passes (£6, £13.90, and £23.50, respectively). Other areas are covered by **Wilts & Dorset** (tel. 01722/336855) and **First Southern National** (tel. 01823/272033 for Somerset area, 01305/766393 for Dorset and Devon). Ask about Explorer Passes, valid for a day or a week; for general transport inquiries in Wiltshire, call 0345/090899.

BATH

Bath's history has been shaped by its hot springs, which pour out of the earth at a steady 116°F. In the 1st century AD, the Romans dedicated the township to the goddess Sulis Minerva, named it Aquae Sulis (Waters of Sulis), and constructed an intricate series of baths and pools around the hot springs. Centuries later, Bath became synonymous with elegance, engendering a social scene second only to London's. The Royals have always shown a preference for the town: Queen Elizabeth I brought a certain prestige to the baths with her visit in 1574, while Queen Anne's visits to the waters in 1702 and 1703 established the "Bath season." In subsequent years, architect John Wood (1704–1754) gave Bath its distinctive, harmonious look. Using the yellowish "Bath stone" cut from nearby quarries, he created a city of crescents, terraces, and Palladian mansions, curving through the city like scalloped paper cutouts.

Sadly, you can no longer bathe in the springs, although you can drink the horrible-tasting water if you so desire. The museums, parks, and architecture make a visit worthwhile. Getting a grip on the town's history and its high-society past will make any stay here more enjoyable—try to get your hands on a copy of Jane Austen's *Persuasion,* much of which is set in Bath. As the only city in Britain to be a World Heritage Site in its entirety, Bath will be a must for many—the only caveats about coming here are that lodging is expensive (of course, don't forget it is entirely possible to do Bath as a day trip from London), and you'll hear more American accents than you might have wanted to.

BASICS

The exceptionally efficient **Tourist Information Centre** (Abbey Chambers, Abbey Churchyard, tel. 01225/477101), open Monday–Saturday 9:30–5 (June–September until 6), Sunday 10–4, gets miserably crowded in summer. Come early to book a room (£2.50 fee plus 10% deposit), as the bargains go

ATLANTIC OCEAN

Ilfracombe

Instow

Bideford
Bay

Clovelly

A39

Bude

Bude Bay

B3254

A388

Okeha

Boscastle

B3263

A39

A30

Tintagel

B3314

Camelford

Launceston

Wadebridge

BODMIN
MOOR

Bolventor

Tavistock

Yelverto

Liskeard

B3276

Bodmin

A38

Newquay

A30

A391

Perranporth

Fal

Polperro

Plymouth

CORNWALL

Looe

St. Ives

Truro

A390

Mevagissey

B3306

A30

B3289

Trelissick

St.
Just

Penzance

St. Michael's
Mount

A394

Roseland
Peninsula

Land's
End

Newlyn

A394

B3291

Falmouth

Mousehole

Gweek

GOONHILLY
DOWNS

B3315

Lamorna

Helston

A3083

Porthcurno

Mullion
Cove

B3293

St. Keverne

The Lizard

Coverack

Lizard
Peninsula

TO
ROSCOFF

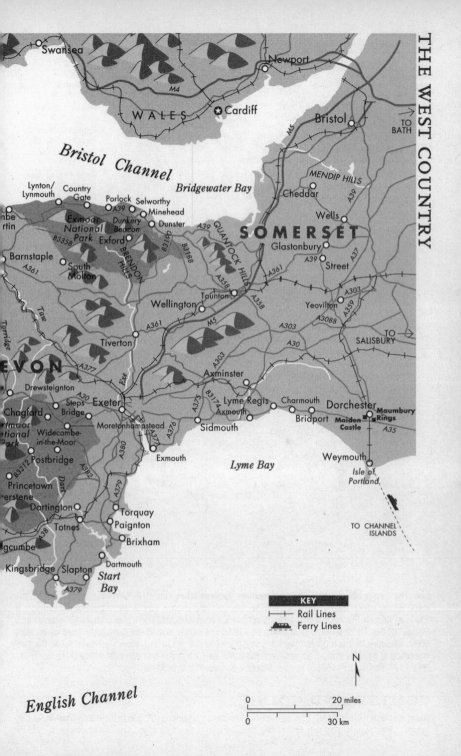

Swansea

Newport

WALES

M4

★ Cardiff

Bristol

TO
BATH

Bristol Channel

MENDIP HILLS

Cheddar

A39

Bridgewater Bay

Lynton/
Lynmouth

Country
Gate

Porlock
A39

Selworthy

Wells

Minehead

Exmoor

Dunster

SOMERSET

National

Dunkery
Beacon

A39

Park

B3358

Exford

Glastonbury

A39

Street

A37

Barnstaple

A361

South
Molton

B3188

QUANTOCK HILLS

A361

A303

Yeovilton

A359

Taunton

A3088

A358

Wellington

A358

A303

DEVON

A361

M5

A303

Tiverton

A30

TO
SALISBURY

A377

Exe

A303

Drewsteignton

Axminster

Steps
Bridge

A30

Exeter

A373

B317

Lyme Regis

Charmouth

Dorchester

Maumbury
Rings

Chagford

Moretonhampstead

A376

Axmouth

Bridport

Maiden
Castle

A35

Widecombe-
in-the-Moor

A382

A377

Sidmouth

Postbridge

B3212

A380

Exmouth

Weymouth

Princetown

A379

Lyme Bay

Isle of
Portland

Dart

Dartington

TO CHANNEL
ISLANDS

Torquay

Totnes

A38

Paignton

Brixham

Kingsbridge

Slapton

Dartmouth

A379

Start
Bay

English Channel

KEY

⊢—⊣ Rail Lines

Ferry Lines

N

0   20 miles

0   30 km

KEY

AE American Express Office

i Tourist Information

fast. The tourist office also holds an **American Express** office (tel. 01225/424416), open during the same hours, which offers regular cardholder services and cashes all brands of traveler's checks for a 1% commission (for cash transactions there's a £2 commission). There's also an AmEx branch at 5 Bridge St. (tel. 01225/444767). **Lockers** on Platform 1 of the station are currently closed as an anti-bomb measure, but you might check anyway. If they're still not in use, leave your bags in the Badger-line office at the bus station, accessible 8:30–4:45, for £2 a day. The main **post office** (New Bond St., BA1 1AA, tel. 01225/445358) is open Monday–Saturday until 5:30 PM.

COMING AND GOING

Great Western makes the 90-minute trip from London's Paddington Station to **Bath Spa Station** for £30 return. Direct trains also run to Cardiff, Salisbury, and Southampton. The ticket office (tel. 0345/

484950) is open 5:30 AM–8:30 PM. **National Express** (tel. 08705/808080) sends 11 coaches daily to and from London for £19.50 return. Buy National Express tickets at Bath's **bus station** (Manvers St., across from train station, tel. 01225/464446). **Bakers Dolphin** (tel. 01934/413000) offers a slightly cheaper service with one bus per day plying to and from London's Marble Arch for £10.50 single, £17.95 open return. Tickets can be purchased by phone with a credit card at least a day in advance, or you can try getting a seat the same day, either by telephone or directly from the driver.

The bus station, which is within striking distance of all Bath's attractions, also dispatches **Badgerline** buses to neighboring towns. If you plan to make day trips from Bath, purchase a **Day Rambler** pass (£5.30), good for unlimited travel on regional Badgerline buses. The blocks surrounding the depot contain bus stops for local routes that fan throughout the city and into the suburbs. Call the **Travel Information Line** (tel. 0117/955–5111) for a comprehensive listing of local bus times throughout the region.

WHERE TO SLEEP

Bath has some delightfully refined hotels. Seek, and ye shall also find, bargains here (so long as you don't mind a short bridge crossing into town or a tramp down a stately hill). Reasonably priced B&Bs are clustered along Pulteney Road in the east, and Charlotte Street and Upper Bristol Road in the west. Note that the more reasonably priced accommodations are invariably outside the city center—often, you will need to take a taxi from the bus or train station (inquire when making your hotel bookings). The tourist office has a bulky accommodations brochure, but the YHA hostel's list of cheap B&Bs is better. In summer, it's wise to book at least two weeks in advance.

Jane Austen's novel, Persuasion, *much of which is set in Bath, is useful for an insight into the town's history and high-society past.*

Badminton Villa. Originally a Victorian-era family house, this hotel of honey-hued Bath stone sits on a hillside with lovely views of the Georgian city. Owners John and Sue Burton are eminently charming hosts, taking great pride in their recent refurbishment of the guest rooms, which run £48 for singles, £58–£65 for doubles (breakfast is complimentary), and include color TV, clock radios, and hair dryers. *10 Upper Oldfield Park, BA2 3JZ, tel. 01225/426347, fax 01225/420393. From station, head south ½ mi along Wells Road, or take a taxi or Bus 14. 4 rooms with bath.*

Bath Tasburgh Hotel. A former residence of an official royal family photographer, some of whose snaps grace the walls, this upmarket hotel (pronounced *Tayz-burra*) sits on acres of well-tended gardens that lead down to the tranquil Kennet and Avon canals. In keeping with its Victorian origins, the redbrick residence has stained-glass windows and marble fireplaces, and a glassed-in conservatory and garden terrace. Owners David and Susan Keeling offer their guests gourmet dinners and picnics for canal-side repasts. Guest rooms run from £48 for singles to £95 for doubles (breakfast included), with color TVs, telephones with data ports, and tea/coffeemaking facilities. *Warminster Rd., along A36, BA2 6SH, tel. 01225/425096, fax 01225/463842. Across the Cleveland Bridge, take A36 exit at the roundabout climbing hill for ½ mi, or take Bus 4. 12 rooms with bath.*

Cranleigh. Standing on the hill high above the city, Cranleigh offers wonderful views over Bath from some of the back rooms. All the comfortable bedrooms have TVs, and one has a four-poster. Excellent breakfasts are served in the dining room, which looks out on the garden, but there are no evening meals. Smoking is not permitted. Doubles are £70 off season, £80 in season. The hotel is about a mile from the city center. *159 Newbridge Hill, along A431, BA1 3PX, tel. 01225/310197, fax 01225/423143, E-mail cranleigh£btinternet.com. By car follow A4 in the direction of Bristol, turn off on A431. From bus station, take any bus toward Bristol or Bitton, ask driver to let you off at Newbridge Hill. 6 rooms with bath or shower.*

Koyro. Don't be alarmed if you're asked to remove your shoes before entering this friendly guest house whose name means "Sunshine" in Japanese. David Smithies and his Japanese wife Sayuri started business here in June 1999 and, hoping to catch the Asian market, have made cleanliness and simplicity the keynotes (that also means no smoking). Breakfast, alas, is resolutely English, but it's better than most. Completely refurbished rooms go for £50. *7 Pulteney Gardens, BA2 4HG, tel. 01225/336712. From stations, walk up Manvers St., turn right on North Parade, cross bridge, turn right on Pulteney Rd., then second left. 3 rooms with bath or shower, 2 singles sharing bathroom. Cash only.*

Membland. Peter Moore goes out of his way to make guests welcome, including picking them up from the train or bus station (evenings only). It's a comfortable Victorian building, with TVs and tea/coffee

THE SQUARE, THE CIRCLE, AND THE CRESCENT

Bath wouldn't be Bath without its distinctive 18th-century Georgian architecture, most of which was conceived by John Wood the Elder, an architect obsessed. Wood saw Bath as a mythical city destined for greatness along the lines of Winchester and Glastonbury. He nurtured the myth that Bath was founded by Prince Bladud (ostensibly with the help of an errant pig rooting in the ground for acorns; Wood later used stone acorns as a motif). Wood sought an architectural style that would do justice to his great concept, and found it in the Palladian style, made popular in Britain by Inigo Jones.

Influenced by nearby ancient stone circles as well as round Roman temples, Wood broke loose from convention in his design for Bath's outstanding Circus, a full circle of houses broken only three times for intersecting streets. After the death of Wood the Elder, John Wood the Younger carried out his father's plans for the Royal Crescent, an obtuse crescent of 30 interconnected houses overlooking Victoria Park—the first row houses in Britain. Stop in at No. 1 Royal Crescent for a look at one of these Georgian homes decked out in period style. Tel. 01225/ 428126. Admission £4. Open mid-Feb.–Oct., Tues.–Sun. 10:30–5; Nov.–early Dec., Tues.–Sun. 10:30–4.

facilities in all rooms, which are £22 per head—though you can negotiate a 10% discount for three nights or more. *7 Pulteney Terrace, BA2 4HJ, tel. 01225/336712. From stations, walk up Manvers St., turn right on North Parade, cross bridge, turn right on Pulteney Rd., then third left. 3 rooms, all with shower. Cash only.*

Woodville House. Tom and Anne Toalster's classic Bath house is ideally positioned near Victoria Park and the Royal Crescent. Basic rooms—the bathroom is shared, but each room has its own wash basin—cost £36, even if you're alone. There's a TV lounge and the no-smoking rule is absolutely rigid. *4 Marlborough La., BA1 2NQ, tel. and fax 01225/319335, E-mail toalster£compuserve.com. From stations, walk to Bath Abbey, turn left on Cheap St., right on Monmouth St. (which becomes Upper Bristol Rd.), right on Marlborough La., or take bus 14a or 14b to Upper Bristol Rd. 3 rooms without bath. Cash only.*

HOSTELS

Bath Backpackers Hostel. Very central, this independent hostel offers cheap beds (£12 in dorms, £15 for a double room), but no breakfast. There's a bar and pool room, no curfew and no lockout, and an amiable, relaxed atmosphere. *13 Pierrepont St., BA1 1LA, tel. 01225/446787, fax 01225/446305, website www.backpackers-uk.demon.co.uk. From stations, walk up Manvers St., which becomes Pierrepont St. 50 beds. Kitchen. Cash only. Open all year.*

Bathwick Hill YHA. This Italianate building has a mellow atmosphere, and the staff has the buzz on what's going on in Bath. The hostel is open year-round, and reservations are essential in summer. Beds cost £10.15. You'll definitely want to take a bus up the steep hill. *Bathwick Hill, Avon BA2 6JZ, tel. 01225/465674, fax 01225/482947, E-mail bath£yha.org.uk. From stations, take Badgerline Bus 18, 418, or 419 directly to hostel. 117 beds. Reception open 7:15 AM–11 PM. Kitchen, laundry.*

CAMPING

Newton Mill Touring Centre. This is the closest campground, 3 mi west of Bath. Sites cost £4.25 per person or £10.95 for two persons, tent, and car (a bit less in winter)—showers included in price. There's a bar, laundry, and restaurant on site, and a shop open in summer. *Newton St., Loe, tel. 01225/333909. From the bus station, take Bus 5, alight at Twerton (ask driver), then walk through playground and down footpath. Showers.*

FOOD

Bath is dotted with many fine restaurants, but you'll also note plenty of burger stands and other bargain eateries around the Theatre Royal, Sawclose, and Kingsmead Square. If you'd rather create your own gustatory masterpiece, there's a **Waitrose** supermarket in The Podium shopping center on High Street and a cheaper **Somerfield** market in the Southgate Shopping Centre behind the bus station. Enhance your meal with some fresh produce, meat, cheese, and pastries from the **Guildhall Market** on High Street.

UNDER £5 • Café Retro. The decor in this mellow and mirrored café/restaurant tends toward art nouveau, but is pared down by simple tables and old wooden chairs. The food is good and reasonably priced with hot panini (£3–£4) and "Smokie Fish Pie" (£5) always available, though things get pricier in the evening, when you can also dine upstairs. *18 York St., near tourist office, tel. 01225/339347.*

Crystal Palace. This "very English" pub is a fine place to enjoy a large range of sandwiches, especially in its garden patio on a sunny day. Other dishes include a hot open-faced prawn sandwich and six versions of ploughman's lunches. *Abbey Green, tel. 01225/423944. From entrance to Roman Baths, turn left and walk less than a min. Cash only.*

Fodder's. Gourmet sandwiches are the specialty at this small takeout in the city center. Choose from prawns in mayo, pâté de campagne, vegetarian fillings, deli meats, and condiments such as garlic olive pâté. *9 Cheap St., near High St., tel. 01225/462165. Closed dinner and Sunday. Cash only.*

You can probably live quite happily without ever sampling the famous "Bath bun," a teatime treat that's degenerated into a tourist curiosity, although locals sometimes indulge. If you feel compelled, Scoffs (20 Kingsmead Sq.) sells them for £1 in an unpretentious atmosphere.

UNDER £15 • Tilley's Bistro. With the land of haute cuisine just across a narrow body of water, it's troubling that good French restaurants such as Tilley's haven't infiltrated the English food scene. You can order entrées such as sautéed medallions of pork in a brandy and Roquefort cream sauce, and vegetarian and vegan dishes. For lunch try a set two- or three-course meal for under a tenner. *3 North Parade Passage, between Abbey Green and North Parade Bridge, tel. 01225/484200. Closed Sun. lunch.*

Wife of Bath. Five rooms in a converted Georgian cellar provide a choice of cozy corners and nifty nooks, with an unhassled ambience. The eclectic menu might include fish from Cornwall, boeuf bourguignonne, and curry. The beefsteak casseroles with shallots are especially recommended, and the puddings are to die for. *12 Pierrepont St., tel. 01225/461745.*

WORTH SEEING

Bath's city center is easily navigable by foot, and a free, comprehensive walking tour is a great way to learn about the city's highlights. Tours leave daily from the Roman Baths entrance (*see below*) in the Abbey Churchyard at 10:30 AM and 2 PM (Sunday at 2:30), and at 7 PM three times a week in summer; confirm times at the tourist office.

BATH ABBEY

In one form or another, Bath Abbey has been around for 1,200 years; what started as a Norman church eventually evolved into this 15th-century Gothic construction. Stained-glass windows at the eastern end portray Christ's life, though the abbey is better known for its spindly, fan-vaulted ceiling—don't forget to look up. If you don't mind the £2 admission, explore the subterranean **Heritage Vaults**, open Monday–Saturday 10–4, with some slightly cheesy exhibits on the abbey's history. In summer, also check for flyers advertising organ recitals in the abbey. *High St., tel. 01225/422462. Admission free, but £2 donation requested. Open Mon.–Sat. 9–6 (in winter until 4:30), Sun. 1–2:30 and 4:30–5:30.*

BUILDING OF BATH MUSEUM

If "Norm" makes you think of *This Old House* instead of *Cheers*, you'll dig the architectural displays at the Building of Bath Museum. If not, the small print and paucity of big pictures make it a bit of a struggle. Check out the huge model of Bath. *The Countess of Huntingdon's Chapel, The Paragon, off Broad St., tel. 01225/333895. Admission £3. Open mid-Feb.–Nov., Tues.–Sun. 10:30–5.*

MUSEUM OF EAST ASIAN ART

Cultivated Bath makes the perfect setting for this amazing museum, which showcases a private collection of East Asian art spanning more than 7,000 years, from 5,000 BC to the 20th century. Since the museum is small, only one-third of the more than 1,500 pieces of jade, gold, silver, wood, bronze, ceramics, and silk (many of which are very rare) that comprise the entire collection can be displayed at a time. The emphasis is on Chinese art but works from Southeast Asia, Tibet, Japan, and Korea are also exhibited. *12 Bennett St., off The Circus, tel. 01225/464640. Admission £3.50. Open Mon.–Sat. 10–6 (Nov.–Mar. until 5), Sun. 10–5 (Nov.–Mar. from noon).*

ROMAN BATHS AND MUSEUM OF COSTUME

The Romans built their luxurious baths here between the 1st and 5th centuries AD, when springs already bubbled from the earth. The bath network is well preserved, and the smell of sulfur, the looming Roman statuary, and the murky green pools make it easy to imagine what it was like being a Roman bather. You can't swim here, but you can sample some vile-tasting mineral water at the overpriced **Pump Room,** above the Roman Baths. Be forewarned: This is one of the most popular attractions in England, and the large crowds can be a bit of a turnoff. The audio-guide handsets help to shut out some of the hubbub, however, and provide an informative commentary along the way. If you have some extra time, buy a combined admission ticket and visit the **Museum of Costume** (Bennett St., tel. 01225/477789), one of the most prestigious and extensive collections of historical costumes in Britain, covering more than 400 years of fashion. It's housed in the Assembly Rooms, a series of elegant chambers built in 1771. *Abbey Churchyard, tel. 01225/477000. Admission £6.70. Combined ticket with Museum of Costume £8.70. Open Apr.–Sept., daily 9–6 (Aug., also 8 PM–10 PM); Oct.–Mar., daily 9:30–5.*

ROYAL PHOTOGRAPHIC SOCIETY GALLERY

This is one of the largest independent galleries devoted entirely to photography and home to the oldest photographic society in the world. The constantly rotating exhibits feature works by up-and-coming and renowned photographers, as well as stock from the society's massive collection of everything from Victorian-era heliogravures to holograms. The society is particularly gifted with its collection of 19th-century photographs from around the world. *Octagon Galleries, Milsom St., tel. 01225/462841. Admission £2.50. Open daily 9:30–5:30 (last admission 4:45).*

ROYAL VICTORIA PARK

If the sun is shining, take a walk through the large open spaces of Royal Victoria Park, south of Royal Crescent. In the east of the park, the beautiful botanical gardens house a vast array of flowers, trees, and plants from around the world. In the summer, free concerts of all sorts are performed throughout the park; for more information check at the tourist office or call Bath Festivals Trust at 01225/463362.

VICTORIA ART GALLERY

If Bath's pricey atmosphere has you feeling monetarily challenged, enrich yourself with some very fine art at the free Victoria Art Gallery. The gallery has a permanent collection of over 6,500 drawings, prints, and paintings, from traditional masters to modern artists. Downstairs, the gallery hosts temporary exhibits ranging from Picasso and Dalí to Sir Matthew Smith, a little-known but highly emotive artist often dubbed as the most "French" of British painters. *Bridge St., tel. 01225/477000. Open weekdays 10–5:30, Sat. 10–5.*

AFTER DARK

Bath's nightlife is lively, if somewhat yup-scale, which explains the £2–£6 cover many pubs charge for live music. For serious out-of-your-head clubbing, you may want to catch the next train to Bristol: A handful of pubs and clubs there have a more relaxed and down-to-earth feel, making them favorites of Bath University students. In Bath, there are several see-and-be-seen options. **The Bell** (103 Walcot St., tel.

01225/460426) is a laid-back and dirty pub with live music three times a week and a back patio. **The Hush** (The Paragon, up from Broad St., tel. 01225/446288) is a cool and casual late-night hangout with club sounds and a small dance area; if you want something a little more sweaty, head for **Po Na Na** (The Basement, 8 North Parade, tel. 01225/401115). The best place to hear live bands is **Moles** (14 George St., tel. 01225/333423), a private club that attracts good acts along with lots of unknowns and techno-playing DJs. **The Bath Tap** (20 St. James's Parade, tel. 01225/448819) is Bath's premier gay bar, with regular cabaret shows including strippers on Friday, and the basement Club Eros for dance grooves.

THEATER

For highbrow theatrics, catch a show (or two) at the old and illustrious **Theatre Royal** (Sawclose, tel. 01225/448844), with plays starring big-name British actors such as Timothy West, Simon Callow, and Pauline Collins. Tickets range from £7 to £25 and the box office is open Monday–Saturday 10–8; standby tickets (£5) are available from noon on the day of the performance. Next-door, the **Ustinov Studio** (same tel.) stages more experimental work at lower prices (£5–£9).

OUTDOOR ACTIVITIES

Though Bath feels like a minimetropolis, its surrounding area is green and lined with paths for walking and biking. Ask at the tourist office for pamphlets about the 80-mi **Avon Cycleway,** which takes you through a string of rural country villages, or the **Bristol and Bath Railway Path,** a 12-mi route along an old railway line, with great views and scenery. Mountain bikes can be rented at the **Avon Valley Cyclery** (Arch 37, rear of train station, tel. 01225/442442) for £14 per day, £18 per 24 hours, £28 per weekend, or £50 for a week. If you want to use your own two feet, pick up a copy of the pamphlet "Country Walks Within 5 Miles of Bath Abbey" from either the tourist office or the youth hostel, which gives *detailed* descriptions of the best local strolls. A great, easy day hike is to follow the River Avon north from Cleveland Bridge and watch as the line between culture and countryside becomes progressively fuzzier. Rowboats and punts on the River Avon cost £4.50 per person for the first hour, £1.50 per person for every subsequent hour, and can be rented until about 6 PM in summer at the **Bath Boating Station** (Forester Rd., tel. 01225/466407); pick up a voucher at the tourist office, giving a whole day's rental for just £5.50.

BRISTOL

Hip and savvy, the harbor city of Bristol could teach you a thing or two about life. The tourist brochures call Bristol "The Great Western City," but hipper elements will know it better as the home of Massive Attack, Tricky, Portishead, and the "trip-hop" scene, the Seattle of England. Although, like Seattle, the buzz has weakened somewhat in recent years, the city still has a vibrant, stomping club scene. Cosmopolitan and multicultural, Bristol is coming into its own, without relinquishing its historic roots dating back to when it was the main port for trade with the New World. While retaining plenty of handsome Georgian architecture, there is none of the precious quaintness of Bath, and no pretense of remaining stuck in a past era—as evidenced by the swirling traffic and acres of modern office blocks.

BASICS

There is plenty to see and do in Bristol, day and night, so visit the helpful **Tourist Information Centre** (St. Nicholas Church, St. Nicholas St., tel. 0117/926–0767, website http://tourism.bristol.gov.uk) for the latest scoop. They offer accommodations bookings for a 10% deposit, as well as staggering amounts of free literature on where to eat, sleep, stroll, shop, and sightsee. The **American Express Travel Service** (74 Queens Rd., tel. 0117/975–0750, and 31 Union St., Broadmead, tel. 0117/927–7788) exchanges traveler's checks for a 1% commission, cash for a £2 commission.

COMING AND GOING

Great Western (tel. 0345/484–950) trains arrive about every 10 minutes at Bristol Temple Meads Station from Bath Spa Station (20 mins, £4.60 single, £4.70 day return) and hourly from London's Paddington Station (1¾ hrs, £30 single, £31 return). Make sure you board a train for Temple Meads, not Bristol Parkway, which is farther out (though still busable). **National Express** (tel. 08705/808080) has hourly coaches to Bristol from London (2 hrs 20 mins, £10 single, £17 return). **Bakers Dolphin** (tel. 01934/413000) buses stop at the Bristol Fashion pub, next to the bus station, and (closer to the TIC and hostel) at the Hippodrome Theatre, six or seven times a day from London's Marble Arch or Victoria Coach Station (£9.95 single, £16.95 open return).

GETTING AROUND

Bristol's sights are spread out across the city. Fortunately, **City Line** (tel. 0117/955–3231) buses follow a complex network of routes around greater Bristol. A free network map is available at the tourist office or the coach station on Marlborough Street. If you plan to do a lot of riding, get a **Dayrider Ticket** (£2.95), good for six journeys after 9 AM on all City Line buses, available from the bus driver.

WHERE TO SLEEP

Central to the major sights of Bristol, the **Naseby House Hotel** (105 Pembroke Rd., BS8 3EF, tel. and fax 0117/973–7859) is Victorian in vintage and situated on a tree-lined street in the heart of Clifton. The comfortable bedrooms have TV and tea/coffeemaking facilities: plushest, and most expensive, are those in the recently refurbished basement, close to the hotel's garden. The lounge is filled with period bric-a-brac, and the breakfast room is also impressive. Doubles range between £55 and £70. As for B&Bs, the best bargains line Bath Road, directly south of Bristol Temple Meads Station, though it's a fairly dull area, and you may prefer something more central. In the university area, **St. Michael's Guest House** sits above a popular café at 145 St. Michael's Hill, and in leafy Clifton, try **K Linton Homes** (3 Lansdown Rd., tel. 0117/973–7326), offering five rooms for £34–£39 a double. The 124-bed **Bristol YHA** (14 Narrow Quay, tel. 0117/922–1659, fax 0117/927–3789, E-mail bristol£yha.org.uk) in the city center is a great place to meet other travelers for £12.15 a night. The University of Bristol's **The Hawthorns** (Woodland Rd., tel. 0117/954–5900) has 120 singles and doubles that it lets out for £17.50–£23.50 per person per night from July through September (a limited number of rooms are available all year).

FOOD

Bristol has an abundance of high-quality eateries—for a real splurge, opt for **Michael's Fusion Restaurant** (129 Hotwell Rd., tel. 0117/927–6190). Informal elegance is the predominant tone at this place sited across Bristol's Floating Harbour from the S.S. *Great Britain*. Aperitifs and post-dinner drinks are taken in a comfortable lounge area, where a log fire provides the centerpiece; next door, culinary delights such as scallops with sweet chili or pan-fried mullet share menu space with exotic Pacific Rim dishes. A prix-fixe dinner will set you back £20. **Belgo** (Queen Charlotte St., tel. 0117/905–8000), housed in a refurbished granary off King St., specializes in Belgian-style moules and frites (mussels and fries) and 101 different beers. The decor is high-tech but the staff is kitted out in Trappist monk's aprons; on weekdays between 5:30 and 7:30 you pay the bill according to the time you order: e.g. order at 6:35 PM and you pay £6.35. On the harborside, the **Mud Dock Café** (40 The Grove, tel. 0117/934–9734) doubles as a bike shop and doles out spicy lamb sausages, "rocket" salads (mixed greens), and tapas at reasonable prices. There's a barbecue on the balcony in summer, and DJs playing loud and strong most evenings. In grungy St. Werburgh's, **The Farm** (Hopetoun Rd., tel. 0117/944–2384) is a country-style pub with a garden where you can down pints and dishes such as pastas and bangers and mash, or just filled baguettes and soups, all for less than £5. For that special evening out, check out **Bell's Diner** (1 York Rd., tel. 0117/924–0357), a converted corner shop in the young and hip Montpelier quarter: A full meal will set you back about £18 excluding bevvies, but it's worth the splash. No smoking in the dining area. For a cheap and cheerful breakfast in Clifton, head down to the **York Café** (1 York Place, tel. 0117/923–9656), an institution among students, builders, and poseurs.

WORTH SEEING

After ditching your bags at the youth hostel, head next door to the **Arnolfini** (16 Narrow Quay, tel. 0117/929–9191), an amazing arts center complete with bar and café. The Arnolfini has a free art gallery, shows films (£3.80), and stages music, dance, and theater performances (£7) nightly. There's a bar and cheap restaurant, and locals and travelers alike sit outside on sunny days and watch the boats go by.

Described by Queen Elizabeth I in 1574 as "the fairest, goodliest and most famous parish church in all of England," **St. Mary Redcliffe** (Redcliffe Way, tel. 0117/929–1962) is well worth a look. Parts of the structure date from 1180, though the stunningly long, narrow nave was built much later. **Bristol Cathedral** (College Green, tel. 0117/926–4879) is a magnificent structure dating back to 1140. Watch for the abrupt changes in architecture resulting from 400 years of construction, and save time to visit the colorfully whimsical **Lady Chapel** (£1 donation requested).

Just down the road from the tourist office, **Castle Park** (High St., at the Floating Harbour) is the result of recent excavations that have unearthed layer upon layer of Bristol history, from the early Saxon settlement of "Bricgstow," to the Norman "St. Mary-Le-Port," to a fashionable 18th-century shopping center destroyed by World War II bombings. A walk through the park's well-marked trails takes you through a thousand years of history. **Clifton,** an area on the west side of town, has some beautiful 18th- and 19th-century houses and the **Downs,** a 450-acre park atop the Avon Gorge. **Clifton Suspension Bridge,** designed by the engineer Isambard Kingdom Brunel, spans the gorge. The outdoor terrace of **Avon Gorge Hotel** (Sion Hill, tel. 0117/973–8955), with a spectacular view of the gorge and the bridge, is a great place for a pint.

AFTER DARK

Bristol's vibrant nightlife is a step up from the somewhat yuppie scene in Bath. For current information on clubs and events, buy a copy of *Venue* magazine (£1.70), available at most newsstands. The best area for clubs is the Stokes Croft area, just north of the bus station. Garage and indie band fans should head for **The Powerhouse** (4 Stokes Croft, tel. 0117/924–4300), which has become one of the hottest venues in town, with entry at about £7. **Lakota** (6 Upper York St., off Stokes Croft, tel. 0117/942–6193) does hard-core techno and up-to-the-minute trance dance; the cover runs high (£6–£12), but it's definitely worth a go. Around the corner, **Club Loco** (Hepburn Rd., tel. 0117/942–6208) attracts almost as big a raving crowd for £7–£10, offering mainly techno and drum & bass on two dance floors. In the center, sweat up a storm for about £6 on the funk/hip-hop/drum & bass/indie dance floors at **Thekla** (tel. 0117/929–3301), a converted freight steamer moored on The Grove. Pre-club pubs and watering holes line King Street, but try the **Llandoger Trow** (5 King St., tel. 0117/926–0783) for a mellower, antique atmosphere. **The Hobgloblin** (2 Byron Pl., tel. 0117/929–9322) is particularly popular with students.

WELLS

Wells took its name from, no surprise, its well: The town lies above small underground streams that surface at St. Andrew's Well on the grounds of Bishop's Palace. The town's centerpiece is the **Cathedral Church of St. Andrew** (tel. 01749/674483), a pure English Gothic cathedral built in the 12th and 13th centuries. Hidden away from the rest of Wells, the lovely west front depicts 297 medieval statues, while inside, the most striking aspect is the so-called "scissor arches," a unique architectural element (vaguely resembling an abstract owl face) designed and built to redistribute the weight of the tower, which had begun to sink and collapse. To the left, a 600-year-old astronomical clock marks off quarter-hours with jousting knights, and a wide staircase leads up to the hexagonal Chapter House. Next to the cathedral is the moat-ringed 13th-century **Bishop's Palace** (Market Pl., tel. 01749/678691), admission £3. Its gatehouse retains the chutes once used to dump boiling oil on intruders. The first-floor hall and Bishop's Chapel are open April–October, Tuesday–Friday 10:30–6 and Sunday 2–6 (daily in August). Nearby is **Vicars' Close,** one of the oldest intact medieval streets in Europe, completed in 1348. The **Wells Museum** (tel. 01749/673477) on Cathedral Green offers unexciting local history and the bones of a "witch" found nearby in the Wookey Hole Caves. Admission is £2.

All signs in Wells point 2 mi away to the **Wookey Hole Caves.** This long series of caverns filled with stalactites and stalagmites has been transformed into a crass amusement park, including a hall of mirrors and a penny arcade. You're probably better off saving the £7 admission and puttering around town, or renting a mountain bike (£9 for one day, £5 per day for subsequent days) at **The Bicycle Company** (80 High St., tel. 01749/675096) and heading for the Somerset countryside.

COMING AND GOING

Wells is only 21 mi from Bath, but hourly Badgerline Bus 173 takes about 80 minutes (£4.50 return), winding its way through the Somerset countryside. From Wells's **Princes Road Bus Park** (tel. 01749/673084), Badgerline also serves Bristol, Cheddar, Glastonbury, Street, Taunton, Shepton Mallet, Weston-super-Mare, and Wookey Hole.

WHERE TO SLEEP

There are a number of B&Bs in town and in nearby homes and farmhouses, with the cheapest averaging £15 per person. The **tourist office** (Town Hall, tel. 01749/672552) is great about noting which accommodations have particular views or special functions such as dairy farming. If you have pastoral dreams à la *Tess of the d'Urbervilles,* head to nearby North Wootton's **Barrow Farm** (tel. 01749/890245), a working dairy farm dating back to the 15th century. They're open March–November for bed-and-breakfast (£17 per person). Eight mi away, the 56-bed **Cheddar YHA** (Hillfield, BS27 3HN, tel. 01934/742494, fax 01934/744724), in a Victorian house on the southwest side of the village, charges £9.15. It's closed Sunday April–May, Sunday and Monday October–November, and Sunday–Thursday December–March (though open daily over Christmas week). Badgerline Buses 126 and 826 serve Cheddar (£2.15 one way) from Wells, 10 mi away. If you're interested in throwing around some serious pounds and pence, **The Crown** (Market Pl., BA5 2 RP, tel. 01749/673457) has been a landmark in Wells since the Middle Ages; William Penn was arrested here in 1695 for illegal preaching. There's a period atmosphere to the place, and several of the rooms have four-poster beds. On site is the Penn Bar and Eating House, which serves up a fine steak-and-kidney pie. Doubles go for around £50 to £60.

FOOD

After you tour the cathedral, stop at the unique **Cloister Restaurant** (tel. 01749/676543). The cafeteria service doesn't quite obliterate the medieval ambience, and they serve a great cottage (meat and potato) pie. If you're hankering for more nutritious food, the **Good Earth Restaurant** (4 Priory Rd., near the bus park, tel. 01749/678600) has baked potatoes, salads, flans, pizzas, and a dish of the day. The restaurant is closed on Sunday.

GLASTONBURY

Auspiciously aligned along ley lines ("invisible axes of spiritual energy that run throughout England," experts tell, and swear, to us), Glastonbury is England's hippie capital and New Age center. Various traditions of spirituality converge, mixing the Christian with the Druidic, the ancient with the New Age. Legends of Arthur still thrive here, contributing to the town's mystique; Glastonbury is supposed to be the mythical Isle of Avalon, where Arthur and Guinevere supposedly died around AD 516. It's also said that the chalice used during the Last Supper is buried in the hill next to **Glastonbury Tor,** a 525-ft-high mound from which you'll catch astounding views of Somerset below. The Tor, seen from miles around, is best reached by the footpath starting off Lambrook Street.

The **Glastonbury Festival,** held somewhat annually a few miles away in Pilton, is the biggest and best of all music festivals in England. For three days over the last weekend of June, the festival hosts thousands of music fans of all tastes and walks of life. Hundreds of MTV-friendly bands such as REM, Pulp, Manic Street Preachers—and even the legendary Billy Bragg—play simultaneously on at least five different stages, though the pleasure is in the smaller marquees and venues, where obscurer and fresher acts perform. Security is tight, with two fences and a roving narc squad, and tickets are steep (£85), but everything except food—tent pitches, wash facilities, and all performances—is included for the three days. To find out who's playing, pick up a June issue of *New Musical Express* or *Melody Maker,* which announce the complete lineup of bands—save a few special guests—or call the festival's PR department at 01749/890470.

No one comes to this otherwise unremarkable town without a mission of sorts: to hear the music; to track down Jesus, Arthur, and Guinevere; or to get in touch with the spirituality that hovers over the town like a nimbus. If you have a mission of your own, catch Bus 163 or 376 (£1.80 single, £2.70 day return) from Wells; they run once or twice an hour. If you're coming from Bath, change in Wells. The **tourist office** (9 High St., tel. 01458/832954) has the usual brochures, will help with accommodations, and sells festival tickets for a small booking fee.

WHERE TO SLEEP

The **Bolt-Hole** (32 Chilkwell St., tel. 01458/832800) is an agreeable little house with clean, basic rooms near the Rural Life Museum. Doubles go for about £35. In the same area, the **Ramala Centre** (Dod La., tel. 01458/832459) is an ashram offering comforts for body and soul, though smokers and carnivores will have to temporarily abstain from their vices. Futon-style beds in double rooms are £25 or £30, including breakfast. In the center of town, **Glastonbury Backpackers** (4 Market Pl., tel. 01458/833353) offers clean, funky colored doubles for £26 with shared bath (£30 private) and dorm beds for £9. There's a cool café, restaurant, and a bar with pool tables where bands occasionally perform; there's no curfew, either. The most convenient campsite is **Isle of Avalon Touring Caravan Park** (tel. 01458/833618), which charges £5.95 per tent and £1.95 per person. To get here, take Northload Street to Godney Road; it's about a 10-minute walk. The nearest YHA hostel is **The Chalet** (Ivythorn Hill, Somerset BA16 0TZ, tel. 01458/442961, fax 01458/442738), about 3 mi from Glastonbury in Street, with sweeping views of the Tor. It's open daily April–August; closed September–March, also Tuesday April–May. Beds go for £8.35. To reach Street, take Bus 376 to Marshall's Elm, and walk about 800 yards.

FOOD

Food is easy to come by in Glastonbury, with a number of take-out places, cafés, and historic public houses. The **Blue Note Cafe** (2–4 High St., tel. 01458/832907) is a laid-back vegetarian eatery where you can enjoy your meal on the incense-scented patio. If you like a little ovo, lacto, or carno in your meal, try **Who'd a Thought It** (Northload St., tel. 01458/834460).

WORTH SEEING

Glastonbury Abbey was started by the Normans, but an earlier church on the site allegedly welcomed Jesus as a visitor, and even King Arthur's grave is said to lie on the abbey grounds. You can peep at the ruins from the end of Magdalene Street near Bere Lane (the entrance is at the other end, near High Street). The grounds take up a major chunk of the town center; the vast remains convey the impressive stature of the original structure. *Magdalene St., tel. 01458/832267. Admission £3. Abbey open daily 9 or 9:30–6 (9:30 or 10–dusk in winter).*

Somerset Rural Life Museum is an interesting interpretive museum that gives a vivid feel for the days of yore. It schedules special events throughout the year, including concerts and a Wassail Evening celebrating Old Twelfth Night on January 17. *Abbey Farm, Chikwell St., tel. 01458/831197. Admission £2.50. Open Tues.–Fri. 10–5 (also Apr.–Oct., weekends 2–6, and Nov.–Mar., Sat. 10–3).*

SALISBURY

The ancient Chalice Well on Wellhouse Lane is associated with both Celtic and Christian mythology and is said to have special healing powers. Take a swig from the lion-headed spout and judge for yourself.

Most Britons equate Salisbury (pronounced sawls-burr-ee) with its massive Gothic cathedral. The cathedral *is* one of Britain's greatest treasures, and the 404-ft-tall spire is indeed impressive (it has a slight tilt, despite Christopher Wren's efforts to stabilize it). However, most foreign tourists use Salisbury, the only true city in Wiltshire, simply as a resting place on their way to Stonehenge, Avebury, and Stourhead—and quite a good resting place it is. In between visiting the surrounding ancient wonders, you can sleep in any number of cheap beds, drink in a great variety of pubs, and wander down roads lined with photogenic Tudor and thatched-roof homes.

BASICS

The **tourist center** (Fish Row, behind Guildhall, tel. 01722/334956) distributes leaflets, changes money for a commission, and books lodgings for a deposit. The office also has info on whirlwind guided bus tours (£15–£20 per person) to Stonehenge and Avebury. There is a **bureau de change** inside the office (maximum £100, with £3 commission), and the banks on High Street change money, as does **Thomas Cook** (18 Queen St., tel. 01722/412787). The main **post office** (24 Castle St., at Chipper La., SP1 1AB, tel. 01722/413051) is open Monday–Saturday 9–5:30.

COMING AND GOING

South West Trains (tel. 01703/229393) arrive at Salisbury Station (South Western Road) direct from London's Waterloo (1 hr, 25 mins); a single ticket costs £21, while a one-month return is £31. The station is an easy five-minute walk east of the city center along Fisherton Road. **National Express** (tel. 08705/808080) buses from London (£16 return), **Stagecoach** (tel. 01256/464501) buses from Winchester (£4.45 day return), and **Wilts & Dorset** (tel. 01722/336855) buses from destinations throughout Wiltshire and Dorset arrive at the main bus station (Endless Street) in the center of town. For general information on transport in Wiltshire, call 0345/090899.

Wilts & Dorset's **Salisbury City** buses serve the city and its environs, but you can hoof it just about anywhere without too much trouble. A good map is essential; the free one from the tourist office is good for the town center. If you want to explore the surrounding villages, Wilts & Dorset sells one-day **Explorer** tickets for £4.80 and seven-day **Busabout** tickets, for which a passport-size photo is required, for £21. The Explorer ticket is a good deal if you plan to tackle Stonehenge and at least one other village on the same day.

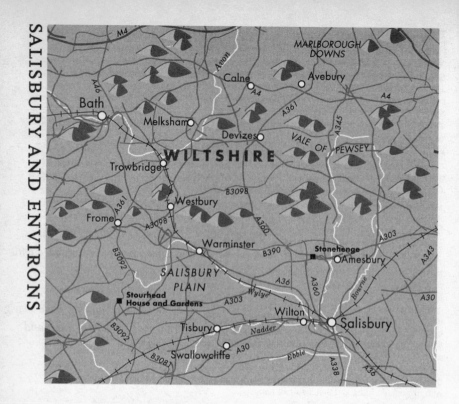

WHERE TO SLEEP

The tourist office used to distribute a free list of all accommodations in town, but with the advent of "Tourism 2000," a tourist board marketing scheme, all lodgings must now pay a hefty fee to be "inspected and approved" for recommendation to tourists. This scheme threatens to hurt small B&Bs, and many have chosen to boycott the measure. Unfortunately, this means that many B&Bs will neither be "officially" recognized nor recommended, requiring a bit of detective work on your part. If you're really stuck, don't be afraid to knock on a few doors on Salt Lane or Belle Vue Road.

Byways House (31 Fowlers Rd., SP1 2QP, tel. 01722/328364) offers friendly service, good value, a quiet location, and a few rooms even have a view of the cathedral—some of the reasons why this double-fronted Victorian house is popular with visitors. The hotel offers large vegetarian or traditional English breakfasts. Doubles with shared bath go for about £45, or £50 with private loo. Farther down on the price scale, **Matt & Tiggy's** (51 Salt La., tel. 01722/327443)—essentially a private hostel—has up to 18 beds spread about two very warped old houses in the center of town. A bed costs £9, sheets 80p, and a self-serve breakfast £1.50. **Mrs. M. Johnson** (94 Milford Hill, tel. 01722/322454) has one double (£32) and one single (£16) in a pleasant house just opposite the youth hostel (*see below*). **Mr. & Mrs. Taafe** (34 Salt La., tel. 01722/326141) run a charming, welcoming B&B with rooms for £15–16 per person. The young, international crowd it caters to has shown their appreciation by plastering the walls with currencies from around the world.

HOSTELS

Milford Hill YHA. This hostel is a warm, convenient place to stay and is usually filled with interesting people. The cafeteria has a license to serve booze and the hostel is open year-round. Beds cost £10.15. *Milford Hill, Wiltshire SP1 2QW, tel. 01722/327572, fax 01722/330446, E-mail salisbury£yha.org.uk. From bus station, turn left on Endless St., left on Milford St. (which becomes Milford Hill after the underpass). 70 beds. Laundry.*

FOOD

Pinocchio (139 Fisherton St., tel. 01722/413069) is a small Italian trattoria near the train station that offers six varieties of veal as well as fish, which finds its way into a homemade fish minestrone. Pizzas are also available, and, for dessert, the tiramisu is sublime. The nearby **Bacon Sandwich Café** (129–131 South Western Rd., tel. 01722/339655) is decked out with '50s-era American car memorabilia. Get the eight-item megabreakfast if you're really hungry; otherwise, try the renowned bacon sandwich or a Knickerbocker Glory (ice-cream sundae). **Thai World** (58 Fisherton St., tel. 01722/414778) serves a nice selection of Thai food, with delectable specials such as roast duck in honey sauce and veggie dishes. **Charcoal Grill** (18 Fisherton St., tel. 01722/322134), open daily noon–midnight, is a Turkish island of taste in a sea of mediocre restaurants. Start with veggie hors d'oeuvres such as artichoke hearts or cucumbers in yogurt; then move on to kebabs or moussaka (a potato, meat, and eggplant casserole)—the house specialty. The cathedral's **Refectory** restaurant (tel. 01722/555172) does a so-so chicken curry and cream teas with scones and jam. Self-caterers can do their shopping at **Tesco** (21–25 Castle Street) or **Safeway** (8–10 Brown Street), both open daily.

WORTH SEEING

SALISBURY CATHEDRAL

The cathedral, begun in 1220, has suffered some serious wear and tear over the past 778 years. Yet it remains, as recorded in the minutes of a government meeting in 1401, "so great a church to the glory of God that those who come after us will think us mad even to have attempted it." The cathedral is an example of architecture at its most grandiose—the spire and tower, built shortly after the rest of the church was completed, are supported by stone columns that weigh an incredible 6,400 tons. The cathedral's **Chapter House** contains one of the four precious original copies of the Magna Carta. Free tours of the cathedral leave at least twice a day—at 11:15 and 2:15—though there are usually a few more starting at irregular times: Check the Visitors Desk for the next one. Tours of the roof and tower (£2.50) currently leave at 2 PM Monday–Saturday, 4:30 Sunday year-round. Up to four additional tours a day (10:30, 11:30, 3, 6:30) are offered during summer and spring; call for schedule. If the tour wears you down, rest your feet and refresh your soul at the daily Evensong service at 5:30 PM. *The Close, tel. 01722/555120. Cathedral admission free; donation of £3 requested. Open daily 7–6:15 (May–Aug. until 8:15). Chapter House admission 30p. Open 9:30–7:45, closes at 5:30 Sept.–Apr. and Sun.*

SALISBURY AND SOUTH WILTSHIRE MUSEUM

This small museum is directly across the lawn from the cathedral's main entrance. Inside you'll find pre-historic, Roman, and Saxon artifacts, as well as displays on the history of Salisbury. *65 The Close, tel. 01722/332151. Admission £3. Open Mon.–Sat. 10–5, also Sun. 2–5 in July and Aug.*

WILTON HOUSE

The ancestral home of the Earls of Pembroke (who hobnobbed with Shakespeare and sundry kings and queens) is built on the site of a 9th-century abbey and is laid out, cloisterlike, around a square court-yard. Major remodeling was done, most notably by Inigo Jones, who brought Palladian architecture to Britain. The tour includes a short film of the house's history. Inside, the most impressive room is Jones's gold-bedecked **Double Cube** room, immortalized in any number of period films, including Emma Thompson's *Sense and Sensibility*, and holding a Cinerama-size Van Dyck painting of the fourth earl's family. Other featured artists are Breughel, Andrea del Sarto, and Rembrandt. *Wilton, tel. 01722/746729. Admission £6.75. Open Easter–Oct., daily 10:30–5:30 (last entry 4:30). From bus station, take Bus 60, 60A, 61, or 61A to Wilton House; or walk west 3 mi on A30.*

AFTER DARK

This small town has a disproportionately high number of pubs per capita, as evidenced by the number of pages on Salisbury in the "Wiltshire Good Pub Guide." Surprisingly, Salisbury's nightlife remains pretty tame, with nary a legless drunk on the street. If you've come to dance and paint the town red, you've picked the wrong canvas. However, if you want to experience the truly wide spectrum of what defines a good English pub, you're in luck. Cheers!

If you want to start with the old and traditional, head for the **Haunch of Venison** (Minister St., tel. 01722/322024), a contender for the oldest pub in England. The comfortable "House of Lords" room in the

OF ART, ALIENS, ELVIS, AND AVEBURY

Between the stone circles, chalk carvings, and crop circles, Wiltshire must be a contender among aliens as the coolest art gallery this side of Andromeda. Indeed, few other places in the world can boast such an astonishing view from an aerial perspective. Of these, the most visually stunning are the crop circles (geometric patterns formed by flattened crops) that have been regularly appearing in the fields around Avebury for the past 50 years. Though some people claim they are natural phenomena—the result of minitornadoes or strange wind patterns—one look at most patterns is usually enough to prove this explanation wrong. Two very human pranksters eventually came forward to claim responsibility for the circles, taking the wind out of the media hype that speculated that aliens (and, by extension, Elvis) were involved in their creation. Supernatural or not, the patterns are creations of pure artistry, and you'll find yourself asking "How?" instead of "Who?" Today, crop circles still appear annually, usually in the summer. Be sure to stop at the Henge Shop on Avebury's High Street for the latest news, or to peek at some of the circles caught for posterity in the books and periodicals dedicated to cerealogy—the study of crop circles.

back is where General Montgomery and the Allies began planning the D-Day invasion. The classy, yet unpretentious **Wig & Quill** (New St., tel. 01722/335665) will warm you with its subdued red tones and live blues on Wednesday nights. On weekends, this is one of the liveliest places in town. On the same street, **Cloisters** (tel. 01722/338102) is another drinking hole with armchairs and low beams and occasional live music and deejays. Although still good for a drink after dark, **Old Mill** (Town Path, tel. 01722/327517) is best experienced on a summer's day when you can sip a pint of Summer Lightning (a local brew) on the riverside terrace. Salisbury's only real club is **Churchill's** (4A Endless St., tel. 01722/337415), with two dance floors churning out everything from house and techno to soul music. Occasional live acts play on Friday nights. Popular music acts are frequently featured at the **Salisbury Arts Centre** (Bedwin St., tel. 01722/321744). The center is also a main venue for the **Salisbury Festival** (tel. 01722/323888), a two-week affair featuring an array of music, theater, and visual arts usually held the last week in May through the first week of June.

OUTDOOR ACTIVITIES

BIKING

Following quiet country lanes and passing through small towns, the **Wiltshire Cycleway,** almost oval with two cross-routes, covers the entire county, the Vale of Pewsey, and the Wylye Valley. The shortest loop is from Salisbury to Horningsham (70 mi), and the longest is the County Route (160 mi). Tourist offices have free leaflets that include a map and detailed directions. For a £25 deposit and £9 per day or £55 per week, you can rent a hybrid or mountain bike at **Hayball Cycles** (The Black Horse Chequer, Winchester St., tel. 01722/411378).

HIKING

Haven't you always dreamed of a nature walk through a firing range? Britain's Ministry of Defense owns about 92,000 acres of **Salisbury Plain** (though only some 30,000 acres are used as a firing range). Actually, the public is allowed in only three well-marked areas, with trails through meadows, forests, and along the River Avon. Call 01980/674695 for info. If you prefer a more peaceful hike, head south along the 34-mi **Avon Valley Path,** known for its wildlife. Pick up a free pamphlet at the tourist office that details the route and describes its highlights. The path roughly follows the River Avon as it flows to the sea at Christ Church passing the New Forest towns of Fordingbridge and Ringwood. If you want to indulge in some serious walking, though, you may as well head into the New Forest itself.

NEAR SALISBURY

STONEHENGE

Stonehenge, that world-famous circle of rough-hewn stones on an exposed expanse of Salisbury Plain, has become something of a national icon. But, when you see it, flanked by two busy roads and surrounded by hundreds of tourists, you may wonder why you bothered to come at all. To appreciate Stonehenge you must have a vivid imagination and a sense of curiosity. What, after all, would possess people in 2800 BC to roll menhirs here from as far away as 130 mi and then heave 7-ton monsters to lay on top as lintels?

> *When you get to Stonehenge, prepare to hear a choral rendition of "It's not as big as I thought it would be."*

It's best to ponder these questions very early in the morning, before the tour buses arrive, or in the evening. At these times, Stonehenge does have a certain mystical quality, and questions keep popping into your head. Why? Why? Why? What scientists think they know is that Stonehenge was started circa 2800 BC, expanded between 2100 and 1900 BC, and redecorated in around 150 BC. The original stones, which make up the inner circles, came all the way from the coast of Wales, probably brought over on rafts and dragged here on rollers. The later menhirs were quarried locally, in northern Wiltshire. The most popular theory holds that Stonehenge was a religious site that was linked to the yearly cycle of the sun.

Vandalism prompted the government to fence off the rocks in 1978. Fact is, you can get as good of a view of Stonehenge from some points on the A344 highway as from the paid area. It pays to hike all about the site, near and far, to get that magical Nikon shot. If you're a romantic, you'll want to view Stonehenge at dawn, dusk, or by a full moon; if you're a druid or crusty, you'll want to participate in the midsummer solstice rumble with the local constabulary—it's become a local tradition. *Tel. 01980/ 624715. Admission £4. Open June–Aug., daily 9–7; mid-Mar.–May and Sept.–mid-Oct., daily 9:30–6; mid-Oct.–late Oct., daily 9:30–5; late Oct.–mid-Mar., daily 9:30–4.*

COMING AND GOING • If you have a car or bike, head north on Castle Road from Salisbury's town center and, at the first roundabout, take the exit toward Amesbury (A345) and Old Sarum. Eight mi later, after a few steep inclines, turn left onto A303 toward Exeter. Signs point in the direction of the entrance, up A344, to the right. It's about 12 mi total, one-way. **Wilts & Dorset** (tel. 01722/336855) Bus 3 leaves from Salisbury's bus and train stations about once an hour for Stonehenge (£4.80 return).

AVEBURY

While it's not as well known, Avebury could whip Stonehenge in a stone-circle popularity contest any day among people who have been to both. Avebury makes less of an initial splash because the 98-stone circle is wide (14 times bigger than Stonehenge) and actually surrounds the tiny village of Avebury. Thus, Avebury needs to be seen one stone at a time, but you can go right up and touch them—for free. No one knows the reasons behind its creation, but it is thought to have been built between 2500 and 2300 BC.

The circle is reckoned to lie at the crossroads of some of the most auspicious ley (spiritual energy) lines in Great Britain and is the centerpiece of a number of ancient sites in the area. Stretching over a mile from the southern end of the ring is **The Avenue,** two parallel rows of smaller standing stones. It is thought to have been a processional route between the main circle and **The Sanctuary,** a building presumably used for religious purposes and whose circular shape can still be discerned from the stone foundations. Less than a mile southwest lies the massive **Silbury Hill**—essentially a 120-ft-high, overgrown, conical pyramid. It is an impressive work of engineering, considering it was built over a 200-year period around 2600 BC. Why it was built or how it was used is a mystery. About ¼ mi past Silbury Hill is **West Kennet Long**

Barrow, a significant burial site consisting of five stone chambers. Work on the site started around 3750 BC, though the tomb wasn't actually sealed for another 500–1,000 years. It was desecrated by so-called doctors and scientists in the 19th century, but, from skeletons that did survive, it has been ascertained most of the dead were traditionally buried *after* the flesh had been stripped from the bones.

If you want to view some art rendered in an unconventional medium, visit one of the seven **chalk figures** of horses carved into the area's landscape. Only the horse in Uffington, northeast of Avebury, is ancient: It is believed to have been carved during the Iron Age. The other six (in Pewsey, Alton Barnes, Westbury, Cherhill, Hackpen, and Marlborough) date from 1778 to 1937 and were mainly cut to commemorate coronations and other grand events. Pick up the pamphlet "A Tour of the White Horses" (45p), which provides historical notes and a map, at the **Henge Shop** (High St., tel. 01672/539229) in Avebury.

The **Alexander Keiller Museum** (tel. 01672/539250), named after the site's principal excavator, gives history and displays artifacts found during the excavations. Admission is £1.70. Next door, the 10th-century **Avebury Manor and Garden** (tel. 01672/539250) is a sight in itself, if you don't mind the £3 admission. The Great Barn, off High Street, holds the **tourist office** (tel. 01672/539425), soon to move to new premises in the vicinity.

COMING AND GOING • Wilts & Dorset buses run between Avebury and Salisbury's bus station three or four times daily. The one-way trip takes about 90 minutes. Buy an Explorer ticket if you plan on doing any more bus travel the same day.

STOURHEAD HOUSE AND GARDENS

Close to the village of Stourton lies one of Wiltshire's most breathtaking sights, Stourhead, a country-house-and-garden combination that has few parallels for beauty anywhere in Europe. Most of Stourhead was built between 1721 and 1725 by "Henry the Magnificent," a wealthy banker by the name of Henry Hoare. The wings of the house (containing the exquisitely elegant library and floridly colored picture gallery—both built for the explicit cultural development of this exceedingly civilized family) were added by his grandson about 70 years later. While the house is a monument to the age of elegance and manners, it must take second place to its adjacent gardens, the most celebrated example of the English 18th-century taste for "natural" landscaping. Temples, grottoes, and bridges have been skillfully placed among colorful shrubs, trees, and flowers to make the grounds look like a three-dimensional Old Master painting. (You'll feel as if you've stepped within a 3-D Poussin.) During the summer there are occasional concerts, sometimes accompanied by fireworks and gondoliers on the lake. Just outside the gates is the Spread Eagle Inn, a pricey and lovely place to overnight and take a pleasant lunch or dinner. Stourhead is 9 mi northwest of Shaftesbury (follow B3081 to B3092), 30 mi west of Salisbury. From London, you can take a train from Waterloo Station to Gillingham, then take a 5-minute taxi ride (which can be shared with other riders). *Stourton, near Mere, tel. 01747/841152. House £4.50; gardens £4.50 (Mar.–Oct.), £3.50 (Nov.–Feb.); house and gardens £8. House open Apr.–Oct., Sat.–Wed. noon–5:30 or dusk; gardens daily 9–7 or sunset.*

THE DORSET COAST

If the stark, white, upright cliffs of the Southeast are any reflection of its conservative nature, one would expect the residents of the Dorset Coast to be a little wild—unpredictably dangerous, yet broodingly calm. Though some may be, it is really the landscape itself that embodies these qualities. On the one hand, Mother Nature has scarred the coast with coves and inlets through the untamed power of her landslides. These coves have "bled" in the more organic hues of golden reds and rich browns and are now occupied by charming, scenic villages, hemmed in by the cliffs and the sea. On the other hand, life inland still remains blissfully unperturbed. Although caravan parks and minimalls have encroached, Dorset has its moments of being utterly provincial and pastoral and at times can feel downright antiquated.

DORCHESTER

Dorchester, the center of "Thomas Hardy Country," is a sleepy town with plenty of old houses, graceful tree-lined walks, and streets that turn alarmingly empty after 6 PM. Hardy immortalized Dorchester as the title town in his novel *The Mayor of Casterbridge*. The Barclays Bank on South Street is the mayor's fictional house; a map next to it highlights other Casterbridge attractions. Dorchester is no longer positioned, as Hardy described it, in the middle of a field "like a chessboard on a green tablecloth," with no "translational intermixture between town and down." It's still provincial, but modern sprawl has softened the edges of the town.

BASICS

The **tourist center** (Antelope Walk, off Trinity St., tel. 01305/267992) books rooms for a 10% deposit and has maps and info on surrounding sights. All banks on South Street have **bureaux de change,** most of which close at 4 PM. Clean your dirty togs at the **launderette** (16C High East Street) for £1.60 a wash, 20p for four minutes in the dryer. The **post office** (43 South St., DT1 1DN, tel. 01305/251093) has Saturday hours until 5:30.

COMING AND GOING

Dorchester is served by two train stations; information for both can be obtained by calling 0345/484950. **South Station** (Station Approach) serves routes from the north, south, and east, including London's Waterloo via Southampton (2½ hrs, £35–£43.30 return) and Weymouth (£2.50 day return). **West Station** (Great Western Road) serves routes from the west such as Exeter (£19.40 single). **First Southern National** (tel. 01305/766393) buses run to Weymouth (£1.30 return) and Lyme Regis (£5 return), while **Wilts & Dorset** (tel. 01722/336855) Bus 184 arrives from Salisbury (3 per day, £4.80 round-trip). Buses leave from stops on either Acland or Trinity streets.

WHERE TO SLEEP

Many B&Bs don't have signs, so stop by the tourist office for a complete list. A five- to ten-minute walk west of the center, **Mountain Ash** (30 Mountain Ash Rd., tel. 01305/264811) is a partially modern, partially late Victorian family house with two rooms for £36 each, facing quiet streets and sharing a bathroom. You can't get much quieter than the residential cul-de-sac harboring **Mrs. B. Broadway** (11 Sydenham Way, off Lancaster Rd., tel. 01305/260248). Very modern, comfortable rooms with flowered bedspreads go for £16–£18 (singles) and £26 (doubles). The **Litton Cheney YHA** (Litton Cheney, tel. 01308/482340, fax 01308/482636), a barn that was once a cheese and milk factory, is the closest hostel to Dorchester, 10 mi west off A35. It's small and very popular, with beds costing £9.15, though only open between April and August. Unfortunately, getting to the hostel is no easy task: Take Bus 31 towards Taunton and ask the driver to let you off near Litton Cheney; then walk 1½ mi to the village and follow the YOUTH HOSTEL signs.

FOOD

If you're of the mind to treat yourself, **Yalbury Cottage** (Lower Bockhampton, tel. 01305/262382) is the place. A thatch roof and inglenook fireplaces enhance the traditional ambience here, just 2 mi east of Dorchester and close to Hardy's own cottage. The three-course fixed-price menu, which changes daily and features English and Continental dishes, might include rack of lamb with cassis and caramelized shallot sauce, or medallions of venison. Complete dinners can run up to £30. And if you have lots of pounds to spare, you can also book one of the eight guest rooms here. Now that you've blown your budget for Dorchester, you'll want to consider the following budget options. **Potter In** (19 Durngate St., tel. 01305/260312) serves big filled rolls, meat pies, and 26 flavors of homemade ice cream. The take-away counter at **Golden Lotus** (5 Trinity St., tel. 01305/266293) has lots of Szechuan and Cantonese dishes for under £5. **Shapla Tandoori** (14 High East St., tel. 01305/269202) offers Indian dishes in a variety of regional styles in a surprisingly elegant atmosphere. For bulk supplies, try the **Waitrose** supermarket (Tudor Arcade, off South Street).

WORTH SEEING

If you've come for a dose of Hardy, the tourist office has a free brochure entitled "Discover the Hardy Country," which gives an overview of Hardy's real and fictitious Dorset. **Max Gate** (Arlington Ave., tel. 01305/262538) is a house designed and built by Hardy while he was still a practicing architect. Hardy returned to live in the house from 1885 until his death in 1928, completing *Tess of the D'Urbervilles, Jude the Obscure,* and much of his poetry while he was there. Tour the house Sunday, Monday, or Wednesday 2–5 for £2.10. The **Dorset County Museum** (High West St., at Trinity St., tel. 01305/262735) exhibits local history and archaeological finds as well as the unavoidable Hardy memorabilia (admission £3). The museum is open Monday–Saturday (and Sunday in July and August) 10–5. On a different note, you may be able to tag along with a group touring Dorchester's most famous brewery, **Eldridge Pope and Co.** (Weymouth Ave., south of The Junction, tel. 01305/251251). Pre-booked tours

WELCOME TO HARDY COUNTRY. NOW GO HOME

In Dorset, and Dorchester in particular, you can't go far without running into something related to Thomas Hardy, the man, the myth, the legend. He was born in Higher Bockhampton, about 3 mi northeast of Dorchester—you can tour his house for £2.60 April–September Sunday–Thursday 11–5 or dusk (tel. 01305/262366)—and attended school in Dorchester itself. Locals are a bit fed up with the man whose name is on every visitor's lips. Many are quick to tell you (a) Hardy was a boob, (b) his books are depressing, or (c) they've never read a word by him and really couldn't be bothered.

(£4) lasting 1¼ hours are given weekdays at 10:30, 12:30, and 7:30, otherwise, just show up Wednesday at 11 or 1.

CORFE CASTLE • Corfe is a satisfyingly tragic ruin that sits in a dent in the Purbeck Hills—an easy hop from Dorchester. Legend has it that young King Edward was killed here by his evil stepmother in 978. Later, as a royalist stronghold, it was partially destroyed by Cromwellians, leaving it as it stands today—a tall, partially crumbled hillside castle. From Dorchester, take one of the hourly trains to nearby Wareham (£4 day return) and then one of a dozen daily buses (60p) to the castle. *Wareham, tel. 01929/481294. Admission £4. Open Apr.–Oct., daily 10–5:30 (Mar. and late Oct. until 4:30); Nov.–Feb., daily 11–3:30.*

MAUMBURY RINGS • First it was a circle of stones used for religious practices by the local Druids. Roman engineers then turned the site into an arena about half the length of a football field. After the Romans left, it went unused until 1642, when Parliamentary troops made it a guard post on the Weymouth Road. Don't expect the Coliseum; this is actually another earthwork—no stone involved. *Weymouth Ave. From tourist office, walk south on Trinity St., crossing over Great Western Rd. onto Weymouth Ave. Admission free.*

OUTDOOR ACTIVITIES

Hardy fans and foes alike will appreciate the beautiful landscape that inspired him. The area and all its walking paths are detailed in *Ordnance Survey Path Finder Maps 1318 and 1332.* In particular, take Bus 184 to Puddletown and meander the 5 mi back to Dorchester via lovely **Thorncombe Woods** and **Higher Bockhampton,** where Hardy was born. You'll traverse some truly beautiful countryside on a walk to **Maiden Castle** (Maiden Castle Road), 2 mi southwest of Dorchester off Weymouth Avenue. Enjoy the scenery along the way and be prepared for the castle's underwhelming construction. Though the English Heritage guide calls it "the finest Iron Age hill fort in Britain," it's just a big pile of earth set in a circle. The tourist office also sells cycling pamphlets (30p) outlining routes in Dorchester and the surrounding countryside. There are other leaflets written by the Thomas Hardy Society that guide you through some captivating scenery. Although written for those with cars, many of the routes are easily biked; try to avoid those on major roads like A35. Bikes can be rented at **Dorchester Cycles** (31 Great Western Rd., tel. 01305/268787) for £10 per day or £50 per week.

LYME REGIS

"A very strange stranger it must be, who does not see the charms of the immediate environs of Lyme, to make him wish to know it better," wrote Jane Austen in *Persuasion.* Judging by the crowds that flock here, most people appear to be not at all strange. Indeed, Lyme Regis is a beautifully scenic little town whose unwavering charm has been drawing people for centuries. The town is famous for **The Cobb,** a serpentine breakwater that was once (unbelievably) England's third-busiest harbor, as well as the fossils embedded in its crumbling seaside cliffs. More recently, Lyme's spectacular scenery was featured in John Fowles's *The French Lieutenant's Woman*. At **Serendip Books** (11 Broad St., tel. 01297/442594) you can buy books signed by Fowles, still a resident and the Honorary Archivist of the Lyme Regis Museum.

In summer, you'll find the crowds hanging out and looking for fossils along the beaches west of town. Until recently, most would have kept out of the sea itself; however, a new sewage treatment plant—an attraction in itself—has made the once-unappetizing water clear and safe. Even dolphins and leatherback tortoises now frequent the area. For indoor diversions, visit the **Philpot Museum** (Bridge St., tel. 01297/443370), built in 1900 by T. E. D. Philpot, a former mayor of Lyme. The museum displays the plaster cast of a skeleton of an Ichthyosaurus platyodon and other fossils found by local Mary Anning (1799–1847). Admission is £1.20. **Lyme Regis Marine Aquarium** (The Cobb, tel. 01297/443678) shows you strange local sea life for £1.50.

BASICS

The main part of town, incorporating Sidmouth Road, Pound Street, and Broad Street, roughly follows the wiggle of the coastline. The **tourist office** (Broad St., tel. 01297/442138), open daily except Sun. in winter, arranges local lodgings for a 10% deposit. With **banks** only open on weekdays, it's a good thing that Midland Bank on Broad Street has an ATM.

Pyne House on Broad Street bears a noncommital sign that says it was "the most likely lodging of Jane Austen" in 1803–1804.

COMING AND GOING

The closest train station is in Axminster, about 6 mi north, with service from London's Waterloo (£32 single) and Exeter (£6 day return). From Axminster's station, you can catch Bus 31 to Lyme. This bus also connects Lyme to Weymouth and Dorchester (both about £4 return). **National Express** (tel. 08705/808080) serves Lyme Regis from London (£24 single, £29 return), and—Saturday only—Exmouth and Bristol.

WHERE TO SLEEP AND EAT

Lyme Regis has plenty of B&Bs for around £15 per person—try **Coombe House** (41 Coombe St., tel. 01297/443849), which has three lovely doubles—including one with a kitchenette—for £16.50 per person. The **White House** (47 Silver St., tel. 01297/443420), a beautiful Georgian house with terrific views over the coast, has doubles only for £19–£21 per person, including a choice of English or Continental breakfast; they're closed October through Easter. **Cliff Cottage** (Cobb Rd., tel. 01297/443334) also has great views of The Cobb, a lovely tea garden/patio, and a good fish restaurant. Rooms are £16.50 per person, and £18.50 with bath. The **Pilot Boat Inn** (Broad St., tel. 01297/443157), near the tourist office, cooks up fresh fish and vegetarian specialties such as seafood pie, bouillabaisse, and delicious whole trout with salad and potato. **Buddles Delicatessen** (1 Coombe St., tel. 01297/443164) has good deli fare as well as some vegetarian options.

OUTDOOR ACTIVITIES

The 3-mi path from Lyme Regis to Charmouth follows the sea cliffs for only part of the way because some of the path crumbled and was rerouted around the cliffside golf course. Between Charmouth and Seaton you can still walk along the stunning cliffs known as the **Golden Cap.** The more ambitious 6-mi walk from Lyme Regis's **Undercliffs** (prominently featured in *The French Lieutenant's Woman*) to Axmouth passes through wooded cliffs and treacherous slopes; it can get narrow, rough, and slippery—be careful. You can walk back the way you came or catch Bus 899 (Bus 378 on Sunday) back to Lyme.

THE CORNWALL COAST

The Cornish simply do not smile enough. It's not that they seriously lack in congeniality or a collective sense of humor, but with the abundance of lush, blue-green seascapes, Iron-Age artifacts, the best of English weather, and a prosperous tourism industry, you'd think they'd be grinning 24 hours a day.

Perhaps the region's economic troubles have something to do with the attitude of the Cornish. Tourism might be booming, but that other, more traditional mainstay of Cornwall's economy, fishing, is in the doldrums, embattled against dwindling fish stocks and restrictive EU fishing quotas. There are no easy answers, but in the meantime, the tourist industry continues to expand relentlessly, so that, while it's becoming increasingly easy for travelers to visit the area, it's more difficult for them to discover the true Cornwall. The quality of light has traditionally attracted artists to **St. Ives** and **Newlyn** (next to Penzance), giving rise to small artists' colonies, and St. Ives is today home to an extension of London's Tate Gallery, its beachside premises a strong inducement to visit. **Penzance** and **Falmouth** are good bases for exploring the south's sandy beaches. In the north, the landscape is more austere and dramatic, and the coast craggy. North or south, you'll have no problems finding beaches for sunbathing and swimming. World-class surfing brings enthusiasts to **Newquay.** Thanks to the winds and tides of the Gulf Stream, the mild climate fosters vegetation—palm trees and semitropical flowers—more typical of the Mediterranean than the English Channel.

COMING AND GOING

Train tracks to Cornwall end at Penzance, with lines branching off to Newquay, Falmouth, and St. Ives. If you don't have a Freedom of the South West pass (*see* Basics, *above*), consider buying a **Cornish Rail Rover,** which allows unlimited travel on trains from Plymouth to Penzance. Passes can be bought for unlimited travel for three out of seven days (£18–£25.50 according to season), or eight out of 15 days (£33–£40.60). **National Express** (tel. 08705/808080) has regular service to all the main towns. For regional bus info, call **Western National** (tel. 01208/79898 in Bodmin, 01209/719988 in Camborne).

FALMOUTH

Falmouth winds up and down steep hills, dropping to beaches on one side and its harbor on the other. It's saved from being just another blah beach town by its great views and rich maritime history, by a strong injection of hipness from the **Falmouth School of Art and Design** (one of Britain's best art schools), and by its proximity to Roseland and the lush and lovely Lizard Peninsula (*see below*).

The city's best and most popular sight is **Pendennis Castle** (tel. 01326/316594), which shares a cliff and incredible views with the hostel. The well-preserved, Tudor-era castle gets lots of attention from English Heritage, who've filled it with historical exhibits. It was originally built to protect the Carrick Roads, the most westerly safe anchorage in the English Channel. Admission is £3.80. **Gyllyngvase Beach** is one of the nicest, but, to escape the crowds, walk the lovely 2½ mi along the coast to much mellower **Maenporth Beach.** For performance pieces, live music of all types, and international independent flicks such as *Fallen Angels,* check out the **Falmouth Arts Center** (Church St., tel. 01326/212300).

BASICS

The **tourist office** (28 Killigrew St., across from The Moor, tel. 01326/312300) hands out free maps and accommodation guides. Next door, **Newells Travel** (tel. 01326/312620) is a National Express and British Rail ticket outlet. The **post office** (The Moor, TR11 3RB, tel. 01326/312525) is open weekdays 9–5:30 and Saturday 9–12:30.

COMING AND GOING

Falmouth is well served by **South Wales and West Railways** (tel. 0345/484950); if you're on the main east–west line, transfer at Truro for the train south to Falmouth. There are two stations in town: **Falmouth Docks** puts you closer to the castle and hostel, while **Falmouth Dell** is closer to The Moor (the central town square where the tourist office and bus stop are located). A return fare from London to Falmouth is £55 (£62.30 on Friday or Saturday). **National Express** (tel. 08705/808080) has daily service from London for £37.50 return (£39.50 if you travel on Friday or Saturday). **Western National** (tel. 01209/719988) covers the immediate area and all of Cornwall; get a comprehensive timetable (20p) at the tourist office.

WHERE TO SLEEP

B&Bs in Falmouth cost more but are of a higher quality than those in Penzance. Melvill Road and its off-shoots, near the Falmouth Dell station, are lined with B&Bs. Nearer the beaches, **Esmond House** (5 Emslie Rd., tel. 01326/313214), on a quiet street has rooms with sea views for £18–£21 per person, and **Chellowdene** (Gyllingvase Hill, tel. 01326/314950) has comfortable rooms 50 m from the sea, costing £25 per person; it's closed October through Easter. At the top of the parallel street, **Gyllingvase House Hotel** (Gyllingvase Rd., tel. 01326/312956) has sea views from two of its fifteen rooms, which go for £24.50 per person; evening meals are available.

HOSTELS • Pendennis Castle YHA. There are 76 beds in this former Victorian military barracks, although accommodations are (mercifully) a lot cozier now. It shares grounds with Pendennis Castle up on a promontory overlooking the sea. From the Falmouth Docks station, follow the road to Castle Street, climb the hill to the left, and follow the signs to the castle—a 20- to 30-minute walk. A taxi ride from the Moor is about £3. Beds cost £9.15. *Pendennis Castle, Cornwall TR11 4LP, tel. 01326/311435, fax 01326/315473, E-mail pendennis£yha.org.uk. Curfew 11 PM, lounge open 10–5. Kitchen, laundry, evening meals. Closed Dec.–mid-Feb. and Sun. and Mon. Oct.–Nov.*

FOOD

High Street/Market Street/Church Street—Main Street by any other name—runs along the Eastern Harbour and is loaded with fish restaurants that are tempting but expensive. One cheaper deal is the **Seafood Bar** (Quay St., tel. 01326/315129), whose window is a fish tank, and offers such dishes as thick crab soup, locally caught lemon sole, and, in summer, turbot cooked with cider, apples, and cream. It's closed lunchtime and Sunday–Monday. On the main drag, try **Bon Ton Roulet** (18 Church St., tel. 01326/319290), a comfortable candlelit place with meals such as lasagna, grilled prawns, and superb seafood crepes. There's also a set-price menu. **Dragon Spring** (Quay St., tel. 01326/314559), one of the best of Falmouth's Chinese restaurants, has good-size dishes.

NEAR FALMOUTH

LIZARD PENINSULA

As the southernmost point of mainland Britain, the Lizard Peninsula is the warmest spot in England (though it's notoriously plagued by gale winds, so pack an anorak with your sunscreen). Surprisingly, apart from a couple of popular beaches, it remains relatively unknown to travelers. Because of the weather, many of Britain's rarest plants grow here and only here. Yellow gorse and daffodils herald the spring, narrow hedgerows bloom with purple orchids in the summer, blackberries and elderberries stain the autumn, and chrysanthemums pierce winter's bleakness.

The **South West Coast Path** circumscribes Lizard, along a coastline owned and protected by the National Trust. The best cliff walks are around Mullion Cove. Inland is **Goonhilly Downs,** one of the oldest nature conservancy areas in the country. At the northern end of the peninsula, in Gweek, is the **Cornish Seal Sanctuary** (tel. 01326/221361), a home and hospital for rescued seals that's open to the public. Near Gweek is **Frenchman's Creek,** a valley owned by the National Trust and immortalized by author Daphne du Maurier. No visit to the Lizard Peninsula is complete without a visit to **Roskilly's Farm** (Tregallast Barton, St. Keverne, tel. 01326/280479) near St. Keverne, brought to you by the same folks who make the sumptuous Roskilly's Cornish ice cream. The working dairy farm is situated on 20 acres of wooded valley, where you can wander the grounds for free, and watch as the cows are milked every evening from 4:15 to 5:15. Finish off your visit at the farm's Croust House and indulge in their homemade ice creams or cream teas. It's open until 6:30, or 8:30 Thursday–Saturday in summer, when there are barbecues available at 6:30.

To reach Lizard Peninsula from Falmouth, take **Western National** Bus 2 to Helston, the peninsula's main hub town, where you'll find the **tourist office** (79 Meneage St., tel. 01326/565431). From Helston, **Truronian** (tel. 01872/273453) runs Bus T1 to The Lizard, the peninsula's southernmost town. Pubs throughout the peninsula ensure an unwavering supply of cheap grub. B&Bs are also plentiful, but the best deal is **Coverack YHA** (Park Behan, School Hill, tel. 01326/280687, fax 01326/280119), a relaxed hostel on the east side of the peninsula with views of the bay and the coastline, and minutes from the South West Coast Path. Its 38 beds are £9.15 and it's closed November–March. To get to Coverack take Bus T2, which runs about five times daily in peak season.

PENZANCE

Penzance's lucrative days of piracy and smuggling are past, and today it's the sloping rows of old stucco houses, the quiet seaside, and the never-ending squawk of seagulls that draw people to this old market town. Penzance and its next-door neighbor **Newlyn** were home to the Newlyn school of painters, who

MINING AND DINING: THE UNIQUE CORNISH PASTY

Savory Cornish pasties were invented by tinners' wives during Cornwall's tin-mining heyday. Originally, these large pocket pies encased not just one filling, but three or four, so that tinners could begin with their vegetables at one end, eat the main course in the middle, and finish with a pudding at the other end. The crusty knobs at the corners were meant for holding the pie, and were not to be eaten, lest the arsenic on the miners' hands get ingested. The modern pasty may bear little resemblance to its tasty original, but excellent pasties can still be found.

recorded local sailing and fishing life in a social-realist style; consequently, the town is home to a museum and some interesting galleries. Penzance is also the best base from which to explore famous St. Michael's Mount, Land's End, St. Ives, and tiny nearby towns like Mousehole. From Penzance you can also sail or fly to the beautiful **Isles of Scilly.** The Isles—with their turquoise waters, sandy beaches, and subtropical plants—seem almost to satisfy a strange British fascination with Spanish holiday islands, while distinctly remaining a microcosm of Cornwall itself.

BASICS

The **Penzance Tourist Information Centre** (Station Approach, near train and bus stations, tel. 01736/362207) has walking guides and lists of accommodations. Pick up a list of area galleries, and ask for the free publication "West Cornwall," which contains useful information about the area. Several **banks** on Market Jew Street change money. The **post office** (113 Market Jew St., tel. 01736/363284) has Saturday-morning hours in addition to its regular weekday schedule. The **luggage storage** at the train station is currently closed.

COMING AND GOING

Great Western (tel. 0345/484950) has frequent service between London's Paddington and Penzance (5½ hrs, £53 single, £54.50 return). **National Express** (tel. 08705/808080) buses from London (7½ hrs, £26.50 single, £37.50 return, £39.50 if traveling on Friday) arrive at Penzance's **bus station** (Wharf Rd., tel. 01736/366055) directly across from the train station. At the bus office, pick up a bus schedule for **Western National** (tel. 01208/79898), which covers Penzance and surrounding areas such as St. Ives, Land's End, Helston, and Newquay.

GETTING AROUND

The train station and bus depot are smack in the center of town. Taxis line up outside the train station and usually charge £2.50 for a ride to the youth hostel. Western National's "Hoppa" buses scoot around Penzance. Several outfits in Penzance rent bikes and mopeds; ask the tourist office for a complete list or try **Bike Bitz** (Albert St., tel. 01736/333243), in an alley between the station and Market Jew Street. They rent standard bikes for a mere £6 a day with a deposit of £50, or a driver's license, or other ID.

The central thoroughfare is busy Market Jew Street (a bad translation of the Cornish phrase "Marghas Yow" or "Thursday Market"). Running roughly parallel is Bread Street, lined with warehouses and small restaurants, and Chapel Street, with some of the town's oldest and most unusual buildings. Pedestrian-friendly Causeway Head, filled with good restaurants, cafés, pubs, and bookstores, forks off Market Jew Street from Market Place.

WHERE TO SLEEP

Penzance is blessed with a youth hostel and an exceptional YMCA. As for B&Bs, those on Morrab and Alexandra roads run a miraculously low £11–£15 per person (although you'll want to stay away from those that are decorated Archie Bunker–style). The best of the bunch is the comfortably furnished, no-smoking **Camilla House Hotel** (Regent Terr., tel. 01736/363771), which stands on a road parallel to the Promenade, close to the harbor. The front rooms have sea views, and the top room is coziest. Bathless singles go for £15–£19.50, doubles £20–£27. The owners are agents for the ferry line and can help with trips to the Scilly Isles. Other B&Bs are on Morrab Road, a notch above those on Alexandra Road. **Kimberley House** (10 Morrab Rd., tel. 01736/362727) has eight comfortable rooms (two with private bath) for £18–£20 per person. **Lynwood Guest House** (41 Morrab Rd., tel. 01736/365871) has seven comfortable rooms with tea/coffeemakers and TVs for £13.50 per person in winter, £16.50 in summer, plus £3 for a private bath. Two mi out of town on Bone Valley Road is the **Bone Valley Caravan and Camping Site** (Heamor, tel. 01736/360313), closed January–February, where it costs £7.50–£8.50 to pitch a tent for two people. Take Bus 11D to the Sportsman's pub and ask for directions.

HOSTELS • Penzance YHA. It's a 30-minute hike from the station (or a bus ride and short walk) to this refurbished 18th-century mansion. The warden is helpful, and the kitchen serves the best pizza you'll ever eat in a hostel. Beds in the standard dorm rooms cost £10.15. *Castle Horneck, Alverton, Cornwall TR20 8TF, tel. 01736/362666, fax 01736/362663, E-mail penzance£yha.org.uk. Take Bus 5B, 6B, or 10B from station to Pirate Inn, then follow signs to hostel (a 5-min walk). 80 beds. Curfew 11 PM. Kitchen, laundry. Closed Jan., Sun. and Mon. in Oct. and Nov.*

FOOD

Between the restaurants on Chapel Street, Bread Street, and Causeway Head, you could eat several great meals in Penzance—somewhat of a novelty in this part of the world. Of course, you can always hit the **Co-operative Pioneer** on Market Jew Street for picnic supplies. **Dandelions** (39A Causeway Head, tel. 01736/367683) is a cool, casual vegetarian café and takeout joint, serving red lentil and vegetable soup, whole-meal deep-pan pizzas, and homemade cakes. It's closed on Sunday. For a delicious pub meal near the waterfront, try the tasty Cornish pasties, daily specials, or homemade treacle tart at the nautical **Dolphin Tavern** (22 Quay St., tel. 01736/364106). The popular **Turk's Head** (49 Chapel St., tel. 01736/363093) serves seafood and veggie entrées, including a tasty fisherman's pie (seafood mushed with mashed potatoes). There are good-priced daily lunch and dinner specials.

WORTH SEEING

Penlee House Gallery, on the edge of beautiful Penlee Park, holds the town's historic collections and a famous exhibit of Newlyn School paintings, as well as displays on social history, fine art, architecture, and natural history. An ongoing refurbishment program promises a major reorganization, and should see the opening of a café on the premises. Check for current opening times. *Morrab Rd., tel. 01736/363625. Admission £2. Open Mon.–Sat. 10:30–4:30, Sun. in July and Aug. 12:30–4:30.*

In AD 495 some fishermen had a vision of St. Michael on the rocky summit of **St. Michael's Mount,** and in the 11th century it became the site of a Benedictine monastery. The 14th-century castle you see now was built on the vertical slate and granite crag, and improved upon by Piers St. Aubyn, an architect and ancestor of the family that has owned the place for three centuries. Follow the dreamlike causeway when the tide is out, or take the ferry (summertime only, 70p return) when it's not. This is a biggie, so you may have to wait in line. *Marazion, tel. 01736/710507. From station, take Bus 2 to Marazion. Admission £4.40. Open Apr.–Oct., weekdays 10:30–5:30 (last admission 4:45), July–Aug., also most weekends 10:30–5:30; Nov.–Mar., as weather permits (call ahead).*

OUTDOOR ACTIVITIES

Step right onto any stretch of the 613-mi **South West Coast Path** for some truly inspirational hiking. Some favorite walks include the 2½-mi section from the tiny fishing village of Mousehole (pronounced mow-zul) to Lamorna, and from St. Just (take the bus out) back to Penzance along the coast (19 mi). From Penzance you can follow **St. Michael's Way,** a traditional pilgrim's route that takes you inland toward St. Ives in the north (7½ mi) or east along the coast to St. Michael's Mount (2½ mi). You can also take a dip in the **Jubilee Bathing Pool** (open 10–5:30 and 6:30–9:30) as you're strolling along Penzance's promenade. The curvaceous pool, built in 1935, follows the contours of the surf.

NEAR PENZANCE

LAND'S END

The afternoon sun bounces off the cars and buses in the full parking lot before you ever see it reflected off the sea beyond. Such is Land's End. Its popularity could only be explained by the Western quest for superlatives (highest, biggest, or, in this case, most western part of England). In any case, visitors flock to Land's End in droves. Your mission: Come for the cliffs and sea and skip the silly hoopla of the tourist-oriented shops and attractions.

An £8.95 charge includes admission to all the **Land's End Attractions** (tel. 01736/871501), which promise, according to the breathless tourist leaflets, "multisensory experiences" explaining the history of Land's End and Cornwall. Alternatively, you can buy individual tickets for each attraction. Parking is £2 extra. If you arrive by bus (from Penzance take Bus 1, 1A, 1B, or, on Sunday, 10A), you can walk for free through the white gates and straight past the Disneyesque hullabaloo to explore the coastline. If you drive here, park down the coast in surfer's heaven, Sennen Cove, and then walk in to avoid being bilked.

The stretches of Coastal Path between Land's End and St. Ives and Land's End and Penzance are notoriously gorgeous. The 18-mi **Tinner's Way,** an ancient walkway along the tops of hills from St. Just (just north of Land's End) to St. Ives, passes close to the stone structures of Zennor Quoit, Lanyon Quoit, and the famous Mên-an-tol. In nearby Porthcurno, 3 mi east of Land's End, check out the cliffside, open-air **Minack Theatre** (tel. 01736/810181), which hosts plays of all genres (about £6.50) May–mid-September. Some regular playgoers prefer the rear seats (£5.50) for the most spectacular views. If you're lucky, you may spot a school of dolphins in the background while watching a play. When plays aren't on, it costs £2 to tour this unusual theater.

WHERE TO SLEEP • Whitesands Lodge. This comfortable guest house and hostel is filled with funky and mellow people and makes a great place to get away from it all. It was once a climbing school and still retains an outdoor-oriented atmosphere: If you want to climb, surf, or mountain bike, they can set you up with all the right people. The South West Coast Path is also only five minutes away. Rates are £10 for a dorm bed (including sheets), £14.50 for a room in the guest house. Breakfast costs £4. It's wise to book early in July and August. On site is a restaurant and bar. *Sennen, Cornwall, TR19 7AR, tel. 01736/871776. From Penzance, take Bus 1, 1A, or 15 toward Land's End; it is the first house on the left as you enter Sennen. 26 beds; 5 rooms, 2 with bath. Kitchen, laundry.*

ST. IVES

As you approach St. Ives, the view will stir you to the aesthetic bone. With waves lapping on one side of the hill and a harbor on the other, you'll wonder why you didn't catch a fast train here to begin with. The yellow lichen that covers most rooftops throughout Cornwall descends on St. Ives like magic gold dust. The water is aqua and deep blue; purple and red umbrellas blossom on the sandy beaches on sunny days and palm trees spike the blue skies. Such beauty attracted folks such as James McNeill Whistler in the 19th century and writer Daphne du Maurier in the 1940s. Virginia Woolf also summered here, incorporating her experiences into her novel *To the Lighthouse* (she especially drew on the view of Godrevy lighthouse from St. Ives). On the downside, this tiny town gets crammed with people seeking sand, sun, and world-class art—so much so that in July and August cars are prohibited from entering the town center.

BASICS

The **tourist office** (Guildhall, off Tregenna Pl., tel. 01736/796297) gives out the free *West Cornwall Accommodations Directory,* as well as a long list of local galleries to explore. **Banks,** scattered along High Street, are open only on weekdays, though there's no shortage of ATMs. The **post office** (1 Tregenna Pl., TR26 1AA, tel. 01736/795004) is open weekdays until 5:30 and Saturday 9–1. At the train station, St. Ives Travel (tel. 01736/795908) sells tickets, changes money, and offers **luggage storage** for £1.50 per bag.

COMING AND GOING

St. Ives is serviced by a **South Wales and West** line that branches off the main Penzance to Paddington line. Trains run several times a day in summer, less in winter. Fares from London are £50–£58 return, while the journey from Penzance is £2.70 single, £2.90 day return. Call 0345/484950 for information. **Western National** Buses 16, 17, 17A, 17B, and 17C from Penzance and, in summer, 57D from Newquay run to St. Ives for about £2.70 return from Penzance, £4.90 return from Newquay. **National Express** (tel. 08705/808080) also serves St. Ives from London (£37.50 return, or £39.50 if traveling on Friday).

WHERE TO SLEEP

B&Bs along Tregenna Terrace, Carthew Terrace, Channel View, and Bedford Road charge as little as £12 per person for sunny rooms near the water. **Garlands** (1 Belmont Terr., tel. 01736/798999) is David and Manya Johnson's sunny, vegetarian-friendly house with good-size rooms for £12–£20 a head. **Horizon Guest House** (Carthew Terr., off Belmont Terr., tel. 01736/798069) is near the South West Coast Path and has five flowery, immaculate rooms for £17 per person; ask for the double with the three-sided view of the ocean. The only campground in St. Ives proper is **Ayr Holiday Park** (tel. 01736/795855), a 15-minute uphill walk from the center of town along Higher Ayr Street. The rates are £6.50 for two people and tent, rising to £10.50 in high summer. It's closed late October–Easter.

FOOD

Grapevine (7 High St., tel. 01736/794030) is a dark, inviting place with both meaty and vegetarian "whole food" dishes for £6–£11. A cheaper option is **Polly's** (14 Fish St., tel. 01736/794928), with specials such as Fish Street Pie. **The Cafe** (Island Sq., tel. 01736/793621) has veggie specials such as mushroom stroganoff and vegetable korma, a mild cream and nut curry. **Tucker Sandwich Bar** (6 Tregenna Pl., tel. 01736/795179) has sandwiches with fillings such as chicken tikka and yogurt, hummus, and Cornish crab. **Roskilly's Cornish Ice Cream** along the wharf has sumptuous flavors—try wild cherry or orange Mascarpone.

WORTH SEEING

Barbara Hepworth Museum, the home and work studio of one of the 20th century's premier sculptors, now houses a small museum run by London's Tate Gallery. The displays are simple, the sculptures and garden sublime. *Barnoon Hill, off High St., tel. 01736/796226. Admission £3.50; joint ticket with Tate Gallery (see below) £6. Open Tues.–Sun. 10:30–5:30, also Mon. 10:30–5:30 in July and Aug., and on national holidays.*

Artists who've spent time in St. Ives include sculptors Barbara Hepworth and Naum Gabo, and painters Peter Lanyon, Mark Rothko, and Helen Frankenthaler.

With enormous local support, London's **Tate Gallery** opened this stunning eponymous offshoot in 1993—a circular glass-and-stucco building with 180° views of turquoise rippling ocean. The permanent collection is spare, but the gallery often has worthwhile temporary exhibits. The rooftop café is one of Cornwall's best locales for a cup of tea and a bun. *Porthmeor Beach, tel. 01736/796226. Admission £3.90. Open Tues.–Sun. 10:30–5:30, also Mon. 10:30–5:30 in July and Aug., and on national holidays.*

NEWQUAY

What do bleached, blissed-out surfers and blue-haired old ladies have in common? They both flock to Newquay, eager for its beaches and promenades, undeterred by its commercialism and significant lack of Cornish charm. World-class waves attract surfers year-round, and the beaches bring families out when school holidays begin in July. The north of town is a wide stretch of sandy beaches from Towan in the west to Lusty Glaze in the east. On Towan, check out **The Island,** an odd towering rock connected to the headland by a suspension bridge. At night, live music emanates from the Red Lion and Victoria pubs near Towan Beach, and the streets are crammed with hearty partyers. The moral: If you didn't come to boogie or boogie board, don't come.

BASICS

The busy **Newquay Tourist Information Centre** (Marcus Hill, tel. 01637/871345) changes money on weekends for a 1.5% commission. It's across the street from the bus station and a five-minute walk up Cliff Road from the train station. The main **post office** (31–33 East St., tel. 01637/873364) has Saturday-morning hours and a row of phones out front. The luggage deposit at the train station on East Street is currently closed.

COMING AND GOING

If you're coming from London (6 hrs, £54 single, £55–£65 return) on the main Paddington-Penzance line, change trains at Par. From here, **South Wales and West** (tel. 0345/484950) scoots to Newquay about four times a day in summer (once on Sunday), only once a day in winter (not Sunday). The ride takes about 50 minutes. You will also have to make one of these connections if you're coming from Penzance (£10.30 single, £11.40 day return). Newquay is also served by **National Express** (tel. 08705/808080) from London (£37.50 return, or £39.50 if traveling on Friday) and Penzance (£4.75–£5.50 return). **Western National** (1 East St., tel. 01209/719988) buses also travel to Penzance (£4.90 return). The **LSA** travel office (tel. 01637/877180), just off the East Street platform, has full rail and bus information. The town itself is easy to navigate. Its main streets—Cliff Road, East Street, Bank Street, and Fore Street (a wobbly street that changes names every few blocks)—run roughly parallel to the seafront. The station café has **left-luggage** facilities (tel. 01637/877837).

WHERE TO SLEEP

The hostels and some B&Bs post signs on the window of Woods the Choc Box smoke shop, just across East Street from the bus depot. One of the better B&Bs is the **Pavilion** (9 Beachfield Ave., tel. 01637/879187), with cozy rooms equipped with armoires, dressers, and TVs for about £15 per person, or £10 for night-only. For £14 you get sea views at **Sea Shells** (55 Fore St., tel. 01637/874582), though the proprietor won't take one-nighters in July–August.

HOSTELS • Get down and very dirty with Australian surfers at the extremely laid-back **Towan Backpackers Hostel** (16 Beachfield Ave., tel. 01637/874668). You'll pay £9.50 for the first night, £8.50 for every night thereafter. A similar deal is offered at **Newquay International Backpackers** (69–73 Tower Rd., tel. 01637/879366), where beds go for about £9. At **Rick's Hostel** (8 Springfield Rd., tel. 01637/851143), Rick's kindly mum cleans every day, making this place an altogether different experience. Beds in tidy, carpeted rooms cost £8–£10, but are rentable by the week only in summer (£60 in August). All hostels have TVs, kitchens, and places to store your surfboard.

FOOD

Newquay isn't exactly known for its fine food, and most of its cafés look very unappetizing. Put together your own meal at **Leo's Supermarket** on Oakleigh Terrace, just off East Street, or at **Gateway,** off Fore Street. One notable exception is the **Lifebuoy Café** (1 Tower Rd., tel. 01637/878076), just up from the beach, which serves all-day breakfasts for £3 (vegetarians pay a little more) and baguettes, which you can munch at outdoor tables. The **Sailors Arms** (15 Fore St., tel. 01637/872838), also one of the more popular nightspots, serves good lunch and dinner at reasonable prices. Try the swordfish steak with salad. Similarly, the very large **Red Lion** (North Quay, tel. 01637/872195) has a good selection of grill items and burgers and often features live music at night.

NEAR NEWQUAY

TINTAGEL

Though references to Tintagel (pronounced tin-ta-jull) as King Arthur's birthplace by Geoffrey of Monmouth, Thomas Malory, and Alfred, Lord Tennyson are vague and unsubstantiated, they cast an Arthurian aura over this tiny north Cornwall village. Even if Arthur never set foot here, something big was afoot in these high rocky cliffs; archaeological finds point to extremely wealthy, perhaps royal folks living in Tintagel as far back as Roman times. Either way, in 1236 the Earl of Cornwall built **Tintagel Castle,** now a formidable windswept ruin perched on a craggy cliff. *Tel. 01840/770328. Admission £2.90. Open daily Apr.–Sept., 10–6 (until 8 mid-July–mid-Aug.); Oct., daily 10–5; Nov.–Mar., daily 10–4. From Fore St. follow signs.*

If you're in the mood for a decent laser show, **King Arthur's Great Hall** has flashing lights, hissing steam, and a disembodied voice reading a synopsis of Thomas Malory's *Morte d'Arthur,* a fictional account of King Arthur's life. Actually, this is a fun, informative little show. Afterward you can sit in a big cement throne and ponder delicately shaded stained-glass windows depicting the life of Arthur, done by an uncredited artist named Veronica Whall (1877–1967). *Fore St., tel. 01840/770526. Admission £2.75. Open daily 10–5 (sometimes until 8 in summer).*

COMING AND GOING • As if to add to the Arthurian mystique, getting to Tintagel (especially in winter) can be like undertaking a search for the Holy Grail. During the summer, bus companies operate excursions to the castle: These aren't guided tours but simply guarantee a ride there and back with adequate time for exploration. From Newquay, **Western National** runs one called "King Arthur's Country" (£3.90) that goes direct to Tintagel at 1 PM on Friday May–September, but you're better off buying a day **Explorer** ticket (£6), which is valid for the trip; check at the bus station for details. Similarly, **Western Greyhound** (14 East St., tel. 01637/873321) operates a half-day tour to Tintagel that leaves Newquay on Wednesday at 1 PM. Fares are £5 or £6.50 return. In winter, be prepared for an epic quest. There is no direct service from Newquay, so you must first get to Wadebridge, serviced by a few National Express buses (X2, 732, 504) in the morning, as well as Western National Bus 56 (which runs daily). From Wadebridge, catch Bus 122, 124, or 125, all running Monday–Saturday, to Tintagel. Buses run about three times a day, but are totally uncoordinated—you may be waiting in Wadebridge for a while. Even with good connections, the total journey can take three to four hours. Check at the bus stations for current times and connection information.

WHERE TO SLEEP AND EAT • Don't miss the chance to sleep in the amiable **Tintagel YHA** (Dunderhole Pt., tel. 01840/770334, fax 01840/770733). It's a fire-warmed, National Trust mining cottage embedded at the top of the Glebe Cliffs, about ½ mi from Tintagel village. Beds cost £9.15. The hostel is closed October–March and Wednesday April–mid-June and September. From the main street, follow the path to St. Materiana's Church, continue on the path toward the cliff, and follow the signs; you won't see the hostel until you're right on top of it. **Ye Olde Malthouse** (Fore St., tel. 01840/770461) is a 500-year-old building with well-furnished rooms for £19.50–£25 per person. There's nary a restaurant or market near the hostel, so stock up on supplies at **Leo's Supermarket** (The Platt) in Wadebridge or at **Londis** on Fore Street.

OXFORD AND THE HEART OF ENGLAND

UPDATED BY ROBERT ANDREWS

The "Heart of England" doesn't really exist; the name is nothing more than convenient travel-guide lingo for an unclassifiable swath of central England just northwest of London. The region does share a few common features, although the adjective "common" doesn't really fit the bill—not when you're talking about countryside so photogenic it practically clicks the shutter on your camera for you, or about those dreamy villages where clocks could have stopped 200 years ago without anyone minding terribly. Within this idyllic realm are two of England's most popular destinations, Stratford-upon-Avon and Oxford. The former is the hometown of one Master William Shakespeare, gentleman; the latter is England's greatest university town.

If you're staying in London for more than a week, leave England in shame if you can't manage a trip to **Oxford,** the region's finest city. Oxford offers the sophistication of an old college town crossed with the hurly-burly of an enormous metropolis—not to mention a thriving club and music scene. If you have more time, discover rural (albeit *wealthy* rural) England in the **Thames Valley,** which stretches east past Oxford toward London. On weekends the villages lining the Thames swell with city dwellers seeking a "quaint" respite from suburbia.

The **Cotswold Hills** get written up in the fancier travel magazines for good reason—it's everyone's ideal of rural England. **Cheltenham** and **Cirencester** are the main urban centers for the Cotswolds; both are attractive, lively, and excellent bases from which to explore secluded villages, such as Bibury, royal Tetbury, and the Slaughters, to name a few. **Stratford-upon-Avon** is at the other extreme: so many Shakespeare lovers pack its streets that, at times, the town becomes tourist hell. We don't recommend ignoring Stratford, but prepare yourself for more than a bit of kitsch—a Shakespeare-head egg-timer, anyone?—and crass commercialism.

OXFORD

Home of the world's first English-language university, Oxford today is bustling and crowded, a vast conurbation expanding outward from the university at its center. Once upon a time, cattle herders led their flocks over this shallow junction of the Thames and Cherwell rivers. These days, however, the horde of

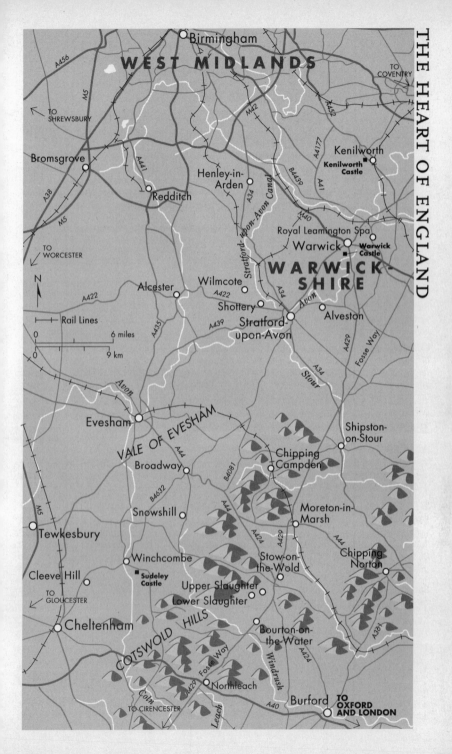

Birmingham

WEST MIDLANDS

TO COVENTRY

A456

M5

TO SHREWSBURY

Bromsgrove

A38

M5

A441

Redditch

Henley-in-Arden

M42

A34

Stratford-upon-Avon Canal

A4177

Kenilworth

Kenilworth Castle

B4439

A41

M40

Royal Leamington Spa

Warwick

Warwick Castle

WARWICK-SHIRE

A34

TO WORCESTER

N

A422

Alcester

Wilmcote

A422

Shottery

A435

A439

Stratford-upon-Avon

Avon

Alveston

A429

Fosse Way

Rail Lines

0   6 miles

0   9 km

Avon

A34

Stour

Evesham

VALE OF EVESHAM

A44

Broadway

B4081

Shipston-on-Stour

Chipping Campden

M5

B4632

Snowshill

A44

A424

A429

Moreton-in-Marsh

A44

Tewkesbury

Winchcombe

Sudeley Castle

Stow-on-the-Wold

Chipping Norton

Cleve Hill

TO GLOUCESTER

Upper Slaughter

Lower Slaughter

COTSWOLD HILLS

Cheltenham

Bourton-on-the-Water

Windrush

A424

A381

Fosse Way

A429

Northleach

Coln

TO CIRENCESTER

Leach

A40

Burford

TO OXFORD AND LONDON

WAR AND PEACE IN OXFORD

Throughout Oxford's history, tensions between the city and the university have often erupted into violence. The most famous and bloodiest event, the St. Scholastica's Day Riots, which took place in 1355, began with a tavern brawl between scholars and a local pub owner. Over the next three days, colleges were sacked and six students were killed. In the end the university gained the upper hand because it had royal backing. Despite several townie attempts to regain control, the university was the heavy in Oxford until the 19th century. Tension still exists today, but the sparring tends to be limited to the occasional sarcastic comment or verbal fisticuffs.

buses and foot traffic in the city center are more comparable to Piccadilly Circus. Contrary to the way it's portrayed in movies, Oxford is not nearly as small and idyllic as Cambridge, England's other ivory tower. Blame the heavy industry on Oxford's outskirts, particularly the large Rover car factory. Even so, street performers and flying troops of bone-rattlers (those shaky bicycles associated with English academics) make Oxford an engaging city, and the food and nightlife rank far above that of quiet Cambridge.

Oxford and Cambridge are the nation's most prestigious universities, and their rivalry is intense. To simplify outrageously, Oxford is better known for the arts, Cambridge for the sciences. Both universities are *names,* and thanks to their legendary old-boy networks, a degree from either, in any field, can translate into a lucrative career. But as in every college town, Oxford student life is a perennial cycle of classes, drinking, more drinking, and frantic bouts of studying.

BASICS

AMERICAN EXPRESS
This office offers the usual cardholder services. Both cardholders and noncardholders pay a £3 commission for currency exchange. *4 Queen St., OX1 1EJ, tel. 01865/792066. Open weekdays 9–5:30, Sat. 9–5, Sun. (June–Sept.) 11–3.*

DISCOUNT TRAVEL AGENCIES
STA Travel (36 George St., tel. 01865/792800), the biggest of Oxford's budget-travel centers, sells ISIC cards, InterRail passes, and bargain plane tickets. When their office gets too busy, stop by **Campus Travel** (105 St. Aldate's, tel. 01865/242067) or the agency inside the **YHA Adventure Shop** (9–10 St. Clement's St., tel. 01865/247948), which offers cheaper transportation fares to those with a hostel card.

LAUNDRY
Safari Launderette (113 Walton St., no phone) is open until 7:30 daily. A medium-size load costs £3 to wash plus 50p per five-minute drying cycle.

MAIL
The busy **main post office** (102–104 St. Aldate's St., OX1 1ZZ, tel. 0345/223344) changes money for a 1% commission (£2 minimum) and handles poste restante. It's open until 6 on Saturday.

VISITOR INFORMATION
Oxford's **tourist office** seems more interested in selling merchandise than in providing helpful guidance. Nearly every map and leaflet costs something. One invaluable source of information that won't cost you a penny is **The Oxford Guide,** issued every June by the *Oxford Mail* and crammed with facts, maps, admission times and prices, pubs and restaurants, and background information on all the colleges. Pick

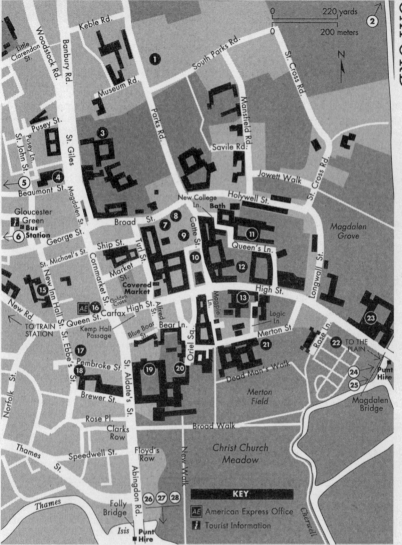

0 220 yards
0 200 meters

N

Keble Rd.

Woodstock Rd.

Little
Clarendon St.

Banbury Rd.

Museum Rd.

South Parks Rd.

St. Cross Rd.

Pusey St.

St. Giles

St. John St.

St. Giles

Parks Rd.

Savile Rd.

Mansfield Rd.

Jowett Walk

Magdalen
Grove

Gloucester
Green
Bus
Station

Beaumont St.

Magdalen St.

George St.

Broad   St.

New College
Ln.

Holywell St.

Bath

St. Cross Rd.

Ship St.

St. Michael's St.

Cornmarket St.

Turl St.

Market
St.

Catte St.

Queen's Ln.

Longwall St.

Covered
Market

Golden
Cross

High   St.

Logic
Ln.

New Inn Hall St.

New Rd.

TO TRAIN
STATION

Carfax

High St.

Alfred St.

Blue Boat
St.

Bear Ln.

Maypole

Oriel Sq.

Merton St.

Rose Ln.

TO THE
PLAIN

Punt
Hire

Magdalen
Bridge

Queen St.

St. Ebbe's St.

Kemp Hall
Passage

Pembroke St.

Brewer St.

Rose Pl.

Clarks
Row

St. Aldate's St.

Dead Man's Walk

Merton
Field

Norfolk St.

Thames

Speedwell St.

Floyd's
Row

New Walk

Broad Walk

Christ Church
Meadow

Thames

Folly
Bridge

Abingdon Rd.

Isis   Punt
Hire

Cherwell

KEY

Ae American Express Office

i Tourist Information

Sights ●

All Souls
College, **12**

Ashmolean
Museum, **4**

Bodleian Library, **9**

Botanic Garden, **22**

Carfax Tower, **16**

Christ Church
College, **19**

Christ Church
Picture Gallery, **20**

Magdalen
College, **23**

Merton College, **21**

Museum of the
History of
Science, **7**

Museum of
Modern Art, **17**

New College, **11**

Oxford University
Museum and Pitt
Rivers Museum, **1**

Pembroke
College, **18**

Radcliffe
Camera, **10**

Sheldonian
Theatre, **8**

St. John's College, **3**

St. Peter's
College, **15**

University
College, **13**

Lodging ○

Brown's Guest
House, **24**

Falcon Private
Hotel, **26**

Isis Guest House, **25**

Mrs. O'Neil, **5**

Newton House, **27**

Oxford Backpackers
Hostel, **6**

Oxford Camping
International, **28**

Oxford YHA, **2**

it up at the tourist office, train and bus stations, and some shops, though it's usually sold out by about Christmas. *The Old School, Gloucester Green, tel. 01865/726871. Open Mon.–Sat. 9:30–5, also Sun. May–end Oct. 10–1 and 1:30–3:30.*

COMING AND GOING

BY BUS

All long-distance buses stop at **Gloucester Green Station,** about two blocks from the train depot. Bus company offices here have info and timetables. **National Express** (tel. 0990/808080) offers service from Oxford to London, Birmingham, Bristol, Cambridge, and Nottingham. The 90-minute journey from Oxford to London's Victoria Station costs £7.50 day return and £9.50 open return, the same prices as **Oxford Tube** (tel. 01865/772250), which runs buses to London every 12 minutes in peak time (at least every hour through the night), and **Oxford City Link** (tel. 01865/785400), with service every 20 minutes. Oxford Tube also operates express buses to Heathrow (£9 single) and Gatwick (£16 single) airports. If you're looking to go to Stratford, **Stagecoach Oxford** (tel. 01865/772250) runs seven buses a day (X50) for £5 day return.

BY TRAIN

Thames Trains (tel. 0345/484950) runs frequent trains from London's Paddington to **Oxford Station** on Botley Road. The trip takes about an hour and costs £12.50 day return, £15.80 five-day return. The train is convenient, but buses are cheaper.

GETTING AROUND

The town of Oxford and its 40 colleges are inextricably intertwined. The jumbled center of it all is **Carfax,** where Cornmarket, St. Aldate's, High, and Queen streets meet, people congregate, and cars battle for space with buses. Beyond Carfax, streets can be hard to figure out, even with a fairly detailed map; invest in an *Oxford A–Z* map (£2.45) if you want to avoid frustration. With so much to see and do, and so much of it spread over a large area, it's wise to make good use of buses; they're fast, frequent, and fairly cheap.

BY BICYCLE

Oxford's flat terrain and extensive network of bike paths make for great cycling. The free *Cycling in Oxford: A Comprehensive Guide* includes detailed maps of all bike paths as well as information on local cycling organizations. Where they exist, bike paths are honored, but biking is always a bit dicey in Oxford (though no more so than in most other city centers). Be extremely careful about leaving your expensive mountain bike locked in the town center—thousands manage to be stolen each year in broad daylight. You can rent bikes from **Bikezone** (6 Lincoln House, Market St., off Cornmarket, tel. 01865/728877) and **Cycle King** (55 Walton St., tel. 01865/516122) for about £12 daily, or £16 per week.

BY BUS

Two main companies, **Oxford Bus Co.** (tel. 01865/785400) and **Thames Transit** (tel. 01865/772250), vie for business on similar routes. Oxford's red double-decker buses and green "Nipper" minibuses run about every seven minutes weekdays and summer Saturdays and at 30-minute intervals at other times. Thames Transit's tan-and-blue minibuses run less frequently but are 5p–15p less expensive. Just about any bus marked CITY CENTER will take you to within ¼ mi of Carfax. Most buses to the suburbs also depart from within two blocks of there. Oxford Bus Co. offers various one-day passes for central zone (£1.80) and beyond, while Thames Transit offers a **City Hopper** pass (£1.80) for one day of unlimited travel within Oxford and an **Explorer** pass (£4.90) for longer journeys including Blenheim Palace. Free route maps are available at the bus station. Be warned that routes and route numbers change frequently—a result of a full-blown war waged between rival bus companies ever since the hasty and ill-considered deregulation of Oxford's transport system. Only some buses, run by **Stagecoach** (tel. 0865/772250), run all night (for example, No. 1 to Blackbird Leys, via Magdalen Bridge and Cowley Road, and No. 7 up Banbury Rd, both every 20 min. There's no all-night service up Abingdon Rd.).

WHERE TO SLEEP

Whether you're a thirtysomething New Yorker looking for a soulmate or just trying to find a budget accommodation in Oxford, the same adage rings true: There are some good ones out there but they're usually taken. With two hostels now open, prospects are improving; however, try to book ahead whenever possible. Peak season lasts from May through August, and arriving unprepared could lead to heartache and serious wallet damage.

UNDER £30 • Mrs. O'Neil. This is one of Oxford's true lodging bargains. The rooms are immaculate, but there are only two of 'em (one single, one double), so make reservations right now. Bed and breakfast costs £12.50 per person, and you get a TV and tea- and coffee-making appliances in your room. *15 Southmoor Rd., OX2 6RF, tel. 01865/511205 or 0401/002845. From Carfax, walk north on Cornmarket St., turn left on Beaumont St., right on Walton St., left on Southmoor Rd. 2 rooms, none with bath. No credit cards.*

UNDER £40 • Isis Guest House. This large college house, just across Magdalen Bridge, is open late June through September, when the students who normally inhabit the Victorian house go home. Modernized doubles go for £38; they're meagerly furnished but generally a fine place to rest your weary head. *45–53 Iffley Rd, OX4 1EB, tel. 01865/741024, fax 01865/243492. From Carfax, take Oxford Bus 4 or Thames Transit Bus 3 toward Rose Hill and alight after Magdalen Bridge.*

UNDER £50 • Brown's Guest House. Brown's is heartily recommended by hostel staff, who often send overflow backpackers here for the comfortable beds, plush rooms, and yummy breakfasts. Try to get a room that doesn't face noisy Iffley Road. Singles are £25, doubles £42 (£50 with bath). There's a 5% surcharge added to bills paid with credit card. *281 Iffley Rd., OX4 4AQ, tel. and fax 01865/ 246822. From Carfax, take Oxford Bus 4 or Thames Transit Bus 3 toward Rose Hill and alight at Howard St. 9 rooms, 2 with bath.*

Oxford University is where Percy Bysshe Shelley was unceremoniously expelled only a few months after arriving and where Hugh Grant perfected his "nervous Englishman" look.

Newton House. A number of bargain B&Bs lurk past Folly Bridge far from the center, and Newton House is the best of them. The spotless rooms all have TVs and plenty of light. Doubles cost £48 (£58 with bath), a bit less in winter. *82–84 Abingdon Rd., OX1 4PL, tel. 01865/ 240561. From Carfax, walk south on Abingdon Rd. or take Bus X3, 16, 30, 31, 32, 32A, 33, or 35. 13 rooms, 8 with bath.*

UNDER £70 • Falcon Private Hotel. This hotel really is a home-away-from-home and definitely worth the splurge. The staff is a bit snooty but the attractive rooms have luxuries such as satellite TV and hair dryers. Singles are £29–£35, doubles £56–£68, triples £72–£84, quads for £88–£98, though prices drop off-season. *88–90 Abingdon Rd., OX1 4PX, tel. 01865/722995. Follow directions to Newton House (see above). 11 rooms, all with bath.*

HOSTELS

Oxford Backpackers Hostel. This hostel is a godsend to budget travelers. The central location, friendly staff, and 24-hour access make it a perfect base for exploring the colleges, pubs, and nightlife (the hostel even organizes a pub crawl on Tuesday). The huge common room includes a pool table and adjoining tropical-style bar open until 2:30 AM on Friday and Saturday. A dorm bed costs from £11 (£10 June–Sept.), including sheets and use of showers and kitchen. *9A Hythe Bridge St., OX1 2EW, tel. and fax 01865/721761, E-mail oxford@yhostels.demon.co.uk, website www.hostels.co.uk. From bus station, turn left on Worcester St., right on Hythe Bridge St. 92 beds. Kitchen.*

Oxford YHA. Clean, comfortable, and expertly managed, the hostel is a model of efficiency with great kitchen facilities, a pool table, and lots of info. Beds fill quickly year-round in this brick Victorian about a mile outside the town center; reserve ahead and check in before 9 PM. Dorm beds cost £10.15. *32 Jack Straw's La., OX3 0DW, tel. 01865/762997, fax 01865/769402, E-mail oxford@yha.org.uk. From Carfax take Bus 10, 13, or 14. 112 beds. Flexible midnight curfew.*

CAMPING

The **Oxford YHA** (*see above*) has a couple of campsites on its yard available for £5 per person. At **Oxford Camping International** (426 Abingdon Rd., tel. 01865/244088) you'll be vying with motor homes, but hey, it's clean, green, cheap, and open year-round. The charges are £3.65 per person, £5.20 in high season, plus a pitch fee of £4.20 per tent. To reach the campground take the Park & Ride Bus, stopping at Carfax every 10 minutes or so.

FOOD

Oxford has great eating options, with all ethnicities and price ranges represented. If you're strapped, head to supermarkets such as **J. Sainsbury** (Westgate Shopping Centre, tel. 01865/722179) and **Tesco** (159 Cowley Rd., tel. 01865/244470), both of which are open on Sunday. At the **Covered Market,** on Market Street a half block east of Cornmarket Street, greengrocers, butchers, and bakers set up shop Monday–Saturday among the clothing and souvenir stands. **Harvey's** (89 Gloucester Green, tel. 01865/ 793963), beside the bus station, has every sandwich combination imaginable. **Heroes** (8 Ship St., tel. 01865/723459) is a bit fancier, with fresh-baked breads and Italian-style subs. For delicious hummus, breads, cheeses, and desserts go to **Gluttons Delicatessen** (110 Walton St., tel. 01865/553748).

UNDER £5 • Café MOMA. This spacious joint is hidden beneath the Museum of Modern Art. By noon it's jumping with the local art crowd, but things quiet down around 3 PM. Chow down on a large salad, or try the vegan "Nutroast," a baked loaf of ground nuts and onions, served with two side dishes of salad. *30 Pembroke St., tel. 01865/722733. From Carfax, walk west on Queen St., turn left on St. Ebbe's St., left on Pembroke St. Closed Mon. and evenings (except Thurs. evening).*

Georgina's Coffee Shop. Toulouse-Lautrec posters line the walls in this hip café hidden within the hectic confines of the Covered Market. Strong coffee complements bagels, pastries, and delicious lunch specials. *Covered Market, above Beaton's Deli, tel. 01865/249527. Closed Sun. and evenings. No credit cards.*

UNDER £15 • Browns. You may have to wait for a table at this popular restaurant patronized by both students and locals. The wide choice of basic dishes includes steak-mushroom-and-Guinness pie and hot chicken salad. Potted palms and mirrors give the otherwise plain rooms some cheer. *5–11 Woodstock Rd., tel. 01865/511995.*

Chang Mai Kitchen. Oxford's best Thai food is served up in a ramshackle Tudor building less than a block from Carfax. Despite the classy wooden-beam surroundings, most dishes are relatively inexpensive. Splurges like the fish in coconut curry go for under a tenner. *Kemp Hall Passage, 130A High St., tel. 01865/202233. From Carfax, walk east on High St., turn right on tiny Kemp Hall Passage.*

News Café. If you want to stay in touch, hunker down here with a stack of newspapers and two TVs tuned to news broadcasts. Breakfasts, bagels, and daily specials (including pastas) make up the menu, as well as beers and wines. It's open till 9 PM daily. *1 Ship St., tel. 01865/247810. From Carfax, walk north on Cornmarket St., turn right at Ship St.*

The Nosebag. This popular upstairs café has been around for more than 25 years. The ever-changing lunch menu features a soup du jour, stuffed baked potatoes, a cold dish, a hot dish, and vegetarian dishes. Dinners are heftier versions of lunch, with more variety. Long lines form for both meals. *6–8 St. Michael's St., tel. 01865/721033. From Carfax, walk north on Cornmarket St., turn left on St. Michael's St. Closed Mon. evening.*

Pizza Express. You'd never know you were in a chain restaurant from the looks of this place. The light, airy building dates back to 1200, when it opened as the Golden Cross Inn. Come for a basic pizza margherita or the fancier Cajun pizza, topped with prawns, mozzarella, tomato, and Tabasco. Or you can sip a glass of wine at the downstairs bar. *Golden Cross, tel. 01865/790442. From Carfax, walk north on Cornmarket St., quick right on Golden Cross.*

UNDER £25 • Cherwell Boathouse. About a mile north of town, this is an ideal spot for a riverside meal. The menus change weekly, but may include mussels in white wine and cream, loin of lamb with red wine, lime, and garlic, or hare with a vinegar and pepper sauce. It's a very friendly spot so be prepared to linger. There are good set menus available for £16.50 and £17.50. *Bardwell Rd. (off Banbury Rd.), tel. 01865/ 552746. From Carfax, walk north up Cornmarket, which becomes St. Giles, bear right on Banbury Rd., walk ½ mi, turn right on Bardwell Rd . Buses 2a, 2b, 2c, 2d run about every 5 min by day, Bus 7 every 20 min at night, from Cornmarket up Banbury Rd. Closed Mon. and Tues. No dinner Sun.*

The Trout. One of Lewis Carroll's favorite places to sup, this creeper-covered, historic, and still excellent Thameside pub is in Godstow, about 2 mi from the city center on the northern edge of Oxford. Its interior, fitted out with sporting prints by "Phiz" and engravings of Oxford by Turner, is remarkable in itself. The dinners can be pricey; trout, of course, is a specialty, while Beef Godstow—fillet cooked in bacon with a black-currant sauce—is a signature dish. Its Stable Bar serves good, moderately priced pub food. Come in the evening for a meal or a drink and watch its peacocks strutting back and forth beside the weir. *Godstow, tel. 01865/302071. Buses to Godstow from bus station.*

WORTH SEEING

Before publicly embarrassing yourself, you should know Oxford University isn't one big campus. The 29 undergraduate colleges, six graduate colleges, four permanent halls, and All Souls College (*see below*) collectively comprise "the university." They're all scattered around town, each with its own dormitories and lecture halls. Many colleges charge a small admission fee to people who want to wander around or take a tour, but there's no harm in trying to pass yourself off as a student by walking determinedly into the colleges. Aside from what we list below, check out the beautiful gardens at **Merton College** (Merton St., tel. 01865/276310) and **St. John's College** (St. Giles, tel. 01865/277300). And definitely don't miss the Bodleian Library, Britain's second largest, and the adjacent Radcliffe Camera, designed by James Gibbs (*see* Museums and Libraries, *below*). For a look at rare and historical woodwind, brass, and percussion instruments, visit the **Bate Collection of Musical Instruments** (St. Aldate's, tel. 01865/276139), free and open weekdays 2–5, term-time Sat. 10–noon. Unless you're game for a silly Disney-esque experience, skip the **Oxford Story** (6 Broad St., tel. 01865/728822) and save the steep £5.50 admission price. Seated at school desks, punters are taken on a patronizing trawl past animations of the university's history, with cameos by famous alumni (Bill Clinton is there), and a film, *The Student Life* (open daily 10–4:30, closes later on weekends and in summer).

BOTANIC GARDEN

In *Brideshead Revisited*, Sebastian Flyte tells Charles Ryder, "There's a beautiful arch there and more different kinds of ivy than I knew existed. I don't know where I should be without the Botanical Gardens." Few gardens are more beautiful or feature a greater diversity of plants than this 300-year-old complex of greenhouses. On a cold day, saunter past the rows of rare tropical plants. *High St., across from Magdalen College, tel. 01865/276920. Admission £2 Apr.–Aug.; free Sept.–Mar. Gardens open daily 9–4:30 (until 5 in summer); greenhouses open daily 2–4.*

> *Vegetarians and those with delicate sensibilities should close their eyes when walking past the butcher shops at the Covered Market; a fresh hare or deer carcass might be strung up by its hindquarters to entice gourmet carnivores.*

CARFAX TOWER

As the last remnant of St. Martin's Church (erected in 1032), Carfax Tower minds the corner all by itself now, marking the passage of time with little mechanical figures that dance every 15 minutes. After the 14th-century St. Scholastica's Day Riots, Edward III ordered the tower lowered to its current 74 ft to prevent townies from showering gownies with rocks, bottles, and flaming arrows. Climb up the tower via the dank stairwell for a good view of the town center. *Admission £1.20. Open Apr.–Oct., daily 10–6; Nov.–Mar., daily 10–3:30.*

THE COLLEGES

Oxford University has been a major player in British history for the past 830 years. The establishment of several monasteries in the early 12th century attracted scholarly clerics, and before long they organized themselves into a *studium generale* offering a curriculum along the same lines as the University of Paris. The turning point for the university came in 1167 when the French expelled all English students from Paris following the assassination of Thomas à Becket, the Archbishop of Canterbury. Thereafter, Oxford multiplied its faculty and student body, gaining immense power and prestige along the way. Oxford University Press was born in 1477, and until 1948 the university had two representatives in Parliament (talk about privilege). Women, however, weren't granted full student status until 1959.

Most colleges will grudgingly allow visitors to snoop around on weekday afternoons between 2 and 5 PM (except during finals, from late May to mid-June). Normally a person at the entrance's lodge or gate collects an entrance fee. Visitors are usually given access to some if not all of the quads, the gardens, and the chapels. Be sure to vacate the grounds by 9 PM: The gates shut at 9:05 on the dot, and some unfortunates have been known to get locked in by accident. The **Oxford Guild of Guides** conducts walks (about £4) daily at 11 and 2. To catch a tour, look for the people in funny hats and bow ties hanging around the tourist office. The well-respected bookshop **Blackwell's** (tel. 01865/792792, ext. 4426) also runs guided walks (£5, for which you also get a £1 book voucher) from outside the shop at 50 Broad Street, currently on Thursday at 11 and Saturday at 11 and 2:30.

ALL SOULS • Possibly the most beautiful college in Oxford, All Souls was founded in 1438 by the Archbishop of Canterbury for spiritual and legal studies. Until the 20th century, All Souls was the only college in Oxford dedicated exclusively to graduate research. The academic program is something of an enigma, but the fellows of All Souls are the best of the brightest; those invited are given academic carte blanche during their seven-year tenure. Today the **North Quad** is a whimsical 18th-century interpretation of Gothic spires and pinnacles, featuring Christopher Wren's sundial and John Hawksmoor's famous twin towers. Sadly, the college doesn't make itself very amenable to tourists; All Souls seems to close "for repairs" every time a light bulb blows out. *High St., tel. 01865/279379. Admission free. Open weekdays 2–4 (closed Aug.).*

CHRIST CHURCH • Founded by Cardinal Wolsey in 1525, Christ Church is never referred to as "Christ Church College." Goodness gracious, no—members call it "The House." In fact, everything seems to have a special name here at The House, which many regard as Oxford's snobbiest college. Professors, called "dons" elsewhere in Oxford, are referred to here as "students." The 6¼-ton bell in the clock tower over the entrance is named **Great Tom,** and the quad over which Great Tom presides is (big surprise) **Tom Quad.** Every night at 9:05, Great Tom rings 101 times, once for each of the original students (not professors); afterward, the college's gates are locked shut. **Tours** of the college kick off from Carfax Tower on weekends at 1:45 PM (£4.50 including admission to college). Near the **Memorial Garden** is Christ Church's 800-year-old **cathedral,** one of the smallest and most ornate in the country. The cathedral's stained glass is exquisite: Some date back to the 14th century, while other pieces are 19th-century works by Edward Burne-Jones and William Morris. The small **Christ Church Picture Gallery** (*see below*) is also part of the campus. *St. Aldate's St., tel. 01865/276150. Admission £3. Open Mon.–Sat. 9–5, Sun. 1–5.*

MAGDALEN COLLEGE • Magdalen (pronounced maudlin) opened its doors to undergrads in 1458 and boasts Oscar Wilde, C. S. Lewis, Peter Brook, and (best of all) Dudley Moore as alumni. The quadrangle is a quiet area enclosed by ancient vaulted cloisters covered with wisteria; beyond it lies a deer park, gardens, and the Cherwell River. At the foot of **Magdalen Bridge,** you can rent punts (*see* Outdoor Activities, *below*). **Magdalen Tower,** one of Oxford's most recognizable landmarks, presides over the college grounds. *High St., tel. 01865/276050. From Carfax, walk east on High St. Admission £2.50. Open daily 2–6.*

NEW COLLEGE • The first college built after the bloody St. Scholastica's Day Riots, New College (officially called St. Mary College of Winchester in Oxenford) incorporated a new design feature—the first enclosed quad—to protect students in the event of another town-versus-gown flare-up. The extra caution proved unnecessary, but founder William of Wykeham (Bishop of Winchester and a wealthy, wealthy man) probably didn't feel like taking chances, considering the shortage of well-educated people after the Black Death outbreak of 1349. Most of the college and its **chapel** were completed in 1386, with further major additions completed in the 17th century. *Queen's La., tel. 01865/279555. From Carfax, walk north on Cornmarket St., turn right on Broad St., right on Catte St., left on New College La. Admission £2. Open daily summer 11–5, winter 2–4.*

UNIVERSITY COLLEGE • To its embarrassment, University is best known for expelling Percy Bysshe Shelley in 1811 because he wrote and distributed a little pamphlet called "The Necessity of Atheism." After he drowned in Italy, the college had second thoughts and erected a monument to him in the **Front Quad.** This is also where a young Bill Clinton sat out the draft and networked like a whirling dervish while a Rhodes scholar. But back to the college: The original foundation dates back to 1249, the earliest extant evidence of any college in Oxford (although Merton claims to be 85 years older). University is not open to the public, unless the students decide to organize tours; call for the latest word. *High St., tel. 01865/276602.*

MUSEUMS AND LIBRARIES

Not only do Oxford's museums house some tremendous collections, but almost all of them are free. The exceptions to the rule are the **Museum of Modern Art** (30 Pembroke St., tel. 01865/722733), which badly needs the £2.50 admission fee (the gallery closes in between exhibitions), and Christ Church Picture Gallery, which doesn't need the £1 fee but takes it anyway. MOMA does offer free admission Wednesday 11–1 PM and Thursday 6–9 PM. All university libraries, with the exception of part of the Bodleian Library, are off-limits to the general public.

ASHMOLEAN MUSEUM OF ART AND ARCHAEOLOGY • The Ashmolean, opened in 1683, is Britain's oldest public museum and boasts artifacts and masterworks ranging from drawings by Michelangelo and paintings by Pissarro to Bronze Age tools and weapons. The Egyptian sarcophagi, Byzantine frescoes, and Islamic pottery downstairs deserve a look, but don't miss the drawings and Rodin sculptures in the upstairs galleries. The prize for Most Bizarre Objet d'Intérêt definitely goes to Oliver Cromwell's death mask. *Beaumont St., at St. Giles, tel. 01865/278000. From Carfax, walk north on Cornmarket St., turn left on Beaumont St. Admission free. Open Tues.–Sat. 10–5, Sun. 2–5.*

THE BODLEIAN LIBRARY AND RADCLIFFE CAMERA • *Camera* means "room" in Latin, and the Radcliffe is one heck of a reading room. So, too, is the library, which owns a copy of every book printed in Britain since printing began—about 5.5 million books, give or take a few. The Bodleian is notoriously stingy about who gets to look at the Big Books, and it takes a full day to retrieve any requested title. Even students can't get inside without a signed letter from their university specifically requesting library access, and then they may still have to haggle. A guided tour (£3.50) is your surest bet; they start at the Divinity School across the street weekdays at 10:30, 11:30, 2, and 3, and Saturday at 10:30 and 11:30 (not weekday mornings in winter). A small exhibition room offers insights into the bookish world. The library's courtyard and the adjacent fan-vaulted divinity school lobby are always open and well worth a peek. Also take a look inside Duke Humfrey's small, churchlike library (1488). *Catte St., tel. 01865/277224. From Carfax, walk east on High St., turn left on Catte St. Exhibition admission free. Open weekdays 9:30–4:45, Sat. 9:30–12:30.*

CHRIST CHURCH PICTURE GALLERY • Early Italian paintings and drawings dominate the small gallery's collection. There are also several Dutch paintings and Inigo Jones drawings. *Oriel Sq., tel. 01865/276172. From Carfax, walk east on High St., turn right at Oriel Sq. Admission £1. Open Mon.– Sat. 10:30–1 and 2–4:30, Sun. 2–4:30, Easter–Sept. until 5:30.*

MUSEUM OF THE HISTORY OF SCIENCE • While it's hardly the Smithsonian, you get to see the blackboard Einstein once used and some impressive Islamic and European astrolabes. The museum is due to reopen with new galleries and visitor facilities in April 2000, thanks to funds from a Lottery grant. *Broad St., tel. 01865/277280. From Carfax, walk north on Cornmarket St., turn right on Broad St. Admission free. Open Tues.–Sat. noon–4.*

Not all of Oxford's colleges are as well off as they look. With ailing endowments and shrinking government funding, colleges such as Pembroke, St. Edmund's, and St. Peter's can use every penny they get.

OXFORD UNIVERSITY MUSEUM OF NATURAL HISTORY • One of the greatest natural-history museums in the world sits 20 minutes north of the town center, in a massive Victorian Gothic building. There are hundreds of exhibits on just about every facet of nature, but the local dinosaur finds attract the most attention. The collection includes the head and left foot of a dodo, a large, flightless bird that has been extinct since the mid-17th century. Lewis Carroll was familiar with the museum's display and cast himself in the role of the Dodo in *Alice's Adventures in Wonderland.* The building itself, designed by Benjamin Woodward, is also worth a gander. *Parks Rd., tel. 01865/272950. Admission free. Open daily noon–5.*

PITT RIVERS MUSEUM • In the same building as the Oxford University Museum (*see below*), the Pitt harbors all sorts of anthropological things: masks, hanging sailboats, wooden clothing—fun for flea market enthusiasts or attic addicts. It also hosts cultural exhibitions highlighting such esoteric areas as string puzzles from around the world to Japanese arts and crafts. Parts of the huge collection are being moved to the Balfour Building (open the same hours at 60 Banbury Rd., tel. 01865/274726), such as the collection of weird and wonderful musical instruments. Cut through an alley at the Lamb and Flag pub on St. Giles to reach the museum from that road. *Parks Rd., tel. 01865/270927 or 01865/270949. From Carfax, walk north on Cornmarket St., turn right on Broad St., left on Parks Rd. Admission free. Open Mon.–Sat. 1–4:30.*

SHELDONIAN THEATRE • Christopher Wren's marble-covered Sheldonian Theatre, built in 1669, was intended as an appropriately sober venue to confer degrees upon graduates. With its painted ceiling, heavy columns, and enormous pipe organ, it does indeed feel like the sort of place everyone should pass through before graduating into "the real world." The cupola provides a decent, if frustrating, glass-enclosed view of central Oxford. You won't miss the front gate: Its stone columns are surmounted by megagigantic heads of the Roman emperors. The theater hosts concerts on Saturday evenings. Call ahead, as the theater often closes for events. *Broad St., tel. 01865/277299. Admission £1.50. Open Mon.–Sat. 10–12:30 and 2–4:30.*

AFTER DARK

Once the sun goes down, drinkers, clubbers, theatergoers, and classical music aficionados keep themselves busy. Otherwise, the main after-dark pursuits are hanging out around Carfax near the kebab vans—pretty dismal. *What's On In Oxford* is an invaluable guide to the club scene, while *This Month in Oxford* covers other events. Both are available free at the tourist office.

THRILLS AND SPILLS

Perhaps to relieve the tension of impending finals, Oxford students get their blood pumping for four days every May during the Eights Week rowing competition. Boats with eight rowers (plus coxswain) set off on the Thames in a single-file line with the aim of bumping a boat in front of their own without being bumped themselves. In short, it's bumper cars on water. Teams who "bump" on each of the four days win blades, which are oars inscribed with the names of their team members. Tradition also dictates that the first team of the first division—"the Head of the River"—burn one of their own boats in celebration. The feisty '95 winners, Pembroke College, created an even bigger spectacle by burning a defeated opponent's boat instead.

PUBS

Most pubs in Oxford stay open through the afternoon for post-tutorial pints. All pubs listed below are open Monday–Saturday 11–11, Sunday noon–10:30.

Head of the River. Oak beams and original stone floors are the setting for this cool hangout. In addition to those who come to eat, drinkers park themselves in the cement "beer garden" to loiter by the riverside and get sloshed before taking out punts. *Abingdon Rd., at Folly Bridge, tel. 01865/721600. From Carfax, walk south on St. Aldate's St. to Folly Bridge.*

King's Arms. The good ales and cosmopolitan clientele make this one of the best traditional pubs in the center of town. Tweedy professor types mix with students, townies, tourists, straights, gays—what have you. The "K. A.," as the locals affectionately call it, also serves vegetarian dishes. *40 Holywell St., at Parks Rd., tel. 01865/242369. From Carfax, walk north on Cornmarket St., turn right on Broad St. (which becomes Holywell St.).*

Turf Tavern. If you can find this tiny 13th-century pub tucked away in a narrow alley, you may never want to leave (which would explain some of the ancient professors lurking in the dark corners). In warm weather, sit on the patio; in winter, try the mulled wine—cinnamon-spiced and guaranteed to lift the spirits of the homesick. Its distinctive style is featured in the *Inspector Morse* television series. *4 Bath Pl., tel. 01865/243235. From Carfax, walk north on Cornmarket, turn right on Broad St., right on Catte St., left on New College La., walk under Hertford's Bridge of Sighs, and take the first quick left.*

CLUBS

Freud. Freud (or FREVD as the sign says) is housed in a 19th-century church with stained-glass windows. Don't ask what the holy builders would think of the enormous selection of cocktails. Live jazz or classical music starts at 11 most nights. *Walton St., at Great Clarendon St., tel. 01865/311171. Cover £1–£4.*

Old Fire Station. This is the ultimate one-stop spot, with a restaurant, theater, bar, and science exhibition all under one roof. DJs play dance music Friday and Saturday; Thursday is for 1970s nostalgists. *40 George St., tel. 01865/794490. Cover £4–£6.*

Zodiac. Members of Britpop bands Radiohead, Supergrass, and Ride are among the shareholders of this hip music venue. Local and big-name bands are featured, along with DJs and club nights. *190 Cowley Rd., tel. 08165/420042. Cover £4–£7.*

THEATER AND MUSIC

Home to the accomplished Oxford Stage Company, the **Oxford Playhouse** (Beaumont St., tel. 01865/798600) hosts first-rate entertainment ranging from Shakespearean drama and Restoration comedy to contemporary dance and musicals. Tickets cost £6–£20. **Apollo Theatre** (George St., tel. 0870/6063500) has a varied program of plays, comedy, opera, ballet, and pop concerts. Tickets usually cost

£5–£20, but can go up to £50 for special performances. In the summer, plays are often performed in the gardens of some colleges; check with the tourist office for venues and ticket prices.

OUTDOOR ACTIVITIES

If you have time, take a stroll through the quiet, tree-lined paths of **Christ Church Meadow** alongside the Thames. When school is in session, college "eights" practice their rowing on the Isis (what they call this section of the Thames).

PUNTING AND ROWING

One of the great Oxford experiences, punting involves propelling a long, flat boat along the Thames River using a 15-ft pole to push off the riverbed; beginners will probably spin around in circles before getting the hang of it. If you find it easier to punt from the front, do so, even if, technically speaking, you're sup-posed to push from the rear. One piece of advice: If your pole gets stuck, LET GO—you can use the smaller paddle to go back and retrieve it. You do not want to end up treading water in the slimy Thames. You can, of course, also get a normal rowboat for the same rate. The friendly **Magdalen Bridge Boathouse** (High St., tel. 01865/202643) rents punts and rowboats for £10 per hour with a £25 deposit and some form of ID. They also offer chauffeured punts if you're feeling lazy (£18 per half hour, including a bottle of plonk—that's cheap wine to you Americans). Punts and rowboats cost £8 per hour with a £25 deposit at **Riverside Boating Co.,** beneath Folly Bridge, though the owner has been known to raise prices dur-ing high-demand periods. Both close for bad weather and boat races.

A handful of literary giants did time at Christ Church, including W. H. Auden, Jeremy Bentham, John Locke, and Charles Dodgson (a.k.a. Lewis Carroll).

NEAR OXFORD

BLENHEIM PALACE

As a reward for his surprising victory over French forces in Blenheim, Germany, in 1704, John Churchill received the title Duke of Marlborough and a great plot of Oxfordshire land from Queen Anne and Par-liament. As any good duke should, Churchill ordered a palace built on the grounds. The dizzying excess of John Vanbrugh's design makes Blenheim one of the greatest, most pleasure-bloated manor houses in England. The baroque design—arches, columns, pediments, and classical statuary—is appropriately complemented by Capability Brown's landscaping of man-made lakes, gardens, forest, and sculpted hedges. In fact, Blenheim claims to have the world's second-largest **hedge maze** (£1), but the hedges are only 4–6 ft high and all paths lead to the exit—Jack Nicholson would catch you for sure.

These days, the 11th Duke of Marlborough and his family hide in an inaccessible wing of the palace. Your appreciation of the interior is enhanced by the snappy, informative guided tour; note the family por-traits by Joshua Reynolds and Van Dyck as you fly by. There's also a small exhibit on Winston Leonard Spencer Churchill—nephew to the eighth Duke of Marlborough—who was born at Blenheim six weeks prematurely in 1874. More intriguing is Winston's quiet grave, beside St. Martin's Church in the village of Bladon, a 1-mi walk from the palace. Another must-do lies just beyond the back gates (actually, the original old gates) of the palace: Woodstock, a quintessentially charming English village. In the postcard-pretty town square, you half expect to see Anthony Trollope taking his morning stroll among the historic inns (The Bear is where Richard Burton popped the question to Liz) and oh-so-chic shops. Bring your camera to capture the quiet corners of this town—they are as lovely as they come. From Oxford's Gloucester Green station, take Bus 20, 20A, 20B, or 20C straight to the palace (30 mins, £2.70 return). *Woodstock, tel. 01993/811325. Admission £8.50; admission to grounds only, £2. House open mid-Mar.–Oct., daily 10:30–5:30; park open daily 9–5.*

WHERE TO SLEEP

Blenheim Guest House and Tea Rooms. The Cinderella of all British hotels, this place sits in one of the most storybook corners in England—the quiet Woodstock cul-de-sac that leads to the back gates of ducal Blenheim Palace. It's a modest, small guest house and tearoom, three stories tall, with its facade still bearing a Victorian-era painted banner that states "Views and Postcards of Blenheim." Guest rooms are unassuming and faux-traditional in furnishings, but the Marlborough room is unique—after all, its bathroom offers a view of Blenheim. Thanks to the cheery staff, breakfast is a delight. Doubles go for about £65. Stay here instead of Oxford and just take the frequent Woodstock-Oxford bus back and forth. *17 Park St., Woodstock, OX20 1SJ, tel. 01993/811467. Follow Park St.—the main artery of the village— till you nearly reach Blenheim's entrance. 6 rooms with shower.*

HENLEY-ON-THAMES

The Thames, England's most famous river, snakes through a series of small, idyllic villages from its source in the Cotswold Hills. Most of the towns follow a simple format: pubs, antiques shops, and riverfront greenery—and Henley-on-Thames is a good example. It's also a convenient exception to the rule that the Thames Valley is not easy to visit without a car, as it's well connected by bus and train. Not that the high society who frequent Henley use such lowly forms of transport. They come out in force for the biggest date on the social calendar over the last weekend of June and the first of July—the **Royal Regatta.** Royalty, zealous fans, and dedicated practitioners of rowing mingle at the most important postcollegiate event of the rowing world. The event dates back to 1839 and takes place on a wide, straight stretch of the Thames just south of Henley Bridge. With no tourist attractions other than the Regatta, Henley is a good place to take pleasant walks by the river, especially if crowded Oxford has you feeling claustrophobic.

BASICS

The folks at the **tourist office** (Town Hall, Market Pl., tel. 01491/578034), open daily April–September 10–7, October–March 10–4, have the goods on the area's numerous manor houses. You might fork out 25p for the *Henley Heritage Trail,* which outlines a walking tour of the town with a basic map and some useful telephone numbers, and pick up a free list of addresses of local B&Bs (many of which don't have signs) and other accommodations.

COMING AND GOING

Stagecoach Oxford (tel. 01865/772250) Bus X39 is the main Thames Valley bus, running between Heathrow Airport and Oxford and stopping en route at Henley. Buses leave hourly from either terminus; from Oxford's Gloucester Green bus station it's £5.70 day return, £7.40 open return. If you're coming from London, you can also take the train (£10.20 single, £10.30 day return) from Paddington Station, change at Twyford, and get off at Henley's small **train station** (Station Rd., tel. 0345/484950).

WHERE TO SLEEP AND EAT

Henley's B&Bs fill up at odd times for no apparent reason, then empty again inexplicably. Most have only two or three rooms, so it's not a bad idea to make reservations through the tourist office (*see above*). At **Alftrudis** (8 Norman Ave., tel. 01491/573099), Sue Lambert's good-humored advice comes along with the three comfortable doubles (£40–£50), in a Victorian house just a couple of minutes' walk from the river, rail station, and center. Second choice is **Avalon** (36 Queen St., tel. 01491/577829), with standard singles for £25 and doubles with shower for £45.

Henley's cuisine proves to be as dull, but plenty of pubs vie with high-priced bistros. The Indian restaurants around the center of town are your best bet for a decent, fair-priced meal. **Henley Tea Rooms** (Thameside, tel. 01491/411412) offers the usual café fare (jacket potatoes, soups, and cheap sandwiches) with unusual flair. The **Angel on the Bridge** (Thameside, tel. 01491/410678) is a centuries-old inn with tables on a riverside terrace. Large lunchtime portions are served to accompany the excellent Brakspear's ale, including stomach-filling wild boar sausage and mash.

ALTHORP

Forty mi northeast of Oxford, Althorp is the ancestral home of Diana, the late Princess of Wales. Her noble family, the Spencers, began the house in 1508, then had architect Henry Holland greatly alter it in 1790. Its Saloon and Picture Gallery are lined with portraits by Van Dyck, Lely, and Reynolds—an incredible record of the Spencer family dating back five centuries. Today, the stately house remains, as Horace Walpole said in 1765, "One of those enchanted scenes which a thousand circumstances of history and art endear to a pensive spectator." Within the estate park, laid out by Capability Brown in the 18th century, is the beloved Princess's grave site—a tiny island in the center of an ornamental lake called the Oval. According to the wishes of Diana's brother, Earl Spencer, the site is only open to the public several weeks a year. Schedules may yet change, so call Althorp to check on the latest info. The house, near the villages of Harlestone and Great Brington, can be reached on Rugby Road, four mi northwest of Northampton, the county town. *Tel. 01604/592020. Admission £9.50; tickets currently available July–Aug., must be booked in advance, either for 9–1 or 1–5.*

STRATFORD-UPON-AVON

To go, or not to go, that is the question. Whether 'tis nobler to suffer the slings and arrows of outrageous prices, or to take arms against a sea of travelers and by opposing end them. To die: of claustrophobia. No more; and by patience we say you'll end the headache and the thousand natural shocks that visitors are heir to: 'tis a resolution devoutly to be wished. To visit: to enjoy. To enjoy? Perhaps to go to the theater. Ay, there's the rub; for in that theater what plays may come, when we have shuffled off the mortifying crowds, must give us peace.

Stratford can become suffocatingly overcrowded—a tourist trap, even—and some say its soul has been sucked dry by mercenary hucksters looking to make a few quid off Shakespeare's good name. If you're really that keen on saying you've "done" Stratford, you won't mind the crowds or the lack of cafés and other forms of cultural life beyond the theater. And while the Royal Shakespeare Company (RSC) stages frequent productions in Stratford, equally prestigious productions run in London—minus the hype. That said, the RSC is the best thing going for Stratford, and we unabashedly recommend it.

Wildness reigns on May Day (May 1), when Oxford celebrates the coming of warm weather. At 6 AM the little boys in the Magdalen College choir sing from Magdalen Tower, and the pubs open at 7 AM.

At the end of the day, the best way to be alone and collect your inspired thoughts in Stratford is to stroll along the River Avon. And Stratford is just fine during winter—the crowds thin out (and the sights become truly enjoyable), the streets become walkable, and the RSC continues its first-rate program of drama. Even so, don't come expecting to find a sprawling Elizabethan town: Apart from a few heavily restored thatched cottages, the streets of modern-day Stratford are lined with high-fashion clothing stores and the ubiquitous McDonald's. The Shakespearean sights have a certain Olde World appeal, but even these have been repeatedly reconstructed and restored. Now that there's a direct train service from London, far more convenient than the slower and less frequent bus service, Stratford is a much easier place to visit, making it a feasible day trip from the capital. To catch Anne Hathaway's Cottage on a crisp October day is an experience few travelers to England would want to miss.

BASICS

AMERICAN EXPRESS
Located inside the tourist office, AmEx changes money, issues traveler's checks, and holds client mail. *Bridgefoot, CV37 6YY, tel. 01789/415856. Open Mon.–Sat. 9–6, Sun. in summer 11–5.*

LAUNDRY
Sparklean Launderette (74 Bull St., at College La., tel. 01789/296075) is near most B&Bs and is open daily 8 AM–9 PM. A wash costs £2, and drying is 20p per five-minute cycle.

VISITOR INFORMATION
The **tourist office**'s multilingual staff and piles of pamphlets may look helpful, but much of the info is geared toward those with money to burn. Come mainly to book a room. *Bridgefoot, tel. 01789/293127. Open Easter–Oct., Mon.–Sat. 9–6, Sun. 11–5, Nov.–Easter, Mon.–Sat. 9–5.*

Guide Friday (The Civic Hall, 14 Rother St., tel. 01789/294466) also has tourist info and free flyers, and the lines are much shorter than at the tourist office. On the downside, they're also trying to sell something: a double-decker bus tour (£8) that stops at all five of Stratford's major sights. Since the price

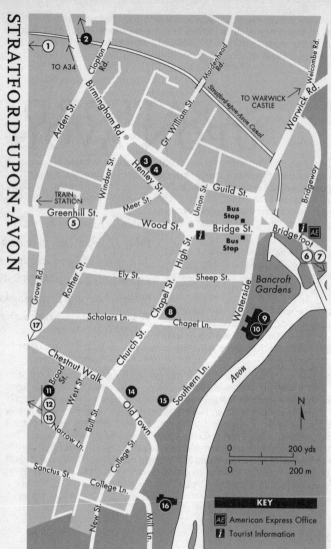

STRATFORD-UPON-AVON

Sights ●

Anne Hathaway's Cottage, **11**

Hall's Croft, **14**

Holy Trinity Church, **16**

Mary Arden's House, **2**

New Place (Nash's House), **8**

The Other Place Theatre, **15**

Royal Shakespeare Theatre, **9**

Shakespeare Birthplace, **4**

Shakespeare Centre and Library, **3**

Swan Theatre, **10**

Lodging ○

Elms Camp, **7**

The Garth House, **13**

Newlands, **12**

Penshurst, **17**

Stratford YHA, **6**

Stratford Backpackers Hostel, **5**

Victoria Spa Lodge, **1**

KEY

AE American Express Office

i Tourist Information

doesn't include admission to the sights and most are within walking distance, it's not worth it unless you're lazy. Take the pamphlets and run.

COMING AND GOING

BY BUS

Buses stop on Bridge Street at Waterside either directly in front of the McDonald's or across the street. **National Express** (tel. 0990/808080) sends three buses per day to London (£14 return, £17 on Friday) and vice-versa. Buy tickets at the travel desk inside Stratford's tourist office (closed Sunday), and at London's Victoria Coach Station. **Stagecoach Oxford** (tel. 01865/772250) runs a bus service to Oxford for £3.75 single, £6.50 return.

BY TRAIN

Direct **Thames Trains** (tel. 0345/484950) leaving hourly from London's Paddington take about 2 hours to reach Stratford's station on Alcester Road (tel. 0345/484950), costing £35 for an open return (or £22 with restrictions). From Birmingham, Central Trains run to Stratford in less than 50 minutes (£4.70 single, £5.30 day return).

GETTING AROUND

Most local bus services are handled by Newmark (tel. 01789/292085), though Guide Friday (tel. 01789/294466) also runs a handy minibus service around the main sights.

Rent a bike from YHA hostel and wheel around town; it's the best way to avoid the congested sidewalks, though the roads aren't much better. **Stagecoach Midland Red** buses cover the main sights around Stratford: Bus X16 runs to Warwick (£2.80 return) and Kenilworth (£3.50 return), as does the slower X18. Bus X20 runs hourly to Birmingham, and Bus 18 runs to the YHA hostel (£2.60 return) from Wood Street.

WHERE TO SLEEP

As one of the leading tourist meccas of England, Stratford has no shortage of B&Bs. The hard part is finding a cheap one. No matter what, reserve space *at least* a few days in advance. Stratford has three concentrated pockets of B&Bs: on **Grove Road** near the train station; around **Evesham Road,** the southern extension of Grove Road; and on **Shipston Road,** across the River Avon from the center of town.

The Bear (Alfred St. and Bear La.) is a magnificent 13th-century pub with walls covered by thousands of ties. You get a free pint if you donate your school, regiment, sporting, or dress tie— assuming they haven't yet got one.

Garth House. Unlike most B&B proprietors, Louise Thomas actually caters to backpackers. The double with bath is especially quiet. Doubles cost £32 (£36–£40 en suite). *9A Broad Walk, CV37 6HS, tel. 01789/298035. From the rail station, walk toward town, turn right on Grove Rd. (which becomes Evesham Pl.), left on Broad Walk. 3 rooms, 1 with bath. No credit cards. Closed weekdays Oct.–Mar.*

Newlands. This unpretentious B&B is wonderfully quiet, and the rooms are surprisingly large. Proprietor Sue Boston is a sweetheart who loves to give advice on the best plays to see in Stratford. Rooms cost £20–£24 per person. *7 Broad Walk, CV37 6HS, tel. and fax 01789/298449. Follow directions to Garth House (see above). 4 rooms, 3 with bath.*

Penshurst. There's nowhere better to stay in Stratford than this pretty, centrally located B&B. The owner is an absolute treasure, and there are flexible breakfast hours to suit early birds and lazy sloths alike. The rooms are named after Stratford's historical streets and each contains a book on the history of the corresponding street. Singles start at £16, doubles run £18–£20 per person. *34 Evesham Pl., CV37 6HT, tel. 01789/205259, fax 01789/295322. From rail station, walk toward town, turn right on Grove Rd. (which becomes Evesham Pl.). 8 rooms, all with bath. No credit cards.*

Victoria Spa Lodge. This upscale, no-smoking B&B lies just outside town, about 20 minutes' walk along the towpath. Draped with clematis, the listed building dates back to 1837 and sports Queen Victoria's coat of arms in two of its gables. Crunch your cornflakes in a grand lounge/breakfast room with tall windows and sofas and chairs for relaxing. Spacious rooms, some with fireplaces, go for £60, or ask for the lone smaller one for £55. *Bishopton La., Bishopton, CV37 9QY, tel. 01789/267985, fax 01789/204728. From rail station, walk toward town, turn left on Arden St., cross Birmingham Rd. to Clopton Rd., turn left on towpath: You'll see the Lodge after about 10 mins. 7 rooms with bath.*

HOSTELS

Stratford Backpackers Hostel. Friendly staff and 24-hour access make this a perfect overnight stop, just a few minutes from the train station. The six rooms have six, eight, or ten pine bunk beds with fluffy duvets and four of them have attached bathrooms, so spartans can look elsewhere. Rates are £12 a head; there's a £5 key deposit and a surcharge on payments by credit card. *Greenhill St., CV37 6LE, tel. and fax 01789/263838, E-mail stratford@hostels.demon.co.uk, website www.hostels.co.uk. From train station, turn left on Alcester Rd., which becomes Wood St., Bridge St., and Greenhill St. 92 beds. Kitchen, café, laundry (£3 wash and dry).*

Stratford YHA. If you have the time, you should definitely walk the 2 mi to the village of Alveston, where this hostel is—you'll pass some beautiful Tudor homes that aren't on the bus route. It's one of the few hostels in Britain with cafeteria-style meals for dinner, so if you only want a pot of tea, you can buy it separately without paying for a full meal. Clean rooms and helpful management make the price (beds £10.70 for under-18s, £14.25 for everybody else), which includes breakfast, an even better value. Definitely reserve ahead. *Hemmingford House, Alveston, Warwickshire CV37 7RG, tel. 01789/297093, fax 01789/205513, E-mail stratford@yha.org.uk. Take Bus 18 from Stratford (£1.70 return). 148 beds. Midnight curfew. Closed mid-Dec.–early Jan. and Mar. 1–13.*

CAMPING

Riverside Park. It's a great alternative to the local lodging scene and closer to Stratford than the YH hostel. The nearby village of Tiddington has a pub and market. Sites are £5–£9 per person per night. As always in Stratford, reserve in advance. On site are a shop, showers, and laundry. *Tiddington Rd., Tiddington, CV37 7AB, tel. 01789/292312. Take Bus 18 or X18 from Stratford to Tiddington, then follow signs. 50 sites. Check-in by 9 PM. No credit cards. Closed Nov.–Mar.*

FOOD

Finding a reasonably priced, tasty meal in Stratford is nearly impossible. Pubs and greasy fast-food stands will cheaply plug the hole in your stomach, but if you want a full dinner, you'll be eating alongside other tourists and paying heavily inflated prices. Try your luck on **Sheep Street,** one block south of the train station. Nearby **Marco Italian Deli** (20 Church St., tel. 01789/292889) sells sandwiches during the day. Slightly removed from touristy ground zero, **Stratford Health Foods** (tel. 01789/292353), open daily, sells bulk groceries and food to go, on Greenhill St., near the train station; there are few other reasonable places hereabouts.

Garrick Inn. A traditional English establishment, the Garrick Inn, built in 1595, still has the cramped feel of an Elizabethan pub, albeit with multilingual tourists. Surprisingly, the food isn't expensive: Chicken-and-mushroom pie and scampi with chips and peas are bargains by Stratford standards. There are good brews on tap, too. *25 High St., tel. 01789/292186.*

The Opposition. An encouraging mix of locals and visitors gives a lively feel to this cozy bistro on Stratford's main restaurant strip. Like most of the dining places in the center, it stays open late. The soups, quiches, and lasagna won't do you wrong, and the service is friendly. *13 Sheep St., tel. 01789/269980.*

River Terrace. At this informal cafeteria in the Royal Shakespeare Theatre, the meals and snacks are crowd pleasers. They include lasagna, shepherd's pie, salads, sandwiches, and cakes, with wine and beer available. *Royal Shakespeare Theatre, Waterside, tel. 01789/293226. No credit cards. Closed when theater is closed.*

Slug and Lettuce. Don't let the name put you off—this pine-panel pub serves excellent meals. Long-standing favorites are chicken breast baked in avocado and garlic, and poached cushion of salmon. *38 Guild St., tel. 01789/299700.*

Vintner Cafe and Wine Bar. An eclectic group of families, twentysomethings, and Europeans crowd one of Stratford's few cool places. Huge candles stuck in wine bottles dominate the small tables, leaving little room for the plates of fish pie or the vegetarian dish of the day. *5 Sheep St., tel. 01789/297259.*

WORTH SEEING

The Shakespeare Birthplace Trust sells a convenient **all-inclusive ticket** (£11) to the five major sights listed below, not including **Holy Trinity.** If you want to skip Anne Hathaway's Cottage and Mary Arden's House, buy the **three-in-town** ticket (£7.50). You can get information about any of the Shakespeare Trust properties by calling 01789/204016. For those seriously interested in the work of the writer, the **Shakespeare Library** (Henley St., tel. 01789/204016) has original Shakespeare folios and a wealth of material on the Bard's life, though casual visitors are not encouraged and the emphasis is on study.

ANNE HATHAWAY'S COTTAGE

Anne Hathaway lived in this thatched cottage in nearby Shottery prior to her marriage to William Shakespeare on November 27, 1582. At the time, Will was only 18 years old, and his betrothed, 26; count backwards from the birth of their child Susanna on May 26, 1583, and the phrase "shotgun wedding" comes to mind. The Tudor furniture pales in comparison with the lovely apple orchard outside. From

Stratford it's a 15-minute walk west through open fields; follow the signs from Evesham Place or take a bus from the Bridge Street bus stop. *Shottery. Admission £3.90. Open mid-Mar.–mid-Oct., Mon.–Sat. 9–5, Sun. 9:30–5; mid-Oct.–mid-Mar., Mon.–Sat. 9:30–4, Sun. 10–4.*

HALL'S CROFT

This sight has a tenuous connection, at best, to the Bard's dramatic life. It was the home of his daughter, Susanna, and her husband, Dr. John Hall. Of the 17th-century antiques on display, Dr. Hall's medical instruments are certainly the most intriguing. *Old Town. Admission £3.30. Open mid-Mar.– mid-Oct., Mon.–Sat. 9:30–5, Sun. 10–5; mid-Oct.–mid-Mar., Mon.–Sat. 10–4, Sun. 10:30–4.*

HOLY TRINITY CHURCH

The remains of Shakespeare lie buried underneath the altar of this traditional Gothic church—not in Westminster Abbey's Poets' Corner, as many think. Will's wife and family rest in peace next to him; above hovers a bust made immediately after his death in 1616 by Gheerart Jansen. It's believed to be one of only two likenesses created in Shakespeare's time. *Trinity St., at College La., tel. 01789/266316. Admission 60p. Open Mar.–Oct., Mon.–Sat. 8:30–6, Sun. 2–5; Nov.–Feb., Mon.–Sat. 9–4, Sun. 2–5.*

MARY ARDEN'S HOUSE

Mary Arden probably didn't live here, and the "home" of Shakespeare's mother is definitely boring. The mostly undecorated Tudor farmhouse has been expanded, however, to include the slightly more interesting **Glebe Farm,** where falconers display their art with live birds, all day, every day. To reach the house and farm, take the train from Stratford to Wilmcote (5 mins, £1.30 return) and follow the signs from the station. *Wilmcote. Admission £4.40. Open mid-Mar.–mid-Oct., Mon.–Sat. 9:30–5, Sun. 10–5; mid-Oct.–mid-Mar., Mon.–Sat. 10–4, Sun. 10:30–4.*

Shakespeare's birthday is traditionally assigned to April 23, 1564. More than 400 years later, it's one of the worst days to look for cheap lodging in Stratford.

NEW PLACE (NASH'S HOUSE)

Shakespeare bought the place in 1597 for £60 (big money at the time) and died here in 1616 at the age of 52. It's called Nash's House after the man who married Shakespeare's granddaughter. Inside, a small museum features artifacts from prehistoric Stratford; the attached garden is much more interesting. *Chapel St., at Chapel La. Admission £3.30. Open mid-Mar.–mid-Oct., Mon.–Sat. 9:30–5, Sun. 10–5; mid-Oct.–mid-Mar., Mon.–Sat. 10–4, Sun. 10:30–4.*

SHAKESPEARE'S BIRTHPLACE

The birthplace of the Bard has become an unruly shrine of vicious, camera-snapping pilgrims trying to elbow their way in and capture that Kodak moment. This small, heavily restored home is usually too crowded to allow for a casual stroll—which is frustrating since the biographical material is actually interesting. **Shakespeare Centre,** adjacent to the house, contains exhibits based on themes such as recent Stratford productions of Shakespeare plays, local Stratford artists, local history, etc. (open weekdays 10–5, Sat. 9:30–noon). *Henley St. Admission £4.90. Open mid-Mar.–mid-Oct., Mon.–Sat. 9–5, Sun. 9:30–5; mid-Oct.–mid-Mar., Mon.–Sat. 9:30–4, Sun. 10–4.*

AFTER DARK

Stratford's nightlife *is* the Royal Shakespeare Company, which presents nightly performances on two main stages, the **Royal Shakespeare Theatre** and the **Swan Theatre.** In any given week there are five or six different plays (not all of them written by Shakespeare)—even during the company's annual hiatus (Oct.–Nov.) when visiting companies take the stage. Down the road, a third stage, the **Other Place,** runs smaller, more modern productions during high season. If you don't mind standing during a performance, you can buy tickets for as little as £5; balcony tickets start at £7.50 in low season, £10 in high (July–Aug.). Students can get £7 standbys for press nights and previews, and early risers can grab one of the few tickets held for day-of-performance sales; be there when the box office opens at 9:30 AM.

The RSC conducts **backstage tours** (tel. 01789/296655, ext. 421) year-round; tickets cost £4. Try to book in advance, as groups fill the tours quickly. Otherwise, meet at the stage door following the evening's entertainment for a 30-minute **post-performance tour** (£3). *Southern La., tel. 01789/295623 box office, 01789/269191 ticket info. Performances usually held Mon.–Sat. at 7:30 PM; additional matinees Thurs. and Sat. at 1:30 PM.*

NEAR STRATFORD-UPON-AVON

WARWICK CASTLE

Built on a cliff overlooking the River Avon, the impeccably preserved Warwick is one of England's biggest and most expensive castles. Alfred the Great's daughter, Ethelreda, built a fortress on this site in the 10th century, and since then a number of additions and restorations have gradually expanded the castle. Moss-covered stones add to the organic feel of Warwick, giving the impression that the castle lives and breathes. Don't miss the gruesome dungeons in **Caesar's Tower.**

Capability Brown's 18th-century landscaping around the castle is stunning, and a tour of the garden deserves much more time than the house, though the latter contains some notable artworks among the cheesy noble portraits, plus a formidable collection of armor and weaponry, and opulent furnishings, mainly from the eighteenth and nineteenth centuries. Try to come in the early morning or late afternoon to avoid the crowds—in large part the fault of the Tussauds Group (of wax-museum fame), which owns the castle and rather predictably brought in wax figures dressed in Victorian costume to simulate "A Royal Weekend Party, 1898." *Castle La., tel. 01926/406600. From Stratford, take Bus X16 or the slower X18 from Guild St. to Warwick (£2.80 return). Admission £9.50 (July–Aug. £9.95). Open Apr.–Oct., daily 10–6; Nov.–Mar., daily 10–5.*

KENILWORTH CASTLE

Unlike nearby Warwick Castle, with its lines, noisy tourists, and wax figures, Kenilworth Castle has been passed over by the tourism fairy. Built in 1120, Kenilworth was almost completely destroyed by Oliver Cromwell in the 17th century for being on the wrong side in the English Civil War. The Earl of Leicester had wined and dined Queen Elizabeth here four times, with a particularly smashing weeks-long party in 1565. The red stone remains of the castle lay in complete disrepair when Sir Walter Scott "discovered" and immortalized them in his 1821 novel *Kenilworth.* On a sunny day, it's an idyllic picnic spot and a good place to roam; on a dreary day, the ruins have a brooding, tragic character. *Tel. 01926/852078. From Stratford, take Bus X16 or the slower X18 to Kenilworth (£3.50 return). Admission £3.50. Open Apr.–Oct., daily 10–6; Nov.–Mar., daily 10–4.*

THE COTSWOLD HILLS

A village green. A church steeple. A pond with ducks. A preposterously picturesque cottage wreathed in rose bushes. Ah, to be in England! Well, if that is the England you dream about, the Cotswolds should certainly be at the top of your itinerary. But be prepared to splurge here—after all, this is the playground of platinum card–packing travelers and a region where there's more antiques shops than pubs. Though there are many remote villages whose appeal lies solely in their picture-postcard prettiness, **Cheltenham** and **Cirencester** have a significant youth population and plenty of restaurants peopled with fun-loving and stylish crowds. Outside of the larger towns, public transport is pretty dire and if you find yourself stuck in a random village for a few days waiting for a bus—you've been warned. If all else fails, hitching is a possibility, though, again, it's easy to get stuck. If you like sheep and fresh country air, then rent a bike or sample the great hiking trails of the region. Otherwise, base yourself in one of the historic towns where you can eat, shop, sightsee, and soak in the blissfully rural atmosphere.

BASICS

VISITOR INFORMATION

With so many helpful tourist offices, you'll need to be selective, or you risk collecting a small forest of pamphlets. The free "Connections" guide, which lists every bus that runs through the area, is essential. "Accommodation in the Cotswolds" (50p) is helpful for finding a room. Walkers will want to get *The Cotswold Way* (£4), by Mark Richards, with detailed maps of the area's best hikes, and "Warden's Way and Windrush Way" (£1.50), which details interesting walks between Bourton-on-the-Water and Winchcombe. In Cheltenham, pick up the free "Getting There" pamphlet at the tourist office; it lists public transport options between Cheltenham and other cities such as Broadway, Cirencester, Moreton-in-Marsh, and Oxford.

Not every small village has an information center, and some are only seasonal, but any one of the following offices can guide you through the Cotswolds: **Broadway** (1 Cotswold Ct., tel. 01386/852937), **Cheltenham** (77 The Promenade, tel. 01242/522878), and **Cirencester** (Town Hall, Market Pl., tel. 01285/654180). Several other towns have small offices that can help you plan your trip, but most of them close November–March. These include, among others: **Moreton-in-Marsh** (High St., tel. 01608/650881), **Stow-on-the-Wold** (Hollis House, The Square, tel. 01451/831082), **Winchcombe** (Town Hall, High St., tel. 01242/602925), and **Woodstock** (Hensington Rd., tel. 01993/813276).

GETTING AROUND

Even from transport hubs like Cheltenham, Gloucester, or Moreton-in-Marsh, you'll need to be a bit creative to get around. Pick up free bus and train timetables from a tourist office, or try hitchhiking (which is considered safe enough in these parts). The only easy way to explore the Cotswolds is by car. With some planning, however, bus travelers can save themselves a lot of aggravation.

> *Throw back a pint or two at The Dirty Duck (Waterside, tel. 01789/297312), Stratford's thespian hangout. Everybody from Olivier to Gielgud to Branagh drank here, and nearly all have left signed photographs on the wall to prove it.*

BY BIKE • Though the long-distance walks above are inaccessible to cyclists, there are numerous country lanes to glide along. **Compass Holidays** (48 Shurdington Rd., Cheltenham, tel. 01242/250642) rents bikes for £11 per day, with prices plummeting to £5 per day after five days. They also sell maps and guides, including the *Inside Track to Mountain Biking in the Cotswolds* (£3.95), and will organize cycling holidays.

BY BUS • Regional bus service is sadly limited: Buses often run late, many of them run infrequently (maybe once a week), many stop running in the early afternoon, and buses to some villages have been eliminated as more locals buy cars. At least getting to **Cheltenham** isn't too hard: **National Express** (tel. 0990/808080) provides service from Gloucester, London, Oxford, Birmingham, and Cirencester; **Swanbrook Transport** (tel. 01452/712386) offers frequent service from Oxford (£4). To reach the smaller villages within the Cotswolds, try local lines such as **Castleways Ltd.** (Cheltenham, tel. 01242/602949), **Gloucestershire Public Transport** (Gloucester, tel. 01452/425543), and **Pulhams Coaches** (Bourton, tel. 01451/820369). Pulhams is the area's most user-friendly service, running six–eight times Monday–Saturday between Moreton-in-Marsh and Cheltenham, stopping en route at Stow-on-the-Wold, Bourton-on-the-Water, and other hyphenated places. On Sunday, only two buses cover the same route from May through September only. Castleways Coaches connect Cheltenham and Broadway four times daily except Sunday. Cheltenham's tourist office organizes a series of coach tours round the Cotswolds and beyond. Contact the tourist office (*see above*) for details. One cheap way to see many of the Cotswold villages was to ride with **Ebleys Coaches** (Stroud, tel. 01453/753333), which went out on a "market run" every Friday, leaving Cheltenham's bus station at 11:15 AM, and tracing a wiggly line through some of the prettiest villages on the way to Cirencester, arriving there at around 1:30 PM. Unfortunately, this was discontinued, though locals have roused a spirited campaign to reinstall it, so keep your ears to the ground.

BY CAR • If you're with a group of people, you'll save money by renting a car. Cheltenham's tourist office has a list of local rental agencies. **Apex Self Drive** (Marshall House, Wymans La., Cheltenham, tel. 01242/233084) rents cars at £32 per day. In Moreton-in-Marsh, **Paxford Garage** (Northwick Business Center, just outside the village of Blockley, tel. 01386/700814) has cars starting at £22 per day.

BY FOOT • Many villages are readily walkable from bigger towns; for example, Bourton-on-the-Water and Upper and Lower Slaughter are within five mi of Stow-on-the-Wold. The two main footpaths that run through the Cotswolds are the **Cotswold Way**, a 100-mi walk from Chipping Campden to Bath, and **Warden's Way**, a 14-mi path between Bourton-on-the-Water and Winchcombe that makes for an ambitious but not impossible day hike. More often than not, the only clue to where the path leads is the slightly discolored grass caused by the tread of hundreds of walkers. The Cotswold Way rambles from village to village but isn't particularly backpacker-friendly. There are few hostels and campgrounds near the path, so you'll have to stay in expensive B&Bs.

BY TRAIN • The best way to reach the Cotswolds is by train from London's Paddington Station to **Cheltenham**'s small train station (tel. 0345/484950), just outside town, for £34 return with restrictions. In the other direction, five trains leave daily from Cheltenham direct to London, others involve a change at Swindon. **Gloucester,** near Cheltenham, isn't technically within the Cotswolds but has the region's busiest rail station (Station Approach, tel. 0345/484950), with regular service to Cheltenham (£5 return) and London (from £33 return). Within the Cotswolds, the itsy-bitsy station in itsy-bitsy **Moreton-in-Marsh** (Station Rd., off High St., tel. 0345/484950) amazingly has almost hourly service to London Paddington (1¾ hr; £22 return, with restrictions).

CHELTENHAM

Elegant, Regency-period Cheltenham is way too big to be considered a village, and technically, it falls outside the Cotswold boundaries. But it's the best-equipped town in the area and a lovely place to hang out. Cheltenham has been a popular spa town since the late 18th century, when it was a haunt of George III. These days, it's better known for cafés, pubs, parks, and shopping—big-name stores and little boutiques all overflow with the chic students of "Gloscat" (a.k.a. the Gloucestershire College of Art and Technology). As a result, Cheltenham has a youth-oriented vibe lacking in most Cotswold villages. Pick up the "Cheltenham Events" pamphlet and the "What's On Cheltenham" bulletin for listings of concerts, festivals, plays, and other events in the area. Both are available at the tourist office (see Visitor Information, *above*). Now in its 56th year, the Cheltenham International Festival of Music (tel. 01242/227979) takes place early–mid July and is one of the leading international music festivals in the world. Mostly classical music is featured, as well as some new and experimental work. Events are held at venues throughout town, the most spectacular being the opening night in Pittville Park, and there is a concurrent program of fringe events including dance, music, and theater. Other festivals to look out for are a Literature Festival in October and a Jazz Festival in April. Between June and September, coach tours and a walking tour around Regency Cheltenham highlighting the architecture—Regency (1811–20) and Georgian (1714–1830)—can be booked from the tourist office (see *above*).

The grandly restored **Pittville Pump Room** (Pittville Park, tel. 01242/523852) is one of the few remnants of Cheltenham's halcyon days as a spa for the rich and royal. There are plans to make this a music venue; in the meantime, you can tour the spa on the weekend and sip the incredibly salty alkaline water, a favored elixir of visitors, for free. On Sunday afternoons in summer, live jazz or classical music accompanies the water tasting. To get here from the tourist office, turn left on the Promenade (which becomes Gligh Street) and left on Portland Street (which becomes Evesham Road). You'll think you've died and gone to heaven in the **Imperial Gardens**; it's not surprising Cheltenham has won first place in the Britain in Bloom festival three times. From the tourist office, walk south on the Promenade until the street becomes the store-fronted Montpellier Walk.

WHERE TO SLEEP

From late June until the start of September, the **College of Higher Education** (Suffolk Sq., tel. 01242/532774, fax 01242/543561) rents dorm rooms (£26 per person with private bath) at two of its campuses around Cheltenham, but don't bother unless the B&Bs are full. Head instead to **Parkview** (4 Pittville Crescent, off Albert Rd., tel. 01242/575567), which may well be the best B&B under £20 in England: Outstanding, gigantic Regency rooms cost £18.50 per person, more in high season, but with discounts for longer stays. As good if not better is **Lawn Hotel** (5 Pittville Lawn, near Clarence Rd., tel. 01242/526638), a private place with single and double rooms, each with a TV, starting at £20 per person; it's often booked, so call in advance.

HOSTELS • YMCA. It's terribly convenient, so many rooms are occupied year-round by local students. Reserve early, because the remaining rooms fill quickly. Bed and breakfast is £14 per person, £12.80 after the first two nights. *6 Vittoria Walk, GL50 1TP, tel. 01242/524024, fax 01242/232635, website www.cheltenhamymca.org. From tourist office, turn right on The Promenade, left on Oriel Rd., right on Vittoria Walk. 56 singles, 3 doubles, none with bath. Laundry.*

CAMPING • Longwillows Caravan and Camping Park. About 3½ mi outside Cheltenham, in the small village of Woodmancote, this campground caters mostly to the trailer-driving crowd, with upscale facilities such as a restaurant, laundry, and bar. Still, it's convenient, cheap, and close to good walking trails around Cleeve Hill. Tent sites cost £5. *Station Rd., Woodmancote, GL52 4HN, tel. 01242/674372. From Cheltenham, take Stagecoach Bus 51 to Woodmancote and ask for Longwillows. 80 tent sites. No credit cards. Closed Oct.–mid-Mar.*

FOOD

There are plenty of interesting and reasonably priced cafés and restaurants throughout Cheltenham. The **Axiom** arts centre (*see* After Dark, *below*) serves vegetarian meals for a bargain £1.50 in its café. Even if you're not staying at the YMCA (*see above*), you can eat a decent lunch for £2 at its cafeteria, **Tuck Inn**. The **Rendez-Vous Coffee Shop** (Regent Arcade, Regent St., tel. 01242/578755) serves filled baguettes, bagels, and baked potatoes, and afternoon cream tea, though sitting in a glass-walled bridge above the shopping mall might not be your idea of taking in the sights. **Boogaloo** (16 Regent St., tel. 01242/702259) is a laid-back coffeehouse with a vast choice of bean brews and all-day breakfasts. Comfy sofas, homemade food and relaxing soundtracks should lull you into a mellow mood. A separate smoking floor will put you in touch with like-minded souls.

AFTER DARK

The pubs and bars of Cheltenham are buzzing with activity. **Peppers** (Regent St., tel. 01242/573488) is a popular hangout, with live blues on Friday, jazz on Saturday. For the clubbing crowd, the current hot spot is **Time** (above Buskers Bar off High St., at 33 Albion St., tel. 01242/230–036), playing a mix of hard house and drum & bass. The **Embassy** and **Knight clubs** (St. James Sq., tel. 01242/527700) appeal to a slightly older crowd: Embassy is for over-25s, Knight for the over-30s. 1960s and 1980s music makes a comeback on Friday, when a £10 wristband gets you admission and free drinks all night.

Axiom (57–59 Winchcombe St., tel. 01242/253183) plays the role of alternative cultural center, with theater, live music, and DJs; some events are free, otherwise the cover varies between £3 and £8. Two theaters, **Playhouse Theatre** (Bath Rd., tel. 01242/522852), specializing in biweekly amateur productions, and **Everyman Theatre** (Regent St., tel. 01242/572573), both hold dance performances in addition to plays. Tickets start at £4.50, £6 on Friday and Saturday.

A typical Cotswold direction: "Continue along the hedgerow next to the damp field while veering to your left. Turn right at the dovecote and walk to the fifth oak tree." But what's a dovecote? (Follow the pigeons).

CIRENCESTER

Cirencester (pronounced SI-ren-SES-ter) is as cosmopolitan as the southern Cotswolds get, with pubs, banks, and bus service. In the 1st century AD, the Romans knew it as Corinium, the second-largest town in Britain, and today it stands as a charming blend of the old and the new. The **Church of St. John Baptist** (Market Pl., tel. 01285/653142), a Gothic jewel, dominates the center of town; have a peek inside at Anne Boleyn's Cup, made for her in 1535, and a series of gravestones along the wall dating back as far as 500 years. Behind the church are the lovely **Abbey Grounds,** an expanse of grass right next to a small lake—a perfect spot for reading or picnicking. The **Corinium Museum** (Park St., tel. 01285/655611) has one of the largest Roman collections in Britain, especially worth the £2.50 admission for its mosaic pavements. It's open April–October, Monday–Saturday 10–5, Sunday 2–5, and is closed on Monday November–March.

Brewery Arts Theatre (Brewery Ct., tel. 01285/657181) hosts theater performances, poetry readings, and live music, and the next-door **Brewery Arts Centre** has a cool café (*see below*) and a craft shop where you can buy the products of artists at work on the premises. If you stop by to watch a game of polo at **Cirencester Park Polo Club** (Cirencester Park, off Tetbury Rd., tel. 01285/653225) on summer Sundays at 3:15, you might even see a prince. Matches take place all though the week from May to mid-September—call the office for chukker times. Reach Cirencester from Cheltenham via Stroud Valley Bus 51, which runs five times a day Monday–Saturday.

WHERE TO SLEEP

If the tourist office can't help you book a room, try wandering along **Victoria Road.** At no. 91, the no-smoking **Wimborne House** has a four-poster in one room and evening meals for just £7.50. (91 Victoria Rd., tel. 01285/653890); doubles, all en suite, go for £30–£40. On a quiet street minutes from the center, the **White Lion Inn** (8 Gloucester St., tel. 01285/654053), a 17th-century coaching stop, has doubles with bathrooms for about £50. Good meals and ales are also available. The **Raydon House Hotel** (3 The Avenue, tel. 01285/653485) is a veritable treasure of a hotel, granting ample singles for £20 per person, rising to £30 in high season.

HOSTELS • Duntisbourne Abbots YHA. Five mi northwest of Cirencester, this is one of the few YHA hostels that delivers on its booklet description; it really is an authentic Victorian building set quietly on a green hill. The homemade food served here includes vegetables grown in the hostel's garden. Infrequent buses run to Duntisbourne on weekdays only, but the warden says it's feasible to hitch. Beds are £5.65 for under-18s, £8.35 for everyone else. *Cirencester, Gloucestershire GL7 7JN, tel. 01285/ 821682, fax 01285/821697. 59 beds. Closed Sun. and Nov.–Mar.*

FOOD

Café Bar (Brewery Ct., tel. 01285/658686) serves simple meals of baguettes sandwiches and quiche. Next door, **Brewery Arts Coffee House** (Brewery Ct., tel. 01285/654790) also has low-priced quiches and salads for lunch. You can enjoy a delicious and reasonably priced pub meal at **Slug and Lettuce** (17 West Market Pl., tel. 01285/653206), Cirencester's friendliest, most cosmopolitan pub. In the evenings students and locals make this their home away from home.

STOW-ON-THE-WOLD

Like many Cotswold villages, Stow attracts plenty of Sunday drivers combing for antiques. It's small, but you'd never confuse it with an off-the-beaten-track destination; the central market square teems with pubs and outdoor cafés, all clogged with exhaust fumes from passing tour buses. Stow has some of the narrowest alleyways in Britain—one alley built specifically for wool shearers is the width of one sheep (look for it just off Sheep St., of course). It's even relatively easy to get to Stow: **Pulhams Coaches** (tel. 01451/820369) stop here several times a day Monday–Saturday on the Moreton-in-Marsh to Cheltenham run. Stow is a 15-minute bus ride from the train station in Moreton-in-Marsh (80p), and an hour bus ride from Cheltenham (£1.25). Once in Stow, pick up the "Stow-on-the-Wold Guide" (75p) from the YHA; it details walks, cycling routes, and car tours in the area.

WHERE TO SLEEP AND EAT

Although the biggest town in the central Cotswolds, Stow doesn't have too much in the way of cheap lodging aside from the hostel. On the B&B front, anyone over 6 ft tall should probably avoid **The Pound** (Sheep St., tel. 01451/830229), a striking 16th-century house with low ceilings and plenty of medieval character. The two doubles are £34 (£32 in winter), or £25 for single occupancy; ask about a discount for longer stays. The **White Hart** (Market Sq., tel. 01451/830674), next to the YHA, serves reasonably priced pub food such as chicken and chips (£4.50). A few doors down from the YHA, **Alldays Market** is open until 10 PM Monday–Saturday.

HOSTELS • Stow-on-the-Wold YHA. It's a great base for first-rate walking paths to Bourton-on-the-Water and Upper and Lower Slaughter, and it's right in the middle of town. Beds in mostly en suite dorms cost £10.15, or £6.85 for under-18s. *Market Sq., Stow-on-the-Wold, Gloucestershire GL54 1AF, tel. 01451/830497, fax 01451/870102. 50 beds. Kitchen, laundry. Lockout 10–5.*

UPPER AND LOWER SLAUGHTER

If Stow gets a little too crowded, make an afternoon trip to the gorgeous villages of Upper and Lower Slaughter, which look like sets for a Merchant/Ivory film. No bloody histories here: Depending on who you speak to, Upper and Lower Slaughter got their names from the sloe fruit of the blackthorn shrub that makes sloe gin, or as a derivation from the term "sloh" for a marshy area, or even from an old landholder's name. Lower Slaughter makes a pleasant stopping point on one of the finest stretches of the **Warden's Way**. Few people venture on to Upper Slaughter (only a mile farther on Warden's Way), the more beautiful sister and an absolutely perfect village in which to have afternoon tea—try **Lords of the Manor** (tel. 01451/820243) for tea or coffee with a biscuit, scones, or the full works, with pastries and cream cakes. The nearby **Parish Church of St. Peter** has some surviving Norman stonework and is well worth a visit. In Lower Slaughter, **Old Mill** (Mill La., tel. 01451/820052) is the only place in the village—other than a pricey hotel—to grab a sandwich. Unfortunately, there are no budget accommodations in either Slaughter—they cater to an older, wealthier crowd. Pulhams Coaches Bus 1 from Stow, Moreton-in-Marsh, and Cheltenham stops about ½ mi from Lower Slaughter, and from there it's a nice walk to either village.

BOURTON-ON-THE-WATER

Nestled in the Cotswolds next to the soothing River Windrush is Bourton-on-the-Water, just two mi south of Lower Slaughter and a bit farther from Stow—a handy break point if you're walking the loop. Grab a bite to eat and relax on the riverbanks before continuing your trek through fields and pastures. Though the town caters to an older, upscale crowd, **Mad Hatter** tearoom (Victoria St., tel. 01451/821508) offers the standard fare of sandwiches and lunch combos (quiche, jacket potato, and salad) that won't break the bank. **St. Lawrence's Church** stands in the center of the village on the site of a Roman temple. The crypt dates back to 1120, while the tower dates back to 1784. Do your nose a favor and skip the Perfumery Exhibition, but do visit the **Cotswold Motor Museum and Toy Collection** (The Old Mill, tel. 01451/821255). Housed in an 18th-century water mill, the museum is the home of Brum, a popular BBC personality, and displays vintage cars, toys, motorbikes, and the largest collection of enamel advertising signs in the world. The museum is open February–November, daily 10–6; admission is £2. If you're into trains, **Bourton Model Railway** (High St., tel. 01451/820686) is worth a peek (admission £2), but don't bother with the Model Village—it's a rather pathetic specimen. If you decide to spend the night in Bourton, **Cotswold Carp Farm** (Rye Close, off Rissington Rd., tel. 01451/821795), closed November–Easter, has basic facilities and not much room. Rates are £35 for an en suite double including breakfast, or £6 per vehicle for campers, with free fishing. Farther out, **Folly Farm (tel. 01451/820285) is an incredibly peaceful campground 2½ mi south of Bourton (on A436). The rates are high** (£8 per person), though you can get your money's worth by gawking at what is claimed to be one of Europe's largest collections of domestic waterfowl, scattered around the huge farm. Camping facilities are sparse, but the farm holds a café for light snacks.

EAST ANGLIA

UPDATED BY LUCY HAWKING

East Anglia is the hinterland of England, a large knob of land jutting out into the North Sea. Its flat, arable lands and gentle forests have been spared the overpopulation and urbanization that much of the rest of England suffers from by the simple fact that it's not on the way to anywhere but itself. East of Cambridge, the lush, sleepy landscape is unscarred by any motorway, no major airport deposits plane loads of tourists in its midst, and the bus and train routes are for the patient traveler. Those happy to take life at a pace rarely found in the modern world will delight in the beauty that East Anglia's four counties offer.

The charms of East Anglia are perhaps less obvious than the wonder of the Lake District or the coast of Cornwall, yet no less endearing for their subtlety. In Suffolk, the southernmost county, rich farmlands are dotted with picturesque villages of thatched, pink-washed cottages. Norfolk has its glorious North coast, with miles of golden, sandy beaches, seals bobbing in the sea, wild flowers nestling in the dunes, and dark fir trees guarding the shore line. To walk for hours along the beach and then retire to a country pub for the freshest of fish and chips and a pint of dark ale is to experience this region at its best. Listen out for the singing accent of the real Norfolker, still heard especially among the older generation. Flat-as-a-pancake Cambridgeshire has farmlands mostly at sea level or even below, making it prone to flooding. Graham Swift's fine novel *Waterland,* set in these fens, discusses at length the uniform levelness of East Anglia, broken only by ditches and drains that seem at times "like silver, copper or golden wires across the fields and which, when you stood and looked at them, made you shut one eye and fall prey to fruitless meditations on the laws of perspective."

The gateway to the region is Cambridge, the medieval university center that is probably the most beautiful city in England—it's not called "The Emerald City" for nothing. Cambridge may not be quite as old a center of learning as Oxford, England's other ancient university, but it's every bit as famous. The serenity of the colleges and their perfect lawns and august buildings is enough to inspire the most pedestrian of minds. Despite its cerebral air, Cambridge is very much a modern city. Then there are the great cathedrals of Ely and Norwich (the latter is also a university town that's a hip alternative to stuffy Cambridge) and the time-warp 18th-century town of King's Lynn. Some of the great families of England built magnificent houses in East Anglia, many of which are now open to the public, like Norfolk's stunning Holkham Hall and the Royal family's country retreat, Sandringham.

In the end, though East Anglia has some undeniably superlative sights, half the attraction of the region lies in its unspectacular but subtle landscapes where the beauties of rural England are seen at their enduring best; to rush in search of one or two highlights is to miss the best, which can be enjoyed only by leisurely journeys along the byways.

BASICS

VISITOR INFORMATION

For more info on East Anglia and the neighboring counties of Bedfordshire and Hertfordshire, send a SASE along with a specific request for brochures to the **East of England Tourist Board** (Toppesfield Hall, Hadleigh, Suffolk IP7 5DN, tel. 01473/822922). Because of its remote location, it's not worth a visit in person.

GETTING AROUND

While you'll have no trouble following the yellow-brick road to Cambridge, elsewhere the transportation network can get downright frustrating. Take buses instead of trains if you want to wander from town to town without having to pass through Cambridge each time. Local buses run only a few times a day so always phone in advance to confirm times and prices. The **Norfolk Bus Information Centre** (tel. 0500/626116) runs a hot line from 9 to 5 to help you navigate the area's confusing bus routes; a **Bus Ranger** ticket (available on board the bus) gives a day's unlimited travel on the whole network for £5.50. If you plan to travel around Norfolk and Suffolk at blistering speeds, consider buying a one-day Rail Rover ticket for £7.50 (valid for unlimited travel after 9:30 AM weekdays) from any station in either Norfolk or Suffolk. Seven-day Regional Rover tickets for unlimited travel in the Anglia Railways region are also available: Norfolk (£27), Suffolk (£27), Suffolk and Cambridge (£40), Norfolk and Suffolk (£51), or Norfolk, Suffolk, and Cambridge (£61). For more information and local timetables, call **National Rail Enquiries** (tel. 0345/484950).

OUTDOOR ACTIVITIES

Most towns are linked by long-distance walking paths used by merchants since the Middle Ages. **Peddar's Way** is a 95-mi route that runs diagonally across Norfolk from Knettishall (on the Norfolk/Suffolk border) to Cromer, via Hunstanton; it continues along the Norfolk coast as the **Weaver's Way,** a 56-mi path that stretches from Cromer (directly north of Norwich) to Great Yarmouth and which gets its name from the wool traders who used the path as early as the 11th century. The "Peddar's Way and Weaver's Way" guide (£2.10), available from the East of England Tourist Board (*see above*), describes the routes in detail. Also request their free accommodations guide when you write.

CAMBRIDGE

Ah, Academia! Even the most jaded dropout won't be able to resist the lure of Cambridge's stone walls, massive libraries, and robed fellows strutting about town. Cambridge is best known for producing some of the world's finest scientists (Stephen Hawking, author of *A Brief History of Time,* today occupies the same faculty chair Isaac Newton once held). The register of literary alumni includes John Milton, E. M. Forster, Virginia Woolf, Vladimir Nabokov, and Ted Hughes, among others. Like many English universities, Cambridge is composed of a number of smaller colleges, around 35 of them. Some of the colleges date back to the 13th and 14th centuries, and nearly all have fine examples of architecture from every succeeding age. But for all the echoes of ancient academia, Cambridge has plenty of life left: These days, you're just as likely to see death-rockers as gray-bearded dons, the Cambridge word for working scholars, putting down a pint or two in the town's pubs.

Since the student area is not concentrated on one campus, the center of town, Market Hill, serves as the focal point for the university's social and cultural scene. Unfortunately, Cambridge isn't all open doors for tourists, or even visiting students. University students eat most meals in their respective colleges, and many activities, bars, and facilities are accessible only to them. For those expecting immediate acceptance into the Cambridge family, coming here cold may prove disappointing. If you happen to know any students at Cambridge, even barely, make an effort to contact them. Having a friend here will open all sorts of doors and enhance the scope of your visit immeasurably. Even though reasonably collegiate-looking visitors can wander through the colleges without getting tossed, the budding Byrons and Newtons who call Cambridge home have to deal with hundreds of tourists on a daily basis and are

EAST ANGLIA

CAMBRIDGESHIRE

ESSEX

SUFFOLK

Grantchester
Cambridge
Newmarket
Bishop's Stortford
Harlow
Stansted International Airport
SAFFRON WALDEN
Haverhill
Bury St. Edmunds
Chelmsford
Braintree
Long Melford
Lavenham
Sudbury
Hadleigh
Colchester
Ipswich
Clacton-on-Sea
Harwich
Felixstowe
Halesworth
Aldeburgh

Blackwater
Cam
Stour
Orwell
Deben
Alde
Tunstall Forest

A10
A11
A14
A142
A11
A120
A12
A131
A120
A604
A134
A604
A143
A143
A1088
A140
A141
A133
A45
A12
A1120
A12
M11
M11

KEY
— Rail Lines

N

0   20 miles
0   30 km

200

EAST ANGLIA

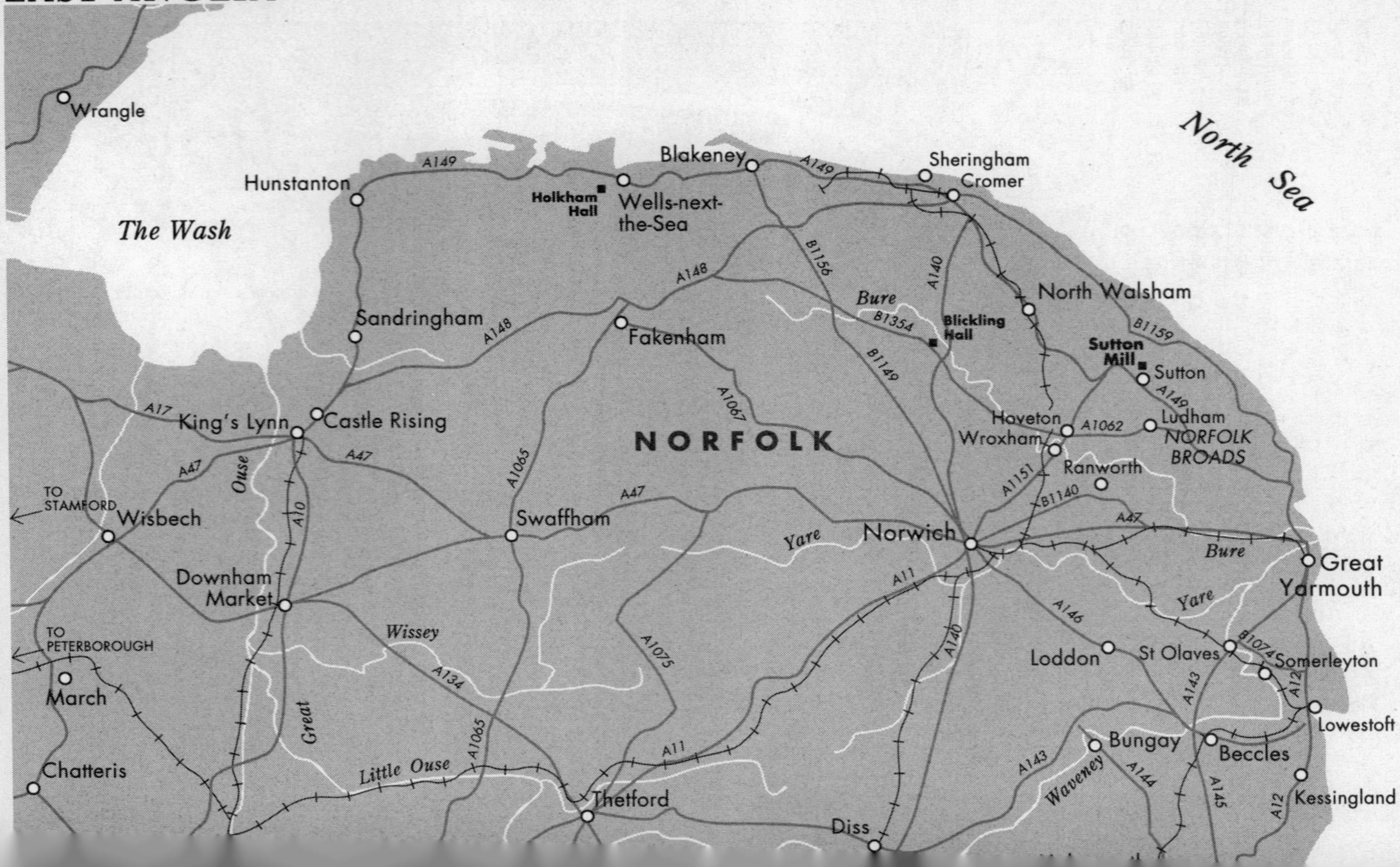

Wrangle
The Wash
Hunstanton
A149
Holkham Hall
Wells-next-the-Sea
Blakeney
A149
Sheringham
Cromer
North Sea
B1156
A140
A148
North Walsham
Sandringham
A148
Fakenham
Bure
B1354
Blickling Hall
B1159
Sutton Mill
Sutton
B1149
A149
A17
King's Lynn
Castle Rising
A1067
Hoveton
A1062
Ludham
NORFOLK
Wroxham
NORFOLK BROADS
A47
A47
Ouse
A1065
Ranworth
A1151
TO STAMFORD
A10
A47
B1140
Wisbech
Swaffham
A47
Yare
Norwich
Bure
Great Yarmouth
Downham Market
A11
Yare
Wissey
A146
A1075
TO PETERBOROUGH
A140
B1074
Loddon
St Olaves
Somerleyton
A134
A143
A12
March
Lowestoft
Great
A1065
Bungay
Beccles
A11
Little Ouse
A143
Waveney
A144
Chatteris
A145
A12
Kessingland
Thetford
Diss

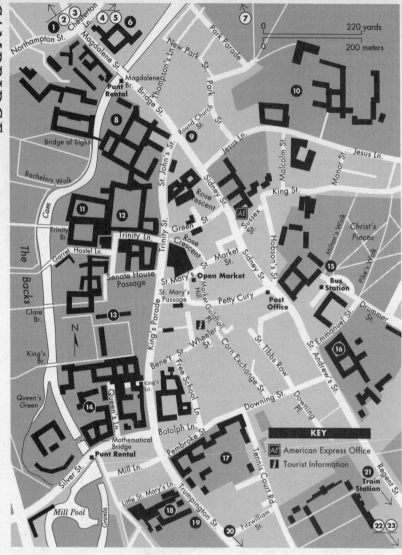

CAMBRIDGE

220 yards
200 meters

Northampton St.
Chesterton Ln.
Magdalene St.
Magdalene Punt Rental
Bridge St.
New Park St.
Thompson's Ln.
Park Parade
Park

Bridge of Sighs
Round Church St.
St. St.
Jesus Ln.
Malcolm St.
Jesus Ln.
Manor St.

Bachelors Walk
St. John's St.
Sidney St.
Rose Crescent
King St.
Christ's Pieces
Milton's Walk
Pike's Walk

The Cam
Backs
Trinity Br.
Garret
Hostel Ln.
Trinity Ln.
Trinity St.
Green St.
Rose Crescent
St. Market St.
Sussex St.
AE
Hobson's St.
Bus Station
Drummer St.

Senate House Passage
St. Mary's
St. Mary's Passage
Market Hill
Open Market
Petty Cury
Sidney St.
Post Office
Emmanuel St.

Clare Br.
King's Parade
King's Br.
King's Ln.
Bene't St.
Wheeler St.
Free School Ln.
Corn Exchange St.
St. Tibbs Row
St. Andrew's St.

Queen's Green
Queen's Ln.
Botolph Ln.
Downing St.
Downing Pl.

Mathematical Bridge
Punt Rental
Pembroke St.
Tennis Court Rd.

Silver St.
Mill Ln.
Little St. Mary's Ln.
Trumpington St.
Fitzwilliam St.
Regent St.
Train Station

Mill Pool
Granta

KEY
AE American Express Office
i Tourist Information

Sights ●
Christ's College, 15
Downing College, 21
Emmanuel College, 16
Fitzwilliam Museum, 19
Girton College, 1
Jesus College, 10
King's College, 13

Magdalene College, 6
Pembroke College, 17
Peterhouse College, 18
Queens' College, 14
Round Church, 9
St. John's College, 8
Trinity College, 12

University Botanic Garden, 20
Wren Library, 11

Lodging ○
Aaron Guest House, 7
Antoni's B&B, 2
Arundel House Hotel, 5
Belle Vue House, 4
Benson House, 3
Cambridge YHA, 23
Cambridge YMCA, 22

understandably impatient. Some colleges have reacted to their incredible popularity by charging entry fees—admission is generally reasonable and the money generated helps maintain the beautiful buildings you're coming here to see. So don't be surprised if a robed man accosts you as you try to walk through an august set of gates and asks you to buy a ticket.

Don't let the exclusiveness keep you from visiting: Cambridge is too beautiful to miss. A narrow, shallow river flows through town, green lawns stretch to infinity, and a mix of architectural styles makes Cambridge one of the most stunning cities in the United Kingdom, if not Europe. For centuries a haven for thinkers, it has now become home to a plethora of rapidly expanding high-tech companies, bringing another influx of intelligence to the already crowded and cobbled streets. Watch out while crossing the road or walking down a side street—pedal-pushers can reach manic speeds. At the first promise of sunshine, many students head to the Botanic Gardens or the banks of the River Cam. On a nice day half the city seems to sit with a pint of beer in a plastic glass watching the ducks float or the punters sink.

BASICS

AMERICAN EXPRESS

This office offers the usual AmEx services. *25 Sidney St., CB2 3HP, tel. 01223/461410. Open weekdays 9–5:30 (Wed. from 9:30), Sat. 9–5.*

DISCOUNT TRAVEL AGENCIES

STA books discount airfares and issues ISIC cards if you can provide £6, a passport-sized photo, and proof of student status (there's a photo booth upstairs at Woolworth's and at nearby Boots the Chemist in Petty Cury). *38 Sidney St., tel. 01223/366966, fax 01223/221802. Open weekdays 9–5:30, (Thurs. from 10), Sat. 11–5.*

LAUNDRY

Clean Machine charges £1.60 per wash, 60p for soap, and 20p per dryer cycle. *22 Burleigh St., tel. 01638/600600. Open daily 7 AM–9:30 PM.*

MAIL

The **main post office** cashes checks, processes film, and even has a photo booth. *9–11 St. Andrew's St., CD2 3HP, tel. 01223/323325. Open weekdays 9–5:30, Sat. 9–5.*

VISITOR INFORMATION

The **Cambridge Tourist Information Centre** is cluttered with flyers, posters, and leaflets; you'll have to buy some of the more useful ones, including maps (20p) of town. Two-hour guided walking tours of the city and colleges leave the office daily, four times a day in summer. Although each tour is different, they are all highly informative—if a bit pricey (£6.25 if the tour includes King's College). The office will book lodging (*see* Where to Sleep, *below*) and, if you're strapped for cash on a Sunday, will give you change in pounds for a purchase made with a traveler's check. *Wheeler St., behind Guildhall, tel. 01223/322640. For advance bookings for lodgings with a credit card, tel. 01223/457581. Open Apr.–Oct., weekdays 10–6, Sat. 10–5, Sun. 10:30–3:30; Nov.–Mar., weekdays 10–5:30, Sat. 10–5.*

COMING AND GOING

BY BUS

One advantage of taking the bus rather than the train to Cambridge is the central location of **Drummer Street Station,** near where St. Andrew's Street becomes Sidney Street. The cramped coach office is hectic, but it does have a good supply of timetables and a helpful staff. **National Express** (tel. 0990/808080) buses run to London—two hours, £9 return—and other cities regularly. **Stagecoach Cambus** (tel. 01223/423554) services the Ely, Bury St. Edmunds, and Newmarket routes, and **Cambridge Coach Services** (tel. 01223/423900) offers a service to Oxford; it's a three-hour trip, and rates are £8 day return, £13 standard return. Buy tickets on board, as drivers often give special return fares the office doesn't offer. *End of Drummer St., tel. 01223/423554. Office open Mon.–Sat. 8:15–5:30.*

BY PLANE

Stansted International Airport (tel. 0800/844844) is as close to Cambridge as it is to London and is serviced by most national carriers. Hourly trains and Cambridge Coach Service's Bus 75 or 79 travel to Cambridge from the airport for about £7 single.

BY TRAIN

Two trains per hour leave for London King's Cross. Travel time on the non-stop Cambridge cruiser is 50 minutes, on the local train 1 hour 5 minutes, and the rate is £13.80 day return, £18.40 standard return, but you must travel after 9:30 AM for these fares. There's regular service to nearby towns like Ely, travel time 20 minutes, rate £4.10 day return; and King's Lynn, travel time 1 hour, rate £7.30 day return, £10.90 standard return, for travel after 9:30 AM. There are a few luggage lockers; large costs £2.50, medium £1.50, small £1, but their availability depends on security measures. To reach town from the station, catch a Cityrail Link bus, or walk 25 minutes: Head down Station Road, turn right on Hills Road (which keeps changing names), and continue straight ahead until you reach the city center. *Station St., tel. 0345/484950.*

GETTING AROUND

It's much easier to get around Cambridge on foot than by car. Much of the city center is off-limits to cars during the day, and traffic on the roads that are open is so bad that the university forbids students to drive cars within 12 mi of the town. You'll get a better sense of the city by walking or cycling—or punting on the River Cam. The layout of the streets is a bit confusing; streets frequently change names and are diverted by the colleges.

BY BIKE

Thanks to the flat terrain and ubiquitous cycling lanes, two-wheelers are the most popular and efficient way of negotiating the city and its environs. **Geoff's Bike Hire** (65 Devonshire Rd., tel. 01223/365629) rents wobbly steeds for £7 a day (with a 10% discount if you're staying at the adjacent YHA hostel)— you'll have to leave a £25 deposit.

BY BUS

For a city overview, hop aboard one of **Guide Friday's** open-top bus tours of Cambridge (tel. 01223/362444), which take in the Backs—the beautiful green parkland that extends along the River Cam— the colleges, and the American war cemetery at Madingley. They operate Easter–September every 15 minutes; October–Easter every 30 minutes. They're a bit (all right, very) touristy, but if you're short on time it's one way to see everything quickly. Tours start from Cambridge train station; tickets, £8, are bought from the driver, the Guide Friday office at Cambridge train station, or the Cambridge Tourist Information Centre (*see above*).

WHERE TO SLEEP

Inexpensive, central lodging is hard to come by in Cambridge. You'd think the university dorms would throw their doors open to visitors, but, no, it doesn't work that way. Though the colleges' rental policies vary, generally those that do have rooms rent them only to large groups. The tourist office's "Where to Stay In and Around Cambridge" booklet, 50p, may be worth investing in. The office can also book lodgings for a 10% deposit and a £3 fee; it's as easy, and cheaper, to make your own calls. The closest budget accommodations to the colleges are the B&Bs on Chesterton Road or Huntingdon Road. Alternatively, the accommodations on Tennison Road and Devonshire Road are closer to the train station; walk down Station Road, hang the first right on Tennison Road, and walk a block or two.

Aaron Guest House. The views of the River Cam and Jesus Green give the Aaron the feel of an English country house that just happens to host a mix of international tourists and visiting professors. It's not the most cheerily run place in the world, and singles will cost you £27, but doubles are a very reasonable £42-£44, rising to a not outrageous £52 for a double with en suite facilities. *71 Chesterton Rd., CB4 3AN, tel. 01223/314723. Take Bus 3 or 5 from train station or walk from bus station across Jesus Green. 5 rooms, 1 with bath. No credit cards.*

Antoni's Bed & Breakfast. This friendly B&B is so centrally located and such a bargain it seems too good to be true. The proprietor is helpful and the rooms are clean and comfortable—each shares a toilet down the hall. Singles range from £13 to £20, doubles from £26 to £40. *4 Huntingdon Rd., CB4 0HH, tel. 01223/357444. From bus station, turn right on Emmanuel St., right on St. Andrews St. (which eventually becomes Huntingdon Rd.). 12 rooms, 8 with shower. No credit cards.*

Arundel House Hotel. This elegantly proportioned Victorian row hotel overlooks the River Cam, with Jesus Green in the background. The bedrooms are all furnished very comfortably with locally made mahogany furniture, and come equipped with TV and tea/coffeemaking appliances; Continental breakfast is included in the room rate. For an overview of the city, you can watch a videotaped tour of it on the hotel's TV information channel. Ask about the hotel's special weekend rates, which are an excellent value. The hotel has a nice restaurant. At the top of our price scale, doubles here run from £75 to £92.50. If arriving by train, note the station is at the south end of the city and this hotel is at the north. *51 Chesterton Rd., CB4 3AN, tel. 01223/367701, fax 01223/367721. From train and bus stations, head north through the city center and turn right on to Chesterton La., which becomes Chesterton Rd. 105 rooms with bath or shower.*

Belle Vue House. Spacious rooms with color TVs and a good location make this very simple B&B a deal. The lone single is £22 and the two doubles go for £35. Call ahead to reserve a room. *33 Chesterton Rd., CB4 3AN, tel. 01223/351859. Follow directions to Aaron Guest House (see above). 3 rooms, none with bath. No credit cards.*

Benson House. Opposite New Hall college, Benson House is a mere 10-minute walk from the town center. With a cheery staff and tasteful decor, this is one of the best budget places to stay in Cambridge. Singles start at £15–£20, while a full range of doubles costs from £34 (standard) to £45 (full en suite). *24 Huntingdon Rd., CB3 0HH, tel. 01223/311594. Follow directions to Antoni's B&B (see above). 9 rooms with shower or bath. No credit cards.*

HOSTELS

Cambridge YHA. The main hostel in Cambridge is a mere three blocks from the train station. Clean beds, powerful showers, a cafeteria, luggage storage, and a mellow international crowd make up for the claustrophobia-inducing bedrooms, but book ahead, as this place fills early. At the very least, phone the moment you arrive; they'll hold a bed until 6 PM if you call in advance. Beds cost £11.15. *97 Tenison Rd., CB1 2DN, tel. 01223/354601, fax 01223/312780. From train station, walk west on Station Rd., turn right on Tenison Rd. 102 beds. Reception open 24 hrs. Lockout 10–2. Kitchen, laundry.*

Cambridge YMCA. This hostel has single rooms available for £20.80 or shared rooms for £17.69 per person, breakfast included. There plenty of bed spaces, but availability varies dramatically, especially in summer when language-school groups descend in droves. There's a gym, exercise classes, and a café here too. *Gonville Pl., on Parker's Piece, CB1 1ND, tel. 01223/356998, fax 01223/312749. From train station, walk west on Station Rd., turn right on Regent St. and right on Gonville Pl. 150 beds. Reception open 24 hrs. Laundry. No credit cards.*

CAMPING

Toad Acre Caravan Park. This well-equipped campsite is frequented by mobile homes, but the grassy strip to the side is peaceful for tent campers, especially when the apple trees are in bloom. The camp closes for the year in mid-September. Sites are £4.50–£5.50 per person. *Mills La., Longstanton, tel. 01954/780939. From Drummer St., take Bus 155 or 157 to Longstanton. 48 sites. Toilets, showers. No credit cards.*

FOOD

Although the students generally eat within their colleges, there are plenty of cafés and restaurants vying to tempt your taste buds. Cambridge's many parks, gardens, and commons are ideal spots for a picnic on a clear day. There are take-away sandwich joints all over the city and in the center of town **Market Hill** has an open market Monday–Saturday with a colorful selection of fruits and vegetables. **Cambridge Health Food** (5 Bridge St., tel. 01223/350433) is the best spot in town to pick up muesli and other whole-food supplies.

Brown's. This huge, airy, brasserie-diner is a classic—and is where students take their parents when they're in town. Stop in for the daily pasta dishes, house hamburgers, breakfast (11–noon), or afternoon tea (3–5:30 PM). It's very busy on weekends, and reservations are accepted only for early evening seatings. *23 Trumpington St. opposite the Fitzwilliam Museum, tel. 01223/461655.*

Clown's. If you like smoky ambiance, strong coffees, and an attractive, young clientele, you'll enjoy this coffee bar with clown memorabilia on the walls. Clown's serves sandwiches and quiches, too, but tends to run out of food around 9 PM. *52 King St., tel. 01223/355711. From bus station, walk across Christ's Pieces to King St. No credit cards.*

Eraina. Crowded at the best of times, this cheap-and-cheerful taverna packs 'em in elbow to elbow on Saturday nights (when no reservations are taken; wait in line with everyone else). It's not all Greek on the

PUNTING ON THE CAM

To punt is to attempt to maneuver a flat, wooden, gondolalike boat through the shallow River Cam along the "backs" of the colleges. (You get a better view of the ivy-covered walls from the water than from the front.) Mastery of this sport lies in one's ability to control a 15-ft pole, used to propel the punt. The Granta Inn Punt Hire (Newnham Mill Pond, Newnham Rd., tel. 01223/301845) rents punts until 10 PM in high summer. Get a bottle of wine, some food, and a small group of people, and you'll find yourself saying things like, "It doesn't get any better than this." One piece of advice: If your pole gets stuck, let go. You can use the smaller paddle to go back and retrieve it.

The lazier at heart may prefer chauffeured punting. Cambridge students wearing Venetian-type straw hats will punt you along the Cam and even give a fairly informative spiel on the colleges. Each chauffeur rents independently so there's no organization to contact; just go down to the dock and wait for the first available boat. Prices are negotiable, though £5 a head is the usual rate. If you choose to get your own punt (which holds up to six people), hourly rentals are around £8; all companies require a deposit of £30. One "dock" for rentals or tours is by the Anchor pub (see below), at the end of Mill Lane near the Silver Street Bridge; another is near the Magdalene Street Bridge.

menu either—pizzas, salads, even curries, are served in monster portions. *2 Free School La., off Bene-dict St., tel. 01223/368786.*

Hobbs Pavilion. Housed in an old cricket pavilion, this cheery place commands views of the playing fields of Parker's Piece, a large open green in the middle of town. Simple but scrupulously prepared food is the bill of fare, with pancakes, both sweet and savory, the main specialty. Three-course fixed-price menus are a special bargain, with soup or salad before, and dessert after, your pancake. The informal atmosphere and reasonable prices appeal to the college community. Expect informal service to match. *Park Terr., tel. 01223/367480. Right on Parker's Piece in center of Cambridge, off Regent St. Closed Sun., Mon., and mid-Aug.–mid-Sept. No credit cards.*

7A Jesus Lane. Scarf down gourmet pizzas (most under £7) in the snazzy former dining room of one of Cambridge's most uptight eating clubs—still a popular place for college students to chat over a long meal. *7A Jesus La., tel. 01223/324033. Turn right off Sidney St. for Jesus La.*

WORTH SEEING

Because of the city's relatively compact size, its main sights are all accessible on foot. For some striking architecture, saunter past the colleges clustered on the west bank of the River Cam, starting perhaps with King's College Chapel and Christopher Wren's library in Trinity College (*see below*). Other colleges worth seeing include **St. John's, Emmanuel, Magdalene, Downing, Jesus, Girton, Pembroke,** and **Christ's.** The list is hard to whittle down, but you'd be insane to attempt to see each of the 35 colleges that make up Cambridge University, especially if you've just come from, or are heading to, Oxford. When you've had your fill of academia, stop by the **Round Church** (corner of St. John's and Bridge streets), built in the early 12th century. It's the oldest of the four remaining round churches in England and now houses the **Cambridge Brass Rubbing Centre,** where you can make rubbings of medieval church brasses in gold, silver, or bronze wax for £2–£15, depending on size. Also, don't miss the views from the tower of **Great St. Mary's**—known as the "university church"—which stands opposite the Senate House on King's Parade. At 113 ft, you get a superb view over the colleges and the marketplace. Admission is £1.50; it's open May–September, Monday–Saturday 9–6; October–April, Monday–Saturday 9–4:15; and Sunday all year after services until 4:15.

THE COLLEGES

Unlike most American universities, Cambridge University has no exact center but is spread over many residential colleges scattered around town. There are only a few large lecture classes, and students spend most of their scholastic careers attending weekly tutorials in the offices of "fellows," the term for an academic who has a permanent position within one of the colleges. And yes, students are required to wear black gowns when attending tutorials. The rest of their time is spent keeping up with the massive reading lists. Bear in mind that many colleges are closed to visitors during final exams, from the fourth week of May until mid-June. The rest of the year, colleges often change their opening hours and close to the public unexpectedly, so call ahead.

Cambridge locals don't always appreciate the way the university is considered synonymous with the town. This town-versus-gown rivalry is as old as the school itself. Much of the friction dates back to the English Civil War, when the university sided with the Royalists while the town's citizens were fiercely loyal to Cromwell (who, incidentally, attended Cambridge's Sidney Sussex College briefly in 1617). The university shares another endless antagonistic tradition with Oxford University: Both rank among the best universities in the world, with Cambridge leading the way in the sciences. To the outside world, the differences can seem quite cosmetic, and Brits not privileged enough to attend either often meld the two names to come up with "Ox-Bridge," a useful adjective.

The huge rivalry between Oxford and Cambridge comes to a head at two annual sporting events: The Boat Race, where their rowing eights race each other down the Thames near Putney; and the rapid rugby match, the Varsity Match, played at Twickenham in London.

KING'S COLLEGE • King Henry VI founded King's College in 1441 and five years later began constructing its greatest monument, **King's College Chapel,** the most glorious flowering of Perpendicular Gothic architecture in Britain. Calling it a chapel seems a bit insulting; it feels more like a cathedral. Completed in 1536, the 289-ft-long structure features the world's longest expanse of fan-vaulted ceiling (the spider-web-style branches supporting the arches). Peter Paul Rubens's Adoration of the Magi hangs behind the altar. During the summer there are public recitals—look for a schedule inside—and on Christmas Eve its famous festival of carols is broadcast worldwide. *King's Parade: College, tel. 01223/331100; 01223/331155 chapel. Admission to chapel £3.50. Chapel open, term time weekdays 9:30–3:30, Sat. 9:30–3:15, Sun. 1:15–2:15; summer, Mon.–Sat. 9:30–4:30, Sun. 1:15–2:15. Access to the college grounds is free but they are closed in the summer term when only the chapel is open to visitors.*

QUEENS' COLLEGE • Queens' College—founded in 1448 by Margaret of Anjou, wife of Henry VI, and later built up by Elizabeth of Woodville, wife of Edward IV—is a ragout of architectural styles. The unspoiled Renaissance cloister court lies beside some ugly, recently constructed buildings funded by Sir John Cripps, owner of the worldwide patent for Velcro. Legend has it that the so-called **Mathematical Bridge** that crosses the Cam to connect both sides of the college was designed and built without screws or fastenings by Sir Isaac Newton. Not true. A local carpenter named James Essex designed the bridge in 1750, more than 20 years after Newton's death. The current bridge is a modern copy, and is supported by bolts and screws. The college allows visitors to stroll through quietly while term is in session, daily 10–4:30. *Queens' La., tel. 01223/335511. Admission £1.*

TRINITY COLLEGE • The largest and richest of Cambridge's colleges, Trinity counts among its graduates Lord Byron, Isaac Newton, William Thackeray, and Prince Charles. Trinity is also the third-largest landowner in Britain—after the Crown and the Church, of course. Once it was literally possible to walk from Cambridge to Oxford and London to Dover entirely on Trinity-owned land. The college's impressive **Wren Library,** designed entirely by Christopher Wren down to the bookshelves and reading desks, contains an astonishing display of valuable books, including one of Shakespeare's first folios and Newton's pocket book. *St. John's St., tel. 01223/338400. Admission £1.75. Open daily 10–5; closed during exams. Wren Library: tel. 01223/338488. Open during school year, weekdays noon–2, Sat. 10:30–12:30; during vacations, weekdays noon–2; closed during exams.*

MAGDALENE COLLEGE • Across Magdalene (pronounced maudlin) Bridge lies Magdalene College, the only one of the older colleges across the river. Magdalene Street itself is narrow and traffic-heavy, but there's relative calm inside the pretty redbrick courts. It was a hostel for Benedictine monks for over 100 years before the college was founded in 1542. In the second court, the college's Pepys Library—labeled Bibliotecha Pepysiana—contains the books and desk of the 17th-century diarist, Samuel Pepys. *Magdalene St., tel. 01223/332100. Admission to library free. Open Apr.–Sept., Mon.–Sat. 11:30–12:30 and 2:30–5:30; Oct.–Mar., Mon.–Sat. 2:30–3:30.*

OTHER COLLEGES • The granddaddy of them all, **Peterhouse College,** has structures dating from the 13th century, when a disgruntled monk from Oxford's Merton College decided to begin a little school of his own. **Emmanuel College,** known as Emma College by the faithful, has a beautiful layout—the chapel and colonnades are by Christopher Wren—and a magnificent duck pond. **St. John's College** (admission 1.50) features the famous Bridge of Sighs, spanning the Cam, built in 1831, and modeled on the original in Venice. **Christ's College,** which educated Milton and Darwin, houses some of Cambridge's best neoclassic architecture, as well as some of the worst architecture; in particular, a notoriously ugly, modern dorm dubbed "The Typewriter" because of its sloping, gridded design.

MUSEUMS AND GARDENS

Fitzwilliam Museum. The permanent collection of this first-rate museum features antiquities from ancient Greece and Egypt in the Lower Galleries, as well as works by Picasso, Degas, Monet, Renoir, Cézanne, Seurat, Brueghel, Constable, Gainsborough, and more in the Upper Galleries. Temporary exhibits range from the fascinating to the truly snooze-worthy, so call ahead to see what's on. *Trumpington St., several blocks south of Peterhouse College, tel. 01223/332900. Admission free, but £3 donation requested. Open Tues.–Sat. 10–5; Sun. 2:15–5; guided tours Sun. at 2:30.*

University Botanic Garden. This is the perfect place to break the musty monotony of cobblestone or to pass time while waiting for a train. Among its many delights are a glass igloo, a limestone rock garden, and flowers, flowers, flowers. *Cory Lodge, Bateman St., tel. 01223/336265. From train station, turn right on Hills Rd., left on Bateman St. Admission £1.50; free Wed. and weekdays Nov.–Feb. Open daily 10–4 or 6, depending on the weather.*

SHOPPING

The developers did their worst in central Cambridge when they plonked modern shopping centers in medieval streets—which is tough on the ambiance on occasion but useful if you're in the market for chain-store goods and services. The heavily signposted **Grafton Centre** and **Lion's Yard** shopping precincts are hard to miss, but more interesting are the small specialty stores found among the colleges, especially in and around Trinity Street, King's Parade, Rose Crescent, and Market Hill.

Bookshops, in particular, are Cambridge's pride and joy. The **Cambridge University Press** bookshop (1 Trinity Street) stands on the oldest bookstore site in Britain, with books sold here since the 16th century. **Heffer's** (20 Trinity Street) is one of the world's biggest bookstores, with an enormous stock of books, many rare or imported. Antiquarian and secondhand books can be found in the serene premises of **G. David** (3 and 16 St. Edward's Passage), which is tucked away near the Arts Theatre (*see* Theater and Film, *below*).

AFTER DARK

Lord only knows what goes on behind the walls of the colleges late at night, and you'll never find out unless you make friends quickly. Still, there's plenty of culture happening outside the college gates: Great rock bands come through Cambridge regularly, and classical concerts are legion, so pick up a copy of *Varsity* (20p) at a newsstand for current listings. Art movies are cheap and abundant, and student theater is excellent. If you have a chance to see a student drama production at the ADC Theatre (*see below*), go. In the summer Cambridge gets festival fever, beginning with the **Cambridge Beer Festival** in May, the **Midsummer Fair** in June, and the **Film Festival, Fringe Festival,** and **Cambridge Folk Festival** in July. Plays are also staged in the gardens of some of the colleges during the month of June.

PUBS

The Anchor. Right along the Cam near the punt rental, this four-story, all-wood pub is filled with locals day and night. The outdoor deck is inviting if and when the sun comes out. *Silver St., tel. 01223/353554.*

Baron of Beef. This small, traditional pub enjoys a good mix of punters (no boating pun intended) and a cheery atmosphere. Real ale is served here along with a no-nonsense attitude toward drinking; do not, on pain of death, ask for a piña colada! *19 Bridge St., tel. 01223/576720.*

The Maypole. The Maypole is the place in Cambridge to overhear pretentious conversation. Thespians hang out here when they're not working on the latest reinterpretation of a Beckett play. Don't leave without trying one of its award-winning cocktails. *Park St., near Jesus College, tel. 01223/352999.*

MUSIC

Look for flyers posted around town to determine what the big show is this week, or pick up a copy of the locally published *Varsity* to see who's playing. You'll find everything from jazz and classical to the *New Music Express*'s flavor-of-the-month band playing at the **Corn Exchange** (corner Wheeler St. and Corn Exchange St., tel. 01223/357851). Tickets usually cost around £8–£12.50. **The Junction** (Clifton Rd., near train station, tel. 01223/511511) is home to local indie bands, hip-hop, house, jazz, and just about everything else six nights a week. Tickets range from £5 for small gigs to £12 for big-name bands. Cambridge has several renowned chamber groups as well as many visiting orchestral concerts and university ensembles who play to a very high standard. Regular musical events are held in the colleges, especially those with large chapels (like St. John's and Trinity). Evensong at **King's College Chapel** (tel. 01223/350411 for information) is held Tuesday–Saturday at 5:30 PM, Sunday at 3:30 PM.

THEATER AND FILM

The **Amateur Dramatic Club (ADC)** (Park St., near Jesus La., tel. 01223/359547 or 01223/352001) presents two different student-produced plays per week, and late-night art house flicks. Ticket prices range from £3 to £7. The city's main repertory theater, the **Arts Theatre** (6 St. Edward's Passage, tel. 01223/519951), built by economist John Maynard Keynes in 1936, juggles a full program of theater, concerts, and events—Derek Jacobi, Ian McKellen, Jonathan Miller, Emma Thompson, John Cleese, Peter Cook, and others too numerous to squeeze onto one stage began their careers here. Tickets for most productions run from £6 to £20. **Arts Cinema** (Market Passage, tel. 01223/504444), affiliated with the ADC, usually shows three different American and European art flicks a day; late-night shows are scheduled about four days a week. Seats are £4.20 from 5:30 PM to 11 PM, £3.20 at all other times.

The Eagle (Benedict St., tel. 01223/301286) pub has a colorful past. It was frequented by scientists Watson and Crick (who announced their discovery of DNA in a back room here), and before taking off for battle, many WWII airmen left their "signatures," on the red ceiling with their standard-issue Zippo lighters.

NEAR CAMBRIDGE

ELY

A warning: Ely (pronounced EE-lee) is for cathedral buffs only. There isn't much else, but what a cathedral! Sited on one of the few ridges in the whole of the Fens, the "Ship of the Fens"—as it is known affectionately—can be seen for miles. If you think all cathedrals are the same, be sure to look up once inside: The spectacular octagon lantern at the crossing of the nave and transepts, built in 1322 to replace a collapsed central tower, is crowned with strongly carved decorative ribs and brilliantly colored stained glass. Its eight massive pillars support some 200 tons of timber, lead, and glass.

The original structure was founded in 673 by St. Etheldreda, Anglo-Saxon Queen of East Anglia, destroyed by the Danes in 870, and reconstructed by the Normans beginning in 1083. The cathedral's nearly all-glass **Lady Chapel,** off the left transept, is probably the sunniest room ever to be found in an English cathedral. Before leaving, check out the **Stained Glass Museum,** admission £2.50; the glass on display ranges from the medieval to the modern, with a focus on Victorian glass rescued from "redundant churches"—former churches that no longer function as such. *Ely Cathedral, tel. 01353/667735. Admission £3.50, free Sun. for services. Open daily Apr.–Oct. 7–7, Nov.–Mar., Mon.–Sat. 7.30–6, Sun. 7:30–5; free guided tour daily at 11:30 AM and 2:30 PM.*

Ely Tourist Information Centre (29 St. Mary's St., tel. 01353/662062) is housed inside Oliver Cromwell's House, but only those with a high threshold for historical marginalia will be impressed. Cromwell and his family lived here from 1636 until 1647, when the tide of history swept them to London. Cromwell's house is disappointing; the tour is ho-hum at best, with a mediocre slide show. If you're still interested, admission is £2.50. Otherwise, pick up a free "Mini-Guide to Ely" and skip the "Fens Drainage Story" video.

COMING AND GOING

Trains for Ely leave all day long from Cambridge, £4.10 day return, and King's Lynn, £4.30 day return. Ely's **train station** (Station Rd., tel. 0345/484950) is south of the cathedral; follow the signs for the city center. **Cambus** (tel. 01223/423554) runs buses from King's Lynn and Cambridge to Ely's Market Street, but stick with the trains; buses are twice as slow and only slightly cheaper.

WHERE TO SLEEP AND EAT

Ely is close enough to Cambridge or King's Lynn to be seen as a day trip, but if you plan ahead you can stay in one of East Anglia's loveliest B&Bs, **Old Egremont House** (31 Egremont St., tel. 01353/663118), a 17th-century oak-beamed house with beautiful views of the cathedral from its two largest rooms. There's a private garden, and the English breakfast includes homemade bread and marmalade. But here's the snag: There are just three rooms—a double costs £40. **The Steeplegate** (16–18 High St., tel. 01353/664731), closed Sunday, near the cathedral, serves teas and snacks; and there's also a café inside the cathedral itself. If you feel like a proper meal and are happy to pay a bit more than usual for it, then head for the **Old Fire Engine** (25 St. Mary's St., tel. 01353/662582), a little traditional English restaurant just by the cathedral. Arguably the best restaurant east of Cambridge, it is also one of the few places you can try fenland specialties such as pike baked in white wine.

KING'S LYNN

King's Lynn is an old port and trading town. Its Georgian town houses, guildhalls, and ancient quayside warehouses are still intact, despite some unfortunate "town planning" done in the 1950s and '60s. The streets have long been worn by tradespeople and sailors such as Captain George Vancouver, as well as by witches and curiosities such as Marjorey Kempe, a 15th-century mystic who wore a hair shirt and who would have gone around kissing male lepers were it not for the intervention of her confessor. These days, the town is somewhat less eccentric, but it does make a very pleasant base from which to travel to nearby historical sights. Travel north, south, or east from Lynn and you're bound to stumble upon a castle or a stately home.

Ten mi north is **Sandringham House** (tel. 01553/772675), now the Norfolk residence of Her Majesty the Queen but purchased by Queen Victoria in 1862 for the future King Edward VII. The house, small museum, and surrounding grounds are open Easter–October, daily 11–4:45 and admission is £5; the house is closed to visitors when the royal family is in residence, usually the last week of July to the first week of August. **Castle Rising** (tel. 01553/631330), 4 mi northeast of Lynn (off A149), boasts of its history as a vital East Anglian fortification and has an elaborate 12th-century keep. It's also the castle where Queen Isabella lived after killing her husband, Edward II. Farther afield near Wells-next-the-Sea (beware: very infrequent bus runs) is one of the most regal of all stately houses, **Holkham Hall** (tel. 01328/710227). Yet it was not built for a duke or a prince. Instead it was the home of a very wealthy merchant, Thomas Coke, who only late in life joined the nobility, becoming the Earl of Leicester. The showpiece of this Palladian palace is the Great Hall, 60 ft high and brilliant with gold and alabaster. Modeled after the Baths of Diocletian, it may be the most spectacular room in Britain (or at least it used to be: an unsightly bannister has defaced the staircase and, sadly, the room's imperial purple rug has been removed). Elsewhere, Gainsboroughs, Van Dycks, and Rubenses abound.

BASICS

The **tourist office** is near the YHA hostel in "Old Lynn," the more interesting part of town. The office organizes guided walks of the old town from May through October—definitely worth the £2 charge. The staff will happily book you a room but will charge you a 10% deposit of your first night's stay, which you will receive back from the lodging. *The Custom House, Purfleet Quay, tel. 01553/763044. From train station, turn right on Blackfriars Rd., left on St. John's Terr. (which becomes Blackfriars St. and New Conduit St., and then Purfleet Quay). Open Apr.–Oct., Mon.–Sat. 9:15–5, Sun. 10–5; Nov.–Mar. Mon.–Sun. 10:30–4.*

COMING AND GOING

King's Lynn's **train station** (Blackfriars Rd., tel. 0345/484950) is the last stop on the Cambridge–Ely line, and to catch a train anywhere, even to Norwich, you must transfer in Ely. Fare is £4.30 day return to Ely, or £7.30 Cambridge day return. Unless you're going directly south, you should probably catch a bus to your destination. The **bus station** (Vancouver Centre, tel. 01553/772343) is more central and services more destinations, including Norwich for £4.55 single, £5.20 day return, and Peterborough, £5 day return, a major rail hub. During summer, Eastern Counties' Norfolk Coastliner service runs buses to Sandringham House—Bus 411, £2.70—and Castle Rising—Bus 410 or 411, £2.10. For Holkham Hall, you must take a bus from King's Lynn to Hunstanton and transfer to another bus (which only runs several days a week). You can store your bags for 50p each at the bus station weekdays 8:30–5, Saturday 8:30–noon and 1–5.

WHERE TO SLEEP

Most of Lynn's B&Bs are a short walk from the city center. Because they often fall into the my-kids-just-moved-out-so-I'll-rent-their-rooms-to-guests variety, they are usually homey and very welcoming. The highest concentration of cheap B&Bs is north and east of the train station; turn left on Blackfriars Road and go left through the park on St. John's Walk, which leads to a number of small B&Bs on Tennyson Avenue and its side streets; Gaywood Road at the northern end of Tennyson Avenue, and Goodwins Road at the southern, both have additional possibilities. Top choices in the area are the **Old Rectory** (33 Goodwins Rd., tel. 01553/768544), no credit cards; **Maranatha Guest House** (115 Gaywood Rd., tel. 01553/774596); and **Fairlight Lodge** (79 Goodwins Rd., tel. 01553/762234), no credit cards—all of which rent attractive rooms for £17–£21 per person. If you're in the market for comfort and joy, the charming **Russet House Hotel** (53 Goodwin Rd., tel. 01553/773098) has what it takes. Singles from £25 and doubles from £40 to £48 are pricey, but all are en suite and include breakfast, and the Victorian house has a garden and bar.

HOSTELS • King's Lynn YHA. Don't bump your head on the low wooden-beam ceilings of this restored 16th-century building, set beside the River Ouse. Beds are £8.35. *Thoresby College, College La., Norfolk PE30 1JB, tel. 01553/772461. 36 beds. Reception open 7–10 and 5–10:30, Curfew 11 PM, lockout 10–5. Closed Sept.–Mar., and Tues. and Wed. Apr.–June. No credit cards.*

FOOD

The city center has plenty of places that serve good, inexpensive meals. **Gifford's Wine Bar** (Purfleet St., tel. 01553/769177), near the hostel, has a healthy menu with plenty of vegetarian options and a nice, candlelit ambiance. For pub food, the best spot is the **Tudor Rose** (St. Nicholas St., tel. 01553/762824), a 15th-century inn just off Tuesday Market Place with treats like steak-kidney-and-mushroom pie and a choice of vegetarian dishes. The **Riverside Rooms** (27 King St., around the back of the guildhall Arts Centre, tel. 01553/773134) is very definitely a splurge option for its swanky dinners (local fish a specialty), but there's an associated coffee shop in the historic undercroft serving coffee, snacks, and pastries.

SHOPPING

King's Lynn market (Tuesday Market Place), held every Tuesday and Friday, is in the great English tradition of open markets: Stalls set up in a large outdoor space, selling everything from cockles and mussels to used Turkish rugs and period bric-a-brac. The atmosphere is bustling and friendly and the savvy visitor can find good deals on just about everything. Looking for a piece of Irish lace, a pound of oranges, or a slightly tarnished set of brass candlesticks? This is the place to go. If you're in the mood, you're also going to enjoy poking around the **Old Granary** antiques center (King's Staithe Lane, off Queen Street), a veritable Aladdin's cave of china, lamps (don't rub them), silver, and jewelry.

WORTH SEEING

Because of its location on the River Ouse near the Wash (a large bay), Lynn has been the region's main market town since the 15th century. Today the markets are held every Tuesday and Friday at **Tuesday Market Place,** where eight roads converge north of the **Guildhall of St. George.** The last witch-burning in Lynn happened right here, and legend has it that the flames forced the poor woman's heart to pop out of her body and splatter against the wall of one of the surrounding buildings. Accordingly, the brick building with the big white door has a heart carved above the door to commemorate the incident. On Saturday, another market is held at **Saturday Market Place,** directly across from the hostel. The Tuesday market features clothes, rugs, jewelry, and food; the Saturday market is mostly fruit, veggies, and fish.

The **Town House Museum of Lynn Life** (46 Queen St., tel. 01553/773450) is an excellent museum that brings to life moments in the social history of Lynn. Everything from children's toys to elaborate toilet bowls is on display, so expertly done it transcends kitsch. **The Trinity Guildhall** (Saturday Market Pl., tel. 01553/763044) has a beautifully checkered stone front; inside is the amusing "Tales of the Old Gaol House," which re-creates a Victorian prison and has displays on Lynn's long, colorful history, chock-full of witch burnings, drownings, whippings, and beatings. For £2, or £2.50 for a combo ticket with the museum, you get a 45-minute Walkman tour—it's entertaining at first, but gets a little silly after a while. The tour ends in the Guildhall's **Regalia Rooms,** housing items associated with the reign of doomed King John, who ruled 1199–1216 and was forced to sign the Magna Carta by his dissatisfied countrymen. The **Guildhall of St. George** (27 King St.)—England's oldest guildhall—sports an Elizabethan stage, now encompassed by the town's respected **Arts Centre** (tel. 01553/764864), which offers art exhibits, plays, and foreign films; call for schedules. During the last two weeks in July, the King's Lynn Festival of Music and the Arts features every sort of performance and exhibitions from around the world. A second arts center, the grand old **Corn Exchange** building (Tuesday Market Pl., tel. 01553/764864) presents dance, drama, rock gigs, and comedy.

SUFFOLK

The landscape of Suffolk has inspired generations of artists, including John Constable and Thomas Gainsborough, with its expanses of heather, sandy coves, peaceful estuaries, and inland marshes densely packed with waterfowl. A county of incredible physical diversity, Suffolk also is home to ancient market towns such as **Bury St. Edmunds.** Originally the site of a Benedictine abbey (founded in AD 945 and rebuilt in the 11th century), Bury is now a sizable town where historic buildings adjoin shops carrying the latest high street fashions. Though most of the abbey was destroyed, the **abbey ruins** are impressive and surrounded by beautiful gardens. The surviving Samson's Tower now houses the **Abbey Visitor Centre** (Abbey Precinct, tel. 01284/763110), open April–October, daily 10–5, with exhibitions and artifacts illustrating the abbey's history. The **tourist office** (6 Angel Hill, tel. 01284/764667), open Monday–Saturday 9:30–5:30 and Sunday 10–3, offers tours of the old town and has plenty of information on nearby attractions.

You can find budget B&Bs in town (ask the tourist office for details), but you may feel Bury is worth treating yourself to something a bit more upscale—if you feel like a true splurge, the **Angel Hotel** (3 Angel Hill, tel. 01284/753926) is the quintessential ivy-clad, historic, market-town hotel. A former coaching inn, with some rooms overlooking the Abbey ruins, it features delightful rooms, one of which hosted Charles Dickens. Doubles cost £86, and breakfast is an additional £11.95. **Ounce House** (Northgate St., tel. 01284/761779) is a friendly, no-smoking B&B, three minutes' walk from the abbey. Rooms start at £80 for a double, but they are large, en suite, very charming, and come with a full breakfast. Don't leave town without visiting **The Nutshell** (The Traverse, tel. 01284/764867). With its bar measuring a minuscule 16 by 7½ ft, it's a cozy place where you'll certainly get to know your fellow drinkers. Bury is accessible by train, £7.70 return, and Bus X11, £4.05 return, from Cambridge.

Seventeen mi south of Bury is the village of **Long Melford,** whose 2-mi-long Main Street features an attractive array of mostly 15th-century half-timber or Georgian buildings—quintessential Suffolk. Once you get away from the customary antiques shops lining the main street, you'll find some excellent sights. Among them are **Melford Hall** (Main St., tel. 01787/880286), a turreted, brick Tudor mansion. An 18th-century owner captured the ship *Santissima Trinidad,* which was loaded with gifts from the emperor of China and bound for Spain. The booty of porcelain and other fine pieces ended up decorating the house. It's open May–September, Wednesday–Thursday and weekends 2–5:30; April and October, weekends 2–5:30; admission £4.20. **Long Melford Church** (Main St.) has stunning stained-glass windows and terrifically detailed flint decoration inside. Walk down the long avenue of lime trees beyond the church to **Kentwell Hall** (Main St., tel. 01787/310207)—open April–June and mid-July–mid-September, daily noon–5—a privately owned Tudor mansion complete with moat, maze, and massive herb garden. Try to visit on weekends in June and July, when history buffs from all over England come to Kentwell to reenact domestic life in Tudor times. Often whole families settle onto the property and perform tasks in the manner of their 16th-century counterparts. Actors dress in costume and play the parts of servants, noblemen, washerwomen and so on, and stay absolutely in character the whole time. There is no food or souvenirs for sale inside the grounds. Admission to Kentwell is £5.25; special events are £7.50–£11.25. Buses leave hourly from Bury St. Edmunds bus station to Long Melford. Frequent buses come from Cambridge and Norwich to Sudbury, where you can catch a bus for the short ride to Long Melford.

NORWICH

Norwich (pronounced NOR-itch) is one of those rare cities that manages to combine the compact, laid-back qualities of a town with the cosmopolitanism of a larger cultural center. The ancient capital of East Anglia, Norwich is the biggest city in Norfolk, but it only feels that way on a few trafficky avenues; otherwise, the pedestrian lanes and winding streets make for pleasant strolling—especially in those city sectors reminiscent of illustrations out of a medieval Book of Hours. The wool and weaving trades once supplied the city's wealth, and local merchants built 30 churches, more than the townspeople could possibly use. In modern times, businesses have taken over a good number of them. It's strange to see the latest camping equipment displayed in the stained-glass window of a so-called "wool" church.

Pre-medieval history of the region includes its early champion, Queen Boudiccea. Where exactly her lands were is not certain, but some think that Norwich was founded on the burial mound of her warrior husband, King Prautagus. After Prautagus' death, the Romans tried to exert their influence over the area by raising taxes. Boudiccea rebelled and went to war against the great Roman Empire. Her victories were brief and Roman wrath eventually destroyed the Icene, Boudiccea's tribe.

Besides the spell of medieval enchantment the town casts—particularly around its famed castle—Norwich is more politically and culturally progressive than most cities north of London. Students from the University of East Anglia and the Norfolk Art and Design School keep the scene from getting stale. Culture and history cohabit with nightclubs and plenty of cheerful drinking holes here. Those put off by Cambridge's occasionally stuffy attitude will find Norwich a welcome and lively alternative.

Norwich has emerged victorious over numerous tragedies in its past. It was pillaged by the Danes in the 11th century, ravaged by the Black Death epidemic in the 14th century, and severely bombed by the Axis powers in 1942.

BASICS

The **tourist office** (Guildhall, Gaol Hill, tel. 01603/666071), open June–September, Monday–Saturday 10–5, October–May, Monday–Saturday 10–4, has the standard official literature, helpful accommodation assistance, and information about the surrounding areas. They also change money for a 3% commission and will store your luggage for £2. At **Norfolk Wildlife Trust** (72 Cathedral Close, tel. 01603/625540) you can pick up leaflets on wildlife reserves and other nature-related attractions, such as the Norfolk Broads.

Several banks with bureaux de change are on London Street, part of Norwich's pedestrian area. The **post office** (9–13 Davey Pl., NR2 1AA, tel. 01603/627171) offers poste restante, changes money, and is open Saturday mornings 9–12:30 in addition to its standard weekday hours. **Clean Machine** launderette (57 Earlham St., tel. 01638/600600) is open daily 7 AM–9:30 PM; a second launderette is at 179 Dereham Road, open Monday–Saturday 8–8, Sunday 8–7.

COMING AND GOING

The city center and all the major sights are clustered around the Guildhall (home to the tourist office). The bus system is fairly good, and you'll need it to reach the hostel, the university, or a campground.

BY BUS

Buses are your best bet if you want to hit nearby sights like the nature reserves of the Norfolk Broads, a network of shallow, reed-bordered lakes where you can rent boats. For local schedules, contact **Eastern Counties** (tel. 01603/622800), the main local carrier, or call or visit the **Norfolk Bus Information Centre (NorBIC)** (4 Guildhall Hill, tel. 0500/626116), open weekdays 8:30–5. A Bus Ranger ticket (available on board any bus) gives a day's unlimited travel on the whole network for £5.50, and is also valid for some routes in Essex. Routes to and from Cambridge are with **Cambridge Coach Services** (*see* Cambridge, *above*). **National Express** goes farther afield, with several daily departures to London—3 hours, £16.75 return, £20 on Friday. To reach the city center from **Surrey Street Bus Station** (tel. 01603/613613), turn left on Surrey Street, right on St. Stephen Street, and continue straight ahead.

BY TRAIN

Norwich's **train station** (Thorpe Rd., tel. 0345/484950), complete with an information kiosk and 24-hour lockers, serves as a major hub for East Anglia. Trains to London (£29.50 return, cheaper if booked at least a week in advance), Cambridge (£15.10 return), and Great Yarmouth (£4 day return) leave throughout the day (above prices are for travel after 9:30 AM). The center of town is a 10-minute walk from the station; turn left on Thorpe Road, cross the river, and continue on Prince of Wales Road to reach Norwich's castle.

WHERE TO SLEEP

Because Norwich is a student center, there's no lack of budget accommodations in town. B&Bs abound in the center, but they tend to be more pricey. The tourist office has a complete list and will help you make reservations. Near the train station along Riverside Road and its side streets are a bunch of small B&Bs that charge about £15 per person—the cheapest B&B rooms you'll find this close to town. Otherwise, it's a slog across town to Earlham Road, 20 minutes west of the center, where you'll find lots more—follow St. Giles St. away from the Guildhall, heading out of town.

The Beeches Hotel. About a mile west of the city center, this attractive family-run hotel is actually two early Victorian houses, set in an extraordinary garden hidden away from the road, known as the Plantation Gardens. All the rooms are simply but pleasantly furnished, and several look out over the gardens, which—with their ornate Gothic fountain and Italianate terrace—are gradually being restored to their original Victorian splendor. Doubles range from £60 to £80 and a restaurant is on the premises. *4–6 Earlham Rd., NR2 3DB, tel. 01603/621167. See Where to Sleep introduction for directions to Earlham Rd. 27 rooms with bath.*

Chalk Hill House. So what if the floral wallpaper doesn't match the psychedelic drapery? This friendly family-run B&B has other assets: a prime riverside location close to the train station, TVs in the rooms, and friendly hosts. Try to get a room not facing noisy Riverside Road. The rate is £17 per night per person with full English breakfast. *1 Chalk Hill Rd., NR1 1SL, tel. 01603/614104. From train station, turn right on Riverside Rd., right on Chalk Hill Rd. 4 rooms, none with bath. No credit cards.*

Midway Guest House. This family-run B&B has cheaper rooms than most of the other places on expensive Aspland Road. The super-friendly Mrs. Bowman will provide tea and coffee and, as a former backpacker herself, may even take pity and do a little laundry for you. She must be the nicest landlady in Norwich. Singles cost £16, doubles £30. *20 Aspland Rd., NR1 1SH, tel. 01603/631752. From train station, turn right on Riverside Rd., right on Aspland Rd. 5 rooms, none with bath. No credit cards.*

HOSTELS

YMCA. Norwich's coed YMCA is just down the street from the Guildhall in the center of town. Bed-and-breakfast costs £12.85 per person in a single room, the only type of accommodation this YMCA now offers. There are budget weekly rates, too (£68.36 B&B) for those who really fall in love with Norwich. Both a cafeteria and a self-service kitchen are on site. *48 St. Giles St., tel. 01603/620269. From tourist office, turn right on St. Giles St. 100 singles, none with bath. Reception open 24 hours. No credit cards.*

CAMPING

Lakenham Camp Site. This site fortunately doesn't allow huge RVs. Even so, reservations are advised during summer. Sites cost £4.70 per person in high season, £3.10 in low season, plus an extra £3.50 pitch charge for those who aren't camping-club members. Bus 9 runs frequently to the site. *Martineau Lake, Lakenham, 2 mi south of Norwich, tel. 01603/620060. 25 tent sites. Toilets, showers. Closed Oct.–mid-Mar. No credit cards.*

FOOD

Budget travelers have it made in Norwich, which has one of the biggest open-air markets in England. The Market Square near the Guildhall, open daily except Sunday, has plenty of cheap and greasy fish-and-chip stands and a wide variety of fresh fruit in summer. Owing to the university, Norwich also has scads of cool student hangouts and vegetarian restaurants. There's also plenty of restaurants, coffee shops, and fast-food joints to choose from.

Bar Tapas. With its wall murals, colorful tablecloths, and Spanish music, Bar Tapas is a lively, cheerful spot to indulge in dishes such as *gambas fritas* (crispy fried prawns with garlic dip), and *patatas a la* *brava* (potatoes with a rich chili sauce). The paella is plenty big enough for two to share. *16–20 Exchange St., tel. 01603/764077. Walk north from the tourist office, up Exchange St. Closed Sun. No credit cards.*

Pinocchio's. A lavish, upscale place with off-white walls and murals, Pinocchio's serves mostly Italian pastas, meat, or fish entrées. A Flamenco guitarist performs every Monday and jazz riffs on Thursday at 8 PM. *11 St. Benedict St., tel. 01603/613318. From tourist office, walk north on Exchange St., turn left on St. Andrew's St. (which becomes Charing Cross and St. Benedict St.). Closed Sun.*

Pizza One and Pancakes Too. The name tells you all you need to know about what's on offer. Neither specialty costs much over a fiver, and it's a nice place to hang out. *24 Tombland, tel. 01603/621583. From tourist office walk along London St., Tombland will be half way along on the left hand side.*

The Treehouse. The second-floor location of this co-op vegetarian restaurant does give it the feel of a tree house, and the pottery plates, produced by local artisans, add to the groovy atmosphere. The informal, friendly staff changes the menu daily. A full meal runs £4.40–£5.90; substantial soups and salads run £2.40–£3.40. Below the restaurant is Rainbow Whole Foods, with whole-food supplies to go. *14–16 Dove St., tel. 01603/763258. From tourist office, walk down Dove St. passageway (look for Tesco Metro on the corner) until you reach Pottergate. Closed Sun. No credit cards.*

Waffle House. To prove their claim that anything tastes better on a waffle, the Waffle House serves them up with everything from ham, cheese, and mushrooms to fresh fish. If you're against the very idea of a tuna and mayo waffle, stick to the more traditional chocolate mousse waffle. *39 St. Giles St., across from YMCA, tel. 01603/612790.*

> *Norwich once manufactured an eclectic mix of things including textiles, beer, shoes, chocolate, and mustard. For more info on the city's trade and industries, visit the Bridewell Museum on Bridewell Alley.*

WORTH SEEING

If you want someone else to decide what's best to see in town, tag along on one of the tourist office's good **walking tours.** They're offered April–May and October, Saturday at 2:30; June–September, Monday, Wednesday, Friday, and Saturday at 2:30 and Sunday at 11. Tours cost £ 2.25 and leave from the Guildhall. Evening tours, June–September at 7 PM only, cost the same but tend to be themed, so you might find out about Georgian Norwich, or merchants and markets in the city. Norwich's blockbuster sights are the castle and cathedral but there are plenty of 20th-century attractions as well. A number of small, free museums house exhibits about life in Norwich, from domestic affairs and church treasures to trade, industry, and the army. The free **Bridewell Museum** (Bridewell Alley, off Bedford St., tel. 01603/667228) and **St. Peter Hungate Museum** (Princes St., tel. 01603/667231), and the **Royal Norfolk Regimental Museum** (Market Ave., tel. 01603/223649), which costs £1.20 admission, are all open Monday–Saturday 10–5. If your palate is dry from too many traditional sights and museums, learn about the history of Norfolk mustard at the free **Colman Mustard Museum** (3 Bridewell Alley, tel. 01603/627889), or stroll among the latest student works in the peaceful gallery of the **Norfolk Art and Design School** (St. George St., tel. 01603/610561). Norwich's **market** sets up Monday–Saturday in Market Square right near the Guildhall. Most of the stalls sell new junk, but lots of alleys within the market have cheap fruit, fresh fish, and bargain clothing.

NORWICH CASTLE MUSEUM

The castle dates back to the 12th century, though restorations have continued since then—the latest being a new American-style mall below the site. Today the castle and castle museum are completely integrated into one altogether strange complex, with unusually fanciful decorations on the exterior walls. The museum's exhibits include a history of William the Conqueror's ascension to the English throne and the subsequent building of castles to secure his position, and works by the Norwich School of painters. London's Tate Gallery also regularly lends a number of exhibitions to the museum. Unfortunately the castle museum will be closed for the whole of 2000 for refurbishment. *Castle Meadows, tel. 01603/223624. Admission to castle and museum £2.30. Open Mon.–Sat. 10–5, Sun. 2–5.*

NORWICH CATHEDRAL

Construction of this amazing cathedral, including the absurdly tall 315-ft tower over the crossing, began in 1096. Highlights include the medieval frescoes in the treasury, beautiful stained-glass windows, and the tall, very Norman vaults in the nave. Look up and you'll see they're adorned with 15th-century "bosses" (carvings) showing the drowning of the Egyptians in the Red Sea and the Crucifixion of Jesus. From June through September, free guided tours of the cathedral leave from the information desk weekdays at 11 AM and 2:15 PM, Saturday at 11. *Tel. 01603/767617. From Guildhall, walk east on London St. (which becomes Queen St.), turn left on Tombland. Admission free (donation requested). Open daily 7:30–6 (until 7 in summer).*

SAINSBURY CENTRE FOR THE VISUAL ARTS

The University of East Anglia's Sainsbury Centre has an ever-expanding collection of sculpture begun by Lord and Lady Sainsbury, who donated their collection in 1973. The hangarlike building houses excellent rotating exhibits and a permanent collection featuring works by Henry Moore, Giacometti, Modigliani, Bacon, and other 20th-century artists. The center also offers lectures and other events relevant to the artists currently on display. Costs range from free to £5, depending on the event. *University of East Anglia, Earlham Rd., tel. 01603/456060. From Castle Meadow, take Bus 4, 5, 26, or 27 (on evenings and Sun., take Bus 3, 4, 26, or 27) and ask for the Sainsbury Centre. Admission £2. Open Tues.–Sun. 11–5.*

SHOPPING

Half the fun of shopping in Norwich is negotiating the medieval lanes, around Elm Hill and Tombland, which contain the best of the city's antiques, book, and crafts stores. You're almost guaranteed to find a special souvenir. **Peter Crowe** (75 Upper St. Giles Street) specializes in antiquarian books, and the **Antiques and Collectors Centre** (in Tombland, opposite the cathedral) is an old house whose little rooms are crammed with shops. There's more fun to be had trawling through the stalls in **St. Michael-at-Plea** (Bank Plain), an ancient church converted into an antiques market.

AFTER DARK

Norwich's city center is like a ghost town from 6 PM until about 10 PM when the pubs swell with crawlers and those in search of a pre-clubbing drink. Last orders are usually at 11 PM though some pubs have an extended weekend license until 12 AM. University happenings (often open to nonstudents, too) are posted around the university or in the free "What's On for the University" pamphlet, available at the Sainsbury Centre (*see above*) and various locations around town.

PUBS AND CLUBS

Set behind the cathedral, **Adam and Eve** (17 Bishopgate, tel. 01603/667423) is the oldest pub in Norwich (founded in AD 1249) and a great place to sit outdoors beside blossoming rosebushes. You'll find an artsy crowd at **Take 5** (St. Andrews St., at Elm Hill, tel. 01603/763099), a mellow café/bar under the same converted church roof as Cinema City (*see below*). The **Finnesko and Firkin** (10 Dereham Rd., tel. 01603/666821) pours a wide range of beers and other drinks. The **Gardener's Arms and Murderers' Café** (2–4 Timberhill, tel. 01603/621447) team up to serve good pub grub and cheap beer to a mix of locals and students; don't miss happy hour, 5–7 PM. The hugely popular **Waterfront** (139–141 King St., tel. 01603/632717) has a DJ spinning dance music and/or live gigs nightly. Consult "What's On" to find out the scoop. **The Loft** (80 Rose La., tel. 01603/623559) is Norwich's principal gay venue and also hosts "Gas Station" on Friday, which attracts a mostly straight crowd. Cover runs £2–£3, £3.50 on Friday.

THEATER

Maddermarket Theatre (St. John's Alley, between Pottergate and Charing Cross, tel. 01603/620917) presents amateur classical and contemporary theater in the summer (though it's closed in August). **Norwich Art Centre (NAC)** (Reeves Yard, St. Benedict's St., tel. 01603/660352), a co-op art house, hosts poetry, music, theater, and most other art media, with special attention given to ethnic cultures. Tickets usually cost £4–£7.50, and there's a good café to boot. **Theatre Royal** (Theatre St., tel. 01603/630000) is Norwich's main theater, featuring opera, musicals, music, dance, and comedy. Ticket prices vary widely, but you can usually get cheap seats for £3–£5. You should also check out upcoming performances at **Norwich Playhouse** (Gun Wharf, St. George's St., tel. 01603/766466), which puts on everything from Shakespeare to world premieres of plays to jazz concerts.

Cinema City (St. Andrew's St., tel. 01603/622047) is the only art movie house in Norwich—or in all of north Norfolk, for that matter. The cinema, housed in a converted medieval church, hosts the nation's longest-running annual tribute to women filmmakers in May. Tickets cost £4.30, though Monday evening and late-night Friday screenings are just £2.50.

NEAR NORWICH

SOMERLEYTON HALL

Somerleyton Hall sits between the towns of St. Olaves and Lowestoft along the River Waveney in the southern Broads. Home to Lord and Lady Somerleyton, the beautiful Victorian mansion makes for a pleasant stop along the Broads; the colorful garden even has a hedge maze. Unfortunately, Somerleyton Hall is difficult to get to; there are no buses from Norwich and buses run sporadically from Lowestoft, Beccles, and Great Yarmouth, while Somerleyton train station (1 mi from the house) is an infrequent stop on the Lowestoft–Norwich line. *Somerleyton, tel. 01502/730224. Admission is £4.20. Open Easter–late Sept., Sun. and Thurs.; July–Aug., Tues. and Wed. House open 1:30–5:30; gardens open at 12:30.*

BLICKLING HALL

Cars often come to a screeching halt when they spot the famed facade of Blickling Hall, looming in the far distance behind a wrought-iron gate, looking for all the world like the Taj Mahal of England, and framed by an imposing allée of two mighty yew hedges: a suitable setting for the house, a perfectly symmetrical Jacobean masterpiece. Blickling belonged to a succession of historical figures, including Sir John Fastolf, the model for Shakespeare's Falstaff, and Anne Boleyn's family, who owned it until Anne was executed by her husband, Henry VIII. The house and famous gardens are located 15 mi north of Norwich via B1354—you can also use Eastern Countries buses, which run from Norwich to Aylesham. From Aylesham it's a 3-mi taxi ride or walk to the hall. *Blickling, tel. 01263/733084. Admission is £5.50. Open Apr.–June and mid-Sept.–Oct., Thurs.–Sun. 1–4:30 (gardens to 5:30); July–mid-Sept., Tues.–Sun.*

7
CENTRAL
ENGLAND

UPDATED BY ROBERT ANDREWS

Most Londoners consider anything between Birmingham and the Scottish border as the "North," so "Central England" is something of a misnomer. The two regions covered here, while contiguous on a map, couldn't be farther apart in reality. The area from Wales to England's eastern shores is often called the Midlands, while the western coast from Liverpool to the Lake District is known as the Northwest. Such distinctions are important, because the Midlands are mostly farmland (plus the extraordinary Peak District National Park), only occasionally interrupted by a sooty city like Nottingham. The Northwest, on the other hand, may seem like one unwieldy, gray metropolis. Most of it has a raw, industrial feel that doesn't encourage visitors, particularly those looking for the England of rural villages and castles (except in the medieval city of Chester). This is Britain's equivalent of America's Rust Belt, a once-proud bastion of heavy industry and blue-collar values. **Manchester, Liverpool,** and **Birmingham** may have been the economic engines that propelled Britannia in the 18th and 19th centuries, but since World War II the engines have decayed—and the region's prosperity has given way to rising unemployment and discontent. Of course, if you are a raging Anglophile raised on *Masterpiece Theater,* you might not want to spend a goodly amount of time in these cities. That noted, these cities often make convenient jumping-off points for traveling to glorious stately houses such as Chatsworth and Haddon Hall, both located in the adjacent Peak District.

Today, many Northwest cities have developed into rich cultural centers with widely respected universities and ever-expanding club and music scenes. As any proud Manchester native or Mancunian (pronounced *man-kyoo-nian*) will tell you, Manchester has become one of Europe's foremost centers of high and low culture, with a youth scene that's probably more progressive than London's. Even Birmingham, a city that, unfairly, has one of the worst reputations in England, is worth a stop—if only to eat at a Balti restaurant (a variety of Indian cuisine) before hitting a few clubs. On the calmer side, **Lincoln** is a worthwhile historical town that shines like a beacon amongst the region's industrial casualties.

"Brummies" (as the people in these parts are known) are acknowledged, however grudgingly, to be among the friendliest in the country. The pace of life is slower here than in the manic environs of London. For the budget traveler, this is a boon—you can sit in a pub and entertain yourself for hours talking to people about any subject. And they just might clue you in on cool local sights you'd never hear of otherwise.

BIRMINGHAM

Owing to its heavy industry and the carryover effects of the German bombing during World War II, Birmingham's true beauty is not instantly evident. The satisfaction of discovering the city's treasures, however, is akin to fishing for one's supper rather than opening a tin of tuna. Birmingham doesn't sanitize and package its history for tourist convenience, and there'll be no kudos back home for saying you've "done" Birmingham. But visit and you'll find an unpretentious city, filled with museums, art galleries, theaters, and a ballet and symphony orchestra—all of which are rapidly challenging London's cultural supremacy. Add to that a veritable bounty of shops, restaurants, a hip night scene, and three accomplished universities, and you'll find a city as refreshing as it is underrated.

BASICS

AMERICAN EXPRESS

Besides this office, there's a second branch at the University of Birmingham (tel. 0121/472–1460). *8 Cherry St., off Corporation St., Birmingham B2 5AL, tel. 0121/644–5555. Open weekdays 9–5:30, Sat. 9–5.*

VISITOR INFORMATION

The **main tourist office** (2 City Arcade, tel. 0121/643–2514, fax 0121/780–4260) is open Monday–Saturday 9:30–5:30, and there is another branch near Chamberlain Square (130 Colmore Row, Victoria Sq., tel. 0121/693–6300), open Monday–Saturday 9:30–6, Sunday 10–4. They book concert and theater tickets and will help you find a room. A **second tourist office** in the city library (Chamberlain Sq., tel. 0121/236–5622), open weekdays 9–5 and Saturday 9–4:30, sells concert and theater tickets and has some information, but doesn't book rooms.

If you arrive by bus or car on the M6 motorway, you may well find yourself entangled in Birmingham's famous Spaghetti Junction—the country's most convoluted highway interchange, which has become a byword for road-planning mania.

COMING AND GOING

In the city center, blue signs point the way to the stations and the main sights. Inevitably these signs funnel you into a shopping mall—proof that city planners are in fiendish collusion with local shopkeepers. Even so, walking through a mall is usually the fastest pedestrian path through Birmingham's convoluted city center.

BY BUS

The **Digbeth Coach Station** is a few blocks from New Street Station via Bull Ring and Digbeth roads. **National Express** coaches (tel. 0990/808080) regularly serve London (2¾ hrs, £13 return) and Manchester (2½ hrs, £11.25 return). Luggage lockers are available. Local buses, including those to Ironbridge and Shrewsbury, leave from the bus terminal inside the New Street Station complex.

BY TRAIN

Getting in and out of Birmingham is straightforward; **New Street Station** isn't simply *in* the center of town, it *is* the center of town. Although there are three rail stations, New Street is by far the biggest and most useful. From here, trains run frequently to London (Euston Station (1¾ hrs, £29.70 return), Manchester (1¾ hrs, £19.50 return), and Liverpool (2hrs, £18 return), among other cities. You'll only need the commuter-friendly **Moor Street Station** or **Snow Hill Station** if you're heading to the suburbs or to Stratford-upon-Avon (50 mins, £3.40 single, £3.50 day return, traveling off-peak). The left luggage office is open at New Street Mon.–Sat. 6.45 AM–9.45 PM, Sun. 11.15 AM–6.45 PM, £2 per item per day. For train info call **National Rail Enquiries** (tel. 0345/484950).

GETTING AROUND

Generally, Birmingham's attractions in the city center are within easy walking distance of each other. As most accommodations are in the suburbs, however, you'll need to become acquainted with the **Centro**

THE VENICE OF THE NORTH

It may come as a surprise that Birmingham has more canals in its city center than Venice. In fact, using waterways from Birmingham, it's still possible to reach the Irish Sea, the Thames, and the Bristol Channel. These canals, which carried 9 million tons of cargo a year in the late 19th century, have undergone extensive renovations in recent years and are now a tourist attraction in their own right. A walk along the canal will bring you to a number of good pubs and cafés, and it's a way to see the city from a new perspective. You can pick up the free "Birmingham, City of Canals" brochure/map, available at the tourist office, which gives information about the canals, and also trail guides for walking along them. In a city that lacks for beauty spots, the canals help cast Birmingham's urban scene in a gentler light.

(tel. 0121/200–2700), the West Midlands' organized and efficient public bus and local train system. Centro produces a free, comprehensive map of Birmingham and the surrounding region that locates bus stops, late-night routes, and rail lines; pick it up at the Centro office inside New Street Station. The most economical way to use the Centro system is with a one-**Day Saver Pass** (£2.50), for use on West Midland Buses only, and available on board, or **Centro Card** (£5), on sale at Centro shops or stations, allowing free travel on all buses and some local train lines at any time, or the **Day Tripper** (£4), which allows the same travel after 9:30 AM on weekdays and at any time at weekends; otherwise, exact fare (85p maximum off-peak) is required. A **weekly Centro Card** (£18.50) is also available.

WHERE TO SLEEP

Inner city accommodations are pricey in Birmingham, which means bargain lodgings are basically to be found on its outskirts. Thanks to the excellent bus system, however, even far-flung locations are no real drawbacks.

One of your best bets for B&Bs is in Edgbaston, a pleasant suburb southwest of the city. **Woodville House** (39 Portland Rd., Edgbaston, tel. 0121/454–0274, fax 0121/457–7180), one of the best B&B deals in town, is a short ride from the city center via Bus 128 or 129. The rooms (£17.50 per person) lack color coordination, but they do come with TVs and a delicious breakfast (vegetarian breakfasts available). Another good area for budget accommodation is Acocks Green, southeast of the center, and a 10-minute train ride from Moor Street or Snow Hill stations on the Stratford line. At **Ashdale House** (39 Broad Rd., Acocks Green, tel. and fax 0121/706–3598), singles are £20, doubles £36 (£25 and £40 for rooms with bath), and good vegetarian and organic breakfasts are offered. This place is about five mi south of the center city; you need to head out on A41 to Warwick Road. By public transport, get off at Spring Road station, turn right, then take the first left for a four-minute walk. If you're out for a pricier set of rooms (to the sizable tune of £67.50 to £77.50 for a double), head for the **Copperfield House Hotel** (60 Upland Rd., Selly Park, Birmingham, B29 7JS, tel. 0121/472–8344 or 0121/415–5655). In a quiet location with secluded lawns, this Victorian family-run hotel is nevertheless convenient to the hustle and bustle of the city center 2 mi away. The restaurant serves good English cooking, including delicious homemade puddings, and you can eat outdoors in summer. From the city center, head south down Edgbaston Road, with a left at the M6, then a right at Eastern Road, then another right at Upland Road.

HOSTELS

YMCA/YWCA. Four coed Ys open their doors year-round to travelers over 18. The two YMCAs (300 Reservoir Rd., tel. 0121/373–1937; 200 Bunbury Rd., tel. 0121/475–6218) charge £15.50 per person,

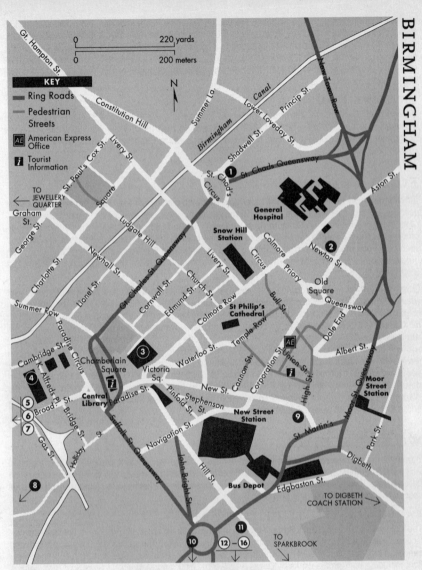

KEY
- Ring Roads
- Pedestrian Streets
- **AE** American Express Office
- **i** Tourist Information

0 — 220 yards
0 — 200 meters

N

TO JEWELLERY QUARTER

Sights ●

Barber Institute of Fine Arts, **10**

Birmingham International Convention Centre, **4**

Birmingham Museum and Art Gallery, **3**

Cadbury World, **8**

Hippodrome, **11**

Rag Market, **9**

St. Chad's Cathedral, **1**

Victoria Law Courts, **2**

Lodging ○

Ashdale House, **16**

Copperfield House Hotel, **12**

University of Birmingham, **13**

Woodville House, **7**

YMCA Bunbury Road, **14**

YMCA Reservoir Road, **5**

YWCA Norfolk Road, **6**

YWCA Stone Road, **15**

plus a £1 membership charge. To reach the one on Reservoir Road, take Bus 102, 104, 105, or 115 from the city center; for Bunbury Road, take Bus 61, 62, or 63. The main **YWCA** (5 Stone Rd., tel. 0121/440–2924) charges £9.50 per night for a bed in a one-bed room; take Bus 61, 62, 63, or 64 from the city center. A second YWCA (27 Norfolk Rd., tel. 0121/454–8134) usually rents beds only by the week (£51), but they will rent for a night (£10) if there's space available (membership 50p); take Bus 9 or 109 from the city center.

STUDENT HOUSING

University of Birmingham. You *must* write ahead to reserve space at the U of B. The University rents out single rooms in five- or six-bedroom flats with shared kitchens for £15 per night, available July–early September. *Contact: Housing Service, University of Birmingham, Edgbaston, Birmingham B15 2TT, tel. 0121/414–3344.*

FOOD

Birmingham's city center is loaded with adequate sandwich places, fast-food joints, and pubs. The most delicious options for inexpensive food in Birmingham, however, are the city's renowned Balti restaurants, most of which are on Stratford Road, Stoney Lane, and Ladypool Road in the suburb of Sparkbrook, just southeast of the city center (take Bus 4 or 6 from the center). Balti is a Pakistani and Kashmir specialty of pan-fried meat and vegetables cooked in curry. Most Balti restaurants aren't open for lunch but stay open fairly late for dinner (usually until midnight), and, as many don't have a liquor license, it's BYOB.

Gorge yourself on first-rate curries and vindaloos—as well as on the largest nan bread you've ever seen—at the stupendous **I Am the King Balti** (230 Ladypool Rd., tel. 0121/449–1170), one of a dozen or so Balti options along busy Ladypool Road. The gaudily bedecked **King's Paradise** (321 Stratford Rd., tel. 0121/753–2212) earns points for being open midday—overload on the lunch special. Full dinners run a few pounds more. In the **Mongolian Bar** (24 Ludgate Hill, off St. Paul's Sq., tel. 0121/236–3849) you can devise your own menu and watch it flash-fried before your eyes; reservations are advised on weekends. For vegan and vegetarian food in a different part of town, or to find out the latest Birmingham happenings, try **Warehouse Café** (54 Allison St., Digbeth, tel. 0121/633–0261), closed most Sundays. On the second floor of the Friends of the Earth building (Birmingham's green center), the Warehouse serves big, cheap meals such as tofu or herb burgers with salad, and leek and cashew crispy loaf with potato wedgies and salad.

WORTH SEEING

Birmingham has a reputation as the flea-market hot spot of central England, but the only one you need visit is the **Rag Market,** at the corner of New Street and St. Martin's Circus, next to the train station. The best days are Tuesday, Friday, and Saturday. It's mostly a textile market featuring factory rejects; the real spectacle is the vicious haggling between vendors and customers.

BARBER INSTITUTE OF FINE ARTS

The University of Birmingham's Barber Institute may be the finest small art museum in England; the collection rivals that of any British museum outside London. While the gallery includes works by such canonical artists as Veronese, Hals, and Bellini, the real strength is the 19th- and 20th-century collection, including high-profile works by Degas, van Gogh, Léger, and Magritte. *University of Birmingham, off Edgbaston Park Rd., near the university's East Gate, tel. 0121/414–7333. From city center, take Bus 44, 61, 62, or 63, get off at Edgbaston Park Rd., cross street, and walk up small hill toward university. Admission free. Open Mon.–Sat. 10–5, Sun. 2–5.*

BIRMINGHAM MUSEUM AND ART GALLERY

You could easily spend a couple of hours browsing the enormous BMAG, which houses an eclectic collection that ranges from stained glass to sarcophagi, insects to watercolors. In addition to a permanent collection of fine art ranging from Bellini's glorious Madonna to Constable, Albert Moore, and pieces by Hockney and Warhol, the BMAG often hosts contemporary exhibits (one recent show was devoted to *Star Trek*). When you approach sensory overload, take a break in the museum's exquisite Edwardian Tea Room. *Chamberlain Sq., tel. 0121/303–2834. From New St. Station, walk left on New St. to Chamberlain Sq. and follow signs. Admission free (small fees for selected exhibits). Open Mon.–Thurs. 10–5, Fri. and Sat. 10:30–5, Sun. 12:30–5.*

CADBURY WORLD

If you've just completed your 12-step Chocoholics Anonymous program, you probably shouldn't risk visiting this shrine to chocolate about 4 mi south of Birmingham. The extensive exhibit begins with the story of chocolate's origins; visitors then head to the factory, don paper hats, and watch the chocolatiers at work. You don't get as much free chocolate as you undoubtedly would like, but you can always buy more in the adjacent chocolate shop. Call ahead, as the factory closes erratically. *Linden Rd., Bournville, tel. 0121/451–4180 or 0121/451–4159 to reserve a ticket. Take the train from New St. Station to Bournville Station, and follow signs from station to factory. Admission £6.50. Open mid-Apr.–Oct., daily 10–5:30 (last entry at 4); call or check brochure for off-season schedule.*

More interesting than the factory tour is the town of **Bournville,** a community created especially for Cadbury workers in the late 1870s. At the time, Bournville was considered an experiment in social reform because it catered completely to the needs of the factory workers and allowed them to buy their own homes. It's a strange mix of capitalism and socialism, all created by the world's unquenchable need for chocolate.

JEWELRY QUARTER

This historic quarter boasts 200 years of jewelry making. The **Discovery Centre** allows you to learn about the skills involved in this painstaking craft, and leads cheery tours to take you back to the glory days of the old Smith and Pepper factory. A departure from your usual run-of-the-mill tourist attractions, the Discovery Centre is both fascinating and fun. *77–79 Vyse St., tel. 0121/554–3598. Follow signs for the Jewelry Quarter from Newhall St. Admission £2.50. Open weekdays 10–4, Sat. 11–5.*

If you meet anyone in England who tells you the North is a gritty, depressing, industrial place, ask them if they've ever been there. Surprisingly, you may find out that many haven't.

ST. CHAD'S CATHEDRAL

St. Chad's was the first Catholic cathedral built in England after the Reformation. Construction of this redbrick edifice, designed by Augustus Welby Pugin (who codesigned London's Houses of Parliament), began in 1839. Located on a busy thoroughfare, St. Chad's has a colorful interior that makes for a welcome respite from the noisy city. The bones of St. Chad, the first bishop of Mercia, rest in the cathedral. *St. Chad's Queensway, tel. 0121/236–2251. From New St. Station, turn right on New St., left on Corporation St., left on Bull St., continue through Colmore Circus and Snow Hill Queensway and look for cathedral on St. Chad's Queensway. Admission free. Open daily 9–5.*

VICTORIA LAW COURTS

If you want to see the English legal system in action and don't mind being frisked, waltz into the Victoria Law Courts and sit in on some hearings. Just about every type of local criminal—from juveniles to murderers—passes through the 25 courts on any given day, so you can move from one court to another if a trial isn't to your liking. The eye-catching, redbrick structure was designed by Messrs. Aston Webb and Ingress Bell. Completed in 1891, it is an incredible work of the Victorian period, with stained glass in the main foyer and underground tunnels (called **The Docks**) linking the courtrooms and prisoners' holding cells. Unfortunately, visitors can't explore The Docks—they're still in use. *Corporation St., tel. 0121/212–6600. From New St. Station, turn right on New St., left on Corporation St., continue past Old Sq., and look for building on left. Admission free. Open weekdays from 9:30.*

AFTER DARK

Birmingham's pubs and clubs are fast and furious, the arts scene is flourishing, and the city's orchestra is world-class. For a useful roundup of the town's cultural calendar, pick up the free *What's On Birmingham* at the tourist office or places around town. Hipper, more underground papers (*Wow* is a good one) list the latest alternative hangouts; look for them at pubs, record stores, and places like the Warehouse Café (*see* Food, *above*). **Birmingham Repertory Theatre** (Broad St., tel. 0121/236–4455) stages first-class dramatic productions by its theater company of the same name. Tickets range from £6.50 to £16.50, with same-day standbys for £4.50. **Crescent Theatre** (Brindley Pl., off Cumberland St., tel. 0121/643–5858) performs a wide selection of plays, with tickets from £7, £6 if booked in advance. The tourist office sells symphony and theater tickets. For an arty cinematic experience, visit **Mac** (Cannon Hill Park, tel. 0121/440–3838), Birmingham's home for alternative films, stageworks, and exhibitions.

PUBS AND CLUBS

Bobby Brown's (52 Gas St., off Broad St., tel. 0121/643–2573) is an expansive warehouse with tons of intimate nooks and crannies. Three dance floors play a variety of music dating from the '50s to the '90s for the over 25s (£5–£7 entry, free before 9:30 and £3 between 9:30 and 10). The **Fiddle and Bone,** (4 Sheepcote St., tel. 0121/200–2223) on the canalside, is owned by members of the City of Birmingham Symphony Orchestra and serves up good grub as well as varied live music—classical to jazz to Celtic—every night and lunchtimes on weekends. **Ronnie Scott's** (258 Broad St., across from the Convention Centre, tel. 0121/643–4525), an offshoot of the pioneering London jazz club and restaurant of the same name, hosts outstanding jazz, blues, and world-music performers every night. If weather permits, you can have a drink outside and hear the music without paying the steep cover of £9–£16. Birmingham University's **Old Varsity Tavern** (56 Bristol Rd., tel. 0121/472–3186) is the third-largest pub in England; what it lacks in character it makes up for in variety—four separate bars fill tankards here nightly.

CLASSICAL MUSIC AND DANCE

Birmingham's **International Convention Centre** (Broad St., tel. 0121/212–3333) is the home of the **City of Birmingham Symphony Orchestra.** The Convention Centre has plenty of concerts, but availability of tickets (£5.50–£31) depends on the event. Call the box office or pick up the bimonthly Symphony Hall Diary for current info. The large stage of the renovated **Hippodrome** (Hurst St., tel. 0121/622–7486) is home to the Birmingham Royal Ballet and also hosts opera, blues, and other entertainment. Tickets usually start at £8.50.

SHREWSBURY

What can you say about a town that has colorful flower pots hanging along the streets instead of lampposts? Shrewsbury (pronounced SHROSE-bur-ee or SHROOS-bur-ee), one of England's most important medieval cities, is filled with 16th-century half-timbered houses, narrow passageways, strange street names (Milk Street, Fish Street), and a multitude of churches. The River Severn cradles the city with its horseshoe-shape path, and many of the streets within the "island" are now reserved for pedestrians only. Unlike many other towns in central England, Shrewsbury has never been defaced by industry; the town has always been wealthy, and its citizens keep things in beautiful shape. Bottom line: Shrewsbury is the perfect stopover between Wales and the north of England.

BASICS

AMERICAN EXPRESS

This office issues traveler's checks and changes money, but if you have mail sent here, they'll make you pay £1 to pick it up. *27 Claremont St., SY1 1QG, tel. 01743/236387. From train station, turn left on Castle Foregate, continue through pedestrian zone, turn right on Mardol, left on Claremont St. Open weekdays 9–5:30 (Thurs. from 9:30), Sat. 9–5.*

VISITOR INFORMATION

The **tourist office** in the Music Hall has a wealth of pertinent info, from budget accommodations to lists of local restaurants and handy maps of town. Pick up the free *What's On Shropshire* for a schedule of local events. *Music Hall, The Square, tel. 01743/350761. From train station, turn left on Castle Foregate, continue through pedestrian zone, turn left on Market St. (which funnels onto The Square). From bus station, turn right on Raven Meadows, left on Mardol, right on Shoplatch, then left on Market St. Open May–Sept., Mon.–Sat. 10–6, Sun. 10–4; Oct.–Apr., Mon.–Sat. 10–5.*

COMING AND GOING

All of downtown seems built on stilts—you'll never cross a street without going under or over it, because New Street Station hurls dozens of trains in every direction through central Birmingham's tunnels and shopping malls.

BY BUS

National Express (tel. 0990/808080) runs a three-times-daily service between London and Shrewsbury (4¾ hrs, £16 return) and Birmingham and Shrewsbury (1 hr 50 mins, £4.50 return). If you're coming from nearby, **Elcock's** offers frequent service on Bus 96 to and from Ironbridge (40 mins, £3 return). Schedules are posted at the station or at the tourist office; you can buy your ticket from the driver. You can get a **Sunday Rover** pass, which will allow you to travel anywhere in Shropshire on a Sunday for £3, or an **Explorer** ticket (£5) which gives you unlimited travel on the **Arriva** network, including Shropshire, Cheshire, and parts of Wales, for one day. Call Arriva, (tel. 01743/344028), or **Telford Travelink,** (tel. 01952/200005) for information.

BY TRAIN

There's no direct service from London to Shrewsbury; take the train from London's Euston Station and change at Birmingham or Wolverhampton. Trains from Birmingham to Shrewsbury (1 hr, £5.40 day return, £10.20 saver return), Wolverhampton to Shrewsbury (50 mins, £5.10 day return, £10.20 saver return), and Manchester to Shrewsbury (1 hr 10 mins, £12.10 day return, £17.90 saver return) run once an hour all day long. Unfortunately, there's no luggage storage at the station. *Castle Foregate, tel. 0345/484950. Info desk open weekdays 5:30 AM–10 PM, Sat. 7:30 AM–8:30 PM, Sun. 8 AM–10 PM.*

WHERE TO SLEEP

There's a string of B&Bs on Abbey Foregate, across the River Severn from the center of town. Make sure you look at the rooms before dishing out money; many face the noisy street. Definitely book ahead in late June and early July, when the **Shrewsbury International Music Festival** (tel. 01743/244255) packs the town. To reach Abbey Foregate from the train station, turn left on Castle Foregate (which becomes Castle Street), left on St. Mary's Street (which becomes Dogpole Street), left on Wyle Cop, and cross English Bridge to Abbey Foregate, keeping Shrewsbury Abbey on your left. From the bus station, turn right on Raven Meadows, left on Mardol, left on Pride Hill, make a quick right on High Street (which becomes Wyle Cop), and cross English Bridge to Abbey Foregate.

Anton Guest House. It's hard to believe that this beautiful Victorian house, with its plush rooms and spacious bathrooms, is actually a B&B. Best of all, Anton's delightful hospitality only costs £18 per person. *1 Canon St., Monkmoor, SY2 5HG, tel. 01743/359275. From Abbey Foregate, left onto Monkmoor Rd., on corner of Canon St. 3 rooms without bath. Cash only.*

Berwyn House. The owners of this no-smoking B&B maintain high standards and low prices, which have made this place one of the best deals in Shrewsbury. Nice rooms, a great shower, and a deli-

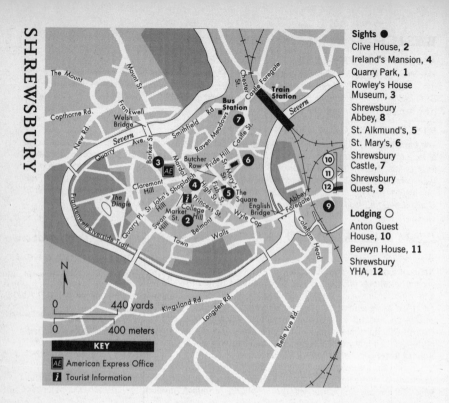

Sights ●

Clive House, **2**

Ireland's Mansion, **4**

Quarry Park, **1**

Rowley's House Museum, **3**

Shrewsbury Abbey, **8**

St. Alkmund's, **5**

St. Mary's, **6**

Shrewsbury Castle, **7**

Shrewsbury Quest, **9**

Lodging ○

Anton Guest House, **10**

Berwyn House, **11**

Shrewsbury YHA, **12**

0 ____ 440 yards

0 ____ 400 meters

KEY

AE American Express Office

i Tourist Information

cious breakfast are included in the £17-per-person rate. *14 Holywell St., SY2 5DB, tel. 01743/ 354858, fax 0797/050–2321. From Abbey Foregate, make first left on Holywell St. 3 rooms, 1 with bath. Cash only.*

HOSTELS

Shrewsbury YHA. The local hostel is a short walk from town and only a few blocks farther than the cluster of B&Bs on Abbey Foregate. The hostel itself is in a converted Victorian structure—a bit musty, but you'll certainly survive. Beds are £8.35. *The Woodlands, Abbey Foregate, at Haycock Way, Shropshire SY2 6LZ, tel. 01743/360179, fax 01743/357423. 60 beds. Curfew 11 PM, lockout 10–5. Open daily mid-Feb.–Oct.; Nov.–Dec., Fri. and Sat. Closed Jan.–mid-Feb.*

FOOD

Installed in a series of 13th-century vaulted brick cellars, the atmospheric **Traitor's Gate** (St. Mary's Water La. and Castle St., tel. 01743/249152) serves freshly prepared, reasonably priced meals. Close to the local castle, the Traitor's Gate gets its name from an incident in the Civil War, when a young Roundhead lieutenant ransacked the Cavalier-held fortress (he was later executed as a traitor). The best bargain lunch in town is at **Subs** (61 Wyle Cop, tel. 01743/241620), with big sub-style sandwiches for under £2. **The Good Life** (Barracks Passage, off Wyle Cop, tel. 01743/350455) serves good-value vegetarian food. **Owen's Café Bar** (18 Butcher Row, tel. 01743/363633) is a stylish place to go for baguette sandwiches, savory croissants, and specialty coffees. Of Shrewsbury's many Balti and Indian restaurants, small and sedate **Ramna Balti House** (33 Wyle Cop, tel. 01743/363170) has the highest quality-to-price ratio in town. Outstanding Balti dishes are under £4; huge nan bread is £1. Locals bring their sweethearts to **The Cornhouse** (59A Wyle Cop, tel. 01743/231991) for a romantic, refined evening. Excellent dinners are served at this restaurant/wine bar, and there's live jazz alternating with bluegrass in the wine bar on Sunday.

WORTH SEEING

Shrewsbury is nothing if not romantic. Most people end up falling in love with the feel of the town. The black-and-white oak-timbered homes, which span the 15th, 16th, and 17th centuries, are brilliantly complemented by Shrewsbury's vibrant flowers. The Horticultural Society has tremendous influence here, prompting people to put an extra effort into their gardens. The best way to experience the town's natural character is to walk the **Frankwell Riverside Trail** (it's signposted around town), which wraps around Shrewsbury parallel to the river. Along the way you'll spot **Shrewsbury Abbey** (Abbey Foregate, tel. 01743/232723), a redbrick oasis of the Benedictines; some of the cloisters now stand across the busy street, courtesy of a Victorian-era road built right through the abbey. The **Shrewsbury Quest** (Abbey Foregate, tel. 01743/243324) is a hokey tourist trap with "medieval" displays and men wandering around in monk's garb saying "Hello, sister," and urging guests to help solve a theatrical reenactment of a murder mystery. The real mystery here is why anybody would shell out £4.50 for this monkish business. Save your money.

In the city center, other historic sights await. **St. Mary's Church** (off Castle Street) has one of the three tallest spires in England, and along with nearby **St. Alkmund's** (St. Alkmund's Place), is worth seeing for its iron-framed stained glass—an indication of the proximity of the Ironbridge Gorge. **Bear Steps** is a cluster of restored half-timbered buildings that link Fish Street with Market Square—look for **Ireland's Mansion,** a massive house with elaborate Jacobean timbering and quatrefoils. **Rowley's House Museum** (Barker St., tel. 01743/361196), housed in a magnificent 16th-century timber-frame warehouse, contains clothing, Shropshire pottery and ceramics, Roman finds from Wroxeter, a reconstructed bedroom with 17th-century furnishings, and other local artifacts of historical interest. On nearby College Hill you'll find **Clive House** (tel. 01743/354811), home of soldier-statesman "Clive of India," who won the Battle of Plassey

Charles Darwin was born in Shrewsbury and attended prestigious Shrewsbury School. Today, however, the scientist's name is splashed across a gaudy shopping mall. Not very evolutionary.

in 1757, thereby avenging the atrocity of the Black Hole of Calcutta (in case you were absent from history class that day). The period rooms here are accented with striking Staffordshire pottery. You can visit both the Rowley House and Clive House for free, but call ahead for hours (both are closed Oct.–Apr.).

THE QUARRY PARK

This huge green expanse south of the city center contains **The Dingle,** a pristine flower garden that attracts hordes of green-thumbers during its famous **Flower Festival** in the middle of August. To reach the park from the tourist office, turn left on Swan Hill, make a right on Murivance, and look for the big park on the left. When you've sniffed one flower too many, cross Porthill Bridge and head to **The Boathouse** (tel. 01743/362965), a pub with a perfect beer garden right on the river.

SHREWSBURY CASTLE

Begun in the 11th century as a stronghold from which the Normans could keep an eye on Wales, Shrewsbury Castle was dismantled during the Civil War and eventually rebuilt by engineer Thomas Telford in the early 19th century. In the early 20th century, the Shrewsbury Horticultural Society took over the small complex and transformed it into a visitor-friendly landmark. The castle contains the **Shropshire Regimental Museum.** *Castle Foregate, tel. 01743/358516. Admission free. Castle and museum open Tues.–Sat. 10–4:30 (also national holidays and Sun. mid-May–late Sept. 10–4). Castle grounds open daily 9–5.*

NEAR SHREWSBURY

IRONBRIDGE GORGE MUSEUM

Shrewsbury is a good point from which to explore Shropshire, a region that served as Smelt Central in the earliest days of the industrial revolution. When 21st-century archaeologists start digging for the crucial artifacts of cultural change in the preceding millennia, the first shovels may well turn Shropshire soil. Capitalizing on the region's industrial history is the **Ironbridge Gorge Museum,** a series of seven museums spread out over 6 square mi just south of the town of **Telford.** The museums were established around the site of the world's first **cast-iron bridge** (1774), which arches magnificently over the River

Severn. Each museum takes a different perspective on the area's development and the environmental beating the land took. The best museum to start with is the **Museum of the River** (tel. 01952/433522), which has audiovisual displays and an enormous model of the gorge as it was 200 years ago. The Museum of the River also contains Ironbridge Gorge's visitor center. Two mi upriver from the Iron Bridge, in the village of **Coalport,** is **Blists Hill Open Air Museum,** a re-created Victorian village with working kilns, wrought-iron works, and offices. Coalport was a famed porcelain center, and its china workshops show how pieces (available to buy) are made. Without a car, you'll probably have to walk between museums, as buses only run on bank holidays. The best way to tackle the entire complex is to buy a **Gorge Passport** (£9.50), which buys entrance to all seven museums. *Ironbridge Gorge Museum, Telford, tel. 01952/433522 or 01952/432166. From Shrewsbury, take Bus 96 (£3 return). Open daily 10–5. Rosehill House, Tollhouse, and Tar Tunnel closed Nov.–Mar. Other museums may have shorter winter hrs, so call ahead.*

WHERE TO SLEEP • The **Ironbridge Gorge YHA** hostel, about ½ mi from the visitor center, has a very helpful staff, and offers a clean, convenient place to crash (you may be sent to an overflow lodging facility in Coalbrookdale, 3 mi away). Definitely call ahead in summer. Beds are £10.15. *81 John Rose Buildings, High St., Coalport Telford, Shropshire TF8 7HT, tel. 01952/588755, fax 01952/588722. 97 beds. Curfew 11 PM.*

THE PEAK DISTRICT

Depending on where you go, you could spend a week in the Peak District and never see another tourist, or you could be trampled to death by a horde of happy snappers within minutes of arriving at Chatsworth House. It's that kind of place, caught between tourist must-dos and miles and miles of fetching landscape. This region contains some of England's most Edenic scenery, charming villages (linked by walking paths established a millennium ago) and—art lovers note—the treasures of several stately houses, including Chatsworth and Haddon Hall, one of the most quintessentially English abodes around. The Peak District is located in the East Midlands, which is easy to get to from London and southern England. Manchester, just west of the region, has an international airport; Nottingham and Sheffield (although not discussed as destinations here) are also transportation hubs. From them, getting to the scenic Peak District is a snap; a bus runs regularly from Manchester to Sheffield directly through the Peaks.

PEAK DISTRICT NATIONAL PARK

When it comes to the Peak District, you should know there's no "peak" here—the highest point in this small national park is only 2,100 ft. What the 555 square mi do offer is more than 4,000 mi of walking trails that wind through some of England's most beautiful hill country. Edged in by the industrial cities of Leeds, Manchester, Stoke, and Sheffield, the Peak District is divided into two distinct parts named for the type of stone found in each region. The northern portion is known as the **Dark Peak,** an area of rugged moors, looming escarpments, and gray millstone grit. To the south, the limestone-filled **White Peak** is a bucolic region of green rolling hills, crumbling stone walls, and tiny villages sheltered in swales and valleys. Here, an extensive system of footpaths and bridleways allows hikers to get away from the roads and into the country. The best time to visit is in late spring, when the northern moors are alive with nesting red grouse, and the southern slopes are dotted with gamboling lambs and drifts of bluebells. If you choose early autumn instead, you'll find the moors topped with clumps of purple heather, fields bristling with corn ready for harvest, and much more room in the hostels.

June and July are peak season; the park's many hostels are filled with rambunctious schoolchildren, and if you haven't reserved a bed, be prepared to camp or stay in a B&B. Because of its rough terrain and limited public transport, the Dark Peak is generally less crowded than the White Peak, especially when you get away from **Edale** and **Castleton,** two villages used as a base by hikers. During the high season, the best way to handle the major villages in White Peak—like **Bakewell, Eyam, Matlock,** and

Buxton—is to enjoy the relative tranquillity of the villages in the early morning and twilight hours, spending the day out and about in the surrounding countryside.

BASICS

VISITOR INFORMATION

It's a good idea to stop in at one of the park information centers to get a feel for what the area has to offer. Each of the four main Peak District Information Centres in the villages listed below can help with specific queries and book accommodations.

Bakewell. *Old Market Hall, Bridge St., tel. 01629/813227. Open Mar.–Oct., daily 9–5; Nov.–Feb., daily 9:30–5.*

Castleton. *Castle St., off High St., tel. 01433/620679. Open Apr.–Oct., daily 10–5:30; Nov.–Mar., daily 10–5.*

Edale. *Fieldhead, tel. 01433/670207. From train station, turn left on road past Rambler's Inn; office is 400 yards ahead on right. Open Apr.–Oct., daily 9–5:30; Nov.–Mar., daily 9–5.*

Fairholmes. *Derwent Valley, tel. 01433/650953. Open Apr.–Oct., daily 10–5; Nov.–Mar., weekends 10:30–4.*

A number of smaller tourist centers are scattered around the park, but they're not affiliated with the Peak District Centre and tend to be more touristy and less outdoorsy. You can find these offices in **Buxton** (The Crescent, tel. 01298/25106), **Glossop** (The Gatehouse, Victoria St., tel. 01457/855920), **Leek** (1 Market Pl., tel. 01538/483741), and **Matlock** (The Pavilion, Matlock Bath, tel. 01629/55082).

Captain Matthew Webb, born and raised just a few miles from Ironbridge, became the first person to swim the English Channel without the use of swimming aids (1875). His daring attempt to swim the Niagara Rapids in 1883, however, cost him his life.

PUBLICATIONS

If traveling by public transport, you need the indispensable "Peak District Bus and Train Timetables" (60p), available at area tourist offices and erratically at the train stations in Manchester and Sheffield. Ordnance Survey maps of the Dark Peak and the White Peak (£6.50 each), or the "Peak District Tourist Map" (£4.50), are also essential for walkers. Tourist offices also stock the following useful publications: *Peakland Post,* a freebie newspaper with a calendar of events for the small villages; numerous cycling trail brochures (£1); Peak National Park guides showing area walks (90p); and a pamphlet on camping and caravanning around the Peak District (free). If tourist offices don't have John Needham's "The Pennine Way Accommodation and Camping Guide" (90p) and "Out and About" (£2)—a yearly guide to events and festivals in the Derbyshire region—you can find them at local bookshops.

COMING AND GOING

The Peak District is the most accessible national park in Britain. Rail and bus lines connect the Peaks with neighboring cities, and the comprehensive (if erratic) bus service is your best option for traveling longer distances inside the park itself. The major entry towns to the Peaks are Bakewell and Matlock in the east, Ashbourne in the south, Buxton in the west, and Glossop in the north. Three regional one-day passes, good for unlimited travel on buses and trains in a limited area (plus discounts on some attractions and bike rental), are available on buses, at most area tourist offices, and at major rail stations. These passes are: the **Wayfarer** from Manchester (£6.50), the **Derbyshire Wayfarer** (£7.25), and the **South Yorkshire Peak Explorer** (£5). For Derbyshire travel information, call 01298/23098, 0161/228–7811 in Manchester, and 01709/515151 in Sheffield.

BY BIKE

Paved bridleways are open to cyclists, although most footpaths are for walkers only. Thankfully, the Derbyshire County Council has joined up with the park to provide the **Peak Cycle Hire.** Each center rents mountain bikes for £8 per day, plus a £20 deposit and you'll need ID. Bikes are available year-round, but advance booking is advised March–October. The centers are in **Ashbourne** (Mapleton La., tel. 01335/343156), **Derwent** (Fairholmes, tel. 01433/651261), **Hayfield** (Information Centre, Station Rd.,

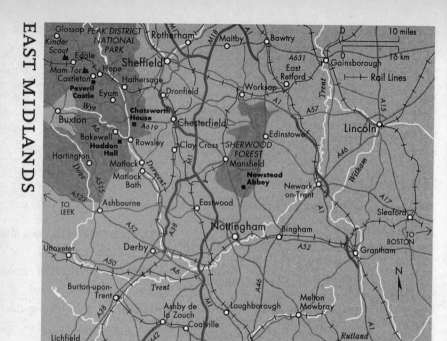

tel. 01663/746222), **Middleton Top** (Visitor Centre, tel. 01629/823204), **Parsley Hay** (tel. 01298/84493), **Shipley Country Park** (tel. 01773/719961), and **Waterhouses** (Old Station Car Park, tel. 01538/308609). Finally, a railway consortium publishes *The Hope Valley Leisure Guide,* which has a calendar of events, details on walks between stations, a listing of trains with folk music, and info on bringing bicycles on the trains.

BY BUS

The most direct route into the Peaks is by **Trent Trans Peak** (tel. 01298/23098) Bus TP, which runs from Manchester through the Peaks to Nottingham, with stops in Derby, Matlock, Bakewell, Buxton, and several other villages. Bus 272 runs from Sheffield to Castleton about 10 times daily (with service once an hour on summer Sundays), stopping en route at Hathersage and Hope. For further info contact **Bus Services** in Derby (tel. 01332/292200). To reach villages elsewhere in the area, buy the comprehensive "Peak District Bus and Train Timetables" (60p), a must for figuring out the confusing schedules.

In Sheffield, the **Pond Street Coach Station,** one block north of the city's rail station, sends National Express buses all around the country, with service to London every two hours.

BY TRAIN

For complete listings, pick up the "Rail Services to and from Derbyshire" pamphlet at a tourist office. Trains run at least once an hour from Manchester to Buxton (£5.15), and many trains run into the park from Sheffield and Nottingham. One of these, the **Hope Valley Line,** crosses the northern part of the Peaks, connecting Sheffield with Manchester via the Peak towns of Hathersage, Hope (2 mi from Castleton), and Edale. This line runs every one or two hours, depending on time of day. In the south, you can reach Matlock from Derby every hour (£3.20).

One of the main transportation hubs to this region is the modern and industrial city of Sheffield. **Sheffield Station** (Sheaf St., tel. 0345/484950) offers direct train service to the Peak District and all major destinations in England, including Manchester, Newcastle, and London's St. Pancras Station.

WHERE TO SLEEP AND EAT

The area has plentiful hotels, hostels, and B&Bs—even so, because the area is especially popular during the summer, it's best to book ahead. If you do arrive without reservations, stop in at the tourist offices, which can provide helpful info: The Peak District Centres stock the free "Destination Derbyshire," which lists camping and youth hostels in the area, and accommodation guides, which list more lodging choices in the Peaks. If you have a sleeping bag, consider staying in **camping barns,** old stone barns converted by farmers into rustic dorms. Each barn has a toilet and a cold-water sink, electricity, but often no heating; you unroll your sleeping bag on a hard wooden platform, or a bunk if you're lucky. It gets cold at night but it's worth the £3.35–£4.50 price. Pick up the free "Camping Barns" brochure at the Peak District Centres; it has a map showing the 12 barns. There are two near Edale, one in Castleton, and one between Buxton and Bakewell. Book ahead by contacting the **YHA** (Camping Barns, 16 Shawbridge St., Clitheroe, Lancs, BB7 1LY, tel. 01200/428366).

BAKEWELL • Bakewell is an excellent base, situated between the light-gray limestone of the White Peak and the millstone grit of the Dark Peak, close to historic **Haddon Hall** and **Chatsworth House** (see Exploring the Peak District, below). A good day to visit is Monday, when the farmers arrive for market. A cordial B&B is Mrs. Westley's **Avenue House** (Haddon Rd., tel. 01629/812467), a gabled, stone Victorian near the river. Rooms are £20–£22 per person, with a fine breakfast included.

The delight of the Peak District is being able to ramble all day in the wilderness but still enjoy civilization and a good pint with locals at night.

The **Wheatsheaf** (Bridge St., across from the visitor center) is a good pub with a big dining room away from the bar. They serve hot food such as homemade soup and fish-and-chips until 9. The **Old Original Bakewell Pudding Shop** (The Square, tel. 01629/812193, open daily 9–6), serves "cream tea": two scones with butter, jam, and cream with an authentic Bakewell pudding and a pot of tea. **Bloomers** (Water La., tel. 01626/818844) sells a similar pudding. **Appleby and Nuthall** (Rutland Bldgs., tel. 01629/812699) has meat pies, quiche, a four-salad lunchbox, and English cheesecake made with cider and Wensleydale cheese.

BUXTON • Although technically outside the park borders, Buxton is an ideal base for exploring the Peak District. (Trains from Manchester run directly to Buxton, so you're likely to start here anyway.) The town is a wonderful mixture of country village and cultural center; it has an opera house, plenty of pubs, and a gorgeous park called the Pavilion Gardens. Buxton has no shortage of B&Bs. Top of the line is the **Lakenham Guest House** (11 Burlington Rd., tel. 01298/79209), a large Victorian structure with a sweeping garden. Potted plants proliferate, while the tastefully decorated bedrooms all have excellent views. Doubles go for around £55–£60. The friendly **Griff Guest House** (2 Compton Rd., tel. 01298/23628) is another Victorian house in a quiet spot, but handy for the center. A double room here will cost you £34. Many moderately priced B&Bs are on Grange Road, a quiet street a short walk from Market Place. For campers, **Limetree Holiday Park** (Duke's Dr., tel. 01298/22988) is 1 mi outside town and has 35 tent spaces from £9.50 for two people in high season. **Spring Gardens,** Buxton's main drag, is lined with bakeries and "chippies," which in Britspeak means a fish 'n' chip takeout, but your grandparents will likely know the word to mean something completely different. You ask them. (And for heaven's sake don't tell them you trolled around town looking for a good one.)

CASTLETON • If you feel like roughing it, **Losehill Caravan Club Site** (tel. 01433/620636) has 30 camping sites open mid-March–early January for £4 per person. The 17th-century **Cryer House** (Castle St., tel. 01433/620244) has rooms for £19–£21 per person, and serves cream tea (£3) in their airy conservatory. **The Castle Hotel** (Castle St., tel. 01433/620578) offers pub lunches and dinners (around £10), and **The Three Roofs Café** (The Island, tel. 01433/620533) serves breakfast, lunch, and dinner daily 10–5:30.

HATHERSAGE • From Hathersage, you can explore both the White and Dark Peaks. Robin Hood's pal Little John is said to be buried unobtrusively here in the graveyard of Hathersage's 13th-century parish church. As if that weren't enough star power, Charlotte Brontë visited Hathersage before writing *Jane Eyre,* and based much of her novel on the town. There are several B&Bs on the upper end of Castleton Road, but they can be heavily booked in summer. Try **Hillfoot Farm** (Castleton Rd., tel. 01433/651673), which has rooms built on to the farmhouse; bed and breakfast here goes for £19–£25 per person. Hathersage has plenty of cafés, pubs, and restaurants. **Peak Fruits** (Main Rd., tel. 01433/650708), open daily, has fresh fruits, vegetables, and salads. **Little John Pub** (Station Rd. off Main Rd., tel. 01433/650225) serves vegetarian meals and large pub lunches such as vegetable lasagna and salad.

WELL DRESSED

Well dressing is an ancient tradition still celebrated today in the Peak District and the rest of Derbyshire (pronounced DAR-be-shure). "Paintings" made of flowers and other organic bits pressed into damp clay are set up around the wells as decorations. Many of the tableaux illustrate Biblical scenes, a holdover from the days when Christian rule didn't allow pagan water-worship and only Christian works were acceptable. The village of Tissington, at the south end of the Peak District, has the most famous ceremony in May on Ascension Day, but there are 62 different blessings in the area from May through September. To find out more or to get a schedule, contact the Chesterfield tourist office (tel. 01246/345777).

HOSTELS

There are 19 YHA hostels in the Peaks. Many lie on major walking trails and are easier to reach on foot than by public transport. Most tourist offices and YHAs in the region carry information on the **White Peak Way,** a 90-mi walk linking seven hostels 9–17 mi apart. Contact the Hathersage YHA (*see below*) for details on the walk.

Castleton YHA. Super-friendly staff and a great location at the base of Peveril Castle make this hostel one of the best in the region. It's incredibly busy April–July, so reserve ahead. Beds cost £10.15. *Castleton Hall, Castleton, Sheffield S33 8WG, tel. 01433/620235, fax 01433/621767. 150 beds. Reception open daily 7 AM–10:30 PM. Curfew 11 PM.*

Edale YHA. A large country house on the moors with many trails nearby, this hostel hosts lots of school groups May–July—book well ahead, especially on weekends. Their Activity Centre plans outdoor excursions ranging from mountain climbing to rafting. Beds are £10.15. *Rowland Cote, Nether Booth, Edale, Derbyshire S33 7ZH, tel. 01433/670302, fax 01433/670243. 139 beds. Reception open daily 1–5. Curfew 11 PM, lockout 10–1. Closed late Dec.–early Jan.*

Eyam YHA. This hostel occupies a Victorian barrister's house built in 1887; note the elaborate tower and excellent views. From April through August *definitely* make reservations in advance. Beds cost £8.35. *Hawkhill Rd., Eyam, Sheffield S32 5QP, tel. 01433/630335. 60 beds. Reception open daily 7:30–10 and 5–11. Curfew 11 PM, lockout 10–5. Open Feb., Mar., and Nov., Fri. and Sat.; Apr.–Sept., daily; Oct., Mon.–Sat. Closed Dec. and Jan.*

Hathersage YHA. The bathrooms in the Hathersage hostel are a bit moldy, but otherwise it's a good place to stay while exploring the town in which parts of *Jane Eyre* are set. Beds cost £8.35. *Castleton Rd., Hathersage, Sheffield S32 1EH, tel. and fax 01433/650493. 40 beds. Reception open daily 5–10:30 AM. Curfew 11 PM, lockout 10–5. Open mid-Apr.–Oct., Mon.–Sat.; Nov. and mid-Jan.–mid-Apr., Fri. and Sat. Closed Dec.–mid-Jan.*

Matlock YHA. This clean, internationally themed hostel is known for the best food in the YHA system. You should always book early, especially June–September. Beds are £10.15. *40 Bank Rd., Matlock, Derbyshire DE4 3NF, tel. 01629/582983, fax 01629/583484. 49 beds. Reception open 7:30–10 and 1–10:30. Lockout 10–1. Closed mid-Dec.–mid-Jan.*

EXPLORING THE PEAK DISTRICT

Like most of Britain's national parks, much of the Peak District is actually private property and farmland. In an agreement with the government, many farmers permit footpaths and bridleways to cross their land, but visitors should remember that they don't necessarily have free run of the hills. Try sightseeing one day, hiking the next, and then resting in a tiny village. Many of the villages are attractions in their own right. The YHA puts together pamphlets (20p) outlining the walks from one hostel to another; many of them are between 10 and 15 mi—perfect for a day hike. Pamphlets are available at YHAs or can be ordered through the YHA Northern Region office (PO Box 11, Matlock, Derbyshire, DE5 3XA).

HIKES

Peak District Centres carry the "Walk With a Ranger" guide, listing free day hikes around the park. For longer hikes, the **Tissington Trail** and **High Peak Trail** follow the routes of old railway lines. Not surprisingly, they don't tackle slopes that are very steep or difficult, but they do pass through some lovely countryside and several nature reserves. Bicycles are welcome, too. The Tissington Trail starts near Ashbourne and runs for 13 mi before joining the High Peak Trail near Parsley Hay. The High Peak Trail runs for 17 mi from Cromford to Dowlow. If you plan to stay in the region south of Bakewell, these are good, easy hikes. Pick up the "Tissington and High Peak Trails" brochure at visitor centers.

Most hikers and climbers stick to the Dark Peak area (near Edale) for rougher treks over rocky, slippery cliffs. The best-known spots for rock climbing are **Stanage, Millstone,** and **Curbar** in the east; and **Roaches, Ramshaw,** and **Windgather** in the west. The **Kinder Scout** is a plateau that rises 2,100 ft above sea level, about as high as you can go in the Peak District. At the western edge of Kinder is the **Kinder Downfall,** a waterfall that drops about 100 ft. On windy days, the water blows upward, splashing onto the top of the rocks; during the winter the rocks are draped with icicles.

The Pennine Way, all 256 mi of it, starts in Edale (at the Nag's Head pub) and demands some serious stamina. The views along the way are amazing, but the Pennine Way is a tough walk—often high, lonely, with no distinct path or way mark. Much of the route is demanding, especially when wet. Walkers should be in shape, and have proper equipment and *plenty* of experience. Make sure you get an updated version of the route before leaving Edale so you can follow detours or other rerouting that may occur. There are 17 hostels along the trail between Edale and the trail's end in Kirk Yetholm, Scotland.

Ask for the recipe of the famous Bakewell tart, and you're likely to get a tart reply instead. The "recipe" actually resulted from a blunder made in the kitchen of the Rutland Arms and is still under lock and key.

HISTORIC SITES AND VILLAGES

CASTLETON • Castleton and the nearby village of Edale are both excellent places from which to explore the northern Peaks. Castleton is also worth a visit to see ruined **Peveril Castle,** founded in the 11th century by William Peverel, one of William the Conqueror's illegitimate sons. Its role in medieval times was to defend the rich lead-mining area in the Peak Forest. Over the centuries, many of the castle's stones have been taken to build the village houses, but the fantastic view of Hope Valley and the Mam Tor ("Mother Mountain" in Gaelic) remains splendid. *Castleton, tel. 01433/620613. Take Bus 272 from Sheffield station. Admission £2. Open Apr.–Sept., daily 10–6; Oct.–Mar., Wed.–Sun. 10–4.*

Castleton has six limestone caves that offer varying assortments of stalactites and stalagmites. At **Speedwell Cavern** (Winnats Pass, Castleton, tel. 01433/620512), motorboats take tourists through water-filled caves daily 9:45–5 (until 4 in winter) for £5.25. You can also take a 40-minute guided tour of **Treak Cliff Caverns** (tel. 01433/620571) to view crystals, veins, and mines, daily 9:30–5:30 (10–4 in winter) for £4.50. Trains run to Hope, about 2 mi east of Castleton (you'll have to walk from there), and buses come to Castleton from nearby towns like Matlock, Bakewell, and Sheffield.

CHATSWORTH HOUSE AND EDENSOR • Chatsworth House, home to the Duke and Duchess of Devonshire, is a place where you spend your money to admire someone else's. Tourists by the thousands come every year to visit the dizzyingly ornate (and rather second-rate, some art historians would whisper) salons during appointed hours, along with thousands of other day-trippers. The house contains a vast collection (well, less than vast—the duke has been selling off numerous treasures to keep the place going) of sculptures and paintings, including works by Canova, Van Dyck, Tintoretto, Gainsborough, and Rembrandt. In the **State Music Room,** check out the trompe l'oeil violin painted by Jan van der Vaart that appears to hang on a mahogany door on the far side of the room, while in the **Blue Room,** you won't want to miss John Singer Sargent's eye-popping *Acheson Sisters* portrait. The noted gardens feature a hedge maze, a grotto, a rose garden, a water cascade, and elegant vistas designed by Lancelot "Capability" Brown, the acclaimed 18th-century "naturalist" landscaper. *Chatsworth, Bakewell, tel. 01246/582204. In Bakewell ask someone at the tourist center which bus to take on any given day to Edensor village, then walk 15 mins on marked path to Chatsworth. Admission to house and gardens £6.50; gardens only £3.75. House and garden open Mar.–Oct., daily 11–5.*

About a half mi from the main house, the village of **Edensor** (pronounced EN-sor) is home to the people who work at Chatsworth House. In the 19th century, the sixth Duke of Devonshire tore down the entire village and rebuilt it in order to create work for the growing number of people on his payroll. He had trouble deciding on the architecture for the new village and eventually built every cottage in a different design. **St. Peter's Church** is quiet and stately, and features an intricately carved tomb and stone skeleton for William Cavendish and his son Henry. A quiet 3-mi footpath leads through the Wye valley from Edensor Lane to Bakewell; it's detailed in the "Bakewell" brochure available at Bakewell's tourist office.

HADDON HALL • Two mi from Bakewell, Haddon Hall has a more intimate feel than Chatsworth and a *much* longer history—part of the house dates back to 1040. In all that time, only two families have ever owned the house: The emblems of the Vernons (peacock) and the Manners (boar) dominate every room. Somewhere along the way, Haddon passed into the hands of the Dukes of Rutland, who, a century ago, awoke this sleeping beauty of a house with a superlative restoration. The inside is utterly magical, a cross between a monastery, a hunting lodge, and an art gallery. The rooms are much less ostentatious than most English country houses, and are all the more English for it. Today, Haddon remains the best-preserved medieval manor house in England because it was uninhabited and unmolested during the 18th and 19th centuries, when other aristocratic homes were altered to fit the changing fashions. Don't miss the museum, the 12th-century chapel, the great hall, the kitchens, and the exquisite courtyard where vines wind over the gray and gold stones, and swallows nest below time-worn gargoyles. Little wonder this is a top location for Hollywood: Films shot here include *The Princess Bride*, Zeffirelli's *Jane Eyre, Moll Flanders,* and *The Prince and the Pauper.* Be sure to take your camera and hike the neighboring hills—from a distance, the house, bristling with towers and castellations, looks like a miniature illumination from a medieval Book of Hours. *Haddon Hall, Bakewell, tel. 01629/812855. From Bakewell, take Trent Bus 61, or Hulley's 171 or 172 straight to the Hall; or walk the scenic mile south along the River Wye. Admission £5.50. Open Apr.–Sept., daily 11–5.*

LINCOLN

As you approach Lincoln by train, the first feature visible over the mounds of rusting scrap metal is imposing Lincoln Cathedral, high atop Steep Hill. The massive, triple-towered Gothic structure is indicative of the church's lasting influence over the city. "On the seventh day, He rested," sayeth the Bible, and every Sunday that's exactly what the locals do. Trying to get a bite to eat on Sunday in Lincoln can be as difficult as hunting live game on the streets of London.

Reaching Lincoln on public bus can be a pain, too, but it's more easily reached by train. Not only is the cathedral one of the most impressive in Europe, but the city itself has a wonderful sense of history. Medieval monuments seem to tumble down the steep lanes leading to the River Witham, and you will come upon vestiges of a time when the Romans and the Danes ruled here.

During the week, the main shopping district is abuzz with thousands of locals and tourists trudging up High Street and Steep Hill to the castle and cathedral. Nevertheless, Lincoln retains a small-town feel that's refreshing after the hurly-burly of central England's sprawling industrial cities.

Lincoln's **tourist office** (9 Castle Hill, tel. 01522/529828) is directly between the cathedral and castle, which is great if you've already climbed the hill but rather inconvenient if you just want a map or listings of B&Bs. They have the free *What's On in Lincoln* calendar of events, and are open Monday–Thursday 9:30–5:30, Friday 9:30–5, Saturday 10–5. The rail station has **lockers** on the platform next to the ticket office; the backpack-size ones cost £1 per day. **Thomas Cook** (4 Cornhill Pavement, tel. 01522/510070), just across from the central market near the stations, changes money at fair rates. Clean those clothes near the cathedral at **Maytag Launderette** (8 Burton Rd., tel. 01522/543498), but BYOS (bring your own soap). The **post office** (tel. 01522/532288) is located off High Street at 19–20 Guildhall Street.

COMING AND GOING

The trickle called the River Witham bisects the city, with the majority of downtown (including the cathedral and castle) lying north of its banks. The bus and train stations lie south of the river—just walk west on St. Mary's Street and turn right on High Street to begin your ascent toward the cathedral. Much of the

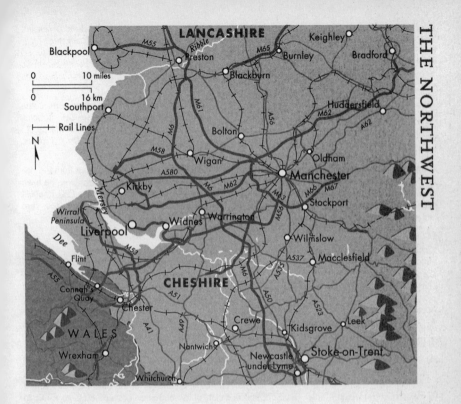

city layout was planned by Roman engineers, who left as evidence of their presence the **Newport Arch** (Bailgate, at Chapel Lane), the old entrance to the city from the north, and a **city wall** that today stands in ruins.

The **Central Rail Station** (St. Mary's St., tel. 0345/484950) has frequent service to all parts of the country—including London King's Cross station, changing at Newark (2 hrs, £47 return), Birmingham (2½ hrs, £24.60 return), and Nottingham (1 hr, £5.70 day return). If those fares seem a little incongruous, it's because of the country's deregulated, market-driven rail system: the more popular the route, the more expensive the ticket, despite the actual distance traveled. The main **bus station** (St. Mary's St., at Broadgate, tel. 01522/534444), directly across the street from the rail station, is where all local and long-distance buses stop. The five-hour coach trip to London costs £22 return, a trip to Leeds £11.25, and a trip to Manchester £14.50.

According to legend, in 1563, heiress Dorothy Vernon slipped away from the ballroom at Haddon Hall and ran down the garden steps to elope with her lover, Sir John Manners. Their descendants have owned the estate ever since.

WHERE TO SLEEP

Although it costs several pounds more to sleep in Lincoln than in the surrounding countryside, Lincoln's excellent B&Bs are worth the extra quid. Many line West Parade, Carholme, and Yarborough roads, about 15 minutes by foot from the stations: Walk west on St. Mary's Street, turn right on High Street, left on Guildhall Street, continue straight to The Avenue, and turn down West Parade, Carholme, or Yarborough Road. Try to book ahead in the summer.

Admiral Guest House. Everything about this B&B is perfect (the £17-per-person rate included)—except its somewhat remote location. Even so, the inviting rooms and fascinating building (actually three older buildings patched together) make it worth the journey. On weekdays the owners will make dinner for £6 per person. *18 Nelson St., LN1 1PJ, tel. and fax 01522/544467. From train station, walk left on St. Mary's St., turn right on High St., left on Guildhall St. (which changes names several times), left on Nelson St. 9 rooms, all with showers.*

Ailsa. This friendly B&B is just a skip and a hop from the castle and city center. The pretty rooms come with sinks and TVs, and you couldn't ask for a more personable proprietor. Singles are £15, doubles £30. *161 Yarborough Rd., LN1 1HP, tel. 01522/534961. From train station turn left on St. Mary's St., right on High St., left on Guildhall St., right on The Avenue (which becomes Yarborough Rd.). 3 rooms. Cash only.*

Bradford Guest House. The Bradford's location can't be beat—it's an easy 10-minute trek from the stations and a short (but steep) walk to the cathedral and castle. Many of the rooms overlook the town below. Neither the hearty breakfast nor the gracious managers will disappoint. Singles are £20, doubles £35. *67 Monks Rd., LN2 5HP, tel. 01522/523947. From train station, walk right on St. Mary's St., turn left up Broadgate, right on Monks Rd. 5 rooms without bath. Cash only.*

HOSTELS

Lincoln YHA. The Lincoln hostel, a large refurbished Victorian mansion, has a comfy lounge, cheerful atmosphere, and friendly staff. Unfortunately, it's literally on the wrong side of the tracks from town, and is a 15-minute walk from the stations. Beds are £9.15. *77 South Park, tel. 01522/522076, fax 01522/567424. From train station, Bus 51 or 51A; or turn right out of entrance and right again, cross Pelham Bridge, turn right at South Park (not South Park Ave.). 51 beds. Open Feb.–Oct. daily; Nov. and Dec., Fri. and Sat. Closed Jan.*

FOOD

High Street (and its continuations, the Strait and Steep Hill) has plenty of fancy establishments, some of them—gasp—within budget range. The **Central Market,** along the river, contains food stalls alongside typical flea-market junk. If you're on your very last penny, fill up cheaply at the **Elite Fish Restaurant** (Moorland Centre, Tritton Rd., tel. 01522/509505); a plate of fish-and-chips costs £2.80 to go, £4.25 to eat in. Otherwise, buy your own supplies at **Tesco** (Wragby Rd., tel. 01522/530306; or Canwick Rd., tel. 01522/520809).

A bit more pricey than most of the other places here is the **Wig and Mitre** (30 Steep Hill, tel. 01522/535190). This interesting downtown pub/café/restaurant stays open all day until 11 PM, offering an extremely wide range of food from breakfast to dinner. Dishes include fresh fish, warming seasonal soups, or classic English roasts. Daily lunch specials at **Pimento Tea Room** (27 Steep Hill, tel. 01522/544880) are usually vegetarian (try the jacket potatoes with bean goulash filling), and are best enjoyed with a spot of their strong coffee or tea. Located on the historic High Bridge over the River Witham, **Stokes of Lincoln** (207 High St., tel. 01522/513825) serves good, cheap food: The Lincolnshire pork sausage, eggs, chips, and tea combo is a mere £4.45. Among the steep streets leading to the cathedral is **The Straits** (9 The Strait, tel. 01522/520814), a second-floor, candlelit wine bar serving pub fare in hefty portions. The huge pies at **Brown's Pie Shop** (33 Steep Hill, tel. 01522/527330) are beautiful to behold—splurge on partridge, apple, and bacon pie or three-cheese and spinach pie. The desserts are every bit their equal.

WORTH SEEING

The two principal sights in Lincoln are right beside one another at the top of Steep Hill. The free "Places of Interest" booklet from the tourist office summarizes the history of over two dozen sites and lists some good outdoor and after-dark activities.

LINCOLN CATHEDRAL

Nothing in this tabernacle is younger than 300 years old. An earthquake in 1185 destroyed most of the original Norman structure, but the West Front and the lower halves of the western towers survived. The rest of the cathedral was built in the structurally stronger Gothic style, while the Angel Choir, chapter house, and cloisters were added during a 13th-century renovation. The humidity-plagued **Wren Library** is the cathedral's newest addition—it dates back to 1674. (If you beg the kind cathedral staff, they may let you have a peek inside its sumptuous Restoration interior during off-hours.) Also check out the Lincoln Imp, a mysterious 15-inch gargoyle perched on a pillar in the left rear of the cathedral. No one, including the priests, claims to know how it *really* got there. *Exchequer Gate, tel. 01522/544544. £2.50 donation requested. Open May–Aug., daily 7:15 AM –8 PM (Sun. until 6); Sept.–Apr., daily 7:15–6 (Sun. until 5). Evensong Mon.–Sat. at 5:15, Sun. at 3:45.*

LINCOLN CASTLE

The sight of the impenetrable walls of Lincoln Castle next to the gargantuan cathedral let the serfs know who was boss. Two years after the Norman invasion in 1066, William the Conqueror razed 166 Saxon homes on top of Steep Hill to make room for this castle, which dominated the surrounding flat countryside. This isn't one of those fairy-tale castles; the fortress has seen some very nasty battles in its time, especially during the Civil War. The castle has acquired one of the three remaining copies of the Magna Carta, formerly in the Wren Library next door. Try to come at opening or closing time to avoid the hordes.

Climb up **Lucy Tower,** named after a countess who ran the place, or **Observatory Tower,** which was used by a Victorian prison warden for stargazing. **Cobb Hall** is a vast, cold, enclosed space whose roof was once the site of hangings. The redbrick buildings are the remains of the **Old County Prison,** and the prison's **chapel** features pews that seem designed to make prisoners as uncomfortable as possible. Through extensive maintenance, two-thirds of the castle wall's catwalk remains usable, so you can see a spectacular view of the city. *Castle Hill, tel. 01522/511068. Admission £2.50. Open May–Aug., Mon.–Sat. 9:30–5:30, Sun. 11–5:30; Sept.–Apr., Mon.–Sat. 9:30–4, Sun. 11–4.*

Plan your day in Lincoln so that you must climb Steep Hill only once. It came by its name honestly.

THE LAWN

Just west of the castle lies the **Lawn** (tel. 01522/560306), a former lunatic asylum whose grounds have been transformed into a kind of executive complex surrounded by a 5,000-square-ft greenhouse, an archaeological center, and a shopping center with a theater and pub. The great view from the top of the hill makes it a perfect place to picnic on warm days, and the paths along the River Witham are wonderful for an afternoon stroll. Five minutes' walk away, the **Museum of Lincolnshire Life** (Burton Rd., tel. 01522/528448) costs £2 to visit (daily 10–5). It's more interesting than it sounds, detailing aspects of the county's industrial, agricultural, and social history. The **Usher Gallery** (Lindum Rd., tel. 01522/527980) houses a fine collection of paintings and sculptures and hosts temporary exhibitions, often of historical significance to the region. It's open daily until 5:30 (5 on Sun.), and costs £2 to get in unless you go on Friday when it's free.

AFTER DARK

Victoria (6 Union Rd., tel. 01522/536048), located conveniently between the Lawn and the castle, serves tasty pub food in the afternoon and a wide range of lagers, ales, and ciders until closing. If you want to drink a pint with the locals, **Adam & Eve Tavern** (25 Lindum Rd., tel. 01522/537108) stays open until 11:30. **Jolly Brewer** (26 Broadgate, tel. 01522/528583) serves beer to both a gay and straight clientele. The groovy **Cornhill Vaults** (Cornhill Exchange, tel. 01522/535113), opposite the Central Market, is a 19th-century grain store that's been converted into an underground pub with small alcoves that get smoky and crowded. **Cheltenham** (Mint Street) is positively heaving with beery lads and lasses on a big night out. The **Theatre Royal** (Clasketgate, tel. 01522/525555) is a Victorian theater offering a mixture of entertainment, including jazz, ballet, and theater. The box office is open 10–6 daily.

MANCHESTER

Thanks to more than 200 years of heavy industry, Manchester doesn't exactly rate in the all-time top-ten Cities of Romance. Indeed, the city's ever-artful native son and '80s feel-bad alter-boy, Morrissey (of The Smiths fame), has called his hometown "ugly, vastly ugly" (he's even less charitable toward its inhabitants). Ostensibly, the downhill spiral toward ugliness began in the 18th and 19th centuries, when the place took off as *the* main city of the industrial revolution, shipping its products to the busy Liverpool ports. One of its main exports was cotton, and Manchester (nicknamed "Cottonopolis") led the modern

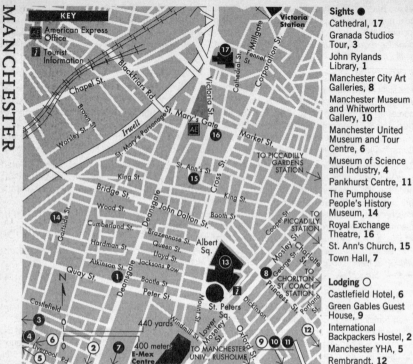

MANCHESTER

KEY

🅰 American Express Office

ℹ️ Tourist Information

Sights ●

Cathedral, **17**

Granada Studios Tour, **3**

John Rylands Library, **1**

Manchester City Art Galleries, **8**

Manchester Museum and Whitworth Gallery, **10**

Manchester United Museum and Tour Centre, **6**

Museum of Science and Industry, **4**

Pankhurst Centre, **11**

The Pumphouse People's History Museum, **14**

Royal Exchange Theatre, **16**

St. Ann's Church, **15**

Town Hall, **7**

Lodging ○

Castlefield Hotel, **6**

Green Gables Guest House, **9**

International Backpackers Hostel, **2**

Manchester YHA, **5**

Rembrandt, **12**

cotton industry for more than 100 years. The city boasts many firsts—the first atom-splitting took place at Manchester University, the first Royce (later Rolls-Royce) was made here in 1903, and in 1980 the city was the first in the world to be declared a nuclear-free zone (Berkeley, California, waited until 1986). Now it actively celebrates the many cultures that exist within its boundaries, with students from three universities (Manchester University, the University of Manchester Institute of Science and Technology—"UMIST"—and Manchester Metropolitan University) adding to the vibrant mix. There's also a visible and active gay community, and local sports facilities get quite a workout—after all, this is the city that will host the 2002 Commonwealth Games, for which a new international-class swimming pool and stadium are currently under construction. All this from a town whose most infamous Smiths song claimed had "so much to answer for."

Manchester's progressive bent dates back many generations. It led the battle against slavery and gave birth to the suffragette movement and Britain's first labor unions and co-ops. Much of this activism can be traced to Manchester's role as the crucible of the industrial revolution. Manchester's cotton mills were the first industry to be fully mechanized. Along with the wealth generated by mass production came appalling factory conditions, long hours, and low pay. The cotton mills, in particular, employed hundreds of children who worked nine- to 15-hour days until social outrage in the mid-1800s forced legislation that put an end to such abuses.

As with other boom cities of the industrial revolution, there is little left from Manchester's medieval days (the Shambles, the Chetham School of Music, and the parish church being the notable exceptions)—but the city's glory is its Victorian-era architecture, including Alfred Waterhouse's stunning **Town Hall** (1877), his **Refuge Assurance Building** (1891) on Oxford Road (now the Palace Hotel), and the Gothic-revival **Midland Hotel** (1898) on Peter Street. Manchester has several distinctive neighborhoods that are within easy reach of the city center. On the southern edge of the city center, the canal-laced **Castlefield** area, where the Romans first took up camp, now has lots of outdoor cafés and museums to explore. Around Charlotte Street near Chorlton Street Coach Station, you'll find **Chinatown,** and behind the coach station along the revitalized Rochdale Canal is the area known as the **Gay Village.** East of central Piccadilly Gardens the Northern Quarter—centered on Oldham Street—continues to develop into a trendy, counter-culture 'hood. Down Oxford Road past Manchester University is **Rusholme,** home to a large South Asian community and the city's cheapest restaurants. Farther southwest is **Hulme,** long a depressed neigh-borhood but now showing signs of improvement as community housing schemes bear fruit—it's still not a place you'd ever go as a tourist. The many places of interest in the city center can be readily reached by foot, and the efficient bus system makes it fairly easy to get into the city's every nook and cranny.

The Mancunian music scene has given a shot in the arm to modern pop: Bands such as Joy Division, the Smiths, the Stone Roses, Simply Red, M People, Oasis, and the flash in the pan boy-band Take That all paid their dues in Manchester clubs. Many of the bands that formed the "Madchester" music move-ment of a few years ago are back in new incarnations, and clubbing is fierce here, with many café-bars packing in the crowds anxious to hear music's Next Big Thing.

BASICS

AMERICAN EXPRESS
This office in the city center provides the usual services. *10–12 St. Mary's Gate, M1 1PX, tel. 0161/833–7301. Open weekdays 9–5:30 (Wed from 9:30), Sat. 9–5.*

DISCOUNT TRAVEL AGENCIES
The busy but well-organized **STA Travel** (75 Deansgate, tel. 0161/834–0668), open weekdays 9:30–5:30 and Saturday 10–3:30, has info on cheap travel deals. **Usit Campus** (in YHA Shop, 166 Deans-gate, tel.0161/273–1721), which also has university campus branches, has good deals on student-ori-ented travel and is open weekdays 9:30–5 (Wednesday 10–5) and Saturday 10–1:30.

LAUNDRY
Show your HI card to use the washers and dryers at the YHA hostel off Liverpool Road (*see* Where to Sleep, *below*). You'll also find several launderettes in Rusholme along Wilmslow Road.

MAIL
Manchester's main post office sells phonecards and has a bureau de change. *26 Spring Gardens, M2 1BB, tel. 0161/839–0687. Open weekdays 8:30–6, Sat. 8:30–7.*

VISITOR INFORMATION
Manchester Visitor Centre, just north of St. Peter's Square, sells the very useful *City Guide* (£1.50) with listings for sights, travel, and food, as well as a city center map. The "Food and Drink Guide" and "Accommodation Guide" are free, as are brochures for arts, sports, and museum events. The office books a variety of guided walks (£3), and sells brochures (starting at 60p) for self-guided walks. *Town Hall Extension, Lloyd St., tel. 0161/234–3157. Open Mon.–Sat. 10–5:30, Sun. 11–4.*

Frontline Books (255 Wilmslow Rd., 2 mi north of center, tel. 0161/249–0202), open weekdays 10–7, Saturday 10–5, and Sunday 1–5, has a selection of brochures that rivals the tourist office's and a bul-letin board jammed with flyers for current happenings. You'll find the biweekly *City Life* (£1.60) here and at most other news agents, an essential events guide, including full club and gig listings.

For advice and info on Manchester's gay scene, call the **Lesbian and Gay Switchboard** (tel. 0161/274–3999)), between 4 and 10 PM daily, which can put you in touch with local groups. Get your hands on a copy of the *Lesbian & Gay Guide to Greater Manchester* (free from bars, clubs, and shops), which lists clubs, bars, gay-friendly lodgings and taxi services, and all sorts of other useful contacts.

COMING AND GOING

BY BUS
Buses leave regularly from **Chorlton Street Coach Station** for Birmingham (£12.50 return), London (£20.50 return), and all other major cities in England. The coach station has the city's only central lug-gage storage (£1 per piece per day), but it closes at 6 PM. *Chorlton St., tel. 0990/808080. Open Mon.–Sat. 7:15–6:15, Fri. until 7:15, Sun. 8:30–6:15.*

BY PLANE
American Airlines, Lufthansa, British Airways, and several other airlines fly into **Manchester Airport** (tel. 0161/489–3000 for general information, 0839/888747 for flight inquiries), about 10 mi from the city

center. The airport has 24-hour lockers, two visitor centers, and a bureau de change. A local train from the airport to Piccadilly station is quick and cheap (£2.35 return after 9:30 AM, or £2.65 single), and runs every 15 minutes between 6 AM and 10 PM, then a reduced service through the night).

BY TRAIN

Manchester has three train stations. **Piccadilly Station** (London Road) provides the most frequent service to cities nationwide, and has lockers available Mon.–Sat. 7–7, Sun. 11–7 (£2–£3 per day, but no overnight storage). The other large station is **Victoria Station** (New Bridge Street), which tends to serve local lines and slow trains to cities to the west and north. Trains pass through both stations at all hours; you can catch a train to most major cities about once an hour. The off-peak return fare to London's Euston is £41, £48.20 on Friday; to Newcastle it's £37, £46 on Friday; and to Liverpool it's £8, £9.20 on Friday. **Metrolink** (see Getting Around, below) stops at both stations. **Oxford Road** station, south of the city center, handles mainly regional and local rail service. **National Rail Enquiries** operates a 24-hour information line (tel. 0345/484950), and handles calls for all stations.

GETTING AROUND

Manchester's city center can be easily covered by foot and the sleek Metrolink tram. Until 11:30 PM, buses are the best way to reach Rusholme, the universities, and outlying areas. Taxis are an affordable late-night option. The **Greater Manchester Passenger Transport Executive** (GMPTE) oversees all local transport routes. It has an info desk at Piccadilly Gardens Bus Station (open Monday–Saturday 7 AM–6 PM, Sunday 10–6pm). A local **travel info hot line** (tel. 0161/228–7811) is available 8–8.

BY BUS

Most local buses converge at **Piccadilly Gardens Bus Station** (Piccadilly, by Portland and Mosley Sts.), though for buses down Oxford Road (for Rusholme restaurants and the Whitworth Art Gallery) it's quicker to use the stops at the bottom of Oxford Road itself, outside the Palace Hotel. Cut-throat competition between the various operators keeps the fares low—the run to Rusholme costs 40p–80p, depending on which bus you catch and the time of day.

BY METROLINK

Metrolink (tel. 0161/205–2000) is Manchester's electric streetcar. While it's mainly useful for traveling north and south throughout the Greater Manchester area, it does link rail stations in the city center as well as outlying neighborhoods, and new extensions will soon serve Salford Quays (for the new Lowry Centre) and the Eastlands sports stadium (being built for the Commonwealth Games). Fares are based on a zone system; just follow the directions on the self-service ticket machines. The streetcars run Monday–Saturday 6 AM–midnight, Sunday 7 AM–11 PM.

WHERE TO SLEEP

Though it doesn't list everything, the free "Accommodation Guide," available at the tourist office, is a good source of lodging info. The outstanding Manchester YHA is a haven for the budget traveler. Since few people live in the city center, most B&Bs are a bus ride away. If you're camping, head to the Peak District (see above); it's only an hour away, and the scenery is refreshingly pastoral.

Castlefield Hotel. This modern beauty on the Castlefield canalside is loaded with facilities—restaurant, bar, leisure club with pool, sauna, and running track—and it's directly opposite the Museum of Science and Industry. Although midweek rates run to £81 per double (including breakfast), weekend rates are a more reasonable £55 (depending on availability), so reserve early. Liverpool Rd., M3 4JR, tel. 0161/ 832–7073, fax 0161/839–0326. Metrolink south to G-Mex station, exit at Castlefield. 48 rooms with bath.

Green Gables Guest House. Lace curtains and embossed wallpaper adorn this large, comfortable Victorian in the tree-lined West Didsbury area. A full English breakfast is included, and you're only a quick walk from a launderette, post office, market, and several pubs and restaurants. Bus 11 from city center stops out front. Singles are £13–£18, doubles £28–£34. Reservations are recommended. 152 Barlow Moor Rd., N20 2UT, tel. 0161/445–5365, fax 0161/445–6363. 27 rooms without bath. Cash only.

Rembrandt. This gay-owned pub and hotel behind Chorlton Street Coach Station serves a mixed clientele. The rooms are small and can get noisy, but many have a view of the waterways. Prices are reasonable for the central location: Singles and doubles are £25 per room. There is an upstairs bar (which hosts a lesbian night on Friday) and a downstairs pub. *33 Sackville St., M1 3LZ, tel. 0161/236–1311. From Chorlton St. Coach Station, turn left on Portland St., left on Sackville St. 6 rooms without bath. Cash only.*

HOSTELS

International Backpackers Hostel. Two converted houses play host to an international backpacking crowd, three mi out of the city center in the Stretford neighborhood, an easy walk from the Old Trafford Metrolink station (call for exact directions). Do your laundry, have a summer barbie in the garden, or just relax. Dorm beds cost £10 a night, but you can reserve singles and doubles (£26). *41–43 Greatstone Rd, Stretford; and 64 Cromwell Rd, Stretford, tel. 0161/872–3499 or 865–9296. Cash only.*

Manchester YHA. This dream-come-true hostel is located in the beautifully redeveloped Castlefield area, just across the road from the Museum of Science and Industry. Rooms, all of which have their own bath, house two to six people, and rates vary—expect to pay £13.55 for a bed, slightly more if you opt for a twin room. There's a restaurant on site. *Potato Wharf, off Liverpool Rd., M3 4NB, tel. 0161/839–9960, fax 0161/835–2054. Metrolink south to G-Mex station, exit at Castlefield; the hostel is behind the Castlefield Hotel. 156 beds. Reception open 24 hrs. Laundry. Cash only.*

STUDENT HOUSING

There's plenty of student housing up for grabs in the summer in Manchester, probably the biggest student center in the country. But most residence halls are out in the suburbs (not always in greatest areas) and short-term stays of just one or two nights may not be viable, as lots of halls charge by the week. Still, if you're interested, contact the **University Accommodation Office** (Precinct Center, Oxford Rd., M13 9RS, tel. 0161/275–2888, fax 0161/275–3213) ahead of time for a list of halls that may have space.

The huge Sanam Sweet House and Restaurant (145–151 Wilmslow Rd., tel. 0161/224–8824) in Rusholme has a wonderfully exotic selection of Indian sweets such as chocolate burfi (35p).

FOOD

Finding cheap food is easy in Manchester, thanks to the enormous concentration of cash-strapped students. For a late-night sampling of Punjabi, Balti, or Persian cuisine, head to the **Rusholme** neighborhood (take virtually any bus going down Oxford Rd.), where around fifty eateries line a mile-long stretch of the road. We recommend few below, but you're bound to find something you like whatever your taste. Another area for (very basic, canteen-style) Indian cafés is in the Northern Quarter, near the **Manchester Craft Centre** (17 Oak St.). **Chinatown** is not especially cheap, but Faulkner Street (between Nicholas and Charlotte Sts.) has a string of reasonable restaurants and bakeries.

UNDER £5 • Café Pop. Just down the street from the trendy Afflecks Palace (*see* After Dark, *below*), this place stands out for its retro decor. Carefully prepared veggie food is served all day, and nostalgic Americans may want to try the Scooby Snax—a huge sandwich "for vegetarian truck drivers." *34–36 Oldham St., between Church and Hilton Sts., tel. 0161/237–9688. Closed Sun.*

Cornerhouse. The city's cool arts centre has a see-and-be-seen downstairs bar (get in those window seats and be nonchalant), where you can grab a cappuccino. Upstairs, the café dispenses goodies like stuffed baked potatoes, soup-and-sandwich deals, bakes, and dips until 8:30 PM most nights. *70 Oxford St., by Oxford Rd. train station, tel. 0161/200–1508.*

Java Bar Espresso. Two locations in town serve up Manchester's best coffee—get your daily latte fix, and munch on the biscotti and big Italian sandwiches. The Northern Quarter branch is the hippest, but the Oxford Road café makes a great pick-me-up stop before hitting the buses down to Rusholme. *Station Approach, Oxford Rd., tel. 0161/236–3656; and Smithfield Building, 55 Oldham St., Northern Quarter, tel. 0161/834–4102.*

On the Eighth Day. This vegetarian café is next to Manchester Metropolitan University's student union. They use fresh ingredients and have a changing menu of freshly made soups, stews, bakes, salads, and lasagna. The adjacent whole-food shop has flyers and magazines on the Manchester green scene. *109 Oxford Rd., tel. 0161/273–4878. Closed Sun. Cash only.*

UNDER £10 • Dimitri's Tapas Bar Taverna. Take your choice of the cozy, yellow dining room or the covered brick arcade, decorated with colorful posters for current art exhibits and long-vanished Edwardian entertainments. The award-winning menu offers everything from chicken satay sandwiches to moussaka. Vegetarian options abound, and there's live jazz on Friday and Saturday nights. *1 Campfield Arcade, off Liverpool Rd., tel. 0161/839–3319.*

Little Yang Sing. You don't have to blow big money in little Chinatown. The Little Yang Sing (it's got a more expensive Yang Sing big brother on nearby Princess St.) is a quality place with one of the best lunch deals in town: mixed appetizers, a main dish with noodles or rice, and tea for under £9. Eating à la carte isn't a huge blow to the wallet either, provided you've come with company to share the cost. *17 George St., tel. 0161/228–7722.*

Mash & Air. As trendy as it gets in Manchester, this converted warehouse by the Gay Village is a big night out for the monied classes. Forget about Air, the high-rolling restaurant on the top floor, and wait in line for space in Mash. It's a microbrewery and informal brasserie, specializing in gourmet pizzas and char-grilled dishes, and while still not exactly cheap, you can get away for under a tenner if you order pizza and a beer. And it is *so* cool. *40 Chorlton St., tel. 0161/661 1111.*

Shere Khan. This popular restaurant in Rusholme has a huge selection of meat and vegetarian dishes, such as chicken curry and *aloo gobhi*, made with potato and cauliflower. The attractive celestial decor will encourage you to stay, but you can also get takeout. *1 IFCO Centre, Wilmslow Rd., at Walmer St., tel. 0161/256–2624.*

WORTH SEEING

Manchester's robust and grand brick buildings bear witness to the might and wealth of the city's Victorian heyday. Among the smoke-smudged byways, you'll find a vital mix of theaters, pubs, and clubs open far into the night. The abundance of superb museums gives you plenty of ways to learn about local history, and most museums are free and easy to reach by foot or bus. Note that the excellent City Art Galleries on Mosley Street are closed until 2001 for major refurbishment. Entertaining tours (£3) often begin at the visitor center at 2 PM—check in to see whether it's canals, Castlefield, or "Feminine Influence" today.

GRANADA STUDIOS TOUR

In an unlikely city center site, the Granada Studios Tour has a lot to offer imaginative children (as well as adults). A British version of the popular Hollywood studio tours, it offers a behind-the-scenes look at television programs. There are backstage tours (including a walk down Sherlock Holmes's Baker Street and along Downing Street), 3D film shows, rides, and other special events. It's from here that Britain's longest-running TV soap opera, *Coronation Street,* is broadcast, and you can even have a drink in the program's pub, the Rover's Return. Get there before 11 AM if you want to see everything and experience a full range of rides and tours in one day. *Water St., tel. 0161/832–4999 for 24-hr info. Admission £14.99. Open mid-Apr.–Sept., daily 9:45–6, last admission at 4; Oct.–mid-Apr., weekdays 9:45–4:30, weekends 9:45–5:30, last admission at 3.*

JOHN RYLANDS LIBRARY

This exquisite neo-Gothic library and museum was built in the twilight of the Victorian era by Mr. Rylands's wealthy widow. To use the library's astonishing collection of books and manuscripts, you must apply for membership (preferably in advance) by presenting ID and a suitable letter of recommendation from a scholarly institution. The library's museum, however, is worth a trip in its own right. Exhibits in the museum use (sometimes ancient) volumes from the library to illustrate the evolution of thought on certain themes, and the tranquil halls are a welcome refuge from Manchester's hectic center. Guided tours (£1) each Wednesday show you the lovely interior. *150 Deansgate, between Quay and Bridge Sts., tel. 0161/834–5343. Admission free. Open weekdays 10–5:30, Sat. 10–1.*

MANCHESTER CITY ART GALLERIES

At press time this museum was closed for a major overhaul and not scheduled to reopen until at least 2001. The collection of British and European art from 1300 to the present is varied, but includes works by Gainsborough, Turner, and the Pre-Raphaelites. Call information for the new phone number (if the one listed is no longer active) as the only bit of information museum officials are sure of at this point is the address. *Mosley St., at Princess St., tel. 0161/236–5244.*

MANCHESTER CATHEDRAL AND CHETHAM'S LIBRARY

The city's cathedral—its finest religious building—has seen quite a bit in the eon or so since its founding. Bombed in the Second World War, and again in 1996 by the IRA, it's a miracle that it still stands.

Originally founded in the ninth century, the only relic of its medieval forerunner is the fourteenth-century arch by the tower, but it's still worth entering to see the widest nave in England (at 114 ft), and the fantastically sculpted misericords. The area around the cathedral is currently being redesigned as a Millennium Quarter, an exhibition area reviewing past millennium and previewing next one. The nearby Chetham's Hospital School trains the cathedral's choristers, and you should hop across the road to see its beautifully carved oak-paneled 17th-century library. Be sure not to miss Karl Marx's old desk in the reading room. *Manchester Cathedral, Deansgate, tel. 0161/833–2220. Admission free. Open daily 7:30 AM–6 PM. Chetham's Library, Long Millgate, tel. 0161/834–7961. Admission free; ask at the porters' lodge. Open weekdays 9–12:30 and 1:30–4:30.*

MANCHESTER MUSEUM AND WHITWORTH GALLERY

Manchester University has two wonderful free museums. Manchester Museum—whose magnificent Gothic-style building was designed by Alfred Waterhouse—explores the complexity of various cultures from around the world and is famous for its pioneering Egyptology exhibit—the mummies are second only to those in the British Museum. Ongoing refurbishment here means that some of its galleries will be closed until 2002, but there's still plenty to see. *Oxford Rd., near Booth St., tel. 0161/275–2634. From Piccadilly Gardens Bus Station take Bus 40–45 or 48. Admission free. Open Mon.–Sat. 10–5.*

The temporary exhibits at Manchester University's **Whitworth Gallery** are as imaginative and involving as any you're likely to see. They ask questions such as "What is art?" and address how certain kinds of creative work are excluded from the traditional definitions. Expect to find exhibits like embroidery and wallpaper on display in ways that will open your eyes. The museum also has a permanent collection of European drawings, paintings, and sculpture. *Oxford Rd., near Denmark Rd., tel. 0161/275–7450. From Piccadilly Gardens Bus Station, take Bus 40–45, 48, 143, 157, 191, or 261. Admission free. Open Mon.–Sat. 10–5, Sun. 2–5.*

MANCHESTER UNITED MUSEUM AND TOUR CENTRE

Football (that's soccer to Yanks) is an integral part of modern British culture, and "Man U" is one of the nation's best-loved teams. While the trophy room and museum are interesting, the 90-minute stadium tour is the real gem. Funny, knowledgeable guides take you on a comprehensive tour—into the press room, police control room, the changing rooms, and through the team's tunnel to the field. Though there's often room with less notice, phone ahead as early as you can to book a spot—March for a July tour is not too early. Tours are not given on match days. *Sir Matt Busby Way, Old Trafford, tel. 0161/877–4002. From Piccadilly Gardens Bus Station, take Metrolink to Warwick Rd. Station (£1.30 return), walk north on Warwick Rd. (which becomes Sir Matt Busby Way). Admission for tour and museum £7.50; museum only £4.50. Open Apr.–Oct., daily 9:30–9; Nov.–Mar., daily 9:30–5.*

Vinyl Exchange Used Record & CD Shop (18 Oldham St., tel. 0161/228–1122) is one of the best record stores outside London. Prices start low (from £1 for CD singles, £9 for full-length CDs and albums) and go down each month.

MUSEUM OF SCIENCE AND INDUSTRY

Set on 7 acres on the site of the world's first passenger rail station (opened in 1830), this hands-on museum encompasses the history of industrial Manchester. Wonderful exhibits on air and space travel, underground Manchester (sewers "complete with sounds and smells"), industrial machinery, and interactive science experiments have won Best of England and Best of Europe awards. *Liverpool Rd., Castlefield, tel. 0161/832–1830. From St. Peter's Sq. (next to tourist office), walk west on Peter St., turn left on Deansgate, right on Liverpool Rd. Admission £5. Open daily 10–5.*

PANKHURST CENTRE

The Pankhurst Centre is located in the former home of Sylvia and Christabel Pankhurst, a mother and daughter who started the Women's Social and Political Union in 1903, devoted to women's suffrage. The museum traces the demonstrations, arrests, and imprisonment of the movement's leaders, and documents the role of women as shapers of British history. Enjoy the Edwardian gardens and have lunch afterwards at the center's exceptional **Café Des Femmes,** with vegetarian entrées for under £5. *Pankhurst House, 60–62 Nelson St., tel. 0161/273–5673. Bus 40–45 or 48 to Nelson St. Admission free. Open weekdays 10–3.*

THE PUMPHOUSE PEOPLE'S HISTORY MUSEUM

The industrial revolution may have brought cheap, mass-produced convenience to the masses, but it wasn't so great for the workers. The exhibits here detail English labor history of the last 200 years: daily life, strikes, cooperatives, as well as cultural and leisure activities. The museum hosts temporary exhibitions as well as lectures and theater throughout the year. *Left Bank, off Bridge St., tel. 0161/228–7212. From tourist office, walk north on Mosley St., turn left on Princess St. (which becomes John Dalton and Bridge Sts.), left on Gartside St. Admission £1, free on Fri. Open Tues.–Sun. 11–4:30.*

ROYAL EXCHANGE THEATRE AND ST. ANN'S SQUARE

Manchester's old Cotton Exchange traded up until 1968, when a new use was found for the handsome premises. Thoroughly restored after a 1996 IRA bombing, the building houses the **Royal Exchange Theatre** (tel. 0161/833–9833). Even if you can't catch a show, you should definitely stroll in to see the theatre-in-the-round resembling a lunar module, or grab an espresso and browse around the craft gallery. Nearby **St. Ann's Church** (tel. 0161/834–0239)—where Thomas De Quincey was baptized—and St. Ann's Square outside the theatre were also badly damaged by the blast, but they too have been restored. The square and its surroundings form part of the adventurous new city-centre plan, which calls for the construction of new public spaces, shops, cafés and bars in the expanse leading up to the cathedral.

TOWN HALL

Just west of the visitor center is this Victorian Gothic marvel designed by Alfred Waterhouse. The exterior is grand, the interior dazzling. Tours (£3) are given regularly and highlight how the history of the city was incorporated into the building's design (a bee mosaic represents Manchester's industry, for example). The Great Hall has 12 gorgeous murals by Ford Madox Brown depicting the city's history from Roman days. The huge pipe organ and Sculpture Hall are also impressive. *Albert Sq., tel. 0161/234–5000. Admission free. Open weekdays 9–5.*

AFTER DARK

If Manchester had a triathlon, the events would be pub-crawling, club-hopping, and ear-bending. Mancunians with seemingly endless energy drink and dance all night before winding up in the early morning hours in café-bars. To keep up with the scene, grab a copy of *City Life,* Manchester's essential biweekly listings guide for everything from jazz to theater to visual arts to clubs, including excellent listings for women and gays. Most restaurants, record stores, and bookstores have a good supply of alternative local magazines, as well as flyers for clubs, raves, and gigs in town. Your best one-stop place for info on the local indie/rave scene is **Afflecks Palace** (52 Church St., at Oldham St., tel. 0161/834–2039).

PUBS AND BARS

Citrus. Behind the Central Library, this spacious, mellow café-bar features relaxing live jazz on Friday and Saturday nights. The long weekend hours make this a good place to get a late-night dish from the ever-changing menu. *2 Mount St., tel. 0161/834–1344. Open Mon.–Thurs. 11–11, Fri. & Sat. 11 AM–2 AM.*

Dry 201. First and trendiest of Manchester's café-bars, the Dry anchors the up-and-coming Northern Quarter and is filled day or night with bright young things checking their E-mail, scoffing tapas, sinking a brewski, or sipping an espresso. *28 Oldham St., Northern Quarter, tel. 0161/236–5920. Oldham St. runs east off Piccadilly Gardens. Open Mon.–Sat. noon–11, Sun. noon–10:30.*

Lass O'Gowrie. This microbrewery brews two beers regularly, LOG 35 and the more potent LOG 42 (both about £1.50 per pint). Order a pint at the gaslit bar, and sit by the parlor fireplace to enjoy the Victorian charm. At times, you may have to squeeze in with the rowdy gangs of students who periodically descend on this place. *36 Charles St., off Oxford Rd., tel. 0161/273–6932. Open Mon.–Sat. 11:30–11, Sun. noon–10:30.*

Manto. It's a major gay scene here—with lots of attitude and dramatics. They serve full meals daily noon–9. The very early (or late, depending on your point of view) weekend hours make this a haven for dazed clubbing refugees. Flyers posted inside will point you to other gay hot spots. *46 Canal St., behind Chorlton St. Coach Station, tel. 0161/236–2667. Open 10 AM–midnight, weekends also 2:30 AM–6 AM.*

Don't Forget To Pack A Nikon.

Nuvis S
The smart little camera in a cool metal jacket.

Slide the stainless steel cover open on the Nikon Nuvis S, and a new world of picture taking is in the palm of your hand. This pocket-sized gem offers a 3x zoom lens, three picture formats, and drop-in film loading. Slide the protective cover over the lens, slip it in your pocket, and you're ready for your next adventure. For more information, visit us at *www.nikonusa.com*

Money From Home In Minutes.

If you're stuck for cash on your travels, don't panic. Millions of people trust Western Union to transfer money in minutes to 165 countries and over 50,000 locations worldwide. Our record of safety and reliability is second to none. For more information, call Western Union: USA 1-800-325-6000, Canada 1-800-235-0000. Wherever you are, you're never far from home.

www.westernunion.com

WESTERN UNION | MONEY TRANSFER

The fastest way to send money worldwide.

Mr. Thomas' Chop House. This Victorian drinking hole, a local favorite, has lots of tiled flooring and burnished wood, a mixed clientele, good food, and great British beer. What more do you want? *52 Cross St., tel. 0161/832–2245. Open Mon.–Sat. 11–11.*

Velvet. Lawks, it's camp in here, but then you are in the heart of the Gay Village. Smooth, cool, stylish—and that's just the clientele, who descend in droves to chill out, listen to the late-night grooves, and discuss their next move. *2 Canal St., Gay Village, tel. 0161/236–9003. Open Mon.–Wed. noon–11, Thurs.–Sat. until 1 AM, Sun. until 10:30.*

CLUBS

We'll never know how many clubs Manchester has, since so many appear and disappear every month. Besides checking the notice boards at Manto, The Cornerhouse (*see below*), and Afflecks Palace, you can try the clubs listed below for surefire entertainment. Many attract a friendly, mixed gay/straight crowd.

Band on the Wall. This small club highlights African, Latin American, indie, and western swing, among other types of music. Cover ranges from £2.50 to £6. *25 Swan St., tel. 0161/832–6625. Open Mon.–Thurs. 8:30 PM–1 AM, Fri. and Sat. 8:30 PM–2 AM, Sun. 7 PM–10:30 PM.*

Holy City Zoo. A regular stop on the Manchester music scene, the Zoo attracts a menagerie of night owls from all over town. With music from house to garage, you may want to move in. Nightly rent is £3 to £10, and it's open most nights 9:30–2. *York St., near Oxford Rd., tel. 0161/273–7467.*

Paradise Factory. This friendly club hosts a mostly gay crowd in the old Factory Records offices. They feature three floors of high camp and handbag house, with oldies thrown in for good measure. Come on Friday (£2) for "Women's Own" on the third floor. Cover varies (£2–£7). *112–116 Princess St., tel. 0161/228–2966. Open Tues.–Fri. 10 PM–2 AM, Sat. 10 PM–4 AM.*

Forgot to pack your clubbing clothes? Afflecks Palace (Church and Oldham Sts.) has four floors of retail shops stocking alternative fashions to help you step out in style. They'll also pierce your hair and give you a nose extension. (Wait! Reverse that.)

Planet K. This Jekyll-and-Hyde venue, where café society meets club culture, opened in 1999 and promises to take over where the legendary Hacienda left off. By day, it's an art gallery where artsy types come to hang out; by night, it's a live music venue hosting big-name acts and a raging dance club where DJs spin everything from hip hop to retro disco. It's open seven days a week; the café/gallery opens at 10 AM, and the club rocks until 2 AM most nights, 3 AM for special occasions. You'll find it in the heart of the groovy Northern Quarter, near the city center. Cover usually runs between £5 and £12. *48–50 Oldham St., tel. 0161/839–9941.*

THEATER AND FILM

The **Green Room** (54–56 Whitworth St. W, tel. 0161/950–5900) hosts fringe and experimental theater, while **Manchester University's Contact Theater** (Devas St., off Oxford Rd., tel. 0161/274–4400) stages innovative contemporary productions; tickets cost £2–£7.50. The **Royal Exchange** (St. Anne's Sq., tel. 0161/833–9833) features the nation's largest theater-in-the-round and presents world premieres as well as classic dramas. **The Cornerhouse** (70 Oxford St., at Whitworth, tel. 0161/200–1500) is Manchester's art center, internationally known for its film, photography, sculpture, and painting exhibits. It has a cinema (tickets £3.80), galleries, and cafés.

LIVERPOOL

Like the rest of the northwest, Liverpool reached its zenith in the 18th and 19th centuries, when it became Britain's major port for products of the industrial revolution. Before that, in the 17th and 18th centuries, Liverpool took an active part in the slave trade. A statue above the entrance to Lewis's department store on Renshaw Street in the city center commemorates this ignoble history. In the early 20th century, the opulent ocean liners of the Cunard and White Star lines set sail from Liverpool, taking rich socialites and poor emigrants to distant ports.

In World War II, Liverpool suffered serious damage when the Germans bombed the city in an attempt to interrupt convoys ferrying material from the United States. Still, the architecture here is incredible—it is second only to London for historically listed buildings and has more Georgian buildings than Bath. The city hosted the Year of Architecture and Design in 1999, and many of the soot-covered buildings (damaged from years of coal-burning) have been cleaned up to spectacular effect, though you'll still come across pockets of dilapidation.

Liverpudlians (also known as Scousers) are among some of the friendliest people you'll ever meet, and you can spend hours talking to a museum attendant or someone you've just met in a pub. Their accent may take some getting used to, but they'll likely have the same problem with yours. The humor of the people and the large university population keep Liverpool from being just another industrial casualty.

BASICS

AMERICAN EXPRESS
54 Lord St. L2 1TD, tel. 0870/600–1060, fax 0151/707–0461. From Lime St. Station, walk left on Lime St., veer right on Elliot St., right again on Church/Lord St. Open weekdays 9–5:30 (Tues. from 9:30), Sat. 9–5.

DISCOUNT TRAVEL AGENCIES
Campus Travel has three offices: one in the YHA Adventure Shop in the city center (25 Bold St., at Concert St., tel. 0151/709–9200), open weekdays 9:30–5:30 (Thursday until 6), Saturday 9–6; one at John Moores University student union (Haigh Bldg., Maryland St., tel. 0151/709–2474), open weekdays 9:30–5 (Thursday 10–5); and one at the University of Liverpool (Guild of Undergraduates, 160 Mount Pleasant, tel. 0151/708–0721), open weekdays 9:30–5 (Wednesday 10–5).

LAUNDRY
There are two launderettes south of the center reachable on buses 35, 80, or 86. The **Liver Launderette** (2b Princes Rd., tel. 0151/709–7414) is open 9–8 weekdays, 9–7 weekends, and charges between £2 and £3 for a wash. The nearby **Pressed for Time** (2a Berkley St., off Princes Ave., tel. 0151 708–8211) charges £1.80 per load and is open weekdays 9–7, Saturday 9:30–6, and Sunday 10–6

MAIL
Both of the main post offices in the city center have bureaux de change and are open Monday–Saturday 9–5:30. The Whitechapel office is at the St. John's Centre and the Lyceum office is at 1 Bold Street. Call 0345/223–344 for information.

VISITOR INFORMATION
Liverpool's two tourist offices are admirably restrained in their promotion of the Beatles and the Liverpool Football Club. Both change money, and the Albert Dock office sells National Express bus tickets. Both offices stock the "Liverpool & Merseyside Visitor Guide" (£1), restaurant and pub lists, and information on entertainment and walking tours. Note that there is currently no listings magazine for Liverpool, so check the daily Liverpool Echo for what's on. The **Merseyside Welcome Centre** (Clayton Sq. Shopping Centre, tel. 0151/709–3631) is open Monday–Saturday 9:30–5:30; from Lime Street Station walk down Lime Street, veer right on Elliot Street, and turn left at Great Charlotte Street. The **Tourist Information Centre** (tel. 0151/708–8854), at the Atlantic Pavilion in the Albert Dock complex near the museums, is open daily 10–5:30. There is also a 24-hour **events hot line** (tel. 0151/708–8838) and a Liverpool and Merseyside Web site (www. merseyside.org.uk).

COMING AND GOING

BY BUS
National Express buses run to London (4 hrs 30 min, £22 return) four times daily, and hourly to Manchester (50 mins, £6 return) via the Express Shuttle. Buses leave from the National Express Travel Office. They have locker storage (£1–£2 per day). *Norton St., tel. 0990/808080. From Lime St. Station, turn right on Lime St., right on London Rd., left on Norton St. Station and info desk open daily 6:30 AM–11:30 PM. Ticket office open Mon.–Sat. 7:15–6:15, Sun. 8:30–6:15.*

BY TRAIN

Trains run from the busy **Lime Street Station** (Lime St., tel. 0345/484950), near the city center. Trains to Manchester (1 hr, £9.20 return) depart every 30 minutes, while trains to London's Euston Station (3hrs, £48.20 return) leave hourly 6 AM–8 PM. The station has luggage storage open daily 7 AM–10 PM (£2 per item), and an information office open daily 8–7.

GETTING AROUND

Despite a population of more than a half million, Liverpool has a relatively small city center, with many pedestrians-only streets. The streets angle in a dozen different directions, making a circuitous route on their way to Albert Dock. Unless you're camping, you should be able to find accommodations and entertainment within easy walking distance of Lime Street Station. If you get lost, look for the tower vaguely resembling Seattle's Space Needle on St. John's Lane north of the Merseyside Welcome Centre, or one of the Liverpool Navigators in blue and yellow uniform, whose job it is to guide lost souls.

Local bus, train, and ferry service is coordinated by **Merseytravel.** For schedule and route info, visit their main office (24 Hatton Garden) weekdays 9–4, or call their **hot line** 8–8 (tel. 0151/236–7676). The tourist offices and bus and train stations also have information. If you plan on doing a lot of touring you may want a **Saveaway** pass, good for one day of off-peak travel on local transport. The **Area C Pass** (£2.10) covers Liverpool, the **Cross-River Pass** (£3.20) takes you across the Mersey and around the Wirral Peninsula, and an **All Areas Pass** (£4.30) covers the whole Merseyside area. Sadly, the passes are not good weekdays 6:30 AM–9:30 AM and 4–6.

You'll see the image of the Liver (rhymes with driver) Bird everywhere—including the top of the famous Liver Buildings. This mythical animal, a cross between the Eagle of St. John and a cormorant, is even the Liverpool football team's mascot.

BY BUS

Almost all local buses leave from Paradise Street Station (near corner of Paradise and Lord Sts.), and the Hood Street crossing and Sir Thomas Street, off Whitechapel near St. John's Shopping Centre. **Smart Buses** cost 40p–50p per journey and run every 20 minutes 7 AM–6 PM, less often at night. Smart Bus 4 will take you around the city center on a circular route; Smart Bus 1 goes to the docks.

BY MERSEYRAIL

Three local Merseyrail train lines travel in a circle around the city center, connect with nearby Stockport and the Wirral Peninsula, or go farther to Chester, Blackpool, and Manchester, depending on the line. Pick up free schedules for all three lines at the Merseytravel information offices (*see above*). Fares vary by distance covered. Merseyrail isn't too useful for intracity travel, but can be a cheap way of getting to nearby areas.

WHERE TO SLEEP

Liverpool has little in the way of cheap, attractive lodgings. If you book a room through the Merseyside Welcome Centre, they may be able to get you a discount; most hotels will charge at least £18 for a bed. **The Belvedere** (83 Mt. Pleasant, below Rodney St., tel. 0151/709–2356) offers a relatively cheap night's sleep (£18.50 per person) in a convenient location near a Smart Bus stop for line 4. The proprietors are kind, the beds clean, and the breakfast good. To get there from Lime Street Station, turn left on Lime Street, and turn left on Mt. Pleasant at the Adelphi Hotel. A step up the hill and in price, the **Aachen Hotel** (89–91 Mt. Pleasant, tel. 0151/709–3477, fax 0151/709–1126) has very good facilities, including hair dryers in all rooms and a pool table (they'll even provide needle and thread to patch your worn socks). You'll need your shades though, to combat the shock of competing patterns of wallpaper, furnishings, and carpets. Single rooms go from £26 and doubles from £40. Slightly cheaper is the **Aplin House Hotel** (35 Clarendon Rd., Garston, L19 6PJ, tel. 0151/427–5047). Built in 1901, this hotel faces a nice park. While 10 minutes by train from the city center, it's just a hop, skip, and a jump from where the Beatles lived and went to school—and, happily, Mrs. Atherton, can give you the low-down on the neighborhood Beatles sights! The five rooms are all comfy, complete with TVs and tea/coffeemakers, and go for around £20 to £36. Take the Northern Line train to Garston, or Bus 80 or 86.

HOSTELS

Embassie Youth Hostel. This friendly independent hostel is considerably more lenient and relaxed than most YHA hostels—there's no curfew or lockout, and you have your own key. It's also a great place to socialize: Stay in and play pool or go out clubbing with your new best friends. Beds are £10.50. *1 Falkner Sq., tel. 0151/707–1089. From Lime St. Station, turn left on Lime St./Renshaw St., veer left on Lecce St. (which becomes Hardman St. and Myrtle St.), cross Hope St., turn right on Catherine St., left on Falkner St. 40 beds. Kitchen, laundry.*

Liverpool Youth Hostel. This brand-new hostel, a stone's throw from the Albert Dock is open round the clock and offers accommodation in rooms that sleep two, four, or six, all with bath. Beds are £14.85, £16.40, or £17. *Wapping, tel. 0151/709–8888, fax 0151/709–0417. Take bus 222 or 224 from Lime St. station or Smart Bus 1. 110 beds. No curfew. Kitchen, laundry, games room. Reception open 7 AM–11 PM.*

STUDENT HOUSING

Like most British universities, the University of Liverpool has a number of separate residence halls, so you have to check with each one for room availability during summer holidays (mid-June–mid-September), at spring break (mid-March–mid-April), and winter break (mid-December–mid-January). Call the **University of Liverpool Conference Services** (tel. 0151/794–6444) to see if they can point you to a particular one. The 166 rooms in **Mulberry Court** (Oxford St., near the Metropolitan Cathedral, tel. 0151/794–3298) come with a kitchen and are £16. **Roscoe & Gladstone Hall** (Greenbank La., tel. 0151/794–6405) is near Penny Lane and Sefton Park, and has B&B service in its 300 singles for £14.50 per night.

FOOD

You'll find decent Indian and Middle Eastern restaurants on Renshaw and Bold streets, Greek restaurants clustered on Hardman Street, and Chinese grub in Liverpool's Chinatown (on Nelson St. between Berry, Great George, and Duke Sts.). Café bars and bistros have made an appearance around Concert Square (with barbecues in summer), Bold Street, and at the Albert Dock. The big mall on St. John's Lane has an enormous market with butcher shops and produce stands. For whole-food groceries and take-out items, try **Holland & Barrett Health Food Store** (17 Whitechapel, tel. 0151/236–8911).

Blue Bar and Grill. Overlooking the Albert Dock, this buzzy and stylish restaurant/bar has a vaulted brick ceiling, crystal chandelier, and dramatic lighting. On Saturday there's big-screen sports. In the daytime drop in for soup and a sandwich, a good deal at £4.95, or in the evening try out the tapas mini banquet, Moroccan lamb, or halibut tagine with apricots. There are plenty of vegetarian options, too. The bar stays open till 12:30 AM during the week and until 2 AM on Friday and Saturday. *Edward Pavilion, tel. 0151/709–7097.*

Far East Restaurant. Perhaps Liverpool's best known Cantonese restaurant, it's large, always thrumming, and serves classic dishes including dim sum. The 11 courses of the Emperor's buffet will set you back a mere £12:30, and on Friday and Saturday you can karaoke your head off in the Dim Sum Wine Bar below the main restaurant. *27 Berry St., tel. 0151/709–3141. From Lime St. Station, turn left on Lime St./Renshaw St. and right into Berry St.*

Jung Wah. One in a row of Chinese restaurants in newly spruced-up Chinatown, this attractive place serves excellent meals. Vegetarian dishes, curries, and entrées like chicken satay with rice make the Hong Kong pop music tolerable. The restaurant stays open extra late on weekends. *36 Nelson St., tel. 0151/709–1224. From Lime St. Station, turn left on Lime St./Renshaw St., right on Berry St., right on Nelson St.*

Metz. Open from noon till late, this modern, Bohemian-style café/bar is great for hot sandwiches at around the £5 mark, and serves a good mix of European dishes, to the accompaniment of mellow music (golden oldies). *Rainford Gardens, Mathew St., tel. 0151/227–2282. From the Welcome Centre take Elliot St., turn right on Church St., right into Whitechapel, and left into Rainford St., which leads to Mathew St.*

Taste. This spot is a useful pit stop perfect for relaxing and water-gazing before or after taking in the Tate. There's decent burger fare and snacks for around a fiver during the day and, at night, a good-value bistro-type menu—mushroom profiteroles mixing with the more prosaic bangers and mash. *The Colonnades, tel. 0151/709–7097.*

WORTH SEEING

Liverpool and the Beatles are nearly synonymous in the minds of most tourists, but even Beatles enthusiasts will feel bludgeoned by the overkill around **Mathew Street.** The tourist office sells maps leading to every site of Beatles minutiae, but seeing **Penny Lane** really won't do anything to increase your appreciation of the song. Those who'd rather not submerge themselves in the shallow shrines to the Fab Four should instead visit Liverpool's well-researched industrial and art museums. Along the River Mersey, Albert Dock (*see below*) is a fancy redevelopment project worth visiting only because some of the city's best museums and restaurants are here. The city has two enormous 20th-century cathedrals, connected by the aptly named Hope Street, that offer remarkably different architectural solutions to the problems of building modern monuments.

ALBERT DOCK

Built in the 1840s when Liverpool was *the* port of the British Empire, Albert Dock was one of the first enclosed warehouse systems. Now that the sun has set on the empire and shipping no longer fuels the city's economic engines, the old working docks have been converted into shops, restaurants—if you've been to New York's South Street Seaport or San Francisco's Fisherman's Wharf, you know what we're talking about—and some excellent museums. *From Lime St. Station, turn left on Lime St., right on Elliot St., jog left across Bold St. and continue west on Hanover St. (which becomes Canning Pl. and dead-ends at Albert Dock). Smart Bus 1, 2, or 5 stops here, 4 nearby on Canning St.*

The Waterfront Pass (£9.50) lets you in to the Albert Dock museums, Tate Gallery, The Beatles Story, and includes the Mersey Ferries Heritage cruise (see below).

TATE GALLERY • A spacious extension of the world-class London museum, the Tate regularly borrows from the permanent collection down south and arranges the works into special thematic exhibits. Young British artists are well represented. There are frequent workshops, and informal gallery lectures are held daily at 2 PM. *Tel. 0151/702–7400, or 0151/709–0507 for 24-hr recorded info. Admission free; special exhibitions £3. Open Tues.–Sun. 10–6.*

MERSEYSIDE MUSEUMS • Your entrance fee allows you one year's unlimited visits (in case you're planning a move) to the Merseyside Maritime Museum, H.M. Customs and Excise Museum, and the Museum of Liverpool Life. The **Merseyside Maritime Museum** features a wide range of exhibits about the Port of Liverpool and its people. Climb aboard a floating exhibit of ships moored on the quayside (summer afternoons only, weather permitting); indoors, don't miss the exhibit on the 9 million immigrants who passed through Liverpool's docks in the 19th and early 20th centuries (this part of the city's history won't be hard to imagine amid the mobs of schoolchildren usually visiting the museum). The most recent addition is a gallery that finally addresses Liverpool's role in the 18th- and 19th-century slave trade. Across the hall is the **H.M. Customs and Excise Museum.** Hands-on exhibits reveal how they spot suspicious people and packages. No need to ask how they catch smugglers who swallow drugs—it's shown with *nothing* held back (maybe even more than you needed to know). They proudly display confiscated goods accumulated by the U.K. customs office. The nearby **Museum of Liverpool Life** reveals the history of the town seen through the lenses of work, culture, and political revolt. *Tel. 0151/207–0001. Admission to all 3 museums £3. Open daily 10–5 (last admission 4:30).*

THE BEATLES STORY • Hardcore Beatles fans won't find much that's new here, but those with a more casual interest might be entertained by the exhibit's videos, posters, text displays, and the replica of the Cavern Club, the Beatles first haunt (now demolished). Chances are this "exciting new multimedia experience" will only please fans who prefer "Hello Goodbye" to "I Am the Walrus." But no Beatles lover will fail to get misty-eyed at the sight of John Lennon's white piano. You may wind up feeling sorry for the lobby staff: They have to listen to the Fab Four's tunes—fabulous as they may be—eight days a week. (Sorry.) *Britannia Vaults, tel. 0151/709–1963. Admission £6.95. Open daily 10–5.*

LIVERPOOL'S CATHEDRALS

Designed by Sir Giles Gilbert Scott, Liverpool's **Anglican cathedral** took 75 years to build and was completed in 1978. It was constructed in the Gothic Revival style in an attempt to duplicate authentically old cathedrals (you know, like Duke University). The only larger cathedrals in Europe are in Vatican City, Milan, and Seville. During World War II, German bombs destroyed a number of windows, but the structure remained unharmed. To give you an idea of how big the place is, it requires two elevator rides and a 108-step climb to get to the top of the 331-ft **tower**, admission £2. A high gallery features amazingly

YEAH, YEAH, YEAH! THE BEATLES' LIVERPOOL

For £1.50 you can buy "Beatles' Liverpool" or "Lennon's Liverpool" maps, or for £4.95 a more detailed "Beatles' Liverpool" book featuring comprehensive self-guided tours that stop by Penny Lane, Strawberry Fields, Menlove Avenue, and many other familiar-sounding places that invariably prove disappointing. You have to take buses to the various points of interest, or you can join the two-hour Magical Mystery Tour (£9.50), which departs daily from the Albert Dock Information Centre at 2:20, and also at 11.50 during school holidays. If you can't find the Beatles knickknack of your dreams, try the Beatles Shop (31 Mathew St., tel. 0151/236–8066).

The truly indefatigable Beatles fan checks out the annual Beatles convention. Known officially as the Mathew Street Festival, unofficially as Beatles Week, it's usually held during the third week in August, when what seems the entire city takes time out to dance, attend John and Yoko fancy-dress parties, listen to any number of Beatle bands from around the world ("There was once a better Beatle band, but they disbanded in 1970," noted the festival press release), and karaoke the night away. For complete info on Beatles Week, contact Cavern City Tours (tel. 0151/236–9091).

detailed Victorian and Edwardian embroidery. A footpath to the left of the entrance gates takes you to a gardenlike cemetery with headstones (not surprisingly) older than the cathedral. *St. James Rd., tel. 0151/709–6271. From Lime St. Station, turn left on Lime St./Renshaw St., left on Leece St., right on Rodney St./St. James's Rd. Or take Smart Bus 4. Admission free, £2.50 donation requested. Open daily 8–6. Evensong held weekdays 5:30 PM, weekends 3 PM.*

As an antidote to all that heritage revival stuff, you might warm to the second of Liverpool's cathedrals, an upside-down funnel shaped construction a few minutes walk along Hope St. from its Anglican counterpart. Affectionately known as "Paddy's Wigwam" or the "Mersey Funnel," the Catholic **Metropolitan Cathedral of Christ the King** was consecrated in 1967 (making it the first cathedral completed in town) after the outbreak of war in 1939 led to the cancellation of the original grandiose design by Sir Edwin Lutyens, whose crypt can now be seen beneath the existing building. Long, narrow, vibrant blue glass windows separate chapels, each with modern works of art and wall hangings, which surround the seating area and central altar. The altar, beneath the red and blue light shed from the glass crown of windows above, is further enhanced by a trickling fountain and potted palms. As a unified whole, it exerts a powerful presence, though the fabric of the building is already undergoing extensive restoration. *Mt. Pleasant, tel. 0151/709–9222. Open daily 8 AM–6 PM. Admission free, donations welcome. From Lime St., walk up Mt. Pleasant or take Smart Bus 4.*

LIVERPOOL MUSEUM

Featuring a truly encyclopedic collection, the museum has a natural history center, aquarium, vivarium, history exhibits, and a planetarium. They also hold one of the only two known carved narwhal horns, once thought to come from unicorns. *William Brown St., tel. 0151/207–0001. From Lime St. Station, turn right on Lime St., left on William Brown St. Admission free, except for planetarium (£1) and temporary exhibitions (£3). Open Mon.–Sat. 10–5, Sun. noon–5.*

MERSEY FERRIES

Gerry and the Pacemakers sang about it in the mid-1960s, but you can still "Ferry 'Cross the Mersey" today. The 50-minute cruise starts off at **Pier Head,** a five-minute walk from Albert Dock, and stops at Seacombe and Woodside, both on the Wirral Peninsula. The views of gray industrial buildup and the shining Victorian buildings are simultaneously stunning and depressing. A return ticket (£3.40) lets you hop off and on at your leisure. If you plan to use the train or underground on the same day as the ferry, buy the Cross-River Pass (*see* Getting Around, *above*). *Pier Head Ferry Terminal, tel. 0151/630–1030, or 0151/236–7776 for 24-hr info. Ferries run daily 10–3, with shuttle service operating between the 3 stops 7 AM–9 AM and 4 PM–7 PM.*

20 FORTHLIN ROAD

This is where it all began, folks. Sir Paul McCartney lived in this modest terraced home between 1955 and 1964 (although it's unclear whether anyone called him "sir" back then), where the Fabs rehearsed their songs and drank numerous cups of, um, *tea.* It's now owned by the National Trust and displays miscellaneous early memorabilia and walls full of photos. A 35-minute audio tour guides you through the kitchen, the front parlor where many of the immortal songs were composed, and Paul's bedroom, hardly a profound or moving experience, but hard-core Beatle-maniacs, devotees of 1950s suburbia, or maybe your mother, might find something of interest in all Paul's (rather banal) yesterdays. Access only by special minibus on a prebooked tour from Speke Hall, on airport road (bus 82C from the city center). Alternatively, buy a £9 combined ticket for this and the Beatles Story, for which you must be at the Beatles Story at 10 (tickets include transport from here at 11:10). *For bookings, tel. 0151/486–4006, Tues.–Sat. 9:30–4:30; 24-hr info line 0870/900–0256. Tours £5. Open Apr.–Oct., Wed.–Sat.; Nov.–mid-Dec. Sat only. Closed mid-Dec.–Mar.*

WALKER ART GALLERY

Two doors up from the Liverpool Museum, the Walker's Pre-Raphaelite section gets the most attention, but the Sculpture Gallery is also worth a look for its alabaster and bronze pieces. For a fun time (just don't let your friends see you), pay 20p for the self-guided quiz tours with themes like "Vive La France" (French art 1300–1900). Posted explanations help put the works in context. *William Brown St., tel. 0151/207–0001. From Lime St. Station, turn right on Lime St., left on William Brown St. Admission free. Open Mon.–Sat. 10–5, Sun. noon–5.*

AFTER DARK

Nightlife in Liverpool is a big deal. During the school year, call the University of Liverpool's **Student Entertainment Office** (tel. 0151/794–4143) or stop by the university on Mount Pleasant if you want to hear about the latest student goings-on; the student union bulletin board also posts current happenings. **The Palace** (Slater St., tel. 0151/708–8515), three floors of trendy shops hustling the latest clubwear, has heaps of flyers and info on the alternative scene. The funkier **Quiggins Centre** (School La., at Peter's La., tel. 0151/709–2462) has similar info and lower prices. The gay-oriented *Boyz* can be picked up at most gay spots for free and lists goings-on throughout the region.

PUBS

Those looking for some nonplasticized Beatles trivia may want to find the cozy, friendly **Ye Cracke** (Rice St., tel. 0151/709–4171) on a skinny street off to the west of Hope Street. John Lennon hung out here before and during the Beatles days, but don't ask anyone to tell you the stories—that was about 30 years ago, and like all sensible people, they've moved on. For a totally different scene, check out **Baa Bar** (43–45 Fleet St., tel. 0151/708–6810)—lots of people come here before clubbing. Sleek, minimalist **Mello Mello** (40–42 Slater St., tel. 0151/707–0898), just down the street from the Cream club, picks up as the night rolls on. DJs spin house music to keep the mood going. The **Philharmonic** (36 Hope St., on Hardman St., tel. 0151/709–1163) is a traditional Liverpool pub whose art nouveau copper and stained glass, tiling, wrought-iron gates, and marble loos are as much of an attraction as the gratifyingly old-fashioned, full-bodied beer. Sink into the antique sofas down in the basement at **Rococomodo** (Concert Square, tel. 0151/709–8832), watch the fish, order a fruit or cream cocktail, and chill out to the jazz and funk. The considerable Irish presence in the city means that there are plenty of genuine Irish drinking holes; some have live music, like **Flanagan's** (Mathew St., tel. 0151/236–1214) and **Guinan's** (Slater St., tel. 0151/707–0834), both with good *craic* (an Irish expression meaning easy good time) with Guinness and conversation flowing free.

CLUBS

Cream/Nation. The **Nation** hosts one of England's top-rated clubs, **Cream,** Friday and Saturday at its massive Parr Street location. You've got a choice of three rooms—the main, the courtyard, and the annex with the bar zoo—all in what appears to be a couple of warehouses stuck together. Catch the top DJs, but watch out for the £11–£13 cover charges. During the day, pick up *Club On,* the free national club listings mag, and other flyers at the **Cream shop** (tel. 0151/708–9979) next door and check out the low-down on inexpensive coach travel to the club. *Parr St., north of Slater St., tel. 0151/709–1693 or during daytime 0151/709–7023.*

Garlands. Garlands is host to a mostly young, gay, and gay-friendly crowd (both men and women)—expect high camp, especially on Saturday. the first three Fridays of the month it's Thank God It's Friday and the last Friday is an all-night affair. Pints of lager go for £1.50. Look for the white and pink sign. *8–10 Eberle St., off Dale St., tel. 0151/236–3307. Cover £4.*

Lomax. This is the current in-place to catch indie bands on their way to becoming the next Oasis—or to disappearing without a trace. It's become so popular that the more established bands also give this place a whirl. Cover is usually around £3. *34 Cumberland St., off Victoria St., tel. 0151/236–6458).*

CONCERTS

The **Royal Liverpool Philharmonic Orchestra** (Philharmonic Hall, Hope St., tel. 0151/709–3789) plays a wide-ranging menu of classical music through the year. The hall also hosts folk and jazz artists and runs the occasional film and in summer there's a program of light classical concerts by the RLPO, in a marquee at King's Dock. Smart Bus 4 stops right outside. The acoustics at the **Anglican Cathedral** (tel. 0151/709–6271) are perfect for the classical concerts there; check out the organ recitals, too.

THEATER

Tucked away in a gorgeous redbrick building in the city center, **Bluecoat Arts Centre** (School La., tel. 0151/709–5297) is host to innovative performances ranging from modern dance and live jazz to poetry, Asian traditional music, animation, and occasional events in the courtyard. You'll also find a gallery, café, and craft/design shop open during the day. The **Everyman Theatre** (1 Hope St., tel. 0151/709–4776) offers a wide range of drama, dance, and musical performances, including lunchtime concerts. Call for more information. **Liverpool Empire Theatre** (Lime St., tel. 0151/709–1555), recently restored to its former glory, is Liverpool's largest theater venue and plays host to opera companies, West End productions, comedy and concerts. Tickets start at around £10. **Unity Theatre** (Hope Pl., off Hope St. between cathedrals, tel. 0151/709–4988) is a lively, small-scale venue hosting a variety of shows. Tickets are £1–£8.50.

CHESTER

Despite attracting a fair number of visitors, Chester manages to rise above the deadening effects of the well-trodden tourist trail. It's a city that still belongs to the locals, who will treat you with an easy amiability and unforced hospitality. As such, Chester makes a good day out from Liverpool or Manchester, and also a good stopping-off point if you're heading to or from north Wales.

It's not hard to like this city, whose medieval layout Henry James found to be "a perfect feast of crookedness." On its quirkily picturesque **Rows,** you'll find arcaded, half-timbered shops set above street-level along the four arms that lead from the **Cross,** the central crossroad of the city. Dating back to the 13th-century, this medieval version of a shopping mall is guaranteed to melt the hardest of anti-shopping hearts, and the numerous "olde" (they can use the superfluous "e" since they've been around so long) inns and patisseries along the way should help as well. Check out Brown's, the Harrod's of the north, if only to window gaze.

Everything in this city seems to warrant superlatives—the largest amphitheater in Britain, the biggest tea rooms, the oldest shopfront, racecourse, crypt—you know the score. Yet don't begrudge Chester this small indulgence: after all, it has two thousand years of history to show off. In AD 79 the city was Deva, the largest Roman port and fortress in the country, where silver from the mines of North Wales and olive oil from the Mediterranean was unloaded. Best of all, Chester has the country's most complete set of Roman and medieval walls, girding the city in a two-mi circle, easily walked in an hour or so.

BASICS

AMERICAN EXPRESS

12 Watergate St., CH1 2LA, tel. 0870/600–1060. Open weekdays 9–5:30 (Wed. from 9:30), Sat. 9–5. Watergate St. is opposite Eastgate St. on the Cross.

VISITOR INFORMATION

There are two **tourist offices,** both dispensing the usual information, including the free *What's On in Chester* booklet for all local events. The office at the **Town Hall** lies very close to the cathedral on Northgate St., open Monday–Saturday 9–5:30 and from May through October also Sunday 10–6. The **Chester Visitor and Craft Centre** (Vicar's Lane, tel. 01244/402111) overlooks the Roman amphitheater and is open daily year-round, usually until at least 5 PM. Upstairs there's a craft center where you can watch candle-making. *From the Frodsham St. bus stop cross to St John St. then turn left into Little St. John St., which leads into Vicar's Lane.*

If you're at the Cross in summer, don't be alarmed if you hear a bell and the shouts of "Oyez! Oyez!" It's only the town criers, a unique British husband and wife team in action.

COMING AND GOING

BY BUS

National Express (tel. 0990/808080) runs coaches ten times daily between Chester (Delamere St.) and London (5 hrs 20 mins, £22 return), four times daily to Birmingham (2½ hrs, £10 return), and three times daily to Manchester (1 hr 10 min, £5.75). Coming from Liverpool, **Crosville** (tel. 01244/602666) runs an hourly bus service X6 (£3.15 return) from Queen's Square, which takes about an hour. An **Explorer** ticket (£5) will give you one day's unlimited travel on the Arriva network, throughout the Cheshire region. Call 0345/056005 for more information.

BY TRAIN

There are only two direct trains from London Euston to Chester a day, but there's hourly service changing at Crewe (2½ hrs, £48.20 saver return); trains run frequently from Manchester (1hr, £8 day return, £9.70 saver return), and every half hour from Liverpool (45 mins, £3.30 day return). Note that there's no luggage storage at the station. *Station Rd, tel. 0345/484950. Ticket office open Mon.–Sat. 5:30 AM–12:30 AM, Sun. 7:45 AM–midnight.*

WHERE TO SLEEP

Make sure you book ahead if you plan on staying in Chester in summer, as the cheaper and more characterful accommodations fill up quickly.

Castle House. Up a notch and right in the center of town, this 16th-century holdout has true antique charm and truly charming owners (not antique). Take your breakfast in a black and white beamed room full of horse brasses, overlooking a small garden stuffed with plants. Rooms go for £23 per person. *23 Castle St., CH1 2DS, tel./fax 01244/350354. From the Cross take Bridge St. which continues into Lower Bridge St., turn right into Castle St.*

Grove Villa. Sleep in period style in either a four-poster or an antique half-tester (canopied) bed for only £20 per person. Beautifully situated on the banks of the River Dee, this smoke-free accommodation offers all suites, most with a river view. No smoking. *18 The Groves, CH1 1SD, tel.01244/349713. Take Little St. John St. from the Visitor Centre, turn left into Souters Lane and left again into The Groves. Alternatively walk down through the well-kept park from Vicar's Lane. Cash only.*

Ormonde Guest House. Five minutes' walk from the train station, you'll come across a clutch of budget accommodations, the best of which is this mock Tudor with £30 doubles and £16 singles. *126 Brook St., CH1 3DU, tel. 01244/328816. Turn right out of station onto Station Rd. which becomes Brook St.*

HOSTELS

Chester YHA. The well-equipped hostel, converted from a large Victorian house and near a large park, is a 20-minute walk from the center. Beds go for £10.15. *Hough Green House, 40 Hough Green, Chester, CH4 8JD, tel. 01244/680056, fax 01244/681204. 130 beds. Reception open 7 AM–10 AM and 3 PM–10:30 PM. No curfew. Closed late Dec.–early Jan. Follow Bridge St. and Grosvenor St., cross Grosvenor Bridge and turn right at the roundabout into Hough Green.*

FOOD

There's no shortage of places for being fed and watered in Chester, ranging from atmospheric old pubs and tea-rooms to modern café/bistros. For full meals, **Mamma Mia** (St. Werburgh St., tel.01244/314663), practically next door to the cathedral, serves good, garlicky pizza and pasta dishes and is always humming. Don't be fooled by the half-timbered building housing **Francs** (14 Cuppin St., off Grosvenor St., tel. 01244/317952); it conceals a very French interior, and delivers an authentically Gallic three-course lunch menu at £6.95, and an all-day Sunday menu at £8.95. If you hanker for something a tad more English, the **Cathedral Refectory** (St. Werburgh St., tel. 01244/313156) should fit the bill. This really was where the brothers ate their monkish fare, but nowadays you're more likely to hear a tinkling piano than holy utterances as accompaniment to your soup of the day. In true monastic fashion, however, it's closed in the evening and gives credit to the Creator only—everyone else pays cash.

Don't miss a tea and a scone in **Katie's Tea Rooms** (Watergate St., tel. 01244/400322), vaunted the largest tea room in the country, taking up three floors and supposedly held up by thousand-year-old oak beams. At the other extreme, the modern and minimalist **Bar Coast** (Music Hall Passage, tel. 01244/354041) serves an all-day brunch, toasted sandwiches, and snacks. Thursday through Sunday DJs spin until 2 AM, and there's a £4–£5 cover after 10 PM on weekends. **Espresso** (60 Northgate St., tel. 01244/343657) is run by clamorous Italians who concoct good-value sandwiches, but aren't so hot in the cappuccino department. **Boulevard de la Bastille** (39 Bridge St. Row, tel. 01244/348708) is a great place to sit out in the Rows and indulge in a mouth-watering pastry.

WORTH SEEING

If you feel like a running—or strolling—commentary from people who know their oats (as opposed to commentary from people who are *feeling* their oats), take one of the **walking tours** round the city (tel. 01244/402445) daily at 10:30 May–October, weekends November–April (£3), which leave the Visitor Center. Or go by yourself on the two-mi trip around the Roman and medieval **walls**, past **King Charles Tower** (where King Charles I witnessed his army's defeat at the battle of Rowton Moor during the Civil War), and the **Roodee,** the oldest racecourses in the country. The filigree wrought-iron **Eastgate Clock** on a sandstone arch above Eastgate St. commemorates Queen Victoria's Jubilee in 1897. If the weather is fine, spend an hour or so messing about on the river; rowing boats can be hired at the Groves for about £4 per hour.

CHESTER CATHEDRAL

Skip the piped music in the exhibition foyer and get down to the sandstone Gothic cathedral itself, begun in Norman times and finished in 1490. The best things to see here are the choir where you'll see scaly winged beasts on the intricately carved misericords (ledges for weary monks); the colorful ceiling dates from 1880. The 16th-century cloisters enclose a small garden that contains a startling contemporary bronze sculpture of Jesus and the Woman of Samaria, reminiscent of dribbling ectoplasm (*you* try to describe it). The cathedral offers free guided tours daily at 2:30 from May through August. *St. Werburgh St., tel. 01244/324756. Admission free, £2 donation requested. Open daily 7:30 AM–6 PM. Evensong weekdays at 5:30, Sat. at 4:15, Sun. at 3:30.*

DEWA ROMAN EXPERIENCE

The pretend Roman vessel, flickering lights, and pungent aromas are intended to convey the spirit of Roman Chester, but you'll probably get more thrills from handling the archaeological odds and ends, trying on (fake) Roman armor, and playing Three Man's Morris—a Roman version of noughts and crosses. You can see part of Chester's original Roman foundations here, or you can save your bucks and view the excellently preserved Roman hypocaust (a kind of early central-heating system) across the street. In the basement. At "Spud-u-like." No kidding. *Pierpoint Lane, off Bridge St., tel. 01244/343407. Admission £3.95. Open daily 9–5.*

GROSVENOR MUSEUM

Chester's town museum, scheduled to reopen in April of 2000 after renovations, includes the Roman Stones Gallery, which claims to be the largest collection of tombstones from any single site in Britain. These and sundry other items of the same period will give you a sense of daily civilian and military life in Roman times. Other parts of the museum incorporate a creaky Georgian house with period rooms furnished in Georgian, Victorian, and Edwardian styles, a review of nightshirts through the ages, and a stenciled Edwardian shower. *27 Grosvenor St., tel. 01244/402008. Open Mon.–Sat, 10:30–5, Sun 2–5. Admission free, donations invited.*

CHESTER HERITAGE CENTRE

The center gives a good explanation of the Rows, offers the chance to do your own brass rubbing, and divulges the age-old mystery of wattle and daub. (We're not telling you.) *Bridge St., tel. 01244/402008. Admission £2. Open Sat. 11–5 and Sun. 2–5.*

AFTER DARK

In the evening head for **Alexander's Jazz Theatre and Café Bar** (2 Rufus Court, off Northgate St., tel. 01244/340005) for either stand-up comedy or live jazz (admission charge some nights) and a good range of tapas, "jazz banquets," and malt whiskies. **Watergates Wine Bar** (Watergate St., tel. 01244/320515) says it's in England's oldest crypt; the atmosphere's Gothic, with candles dripping into wax stalactites, but the food's Mediterranean. The **Falcon** (Lower Bridge St., tel. 01244/314555) and the **Boot** (Eastgate St. Row, tel. 01244/3145400) are good traditional pubs, with dark-wood beams and smoky yellow ceilings.

THE LAKE DISTRICT

UPDATED BY JULES BROWN

E ven if you aren't a fan of Wordsworth and can't tell a daffodil from a dandelion, the Lake District is an unforgettable area to explore. As a place of natural beauty it has no equal in Britain: sixteen major lakes, and countless smaller stretches of water known as tarns, combine in a mesmerizing landscape of jagged mountains, waterfalls, babbling streams, grassy clearings, wooded valleys, and stone-built villages. England's highest mountain peaks—Scafell Pike, Scafell, Helvellyn and Skiddaw—are over 3,000 ft high and are joined by myriad other more modest hills and mountains. The area is a candy store for avid outdoor enthusiasts who hike, climb, and scramble on the ridges and valley walls.

Dreamers and poets have been entranced by the beautiful shores of Lake Windermere and Coniston Water for centuries. Barring the hordes of tourists invading Grasmere, Keswick, and Ambleside, the area can be pretty relaxing if you have the patience to understand the bus schedule and the time to wander without hurrying. Maybe you'll get some artistic/philosophical inspiration from this pastoral land—heck, it worked for William Wordsworth, Thomas De Quincey, and Beatrix Potter, all of whom made their home in this once-undiscovered Eden. Nowadays, most of the lakes and surrounding villages are about as tranquil as Victoria Station, but a short walk out of the villages will put you in the company of only a handful of other robust adventurers. In fact, if you're an impulsive backpacker and willing to take off in search of a few days or weeks of Wordsworthian wandering among hills, vales, and somnolent villages, you can still count on enough tranquillity in which to recollect a whole lifetime of emotion. Especially if you head north or west, you'll find unspoiled valleys where sheep far outnumber tourists.

The region was put on the map by the Lake Poets in the early 19th century. It probably all started that lovely April day in 1802 when Wordsworth and his sister Dorothy were ambling through the woods of Gowbarrow Park just above Aira Force, and Dorothy happened to remark that she had never seen "daffodils so beautiful"—thereby inspiring one of the best-known poems in English, "I Wandered Lonely as a Cloud." The poet's lyrics seemed to capture the quintessence of the entire area, which appeared to be bathed perpetually in that romantic "light that never was on sea or land"; following Wordsworth, the region has been consecrated by other noted writers, such as Thomas Gray, Samuel Taylor Coleridge, Thomas De Quincey, John Ruskin, Hugh Walpole, and Matthew Arnold. Some of their homesteads are now leading attractions, but don't worry too much about a sightseeing itinerary: The Lake District's organized sights are no match for the natural beauty of the area.

Since 1951, the region has been maintained as the Lake District National Park and most of what people come to see—including virtually all the famous mountains, literary sights, and beauty spots—lies within its boundary of 35 square miles. The park itself has no official entrances or checkpoints and sits within the larger county of Cumbria, which was cobbled together in 1974 from the historic counties of Cumberland and Westmorland, and the northern segment of old Lancashire. Some of the more popular towns, such as Kendal, Cockermouth, and Penrith, lie just outside the park boundary.

In practice, none of this makes the slightest difference to the visitor. What you do have to figure out (and quickly) is Lake District terminology. If someone gives you directions to walk along the "beck" to the "force" and then climb the "fell" to the "tarn," you've just been told to hike along the stream or river (beck) to the waterfall (force) before climbing the hill or mountain (fell) to reach the lake (tarn). Moreover, town or village place names in the Lake District can also refer to the lake on which they stand: Thus, there's a Coniston village on Lake Coniston, and a town called Windermere on Lake Windermere. And just to really confuse matters, locals would never say "Lake Windermere", but just Windermere, since "mere" means lake in Old English (whence all the other dialect words above derive).

The park's southern region (around **Windermere, Ambleside,** and **Coniston Water**) is the most popular target, but the scenery is more dramatic in the slightly less-explored areas to the west and north (around **Keswick** and **Ullswater**). To reach the lakes, you'll probably pass through Windermere or Ambleside, both of which have markets and equipment stores where hikers and campers can stock up. During July and August, when most of the hostels are open and buses run more regularly, you can explore some fairly remote sights. During the winter as well as in spring and fall, you'll be limited by infrequent public transportation and wet, wet, wet weather (the Lake District gets more rainfall annually than any other region in England). Most of the hostels, attractions, and tourist offices are closed November–Easter, but B&Bs give off-season discounts, and the hardy traveler will find winter's snowy mountains and frozen waterfalls bewitching.

High-rollers can indulge in luxury hotels and blue-chip escorted tours, but the Lake District is also affordable. There's a plethora of guest houses and youth hostels offering reasonably priced accommodations, a busy bus network geared to the needs of travelers and, of course, the greatest travel bargain of all—free views.

BASICS

PUBLICATIONS
Essential maps for hikers are the yellow Outdoor Leisure (1:25,000) series—£5.95 each—which cover the whole Lake District in four separate maps. For an overview of the area, Paul Buttle's *The 12 Best Walks in the Lake District* is a good buy, though the most famous hiking guides are known everywhere simply as "Wainwright's"—a series of beautifully drawn pictorial guides by A. Wainwright to every fell and mountain (each £10.99) in the Lake District (that's over 3,000 peaks for all you mountain-baggers). Jim Watson's guide to *The Cumbria Way and Allerdale Ramble* (£6.99) is the best-written and most widely available guide to the region's two premier long-distance footpaths.

For a general look at the region, Hunter Davies's *The Good Guide to the Lakes* (£5.80) is extremely comprehensive, and a lot of fun, to boot. Every bookshop in the region sells at least a selection of all these books and guides, as well as endless volumes of poetry and writing inspired by the Lakes—look for works by local poet Norman Nicholson, or novels by authors as diverse as Hugh Walpole and Melvyn Bragg, and not just the omnipresent Wordsworth and Coleridge.

VISITOR INFORMATION
Take a large backpack—you're soon going to be weighed down with books and brochures. If you write or fax before your arrival, the **Cumbria Tourist Board** (Ashleigh, Holly Rd., Windermere, Cumbria LA23 2AQ, tel. 015394/44444, fax 015394/44041) or **Lake District National Park Authority** (Murley Moss, Oxenholme Rd., Kendal, Cumbria, LA9 7RL, tel. 01539/724555, fax 01539/740822) will send any info you request. All larger tourist offices carry the annually updated publications "Where to Stay in South Lakeland," "Where to Stay in Eden," (for Penrith, Ullswater and the Eastern Lakes) and "Keswick on Derwentwater and the Northern Lakes Visitor's Guide" (£1 each), which list each town's hotels and B&Bs. Most tourist offices also hand out free lists of local campsites, eateries, and seasonal events, and sell specialist guides to subjects as diverse as veggie restaurants, mountain bike trails, and local walks.

COMING AND GOING
Lancaster to the south and Carlisle to the north are the major points of approach to the Lake District, though the region doesn't properly begin until the gateway towns of Penrith or Keswick (north) or Kendal

N

Rail Lines

0

0

6 miles

9 km

Irish Sea

Isle of Walney

Barrow-in-Furness

A5087

A590

A5087

Duddon Sands

A595

A5093

Broughton-in-Furness

A593

A595

A593

Ravenglass

A5093

at Coniston

Seathwaite

A5084

Coniston Water

Coniston

Brantwood

Hill Top

Near Sawrey (Hilltop)

Winderm

Bowness

A591

B5285

Ulverston

A590

Haverwaite

Lake

Cartmel Sands

B5278

Grange-over-Sands

Hampsfield Fell

Lakeside

A590

Morecambe Bay

Morecambe

Lancaster

Carnforth

Arnside

M6

Kent

Kendal

Oxenholme

LANCASHIRE

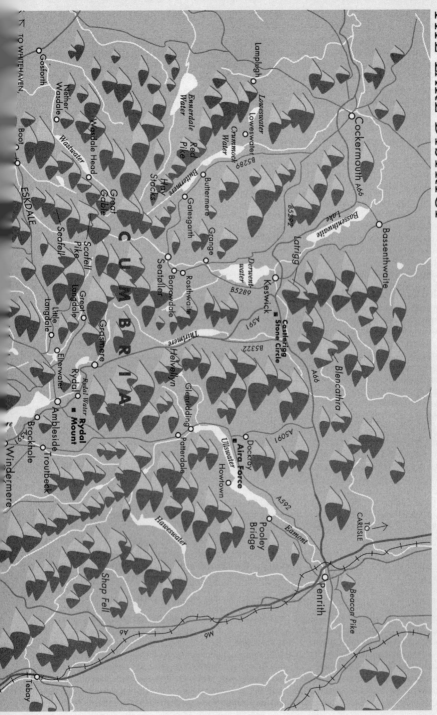

TO WHITEHAVEN

Gosforth

Nether
Wasdale

Boot

Lamplugh

Ennerdale
Water

Loweswater

Loweswater

Red
Pike

Crummock
Water

Cockermouth A66

B5289

B5292

Larrigg

Bassenthwaite
Lake

Bassenthwaite

Wasdale Head

Wastwater

ESKDALE

Great
Gable

Hay
Stacks

Buttermere

Buttermere

Gatesgarth

Grange

C

U

M

B

R

I

A

Scafell
Pike

Seafell

Seatoller

Borrowdale

Rosthwaite

Derwent-
water

B5289

Keswick

A591

Castlerigg
Stone Circle

B5322

A66

Blencathra

Great
Langdale

Little
Langdale

Grasmere

Thirlmere

Helvellyn

Elterwater

Rydal
Rydal Water

Rydal
Mount

Glenridding

A5091

A66

Brockhole

Ambleside

Troutbeck

Potterdale

Ullswater

Aira
Force

Dockray

Howtown

Pooley
Bridge

Eamont

A592

TO
CARLISLE

Windermere

Haweswater

Shap Fell

Penrith

Beacon Pike

A6

M6

Teebay

(south). While trains are probably the easiest way to get to the Lake District, buses provide the best service for travel within the region (*see* Getting Around, *below*).

BY BUS • The **National Express** (0990/808080) bus from London's Victoria Coach Station makes the trip to Windermere (7 hrs, from £30 return) twice daily. The bus continues on from Windermere to Ambleside, Grasmere, and Keswick. From Manchester's Chorlton Street Station there's one bus per day to Windermere (3 hrs 30 mins, £16 return, £19.25 on Friday) that stops in Ambleside, Grasmere, and Keswick.

If you're coming from Carlisle, Lancaster, or York, **Stagecoach Cumberland** (tel. 01946/63222) buses offer cheap transport to the lakes. Bus 555/556 runs twice daily from **Carlisle** to Ambleside and Windermere and also connects **Lancaster** to Kendal, Windermere, Ambleside, and Keswick every hour. Your best deal for these journeys is an **Explorer Pass** (*see* Getting Around, By Bus, *below*). From **York,** Cumberland Bus X9 runs daily (except Sunday) from the end of April through August to Ambleside at 3:35 PM (£11.99 return). It also drops off at Keswick on Saturday. The Ambleside YHA hostel is a pick-up/drop-off point for the **Stray Travel** coach (*see* Bus Travel, *in* Chapter 1), with service from Stratford-upon-Avon through the Lakes to Edinburgh. Buy tickets at the hostel.

BY TRAIN • Trains from London's Euston Station depart for **Kendal** and **Windermere** about 10 times daily; the four–five-hour trip costs from £44 round-trip, and as much as £62 if you travel on a Friday (book at least seven days in advance for the cheaper fares). You take the main line service to Carlisle, Edinburgh, or Glasgow and change at Oxenholme for the branch line service to Kendal and Windermere. If you're heading for Keswick, you can either take the train to Windermere and continue from there by bus (*see below*) or stay on the main London–Carlisle train to Penrith station, from which buses also run to Keswick. Direct trains from Manchester depart for Windermere (2 hrs, £19.50–£22.50 return) five times daily. For more information call **National Rail Enquiries** (tel. 0345/484950).

GETTING AROUND

If you don't have a car—and if you do, shame on you for clogging up the tiny region's roads—the main transportation in the Lakes is the bus network. Local **Stagecoach Cumberland** buses converge in Windermere, Ambleside, and Keswick, with lines fanning out to villages like Hawkshead, Coniston, Grasmere, and Cockermouth. Pick up a free "Lakeland Explorer" timetable from tourist offices to plan your maneuvers—"plan" is the key word, since most buses stop running in the late afternoon, and you could find yourself stranded in some village for the night. If you enjoy walking, hoof it from one village to the next—there's no better way to get a feel for the region. Ambleside and Windermere are only about 3 mi apart; Ambleside to Grasmere only 2½ mi. Some hikers walk from one B&B or youth hostel to the next. *Inter-Hostel Walks in the Lake District* (£2), available at YHA hostels in the region, gives full details.

BY BIKE • Tourist info centers have all sorts of books, cheap and costly, describing trails of varying difficulties and distances. The **C2C cycle route** goes 140 mi between Workington and Newcastle; **Cumbria Cycle Way** circles Cumbria County; and the **West Cumbria Cycle Path** stretches a mere 10 mi between Whitehaven and Ennerdale. Bike rental generally costs £10 per half day, £12–£15 per day, and £55–£105 per week; be prepared to leave a deposit. Some rental companies offer discounts to YHA members. Around the Southern Lakes, places to try are: **Summitreks** (14 Yewdale Rd., Coniston, tel. 015394/41212), **Ghyllside Cycles** (The Slack, Ambleside, tel. 015394/33592), **The Croft** (Croft Caravan and Campsite, Hawkshead, tel. 015934/36374), and **Windermere Cycles** (12 Main Rd., Windermere, tel. 015394/47779). The best place to rent bikes in the north is at **Keswick Mountain Bike Centre** (Southey Hill, Keswick, tel. 017687/75202).

BY BUS • Buses serve most towns and villages, and most offer frequent service between late April and mid-August, with the best service in July. Service comes to a virtual standstill November–late April, when the roads are often snowy and icy. **Stagecoach Cumberland** is the largest company, whose **Explorer Pass** (£5.50 per day, £13.60 for four days), available on any bus, is good for travel on all the Cumbrian lines. The pass is a good deal if you're going to more than two towns, or traveling to or from Carlisle or Lancaster. For more info call the Stagecoach Cumberland **Bus Help Line** (tel. 01946/63222).

Stagecoach Cumberland Bus 599 goes from Grasmere to Ambleside, Windermere, and Bowness, and Bus 555/556, known as the **Lakeslink,** will take you north from Kendal, Windermere, and Ambleside to Keswick, continuing on to Carlisle. During the summer, Bus 505 or 506 (a.k.a. the **Coniston Rambler**) leaves Bowness about every hour from 9 to 5, stopping in Brockhole, Ambleside, Hawkshead, and Coniston. In the north, Bus X5 makes the half-hour journey between Keswick and Cockermouth eight times daily (four times on Sunday). Bus X5 also continues east to Penrith. The 79 Borrowdale bus runs from Keswick along the eastern shore of Derwentwater, past Lodore (where there are some lovely waterfalls), and on to Seatoller. Bus 77 (a.k.a. the **Honiston Rambler**) goes through Keswick, Buttermere, the Honister YHA, and Seatoller, returning to Keswick via Grange Bridge. The entire central and western region is less easily reached by bus, though useful services include the 516 (Ambleside to Elterwater and the Langdale valley) and cross-region buses to towns like Workington, Ulverston, and Barrow.

The YHA operates its own **shuttle bus** service between popular hostels (Easter–Oct., £2); call the Ambleside hostel (*see* Where To Sleep, *below)* for more information. The National Trust also offers free summer buses to beauty spots like Tarn Hows (near Hawkshead), and Watendlath in Borrowdale—local tourist offices have all the details.

BY CAR • If your time is limited or you're traveling during the off-season when buses don't run frequently, renting a car may actually be a necessary investment. Often you must be over 21, though some agencies do rent to the 18–20 crowd for a small additional fee—be sure to ask. **Cumbria Car Hire** (Brantfell Garage, Kendal Rd., Bowness, tel. 015394/44408) will deliver a car to you in Ambleside or Windermere from £31 per day. **Europcar** in Carlisle (Lancaster St., tel. 01228/515710) charges from £40 per day. Other local agencies include **Avis** (Station Rd., tel. 01539/733582) in Kendal, and Keswick's **Keswick Motor Company** (Lake Rd., tel. 017687/72064). Or ask at any local tourist office (*see* Visitor Information, *in* Southern Lakes or Northern Lakes, *below)* about reservations and discounts.

BY TRAIN • Train connections are good around the edges of the Lake District, especially on the Oxenholme–Kendal–Windermere line and the Furness and West Cumbria branch line from Lancaster to Grange-over-Sands, Ulverston, Barrow, and Ravenglass. However, these services aren't of much use for getting around the central Lakeland region (where you'll really need to take a bus or walk), and services on these lines are reduced, or nonexistent, on Sunday. Seven-day regional **North West Rover** tickets (£45) are valid for unlimited travel within the area, but it's unlikely that they would be worth it on most itineraries. Two private lines run short distances long on nostalgia. **Lakeside & Haverthwaite Steam Railway** (tel. 015395/31594) runs from Haverside to Lakeside along the eastern side of Lake Windermere (£3.40 return). The line does not run in winter. **Ravenglass & Eskdale Railway** (tel. 01229/717171), still going strong on England's oldest narrow-gauge rails, travels from Ravenglass (on the West Cumbria branch line) on the west coast to Dalegarth, near Boot in Eskdale, at the foot of the Lakeland's highest hills. Trains run year-round—about once an hour in summer, much less frequently (usually weekends only) in winter—and the trip costs £6.50 return.

SOUTHERN LAKES

You didn't come here just to contemplate the specter of Beatrix Potter, did you? That's good, because the Southern Lakes has so much more to offer than the cutesy Potter sights and overrun villages of **Hawkshead, Windermere,** and **Hill Top.** True enough, these places are all handsomely sited—glistening water, wood-fringed shores, and green fells are always within view wherever you go. And in cobble-path, ivy-clad, stone-built Hawkshead, you have one of the single most attractive villages in the entire region. But the relative ease of access, and the abundance of literary sights (the Wordsworth shrines included), means that the Southern Lakes suffers from chronic overcrowding in the summer, especially during the school holidays. That said, many excellent walks begin right in the center of a village, pass by a youth hostel or two, climb to some uninhabited place with a spectacular vista, and then return to the village. Even around busy Windermere, you can always find some solitude by striking off to the less-visited southern and western shores. The town of Windermere (with its train station) and adjacent lakeside Bowness are best appreciated as stopovers to grab some food and equipment before moving on. Although it's just as busy, **Ambleside**—at the northern end of Lake Winderemere—makes a good base for touring the Southern Lakes; most local buses make connections here, and cheap accommodations abound. Elsewhere, **Coniston** village, while not in the same picturesque league as **Grasmere** or Hawkshead, is another great base for walks in the dramatic mountain surroundings.

BASICS

BUREAUX DE CHANGE
Banks in Windermere change money during normal bank opening hours, as does the post office (*see* Mail, *below).* The National Park Information Centres in Coniston, Bowness, Grasmere, Hawkshead, and Waterhead will also change money for a flat £3 fee (*see* Visitor Information, *below).*

LAUNDRY

Take care of your underwear and socks at **Ambleside Launderette** (Kelsick Rd., tel. 015394/32231; closed Thurs.). If you're staying at the hostel, the laundry and drying facilities there are handy. In Windermere try **Windermere Launderette** (19 Main Rd., tel. 015394/42326).

LUGGAGE STORAGE

Windermere Rail Station has a luggage-storage desk, open Monday–Saturday 10–5 and Sunday 10:45–5; the charge is £1.50 per bag.

MAIL

The post offices in **Windermere** (21 Crescent Rd., LA23 1AA, tel. 015394/43245) and **Ambleside** (Market Pl., LA22 9AA, tel. 015394/32267) both have a bureau de change.

VISITOR INFORMATION

There are two kinds of tourist offices in the Lake District: tourist information centers run by local tourist boards, and National Park Visitor Centres. Both often have offices on the same premises, so you'll usually be able to glean all the information you need in one stop. If you're interested in the outdoors, your best bets are the park centers, the most comprehensive of which is in Brockhole, though the offices listed below in Bowness, Coniston, and Grasmere are also particularly useful.

Most of the following offices are open daily 9:30–5:30 April–October; many offer currency exchange for a £3 fee: **Ambleside** (Central Buildings, Market Cross, tel. 015394/32582), also open November–March, daily 9–5; **Bowness-on-Windermere** (Glebe Rd., off A5074, tel. 015394/42895); **Brockhole National Park Visitor Centre** (on A591 between Ambleside and Windermere, tel. 015394/46601); **Coniston** (Ruskin Ave., tel. 015394/41533); **Grasmere** (Redbank Rd., tel. 015394/35245); **Hawkshead** (Main Car Park, tel. 015394/36525); **Waterhead** (Main Car Park, Borrans Rd., near Ambleside YHA hostel, tel. 015394/32729); and **Windermere** (The Gateway Centre, Victoria St., tel. 015394/46499), open year-round.

WHERE TO SLEEP

B&Bs in Ambleside and Windermere run from about £16 per person and should be reserved well in advance if you plan to visit in July or August. At other times of the year you'll survive without advance reservations. Anyone on a really tight budget might have to miss out on the prettiest of the lakeland villages unless they've made a hostel reservation—in places like Coniston and especially Grasmere, B&B prices can start at around £20. A bewildering lack of convenient campgrounds in the Windermere and Grasmere areas makes things difficult for the carless masses who want to sleep outdoors. Plan on long walks or bus rides to reach campsites. For more suggestions you can also pick up from a tourist office "Where to Stay in South Lakeland" (*see* Visitor Information *in* chapter Basics, *above*), which lists officially inspected properties.

AMBLESIDE • Ambleside YWCA (Iveing Cottage). Beds aren't any cheaper than at a regular B&B, but the dining room with white wooden tables and French windows is classy, the proprietors are helpful, and the rooms are clean. Singles, doubles, and dorm beds go for £13.50 per person. Both sexes are welcome (though the dorms aren't coed). *Old Lake Rd., LA22 0DT, tel. 015394/32340. From bus stop, turn left on Kelsick Rd., right on Lake Rd., veer left on Old Lake Rd. 35 beds. Curfew 11:30 PM. No credit cards.*

Linda's B&B. This place is an especially good deal if you're lucky enough to book the attic room, which sleeps three and costs a mere £8 per person. The other singles and doubles are £13 per person, though for a couple of pounds less, you can opt for a stay without breakfast. You can use the kitchen if you ask. *Shirland House, Compston Rd., LA22 9DJ, tel. 015394/32999. From bus stop, turn right on Kelsick Rd., right on Compston Rd. 5 rooms, none with bath. No credit cards.*

3 Cambridge Villas. In this lofty Victorian house in the heart of town, you can get a bright, charming room furnished with antiques for £16 per person, £18.50 with bath. English or vegetarian breakfast is included, and the spacious lounge has plenty of books. *Church St., LA23 9DL, tel. 015394/32307. 8 rooms, 4 with bath. No credit cards.*

CONISTON • The spacious, pretty rooms with private bath at **Orchard Cottage** (18 Yewdale Rd., tel. 015394/41373) can cost £21 per person in summer, no credit cards, though prices fall a little out of season. It's a similar story at **Shepherd's Villa Guest House** (Tilberthwaite Ave., tel. 015394/41337), a stone country house with a prime location on the edge of the village. Rooms run £16–£21 per person, depending on whether you want your own private shower; packed lunches are available for hikers and there's a garden for summer relaxing.

GRASMERE • Banerigg Guest House (Banerigg GH, Grasmere, tel.015394/35204) sits on the lake, ten minutes' walk from the town, a smashing no-smoking place with doubles for £40–£48, no credit cards. Other B&Bs in the center tend to cost £6–£10 or so more per room; the information office can let you know about vacancies.

HAWKSHEAD • The Queen's Head. One of the Lake District's prettiest villages also holds one of the Lake District's prettiest old inns, the black-and-white, timbered Queen's Head, sporting low-beamed ceilings, paneled walls, and cozy rooms that shout its 16th-century credentials. All the real atmosphere is downstairs—in the welcoming bar, or outside at tables fronting the sunny, traffic-free street. A splurge proposition, doubles here go for £70 to £80. *Main St., Hawkshead, LA22 0NS, tel. 015394/36271. From the parking lot and tourist office, follow the only road into Hawkshead, which becomes Main St. 13 rooms, 11 with bath.*

WINDERMERE AND BOWNESS • In Windermere, rows of B&Bs line the streets off Crescent Road; from the train station, walk left past the tourist office, turn left on Victoria Street, hang another left on Crescent Road, and start scouting on Beech, Birch, Oak, and Broad streets. Another good place to try is College Road. The tourist office can also help with securing lodging or letting you know who's got rooms available. B&Bs in neighboring Bowness, a large number of which are on Lake Road (the main road from Windermere) and its side streets, cost a bit more than those in Windermere. You can walk from the train station to Bowness in about 20 minutes, but look out for Bus 599, which runs between the two every 20 minutes in summer, hourly the rest of the year—jump on to save your legs.

Brendan Chase. This comfortable, well-maintained B&B is conveniently near the train station. The rooms are furnished with antiques, and some have views of the lake. Rooms cost £13.50–£25 per person, including English or vegetarian breakfast. *1–3 College Rd., LA23 IBU, tel. 015394/45638. From train station, turn left and walk downhill to Methodist Chapel. 8 rooms, 3 with bath. No credit cards.*

Broadlands Guest House. You'll find this house near the Queen's Park and the train station neat as a pin. Rooms cost £16–£20 a person, and the kitchen will cook breakfasts for vegetarians. *19 Broad St., LA23 2AB, tel. 015394/46532. From train station, turn left on High St., left on Main Rd. (which becomes Broad St.). 5 rooms, 3 with bath.*

The Haven. The location of this small no-smoking B&B is great—very close to town and the train station. Rooms are £16 per person, and one has its own shower. *10 Birch St., LA23 1EG, tel. 015394/44017. From train station, turn left on Victoria St., left on Crescent Rd., left on Birch St. 4 rooms, none with bath. No credit cards.*

Mortal Man. A lovely splurge, this 17th-century inn lies in a magnificent valley north of Windermere, well away from the bustle of the town. Guest rooms are fairly simple, but pleasantly decorated, and there's a relaxed atmosphere that's hard to beat, helped along by the welcoming staff. Doubles are £120, but the stiff price includes a full lakeland breakfast and dinner. *Troutbeck, 3 mi north of Windermere, LA23 1PL, tel. 015394/33193. Take the bus to Troutbeck from Windermere Station. 12 rooms with bath. Closed mid-Nov.–mid-Feb. No credit cards.*

HOSTELS

The Southern Lakes seem to have a hostel around every bend, so you'll never be far from a cheap bed if you plan ahead—definitely reserve ahead in summer or risk shelling out for a B&B. Some hostels close for the winter and for one or two days per week during spring and fall. Most of the Lakeland villages are so small that you won't have a hard time finding the signs pointing to the hostel. YHA also runs a shuttle service to its most popular hostels; call the Ambleside YHA (*see below*) for more information.

In addition to the hostels listed below, other YHA hostels in the area are **Coniston Coppermines** (Coppermines House, tel. 015394/41261); **Elterwater** (tel. 015394/37245); **Eskdale** (Boot, Holmrook, tel. 019467/23219); **Grasmere "Butterlip How"** (Easedale Rd., tel. 015394/35316); **Hawkshead** (Esthwaite Lodge, tel. 015394/36293); **High Close/Langdale** (Loughrigg, tel. 015394/37313); **Kendal** (118 Highgate, tel. 01539/724066); and **Patterdale** (Goldrill House, tel. 017684/82394).

Ambleside YHA. This hostel has the best amenities of the Lakelands hostels. Once a hotel, the hostel is large and noisy but amazingly well maintained. Each room has its own lock and you get your very own key. The Stray Travel coach (*see Bus Travel, in Chapter 1*) stops here four times a week in summer on its way to Edinburgh. Beds are £11.15. On site are a common room, luggage storage, snack shop, and a bike rental facility. There's a kitchen, too, plus a café serving cheap evening meals, though it's often full of school groups. *Waterhead, Cumbria LA22 0EU, tel. 015394/32304, fax 015394/34408. From tourist office, walk SE on Kelsick Rd., turn right on Lake Rd., and continue south 1 mi toward Waterhead; or take Bus 555/556 or 599 from Windermere and ask driver to stop at the hostel; or take free YHA shuttle bus from Windermere station. 226 beds. Reception open 7 AM–midnight. Curfew 11:30 PM. Laundry.*

Coniston (Holly How) YHA. Believe it or not—it's a quiet hostel! The rooms offer great views of the hills, and the setting in Coniston is very peaceful. They serve yummy vegetarian dishes in addition to traditional English grub. Beds cost £9.15. *Far End, Cumbria LA21 8DD, tel. 015394/41323, fax 015394/ 41803. From Coniston village, follow main road north toward Ambleside for ¼ mi; or take Bus 505 or 506. 60 beds. Reception open 8 AM–10 AM and 5 PM–10 PM. Curfew 11 PM, lockout 10–5. Closed Dec.– mid-Jan.; also mid-Jan.–Mar., May–June, and Oct.–Nov., open Fri.–Sun. only.*

Grasmere (Thorney How). This is the better of Grasmere's two hostels: It's smaller and twice as friendly. The building is the first hostel the YHA bought in 1931, and it's 335 years old. Friendly wardens with local info lend maps and make excellent sticky toffee pudding. Fall asleep on the lounge's couch— sigh—in front of a log fire. Beds are £9.15. *Easedale Rd., Thorney How LA22 9QW, tel. 015394/35591, fax 015394/35866. Walk ½ mi past Butterlip How Hostel, turn right at sign, and follow path for ¼ mi (the hostel is to left). 48 beds. Reception open 8:30 AM–10 AM and 5 PM–10:30 PM. Curfew 11 PM, lockout 10–5. Closed Jan.–mid-Feb.; also mid.-Feb.–mid-Mar. and Oct.–Dec., closed Tues. and Wed.*

Windermere YHA. The name's misleading: This hostel is actually in pretty Troutbeck Bridge, between Windermere and Ambleside. Large, bright rooms and gorgeous views of the lake and mountains are the hostel's best features; the bus ride from Windermere and the ¾-mi walk uphill are the bummers. Dorm beds cost £9.15. *High Cross, Bridge La., Troutbeck, Cumbria LA23 1LA, tel. 015394/43543, fax 015394/47165. From train/bus station, take Bus 555/556 to Troutbeck Bridge, then walk down main road, turn right at hostel sign, and climb uphill. 73 beds. Reception open 8 AM–10 AM and 5 PM–10 PM. Curfew 11 PM, lockout 10–1. Closed Nov.–Dec.*

CAMPING

The YHA has a camping barn network throughout the park—ask for a free brochure at National Park Information Centres or call 017687/72645 to check on availability. Camping barns provide out-of-the-way shelter for trekkers and campers. Basically just a dry place to sleep, these renovated barns have perks like coin-op electricity, running water, and toilets, as well as fresh milk and eggs! Prices start from £3.35 per person per night. Otherwise, farmers commonly set up campgrounds and charge a £1 or £2 usage fee. The "Caravan & Tent Guide to Cumbria and the Lake District," available at National Park Information Centres, gives comprehensive info and directions for official campgrounds in the area, all of which tend to cost quite a bit more, from £3–5 per person.

Coniston Hall Camp Site. It's not exactly in the wilderness, but this camping and caravan park on the edge of Coniston Water has a wide range of amenities, including hot-water taps, a food shop, laundry facilities, and canoes. The tent sites are £3 per person. *Coniston Hall, tel. 015394/41223. From the Catholic church, walk toward the lake and follow the signs. 200 sites. Toilets, showers. Closed Nov.–Mar.*

The Croft. This caravan and camping site near Hawkshead is so close to the village that many travelers head here first; as a result, it's often crowded and noisy. Tent sites (for two people) cost £9.50. A shop and laundry are on the premises. You can also rent mountain bikes here and explore the nearby Grizedale Forest. *N. Lonsdale Rd., tel. 015394/36374. From tourist office, walk east past parking lot. 85 sites. Toilets, showers. Closed mid-Nov.–mid-Mar.*

Low Wray. About 3 mi southwest of Ambleside on the road to Hawkshead, this campsite gets crowded, but it only costs £3 per person, and nearby Wray Castle (built in 1840 and now a college) lends a slight mystique to the grounds. *Wray Rd. End, tel. 015394/32810. From Ambleside, take Bus 505 or 506 to Wray Rd. End, which is ¾ mi from the sites (ask the driver—sometimes buses don't stop here, especially on weekends). 200 sites. Toilets, showers. Closed Oct.–Easter.*

FOOD

In Grasmere, **Langman's Delicatessen & Bakery** (Red Lion Sq., tel. 015394/35248) is a good place for fresh-baked goods, sandwiches, and coffee. And you can't leave without sampling the goods at **Sarah Nelson's Gingerbread Shop** (no phone), housed in a tiny cottage by the gate to the village church. Fine gingerbread is made from a 150-year-old recipe (the recipe is kept in a local bank vault). In Coniston,

Bridge House Café (Broughton Rd., tel. 015394/41278) serves homemade soups, pizzas, and salads until 5 PM, while the public bar at the **Sun Hotel** (tel. 015394/41248)—200 yards out of town, uphill from the bridge—has the best pub meals in or out of town. In Hawkshead, **Whig's** (The Square, tel. 015394/36614), closed Thursday and January, serves (what else?) *whigs*—delicious seeded rolls baked from a centuries-old recipe—plus a variety of breakfasts and light lunches. The 16th-century **Queen's Head** (tel. 015394/36271) is bang in the center of the village, too, and though its rooms are pricey (*see above*), the inn's bar meals, served on garden seats outside in summer, are a good deal.

AMBLESIDE

Market day in Ambleside is Wednesday, so stock up on picnic supplies straight from the food stalls. Otherwise, visit Ambleside's **Spar** supermarket, open daily until 10 PM, on Compston Road, where it turns into Rydal Road. **Pippins** (10 Lake Rd., tel. 015394/31338) serves English breakfasts, filled baguettes, and burgers. **Apple Pie Eating House & Bakery** (Rydal Rd., tel. 015394/33679) is one of those fun-lovin', plate-clankin' joints with a line stretching out the door. Lunch items include spicy chicken and a long list of yummy pastries. **Zeffirelli's Wholefood Pizzeria** (Compston Rd., tel. 015394/33845) creates vegetarian pizzas in addition to running the only movie theater in town—ask about their all-in-one dinner-and-cinema ticket. The best place to treat yourself in town is the **Glass House** (Rydal Rd., tel. 015394/32137), an old mill converted into a trendy restaurant. Dinner costs upwards of £15–20 a head, though early bird and lunch deals cut the price. Hikers should fuel up with great bar meals at Elterwater's **Britannia Inn** (tel. 015394/37210), an old pub 4 mi west of Ambleside on the B5343. Two miles farther along B5343, the **Old Dungeon Ghyll Hotel** (Great Langdale, tel. 015394/37272) is one of the most picturesque hostelries in the region. Once hikers finish off their homemade soup or hearty pie or stew, the stone floor and wooden beams echo to the clatter of boots. Bus 516 from Ambleside comes out past Eltwerwater to Langdale two or three times a day.

BOWNESS AND WINDERMERE

In Bowness, **Rastelli** (Lake Rd., tel. 015394/44227), closed Wednesday and February, serves the best pizzas in town. For filling pub food you can't beat the **Hole in t'Wall** (Fallbarrow Rd., tel. 015394/43488), an atmospheric joint with flagstone floors, Cumbrian ales, and home cooking. Restaurants in Windermere tend to be expensive, but **Renoir's Coffee Shop** (Main Rd., tel. 015394/44863) is a cheerful little blue-and-yellow café with big cappuccinos and plenty of lunch specials; try the turkey breast with red-currant relish, roll, salad, and coleslaw. For fresh fruit and vegetables, join the local mob at **Booths** supermarket (tel. 015394/46114), right outside the train and bus depot.

EXPLORING THE SOUTHERN LAKES

Easy access to the trails is probably the best aspect of the Southern Lakes, but make sure you have waterproof clothing and hiking boots before you set off. If you don't feel like exploring alone or would like to learn about the area as you go, the National Park Information Centres are the place to find out about free or cheap (£3–£4) guided walks and bicycle tours, as well as other events.

WORTH SEEING

Although the Southern Lake District has an ample share of museums and historic sites, the real attractions are the lakes, rivers, fells, valleys, and crags; Wordsworth himself refused to keep a desk, and composed his poetry out-of-doors, much of it in this region. Hikes through sheep pastures and over mountains will lead you away from the summer crowds—at the height of the season, the Wordsworth sights around Grasmere are tour-bus-arama and you may be better off reading his poetry and closing your eyes. Note that even July has occasional rainy days, which might make the museums and tea shops seem more appealing.

BROCKHOLE • A magnificent lakeside mansion with terraced gardens sloping down to the water houses the official **Lake District National Park Visitor Centre** at Brockhole, 3 mi northwest of Windermere. The center offers a fine range of exhibitions about the Lake District, including useful interpretative displays on local ecology, flora, and fauna. The gardens are at their best in the spring, when daffodils cascade over the lawns and the azaleas bloom. Park activities include lectures, guided walks, and demonstrations of fascinating, traditional lakeland crafts like dry-stone-wall building. There's also a well-stocked bookstore—just the place to pick up hiking guides and maps—and a café-restaurant. *Ambleside Rd., near Windermere, tel. 015394/46601. Take Bus 555/556 from Windermere train station or the ferry from Ambleside, the service operated by Windermere Lake Cruises (tel. 015394/43360, £3.40 return). Admission free. Open Easter–late Oct., daily 10–5.*

POETRY, PROSE, AND THE LAKES

The beauty of the Southern Lake District whetted the creativity of many a famous poet and artist. Here's a quick rundown of some of the writers about whom you will hear—again and again—in your wanderings:

William Wordsworth (1770–1850), one of the first English Romantics, redefined poetry by replacing the mannered style of his forerunners with a more conversational, succinct, and emotional style. Many of his greatest works, such as "The Prelude" and "Tintern Abbey," draw directly from his personal experiences of the Lake District, where he spent the first 20 and last 50 years of his life. Wordsworth was incredibly influential, having a great impact on Keats, Shelley, Byron, and countless others.

John Ruskin (1819–1900) was to art criticism what Thomas Carlyle was to historicism: an impassioned champion of new ways of seeing. He defended contemporary artists like William Turner and the Pre-Raphaelites despite the widespread scorn of his peers. His three volumes of Modern Painters changed the role of the art critic from that of approver or naysayer to that of interpreter.

Thomas De Quincey (1785–1859) wrote essays whose impressionistic style influenced a host of 19th-century writers, including Poe and Baudelaire. His most famous work, "Confessions of an English Opium Eater" (1822), is an imaginative and comic memoir of his young life, which indeed included a massive opium addiction. He settled in Grasmere in 1809.

Beatrix Potter (1866–1943) never had a formal education; instead she spent her childhood studying nature. Her love of biology and the outdoors, and Lakeland scenery in particular, influenced her best-known, charmingly illustrated children's books, The Tale of Peter Rabbit, The Tale of Jemima Puddle-Duck, and Johnny Town Mouse.

CONISTON • Coniston provides a welcome refuge from the commotion of other Southern Lake villages, and the lake itself is a good place to rent a rowboat and while away a few hours. Many come to climb the famous **Old Man of Coniston** (2,635 ft), and tracks lead up from the village past an old mine to the peak, which you can reach in about two hours, though longer routes are also possible (*see* Outdoor Activities, *below*). The fierce writing of radical John Ruskin, Coniston's most famous visitor and resident, appeals to fewer souls than the poetry of Wordsworth, which means that few tour groups clutter the village, and you can see things at a relaxed pace. Ruskin's grave lies in the village churchyard, identified by a well-worked Celtic cross. In summer between 9 and 5, the Coniston Rambler (Bus 505 or 506) lumbers along to Coniston from Windermere or Ambleside, about once every half hour.

Across the lake from Coniston village, John Ruskin's house, **Brantwood,** contains many of his personal belongings, writings, drawings, and watercolors. A video on his life shows the lasting influence of the revolutionary thinker. The peaceful view of Coniston Water from Brantwood and the woodland walks through the 250-acre grounds are worth the trip, and it's not surprising that Ruskin boasted his estate had the best prospect in the district. He lived here until his death in 1900. Unfortunately, the house itself, while enlivened with a lantern window and some neoclassic ornaments, is a bit on the dull side. The on-site **Jumping Jenny** tearoom and restaurant (named after Ruskin's boat) serves homemade pastries and has a gorgeous view from the terrace, and the upstairs **Coach House Gallery** features local artists' work. To get here from Coniston Pier take the MV *Ruskin* ferry (£3.60 return) or the lovely antique steam yacht *Gondola* (£4.50 return). Otherwise, Bus 505 or 506 from Hawkshead stops at Coniston; from here follow signs for 1½ mi to Brantwood. *Coniston, tel. 015394/41396. Admission to house and gardens £4, gardens only £2, or combined house, gardens, and ferry £7. Open mid-Mar.–mid-Nov., daily 11–5:30; mid-Nov.–mid-Mar., Wed.–Sun. 11–4.*

GRASMERE • A ghost town in the winter, Grasmere metamorphoses into Wordsworthland—a hive of buses and duty-bound ex-poetry students—in the summer. This was Wordsworth's home during his most creative periods, and let's just say you won't be wandering lonely as a cloud through his former haunts. You shouldn't miss out on a visit though, since its grey-stone houses, riverside setting, and shady churchyard are all extremely appealing, while the lake itself is only a short walk from the village. The four-mile circuit of the lake and neighbouring Rydal Water is one of the finer walks in the Southern Lakes. Budget accommodations in town are hard to come by, so unless you've lucked into an especially good deal or are booked at one of the two hostels, Grasmere is best seen on a day trip.

Dove Cottage and Wordsworth Museum. This two-building complex was originally an inn called the Dove and Olive Branch when it was built in 1600. Wordsworth spent his "lyric years" here, from 1799 to 1808, along with his sister Dorothy, who was also a writer; his wife Mary; her sisters Sara and Joanna; three children (two of whom died here); extended houseguests Samuel Coleridge and Thomas De Quincey; and miscellaneous visitors. The seven-room house was constantly bustling and overflowing with people until Wordsworth decided to move to a larger one in 1808, leaving the place to De Quincey, who moved in with his thousands of books. Inside the house, which has some interesting 19th-century household features (like a pantry that's still kept cold by a stream running beneath the slate floor), are some of Wordsworth's personal items. Both the cottage and adjacent museum are painstakingly cared for by a young staff well versed in all things Wordsworthian, and your visit to the cottage begins with a guided tour. One ticket admits you to both Dove Cottage and the Wordsworth Museum, and gives you a 15% discount to Rydal Mount (*see below*) and Wordsworth House (*see* Cockermouth, in Northern Lakes, *below*). In summer there are free poetry readings and lectures. *A591, Grasmere, tel. 015394/ 35544. From National Park Information Centre, turn right on Red Bank Rd., right on Stock La., right on A591. Bus 555 between Ambleside and Keswick runs past. Admission to cottage and museum £4.80. Open mid-Feb.–mid-Jan., daily 9:30–5:30.*

Rydal Mount. The original 16th-century cottage on this site was rebuilt in the 18th century and eventually became Wordsworth's last home: Between 1813 and 1850, Rydal Mount saw Wordsworth become Poet Laureate, a conservative, and locally employed as Distributor of Stamps. Wordsworth himself designed the gardens and dedicated some verse to them. Admission includes a 20% discount for Dove Cottage (*see above*). *A591, between Grasmere and Ambleside, tel. 015394/33002. From Grasmere, take Bus 555 and alight at first stop. Admission £3.50. Open Mar.–Oct., daily 9:30–5; Nov.–Feb., Wed.–Mon. 10–4. Closed 3 wks in Jan.*

HAWKSHEAD • Hawkshead is a picturesque village that, nevertheless, feels like one big souvenir shop. Figurines of farm animals in Victorian clothing appear in every shop window, delighting the Potter pilgrims who tread the cobblestone streets almost year-round. The "Coniston Rambler" (Bus 505 or 506) stops here en route from Coniston to Ambleside.

Beatrix Potter Gallery. This small shrine to the creator of Peter Rabbit is in the former office of her husband, attorney William Heelis. On display is a rotating collection of Potter's original drawings and illustrations, as well as excellent biographical displays. *Main St., see directions for Queen's Head, above, tel. 015394/36355. Admission £2.90. Open Easter–Oct., Sun.–Thurs. 10:30–4.*

Hawkshead Grammar School. This school was founded in 1585 and closed in 1909—and guess what? William Wordsworth was one of its illustrious alums. The little vandal even carved his name into one of the desks. Some of the young scholar's works are under glass on the second floor. *Main St., across from tourist office, tel. 015394/36525. Admission £2. Open Easter–Oct., Mon.–Sat. 10–12:30 and 1:30–5, Sun. 1–5.*

Hill Top. This was the first and probably most beloved of Beatrix Potter's 15 houses and farms in the Lakelands. Many of Potter's domestic possessions remain, giving visitors a fairly authentic picture of her life here, during which time she wrote many of the Peter Rabbit stories. Don't leave without taking a peek at the garden, glorious in bloom during spring and summer. The house is in Near Sawrey, about 2 mi south of Hawkshead. From Hawkshead, Ambleside, Windermere, Coniston, or Waterhead, take Bus 505 or 506 to Hilltop; from April through October there are hourly buses from 9 AM to 5 PM. *Near Sawrey, tel. 015394/36269. Admission £4. Open Easter–Oct., Sat.–Wed. 11–4:30.*

OUTDOOR ACTIVITIES

Hiking and walking are the area's great draws, even though there is no such thing as a guaranteed rain-free day. Tourist offices have plenty of maps and suggestions for local walks; you should definitely tap into their resources. Most trails are well marked and near hostels and major villages. For recommended guides *see* Publications *in* Basics, *above*. Mountain biking is permitted only on bridleways and not on public footpaths. Biking guides are available in most bookshops and tourist offices, or ask at one of the cycle rental outfits (*see* Getting Around, *above*) about bike tours.

AMBLESIDE

Ambleside is the base for some of the region's best—and most difficult—hikes. Most are highlighted in the Footprint Guides' *Walks Around Ambleside* (£3), available at the tourist office. The trails head off in all directions and interconnect, so the options are endless; it's a good idea to arm yourself with a detailed map. The 6½-mi circular walk from Ambleside north to the bare slopes of **Loughrigg Fell** (1,100 ft) goes right by Wordsworth's home in Rydal and takes three to four hours. Near Loughrigg Fell, you'll get a ter-rific 360-degree view of Lake Windermere, Rydal Water, and Ambleside. Hardier hikers head out west to the **Langdale Pikes,** offering some incredible views from its high ridge; the circuit stretches almost 5 mi and ascends 2,400 ft. The three- to five-hour hike begins at the New Dungeon Ghyll Hotel, located on B5343 (take Bus 516 from Ambleside to Dungeon Ghyll).

CONISTON

The Footprint Guides' *Walks Around Coniston* (£3) outlines a variety of walks around the town of Conis-ton and Coniston Water. The most challenging is the 9-mi round-trip path from the village center that climbs up past Coniston Coppermines YHA hostel (*see* Where to Sleep, *above*) to Coniston Fell's three main summits—the **Old Man, Swirl How,** and **Wetherlam.** What starts as a gentle valley walk soon becomes much tougher as you climb up the rocky side of the Old Man, passing defunct mines and a scintillating small tarn before reaching the craggy summit. The views from the Old Man are magnifi-cent—on a clear day, as far south to the coast as Morecambe Bay. From here it's a relatively easy walk along the windswept grassy tops of Swirl How and Wetherlam, before you descend a steep, boulder-strewn valley to Coniston. This route could easily take up a whole day of slow rambling.

GRASMERE

Several fun, short-distance hikes begin just north of Ambleside in Grasmere. The steep 3½-mi round-trip trail to the rocky summit of **Helm Crag** takes about two hours and is easily reached from either of Grasmere's hostels. From the Grasmere bus stop, walk east on Easedale Road past the old quarries to the peaks—successively known as The Lion and the Lamb, Lady at the Organ, and The Lion. The 4½-mi round-trip path to **Easedale Tarn,** a still-water pond, follows the first part of the Helm Crag route and continues past Easedale Tarn and the Sour Milk Gill waterfall. Quick walkers can do the relatively easy circuit in about three hours.

WINDERMERE AND BOWNESS

Windermere and Bowness are usually bustling with people just passing through; most hikers base themselves in Ambleside. Still, the Windermere/Bowness area has a few good walks with terrific views of Lake Windermere. The 2½-mi round-trip climb from Windermere to **Orrest Head** (784 ft) is the sim-plest hike in the area and offers a fine panorama of the lake and the villages along the shore. The walk begins at the Windermere tourist office. About five marked walks begin in Bowness, one of the nicest being a 6-mi circuit south along the shore to **Rosthwaite Farm,** east to Winster, and north back to Bow-ness Bay. Much of the walk is through secluded pastures. To get out on the lake itself, head down to the piers at Bowness and jump on one of the cruise boats run by **Windermere Lake Cruises** (tel. 015394/43360), which connect with the visitor center at Brockhole, and Ambleside, among other places. Ticket prices vary, but a Freedom-of-the-Lake ticket (£9.50) gives you unlimited travel on any Windermere ser-vice for 24 hours.

NORTHERN LAKES

If the Southern Lakes strike you as a tad too crowded, you'll welcome the Northern Lakes' wide-open spaces, wonderful hiking trails, and slower pace. The remote region also has England's richest topography: The mountains are the nation's highest, and the lakes are its deepest. Fern-fringed streams, wild purple foxgloves, hedgerows full of dog roses, and green-slate cottages add their quiet charm to the landscape. The beautiful, well-equipped town of **Keswick** (pronounced KES-ick) is a popular base from which to explore the area, particularly the spectacular valley of **Borrowdale,** to the south, whose steep fells are a dramatic sight. **Cockermouth** is an attractive town, much less visited than Keswick, whose cheap and charming B&Bs make it a good alternative. Public transportation in the region is adequate, but if you want to reach some out-of-the-way lakes and hills, prepare to hike.

BASICS

BUREAUX DE CHANGE

You can change money at Keswicks' banks, the Keswick tourist office (*see* Visitor Information, *below*), and at the post office in Cockermouth (*see* Mail, *below*).

LAUNDRY

In Keswick, there's **Keswick Launderette** (James Ct., next to Co-op supermarket, no phone), though most hikers use the town youth hostel's laundry and drying room.

Don't forget proper hiking aids—if you're doing some rock-scrambling, mud-wading, or toe-wedging fell climbing, you should have an Ordnance Survey map and a compass (and biscuits).

MAIL

The post office in **Keswick** (48 Main St., CA12 5JJ, tel. 017687/72269) has a bureau de change, a color copier, and fax and E-mail facilities, and sells Stagecoach and National Express bus tickets. It's open Monday–Saturday 8:30–8, Sunday 10:30–5; shorter hours January–March. In **Cockermouth** the post office (18 Main St., tel. 01900/822277) is open Monday–Saturday 9–5:30.

VISITOR INFORMATION

Keswick's combined National Park Visitor Centre and Tourist Information Centre (Moot Hall, Market Sq., tel. 017687/72645) is open year-round, daily 9:30–5, July and August until 7. The "Keswick Visitors Guide" (£1) has local accommodations details, and a map of town costs 20p. The office also has valuable suggestions on the best ways to explore the area or can book you onto one of their guided walks (from £4 per person) led by local experts (Easter–Oct., daily at 10:15 AM from the tourist office). **Cockermouth Tourist Centre** (Town Hall, Market St., tel. 01900/822634) is not connected with a National Park Visitor Centre but has a friendly staff and some useful information. Smaller settlements with joint info centers include **Pooley Bridge** (The Square, tel. 017684/86530), **Seatoller** (Seatoller Barn, tel. 017687/77294), and **Ullswater** (Main Car Park, Glenridding, tel. 017684/82414).

WHERE TO SLEEP

Unless you plan to stay in one of Keswick's cheaper B&Bs, you'll save money by booking ahead at one of the numerous hostels in the Northern Lakes. Get the free "Cumbria Western Lakes and Coast Accommodation Guide" for information on B&Bs in the remoter areas.

BORROWDALE • The two youth hostels (Derwentwater and Borrowdale, *see* Hostels, *below*) are the least expensive options in beautiful Borrowdale, but there are also a few homely B&Bs on the B5289 road, south of Keswick. The tiny hamlet of Rosthwaite has the most choice, plus the excellent **Royal Oak Hotel** (tel. 017687/77214). The Royal Oak relieves you of £40–£43 per person, but then hands over a comfy room with shower, use of the cozy lounge and bar, an egg-and-bacon breakfast, *and* a three-course dinner.

COCKERMOUTH • Although it's quite far from any lake, the historic small town of Cockermouth has both Wordsworth's birthplace and the Jennings Brewery, as well as some affordable accommodations. **Manor House** (23 St. Helens St., tel. 01900/822416) is a lovingly restored 1712 house, just a minute's walk from town center. The charming rooms are £17 per person, no credit cards, and Belinda will gladly cook a special breakfast for fellow vegetarians.

KESWICK • The cheaper B&Bs in Keswick cluster around the corner of Southey and Blencathra streets, about ¼ mi from Main Street; from the tourist office, walk up St. John's Street, turn left on Station Street, then right on Southey Street. A higher class of B&Bs (£15–£20 per person) lines Stanger Street; from the bus stop on The Headlands, turn left on Tithe Barn Street, right on Main Street, and left on Stanger Street.

Bluestones Guest House. Bluestones's convenient location and spotless rooms are a welcome sight after a day of hiking, though the beds aren't the best. Rooms start at £15 per person, £19 en suite. *7 Southey St., CA12 4EG, tel. 017687/74237. From St. John's St., turn left on Station St., right on Southey St. 5 rooms, 1 with shower. No credit cards.*

Bridgedale Guest House. Check into the Bridgedale for a cheap sleep in clean rooms in an 18th-century cottage. Various prices let you stick to your budget—from a bed-only rate (£12) to top-of-the-range room-with-shower-and-breakfast (£18). *101 Main St., opposite Co-op market, tel. 017687/73914. From bus stop, turn left on Tithe Barn St., left on Main St. 7 rooms, 1 with bath. No credit cards.*

Lane's End Guest House. On a quiet corner just seconds from the town center, John and Wendy Harvey and two cats keep a small, congenial house with all sorts of modern conveniences—TVs, tea/coffeemakers, and your own shower (in the corner of your room). At £16.50 per person, you'll be glad you passed the flurry of B&Bs on Station Road. *4 High St., CA12 5AQ, tel. 017687/74436. From tourist office, walk east on Main St. (which becomes St. John's St.), turn right on High St. 3 rooms, 1 with bath. No credit cards.*

LOWESWATER • **Kirkstile Inn.** This 16th-century inn stands 7 mi south of Cockermouth in lovely, quiet surroundings. There's a cozy pub downstairs, with a roaring fire in winter, and 10 rooms upstairs, arranged along a long, oak-beamed corridor—you'll pay £50–£60 per room, depending on the time of year. The rooms are all simple, with rather garish floral carpets, but they're cool in summer, and well-heated in winter, while the beds are supremely comfortable—just the thing after a day's walking. There's decent food available in the bar, and you better enjoy it because there's nowhere else to eat nearby. The inn is quite tricky to find, so phone for directions. *Loweswater, CA13 ORU, tel. 01900/85219. 10 rooms, 7 with bath.*

HOSTELS

It's always wise to phone ahead, either to book a bed during the summer when backpackers and bus-loads of screaming school kids fill the Northern Lakes' hostels, or to make sure the hostel is open during the other seasons. Besides what's reviewed below, other YHA hostels in the area include: **Carrock Fell** (High Row Cottage, Haltcliffe, tel. 016974/78325); **Honister Hause** (Seatoller, tel. 017687/77267); **Keswick YHA** (Keswick, tel. 017687/72484); and **Thirlmere** (The Old School, Stanah Cross, tel. 017687/73224). Some are unreachable by car but lie right along long-distance hiking routes; tourist offices can help you figure out which ones are close to where you'll be.

Borrowdale (Longthwaite) YHA. The sunny dining room and comfortable lounge testify that this hostel was designed and built as a hostel, rather than being converted from old stables or something worse. The red-cedarwood construction and the laid-back staff will remind you of summer camp. Beds are £10.15. *Longthwaite, tel. 017687/77257, fax 017687/77393. From Keswick, take Borrowdale Bus 79 to the hostel turnoff just outside Longthwaite; or follow riverside path from Seatoller parking lot. 91 beds. Reception 8 AM–10 AM and 5 PM–10 PM. Curfew 11 PM, lockout 10–1. Closed Jan.–mid-Feb.*

Buttermere YHA. The building's quiet rooms overlook Buttermere and the Scale Force (a waterfall). Bring food—the shop has mainly canned food, and Buttermere consists of a café and two pubs. Beds are £9.15. *King George VI Memorial Hostel, Cumbria CA13 9XA, tel. 017687/70245, fax 017687/70231. From Keswick, take Honister Rambler Bus 77 or 77A to Buttermere and walk south on B5289; building is on the left 50 yards up the hill. 71 beds. Reception open 5 PM–10:30 PM. Curfew 11 PM, lockout 10–5. Open daily Apr.–Aug.; Sept.–Oct., closed Mon.; Jan.–Mar., closed Sun. and Mon.*

Cockermouth YHA. This spotless, cheerful hostel is within a 17th-century water mill, set of course on a picturesque wooded riverbank. Evening meals and packed lunches are available, or you can use the kitchen to make your own. The peaceful retreat has beautiful views, an easygoing warden, and few school groups. Beds are £7.50. *Double Mills, Cockermouth, Cumbria, CA13 ODS, tel. 01900/822561. From town center, take footpath north along the river. 28 beds. Reception open 8 AM–10 AM and 5 PM–10 PM. Curfew 11 PM, lockout 10–5. Kitchen. Closed Nov.–Feb. and closed Wed. throughout the yr.*

Derwentwater YHA. This hostel on the lake occupies a grand 200-year-old mansion. With 15 acres of grounds in a choice location midway between busy Keswick and the village of Grange, in Borrowdale, it's a primo place to crash for a day or two. Beds cost £10.15. *Barrow House, Borrowdale, Cumbria CA12 5UR, tel. 017687/77246, fax 017687/77396. From Keswick walk south 2 mi on B5289 toward Borrowdale; or catch Stagecoach Cumberland Bus 79. 95 beds. Reception open 8 AM–10 AM and 1 PM– 10 PM. Curfew 11 PM, lockout 10–1.*

Wastwater YHA. Once you finally arrive—Gosforth, the nearest bus stop, is 5 mi away—plan to stay for a while to enjoy the quiet, take a dip into the Lakelands' deepest waters (brrrrr), or climb England's highest peak (Scafell Pike). This hostel makes the best base for serious hikers and climbers planning to tackle Scafell and the Gables. The half-timber building, which dates back to 1829, has comfortable beds for £9.15. The warden has accumulated a 3,000-book library, in case you should get bored on a rainy day. *Wasdale Hall, Wasdale, Cumbria CA20 1ET, tel. 019467/26222. From Gosforth, walk, drive, or hitch east on the road to Nether Wasdale. 50 beds. Reception open 8 AM–10 AM and 5 PM–10 PM. Curfew 11 PM, lockout 10–5. Closed Nov.–Dec., and Tues.–Wed. Jan.–Mar. and Sept.–Oct.*

CAMPING

It's easier to find a quiet, out-of-the-way place to pitch a tent in the Northern Lakes than in the southern region. Apart from the sites listed below, and all the other official sites in the region, many farmers allow you to camp on their land, provided you're quiet, discreet, and clean; always ask local farmers before setting up and expect to pay a pound or two for the night.

Castlerigg Hall Caravan and Camping Park. Bus 555/556 brings you to this well-equipped campsite away from the frenzy. The site has a shop, showers, and thrilling views of Derwentwater from the high slopes of Rakefoot. They serve a full breakfast for £3. Sites are £3.60 per person. *Castlerigg Hall, near Keswick, tel. 017687/72437. From Rakefoot Rd. bus stop, walk ⅓ mi uphill to Castlerigg Hall (it's on your right). 120 sites. Toilets, showers. Closed mid-Nov.–Easter.*

Gatesgarth Farm. The rugged mountaineer will find this a great base for venturing to Hay Stacks, Fleetwood Pike, and the Gables. Less rugged types can just hang out in the valley stream with the black lambs. Sites cost £2 per person. *Tel. 017687/70256. From Buttermere, follow lakeside path to Gatesgarth; or walk 2 mi south on B5289 and turn right on path just before farm parking signs. 15 sites. Closed Nov.–Mar.*

Wasdale Head. This National Trust campground is the perfect base for climbing Scafell Pike. A little shop, a telephone, and a shower/toilet/laundry facility mean that you don't have to absolutely rough it. Sites are £3 per person. No reservations are accepted. *Tel. 019467/26220. From Ravenglass, take Ravenglass & Eskdale Rail to Eskdale (Dalegarth), walk north on Giggle Alley Walk to Wasdale Head, then walk along western bank of Wastwater to Wasdale Head. 120 sites. Toilets, showers. Closed Nov.–Mar.*

FOOD

Keswick offers the greatest variety of dining options in the Northern Lakes. In the smaller villages, you'll need to choose between a pub, a tea shop, or the greengrocer.

COCKERMOUTH

Norham Coffeehouse and Restaurant. The ample menu includes brie-and-kiwi sandwiches, various soups, and home-baked treats. On the rare sunny day, you can lunch in the garden courtyard. *73 Main St., tel. 01900/824330. Closes at 5 PM, closed Sun.*

KESWICK

Keswick is the Northern Lakes' equivalent of a sprawling metropolis and has the area's best restaurants and markets. If you're here on Saturday, visit the bustling market, opposite the tourist center, for fresh food straight from the farm. **Lakes Shopping** (tel. 017687/72715), a well-stocked though somewhat pricey grocery store, is right next to the town's bus stop. You'll find a great selection of staples and dried fruit at **Sundance Wholefoods** (33 Main St., tel. 017687/74712). The best restaurants are right in the center of town along Main Street and on Lake Road just off Borrowdale Road.

Abraham's Café Tea Room. Inside George Fisher's outdoor equipment shop, this casual eatery is open daily for nourishing snacks and meals (including a vegetarian choice). *2 Borrowdale Rd., tel. 017687/ 72178. Borrowdale Rd. runs off from the central Market Place.*

Lake Road Inn. This cozy, old-fashioned pub has a surprisingly varied menu. The usual fare includes a prawn and apple platter, locally caught Borrowdale trout with white wine and parsley sauce, and inventive pasta dishes, all for under a fiver. *Lake Rd., tel. 017687/72404. From tourist office, head south on Borrowdale Rd., turn right onto Lake Rd.*

Loose Box Pizzeria. The name refers to the fact that the building was formerly a horse stable. The pizza quattro stagioni and the salmon-and-spinach lasagna are especially excellent. *King's Arms Courtyard, tel. 017687/72083. Off Main St., just SW of tourist office.*

Maysons. Friendly and casual Maysons has the tastiest cheap food in the Northern Lakes. Satisfying dishes include the garlic, mushroom, and broccoli bake and the vegetarian pizza. They also serve a variety of curries and specialty salads to please carnivores, vegetarians, and vegans alike. *33 Lake Rd., tel. 017687/74104. From tourist office, head south on Borrowdale Rd., turn right on Lake Rd. Closes at 5 PM; June–Sept. at 9 PM*

OUTDOOR ACTIVITIES

Typical tourist attractions are nearly nonexistent in the Northern Lakes as people come to walk, hike, and explore the countryside instead. Because most buses stop in Keswick, you'll probably have to stop here at some point. Luckily, there are good hikes in the surrounding mountains.

The Northern Lakes have longer, more ambitious hikes than the village-oriented Southern Lakes. National Trust trails are generally well marked and easy to follow, but a good trail map definitely helps. The "Footprint" maps (£3 each) give detailed descriptions of the best hikes in the area. The "Lakeland Leisure Walks" series (25p each) shows easy walks and nature trails. Paul Buttle, local fell expert and eccentric, has also published several books with excellent hiking info.

The highest peaks in England—**Scafell Pike, Scafell, Great Gable,** and **Green Gable**—are best accessed from **Seathwaite** (a 1½-mi walk from Seatoller, accessible on Stagecoach Cumberland Bus 79) or **Wasdale Head** (at the north end of Wastwater, unreachable by public transport). This largely volcanic area west of the major villages has a stark character that brings out serious hikers. Even more remote and untrammeled are the pristine lakes **Ennerdale Water** and the smaller **Loweswater,** both offering a reprieve from civilization—no cars can come within 3 mi of Ennerdale Water. To reach Ennerdale from Buttermere, hike a half mile west over Red Pike through Ennerdale Forest to Gillerthwaite (site of the Ennerdale hostel). To reach the hamlet of Loweswater (and its splendid Kirkstile Inn, *see* Where To Sleep, *above*), walk 4 mi north from Buttermere along the western shore of Crummock Water (which, incidentally, has the Lake District's best swimming).

BUTTERMERE

For an easy, extremely enjoyable walk with views of **Buttermere's** many waterfalls and prominent peaks, take a stroll around the lake. Though it requires a little scrambling over rock piles and splashing through little streams, most of the path is smooth. The 4-mi circuit takes about two hours. The medium-difficulty, circular, 6-mi hike to **Hay Stacks,** a series of hills named for their resemblance to Monet's paintings, heads south from Buttermere and goes by some nifty waterfalls. After passing the Hay Stacks' plateau, the path descends through **Scarth Gap** down to Buttermere. You can return by walking to the farm at **Gatesgarth** or heading north along the lakeside to Buttermere. Another path ascends from Buttermere village to **Red Pike, High Stile,** and **High Crag,** which form an imposing peaked ridge southwest of the village. The steep trail is rocky, slippery, and made up of loose shale in some places (wear strong boots). Some say the view from Red Pike is the best in the valley.

COCKERMOUTH

Though it's not on one of the lakes, Cockermouth wins points as a handsome, historic town with scenic surroundings and few tourists. Pick up the "Walks Around the Town" (50p) or "Walks from Cockermouth" (50p) brochures from the tourist center for details of walks around the area. While in town, you can visit **Wordsworth House** (Main St., tel. 01900/824805), where the poet and his siblings were born; admission is £2.80 and the house is open Easter–October, weekdays 11–5; also Saturday 11–5 during July and August. The 1½-hour tour of **Jennings Brewery** (Brewery Lane, tel. 01900/823214) will demystify things like the *mash tun* and *hop back,* and will introduce you to their potent *sneck lifter.* Tours cost £3 per person, and you should book in advance.

KESWICK

The 4-mi walk from the Keswick tourist office to **Castlerigg Stone Circle** and back takes about 2½ hours. It's a brooding, dramatic spot, ringed by peaks and ranged by sheep, with the stone circle itself about 100 ft in diameter and 5,000 years old. The stone alignment suggests it may have been a calendar, but its origins remain a guessing game. The "Lakeland Leisure Walks" brochure KW-4 (25p) is a good way to plan your trip.

The 3-mi, 1½-hour walk to **Friar's Crag** from Keswick's tourist office takes you along the Derwentwater Lake and up the 530-ft Castlehead. Saint Herbert lived on an island in the lake and, after his death, Friar's Crag became the launching point of pilgrimages by monks. "Lakeland Leisure Walks" brochure KW-1 (25p) is a useful guide here.

The 6-mi walk from **Hawes End** to **Cat Bells, Maiden Moor,** and **High Spy,** ending in the village of **Rosthwaite,** often gets crowded, but it's a lovely ridge hike all the same. Cat Bells rises 2,200 ft above Derwentwater (Maiden Moor and High Spy are slightly smaller peaks). Take a 15-minute Keswick Launch ferry (75p single) from Keswick to Hawes End. Begin the hike there and return via the Seatoller–Keswick Bus 79.

ULLSWATER

Ullswater, a beautiful, elongated lake north of Windermere, is blissfully free from crowds. Bus 517 (a.k.a. the Kirkstone Rambler) travels from Bowness to Penrith through Glenridding and Patterdale and along the north shore of Ullswater. You can ask to be let off anywhere along the route. The village of **Glenridding,** at the southwestern corner of the lake, is the

The daffodils immortalized in Wordsworth's famous poem can be found in Gowbarrow Park on the west side of Ullswater.

best place to begin. The easy walk south to **Lanty's Tarn** (Lanty is a local nickname for Lancelot) takes less than an hour, though you can continue all the way up beautiful Grisedale to the far bigger **Grisedale Tarn,** 3 mi from Glenridding. On the northern side of Ullswater, the 65-ft waterfall **Aira Force** sits within a forestlike glen on a 3-mi path from the village of **Dockray.** For directions to Aira Force and other waterfalls, pick up the leaflet "Walks to Lakeland Waterfalls" (60p). Don't miss a cruise on the **Ullswater Steamer** (tel. 01539/721626), with several departures a day (Easter–Oct.) from Glenridding to Howtown (£2.75 one-way)—from where you can walk back in 3 hours—or to Pooley Bridge (£3.30), which has a couple of pubs. A round-the-lake cruise costs £5.50.

Helvellyn Peak, the third-highest in the Lake District at 3,116 ft, isn't hard to reach thanks to its convenient location between Ullswater and Thirlmere; consequently, it has become the most-climbed peak in the Northern Lakes. That doesn't mean it's easy, though. The 9½-mi round-trip hike takes 6½ hours and takes you along **Striding Edge,** a steep, serrated ridge. Begin from the Glenridding tourist office (which has trail maps) and follow the signs toward Gillside Farm to reach the main trail.

YORKSHIRE

UPDATED BY JULES BROWN

ention Yorkshire and it's not hard to imagine Emily Brontë's Heathcliff from *Wuthering Heights* running through the heather-covered moors with his beloved Cathy. Remember Laurence Olivier and Merle Oberon in the classic 1940s film? This vision remains Yorkshire in all its Hollywood grandeur. No doubt, you, too, may come to track Heathcliff's shadow across the moors and to visit Haworth, the little town where Emily and her sisters, Charlotte and Anne, lived. While a visit to Brontë Country can be a highlight of your Yorkshire sojourn, there are many other regional must-dos. To name just a few: **York**—site of York Minster, the largest Gothic cathedral in Northern Europe, and probably the best preserved medieval city in England; **Castle Howard,** that most photogenic of stately houses—it starred in the TV series of *Brideshead Revisited* and *The Buccaneers;* Georgian **Whitby,** the time-stained British setting for Bram Stoker's *Dracula;* the idyllic **Yorkshire Dales,** where both Eric Knight's *Lassie Come- Home* and James Herriot's *All Creatures Great and Small* were set; and historic abbeys such as **Rievaulx,** all the more romantic for their often ruinous state. In Yorkshire, you'll find it's easy to be swept away—by *both* the wind and the native sights and wonders.

Until recent years, woolens and coal brought in Yorkshire's principal profits. From the 12th through the 15th centuries, the Cistercian monks of **Fountains Abbey** oversaw vast farmlands; their success as wool producers and exporters formed the cornerstone of that industry. Today, profits from wool sales barely cover the cost of the shearing. Though the coal mines once kept many employed, the decimation of the mining industry in the 1980s and 1990s has made the Yorkshire miner an historical figure. Despite these difficulties, the people of Yorkshire remain some of the friendliest and most outgoing in England. Spend some time in pubs, or with your B&B host, learning about the area's hidden gems.

The splendid city of York is the heart of the historic county, drawing trainloads of visitors to its ancient, winding streets and superb museums, but there are plenty of other finds scattered throughout the countryside. You can tour stately homes, take nature walks along canals, attend cricket matches, dance in some great clubs, root for your favorite purebred collie in a dog show (don't forget that Lassie was born and bred in Yorkshire), or bend an elbow in one of the region's ancient inns.

BASICS

VISITOR INFORMATION

Yorkshire Tourist Board (12 Tadcaster Rd., York YO2 2HF, tel. 01904/707961, fax. 01904/701414) isn't open to the public, but write ahead and they'll send info and advice. For information on specific towns, contact the local tourist boards.

COMING AND GOING

There are fast and frequent trains from London and Manchester to Leeds, York, and other Yorkshire cities. In South and West Yorkshire, around Sheffield, Bradford and Leeds, the regional railway and bus system is exceptional, but all across the county there are good connections. A few areas offer one-day travel passes: the most useful for the sights covered in this chapter is the **Explorer** (bus only; not valid on National Express services) in the northeast, which costs £4.95 and is valid on most local routes including the coastal route between Scarborough and Whitby. National Express **buses** connect the major towns throughout Yorkshire and are almost always cheaper than the equivalent train rides—though the journeys can take several Brontë chapters longer. If you plan to visit the national parks and don't want to deal with the unreliable public transportation, splurge and rent a car in York or Leeds. Note that Leeds isn't explored as a destination in this chapter, but the city is a significant transportation hub for the region; for information, *see* Coming and Going in Haworth, *below*.

Yorkshire is not just stuck in the past but is busy greeting the 21st century: Immigrants from India, Pakistan, the West Indies, Jamaica, Vietnam, and many other countries have injected great new energy into both the cultural and dining scenes.

OUTDOOR ACTIVITIES

Without question, the many pedestrian pathways offer the most thorough and exciting way to see the area. The **Cleveland Way** (*see* Exploring the North York Moors, *below*), a circular path that runs through North York Moors National Park, pitches and yaws along the beautiful Yorkshire coast and through wide-open inland dales. Cyclists love the gentle slopes and flat stretches in the southern part of Yorkshire.

Only for the stalwart walker, the **Coast to Coast Walk** may get it out of your system once and for all. This 190-mi walk starts on the western shore at Saint Bees and passes through the Lake District, the Yorkshire Dales, and the North York Moors, ending up at Robin Hood's Bay. Designed in 1972 by naturalist A. W. Wainwright, the walk eschews civilization as much as possible. Consult Ordnance Survey Outdoor Leisure Maps 33 and 34 or Wainwright's *A Coast to Coast Walk* for more information. The **Pennine Way**—most celebrated of all Britain's long-distance hikes—also passes through the Yorkshire Dales, on its way from the Peak District to Scotland.

YORK

One of England's busiest and most gorgeous cities, York invites you to jump in with both feet and enter the fray. The capricious medieval streets, teeming with pubs and people, lead you everywhere you wanted to be but didn't know it—to a "redundant" church, a shop-lined cobblestone "snickleway," a museum, or a postcard-perfect garden. York's museums display a vaunted stock of relics and art, but it can be more fun just to wander the crooked streets. York's richly layered history is manifest in its magnificent architecture, from its ancient Roman foundations and encircling Norman city walls, to its towering Gothic Minster. In AD 71, York (then called Eboracum) became the military capital of Roman Britain; a ghostly lost legion is said to haunt the Treasurer's House, built over a Roman road. In the 7th century, the city became a Christian center of learning under the Saxon King, Edwin. In the 9th and 10th centuries, Vikings ruled the prosperous trading hub, and the suffix "-gate" in street names may as well be their graffiti, claiming they were here ("gate" was the Viking word for street). Wool was the principal commodity in Norman days, while Rowntree's chocolate sweetened the till in the 19th century.

On a busy day it seems that York has a million visitors and only 40 residents. But as heavily beaten paths go, York ranks with the best in Britain. Take a walk along the paths that crown the city walls, meditate within the hallowed beauty of the Minster, and lose yourself again in the elegant labyrinth of York's twist-

Richmond

Swale
A6108
B6270
Muker
SWALEDALE

A684
Askrigg
Hawes
Bainbridge
Redmire
Leyburn
WENSLEYDALE
A684
Aysgarth
Ure
Yorkshire
Dales
National
Park
A6108
B6255
B6160
Masham
TO COWGILL
TO INGLETON
Hudderholme
Buckden
P
E
N
N
LITTONDALE
I
Arncliffe
N
Gouthwaite
Res.
E
Stainforth
Malham
Tarn
B6160
Grassington
S
Pateley
Bridge
Settle
Malham
Threshfield
Linton
B6265
B6165
Calton
Cracoe
Wharfe
Hetton
A65
B6265
Blubberhouses
A59
Bolton
Abbey
A59
Skipton
Ilkley
Askwith
A6
29
77
AIREDALE
WHAREFDALE
A682
A65
Keighley
A650
Aire
Haworth
A629
Saltaire
B6144
N
Bradford
TO MANCHESTER
0   Rail Lines   6 miles
0   9 km

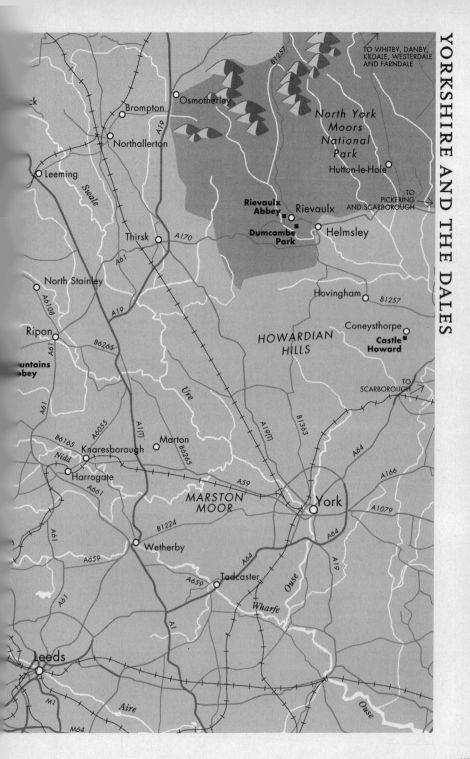

TO WHITBY, DANBY,
KILDALE, WESTERDALE
AND FARNDALE

Osmotherley

Brompton

Northallerton

North York
Moors
National
Park

Hutton-le-Hole

Leeming

Swale

A19

A19

A61

TO
PICKERING
AND SCARBOROUGH

Rievaulx
Abbey

Rievaulx

Thirsk

A170

Dumcombe
Park

Helmsley

North Stainley

A6108

A61

Hovingham

B1257

Coneysthorpe

Castle
Howard

Ripon

A61

B6265

HOWARDIAN
HILLS

untains
bey

A61

B6165

Ure

A6055

A1(T)

B6265

B1363

A19(T)

TO
SCARBOROUGH

Nidd

Knaresborough

Marton

A64

Harrogate

A661

A59

A166

MARSTON
MOOR

York

A1079

B1224

A64

Wetherby

A659

A64

A19

A61

A659

Tadcaster

Onse

Wharfe

A1

Leeds

M1

Aire

Ouse

M64

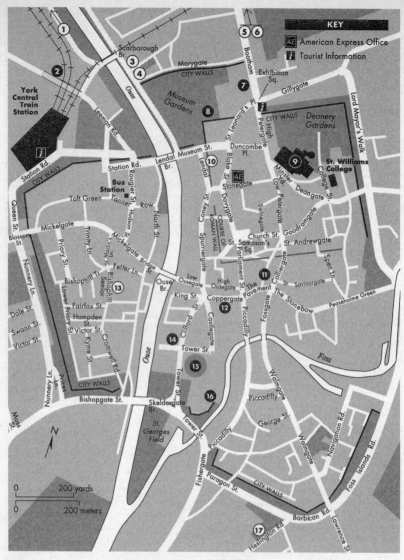

KEY

A̲E̲ American Express Office

i̲ Tourist Information

Scarborough Br.

Marygate
CITY WALLS

York Central Train Station

Museum Gardens

Exhibition Sq.

Gillygate

Bootham

St. Leonard's Pl.

High Petergate

Duncombe Pl.

CITY WALLS

Deanery Gardens

Lord Mayor's Walk

Station Rd.

Museum St.

Lendal Br.

Lendal

Blake St.

Stonegate

Minster Yd.

Low Petergate

Deangate

St. Williams College

College St.

Station Rd.

Kougler St.

Tanner Row

Toft Green

Bus Station

Hudson St.

North St.

Mickelgate Bridge

Coney St.

Davygate

Swinegate

Church St.

St. Sampson's Sq.

Goodramgate

St. Andrewgate

Mickelgate

Trinity Ln.

Priory St.

Fetter Ln.

Spurriergate

COURSE OF ROMAN WALL

St. Saviourgate

Colliergate

Peaseholme Green

Bishophill Jr.

Bishophill Senior

Ouse Br.

King St.

Low Ousegate

High Ousegate

Coppergate

The Pavement

Fossgate

The Stonebow

Fairfax St.

Hampden St.

Victor St.

Cromwell Rd.

Kyme St.

Castlegate

Piccadilly

Foss

Dale St.

Swann St.

Victor St.

Tower St.

Navigation Rd.

Foss Islands Rd.

Nunnery Ln.

Prices

CITY WALLS

Bishopgate St.

Skeldergate Br.

St. Georges Field

Tower St.

Walmgate

George St.

Piccadilly

Walmgate

Moss St.

Fishergate

Paragon St.

Piccadilly

CITY WALLS

Barbican Rd.

Lawrence St.

Heslington Rd.

N

0   200 yards
0   200 meters

Sights ●

Castle Museum, **16**

Clifford's Tower, **15**

Fairfax House Museum, **14**

Jorvik Viking Centre, **12**

National Railway Museum, **2**

The Shambles, **11**

York City Art Gallery, **7**

York Minster, **9**

Yorkshire Museum, **8**

Lodging ○

Abbey Guest House, **4**

Arnot House, **3**

Fairfax House, **17**

Inglewood, **5**

The Judge's Lodging, **10**

Queen Anne's Guest House, **6**

York YHA, **1**

York Youth Hostel, **13**

ing streets. If you plan ahead, you can catch one of York's annual festivals—the **Viking Festival** (February) plays on its Viking past; **Bonfire Night** celebrations on November 5 have added piquancy, since the notorious 16th-century conspirator Guy Fawkes was a native son; and an **Early Music Festival** is held each summer. While you're here make arrangements for the next quadrennial performance of the medieval **York Mystery Plays,** which will take place in the summer of 2000 (June 22 to July 22) and again in 2004. The millennium performance is sure to be oversubscribed, so if you haven't made advance reservations, you're unlikely to score a ticket (or a room in town for that matter). For details, call the Festival Office (tel. 01904/658338) or one of the tourist information centers in York (*see* Basics, *below*).

BASICS

AMERICAN EXPRESS

This office in the city center provides the usual services. *6 Stonegate, YO1 2AS, tel. 01904/670030. Open weekdays 9–5:30 (Wed. from 9:30), Sat. 9–5; also Apr.–Oct., Sun. 10:30–4:30.*

LAUNDRY

York has a dozen launderettes scattered about the city center and the tourist information centers can point you to the nearest one. If you're staying in either of the York youth hostels (*see* Where to Sleep, *below*), you'll be able to wash and dry your gear there.

MAIL

This center city post office is near the river, between Museum Street and Stonegate. *22 Lendal, YO1 2DA, tel. 01904/617285. Open weekdays 9–5:30, Sat. 9–12:30.*

VISITOR INFORMATION

York has three **tourist information centers,** all offering broadly similar services—they'll exchange money, book sightseeing tours, and make accommodations reservations for a £2.90 fee, plus 10% deposit for the first night's stay. Make sure you pick up the *York Visitor Guide,* a free brochure full of useful listings, opening times, and other information. The most helpful office is operated by the **York Tourism Bureau** (20 George Hudson St., tel. 01904/554488), open April–October, Monday–Saturday 9–6, Sunday 10–4; November–March, Monday–Saturday 9–5, closed Sunday. The tour company **Guide Friday** (tel. 01904/621756) runs offices at the **De Grey Rooms** (Exhibition Sq.), open April–October, daily 9–6; November–March, Monday–Saturday 9–5, Sunday 9:30–4; and at the **Railway Station** (Outer Concourse), open May– October, Monday–Saturday 9–8, Sunday 9–5; November–April, Monday–Saturday 9:30–5, Sunday 10–4.

COMING AND GOING

BY BUS

Buses converge on **Rougier Street,** off Station Road between the train station and Lendal Bridge. **Yorkshire Coastliner** (tel. 01653/692556) serves Leeds (£4 day return, £5.60 period return) and outlying Yorkshire areas like Scarborough and Whitby (both £6.80 day return, £8.60 period return). **National Express** (tel. 0990/808080) covers destinations throughout England, and runs three daily buses from York to London's Victoria Coach Station. The ride takes 4½ hours and costs £26.50 return. Any of the tourist offices can provide up-to-date timetables.

BY CAR

Many of York's streets are accessible to pedestrians only, especially within the 2-mi circumference of the city walls. If you plan to use York as a jumping-off point, you can rent a car from **Hertz** (inside train station, tel. 01904/612586), **Budget** (Station House, Foss Islands Rd., tel. 01904/644919), or **Kenning** (Mickelgate Bar, tel. 01904/659328). Rental costs start around £33 per day, £160 per week, plus a £100 deposit. Book ahead.

BY TRAIN

York Central Train Station, a brick and glass marvel built in 1875, serves the entire country. Trains run from London's King's Cross about twice an hour. The ride is two hours, and costs from £44 off-peak return, £51–£59 standard return, and even more on Friday. There are 19 trains to Edinburgh, costing from £44 off-peak return on weekdays, more on weekends. The station has an info center, bureau de

TRAINSPOTTERS

Look carefully in train stations and you may glimpse a trainspotter—an olive anorak-clad person perched on a portable stool, clutching a tea-filled thermos, and scribbling the type and number of the arriving trains into a notebook. Like the American nerd stereotype, people snort at the mention of trainspotters, who are hobbyists with a special devotion. Even the success of the cult Scottish movie, "Trainspotting," failed these people—the title was merely a metaphor, for it was a film noticeable for its complete absence of trains or trainspotting. But trains hold a special place in many British hearts, and trainspotters live in hope of sighting a rare engine to record faithfully in their books. The world champion noted 79,500 different engines in 40 years.

change, luggage storage office, and 24-hour lockers, which cost £1.50–£3.50. *Station Rd., tel. 0345/ 484950. Ticket and info counter open Mon.–Sat. 8–7:30, Sun. 9–7:30. Station open 24 hrs.*

GETTING AROUND

York is a compact city and you can easily walk to most of the sights. If you do need to take the bus, **First York** (7 James St., tel. 01904/435600) provides service throughout the York area. They sell a **Minstercard** for £9, good for a week's worth of unlimited rides. York is also known as one of the most cycle-friendly cities in England. **Cycle Scene** (2 Ratcliffe St., tel. 01904/653286) and **York Cycleworks** (14–16 Lawrence St., tel. 01904/626664) both rent bikes for about £10 per day, plus a £50 deposit. Bring your ID.

WHERE TO SLEEP

York may have a wealth of B&Bs, but large hotels are few and far between. This unfortunately means you can have a frantic time trying to book a room in this teeming tourist town. So, be on the safe side and make reservations as far in advance as possible. The best B&B deals can be found along Bootham (which becomes Clifton) and its side streets, such as Queen Anne's Road, just northwest of the city walls. To get there from the train station, go left on Station Road (which turns into Museum Street across the bridge), turn left on High Petergate, and follow Bootham through Bootham Bar, one of York's old gates. There's another cluster of B&Bs along Scarcroft and Southlands roads; from the train station, turn right on Queen Street (which becomes Nunnery Lane), then right on Bishopthorpe Road. Scarcroft and then Southlands will intersect on your right.

UNDER £40 • Abbey Guest House. This pretty, no-smoking, terraced guest house— formerly an artisan's house—is a 10-minute walk from the train station and town center. It's very clean and friendly, and the real bonus is being able to hang out in the peaceful garden right on the river, with ducks puttering about nearby. Rooms cost £18 per person; those with en suite shower can be as much as £25 per person in summer. *14 Earlsborough Terr., Marygate, YO30 7BQ, tel. 01904/627782. From Minster, walk north on High Petergate (which becomes Bootham), turn left down Marygate, and right at the end, by the river. 7 rooms, 3 with bath.*

Inglewood. Five minutes from the banks of the River Ouse and a 15-minute walk from the city center, Inglewood is typical of York B&Bs: spotless rooms, a carefully decorated interior, and good-natured hosts. Singles for £25, cheaper out of season, are not as good a deal as doubles, which range from £17.50 to £22.50 (with bath) per person. *7 Clifton Green, YO30 6HL, tel. 01904/653523. From Minster, walk north on High Petergate (which becomes Bootham), turn left on Clifton Green. 9 rooms, 4 with bath. No credit cards.*

Queen Anne's Guest House. This B&B is a real bargain. The rooms are immaculate and quiet, the location (a 10-minute walk from the Minster) is convenient, the bathrooms are huge, and the hospitality will entice you to stay all day. Rooms (there's just one single) run around £16 to £17 per person. *24 Queen Anne's Rd., off Bootham, YO30 7AA, tel. 01904/629389. 7 rooms, 4 with shower. No credit cards.*

UNDER £55 • Arnot House. Look no further for a comfortable berth overlooking Bootham Park and the tower of the Minster in the distance. This attractively decorated late-Victorian B&B has TVs and tea/coffeemaking facilities in all rooms, which cost £50—£55 if you want to sink into a four-poster at the end of a hard day. There's no smoking, and vegetarian breakfasts are served on request. *17 Grosvenor Terr., YO3 7AG, tel. 01904/641966. From Minster, walk north on High Petergate (which becomes Bootham), turn right on Grosvenor Terr. at the railway line. 4 rooms with bath.*

UNDER £110 • The Judge's Lodging. Easily the prettiest hotel in York—and definitely in the "I'm worth it" category—this picturesque mansion used to be a judges' lodging, providing accommodations to justices when they traveled up north from London's Inns of Court. Past the elegant gates and charming front yard, you mount an imposing staircase to enter a Georgian town house. Beyond the lovely, somewhat shabby-genteel lobby is the main salon—a cozy cocoon of Queen Mum pastels, overstuffed chairs, and gilded mirrors. Upstairs, the decor continues in the same vein: One room is called the Queen Mother and another grand suite, the Prince Albert (who actually stayed here) is a special treat. Downstairs, there's a cellar bar. Doubles range from £100 to £150 and include breakfast. All in all, pretty as only a time-burnished 19th-century picture can be. *9 Lendal, YO1, tel. 01904/638733. 15 rooms with bath.*

HOSTELS

York YHA. Although it's more expensive than most other hostels, this place is worth it. The facilities are terrific, the rooms are clean, the staff is wonderful, and the on-site café serves cheap vegetarian meals. There's also cycle and luggage storage. It's a 15-minute walk from the city center, or you can get a taxi for around £3. Beds cost £15.25 (including breakfast). Book ahead for summer. *Water End, Clifton, YO3 6LT, tel. 01904/653147, fax 01904/651230. From train station, walk left on Station Rd. to Leeman Rd., go right over railway bridge, then follow path left along River Ouse to Water End. 150 beds. Reception open 24 hrs. Kitchen, laundry.*

York Youth Hotel. Dorm beds in this independent hostel aren't as comfortable as at the official YHA, but they're a good bit cheaper—prices start at £9, singles £14, and doubles £26, with breakfast another £1.50–£2.50; take a pound off if you're staying more than a couple of nights. If you don't have your own sleeping bag, you'll be stung for another £1 to rent one. On premises is a bar, and there is a nice bike rental facility. *Bishophill House, 11–13 Bishophill Senior, tel. 01904/625904, fax 01904/612494. From train station, turn right on Queen St., left on Mickelgate, go under Mickelgate Bar to St. Martin's La., and follow to Bishophill Senior. 120 beds. Reception open 24 hrs. Kitchen, laundry.*

STUDENT HOUSING

Fairfax House. An excellent option during University of York vacations, July– September and around Easter, Fairfax House is just a 15-minute walk south of the city center. Sleep in the Georgian-era dorms and feel like a student, or stroll the 2 acres of private grounds and feel like a lord. Single rooms, with desks, cost £20 per person between the beginning of July and the end of September. *99 Heslington Rd., tel. 01904/432095. Information and bookings available weekdays 9:30–4:30. From Minster, turn left on Low Petergate and continue past the city walls; turn right on Barbican Rd., left on Heslington Rd. 93 rooms, none with bath. Laundry. Closed Oct.–June. No credit cards.*

CAMPING

Campgrounds are plentiful around York, especially in the Acaster (pronounced AY-cast-er) Malbis area 4 mi south. All the main sites are listed in the *York Visitor Guide* (*see* Basics, *above*); one that isn't is **Poplar Farm Caravan Park** (Acaster Malbis, tel. 01904/706548), near the River Ouse, which has 30 sites. It costs £8.50 for two people and a tent, and is closed November–March. To get here take **Sykes** (tel. 01904/774231) Bus 192—four daily between 8:30 and 5:45—from Skeldergate Bridge, by the river.

FOOD

York offers surprising culinary variety, with a particularly good range of tea shops and cafés as well as upscale restaurants and cheaper ethnic choices. At **Newgate market** (between Market Street, The Shambles, and Parliament Street) you can buy fruit, vegetables, meats, sweets, eggs, china—you name it—every Monday–Saturday.

UNDER £5 • Blake Head Vegetarian Café. This paradise for health-conscious eaters is tucked behind an excellent bookstore. Sit on the patio, enjoy the fresh air, and tackle the quiche of the day, with potatoes, and salad. *104 Mickelgate, tel. 01904/623767.*

Spurriergate Centre. Come to this deconsecrated 15th-century church to receive your daily bread. St. Spurriergate has now been resurrected as a cafeteria by a religious organization, a favorite spot for tired tourists and mothers-with-strollers. The Lord seems to be quite near, as the decor is magnificently medieval, with crucifixes and shrines all around. Order double rations of the cream scones, which are "smacker lipstastic." If you can enjoy your lunch dining over the floor's inlaid stone graves ("Is it good to eat on dead bodies?" inquired one tot), this can be a delightful experience—just the spot for some bizarre photo ops. *Spurriergate, tel. 01904/629393. Closed Sun.*

Taylors Tea Rooms. If Betty's (*see below*) is bursting at the seams, then try here—owned by the same people and with the same classic old-style ambiance, teas, coffees, cakes, snacks, and light meals for the gentry. *46 Stonegate, tel. 01904/622865.*

UNDER £10 • Betty's. At the opposite end of Stonegate from the Minster, Betty's, arranged elegantly across two large floors in a beautiful Art Nouveau building, has been a York institution since 1912. Best known for its teas, served with mouthwatering cakes (try the "fat rascal," a plump bun bursting with cherries and nuts), Betty's also turns out light meals and a splendid selection of expensive, exotic coffees. Grab a table on the upper floor if you can, next to the floor-to-ceiling picture windows. *6–8 St. Helen's Sq., tel. 01904/659142.*

La Piazza. You can have a fine, fresh Italian meal in the 14th-century Tudor house or the back garden. Pizzas and pasta all cost under £6; steak and fish entrées cost more like £9 or £10. *45 Goodramgate, tel. 01904/642641.*

Pierre Victoire. Saunter in to this airy brasserie at lunchtime and you can feast on a set two-course menu of simple French food for just £5.90, one of the city's best bargains. At dinner, prices increase, but not outrageously so—choose that old brasserie standby, *moules marinière* (mussels in white wine). *2 Lendal, tel. 01904/655222.*

Pizza Express. The successful London chain has found another fine building in which to serve its pizzas, this time the River House at Lendal Bridge. You eat in the grand salons of what used to be the York Gentleman's Club; a piano serenades evening diners from the lounge; even the rest rooms are fancy. The pizzas are not always all they could be, but lap up the good house wine and the upscale ambiance and all is forgiven. *River House, 17 Museum St., tel. 01904/672904.*

Rubicon. This vegetarian restaurant offers great fixed-price meals—two-course lunches cost £6, two-course dinners cost £10 and adding dessert won't break the bank. It's now licensed so you can order wine with your meal. Eggplant couscous and nut roast are typical dishes. *5 Little Stonegate, off Stonegate, tel. 01904/676076. Closed Sun. lunch.*

WORTH SEEING

As York is immensely popular, minimize collisions by sightseeing in the morning or late afternoon. Get a good map, walk the 2-mi circuit of the walls and gates, and then explore the city itself. Take your pick of the city's superlative museums and historic sites, but don't miss the magnificent **York Minster.**

CASTLE MUSEUM

From the 1890s to the 1920s, a rural doctor collected everyday things that he knew would become rare. In 1935 he gave his collection to York and thus began this museum, which is an excellent way of learning about Yorkshire life from the 1800s to the present. This huge ex-prison includes reconstructed period streets and interiors as well as displays of costumes, arms and armor, children's toys, farm equipment, and home-front memorabilia from World War II. *Clifford St., tel. 01904/653611. Admission £4.75. Open Apr.–Oct., Mon.–Sat. 9:30–5:30, Sun. 10–5:30; Nov.–Mar., Mon.–Sat. 9:30–4, Sun. 10–4.*

CLIFFORD'S TOWER

Clifford's Tower is all that remains of York Castle and, like other ruins in York, it has a layered and often macabre history. The original wooden tower was the site of a massacre of 150 Jews in 1190, during which the tower was burned to the ground. Its replacement was built in the 13th century by Henry de Reyns, who designed Westminster Abbey. The tower served as a garrison for the army of King Charles I during the siege of York in the Civil War. It was burned, perhaps deliberately, in the 1680s, and in the

18th and 19th centuries, it became a picturesque folly in the manor house's garden. It escaped destruction to become a public monument in 1877. The walkway along the tower walls affords splendid views of the city. *Tower St., tel. 01904/646940. Admission £1.80. Open Apr.–Oct., daily 10–6; Nov.–Mar., daily 10–1 and 2–4.*

FAIRFAX HOUSE

In a city known for brutish Norman keeps and cold Gothic towers, it's a delight to find one of the most elegant of Georgian town houses in all England. Now a decorative arts museum, this overlooked treasure was originally built in 1762. The marble dining room and the grand salon—all crystal chandeliers and flaming crimson silk walls—are knockouts and rival anything found at Castle Howard. *Castlegate, tel. 01904/655543. Admission £3.75. Open mid-Feb.–Dec., Mon.–Sat. 11–5, Sun. 1:30–5.*

JORVIK VIKING CENTRE

On an authentic Viking site, archaeologists have re-created a Viking street with astonishing attention to detail. Its "time-cars" whisk you through the streets to experience the sights, sounds, and (the bit you won't like) the smells of Viking England, while excellent displays indicate the extraordinary breadth of the Viking culture and social system. If there's a massive line (and there often is), jump to the front and buy a timed entry ticket instead—you can come back later in the day and avoid hanging around unnecessarily. *Coppergate, tel. 01904/643211. Admission £4.99. Open Apr.–Oct., daily 9–7; Nov.–Mar., daily 9–5:30; last admission 2 hrs before closing.*

NATIONAL RAILWAY MUSEUM

Trainspotters (*see* box, *above*) shouldn't miss this museum, which brilliantly traces 200 years of railway history. The collection of gleaming monsters includes *Mallard*, the world's fastest steam locomotive; carriages used by commuters both royal and common; and a charity-collecting stuffed dog. New exhibits include a viewing platform over the main east coast line, and The Works—an engineering workshop and backstage storage area to explore. Take a walk along the River Ouse when you're done. *Leeman Rd., tel. 01904/621261. Admission £4.95. Open daily 10–6.*

THE SHAMBLES

One of York's most picturesque streets, The Shambles served as butcher's row in the medieval era, and you can still see the meat hooks on the half-timber walls. Today, its leaning homes and cobblestone streets enjoy the jingling sound of modern English commerce as the street brims with buskers, peddlers, and shoppers. Shops in the Shambles are open Monday–Saturday 9–5. After dusk, it's a truly lovely place to take a quiet stroll. To get here from the Minster, follow Low Petergate south to Colliergate.

YORK CITY ART GALLERY

In addition to innovative contemporary shows, the gallery houses an internationally respected collection of mostly English paintings. Illuminated stained-glass windows are also on display. Important to note is the pottery from the pioneer studio—an alternative to the conventional pottery mass-produced in factories in the first half of the 20th century. *Exhibition Sq., tel. 01904/551861. Admission free. Open Mon.–Sat. 10–5, Sun. 2:30–5.*

YORK MINSTER

No matter how many cathedrals you've seen, your first glimpse of York Minster will awe you. Imposing and glorious, the Minster is the largest medieval cathedral in northern Europe. The building's foundations date back to AD 627, when it was the site of a wooden chapel built for the baptism of the king of Northumbria. It has since undergone at least three major reconstructions, with the present building dating from 1220 to 1472. In 1967, the two west towers and the east end underwent extensive—and astoundingly difficult—work to prevent collapse. The oldest glass in England (circa 1150) forms part of the west aisle windows, while the **Great East Window** (1405–1408), the world's largest expanse of medieval stained glass, depicts scenes of creation and apocalypse from Genesis and Revelation.

The 13th-century **Chapter House** still functions as the meeting place for the Dean and Chapter, the governing body of the cathedral. More than 250 carved stone heads and nearly 300 capitals and pendants are on display. The **treasury** contains pieces from the 11th through the 20th centuries, including the Horn of Ulf, dating from around 1000. You can compare the constructions of Roman, Norman, and medieval engineers in the **foundations** underneath the Minster. The **crypt** shows skeleton-faced devils, a Madonna without a head, and the shrine of St. William of York. The **central tower** offers a fabulous view of York for those willing to climb 200-plus stairs. *Duncombe Pl., tel. 01904/624426. Admission to Minster free, but £2 donation requested, Chapter House 70p, foundations (including treasury) £1.80,* *crypt 60p, central tower £2. Open daily 7–5 (during summer 7 AM–8:30 PM); evensong held weekdays at 5 PM, weekends at 4 PM.*

YORKSHIRE MUSEUM AND MUSEUM GARDENS

The Yorkshire Museum is built around and within the ruins of St. Mary's Abbey, a monastery founded by the Benedictines in 1080 and flattened by Henry VIII in 1539. It covers the natural and archaeological history of the whole county. Exhibits range from Roman grave goods and Saxon farming implements to the 15th-century Middleham Jewel, a pendant resplendent with a large sapphire and the best piece of Gothic jewelry found in England this century. If the narrow snickleways of York make you claustrophobic, the 10 acres of botanical gardens surrounding the museum offer a breath of fresh air. In these atmospheric gardens, with their crumbling medieval columns and blaze of summer flowers, the city's cycle of mystery plays is performed every four years. The museum lies just outside the walled city, through Bootham Bar. *Museum St., tel. 01904/629745. Admission £3.60, garden admission free. Open daily 10–5 (Nov.–Mar., Sun. 1–5).*

SHOPPING

The new and secondhand bookstores around Petergate, Stonegate, and the Shambles are excellent. **Blackwell's** (32 Stonegate), has a large stock of new titles and a convenient mail-order service. For secondhand books, old maps, and prints, head for the Minster and the musty old **Minster Gate Bookshop** (8 Minster Gate). York is also awash with antiques shops, crystal and china stores, old-style clothes outfitters that sell tweed suits and skirts, formal hats, silk ties and the like, and chichi New Age emporiums. A good place to browse is the **York Antiques Centre** (2 Lendal), which has 34 shops on two floors selling antiques, bric-a-brac, books, and jewelry. Most Saturdays throughout the year, antiques fairs are held inside the **Merchant Adventurers' Hall** (Fossgate), a medieval half-timber hall.

AFTER DARK

In addition to the usual pub and club fare, York (allegedly the most haunted city in Europe) offers a variety of guided ghost walks. The tourist offices have current schedules, or call the **Original Ghost Walk** (tel. 01759/373090), £3.50, which features master thespian Ray Alexander's amusing narrative. It starts at 8 PM from the King's Arms pub (*see* Pubs, *below*) and is spookiest in autumn and winter.

PUBS

You'll find a mass of popular pubs around Stonegate, where the summer crowds usually flow out onto the streets. With outdoor tables along the River Ouse, **King's Arms** (Kings Staith, tel. 01904/659435) gets packed during the summer. The pub floods four to five times each winter, though it stays open until the water reaches the height of your wellies. The **Punch Bowl Inn** (Stonegate, tel. 01904/622305) caters to a hip crowd with live music—usually jazz and blues. York's oldest pub, **Ye Olde Starre Inn** (40 Stonegate, tel. 01904/623063), opened in 1644 and still rates highly with locals. Drink inside if you like low ceilings and wooden beams or out in the beer garden if you want to catch some rays. They even serve good meals for under £5. Serving lunch, dinner, and drinks, **The York Arms** (26 High Petergate, near York Minster, tel. 01904/624508) has an ideal location in one of York's original 18th-century coffeehouses. Another historic site is the **Judge's Lodgings** (9 Lendal, tel. 01904/638733), an 18th-century house for the York judiciary, now a hotel but with a great cellar bar open to anyone.

MUSIC AND THEATER

Pick up a York "What's On" or "York Diary" for weekly listings of musical events. The monthly *YorKmusic* lists music happenings throughout Yorkshire. **Black Swan Folk Club** (Peasholme Green, tel. 01904/632922), **Bonding Warehouse** (Skeldergate, tel. 01904/622527), and **Fibbers** (Stonebow House, tel. 01904/651250) all host live music weekly, from folk to jazz. **York Arts Centre** (Mickelgate, tel. 01904/627129) offers adventurous works that travel all the boundaries of performance; frequent events range from classical to theater to comedy to Jamaican poetry rap. The **University of York Department of Music** hosts orchestral and chamber concerts October–June; call the university at 01904/432–439 for info and tickets, which sell for £3–£11. The main theater is **Theatre Royal** (St. Leonard's Pl., near the tourist office, tel. 01904/623568), which presents a full program of rep and touring productions.

NEAR YORK

CASTLE HOWARD

Castle Howard, well known to PBS junkies as the setting of *Brideshead Revisited* and *The Buccaneers*, is Yorkshire's best example of sheer opulence. Built as a hideaway for the third earl of Carlisle over a 60-year span beginning in 1699, this spectacular estate was designed by Sir John Vanbrugh, author of some bawdy morality plays, as his first architectural project. Without question he drew better plans than plots. A Baroque-era extravaganza, the house is complete with massive dome, sculpted figures, a plethora of Palladian pilasters, and any number of obscenely gorgeous rooms (still housing the Howard family, once bearers of the Carlisle title). Better, the house is set in a true 18th-century fantasyland, studded with marble temples, pyramids, a spectacular fountain of Atlas, a lake, and formal rose gardens. Clearly, the resident peacocks live better than dukes. You'll find views of the family mausoleum—so perfect a neoclassic structure Horace Walpole was inspired to write "that all who view it would wish to be buried alive"—from the Temple of the Far Winds. *Coneysthorpe, tel. 01653/648333. Admission £7. Open mid-Mar.–Oct., daily 11-4:30.*

COMING AND GOING

Castle Howard is 15 mi from York. From the beginning of May until the beginning of October, there are two daily Yorkshire Coastliner bus services from York's train station (No. 840 or 842, toward Pickering/Whitby, £4 day return), currently departing at 11:10 AM and 3:10 PM. These take 40 minutes to reach the stop just outside the gates at Castle Howard. The return services are at 3:25 PM and 5 PM. Believe it or not, this magical destination can also be done as a day trip from London—catch the 8 AM super-express train from King's Cross to York, and get on the 11:10 AM Yorkshire Coastliner. Leave on either of the afternoon return bus services for York station, catching trains back to London at around 4:30 PM or 6 PM. You'll be exhausted but it will have been worth it.

NORTH YORK MOORS NATIONAL PARK

About 25 mi north of York, the North York Moors contain some of the most varied and dramatic landscape in England. In the park's 553 square mi, you'll find wind-worn plateaus cut by steep gorges, sloping valleys carved by ancient lakes, and ruins of castles and abbeys. The many stone crosses throughout the moors are of unknown origin and age, but may have been used by pilgrims or *drovers* (herders) as markers. Tradition holds that travelers who place a coin atop these crosses will be protected. Heavily wooded valleys, small farms, and untouched villages punctuate the high plains. Romantics will love the dramatic skies, the moorland mists, and the vast expanses of heather, which flower purple in the summertime. Others may find the area too foggy and boggy for their taste.

The park boundary runs from Scarborough in the southeast to Thirsk in the southwest, and from near Middlesbrough in the northwest corner to Whitby (a good base for exploring) in the northeast. The relatively large towns of Pickering and Helmsley (both also good bases) lie along the southern boundary of the park and are easily accessible from York. The long-distance **Cleveland Way** (*see* Exploring the North York Moors, *below*) circles the outer boundary of the park; the coastal stretch from Whitby to Scarborough, passing right along dramatic, windy cliffs, is especially beautiful.

BASICS

BUREAUX DE CHANGE

In **Pickering**, Midlands Bank (15 Market Pl., tel. 01751/472534) has a Thomas Cook branch inside; other banks are just down the street. **Helmsley** also has a Midlands Bank (12 High St., tel. 01439/735353). Banks are ubiquitous in Whitby and Scarborough, but if you're heading off the beaten track make sure you have enough cash to see you through—and don't count on being able to use your credit card in out-of-the-way B&Bs and cafés.

PUBLICATIONS

Survival in the moors requires a **"Moors Connections,"** a free bus and train schedule, and a copy of the *Visitor* newspaper (50p), a superb source for sightseeing information, lodging, and restaurants. **"Waymark Walk"** pamphlets (30p each) cover more than 40 trails—each 2–5 mi long—that crisscross the park. All the above publications—as well as the free guides "Information for the Disabled Visitor" and *Summer Events,* which lists guided walks, workshops, exhibitions, and other fun, cheap stuff—are available at most tourist offices. Serious hikers will need Ordnance Survey Outdoor Leisure Maps 26 and 27.

VISITOR INFORMATION

Because you can enter the North York Moors from a number of small towns, tourist offices abound on the park's edges. The **Moors Centre** in **Danby** (Lodge La., Danby, Y021 2NB, tel. 01287/660654) is the headquarters, but any other office can provide basic info and help you book lodgings. **Pickering's** excellent tourist office (Eastgate parking lot, tel. 01751/473791) is the best place to get started on your Moors visit. They have an endless array of pamphlets and brochures, and the extra-friendly staff will phone other sources if they can't answer your questions. The **Whitby** tourist office (Langborne Rd., tel. 01947/602674) is also helpful, though they stock fewer hiking publications. Additional tourist offices are at **Great Ayton** (High Green parking lot, tel. 01642/722835), **Helmsley** (Town Hall, Market Pl., tel. 01439/770173), **Scarborough** (Pavilion House, Valley Bridge Rd., opposite the train station, tel. 01723/373333), and **Sutton Bank** (on A170, near Thirsk, tel. 01845/597426). During the winter most offices close or are open only on weekends, so call ahead.

COMING AND GOING

Transportation to the North York Moors is fast and frequent. As usual, it's cheaper to travel by bus than by train. Pickering and Whitby are the best launchpads for trips into the moors, since bus connections to Pickering (via Malton) or to Whitby (via Scarborough) are particularly good.

BY BUS

Yorkshire Coastliner (tel. 01653/692556) Bus 840 or 842 runs every hour from York (originating in Leeds) to Malton in 45 minutes, and to Pickering in 1½ hours; these buses travel on to Whitby three or four times a day. From York you can also take Bus 843 to Scarborough, via Malton. **Stephensons** (tel. 01347/838990) runs buses from York to Helmsley, in the southwest corner of the park, three times a day Monday–Saturday. **Scarborough & District** (tel. 01482/327164) has daily services from Scarborough to Pickering and Helmsley. **Arriva** (tel. 0345/124125) Buses 93, 93A, and X93 travel from Middlesbrough to Scarborough (with stops in Whitby and Robin Hood's Bay) every one to two hours. **National Express** (tel. 0990/808080) Bus 563 runs between York, Scarborough, and Whitby once daily.

BY CAR

From York, take A1036 to A64 north to Malton. From Malton, you can stay on A64 and head east, but you'll end up in Scarborough, a garish seaside vacation spot, complete with carnival rides. Instead, take A169 north from Malton to Pickering, or continue north to Whitby (connecting with A171 east). The A169 cuts directly through the middle of the moors and offers some stupendous views. To reach Helmsley, the most direct route is to take the A170, which runs west from Pickering, though if you have the patience and a decent road map, you'll be able to make your way to the town on a succession of minor moorland roads either from York to the south, or from Whitby and the Esk Valley to the north.

BY TRAIN

Trains run almost every hour from York to Scarborough (£10.70 day return, £12.90 period return) and Middlesbrough (£7–11 day return, £17.20 period return, £19 if traveling on a Friday); for the latest timetable and ticket information, call 0345/484–950. However, coming from York, the train won't take you to the park's interior; instead, it's better to take a bus directly from York to Pickering, Helmsley, or Whitby.

GETTING AROUND

It's really not that hard to get around this area by bus or train. Get hold of the free "Moors Connection" guide to help you master the bus lines. The best place for car rental is York (*see* Coming and Going, *above*) since, although there are local rental outfits in places like Pickering, Helmsley and Whitby, availability (or choice) can't be guaranteed.

BY BIKE

Biking is an excellent way to explore the Moors, and cyclists of any ability can handle the varied terrain. Bike rental in the region runs £8–£12.50 per day for mountain bikes. Some places will deliver bikes to you or offer guided tours, so call to check on weekly deals. Contact local tourist offices for bike rental outfits, or call **Trailways Cycle Hire** (The Old Railway Station, Hawsker, tel. 01947/820207), for a relatively easy cycling day out on the old Scarborough–Whitby rail track, which runs through a really scenic part of the coast. More serious off-roaders can rent mountain bikes from **Footloose in North Yorkshire** (Borogate, tel. 01439/770886), based in Helmsley, or **Wardill Brothers** (The Square, tel. 01751/474335) in Thornton-le-Dale, 2 mi east of Pickering.

BY BUS

Buses = confusion, given the many private lines and changing seasonal schedules. Once again, you definitely need the "Moors Connection" guide to avoid getting stuck somewhere. Scarborough & District's Bus 128 travels about once an hour between Scarborough's train station and Pickering, with connections from Pickering to Helmsley every two hours. An Arriva **Explorer Pass** (£4.75) allows a day's worth of unlimited travel on routes between Middlesbrough, Whitby, and the coastal areas. Best of all, the North York Moors National Park Authority (tel. 01439/770657) operates the **Moorsbus** on Sunday and bank-holiday Mondays April–October, with a daily service in August. Various routes operate in the park between Pickering, Helmsley, and all the major sights, about every 30 minutes 9–5, and an all-day pass is only £2.50.

BY TRAIN

Two railways operate within the park. Regional Railways North East's (tel. 0345/484950) **Esk Valley Line** runs across the northern boundary of the park from Middlesbrough to Whitby on the coast (£8–£10 return). Trains run four or five times per day, stopping in Great Ayton, Danby, and Grosmont, among other villages. The last train back to Whitby from Grosmont leaves at 6:41 PM. The dramatic steam engine on the **North Yorkshire Moors Railway** (tel. 01751/472508) runs in a north–south direction from Pickering to Grosmont, near Whitby. The views will take your breath away and, unfortunately, so will the price (£9.20 return).

WHERE TO SLEEP

The North York Moors National Park publishes an annual Accommodation Guide listing detailed information on all types of accommodations. This, and the "Ryedale Holiday Guide" covering accommodation in Pickering, Helmsley, and surrounding areas, are both available from any local information office. Most towns near the park are filled with B&Bs (about £15–£25 per night), and plenty of campgrounds, hostels, and B&Bs are easily accessible from footpaths in the park. In busier towns like Whitby, Pickering, and Scarborough, the hostels are often full, so book ahead. The tourist offices do a great job helping travelers find affordable shelter for the night, and in many places no booking fee is charged—just tell them how much you want to pay and they'll do the rest.

Camping barns, always a good option during warm weather, have been rapidly multiplying in the park. Even on summer evenings, be prepared for a cold snap. The barns provide simple cover, a place to roll out your sleeping bag, a toilet, and cold-water taps for under £3.50. The YHA brochure "Stay in a Camping Barn," available at many tourist offices and hostels, details many in the North York Moors and Yorkshire Dales parks. There are currently nine barns in and around the park, including those in **Brompton-on-Swale, Farndale, Kildale, Lovesome Hill, Sinnington,** and **Westerdale.** Book well ahead through the YHA's Camping Barns Reservations Office (16 Shawbridge St., Clitheroe, Lancs, BB7 1LY, tel. 01200/428366).

HELMSLEY

Helmsley is the best base for the central park area: it's got regular Moorsbus service to most destinations and marks the start of the Cleveland Way—which explains all those big-booted, weighed-down hikers rambling around town. If you want to join them at the **Helmsley YHA** (Carlton Lane, tel. 01439/770433), where beds cost £8.35, put on your track shoes—it fills quickly. Otherwise, look for cheap B&Bs along Ashdale Road, up Bondgate from the Market Place and on the right. There are some really nice old **inns** in the town center—like the Feathers or the Black Swan—but rooms are very pricey. The Feathers goes for about £60 a double, the Black Swan for over £100. No one can stop you strolling in for a drink though.

PICKERING

Pretty Pickering is a fine base for exploring the eastern sector of the park: Public transportation is frequent, the town lies right on A169 (which runs through the park), and there are banks, launderettes, and markets. It also has a ruined 14th-century castle and a Norman-Gothic church with the best-preserved medieval wall paintings in England. The **youth hostel** is the best deal around—unfortunately, it's five mi northeast of town off the A169 at the **Old School,** Lockton (tel. 01751/460376)—two mile's walk from the NYMR station at Levisham, or you can ask to be dropped at the turnoff by the Whitby bus. Beds cost £6.10 a night, and the hostel is closed from October through March. In town, look for B&Bs down Eastgate (the Scarborough road), or at **Eden House** (120 Eastgate, tel. 01751/472289) and **Heathcote House** (100 Eastgate, tel. 01751/476991). Rooms at either cost £20–£21 per person, and both are only a short walk from the tourist office. About 1½ mi south of Pickering, **Upper Carr** (tel. 01751/473115), closed November–February, is a great campsite with chalets to rent, as well as tent space. The Black Bull pub opposite the main entrance serves cheap bar meals. Campsite and pub are on the Malton road out of town; any bus to York runs that way.

WHITBY

Whitby has plenty of accommodations, except during the Regatta and Whitby Folk Week, usually the last two weeks in August. Rows of B&Bs line Hudson Street and Normanby Terrace, off Belle Vue Terrace, about ¼ mi from the bus and train station. To reach the B&Bs, turn right on New Quay Road, left on Flowergate opposite the bridge, and right at Skinner Street (which becomes Belle Vue Terrace). Most cost £15–£20 per person and are within a 10-minute walk of the beach—in high season, it's just a matter of walking the streets, finding one with a "Vacancy" sign in the window. In the heart of this B&B district the very friendly hosts at **Number Five** (5 Havelock Place, tel. 01947/606361) cook a fine breakfast. Rooms cost from £15 per person, no credit cards. Moving a little upmarket, there are two excellent accommodations in the cobbled old town, on the east side of the river. The **Shepherd's Purse** (95 Church St., tel. 01947/820228) has en suite rooms in its galleried courtyard behind a whole-food café and health food store. It costs £25 per person, no credit cards, though there are two less expensive bedrooms above the store. Just down the street and even more atmospheric is the **White Horse and Griffin** (Church St., tel. 01947/6048570), in an easygoing 18th-century coaching inn. Here you'll find a characterful old building, a roaring fire in the grate, food to thrill in the fine restaurant, and a fabled guest list: Charles Dickens once overnighted and railway pioneer George Stephenson lectured here. En suite rooms are a fabulous £45 double.

HOSTELS • Whitby YHA. At the top of the famous 199 Steps, beside an 18th-century graveyard and photogenic Whitby Abbey (*see* Historic Sites, *below*), this hostel has haunting views of the abbey (especially at night) and of the town and harbor. The simple, clean facilities were once horse stables. Ask the staff for tips on hiking in the moors. Beds are £8.35. *East Cliff, YO22 4JT, tel. 01947/602878, fax 01947/ 825146. From bus/train station, turn right on New Quay Rd., cross bridge, turn left on Church St., follow curve to 199 Steps, climb them, and turn right through gateway. 66 beds. Reception open 5 PM–11 PM. Curfew 11, lockout 10–5. Closed Sun., Apr.–mid-May and mid-Sept.–Oct.; closed weekdays Nov.– Mar.*

CAMPING • Sandfield House Caravan Park. This is the nearest grounds to Whitby, but call ahead since it only has five tent sites (£3.50–£6.75, depending on size). *Sandsend Road, tel. 01947/602660. 5 sites. Toilets, showers. Closed Nov.–Easter.*

Whitby Holiday Village. The sprawling campsite has spots for £7–£11 and practical amenities such as laundry, a shop, bar, game room, and live music. Unfortunately, no buses run here from Whitby, so you'll have to walk or take a taxi. *Saltwick Bay, tel. 01947/602664. 1½ mi south of Whitby on the Cleveland Way. Toilets, showers. Closed Nov.–Easter.*

FOOD

In relation to the rest of the moors, Pickering and Whitby are positively cosmopolitan. Outside these towns you'll find little more than pub grub and fish-and-chips, if anything. Be sure to stock up on food and water before embarking on any lengthy hike.

PICKERING

Mulberries tearoom (5 Bridge St., tel. 01751/472337) serves classy but inexpensive food such as mushroom and asparagus pancakes (£2.90) and curried chicken with rice (£4). One of the few ethnic eateries in hiking areas, the **India Garden Tandoori Restaurant** (7 Eastgate Sq., tel. 01751/477039) serves up spicy chicken tandoori. The town's massive **Safeway** is hidden on The Ropery, the southern extension of Park Street. The **White Swan** (Market Place, tel. 01751/472288) sells the town's best pub grub, though it's somewhat pricey. For cheaper deals, try the **Black Swan** (18 Birdgate, tel. 01751/472286).

WHITBY

Whitby has more fish-and-chip shops and cafés than you can shake a stick at, and most are pretty good—a huge plateful of battered fish, chips, bread, and tea or coffee rarely costs more than £4. The two places where it costs considerably more just happen to be the two best fish-and-chip restaurants in England, so indulge yourself at either the diner-style **Trenchers** (New Quay Rd., opposite the train station, tel. 01947/603212), closed mid-November–mid-March, or at the more traditionally English **Magpie Café** (14 Pier Rd., tel. 01947/602058), past the swing bridge toward the beach. A fish-and-chip meal in either will set you back around £8–£9, but you'll be spoiled for life. Fish-and-chips aside, top marks go to **Grapevine** (2 Grape La., tel. 01947/820275), a friendly café and bistro (open evenings in summer) serving daily tapas specials like vegetarian tacos with salsa or Spanish-style chicken with chorizo sausage—you'll be able to fill up for under £6, a bit more if you snag a beer or glass of wine. The **Shepherd's Purse** (see Where to Sleep, above) has vegetarian lunches at similar prices, and sells a range of homemade take-out snacks. It also opens for dinner, when its menu concentrates on fish and vegetarian specials; most dishes cost well under £8. Of the myriad pubs serving food, the only one worth the bother is the popular **Duke of York** (Church St., at bottom of 199 Steps, tel. 01947/600324), which has a harbor view and serves lunch and dinner—a fresh crab salad costs £5.95, and prices go down from there. Two big supermarkets, the **Co-op,** across from the tourist office, and **Safeway,** on Flowergate (the hill opposite the bridge), provide all the picnic supplies you could need.

Aelred, the 12th-century abbot of Rievaulx, found in it "a marvelous freedom from the tumult of the world." And we thought the 20th century was harsh.

EXPLORING THE NORTH YORK MOORS

LONG-DISTANCE WALKS

THE CLEVELAND WAY • Britain's second-longest footpath meanders for 110 mi in a horseshoe loop along the outskirts of the park, from Filey to Saltburn-by-the-Sea and south by Rievaulx Abbey to Helmsley. The entire route is marked by acorn-shape signposts—as pioneering naturalist A. W. Wainwright said, "only a genius could get lost." Although well maintained, the path follows the swiftly changing terrain across from some of the highest cliffs in England, so a day's journey involves a lot of ups and downs. You can tackle the Cleveland Way in distinct sections: From Filey to Saltburn the path follows the impressive cliffs along the coast, via Scarborough, Robin Hood's Bay, and Whitby; from Saltburn to Helmsley the path takes you through the western moors. There are countless booklets and guides to the route, available in all local bookshops and tourist offices, but an indispensable one is the "Cleveland Way National Trail Accommodation and Information Guide," which recommends maps, public transport, accommodations, and restaurants. It's available at tourist offices (who sometimes collect a small charge for it), or direct from the National Park Office at the Helmsley tourist office (see Basics, above). If you want to hostel-hop, call the YHA Booking Bureau (tel. 01629/581061), which can organize the walk by booking your hostel accommodation and meals in advance. Long-distance walkers should consider picking up Ordnance Survey Outdoor Leisure Maps 26 and 27 or Ian Sampson's The Cleveland Way National Trail Guide (Aurum Press, £10.99).

THE LINK • When connected with the Cleveland Way, this 48-mi walk makes up the southern perimeter of the North York Moors National Park. Most walkers take about four days to complete the trek, beginning at Helmsley, passing through the **Tabular Hills,** and ending at Scarborough. The limestone soil of the Tabular Hills is host to a large number of wildflowers and plants, and you'll likely see gray squirrels and rabbit droppings (though probably not any actual bunnies) as you pass through forest areas. The open-air **Ryedale Folk Museum** in the gorgeous, rustic hamlet of Hutton-le-Hole (tel. 01751/417367), admission £3, is on the way, as are rolling farm and moorlands, and the impressive swathe of Dalby Forest, with its wind-sculpted rock outcrops. The walk is clearly marked, and there is a Regional Route (£4) guide to the area.

SHORTER WALKS

Tourist offices sell "Waymark Walk" leaflets (30p each) describing more than 40 walks within the park, each lasting anywhere from 45 minutes to four hours. The "Walks from the North Yorkshire Moors Railway" (60p) pamphlet, available at most tourist offices, details some especially beautiful hikes from stops along the North Yorkshire Moors Railway. **Newtondale,** the most dramatic valley in the moors, is easily reached from the station at **Newtondale Halt.** Three circular walks of 3–5 mi also begin at the station; they're well marked and easy to follow. Check the rail schedule so you don't miss the last train out.

If you don't have much time or equipment, Waymark Walk Number 15 is a good trek near the village of **Goathland.** This 3-mi circular path leaves from near the Goathland train station and leads to **Beck Hole** and the 70-ft **Mallyan Spout** waterfall. There's a fantastically tiny pub-that-time-forgot at Beck Hole, the **Birch Hall Inn,** where you can get a pint and a sandwich—if you can squeeze through the door to the microscopic bar room. The return route follows yellow and blue arrows along the track bed of the original Whitby–Pickering railway.

HISTORIC SITES

RIEVAULX • Considered one of England's most beautiful abbey remains, **Rievaulx Abbey** (pronounced REE-vo) near Helmsley, is a vision at once massive and delicate, with lofty stone walls and pointed arches. Originally an austere structure housing the plain-living Cistercian monks, the abbey became increasingly ornate during the 13th century as monastic life grew more luxurious; one abbot converted the large infirmary into his personal quarters. The open fields surrounding the abbey are bewitching—bring a picnic. If you want to stay near the abbey, **Helmsley YHA** (*see above*) is near the town center. *Rievaulx Abbey, tel. 01439/798228. From Helmsley, take the well-marked Cleveland Way 2 ½ mi through the woods, or catch the Helmsley–Stokesley bus or the Helmsley–Rievaulx–Sutton Bank Moorsbus. Admission £2.90. Open Apr.–Sept., daily 10–6; Oct.–Mar., daily 10–4.*

The nearby **Rievaulx Terrace and Temples** were built in 1758 as a contrast to the more rigid arrangement of the terrace at Duncombe Park (*see below*). The terrace has a panoramic cliff view that includes the abbey; there's also a small Tuscan rotunda at one end and an Ionic temple at the other. *Tel. 01439/798340. Admission £2.80. Open Apr.–Oct., daily 10:30–6.*

DUNCOMBE PARK • Designed in 1713, Duncombe Park is most famous for its 30 acres of lush classical landscaping along the River Rye. The house, much of which was added in 1843, has weathered a serious fire (1879) and use as a girls' school (1916–1985). Duncombe's descendant Lord Feversham is restoring the building and gardens. The aromatic garden is heavenly on a warm evening. The excellent woodland and riverside walks, each about an hour's length, will introduce you to peacocks, foxes, and magnificent views. *Helmsley, tel. 01439/770213 or 01439/771115. Admission to house and grounds £5.50, grounds only £3.50. Open May–Sept., Sun.–Fri. 11–4:30; Apr. and Oct., Sun.–Thurs. 11–4:30. Closed certain dates each month; call to check.*

WHITBY ABBEY/ST. MARY'S PARISH CHURCH • These majestic ruins are particularly haunting, so it's little wonder author Bram Stoker found them the perfect setting for Dracula's arrival in England. Sitting on a tall headland above Whitby's beach, Whitby Abbey has an evocative silhouette that looms over the lively harbor and town. The present structure was begun in 1220 on the site of a 7th-century monastery; only the three-tier choir, north transept, west doorway, and part of the nave remain. The abbey shares the cliff with St. Mary's, an 870-year-old parish church ringed by masses of wind-worn, blackened tombstones. The abbey, graveyard, and cliffside path are mentioned in Bram Stoker's *Dracula* (1897), three chapters of which are set in Whitby. For more information on the Stoker connection, pick up the "Dracula Trail" pamphlet (30p) from the local tourist office. *Abbey La., East Cliff, tel. 01947/603568. From Whitby, turn right on New Quay Rd., cross bridge, turn left on Church St. to 199 Steps. Admission to abbey £1.80, free admission to church. Open Apr.–Sept., daily 10–6; Oct.–Mar., daily 10–4.*

WHITBY MUSEUM/CAPTAIN COOK MEMORIAL MUSEUM • These two small museums in Whitby will give you a bit of insight into the region and shield you from the tourist trappings of the city. The **Whitby Museum** has exhibits in archaeology, geology, and natural history that cover the town's past, including Whitby jet (black) stones and local hero Captain Cook. If you want more of the Captain, the **Captain Cook Memorial Museum** details the historical and scientific impact of his voyages in the house where the young James Cook served as an apprentice. An evocative collection of letters, sketches, paintings, and artifacts are accompanied by models of ships that Cook sailed in. *Whitby Museum: Pan-*

nett Park, tel. 01947/602908. Admission £1. Open May–Sept., Mon.–Sat. 9:30–5, Sun. 2–5; Oct.–Apr., Mon.–Tues. 10:30–1, Wed.–Sat. 10:30–4, Sun. 2–4. Captain Cook Memorial Museum: Grape La., tel. 01947/601900. Admission £2.20. Open Easter–Oct., daily 9:45–5; Mar. and Nov., weekends 11–3.

SCARBOROUGH CASTLE • The ruins of Scarborough Castle dominate the promontory, which is reached by paths from the harbor. Dating from Norman times, the castle was built on the site of a Roman signal station and near a former Viking settlement. There are spectacular views across the North Bay, and to the town's wide sandy beaches and landscaped shore gardens. On the way back down into town, pop into Scarborough's little medieval church of **St. Mary,** where in the churchyard you'll find the grave of Anne, the youngest Brontë sister, who died in 1849; she was taken to Scarborough from Haworth in a final desperate effort to combat sickness with the sea air. *Castle Rd., tel. 01723/372451. Admission to castle £2.20. Open Apr.–Sept., daily 10–6; Oct.–Mar., Wed.–Sun. 10–1 and 2–4. Church also on Castle Rd., tel. 01723/371354. Admission free. Churchyard always open.*

YORKSHIRE DALES NATIONAL PARK

The Yorkshire Dales National Park in the central Pennines encompasses an amazing variety of sights, most of which are accessible by public transportation. The villages here display distinctive architecture that has changed little over the centuries. Some of the field barns and drystone walls (made *without* mortar) are more than 200 years old and still in use. The dales are home to woodlands, grit-stone moorlands, flowering meadows, and wildlife of all kinds. Some of the limestone outcroppings and caves can be explored safely even by city slickers. Heather, streams, and sheer valleys characterize the landscape, and sheep outnumber people over long stretches of the park. The bright months from April through October show off the best colors of the moors and fells, and the spring bloom is especially beautiful. One of the most intriguing phenomena is found in Malham and the **Malham Tarn** ("tarn" means a mountain lake). The lake's high elevation and lime saturation provide a specialized environment for unique flora and fauna. Popular walks like the challenging **Pennine Way** and **Three Peaks Walk** are complemented by gentler, shorter walks from the villages. The best place to start your visit is south of the park in the historic town of **Skipton,** which has the best connections to the rest of the country, or in **Ingleton,** on the western edge near Ingleborough—one of the Three Peaks.

BASICS

PUBLICATIONS

You'll need the free **"Dales Connections"** schedule to help you get around, available from most local information offices. It lists local train and bus services, which can be hit-or-miss. Service changes during the year, so the guide is published biannually—be sure to get the latest one. The free **"Yorkshire Dales Accommodation Guide,"** available at area tourist offices, has exhaustive listings from bunkhouses to luxury hotels. The extremely helpful *Visitor* newspaper (free) is a treasure trove of information, including schedules for guided walks and special events and information for disabled travelers. More detailed hiking information is available in any one of dozens of different guides to the region. Malham and the other National Park Centres stock a good range; ask for advice before buying, since not all are updated annually.

VISITOR INFORMATION

Before exploring the park, contact one of the six **National Park Centres,** most of which are closed November–March: **Aysgarth Falls** (tel. 01969/663424), **Clapham** (tel. 015242/51419), **Grassington** (Hebden Rd., tel. 01756/752774), **Hawes** (Station Yard, tel. 01969/667450), **Malham** (tel. 01729/830363), and **Sedbergh** (72 Main St., tel. 015396/20125). The biggest regional tourist office is in **Skipton** (Old Town Hall, 9 Sheep St., tel. 01756/792809), though it's still pretty small. Other offices are in **Ilkley** (Station Rd., tel. 01943/602319), **Richmond** (Friary Gardens, Victoria Rd., tel. 01748/850252), and **Settle** (Town Hall, Cheapside, tel. 01729/825192).

COMING AND GOING

BY BUS

Skipton is the main point of entry to the Dales; its bus station is in the center of town on Keighley Road, at the bottom of High Street. **Leeds City Link** (tel. 0113/245–7676) runs Bus X84 from Leeds to Skipton (no service on Sunday). **Cumberland** (tel. 01946/63222) Bus X9 goes from Ambleside and Windermere to Skipton, and from York to Skipton, Settle, and Ingleton once per day on Wednesday, Friday, and Saturday. However, there are also bus services from towns such as Richmond, Ripon, and Harrogate to various points in the Dales—the "Dales Connections" timetable (*see above*) is invaluable.

BY TRAIN

Trains on the Leeds–Settle–Carlisle line traverse the western side of the park along the Pennine Way, with stops in Skipton, Kirkby Stephen, and Dent, and in several other more remote villages. Trains from Leeds to Skipton (£4.80–£6.60 return; 45 mins) and Settle (£7.30 day return; 1 hr) depart every one to two hours (fewer services on Sunday). A Settle–Carlisle Day Ranger ticket (£18) provides unlimited travel between the two stations, allowing you to stop off for some isolated walking before picking up the train again. *Central information, tel. 0345/484950.*

GETTING AROUND

Trains will get you almost nowhere in the park, so you'll have to familiarize yourself with the "Dales Connections" schedule to understand the myriad bus lines operated by private bus companies. Plan to do a lot of walking if you don't have a car.

BY BIKE

Cycling has become so popular in the Dales that advance booking, especially in the summer, is a must. Rental prices average £10 per day, £40 per week. In Skipton try **Dave Ferguson Cycles** (1 Brook St., tel. 01756/795367); near Reeth in Swaledale, the **Grinton Lodge YHA** (tel.01748/884206) rents out bikes and provides route maps.

BY BUS

Several private bus companies serve the park's interior, but services and route names and numbers change frequently so always double-check with the nearest tourist office. **Keighley and District** (tel. 01756/753123) Buses 71, 72, and 272 run from Skipton to **Grassington** hourly 8–6. From Skipton to **Malham,** catch **Pennine Motors** (tel. 01756/749215) Bus 210, which runs two or three times per day weekdays. Getting to and from **Hawes** requires either luck or persistence. Bus 800 runs from Grassington to Hawes only during the summer, and only on weekends—once on Saturday and twice on Sunday, with an additional bus on Tuesday from late July to late August. It's easier to approach from Richmond in the north: **Arriva** (tel. 0345/124125) Bus 156 or 157 runs to Hawes twice a day, but not on Sunday. Pennine Motors Bus 580 runs between Skipton and **Settle** about once an hour; on Saturday only, every two hours; there's no Sunday service. In addition, special summer services—often at weekends only— connect the more remote villages of Swaledale and Wharfedale. Each bus company has its own one-day bus pass for about £5, but unless you're traveling on one line exclusively you won't save much money.

WHERE TO SLEEP

The "Yorkshire Dales Accommodation Guide" (free at National Park Centers and tourist offices) is a fairly comprehensive listing of lodgings from B&Bs to campgrounds. B&Bs in the area charge £15–£20 per person, but they are not your only option, since hostels are ubiquitous and usually good. Most of the area's campgrounds tend to be near towns, so don't get stranded on a moor expecting to find a campsite—you may find yourself clinging to a sheep for warmth.

SKIPTON

Skipton's cheapest B&Bs are on Gargrave Road; to get there from the train station, turn right on Belmont Street and left on Brook Street, which meets Gargrave Road. **Peace Villas** (69 Gargrave Rd., tel. 01756/790672) offers simple accommodations and an English or vegetarian breakfast for £16 per person, no credit cards. **Bourne House** (22 Upper Sackville St., off Keighley Rd., tel. 01756/792633) has rooms for £15 per person, no credit cards; £17 if you want en suite facilities.

ELSEWHERE IN THE YORKSHIRE DALES

You might get the least expensive room in Skipton, but it's not exactly in the rural heart of the Dales. You tend to pay more out in the sticks, but it's worth it. In the tiny village of **Airton,** 10 mi northwest of Skipton and just 3 mi from Malham Cove, **Lindon House** (tel. 01729/830418) has beautiful views of the limestone country and provides comfortable rooms for £18 per person, no credit cards. In **Malham** itself, there are only a few central B&B options, like **Beck Hall** (tel. 01729/830332), charging from £16–£21 per person, no credit cards. Or you could stay at the **Riverhouse Hotel** (tel.01729/830315), whose standard doubles are a stretch to £42 (but £54 en suite). **Grassington** is a shade bigger and has a few more B&B options, like **Kirkfield** (Hebden Rd., tel. 01756/752385), where rooms are £17.50–£20 per person, no credit cards. The well-run **Ashfield House** (Summers Fold, tel. 01756/752584) is an amenable guest house just off the main street. Doubles are a pricey £64, but the rooms are en suite and the breakfast is excellent. It's closed mid-November–mid-February. Nearly all local **pubs** have rooms to rent and while you might pay £45–£50 for an en suite room (though sometimes less), you don't have very far to stagger for a cozy fireside drink and bar meal.

HOSTELS

The Yorkshire Dales has a well-planned hostel setup, meaning you can walk from one remote hostel to the next without too much trouble. Beds usually cost £7.50–£9.15. Most area maps indicate where the hostels are—make sure you pick one up before heading into the wilds. Hostels in Yorkshire Dales National Park include **Aysgarth Falls** (Aysgarth, tel. 01969/663260); **Dentdale** (Cowgill, tel. 015396/25251); the highly recommended hostel in **Hawes** (Lancaster Terr., tel. 01969/667368); **Ingleton** (Greta Tower, Sammy La., tel. 015242/41444); remote **Keld** (Keld Lodge, Upper Swaledale, tel. 01748/886259); **Kettlewell** (Whernside House, tel. 01756/760232); the peaceful and relaxing hostel in **Linton,** near Grassington (Old Rectory, Linton-in-Craven, tel. 01756/752400); **Malham** (John Dower Memorial Hostel, tel. 01729/830321); and **Stainforth** (Taitlands, Stainforth, tel. 01729/823577). Note that many close in the winter, either for a few months at a stretch, or for a day or so a week—always call to check.

CAMPING

For info on camping barns in the Yorkshire Dales, contact the tourist centers or **Camping Barns Reservations Office** (16 Shawbridge St., Clitheroe, Lancashire BB7 1LY, tel. 01200/428366). The YHA brochure "Stay in a Camping Barn" details many in the Yorkshire Dales park and is available at many tourist offices and hostels. Pick up a "Yorkshire Dales Caravan & Camp Sites" pamphlet (10p) for extensive listings of all the campgrounds in the area. The Skipton tourist office also has a free handout on local camping sites. Near Skipton is **Tarn House Caravan Park** (Stirton, tel. 01756/795309), offering showers and a tent site for £5. Stupendous views and a convenient location ½ mi from Hawes make **Bainbridge Ings** (off A684, tel. 01969/667354) one of the best campgrounds in the center of the park—so much so that it's often booked up with long-term campers. Basic facilities include showers and toilets, and a stone wall provides shelter from the cold, cold wind. Sites are £2–£2.50 per person. Near the Aysgarth Falls National Park Centre is **Westholme Park** (Aysgarth, just off A684, tel. 01969/663268), closed November–Easter, well-stocked with toilets, showers, a laundry, shop, bar, and lots of trees and footpaths. Call ahead to book a tent site, which costs £3–£4.40.

FOOD

SKIPTON

Skipton has plenty of pubs, cafés, and tea shops, as well as restaurants serving Indian and Chinese food, kebabs, and pizza. **Herbs** (10 High St., tel. 01756/790619), closed Tuesday and Sunday, has the only strictly vegetarian menu and whips up tasty salads, sandwiches, and teatime snacks. The entrance to Herbs is through **Healthy Life Natural Food Centre,** which sells juices, dried fruit, and nuts. For takeout sandwiches made to order, go to **Jacques Simons Tea Rooms** (6 Victoria Sq., no phone) in the Victoria St. shopping area. The best bar meals are at the **Woolly Sheep Inn** (38 Sheep St., tel. 01756/700966), a jolly old 17th-century inn near the tourist office—it has rooms, too (around £20 per person) if you can't pry yourself away.

ELSEWHERE IN THE YORKSHIRE DALES

There are several tearooms and cafés in **Grassington,** but the best meal hereabouts is actually 1 mi west of the village: The **Old Hall Inn** in Threshfield (tel. 01756/752441), closed Monday and dinner Sunday.

A stone-flagged, rustic country pub, it has an out-of-the-ordinary menu that draws people from miles around—most things go for under £7. In Grassington itself, give the **Dales Kitchen** (51 Main St., tel. 01756/753208) a whirl: English and European cooking during the day and themed dinners once a month. At Linton, opposite the youth hostel, the **Fountains Inn** (no phone) on the green has good Yorkshire beer and above-average bar food, including roast lamb. In **Hawes, Laburnham House** B&B (The Holme, tel. 01969/667717) has a tea room attached, and a little terrace for summer dining, or head out to the **Wensleydale Creamery** (Gayle La., tel. 01969/667664), where they make the famous Wensleydale cheese. There are tours of the plant for £2, cheeses to sample in the shop, and light meals and snacks in the *Buttery,* formerly the butter-making room. **Malham** is short on places to eat, but you don't need to look any farther than the central **Buck Inn** (tel. 01729/830317), a welcoming pub with a hikers' bar and good food. For those with a car, make for Hetton's **Angel Inn** (5 mi north of Skipton, off B6265, tel. 01756/730263), a tiny hamlet that holds a pub-restaurant with a big reputation—fish is a specialty.

EXPLORING THE YORKSHIRE DALES

The Dales can be roughly divided into two terrains. The south is characterized by millstone grit, a dark-gray rock formerly used to make, yes, millstones. There's more dirt near the earth's surface here than in the north, and the landscape is subtler—freshly mown fields, lush forests, and shaggy grass. It's more industrialized than the north and transport is easier to find. The north (northwest of the Craven fault line) contains the best limestone sights in the country and is very dramatic; velvety grass is the only major vegetation you'll find. Here's where you'll see the pavements and potholes that limestone, a porous stone, becomes. Traveling from east to west is not so difficult in the park, though north to south is tough unless you use the Settle–Carlisle train. Go to a tourist office and plan your route carefully and well in advance, as transportation is infrequent. Be prepared to do a lot of walking. In Dent, for example, the village is 4 mi from the bus station.

HIKING

Before undertaking a hike, pick up one of the helpful "National Park Trail Series" brochures for 30p–40p each from any tourist office. You won't have to wander aimlessly on the moors since there's dozens of books and maps covering the popular but difficult **Pennine Way,** which runs south–north through Malham and Hawes on its way to Scotland. Other hiking trails such as **Three Peaks, Dales Way,** and **Ribble Way** provide an intermediate challenge. The 70-mi Dales Way, in particular, is a perfect trail to section off into several day hikes. It runs from Ilkley to Bowness, linking Leeds and Bradford with the Dales and the Lake District. *The Dales Way Route Guide,* available at the Skipton tourist office, provides excellent directions.

NEAR SKIPTON AND SETTLE • Not many trails begin in Skipton, but a short bus ride takes you into prime hiking territory. A 7-mi stretch of the Pennine Way near Malham traverses some rocky, uneven areas and passes **Malham Tarn,** a lime-rich lake, and **Malham Cove,** a natural amphitheater surrounded by 70-ft-high cliffs. The hike begins at Malham National Park Centre; to reach Malham, take Pennine Bus 210 from Skipton.

There are two routes you can follow through high limestone country from **Stainforth** to **Cattrig Force** and **Langcliffe:** the easy way (4 mi), or the easier way (2½ mi). Both pass two of the area's prettiest waterfalls. The hikes begin at Stainforth Car Park, 1 mi north of Settle off B6479. The guide "Walks in Ribblesdale No. 2" provides hair-splitting detail and some good background info on the walks.

Another nice amble is the 5-mi walk from Settle to **Victoria Cave,** where 120,000-year-old mammoth bones and some Roman artifacts were found earlier this century. The path is marked fairly well, so you may not need a guide; if you don't want to chance it, obtain "Walks in Ribblesdale No. 3."

NEAR HAWES AND AYSGARTH • **Hardraw Force,** the highest unbroken waterfall (100 ft) in England, is only about 2 mi from the village of Hawes. The waterfall is most impressive after a heavy rain; if there's been a dry spell, the torrent is reduced to a trickle. The walk begins from the National Park Information Centre in Hawes and is easy to follow.

The village of Aysgarth, about 8 mi east of Hawes, is the starting point for the 7-mi hike to **Castle Bolton,** a onetime prison for Mary, Queen of Scots, during her involuntary 16th-century tour of Northern England. The hike begins at the Aysgarth Park Information Centre. Another walk leaving from the Park Information Centre takes you by **Aysgarth Falls** through amazing hazel woodland. Turn right outside the car park and follow the old train tracks, crossing the road and turning right to enter Freeholder's Wood.

Then follow posts numbered one through seven to loop back to the trailhead. You'll pass by the Lower and Middle Falls, and precious marshland. The walk takes about an hour.

HISTORIC SITES

FOUNTAINS ABBEY AND STUDLEY ROYAL WATER GARDEN • Northeast of Skipton are the vast ruins of Fountains Abbey, surrounded by some of the most gorgeous neoclassic gardens in Europe. At the height of its glory in the 14th century, the abbey's wealthy Cistercian brotherhood profited from an extensive system of granges, farms, mills, and mines. In the 18th century the ruined abbey became a picturesque feature of the elaborately landscaped gardens, which include ponds, waterfalls, temples, and wooded walks. Among the other historic buildings in the gardens are **Fountains Hall,** a Jacobean mansion built with stones from the abbey, and **St. Mary's,** a richly decorated Victorian church on the edge of a medieval **deer park.** Bring some bread crumbs for the ducks, swans, and pheasants. *Fountains Abbey, tel. 01765/608888 or 01765/601005 (weekends). From Skipton, take B6265 toward Ripon. Admission £4.30. Open Jan.–Mar., daily 10–5 (or dusk); Apr.–Sept., daily 10–7; Oct.–Dec., daily 10–5 (or dusk). Closed Fri. Nov.–Jan.*

SKIPTON CASTLE • Built in the 11th century, Skipton Castle is in fine shape despite the beating it took from Cromwell's troops in 1645; when Lady Jane Clifford was restoring the castle in the 1650s, she was given permission to replace the roof, as long as it wasn't made strong enough to bear cannons. "Desormais," (Henceforth!) the Clifford family motto, greets you at the front gates. One of the most striking views of the castle is from below, from the wooded tow road between the canal and Eller Beck. *North end of High St., off the Bailey, tel. 01756/792442. Admission £4. Open Mar.–Sept., Mon.–Sat. 10–6, Sun. 2–6; Oct.–Feb., Mon.–Sat. 10–4, Sun. 2–4.*

BRONTË COUNTRY

HAWORTH

After the three Brontë sisters spun passionate novels out of their provincial lives, what was once a sedate Yorkshire handweavers' village was permanently engraved on the map of England. Here in Haworth, a gray west Yorkshire village, Charlotte Brontë wrote *Jane Eyre,* Anne, *The Tenant of Wildfell Hall,* Emily, and the incomparable *Wuthering Heights.* The steep and cobbled main street of Haworth (pronounced HOW-weth) will lead you past innumerable tea shops and B&Bs up to the 19th-century church where Charlotte and Emily rest, and to the **Brontë Parsonage Museum** (tel. 01535/642323), which draws literary pilgrims from around the world. The parsonage has been restored to its 1850s appearance and contains countless pieces of Brontëana, including clothing, portraits, letters, and sketches. Admission is £3.80, and it's open April–September, daily 10–5:30, October–March, daily 11–5; closed mid-January–early February.

Year-round, buses bring flocks of British students and foreign tourists to Haworth, who walk through the museum, have tea, and then leave town. The best way to enjoy Haworth is to stay over in one of the quaint B&Bs and allow a full day for walking across the solitary, heather-covered moors that Emily often escaped to. "My sister Emily loved the moors," Charlotte Brontë wrote of her sibling. "Flowers brighter than the rose bloomed in the blackest of the heath for her; out of a sullen hollow in a livid hillside her mind could make an Eden." Some people, dwellers in the north of England included, find the wildness of these moors rather oppressive, but all fans of Heathcliff and his Cathy will rejoice in them. "She found in the bleak solitude many and dear delights," Charlotte continued. "Liberty was the breath of Emily's nostrils; without it she perished." The nearby **tourist office** (2–4 West La., tel. 01535/642329) can help you with accommodations and has loads of maps and books on the Brontës. They also sell inexpensive leaflets with maps to help you find your way to sites associated with Emily Brontë's *Wuthering Heights,* including **Top Withens** (Wuthering Heights), **Ponden Hall** (Thrushcross Grange), and **Ponden Kirk** (Penistone Crag). The 25p "MiniGuide to Haworth and Brontë Country" also has a useful map and lists attractions and travel info. The trails are well marked, but you should bring windproof/waterproof clothing and sturdy shoes.

COMING AND GOING • To reach Haworth, take the Metro train from Leeds to Keighley. There are about three hourly. From Keighley, take **Keighley and District** (tel. 0113/245–7676) Bus 663, 664, or 665 to Haworth; one leaves every hour during the day. The same buses make the direct journey from Bradford, also every hour.

Leeds City Station is a major junction for trains to this region of Yorkshire. Routes from Leeds run to Edinburgh (from as little as £24 if you book a week in advance, otherwise £42–£47 standard return), Manchester (£9.30 day return, £11.80 standard return), and York (£6.80–£8.70 day return), as well as other major cities in northern England. Metro trains provide cheap local service to York, Hull, Sheffield, Manchester, Liverpool, Blackpool, and Skipton. *New Station St., across from City Sq., tel. 0345/484950. Open Mon.–Sat. 8–8, Sun. 9–8.*

Stop by **Gateway Yorkshire,** a huge tourist center inside the train station, for free maps and tourist guides, and bus and train schedules. They also book accommodations, provide information on car rental, and sell phonecards and stamps. *The Arcade, City Station, tel. 0113/242–5242; 0891/137–400 24-hr information line. Open Mon.–Sat. 9:30–6, Sun. 10–4.*

The **National Express Coach Station** in Leeds is permanently busy with buses crisscrossing England; Leeds is a frequent stopover point for buses bound for Edinburgh (£29 return, £35 if traveling on Friday), Newcastle (£14.50 return), and Manchester (£6 return). *City Bus Station, St. Peter's St., tel. 0990/808080.*

WHERE TO SLEEP AND EAT • More than 20 guest houses, B&Bs, and hotels surround the village, and they are all listed in the tourist office's free accommodations booklet. Just across from the church and the parsonage, **Apothecary Guest House** (86 Main St., tel. and fax 01535/643642) has single, double, and triple rooms (all with private bath) for £19 per person including a full English breakfast. The rooms are lovely, and Mr. Sisley will gladly give you a vegetarian breakfast, if you wish. **Heather Cottage** (25–27 Main St., tel. 01535/644511), at the bottom of the hill, is a pretty B&B in an 18th-century weavers' cottage. They have rooms for £16 per person and also serve cream tea and hot meals. For a top-priced accommodation, try the **Old White Lion Hotel** (6 West Lane, tel. 01535/642313), next door to the church where Patrick Brontë preached and not far from the family parsonage. The place is cheery, comfortable, and filled with antique accents. Rooms go for £55 to £65 and the kitchen can provide filling dinners. **Weaver's** (15 West Lane, tel. 01535/643822) is the best restaurant in Haworth, an informal and inviting place that serves up some native specialties such as Gressingham duck. If you're lucky, you'll land one of the four guest rooms, which run about £70 for a double. For pub food, try the **Black Bull** (Main St., tel. 01535/642249), which is where the Brontës' scapegrace brother, Branwell, drank himself into an early grave. You can overnight here from £23 per person.

Call ahead before taking the ½-mi hike from the train station if you intend to stay at **Haworth YHA,** located in a beautiful Victorian mill owner's home. Beds are £9.15. *Longlands Hall, Longlands Dr., Lees La., BD22 8RT, tel. 01535/642234. From railway station, head east along Mill Hey Rd. until it becomes Lees La.; just before roundabout, turn left onto Longlands Dr. Reception open 7 AM–11 PM. Lockout 11 PM. Closed Jan., and Sun. Oct.–Mar.*

NORTHUMBRIA

UPDATED BY JULES BROWN

ind-blasted castles, raging Celtic saints, rampaging Roman emperors, and stony fortress-cathedrals—with this cast of characters and settings no wonder there's a feeling of deeply entrenched history throughout Northumbria. Originally the region's name meant "Lands North of the River Humber," when, centuries ago, it was an Anglo-Saxon kingdom. Now Northumbria consists of three main counties: Durham, Tyne and Wear, and Northumberland—alike in their numberless historic associations and monuments of a vigorous warlike past, starting, of course, with the ancient Roman stones of **Hadrian's Wall,** snaking away across the landscape, and continuing through the mystic rocks of **Holy Island.** Amazingly, Northumbria is still reminiscent of the days when emperors and kings passed along its roads as their armies battled in the backwards and forwards surges of warfare. For those intrepid travelers that come to this part of Britain, a landscape of untamed natural beauty awaits—a prime place for hiking, that fabulous freebie of activities. And since tourism has never gained much of a hold up here, the good news is that prices for hotels and restaurants can be 10%–15% lower than elsewhere on the sceptered isle.

Northumbrian history is bookended by two groups: the Romans and the Reivers. From the 1st until the 5th century, the Romans occupied Britain, and for most of that era, Northumbria was the well-patrolled northern frontier of their empire. From the 14th century until the union of the Scottish and English parliaments in 1704, fierce border wars were ceaselessly waged upon Northumbrian soil; a border town like Berwick-upon-Tweed could be English one year and Scottish the next. The region's conflicts were civilian as well as military: From the rugged cliffs of the North Sea coast westward through the **Cheviot Hills,** bandit gangs known as Reivers, who were allied with influential families, pillaged the countryside almost unchecked—except by other bands of Reivers.

The region's turbulent, often violent, history has left a wealth of grand and battered monuments to create snapshots within these more peaceful times. The imposing ruins of Hadrian's Wall, built in the 2nd and 3rd centuries by Roman soldiers, traverses some of the most striking scenery of Northumberland National Park. Along the windswept eastern shore, magnificent castles abound, including ruined **Warkworth Castle** and richly furnished Alnwick Castle. Holy Island, once a cradle of Christian learning, still bears the ruined arches of **Lindisfarne Priory,** reachable only when the North Sea retreats, granting the island a tenuous union with Northumbria's shore.

Only a few of **Newcastle's** historic buildings escaped the wrecking ball in the 1960s, though its "new castle" did—now over 900 years old and still going strong. The rest of the brash industrial city is under-

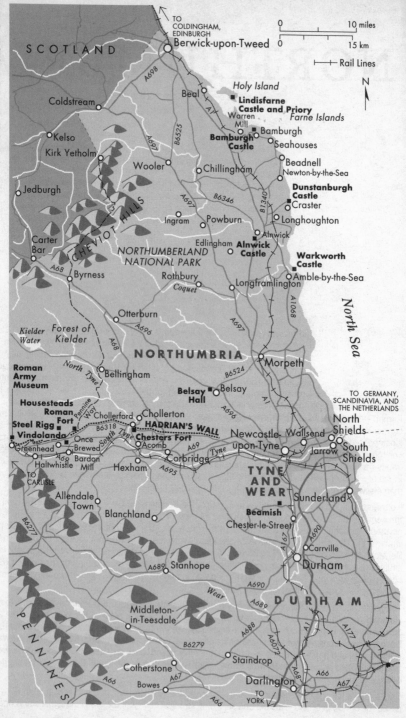

0   10 miles

0   15 km

⊢—⊢ Rail Lines

N

TO COLDINGHAM,
EDINBURGH
Berwick-upon-Tweed

SCOTLAND

Holy Island

Lindisfarne
Castle and Priory   *Farne Islands*

Beal

Warren
Mill   ○ **Bamburgh**
Bamburgh
Castle   Seahouses

Coldstream

○ Kelso
Kirk Yetholm   Wooler   ○ Chillingham   Beadnell
Newton-by-the-Sea

○ Jedburgh

CHEVIOT HILLS   **Dunstanburgh**
Castle
○ Craster

Ingram   ○ Powburn   Longhoughton

Carter
Bar   **NORTHUMBERLAND**
NATIONAL PARK   Edlingham   **Alnwick**
Castle   **Warkworth**
Castle

A68   Byrness   Rothbury   Amble-by-the-Sea

Coquet   Longframlington

○ Otterburn

Kielder
Water   *Forest of*
Kielder   **NORTHUMBRIA**

North Tyne   Bellingham   Morpeth

North Sea

Roman
Army
Museum   **Belsay**
Hall   ○ Belsay

Housesteads
Roman
Fort   Chollerford   ○ Chollerton
Steel Rigg   **HADRIAN'S WALL**   TO GERMANY,
SCANDINAVIA, AND
THE NETHERLANDS
Vindolanda   **Chesters Fort**
Once   Acomb   North
Greenhead   Brewed   **Newcastle**   Wallsend   Shields
Bardon   *South Tyne*   Corbridge   upon-Tyne   Jarrow   South
Haltwhistle   Mill   ○ Hexham   Shields
TO CARLISLE

Allendale
Town   Blanchland   **TYNE**
AND
WEAR   Sunderland

Beamish
Chester-le-Street

Stanhope   Carrville

Wear   **Durham**

Middleton-
in-Teesdale   **D U R H A M**

PENNINES   Cotherstone   Staindrop

Bowes   Darlington

TO
YORK

going something of a renaissance, with a party zone of bars and restaurants developing on its renovated Quayside. Most foreign visitors, though, still see Newcastle as basically a transportation and retail hub, and focus on the medieval castle and cathedral at nearby **Durham** instead. This university town, which rests beside the River Wear, has a real air of elegance and quickly becomes many people's favorite northeastern city. But despite its rich historical legacy and outgoing locals eager to show off their homeland, Northumbria remains a little-traveled and relatively unspoiled corner of England.

GETTING AROUND

Newcastle-upon-Tyne, referred to commonly as Newcastle, is the area's main transport hub; there's main-line train service from London and Manchester through Durham and Newcastle and up into Scotland. To reach other towns in Northumbria by train, you must change to local lines in Durham or Newcastle. National Express buses connect these two cities to the rest of the country; a host of private bus companies provides local service. To understand how it all works, pick up the **"Northumberland Public Transport Guide"** (£1) from a local tourist office—it will help you avoid depending on a bus that comes only once a week. It's also available by mail (send £1.80) from the Public Transport Team, Environment Department (Northumberland County Council, County Hall, Morpeth, NE61 2EF, tel. 01670/533128). A one-day **North East Explorer Pass** (£4.95), available directly from bus drivers, allows unlimited travel on most of the region's *local* bus lines (not National Express lines), from the Scottish border at Berwick, south to Scarborough and west to Carlisle. Newcastle and the Tyne and Wear region, south of Northumbria, have their own series of travel passes, though you won't need them for any of the sights that we cover. But if you fancy a day out in the city, call Newcastle's **Nexus Travel Line** (tel. 0191/232–5325), open Monday–Saturday 8–8, Sunday 9–5. Note that the North East Explorer pass is also valid on Newcastle's metro and the Shields Ferry. Seriously consider renting a car if you plan to visit the coastal castles; buses are sporadic and hard to coordinate.

The bleak moors, gray cliffs, and sturdy castles of Northumbria have appeared in several major movies: Mel Gibson filmed Hamlet at Dunstanburgh, while the 1999 Oscar-winner Elizabeth used Alnwick and Warkworth castles to great effect.

DURHAM

Durham remains one of northern England's most attractive cities, despite its long mining history and its location midway between the industrial cities of Darlington and Newcastle. Dramatically sited, the heart of the ancient city stands on a rocky promontory above a loop of the River Wear (it rhymes with "beer"). In summer, the gray medieval stones of Durham's castle and famous cathedral contrast with the green hills surrounding the town; in winter, the willow trees along the frozen river conjure the perfect setting for a fairy tale.

The Normans and the Scots fought repeatedly for control of Durham, which was ruled for nearly 1,000 years by powerful prince-bishops. They kept the city and county on a tight rein, coining their own money, raising their own taxes, and maintaining their own laws and courts; not until 1836 were these rights finally restored to the English Crown. The town's centerpiece is Durham Cathedral, probably the finest piece of Norman architecture in Britain. The view of the cathedral from the Elvet Banks on the far side of the river is memorable; make the effort to see it. Durham Castle, built on the highest hill in the center of town, testifies to the prince-bishops' dual roles as religious and political leaders. Today, the castle houses University College, one of the colleges that comprise Durham University, which is the third-oldest in England after Oxford and Cambridge. You'll soon realize that Durham is more than just its cathedral and castle. It's a great place to explore, with steep, narrow streets overlooked by perilously angled medieval houses and 18th-century town houses. The most attractive part of the city is near the Castle Green and along the banks of the river, where families go boating, anglers cast their lines, and lovers stroll hand-in-hand along the shaded paths.

BASICS

MAIL

Durham's post office offers poste restante and has a bureau de change. *33 Silver St., DH1 3RE, tel. 0191/386–4644. Open weekdays 9–5:30, Sat. 9–7.*

VISITOR INFORMATION

The tourist office distributes free city maps and has lists of accommodations posted by the window for late arrivals. They stock a number of helpful publications, including "What's on in Durham" (free), "Cycling in County Durham" (£1.95), and packs of city walks (four for £1). The huge, free *County Durham Holiday Guide* lists attractions and lodging, and the "County Durham Attractions" sheet gives transport information. The staff also books rooms for free and leads free 90-minute city walks Wednesday and Saturday at 2:15, June through September. *Market Pl., tel. 0191/384–3720. From bus station, turn right on North Rd., cross Framwellgate Bridge, and continue up Silver St. to Market Pl. From train station, walk east on Leazes Rd., turn left at St. Nicholas' Church. Open July–Aug., Mon.–Sat. 9:30– 6:30, Sun. 2–5; June and Sept., Mon.–Sat. 9:30–5:50; Oct.–May, Mon.–Sat 10–5.*

COMING AND GOING

Durham is on the main London–Edinburgh rail line, three hours north of London and two hours south of Edinburgh. For info on the area's public transport, call County Durham's **travel hot line** (tel. 0191/383– 3337) weekdays 9–5. Durham's train and bus stations are about two blocks apart and about ¼ mi west of the cathedral and castle. To reach the latter two sights, walk down North Road, cross Framwellgate Bridge, veer left on Silver Street, cross Market Place, then turn right on Saddler Street; the castle and manicured lawn of the cathedral are dead ahead.

BY BUS

National Express coaches (tel. 0990/808080) to Durham depart every two hours from London's Victoria Coach Station (£27 return) and Edinburgh (£21 return). Buses in Durham all stop at the North Road bus station. Several different companies operate out of here; the tourist office (*see above*) has information and timetables. If you're traveling from Durham to Newcastle, trains are much faster than buses (20 minutes as opposed to 50) and only very slightly more expensive.

BY TRAIN

There is hourly rail service to Durham from London's King's Cross Station (from as low as £31 return if you book at least 2 weeks in advance, otherwise £66–£77 return). Trains leave from Durham for Edinburgh every two hours, for Newcastle and York every 30 minutes. Lockers inside the station cost £1.50 per 24 hours. *North Rd., tel. 0345/484950. Open 6 AM–midnight.*

WHERE TO SLEEP

Most of the town's inexpensive B&Bs are on Claypath/Gilesgate and its side streets, about ¼ mi northeast of the city center. To get there from the tourist office, turn left (away from town center) and cross the overpass to Claypath. Be sure to book ahead for late June, when the town fills up for graduation. Since the closure of the city's youth hostel, Durham's cheapest option is camping—and it's worth your while to endure the 2-mi bus ride to **Grange Camping and Caravan Site** (Meadow La., Carrville, tel. 0191/384–4778), with wide-open, manicured meadows and a food shop. The 14 tent sites are £3.50 per person. Take Bus 220 or 222 (to Sunderland) from the bus station to Carrville High Street; they run every 15 minutes during the day and until 11 at night. In July or August, you won't have much trouble finding lodging in one of Durham University's residence halls—a savings for the high-season traveler.

Castle View Guest House. This 25-year-old building, in the heart of the old city near St. Margaret's Church, has a magnificent view of the cathedral and—surprise, surprise—the castle, too. Double rooms run £40–£50 (the more expensive ones have their own private facilities). *4 Crossgate, DH1 4PS, tel. 0191/386–8852. See Georgian Town House below for directions. 6 rooms, 3 with bath.*

Georgian Town House. Exactly as the name suggests, this well-sited little hotel, at the top of a cobbled street overlooking cathedral and castle, makes the best of its Georgian exterior and fittings. You pay your money (£45–£50 double), and you get your view of the cathedral. *10 Crossgate, DH1 4PS, tel. 0191/*

386–8070. From bus station turn right on North Rd., right on Neville St., and Crossgate and the hotel is straight ahead at the top of the hill. 6 rooms with bath. Cash only.

STUDENT HOUSING

The tourist office has a free list of all 12 colleges that rent rooms July through September; some also rent rooms during the students' Easter holiday and at Christmas.

College of St. Hild and St. Bede. This massive college prides itself on its first-rate facilities, including tennis and squash courts, a big bar, and TV lounges. The buildings themselves date back "only" to the 18th century. A simple bed and breakfast in a student room with wash basin costs £19 per person. *Leazes Rd., tel. 0191/374–3069, fax 0191/374–4740. From Market Pl., walk south on Saddler St., turn left on Elvet Bridge, left on New Elvet Bridge, and right on Leazes Rd. 400 singles and 80 doubles, none with bath. Laundry. Closed Oct.–June (except Easter holiday). Cash only.*

University College. It's housed in Durham Castle, which means you get to eat in the beautiful 13th-century Great Hall. Beds cost £19.50 (£27.50 with bath) per person, including breakfast. *Durham Castle, Palace Green, tel. 0191/374–3863. From Market Pl., walk south on Saddler St., turn right on Owengate. 100 singles and 50 doubles, 6 with bath. Cash only. Closed Oct.–June. (except Easter holiday).*

FOOD

The best times to search for a hearty meal are lunchtime and early on weekday evenings, when otherwise pricey restaurants lure hungry students with happy-hour specials. There are sandwich bars, tearooms, and greasy cafés all over the city center, while the ornate **Market Hall,** open Thursday and Friday 9–4, Saturday 9–4:30, is the place to pick up fresh fruit and veggies.

Almshouses Café. Look out the windows onto Palace Green while chowing down on loads of excellent vegetarian dishes. They also serve meat and fish dishes, and the menu changes daily. *Palace Green, tel. 0191/386–1054. From Market St., turn right on Saddler St., right on Owengate. Closes at 8 PM (Oct.–Apr. at 5 PM).*

Pizzeria Venezia. This cheery Italian trattoria-pizzeria offers real bargains at lunch when pizzas and pastas sell for around £4. Things don't increase much in price at other times either, so go for the full feast and you'll eat for less than £10. *4 Framwellgate Bridge, tel. 0191/384–6777. Closed Sun.*

Shaheen's Indian Bistro. Durham's former post office now houses a mouthwatering Indian restaurant. The fiery tandoori chicken is especially good. Seafood dishes cost a few quid more. Reservations are advised. *48 North Bailey, tel. 0191/386–0960. From Market Pl., walk south on Saddler St. (which becomes North Bailey). Closed Sun.*

Vennel's Courtyard Cafe. This centrally located cafeteria attracts Durham's students with a great variety of meat and vegetarian entrées, plus sandwiches, quiches, and homemade cakes. *Saddler's Yard (behind 71 Saddler's St.), no phone. Closes at 5 PM.*

WORTH SEEING

On the peninsula created by the River Wear, the castle and cathedral are the historic and aesthetic heart of Durham. Many people never leave this green kernel during their stay; a circular walk along the river banks can take an hour or a whole day, depending on your mood. For further contemplation, pay your pound entrance fee and stroll around the 18 acres of gardens at **Durham University Botanic Garden** (Hollingside La., off South Rd., tel. 0191/374–7971), about a 30-minute walk from the center of town. Or, on one of those rare days when the sun shines long and brightly, try and race the college boat crews on the river in your own dumpy rowboat—available from **Brown's Boat House** (Elvet Bridge, tel. 0191/386–3779), from April to early November, for £2.50 per person an hour. Summer cruises (£3) on the Prince Bishop leave from the bridge, too, while the Durham Regatta in June (book accommodations well in advance if you're coming then) sees the bridges and river banks packed with spectators.

DURHAM CATHEDRAL

Cradled on the west end by the River Wear, Durham Cathedral enjoys the most beautiful setting of any English cathedral. The Saxons built a small church near this site in 998, but it was destroyed completely to accommodate the present structure, built between 1093 and 1279. The impressive exterior influenced many subsequent Gothic structures, and the cathedral's **choir** features the earliest use of rib vaulting in Western architecture. The beautiful, 15th-century **Galilee Chapel** contains the tomb of the Venerable Bede, author of the first historical text in English. The **Chapel of the Nine Altars** at the east end houses the shrine of St. Cuthbert, whose relics were brought here in 995. Climb the 325 steps of the **tower** for a panoramic view of Durham. On the cathedral's north entrance is a replica of a 12th-century bronze knocker shaped like the head of a beast. By grasping the ring, medieval criminals could claim sanctuary; cathedral records show that 331 felons sought this protection from 1464 to 1524. The original door knocker is in the **treasury,** which also contains the coffin of St. Cuthbert, vestments, manuscripts, plate, and parish treasures. *Palace Green, tel. 0191/386–4266. Admission to cathedral free but £2 donation suggested, tower £2, treasury £2. Cathedral open May–Sept., daily 9:30 AM–8 PM; Oct.– Apr., daily 9:30–6; tower open Mon.–Sat. 9:30–4; treasury open Mon.–Sat. 10–4:30, Sun. 2–4:30. Tours, May–Sept., Weekdays at 10:30 and 2, cost £2.50.*

DURHAM CASTLE

Durham Castle served as the palace of Durham's prince-bishops for 800 years until 1832, when the bishops turned it over to become Durham University's University College. Parts of the castle date back to Norman times, but much of the structure was rebuilt in the 18th century by architect James Wyatt in a Romanesque vein. The original keep crumbled and was replaced by the present structure in 1840 for use as dorm rooms. The **Great Hall,** built in the late 13th century, houses two thrones that symbolize the bishops' dual functions as princes of church and state. The room now serves as a stately dining hall. *Palace Green, tel. 0191/374–3800. Admission, by guided tour only, £3. Guided tours offered Easter and July–Sept., Mon.–Sat. 10–12:30, 2–4, Sun. 10–noon, 2–4; Oct.–June, Mon., Wed., and Sat. 2–4.*

MUSEUM OF ARCHEOLOGY

This wonderful little museum provides a perfect excuse to take a walk along the river. Tucked into an old mill, it has a splendid collection of local artifacts, including Romano-Celtic stone altars inscribed to Cybele, Fortuna, and the Mother Goddesses and a "Hidden Durham" display that points you to easily missed 14th- to 17th-century buildings still in use throughout the city. The upstairs gallery hosts touring exhibits. *The Old Fulling Mill, The Banks, tel. 0191/374–3623. Admission £1. Open Apr.–Oct., daily 11– 4; Nov.–Mar., Wed.–Fri. 12:30–3, weekends 11:30–3:30.*

AFTER DARK

Most of the nightlife in downtown Durham is aimed squarely at the student pound, and you'll have to look hard for a venue that's free of collegiate sweat. Of the pubs, the **Hogshead** (58 Saddler St., tel. 0191/386–4134) is a real student haunt. The high-profile **Coach and Eight** (Bridge House, Framwellgate Bridge, tel. 0191/386–3284) can be just as rowdy, but in summer the outside seating makes it more appealing. The **Swan and Three Cygnets** (Elvet Bridge, tel. 0191/384–0242) is another riverside pub, with views. For more cerebral goings-on, check out the concerts and events at the **Durham Light Infantry Museum and Art Gallery** (Aykley Heads, tel. 0191/384–2214). Student Union gigs take place throughout the academic year and you can see decent touring bands as well as local hopefuls. Call 0191/374–3310 for information. Regular choral and classical concerts take place in the Cathedral (*see* Worth Seeing, *above*).

HADRIAN'S WALL

Dedicated to the Roman god Terminus, the massive 73-mi span of Hadrian's Wall once marked the northern frontier of the mighty Roman empire. For more than 250 years, the Roman army used the wall to control travel and trade and to fortify Roman Britain against the barbarians to the north. At Emperor Hadrian's command (he ruled from 117 to 138), three legions of soldiers began building the Wall in AD 122. Around AD 200 Emperor Severus had the wall repaired and rebuilt. During the Roman era, the wall stood 15 ft high and 9 ft thick; behind it lay the vallum, a ditch about 20 ft wide and 10 ft deep. Spaced at 5-mi intervals along the wall were 3- to 5-acre forts (such as those at Housesteads and Chesters), which could hold 500 to 1,000 soldiers. Every mile was marked by a thick-walled milecastle (a smaller fort that housed about 30 soldiers), and between each milecastle were two smaller turrets, each lodging four men who kept watch from the tower's upper chamber.

Hadrian's Wall originally stretched from *Pons Aelius,* the present site of Newcastle, to *Maia,* near Bowness-on-Solway on the Solway Firth. During the Jacobite Rebellion of 1745, the English dismantled much of the Roman wall and used its stones to pave the new Military Road (now B6318). Some old Northumbrian farmhouses are also built of stones pulled from the wall. The most substantial stretches of the remaining wall are between Housesteads and Birdoswald. Running through the southern edge of Northumberland National Park and along the sheer escarpment of Whin Sill, this is also an area of dramatic natural beauty. The ancient ruins, rugged cliffs, dramatic vistas, and spreading pastures make this an excellent region for walking. The fine museums and information centers and the perpetually friendly Northumbrians will add to your enjoyment of this beautiful, sparsely touristed region. Haltwhistle and Bardon Mill make the best bases for exploring the wall, especially if you don't have a car.

BASICS

VISITOR INFORMATION

The best tourist office for Hadrian's Wall is at **Once Brewed** (Military Rd., a.k.a. the B6318, tel. 01434/344396), closed January–mid-March. It's just a short walk from the most striking portion of the wall and has an excellent staff and plenty of books and leaflets. Once Brewed takes its name from the nearby youth hostel, founded by a teetotaler benefactor who hoped that only "once-brewed" tea or coffee would be served here. Incidentally, the hostel and tourist office is very close to the Twice Brewed Inn, whose name has a much older heritage. While building the Military Road in 1751, workers complained about the weakness of the local beer and insisted it be "twice brewed." There is a smaller tourist office in **Haltwhistle** (at the train station, tel. 01434/322002) and others in **Hexham** (The Manor Office, Hallgate, tel. 01434/605225) and **Carlisle** (Old Town Hall, Green Market, tel. 01228/625600) at the western end of the wall.

In 1802, at the age of 78, William Hutton decided to take a stroll along the entire length of Hadrian's Wall, with an additional 525 mi for good

COMING AND GOING

BY BUS

Your best companion for planning travel here is the "Northumberland Public Transport Guide" (£1), available for purchase or reference at some tourist offices. The main bus service is the excellent **Hadrian's Wall Bus,** stopping at Hexham bus and train stations, Chester's Fort, Housesteads, Once Brewed, Vindolanda, Haltwhistle, the Roman Army Museum, Greenhead, and Carlisle; single fares are £3 or less, but if you plan to do a lot of traveling, buy a **Day Rover** (£5) on the bus—holders of either the North East Explorer or Stagecoach Cumberland Explorer pass can claim 50% discount on travel. The service operates from the end of May to the end of September, three to four times a day in either direction. There's a winter service, too (from mid-Oct. to late-May), but this runs only between Carlisle and Housesteads, via Brampton and Haltwhistle, and there are no winter services on Sunday. The "Hadrian's Wall Bus" brochure, available at tourist offices, explains the routes and lists connecting transport info. To inquire about schedules or any of the other piecemeal lines traversing the region, contact **Northumberland County Council Transport Enquiries** (tel. 01670/533128) or **Cumbria County Council Journey Planner** (tel. 01228/606000).

BY TAXI

Local taxi firms in Hexham and Haltwhistle offer return fares to sections of the wall, starting at around £10, which isn't a bad deal if you're traveling in a group. Local tourist offices have contact numbers, or try **Batey's** in Hexham (tel. 01434/602500) or **Henshaw Garage** in Haltwhistle (tel. 01434/344272).

BY TRAIN

The scenic **Tyne Valley Line** travels the Newcastle–Corbridge–Hexham–Bardon Mill–Haltwhistle–Carlisle route once an hour Monday–Saturday, every other hour on Sunday. Call 0345/484–950 for exact times. Fares to Hexham from Carlisle or Newcastle are £7.50 return. Although the rail line runs parallel to the wall, you can't see much of it from the train. Not all trains stop in Bardon Mill and Haltwhistle, which are only 2 to 3 mi from the wall, so check beforehand. If you're coming from York to Hexham, which is 5 mi from the wall, you'll need to change trains in Newcastle-upon-Tyne.

A main transportation gateway to the Hadrian's Wall region is the city of Newcastle. From Newcastle's **Central Station** (Neville St., tel. 0345/484950), trains to Durham, York, and London depart every 30 minutes, to Edinburgh every hour.

WHERE TO SLEEP

Haltwhistle is the closest village to the densest area of Roman sites and the best sections of Hadrian's Wall; it's on rail and bus lines and has affordable B&Bs, which can be booked through any tourist center in the area. The town of Hexham has a much wider range of accommodations, and though it's 5 to 10 mi from most of the Roman structures, including the wall, the Hadrian's Wall Bus service gets you there quickly. There are also three youth hostels and several campgrounds within striking distance of Hadrian's Wall.

In Haltwhistle, the outstanding **Ashcroft Guesthouse** (Lantys Lonnen, near the tourist office, tel. 01434/320213) is a grand Victorian house with huge, comfortable, and attractive rooms. Rooms are £22.50 per person, and there's a four-poster room for £50. Out of town, at the town's eastern end, just a mile from the wall, **Ald White Craig Farm** (Haltwhistle, tel. 01434/320565) is also recommended—the breakfasts are great and the comfy rooms go for £48 double, cash only. Corbridge is also worth a stopover for its Roman site and the charm of the village. The **Riverside Guest House** (Main St., tel. 01434/632942), just over the bridge from the station, opposite the fancy Angel Inn, is a good choice for £40 double, cash only. A mile out of Greenhead village, **Holmhead Guest House** (Greenhead, off A69, tel. 01697/747402) is an absolute gem, featuring stone arches, exposed beams, and antique furnishings; there's open countryside in front and a ruined castle almost in the backyard. En suite doubles are £56 (with small discounts for longer stays) and in addition to "the longest breakfast menu in the world," a set dinner (£17, and worth every penny) is served at the farmhouse table. In Hexham, you'll have no trouble finding comfortable lodgings in places with silly names. For around £40–£45 double (depending on the season), you can cozy up at **Topsy Turvy** (9 Leazes Lane, tel. 01434/603152), or at **Kitty Frisk House** (Corbridge Rd., tel. 01434/601533), both cash only. The splurge option in town is the **Royal Hotel** (Priestpopple, tel. 01434/602270), an old coaching inn with a smashing restoration job. A double room and breakfast goes for £60, and there's a great brasserie (*see Food, below*).

HOSTELS

Greenhead YHA. Only 1 mi south of Hadrian's Wall and close to the Pennine Way and Northumberland National Park, Greenhead's hostel makes a good starting point to explore the middle section of the wall. Beds in the converted Methodist chapel are £7.50. *Greenhead, tel. 016977/47401. From Newcastle (Eldon Sq.) or Carlisle, take Bus 685 to Greenhead. 40 beds. Reception open 7–10 and 5–11. Curfew 11:00, lockout 10–5. Closed Nov.–Mar.; Sun., Apr.–June; Wed.–Thurs., Sept.–Oct.*

Hadrian's Lodge. This independent hostel-cum-bunk-house is a nice step up from the nearby Once Brewed YHA. The bunk beds are a tenner a night, or there's twin bed rooms for about twice that. The grounds have a sort of campground-style setup with a bar and café, bike rental, fishing, and drying room. If you're in a group of four or five, the five self-catering cottages for rent here can be a steal, at least out of season when three nights costs £120–£150 (more than twice as much in summer, when minimum rental period is one week). Unless you walk from Haydon Bridge or the wall, you'll need a car to get here. *North Rd., tel. 01434/688688. It's just under two mi north of Haydon Bridge—from the wall and the B6318, take the turning for Haydon Bridge, about a mi east of Housesteads. Open year-round, though call first in winter.*

Once Brewed YHA. Beware the invading armies of teenage school kids in summer at this clean, characterless hostel. Once Brewed has no services except for a tourist office and this shelter, but it's only a 10-minute walk to one of the best stretches of Hadrian's Wall. Your only chance to catch a direct bus to the hostel (the Hadrian's Wall Bus) is between May and September. Beds are £10.15. *Military Rd., Bardon Mill, tel. 01434/344360, fax 01434/344045. From Newcastle (Eldon Sq.) or Carlisle, take Bus 685 or the train to Bardon Mill; Once Brewed is 2½ mi NW. 87 beds. Reception open 7–10 and 1–11. Curfew 11 PM, lockout 10–1. Open Apr.–Oct. daily; Feb.–Mar. and Nov., Mon.–Sat. Closed Dec.–Jan.*

CAMPING

Tourist offices carry several brochures on camping near Hadrian's Wall. The lush **Fallowfield Dene Caravan Park** (Acomb, tel. 01434/603553), closed November–February, has a flowing stream, greenery to spare, and wonderful facilities, including a laundry room with real washers and dryers. Sites cost £6.50 for a tent with two people. **Winshields Camp Site** (Winshields Farm, west of Once Brewed, tel. 01434/

344243) is in the front yard of a farm, right on B6318. You, the sheep, and the cows enjoy the grassy fields in perfect harmony—though the road isn't exactly quiet. Sites are £2 per person and the grounds are closed from November through March. **Haltwhistle's campsite** (Burnfoot, tel. 01434/320106) is on the southeastern edge of town. All the campsites have toilets and showers.

FOOD

You'll find the usual pub fare and bakery shops in the towns near the wall, but very little else. Hexham has the most variety, with several budget restaurants on Priestpopple, the street with the bus station. Best choice here is the **Priestpopple Brasserie** (in the Royal Hotel, Priestpopple, tel. 01434/602270), an airy, sit-around-all-day kind of place, with good coffee, a changing blackboard menu, and lunch deals for around £7. For cheaper eats try **Mrs. Miggin's Coffee Shop** (St. Mary's Wynd, off Beaumont St., opposite Queen's Hall, tel. 01434/605808) for coffee and homemade cakes served on pine tables. The **Hexham Tans** (11 St. Mary's Chare, tel. 01434/604040) is a whole-food vegetarian café, that closes around 4 PM. **Hexham Market,** west of the tourist office, is a good place to get produce. In Haltwhistle, **Manor House Hotel** (Main St., near the tourist office, tel. 01434/322588) serves salad, meat, and vegetarian entrées. The town also has several pubs that serve bar meals, including the **Spotted Cow Inn** (Castle St.), and three supermarkets with late closing hours at least one day a week. In Corbridge the **Watling Coffee House** (Hill St., no phone), just off the square, is the place for all-day snacks and light meals. Two pubs near the wall on B6318 (Military Rd.) do the honors: **Twice Brewed Inn** (tel. 01434/344534), next to Once Brewed, has leek, cheese, and onion hotpot and a variety of sandwiches, while the isolated **Milecastle Inn** (near Cawfields, tel. 01434/320682) is known for its homemade pies.

If you find the weather inclement, you may want to leave an offering at the temple of Mithras, the Sun God (off B6318, east of Housesteads).

WORTH SEEING

While the main sight is Hadrian's Wall itself, a number of other impressive ruins, reconstructions, and informative museums help give a detailed picture of Roman military life. Hexham itself is worth a morning of your time before hitting the wall. Not only does Hexham Abbey stand proud here, but you could check to see what's on at the town's **Queen's Hall Arts Centre** (Beaumont St., tel. 01434/607272), one of the Northeast's most adventurous arts venues. In reviewing the sights below, we start at Hexham and head west toward Carlisle. For the most spectacular views of the wall, take the 3-mi walk from **Steel Rigg** to **Housesteads Roman Fort,** beginning near Once Brewed. The full walk is about 2½ hours of athletic walking up and down hills, but there are no museums or admission charges along this stretch of the wall, and your effort will be rewarded by dramatic prospects from the high, rocky ridge.

HEXHAM ABBEY

Ancient **Hexham Abbey,** a tranquil place of Christian worship for more than 1,300 years, forms one side of the town's main square. The original Benedictine abbey was replaced in Norman times by an Augustinian priory, of which only segments now remain intact. Inside, you can climb the 35 worn stone "night stairs," which once led from the main part of the abbey to the canon's dormitory, to overlook the whole ensemble. Most of the present building dates back to the 12th century, and much of the stone was taken from the Roman fort at Corstopitum (Corbridge) a few miles northeast. This explains the most impressive relic, the 1st-century tombstone near the main entrance, dedicated to Flavinus, a 25-year-old Roman standard-bearer who met his death far from home. *Beaumont St., tel. 01434/602031. Admission free, but £2 donation suggested. Open June–Sept., daily 9–7; Oct.–May, daily 9–5. No tours during services.*

CORBRIDGE ROMAN SITE

The excavated remains of the Roman garrison town, Corstopitum, on the ancient Stanegate Road include the foundations of granaries, temples, and houses. This once-prosperous town was where soldiers stationed at the wall came to spend their leave and their money. An excellent taped guided tour of the site is free with admission. The small museum contains sculpture, armor, and other excavated items. The site is about ½ mi northwest of Corbridge (follow the signs from town). Bus 685 from Carlisle and Newcastle stops in Corbridge. *Tel. 01434/632349. Admission £2.80. Open Apr.–Oct., daily 10–6; Nov.–Mar., Wed.–Sun. 10–1 and 2–4.*

CHESTERS FORT

Built beside the wall, Chesters Roman cavalry fort has been extensively excavated and includes a bathhouse, a bridge across the Tyne, and a museum displaying Roman sculptures found around the fort. A typically innovative Roman structure, it has a sophisticated system of underground heating ducts. *Chollerford, tel. 01434/681379. ½ mi west of Chollerford on B6318. Take Hexham Bus 880 or 882 to Humshaugh Village, ½ mi north of Chollerford, or catch the Hadrian's Wall Bus to the gate. Admission £2.80. Open Apr.–Sept., daily 10–6; Oct.–Mar., daily 10–4.*

HOUSESTEADS ROMAN FORT AND MUSEUM

If you have time to visit only one Hadrian's Wall site, Housesteads Roman Fort is your best bet. It offers an interpretive center, views of long sections of the wall, the excavated 5-acre fort itself, and a museum. It's a steep, 10-minute walk up from the parking lot by B6318 to the site, but it's worth the effort, especially for the view of the wall disappearing over hills and crags into the distance. The vast remains include altars, hospitals, latrines, and a circular outer wall. The tiny museum features a collection of carved stone altars. *Tel. 01434/344363. 3 mi NE of Bardon Mill on B6318. Train and Bus 685 from Newcastle and Carlisle stop in Bardon Mill. From here, take the Hadrian's Wall Bus, or walk, take a cab, or hitch a ride to the fort. Admission £2.80. Open daily, Apr.–Sept. 10–6; Oct.–Mar. 10–4.*

VINDOLANDA ROMAN FORT AND MUSEUM

Of all the area's Roman sites, Vindolanda offers the richest variety of exhibitions. In the midst of beautiful countryside, you'll find the ruins of the military fort and civilian settlement and replicas of a timber mile castle and stone turret from the Roman wall. In the gardens, the open-air museum has reconstructions of a Roman shop, temple, and house and an 18th-century tenant farmer's croft, all with audio presentations describing daily life in the area. The indoor museum has an extensive collection of jewelry, weapons, shoes, household items, and personal letters. Vindolanda's wooden tablets contain the earliest known writing by a woman in Western Europe—an invitation to her birthday party. *Tel. 01434/344277. Between A69 and B6318. Take Bus 890 or 682 to Vindolanda. Admission £3.80. Open May and June, daily 10–6; July and Aug., daily 10–6:30; Apr. and Sept., daily 10–5:30; Mar. and Oct., daily 10–5; first half Nov. and last half Feb., daily 10–4; last admission ½ hr before closing. Closed mid-Nov.– mid-Feb.*

ROMAN ARMY MUSEUM

Don't miss the **Roman Army Museum,** at the garrison fort of Carvoran, near the village of Greenhead. Full-size models and excavations bring to life this remote outpost of empire; you can even inspect authentic Roman graffiti on the barracks' walls. The gift store stocks, among other unusual items, Roman rulers (1 ft = 11.6 inches) and Roman cookbooks. Opposite the museum, at Walltown Crags on the Pennine Way, are 400 yards of the best-preserved section of the wall. *1 mi northeast of Greenhead, off B6318, tel. 016977/47485. Take the Hadrian's Wall Bus to the museum. Admission £3, joint admission ticket with Vindolanda £5.60. Open May and June, daily 10–6; July and Aug., daily 10–6:30; Apr. and Sept., daily 10–5:30; Mar. and Oct., daily 10–5; first half Nov. and last half Feb., daily 10–4. Closed mid-Nov.–mid-Feb.*

OUTDOOR ACTIVITIES

The best way to experience Hadrian's Wall is to follow any of the several well-marked paths that crisscross the area. If you plan to go on one of the longer walks, bring some sturdy hiking shoes to scale the steep slopes around the wall. The circular 3-mi walk from **Cawfields** (near Once Brewed) covers one of the wall's best-preserved sections and goes along the Whin Sill, a rock ridge created 30 million years ago. Pack a lunch for the two-hour trek. From **Once Brewed** another circular walk wanders through wide-open fields to Melkridge Tilery (a small factory and mine) and along the highest stretch of the Winshields Crags, offering unforgettable views of the hills. The 4-mi walk begins at the Once Brewed Information Centre (*see* Basics, *above*), takes about three hours, and climbs some steep slopes.

NORTHUMBRIAN COAST

For those who like their scenery broodingly romantic, several impressive castles dot the Northumbrian coastline between Newcastle and the Scottish border. Some are little more than ruins, reminders of the region's bloody past as a battleground between the Scots and the English. Others, especially Alnwick and Bamburgh, are so idyllic they deserve etchings in the dictionary beside the definition for "castle." The landscape up here can seem lonely and bleak—a biting wind blows off the North Sea, over rocky cliffs and heathered moors—but it is also ruggedly beautiful, filled with flocks of rare birds, and largely untouristed. Bring a warm jacket even in summer, especially if you plan to walk much. Of course, if you don't plan your route carefully, you'll do a lot of walking whether you want to or not—public transportation can be a real pain along the coast.

Tourist offices in **Berwick-upon-Tweed** (The Maltings, Eastern Lane, tel. 01289/330733) and **Newcastle** (Central Station, Neville St., tel. 0191/230–0030 and Central Library, Princess Sq., tel. 0191/261–0610) have info on the coastal castles; Berwick's office also has miniguides (25p) about the town's architecture, history, and riverside walks. Smaller offices in between also have useful pamphlets: Try the ones in **Alnwick** (The Shambles, tel. 01665/510665), and **Seahouses** (Seafield Rd. Car Park, tel. 01665/720884), closed November–April.

One letter found at Vindolanda documents a parcel of desperately needed articles sent to a soldier at a lonely frontier outpost of the wall: socks and underclothing.

GETTING AROUND

Main-line trains run up the coast, but they don't go near the main sights (except for Berwick, which all Scotland-bound trains pass through). Instead, it's better to start in Newcastle or Berwick and tour the area by bus. Centrally located Alnwick also makes a good base. We cannot overstate the importance of the **"Northumberland Public Transport Guide"** (£1), available in Newcastle, Berwick, and some tourist centers in between. It contains bus, train, and ferry schedules, useful telephone numbers, a list of market days and early closing days in the villages, as well as walks and transit routes to attractions. When you're done with the book, make sure to hand it to some stranded soul without one—it's that essential.

If you plan to spend much time on the Northumbrian coast, you'll most likely change trains or catch a bus at least once in **Berwick,** the last stop in England before entering Scotland. Trains to and from Edinburgh and Newcastle (from £10–£14 return) pass through Berwick's **rail station** (Railway St., tel. 0345/484950) every 90 minutes. From Berwick, a whole fleet of companies send buses south toward Newcastle, sweeping by or stopping at several of the coastal castles covered below. For all local bus information and National Express tickets, stop by the **Berwick Bus Shop** (125 Marygate, tel. 01289/307283). It also has info on bus times to Holy Island.

BY BUS

To reach **Belsay** village, a mile from the Belsay estate, take Bus 808 (not Sunday) or 508 (summer Sundays only) from Newcastle. To visit **Warkworth Castle,** catch Bus 518 from Newcastle's Haymarket bus station; a bus leaves almost hourly between 7 AM and 10 PM. The same bus continues on to Alnwick, a short walk from **Alnwick Castle.** If you want to see decaying **Dunstanburgh Castle,** take Bus 401/501 (five daily) from Alnwick to nearby Craster; from Craster you have to walk another 1½ mi to Dunstanburgh, which sounds like a hassle, but it's one of the finest castle approaches in Britain. From Craster, Bus 401/501 continues on to **Bamburgh Castle,** from where Bus 411 heads to Berwick. You could cover three or four of these castles in one day, but not if you're traveling by bus. **Holy Island,** between Bamburgh and Berwick, is accessible only via a skinny causeway that's underwater at high tide. Call Berwick's tourist office or Bus Shop (*see above*) for tide schedules. To reach Holy Island, catch Bus 477 from Berwick; there are two daily in each direction Monday–Saturday in summer; schedules vary with the tides. For most of these trips, you're better off getting a **North East Explorer** pass (£4.95), good for one day of travel in the area from Newcastle to Berwick, Hadrian's Wall, and the Tyne and Wear district. You can buy one on the bus or in advance at bus company offices such as the one in Berwick.

BY CAR

You've got a car? Ah, the world is your oyster. To reach the castle at **Belsay** take A696 north from Newcastle. From here B6524 heads to **Morpeth,** where you can join A1068 coastal route (the road changes numbers to B1339, B1340, and B1342, but it's always signposted COASTAL ROUTE). From **Bamburgh** take B1342 west to A1, which runs north to **Berwick.** Signs on A1 point you to **Holy Island** from Beal a few miles south of Berwick. The best place to rent a car is in Newcastle, where all the major rental outfits are represented—the city tourist offices (*see above*) have a list of contact numbers. You may want to wait until you reach smaller towns like Durham, Hexham, or Berwick, where rates might be a little cheaper (from around £31 per day) but the supply and choice is limited.

WHERE TO SLEEP

Tourist offices have lists of B&Bs in the towns and villages, many of which are surprisingly good value. It's a good idea to make reservations, because although it's not the most touristed region of Britain, accommodations are sometimes in short supply.

In Alnwick, look along Bondgate Without for B&Bs; from Market Place, it's the main road that runs away from the castle, through the old town gate. **Mrs. Givens** (8 Bondgate Without, tel. 01665/604473) has big, nicely decorated rooms in a 300-year-old house for £17 per person, no credit cards, and there are several other similarly priced places nearby. Berwick has the most B&B options—pick up the "Berwick-upon-Tweed Holiday Guide" from the tourist office for extensive listings. There are lots of places on Church Street: Try the modern and clean **Miranda's Guest House** (43 Church St., tel. 01289/306483), with rooms from £16 to £18.50 per person, no credit cards. If you don't mind a short walk from central Berwick, the wonderful **Old Vicarage Guest House** (Church Rd., Tweedmouth, tel. 01289/306909) has eight charming rooms in a 19th-century, stone-walled building from £16 per person, up to £25 for en suite facilities; from the town center, cross Berwick Bridge, turn left on Main Street (which becomes Dock View), turn right on Brewery Bank, and left on Church Road. In Bamburgh, accommodations tend to be more expensive, but **Greengates** (34 Front St., tel. 01668/214535) has rooms for £19.50–£29 per person (depending on the season; no credit cards), and is superbly located—very close to the castle. For real isolation, you can't beat a night on Holy Island, but you'll have to book ahead and grit your teeth—it doesn't come cheap. **Mrs. Patterson** at Britannia House (Holy Island, tel. 01289/389218), has one of the best deals, with rooms around £18–£19 per person, no credit cards. The house is closed from November through February. Otherwise, Holy Island lodgings cost at least £25 per person a night.

HOSTELS

Newcastle-upon-Tyne YHA. Newcastle's city-center hostel makes a convenient launch pad for the castles and towns of the Northumberland coast, most of which can be reached by bus. The hostel is a converted town house in the Jesmond district, just a short Metro ride or 15-minute walk from all the city sights. It's *very* popular so book as far in advance as you can in summer. Beds cost £10.15, and there's a self-catering kitchen, café, bicycle storage area, and shower rooms. *107 Jesmond Rd., tel. 0191/281–2570. From Jesmond Metro station walk along Jesmond Rd.; the hostel is opposite the cemetery. 60 beds. No curfew, hostel open all day.*

Wooler YHA. In the Cheviot Hills on the north side of the park, this modern family-style spot is the only hostel anywhere near the castles. It's accessible by bus from Berwick, Alnwick, or Newcastle. Beds run £8.35 and there's a self-catering kitchen. *30 Cheviot St., tel. 01668/281–365. From Wooler's bus station, turn left on High St., right on Cheviot St. 50 beds. Curfew 11 PM, lockout 10–1. Reception open 5 PM–11:30 PM. Open mid-July–Aug., daily; Apr.–mid-July and Sept.–Oct., Mon.–Sat.; mid-Feb.–Mar. and Nov., Fri.–Sat. Closed Dec.–mid-Feb.*

CAMPING

The campgrounds here are listed in south–north order. On the whole, the coastal campsites are excellent, and mostly sited next to glorious beaches, but you should always be prepared for the weather to turn chilly, even at the height of summer. A drawback is that at **Camping and Caravaning Club** campgrounds, unless you're a camping club member, you'll pay another £4.20 club fee on top of the site fee every time—it pays to join at the first campground. Only in Berwick is it tough to camp—there are local sites, but they're a ways out of town and there's no public transportation.

Dunstan Hill Camping and Caravaning Club Site. This campground near Dunstanburgh Castle has all the modern goods—manicured lawns, tiled bathrooms, showers, and laundry facilities. Tent sites cost

£5.20 per person. *Dunstan Hill, tel. 01665/576310. 1 mi inland, near B1339 and Dunstanburgh Castle. 160 sites. Toilets, showers. Closed Nov.–Mar.*

Beadnell Bay Camping & Caravaning Club Site. This campground is midway between Dustanburgh and Bamburgh on B1339—right on the route of Bus 501. Little stone walls provide wind cover on three different fields, and the facilities are immaculate. The friendly proprietors are reassuring, and there's a lovely beach just across the road. Tent sites are £4.70 per person. *Beadnell, off B1339, tel. 01665/720586. 150 sites. Toilets, showers. Closed Oct.–Mar.*

Waren Caravan Park. Two mi north of Bamburgh, this family-oriented site in Waren Mill overlooks the sea and a gorgeous stretch of white beach. Tenters camp in a small "valley" that helps cut down the wind, which can really howl around here. On site is a laundry, restaurant, and shop. Bus 501 travels five times per day between Bamburgh and Belford; the campground is ½ mi up the road from the bus stop in Waren Mill. Sites run £8–£11. *Waren Mill, tel. 016684/214366. 180 sites. Toilets, showers. Closed Nov.–Mar.*

FOOD

As well as the usual pubs, teahouses, and fish-and-chip shops, the northeastern coast occasionally throws up a gastronomic treat. **Popinjays** (32 Hide Hill, tel. 01289/307237) in Berwick is great for all-day snacks, light meals, and coffee. **Foxton's** just down the road (26 Hide Hill, tel. 01289/303939) is a trendy brasserie with good, if pricey main meals, though sandwiches, lunch specials, and drinks won't break the bank. Best Berwick pub is the **Barrels Ale House** (59–61 Bridge St., tel. 01289/308013), which apart from a changing selection of real ales, also serves tapas at lunch (noon–2). In Bamburgh try **The Greenhouse** (5–6 Front St., tel. 01668/214513) for local fish and gourmet desserts, or the **Lord Crewe Arms** (Front St., tel. 01668/214243), a cozy stone-walled inn with oak beams, open fires, and renowned pub food. It's closed November through February. Having slogged to Dunstanburgh Castle and back, check out Craster's local specialties—kippers at **Craster Fish Restaurant** (opposite the smokehouse near the harbor, open Easter–Sept. only, no phone) or fresh crab sandwiches at the **Jolly Fisherman** pub (tel. 01665/576461).

Holy Island cannot be visited at high tide, when the causeway from the mainland is covered by the North Sea. For tide info call Berwick tourist office at 01289/330733.

WORTH SEEING

For those who love castles, the gray, windswept Northumbrian coast has a richly varied selection, from the desolate, ruined shell of **Edlingham Castle** (between Alnwick and Rothbury) to the lavish splendor of **Alnwick Castle,** home to the regal Percy family, the Dukes of Northumberland. The beaches here are cold but beautiful, and the picturesque villages have friendly natives and some lovely old churches. The following towns and castles are arranged in south–north order, ending in Berwick-upon-Tweed.

BELSAY HALL AND GARDENS

A large estate with an intriguing assemblage of mix-and-match architectural styles, Belsay Hall includes a 14th-century castle from times of border siege, a manor house built in the 17th and 18th centuries when the rich could relax and decorate, and a main hall from the early 19th century. Nobody lives in Belsay; the rooms in the main hall, modeled after the Temple of Theseus in Athens, stand totally empty. Don't miss the fabulous quarry garden, weaving its way through the rock from which the hall was built. Bring a picnic. *Belsay, tel. 01661/881636. From Newcastle (Eldon Sq.), take Bus 808, or the National Express Edinburgh 383/394 service, which stops in Belsay village; on summer Sundays, take Bus 508 from Newcastle. Admission £3.80. Open Apr.–Sept., daily 10–6; Oct.–Mar., daily 10–4.*

WARKWORTH CASTLE

First built as a Scottish stronghold in the 12th century, Warkworth Castle was subsequently owned by the Percy family for 600 years, and the castle and family (including well-known Harry "Hotspur" Percy) appear in Shakespeare's *Henry IV, Part I.* The well-known Magna-Carta writing, Scott-fighting family was elevated to the dukedom of Northumberland in the 18th century, and they're still one of the biggest private landowners in the country. Warkworth Castle has weathered repeated attacks; by 1617 it was in such bad shape that James I, pointing to a sculpture on a tower wall, commented, "This lion holds up this castle." The labyrinthine **keep,** built in 1400, remains perfectly intact (save for the roof and win-dowpanes) and still offers travelers shelter from the chilling winds. A self-guided taped tour (£1.50) details the castle's complicated history. You can also catch a boat (included in the entrance price) to the **Warkworth Hermitage,** a fascinating hall and chapel hewn out of a cliff beside the River Coquet. *Warkworth, tel. 01665/711423. From Newcastle or Alnwick, take Bus 518. Admission to castle £2.40, to Hermitage £1.60. Castle open Apr.–Sept., daily 10–6; Oct.–Mar., daily 10–4; Hermitage open Apr.–Oct., Wed. and Sun. 11–5.*

ALNWICK CASTLE

Opulent Alnwick (pronounced ANN-ick) Castle was overhauled in the 19th century, and its heavily fur-nished, red-walled interiors are more consonant with high-Victorian taste than with the medieval archi-tecture. The original fortress and castle date from the 11th century. The irrepressible Percys—one of the grandest families in England—took up residence in 1309 and still live here today. They now make their living from their huge Northumbrian estates, centered on this castle. The front hall is decked with arma-ments from the Napoleonic wars, while other rooms boast paintings by Titian and Van Dyck, as well as furnishings that are themselves works of art. Capability Brown landscaped the elegant grounds; take a walk along the River Aln east of the castle. *Alnwick, tel. 01665/510777. From Newcastle or Berwick, take Bus 505 (on Sunday it's the 525). Admission £5.95. Open Easter–Sept., daily 11–5.*

DUNSTANBURGH CASTLE

A dramatic and desolate ruin, Dunstanburgh Castle has been in steady decay since the Wars of the Roses (1455–85), a protracted conflict between the royal houses of York and Lancaster. Initially built in 1313 by the Earl of Lancaster, the castle was largely rebuilt in 1372 by John of Gaunt, Chaucer's patron and a notable character in Shakespeare's *Richard II.* The skeletal remains of the castle rise from a cliff 100 ft above the North Sea. *Tel. 01665/576231. Admission £1.80. Open Apr.–Oct., daily 10–6; Nov.–Mar., Wed.–Sun. 10–4.*

BAMBURGH CASTLE

On a great crag overlooking the coast, Bamburgh Castle is hauntingly beautiful, with enchanting views of the sea, Holy Island, and the Farne Islands. Owned by various Norman lords through the middle ages, Bamburgh passed into the Armstrong family in the 1890s; Lady Armstrong lived in the castle until her death in 1999. The pink sandstone walls and keep are Norman, but most of the castle is Victorian Gothic-revival. Its rooms display family china, tapestries, and armor. Skip the dungeon and save the cheese for your picnic at the beach. This is a magnificent sweep that stretches three mi south to the lit-tle port of Seahouses, from where you can take a boat trip out to the nature reserves on the Farne Islands. *Bamburgh, tel. 01668/214515. Admission £4. Open Apr.–Oct., daily 11–4:30.*

FARNE ISLANDS

Regular boat trips from the village of Seahouses head to two of the bleak, wind-tossed Farne Islands (owned by the National Trust), colonized by seabirds, including puffins, kittiwakes, terns, shags, and guillemots. There's also a thriving gray-seal colony. Inner Farne, where St. Cuthbert, the great abbot of Lindisfarne, died in AD 687, has a tiny chapel dedicated to his memory. Trips vary, from a 2½-hour cruise past the islands to a longer trip, during which you'll make landfall. Landing fees differ depending on sea-son, since there's more wildlife to see at certain times of the year. *Seahouses Tourist Information Cen-tre, tel. 01665/720884. Information center open Easter–Oct. Boat trips, tel. 01665/720308. Admission £7–£14; landing fees £3–£3.90 are payable to the wardens. Closed Oct.–March; access restricted dur-ing seal breeding season (May 15–July 15).*

HOLY ISLAND

Once known by the Celtic name of Lindisfarne, Holy Island was one of the first Christian settlements in England, founded in 635. In 698 the monks on this weather-beaten islet produced the illuminated book, the *Lindisfarne Gospels,* one of the finest works of art of the Dark Ages (it's now kept in the British Museum in London). In 793, the Danes plundered the island, which remained unoccupied until 1083, when rebuilding began on **Lindisfarne Priory.** Sadly, the ruins of the medieval priory are sparse, though the red sandstone arch can be a bit haunting on stormy days. The adjoining **museum** has a small exhibit chronicling the priory's history. *Tel. 01289/389200. Admission to museum and ruins £2.80. Open Apr.–Oct., daily 10–6; Nov.–Mar., daily 10–4.*

On the farthest edge of the small island, **Lindisfarne Castle** perches atop rocky Beblowe Crag. Built in the 1500s as a fortress against Scottish attacks, the castle was sadly neglected by 1902, when *Country*

Life magazine founder Edward Hudson hopped over the wall and decided to buy the property. The spare yet elegant interiors were created by Sir Edward Lutyens and are furnished with handsome antiques. From the Upper Battery there are spectacular views of the spreading green sheep farms below, the wheeling gulls above, and the restless, surrounding sea. The island also has a single, small village with pubs, restaurants, B&Bs, and (mostly touristy) shops. *Tel. 01289/389244. From Berwick, take Bus 477, which runs twice daily in summer but is much reduced in winter; departure times vary according to the tides. Otherwise, ask to be dropped off at Beal from any bus that runs between Berwick and Newcastle, though you'll have to walk four mi from Beal to the island. Admission £4. Open Apr.–Oct., Sat.– Thurs. 1–5:30.*

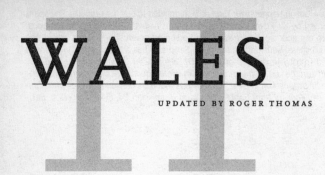

WALES

UPDATED BY ROGER THOMAS

To the outsider, the fiercely independent attitude cultivated by the Welsh people may seem downright curious, if not hopelessly confusing. After all, London is only a few hours away by train, there are no border controls, and Wales seems very much an integral part of the United Kingdom. But that's Wales in a nutshell—a country within a country with its own native language and customs, a strong patriotic pride and a rural, rugged flavor all its own. Wales is called Cymru in Welsh, which is one of the oldest languages in Europe and is still the first tongue in the northwest. It's estimated that 20% of the country's 2.8 million inhabitants still speak it fluently.

In a 1999 national referendum, the Welsh voted by a very narrow majority in favor of partial devolution for the country. A few months later in May, after an election in which a significant proportion of the electorate didn't bother to vote, the new Welsh Assembly was born. Unlike the new Scottish Parliament which came into being on the same day and which was supported more enthusiastically by the Scots, the Welsh Assembly has devolved administrative powers from the Westminster Parliament, but no lawmaking powers. The Assembly will be housed in a prestigious new building on Cardiff Bay.

The Welsh, a Celtic race, inhabited the isolated western shores of Britain long before the Anglo-Normans began their westward expanse in the 12th, 13th, and 14th centuries. The Cambrian mountains, which cover the length of Wales, served as a kind of natural barrier against the Romans, Saxons, and even the Vikings. Yet, as the Anglo-Normans started spreading like a plague, Welsh tribes were pushed even deeper into mountain strongholds. In 1282, the last native Prince of Wales, Llywelyn ap Gruffudd, was killed in battle, squashing any serious hope of Welsh nationhood. Owain Glyndwr̂, another Welsh revolutionary, nearly succeeded in pushing the English out of Wales in 1400. But in an oft-repeated scenario, England's armies prevailed over the disjointed clans of Cymru.

With the exception of the capital, **Cardiff,** and **Swansea,** Wales's second city, Wales has few large urban areas. What it does have from north to south are pretty villages, attractive market towns, traffic-free roads, and wonderful countryside. Few other regions in Britain are as free of 20th-century encroachments, and the wise traveler will head for the wide-open spaces of Wales's three national parks: **Snowdonia, Pembrokeshire Coast,** and the **Brecon Beacons.** If you're interested in castles, then make **Porthmadog** or **Caernarfon** your base. If it's hiking you want, head to **Llanberis.** You won't actually be escaping civilization—plenty of British families come to Wales on holiday. Yet Wales is still largely unknown to many foreign tourists, a true shame, or a blessing, depending on how you look at it. If you like sheep, rolling green hills, wild moor and mountain ranges, lots of sheep, staggeringly beautiful coastline, and more sheep, the country will not disappoint.

BASICS

VISITOR INFORMATION

Wales has more than 60 **Tourist Information Centres.** There's a helpful office in Cardiff (*see below*), together with offices at all major tourist destinations throughout Wales, and some even at quiet spots in the heart of the country. The staff at any office can book you a bed (free for local reservations based on a 10% deposit system, and a £1 fee plus 10% deposit for bookings made further afield). Many offices are closed from the end of October through Easter. Luckily, most offices post a list of B&Bs in their window, along with important emergency numbers. For free brochures or accommodations listings before setting foot in Wales, contact the **Wales Information Centre** (British Visitor Centre, 1, Regent St., London, SW1Y 4XI, tel. 020/7808–3838).

COMING AND GOING

BY BUS • National Express (tel. 0990/808080) buses depart from London's Victoria Coach Station for Cardiff (3 hrs, £20 return), Swansea (4 hrs, £24 return), Aberystwyth (4 hrs, £22 return, £26.50 Friday), and other destinations throughout Wales. Once you arrive, you must hook up with regional or local bus services. The main carriers are **First Cymru** (tel. 01792/580580) and **Stagecoach Red and White** (tel. 01633/266336) in the south, and **Arriva Cymru** (tel. 01970/617951, 01745/343721, and 01492/596969) in central Wales and the north. Arriva Cymru also operates the **Traws Cambria** line, the only north–south connection between Cardiff and Holyhead (1

The name "Wales" comes from the Saxon word "weallas," which means "strangers"—ironic when you consider that the Welsh were here long before the Germanic Saxons conquered Britain.

per day, £20 single, £32 return) via Aberystwyth. Local-line prices are reasonable, but service can be inconsistent—get a schedule from the tourist office or call ahead to avoid being stranded. Also note that many buses do not run on Sunday. If it's maximum efficiency you're after, you may want to rent a car in Cardiff.

BY FERRY • Wales is a major departure point for ferries to Ireland. **Irish Ferries** (tel. 0990/171717) sails from Pembroke Dock to Rosslare and from Holyhead to Dublin. **Stena Line** (tel. 0990/707070) sails from Fishguard to Rosslare and from Holyhead to Dún Laoghaire (near Dublin). **Swansea Cork Ferries** (tel. 01792/456116) obviously sails between Swansea and Cork. For more info on ferries, *see* Coming and Going in the specific towns.

BY TRAIN • Since the demise of British Rail there has been a mushrooming of train operators serving Wales and a correspondingly bewildering array of fares. As in much of the West Country, major southern Welsh destinations on the main London–Swansea line are part of the **Great Western Railway** network. For a brief explanation of the types of fares available, *see* Coming and Going *in* Chapter 4. For routes with such fares we have quoted the Saver return, but if you don't travel on a Friday and/or book seven days in advance, you could save up to 30%–50% on your fare. From London's Paddington Station, Great Western serves Cardiff (2 hrs, £37 return), Swansea (2½ hrs, £52.60 return), and Fishguard (3¼ hrs, £60.20 return).

When traveling in the rest of Wales you'll be riding on **Wales & West/Alphaline,** which runs to and within South Wales and **Central Trains** and **First North Western,** which run to and within Mid Wales and North Wales respectively. Fares generally differ only according to whether you travel at peak or off-peak times and how long your return is good for (one day, five days, one month). From London's Euston Station trains also run to Bangor and Holyhead in the north, while Aberystwyth and central Wales are accessible from Birmingham, which connects with London Euston. Fortunately for the confused traveler the enquiry number for all services is the same—0345/484950. If you plan to travel extensively in Wales, your best option is the **Freedom of Wales Flexi Pass**—one ticket that gives unlimited access to both rail and bus services in Wales. Ticket holders also receive discounted admission to historical sites, travel on narrow gauge railways, and reduced price accommodation vouchers. The 15-day ticket (15 days bus/any 8 days train) costs £92 peak, £75 off-peak. The 8-day ticket (8 days bus/any 4 days train) costs £49 peak, £39 off-peak. A 7-day **Flexi Rover** for South or Mid and North Wales is also available. Tickets can be bought at train stations, travel agents, or by post or phone. Ring 08457/125625 or 01766/512340 for all details.

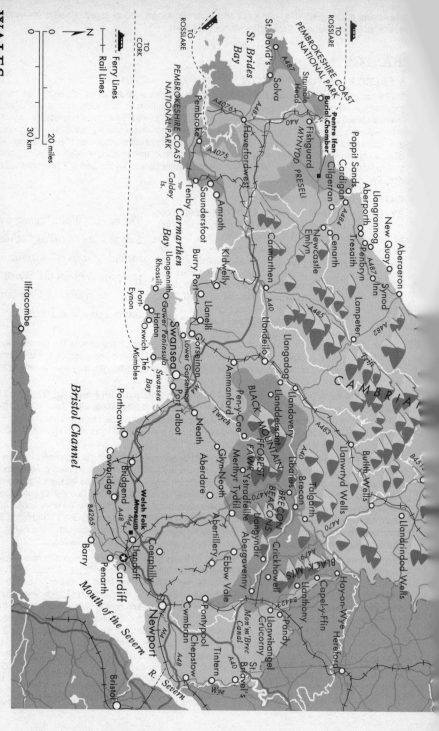

WALES

N

——▲—— Ferry Lines
—|—|— Rail Lines

0
0   20 miles
    30 km

TO
ROSSLARE

TO
CORK

TO
ROSSLARE

PEMBROKESHIRE COAST
NATIONAL PARK

PEMBROKESHIRE COAST
NATIONAL PARK

St. Brides
Bay

St. David's

Solva
A487

Strumble
Head

Pentre Ifan
Burial Chamber

Fishguard
Cilgerran

A40

MYNYDD PRESELI

A4076

Haverfordwest

A4075

Pembroke

Calday
Is.

Tenby

Saundersfoot

Amroth

Poppit Sands

Cardigan
A484

Penbryn
Tresaith

Aberporth

Llangrannog

New Quay

Synod
Inn
A487

Aberaeron

A482

Newcastle
Emlyn

Cenarth

Lampeter

A485

Carmarthen

A40

Llandovery

Llandeilo

A40

Llangadog

A483

A40

A40

A483

A482

A483

CAMBRIA

B451

Llanwrtyd Wells

Builth
Wells

Llandrindod Wells

A470

A479

A483

Carmarthen
Bay

Burry Port

Kidwelly

Llanelli

Gorseinon

Lower Gorseinon

Llangennith
Rhossili

Port-
Eynon

Oxwich
Horton

Gower Peninsula

Swansea
Bay

The
Mumbles

Swansea

Port Talbot

Ammanford

Pen-y-Cae

BLACK
MOUNTAIN

Twrch

FFOREST
FAWR

Merthyr
Tydfil

Ystradfellte

Glyn-Neath

Neath

Aberdare

Llandeusant

Libanus

BRECON
BEACONS

Brecon

Talgarth

Hay-on-Wye

Capel-y-Ffin

Crickhowell

Llanthony

Pandy

Hereford

Llangynidr

Abergavenny

BLACK MTS

Porthcawl

Cowbridge

Bridgend
A48

A4265

Barry

Welsh Folk
Museum

Llandaff

Cardiff

Penarth

Caerphilly

M4

Newport

Cwmbran

Pontypool

Ebbw Vale

Abertillery

Mon'/Brec Canal

Crucorny
Llanvihangel

St.
Bridge's

A40

Chepstow

Tintern

Wye

M4

A48

R. Severn

Bristol

Mouth of the Severn

Bristol Channel

Ilfracombe

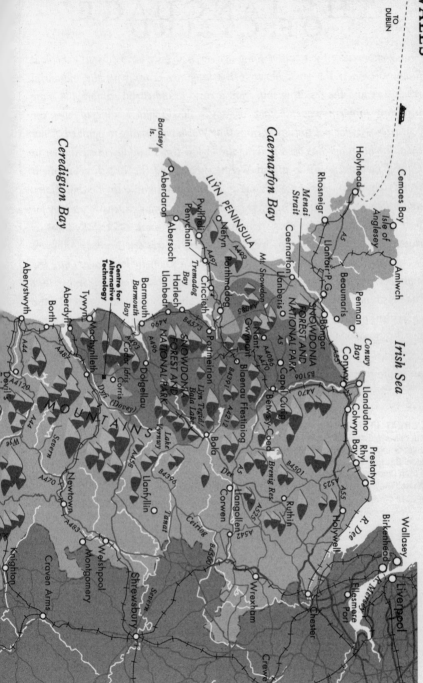

WALES

TO
DUBLIN

Irish Sea

Cemas Bay
Isle of
Anglesey
Amlwch
Holyhead
Penman
Bay
Conwy
Bay
Penman
Beaumaris
Colwyn
Llandudno
Colwyn Bay
Rhyl
Prestatyn
Holywell

Rhosneigr
Menai
Strait
Caernarfon
Bangor
Llanberis
Llanfair-P.G.
A5
B5106

Caernarfon Bay

Bardsey
Is.
Aberdaron
LLŶN PENINSULA
Nefyn
Pwllheli
Penychain
Abersoch
Tremadog
Bay
Criccieth
Porthmadog
Mt Snowdon
Nant
Gwynant
Capel Curig
Betws-y-Coed
Brenig Res.
Ruthin
Llandudno
Colwyn Bay

Centre for
Alternative
Technology
Barmouth
Harlech
Llanbedr
SNOWDONIA
FOREST AND
NATIONAL PARK
Blaenau Ffestiniog
Dee

Ceredigion Bay

Aberystwyth
Borth
Aberdyfi
Tywyn
Machynlleth
Cader Idris
Corris
(Dovey)
Dolgellau
Llyn Tegid
Bala Lake
Bala
Lake
Vyrnwy
Llangollen
Wrexham
Chester
Crewe

MOUNTAINS
Wye
Severn
A470
Newtown
Llanfyllin
Corwen
Welshpool
Montgomery
Shrewsbury
Knighton
Craven
Arms

Ellesmere
Port
Wallasey
Birkenhead
Liverpool
R. Mersey

R. Dee

THE LANGUAGE OF CYMRU

The Welsh revere their native language, even if only 20% can still speak it fluently. One of the great blows to the language came with the industrial revolution and the resulting shift from a rural to industrial economy. A more insidious problem was the lack of status the language suffered over the centuries—it was not until the 1960s that Welsh was legally recognized. Since then, the language has been making up for lost time. Middle-class children in Cardiff now queue up to attend Welsh schools, and the British government spends tens of millions of pounds a year for bilingual signs, tourist publications, and public broadcasting. The effort constitutes a fittingly expensive apology for past wrongs, and Welsh does seem to be surviving more successfully than its closest Celtic cousin, Breton, which is spoken in western France. Although Welsh may look impossible to pronounce, it is a phonetic language. Once the alphabet is learned, pronunciation is quite straightforward. Remember that "dd" is sounded like the "th" in they; "f" sounds like "v" as in save and "ff" is the equivalent of the English "f," as in forest. The most difficult sound to master is the "ll" sound which, has no English equivalent. "Speak Welsh" suggests you try resting the tip of the tongue against the top front teeth and emit a sharp burst of air without making a noise in the throat.

BY GREAT LITTLE TRAIN • Wales is famous for its so-called Great Little Trains, narrow-gauge steam railways that chug "I think I can, I think I can" style through scenic, rural landscapes from April through October, with some limited winter services. The most commonly used lines include the **Vale of Rheidol Railway,** which travels from Aberystwyth to Devil's Bridge; and the **Ffestiniog Railway,** with service from Porthmadog to Blaenau Ffestiniog. For info and detailed schedules contact **Great Little Trains of Wales** (The Station, Llanfair Caereinion, Powys SY21 0SF, tel. 01938/810441). The eight Great Little Trains are covered by their own **Wanderer** ticket, which gives you unlimited travel on any four days in eight (£32) or eight days in 15 (£42).

CARDIFF

Despite its Welsh street signs and red dragon souvenirs, Cardiff feels like just another British town filled with English speakers and middle-class retail stores. On the other hand, the city somehow retains the charm of grander days with its numerous Victorian office buildings, department stores, and arcades—structures that have been lost, bombed to eternity, or demolished by short-sighted town planners in many English cities. Look behind the facades and you'll find a vibrant culture that keeps Cardiff moving and supports a surprisingly active nightlife. Cardiff, which became Wales's capital city in 1955, is certainly worth a couple of days' exploration—and it makes a good base for exploring the nearby coast and country, where you'll find the "true" Wales.

Cardiff has existed since Roman times but did not expand until the industrial revolution, when it became the most important coal-shipping port in the world. Between 1801 and 1911, the population boomed from 1,000 to 180,000 residents. The newcomers were mostly Brits, Scots, and northern Welsh who came to work in the burgeoning factories and to construct the buildings that stand as reminders of Cardiff's past prosperity. Following World War I, trade dropped off as coal mines around Wales began to close down. Cardiff hit a major low point during the 1930s and '40s, when unemployment peaked at 65% and poverty was rampant. Nowadays, the city is on the upswing. Forecasters have identified it as one of the top cities for "quality of life" for the new century, and the old docklands are being completely redeveloped as part of the huge Cardiff Bay regeneration scheme that will give the city 8 mi of waterfront housing, hotels, restaurants, museums, and a new opera house. At the heart of the development is the specially commissioned Welsh Assembly building. The debating chamber will open in the spring of 2001.

BASICS

AMERICAN EXPRESS

The office changes traveler's checks for a 1% commission, and all foreign currencies for £3. *3 Queen St., near Cardiff Castle, CF1 4AF, tel. 02920/668858. Open weekdays 9–5:30, Sat. 9–5.*

LAUNDRY

Launderama is within easy striking distance of the Cathedral Road B&Bs. There's no self-service but a wash, dry, and fold costs £4.50. *60 Lower Cathedral Rd., tel. 02920/228326. Open Thurs.–Tues. 9:30–4:30*

MAIL

The main **post office,** near Cardiff Central Station, will hold mail. *2–4 Hill St., The Hayes, CF1 2ST, tel. 02920/345286. Open weekdays 9–5:30, Sat. 9–12:30.*

MEDICAL AID

In the event of a medical emergency, go to the **University Hospital of Wales** (Heath Park, tel. 02920/747747). Cardiff's pharmacies take turns staying open late; check the daily *South Wales Echo* newspaper for current schedules.

VISITOR INFORMATION

Cardiff Tourist Information Centre has maps and bus schedules and will book you a bed in Cardiff or anywhere else in Wales for a 10% deposit plus a £1 fee. *Cardiff Central Station, tel. 02920/227281. Open Mon.–Sat. 9–6:30, Sun. 10–4.*

COMING AND GOING

BY BUS

National Express serves Cardiff seven times per day from London's Victoria Coach Station (3 hrs, £20 return) and Birmingham (2½ hrs, £17.50 return, £21 Friday). These and other buses converge at the bus station, across from the train station. *Wood St., tel. 0990/808080.*

BY CAR

You'll save time and aggravation by taking the train from London to Cardiff and then renting a car from here—though with the high price of train fares, you may save money by renting a car with a friend in London. The best rates within Cardiff are available at **Day's Hire** (Trade St., tel. 02920/237771), with compact cars from £32.08 per day, £151.60 per week, including insurance, VAT, and unlimited mileage. For a few pounds more try **Hertz** (9 Central Sq., tel. 02920/224548) or **Alamo** (Cardiff International Hotel, Mary Ann St., tel. 02920/222098).

BY TRAIN

From **Cardiff Central Station** there's hourly service to London's Paddington (2 hrs, £37 return), Swansea (1 hr, £9 day return, £13.30 period return), Abergavenny (40 mins, £8.50 return), Bath (1 hr, £13 day return, £15.70 period return), and Fishguard (2¼ hrs, £18.60 period return). *Wood St., tel. 02920/228000. Open daily 5 AM–11 PM.*

GETTING AROUND

Cardiff's center is very compact and walkable. The main street, known as St. Mary Street to the south and High Street to the north, runs between the train station and Cardiff Castle. Queen Street, the main pedestrian district, extends east from the castle; to reach the university from here walk about a ½ mi north on Park Place. Running east from the end of St. Mary Street is the Mill Lane Café Quarter, where you'll find a good choice of sidewalk cafés, shops, pubs, restaurants, and nightclubs. You may want to take a bus or taxi to reach the hostel and cheaper B&Bs. A cab from the city center to the B&Bs on Cathedral Road should cost no more than £3.50. Catch cabs at the train station or at ranks on The Hayes or Westgate Street. Otherwise, call **Capital Cabs** (tel. 02920/777777) or **Castle Cabs** (tel. 02920/344344).

BY BUS

The main bus station is right across from Central Station, though many buses also leave from Wood Street behind the bus station and Castle Street near the castle. The very orange fleet of **Cardiff Bus (Bws Caerdydd)** serves the city and environs about 7 AM–11 PM (limited late- night service is available). Fares are 55p–£1.40 during peak hours, 45p–£1.05 off-peak, depending on how far you travel. The **Capital Day Out Ticket** allows one, two, or three days' unlimited bus travel for £3.30 per day. All tickets can be bought on the bus; exact change is required. *Main office: Wood St., tel. 02920/396521. Open Mon.– Sat. 8:30–5:30.*

WHERE TO SLEEP

There are plenty of B&Bs on Cathedral Road (northwest of the station) and its neighboring streets, such as Plasturton Place and Pontcanna Street, and on Newport Road (northeast of the station). Both are 20- to 30-minute walks (or short bus rides) from the city center. To get from the train station to the land of B&Bs, walk northwest on Westgate Street, cross the bridge to the left, and turn right on Cathedral Road (or take Bus 25, 32, 62C, or 65C from the center of town). For Newport Road, take Bus 47, 48, 50, 61, 61A, 62, 62B, 62C, 65, 65B, or 65C from the stations.

During school holidays—usually April and mid-June–September—**Cardiff University** residence halls are a particularly inexpensive option, from £15. It's usually necessary to book at least a day in advance. Facilities include shops, launderettes, sports complex, and bars (58 Park Pl., tel. 02920/874027, fax 02920/874990).

UNDER £35 • Amberley Guest House. Just off Cathedral Road, Amberley is cheap and quiet, and some of the spacious rooms overlook a miniature park across the street. The cheery owners add to the comfort. Singles are from £15, doubles £32. *22 Plasturton Gardens, tel. 02920/374936. 7 rooms, 1 with bath.*

Austins Hotel. This friendly, family-run hotel overlooks the River Taff and is close to Cardiff Castle and all city center amenities. Singles cost from £16, doubles £30. *11 Coldstream Terrace, City Center, tel. 02920/377148. 11 rooms, 4 en suite.*

UNDER £45 • The Beeches Hotel. This family-run hotel overlooks Roath Park with its lake and attractive gardens. Although in a quiet residential area, it's a good base for exploring the more lively area of Albany Road with its wealth of pubs, restaurants, and take-out joints. The city center is only a 15-minute walk away. Singles cost £25, doubles from £35. *73 Ninian Rd., Roath Park, tel. 02920/491803. 10 rooms, 2 en suite.*

Penrhys Hotel. In addition to spacious singles (£32) and doubles (£42), all with private shower/bath, phone, and TV, the Penrhys has a fancy dining room, bas-relief wainscoting, and carved detail on the staircases. *127 Cathedral Rd., tel. 02920/230548 or 02920/387292, fax 02920/387292. 20 rooms, 14 with shower/bath.*

St. Hilary Hotel. A display case of trophies and rugby jerseys and team pictures of burly men confront you when you enter the door. Thankfully, the rest of the house is much more toned down with comfortable wood- and lace-filled singles (£18–£25) and doubles with bath (£34), plus larger rooms with four-poster beds (£38). *144 Cathedral Rd., tel. 02920/340303. 12 rooms, 8 with bath.*

HOSTELS

Cardiff Backpackers. This bright yellow and purple building is close to all city-center amenities and is Cardiff's first independent backpacker's hostel. Facilities include a bar and lounge. Prices start at £12.50 per person. *99 Neville St., Riverside, tel. 02920/345577. 50 beds. Kitchen.*

Cardiff YHA. This functional, noisy place—several busy streets and a train line practically run through the rooms—is the only cheap sleep in town. The 2-mi urban hike to the hostel may be a bit much with a pack, so take Bus 78, 80, 80B, or 82 from Cardiff Central. Beds are £10.15. *2 Wedal Rd., Cardiff, CF2 5PG, tel. 02920/462303, fax 02920/464571. 68 beds. Check-in after 3 PM. Curfew 11 PM, lockout 10– 3. Kitchen, laundry. Closed Dec.*

CAMPING

If you want to camp, you might as well head to the beautiful Brecon Beacons (only an hour away to the north), since campgrounds are far from the city and inconvenient for those without cars. **Lavernock Point** (tel. 02920/707310), 4 mi from Cardiff, is your closest option. It's closed November–Easter and costs £3 per person. From Wood Street, take Bus P4, P4A, P5, or P8 to Fort Road, then follow the signs for ½ mi.

FOOD

While there are many good eateries in Cardiff, you're just as likely to stumble across some rather unimaginative ones. Morning teas and lunches generally run less than £6, but dinners can cost £12 unless you resign yourself to pub grub. **St. David's Centre** (Queen St.) has a good outdoor produce market, and the nearby indoor **Central Market** (St. Mary Street) is filled with shops selling pastries, cheese, and meats. There are also many small eateries and take-away stands in the shopping arcades along **St. Mary Street** and **High Street.**

"We Serve Brains" doesn't mean what you might think. Brains is the local brew of choice—and there are nine varieties to do your head in.

Canadian Muffin Company. Close to Cardiff Castle, this vibrant little café and take-away offers an inspirational menu and wonderful coffee. A huge variety of muffins, both savory and sweet, are on offer, plus soups, baked potatoes, a range of filled baguettes and ciabatta, and hot dishes with plenty of fish and vegetarian choices. *13 High St., tel. 02920/232202. Open daily 8– 6, Sun. 11–4.*

Celtic Cauldron. Come for traditional Welsh food and a wide variety of vegetarian dishes at decent prices. Try the *laverbread* (seaweed mixed with oatmeal on toast) with salad or the Glamorgan sausage (a veggie "sausage" of cheese, eggs, herbs, and onions). *47–49 Castle Arcade, across from castle, tel. 02920/387185. Closed Sun.*

Hullaballoos. Housed in an old bank in the center of Cardiff, this is a lively and spacious restaurant with round tables and bright lighting. You can bring your own wine and enjoy a set lunch for £5.99 or an early supper for £7.99. Try the salmon-and-asparagus terrine or blackened chicken with lime. *92 St Mary's St., tel. 02920/226811.*

WORTH SEEING

Signs throughout the city center point the way to Cardiff's main sights, and with everything oriented around Cardiff Castle, it's difficult to get lost. For a quiet, relaxing afternoon, take Bus 78, 80, 80B, or 82 northeast to **Roath Park**, with a riotous rose garden, a conservatory (70p), and a lake where you can rent rowing skiffs and paddle boats (£3.35 per hr). For a taste of local politics, you can waltz right into the Lord Mayor's office at **City Hall** (Blvd. de Nantes) for free when he's not around. City Hall also has a statue gallery known as the "Welsh Hall of Heroes," where the likes of Llywelyn and Owain stare down at you.

CARDIFF BAY INNER HARBOR

A lively and up-and-coming area of Cardiff is the revitalized Cardiff Bay docklands, 1 mi from the city center, with attractive promenades, views across the bay to Penarth, and various attractions. Visit the **Norwegian Church Arts Centre** (Harbour Drive, Waterfront Park, tel. 01222 /454899), a pretty white-timbered building where children's author (James and the Giant Peach) Roald Dahl was baptized. Call in at the futuristic **Cardiff Bay Visitor Center** (Harbour Drive, Waterfront Park, tel. 01222/463833), known locally as "the Tube," which tells the story of the docklands regeneration project. Whatever your age, you'll be fascinated by the hands-on exhibits, Science Theater, and Planetarium at **Techniquest** (Stuart St., tel. 01222/475475), one of Britain's leading Science Discovery Centers. Admission is £5. For entertainment there's **Atlantic Wharf Leisure Village** (Hemingway Rd., tel. 01222/471444) with a 12-screen cinema, 26-lane Hollywood Bowl, nightclub, restaurants, cafés, and bars all under one roof.

CARDIFF CASTLE

One of the most extraordinary sights in Wales is this famous castle—showpiece of the city and the perfect expression of the anything-goes Victorian spirit prevalent in the mid-19th century. In classic leisure-class style, the third marquess of Bute went all out back then to renovate Cardiff Castle, transforming it into a sumptuous place where he might spend a few weeks each summer. While there's a length of wall dating from the Roman period and several Norman towers, most of the castle is the work of William Burges, a 19th-century architect who had an addiction to the French Gothic style. Obsessed with whimsical flights of fancy, he created spectacular chambers and halls that look for all the world like stage sets for a fairy-tale King Arthur. The view of the city isn't terribly inspiring from the castle, but all in all it's one heck of a Victorian ego trip. Call for information about the medieval banquets occasionally offered on site. *Castle St., tel. 02920/878100. Guided tour of the castle £5. Open Mar.–Oct., daily 9.30–6; Nov.–Feb., daily 9:30–4:30; call for tour times.*

NATIONAL MUSEUM OF WALES

This huge, stately museum covers Wales's history with comprehensive exhibits of local archaeology, industry, botany, geology, and zoology. There's also a permanent collection of painting and sculpture, featuring lesser-known works by European heavyweights like Rodin, Cézanne, and Rembrandt as well as works by beloved Welsh artists such as Richard Wilson and Augustus John. *Cathays Park, tel. 02920/397951. From castle, walk left on Kingsway, turn right on Blvd. de Nantes. Admission £5.50. Open Tues.–Sun. 10–5.*

AFTER DARK

Pubs and clubs seem to be around every downtown corner, concerts and films are relatively cheap, and even after a few pints the city is simple to navigate. The free *Buzz* magazine, available at the tourist office and some pubs and clubs, has detailed info on all the hot spots and a listing of what's on for the month. Nightly listings can also be found in the "What's On" section of the *South Wales Echo,* the local paper.

PUBS AND CLUBS

The Borough (72 St. Mary St., tel. 02920/221343) has a great traditional atmosphere, and **Sam's Bar** (63 St. Mary St., tel. 02920/345189) is a lively spot, which is open till 4 AM on Sat. morning. Jazz fans will love **Café Jazz** (21 St. Mary St., tel. 02920/387026), which has live jazz six nights a week with TV screens in the restaurant and bar so you can view the action on stage. For something uniquely Welsh, try **Clwb Ifor Bach** (Womanby St., tel. 02920/232199). The biggest nights are Wednesdays, with three floors of music to choose from—Funk & Disco, Popscene, and Breaks 'n' Beats. Gay bars congregate around the Charles Street area; **Minsky's Show Bar** (42 Charles St., tel. 02920/233128) serves up music from the '70s to the '90s.

OPERA, THEATER, AND FILM

The Welsh National Opera, one of Britain's four major opera companies and its most adventurous, is based at the New Theater. The company is often touring; call 02920/464666 for schedule information. **St. David's Hall** (The Hayes, tel. 02920/878500) is Wales's premier national concert hall, drawing first-class performers of everything from rock to ballet. Cult and art-house films play at **Chapter Arts Centre** (Market Rd., tel. 02920/399666), which also hosts cheap plays and dance events; take Bus 12, 16, 17, 18, 33, 33A, or 133 west from the city center.

NEAR CARDIFF

CAERPHILLY

Caerphilly is the largest (with over 30 acres of grounds) and possibly most impressive fortress in Wales. The original 13th-century Norman construction was remarkable for its time, with a fourfold concentric fortification surrounded by two seemingly impregnable, man-made moats (medium-size lakes, really). Caerphilly is no longer on guard; some walls have toppled and others lean haphazardly. Exhibits trace the castle's turbulent 700-year history. Of all the sights near Cardiff, Caerphilly ranks among the very best. *Caerphilly, tel. 02920/883143. From Cardiff Central Station, take a train (20 mins, £3.60 return) or Bus 26, 71, or 72 (35 mins, £2.10 return) to Caerphilly. Admission £2.50. Open late Mar.–late Oct., daily 9:30–6:30; late Oct.–late Mar., Mon.–Sat. 9:30–4, Sun. 11–4.*

TINTERN ABBEY

When Wordsworth penned "Lines Written a Few Miles Above Tintern Abbey," he had no idea that tourists, who didn't quite grasp the poem's meaning, would flock to Tintern to gawk at said abbey. Beautiful as it is, Tintern's appeal is vastly diminished in summer because of the crowds. After gazing at the sky through the roofless cloister, take advantage of the marked walks in the nearby woods of the **Wye Valley,** especially the Offa's Dyke Path. Ambitious walkers should try the 5-mi hike from the nearby YHA hostel (tel. 01594/530272) at the St. Briavels Castle, once a Norman castle used by King John. Pick up walking guides at the tourist office near Tintern Abbey. *Tintern, tel. 01291/689251. From Cardiff Central Station, take any train east to Chepstow, then Stagecoach Red and White Bus 69 (every 2 hrs, £2.45 return). Admission £2.40. Open late Mar.–late Oct., daily 9:30–6:30; late Oct.–late Mar., Mon.–Sat. 9:30–4, Sun. 11–4.*

MUSEUM OF WELSH LIFE

This excellent open-air museum celebrates Wales's rich rural culture on some 100 acres of open parkland—it's a complete Welsh village with dwellings imported from around the country. There's a bakery, a tollhouse, a wool and flour mill, plus farm animals clucking about. The Elizabethan mansion, built within the walls of St. Fagan's Castle, has particularly gorgeous gardens. If you're visiting in spring or fall, look for reenactments of medieval festivals such as May Day and the Harvest. *St. Fagan's, tel. 02920/ 569441. From Cardiff Central Station, take Bus 32 (30 mins, £1.45 return). Admission £5.50; Nov.– Easter £4.50. Open daily 10–5 (July–Sept. until 6).*

BRECON BEACONS NATIONAL PARK

The grassy, sandstone Brecon Beacon mountains make up only part of this huge national park, a vast playground for hikers, cyclists, and spelunkers. If your ideal image of Wales is one of sheep-flecked hills, gently sloping valleys, and rural villages, this superb national park will not disappoint.

Brecon Beacons extends over 519 square mi and encompasses four distinct areas. In the east, the **Black Mountains** are considered the most "civilized" part of the park, as they are close to a number of towns and rife with religious and historical monuments. In the middle of the park are the popular **Brecon Beacons** themselves, a spectacular series of 2,000-ft peaks characterized by huge glacierlike curving ridges. Just west, **Fforest Fawr,** with its open, high moorland and conifer forests, contains the distinctive little pocket of the park known as the Waterfall Region, with its limestone gorges, falls, and caves, centered around the hamlet of Ystradfellte. In the west, **Black Mountain** (singular, not to be confused with the Black Mountains) is actually a series of peaks and open moorland particularly devoid of roads and towns, making it one of the most inaccessible regions, but also the quietest and most unspoiled.

Public transport within the park is neither terrible nor great. Fforest Fawr and Ystradfellte, for example, are both inaccessible without a car. On the other hand, **Brecon** in the north, **Abergavenny** in the southeast, and **Hay-on-Wye** in the northeast are accessible by a combination of train and bus (Abergavenny is the only one on a rail route) and are therefore prime bases for backpackers. To spend a solid week exploring the park, you'll need a good pair of hiking books and/or a car to call your own. Otherwise, you can make short excursions from the above three towns without too much hassle.

BASICS

VISITOR INFORMATION

The main park visitor center, **Brecon Beacons Visitor Centre** (Libanus, tel. 01874/623366), open daily year-round, is in the middle of nowhere, but the views are grand and the tourist pamphlets plentiful. It's a long trek if you lack a car, but if you can get to the center, you'll walk away with armloads of park information. They don't, however, book lodgings. From April through September, park information offices are also open in **Abergavenny** (Monmouth Rd., tel. 01873/853254), **Brecon** (Cattle Market parking lot, tel. 01874/623156), **Llandovery** (King's Rd., tel. 01550/720693) in the west, and **Pen-y-Cae** (Craig-y-Nos

Country Park, tel. 01639/730395) in the southwest. All are loaded with pamphlets and walking guides and reserve rooms for a 10% deposit. There is also a tourist information center in **Hay-On-Wye** (Oxford Rd., tel. 01497/820144), which, though not an actual park office, can supply you with some maps and hiking info, and will book rooms.

Unrelated to park and city offices but nonetheless friendly, the **Garwnant Forest Centre** (Cwm Taff, Merthyr Tydfil, off A470, tel. 01685/723060) offers waymarked footpaths, mountain bike hire, a Discovery Centre full of environmental information, organized events and activities, and pleasant tearooms.

PUBLICATIONS

Most of the park is covered by the Landranger series of maps (Nos. 160 and 161 are the most useful) available at many tourist offices. If you're really serious, get Ordnance Survey's "Outdoor Leisure Maps" No. 11, 12, or 13. Aside from the numerous free trail pamphlets, you can also get "postcards" (40p) featuring a map and description of individual walks, and leaflets (20p–25p) detailing activities like hiking, biking, boating, and riding. Also helpful are the "Walks in the Brecon Beacons" and "Usk Valley Walks" booklets (50p–£2). For serious trailblazers, there are extremely detailed books with excellent maps such as the Ordnance Survey's *Offa's Dyke Path South* (£10). Safety should never be underestimated on the peaks; dozens of people who "knew what they were doing" are rescued each year. A major factor is the notoriously changeable weather. If you want to be truly informed, pick up *Brecon Beacons, Its Climate and Mountain Weather* (£4.50).

COMING AND GOING

Do yourself a favor and throw away any notions of efficiency in Brecon Beacons. Getting from Point A to Point B is half the fun, and if you're not that kind of traveler, rethink your Brecon Beacons itinerary. Transportation within the park is limited, and you'll be dependent upon local buses—definitely stop into a tourist office and acquaint yourself with the bus companies' complicated schedules. Hitchhikers may get lucky, but then again, may not. Major roads make the park easy to access by car, and the best place to rent is in Cardiff (*see* Coming and Going *in* Cardiff, *above*).

BY BUS

National Express runs one direct bus between Cardiff and Brecon per day, which leaves Cardiff at 5 PM. The bus is not run for tourists' convenience but rather for locals either shopping or working in Cardiff. If you miss it, you can take the train to Merthyr Tydfil and hop on the connecting **Stagecoach Red & White** (tel. 01633/266336) Bus 43, which runs to Brecon six or seven times per day (twice on Sunday). Stagecoach Red & White also sends Bus 63 between Brecon and Swansea two or three times a day (twice on Sunday) and is a major provider of essential bus services throughout the park: Bus X4 (hourly) runs between Cardiff and Abergavenny; Bus 21 (six per day, no Sunday service) runs between Brecon and Abergavenny; and Bus 39 (five per day, with two on Sunday) runs from Brecon to Hay-on-Wye on its way to Hereford, a major stop on the Cardiff–Shrewsbury train line.

BY TRAIN

You can reach **Abergavenny,** on the park's eastern edge, from both Cardiff (1 hr, £8.50 day return) and London (via Newport) by train. You can also reach **Merthyr Tydfil** (£5.20) from Cardiff. If you're coming from western England, the **Heart of Wales Line** runs from Craven Arms to Swansea, with stops in **Llandeilo** and **Llandovery,** both on the park's western fringe. For train info call 0345/484950.

The only train that runs within the park is **Brecon Mountain Railway** (tel. 01685/722988) near Merthyr Tydfil. It operates Easter–October and costs £6.20 for a return sightseeing excursion. The vintage steam train is one of those Great Little Trains (*see* Chapter Basics, *above*) and is more of a tourist attraction—albeit a pleasant one—than a means of getting around.

WHERE TO SLEEP AND EAT

Brecon, which lies within the park's official boundaries, has B&Bs aplenty, good hostels, and nearby campgrounds. All in all, it's a great base for day hikes within the park proper. **Abergavenny** and **Hay-on-Wye** lie just outside the park but are close enough to serve as bases for hiking. And remember, no matter where you stay, you're never that far from a good hike.

ABERGAVENNY • The B&Bs here, many of them crowded along Monmouth Road near the train station, vary wildly in price—from £14 to £25 per person. The tourist office only books "officially approved" rooms, so you might want to wander through town on your own, as many "unapproved" B&Bs have signs in their windows. The cheapest and most central B&B in town is **Mrs. Bradley's** (10 Merthyr Rd., tel. 01873/852206), with large doubles for £20, including tea and toast (£26 with full English breakfast); no credit cards. At the opposite end of town from the train station, **Ivy Villa Guest House** (43 Hereford Rd., tel. 01873/852473) offers simple, clean rooms with TVs and a full English breakfast for £15 per person, no credit cards. The tourist office also lists farmhouses where you can camp cheaply. In the Abergavenny area, many farmhouse owners will even drive into town and pick you up if you're auto-less.

Tuesday is Abergavenny's market day, when the country folk bring in butter, eggs, and other fresh produce. Several stores fill in the gaps, notably **Cornucopia Health Shop** (Market St., tel. 01873/855346), with dried fruit, tofu, and all things herbal. Sit down, take off your shoes (unless you've been hiking), and enjoy a tasty Chinese meal at the **Peking Chef** (59 Cross St., tel. 01873/857457) or choose from a wide range of inexpensive homemade lunches, soups, sandwiches and cakes at **Focus** (53 Frogmore St., tel. 01873/853530). For a solid, cheap dinner, order the homemade chicken and mushroom pie at the pub in the **Swan Hotel** (Cross St., tel. 01873/852829). **Thimbles** (St. John St., off High St., tel. 01873/853134) sells Welsh fudge, and homemade candies for under £1.

BRECON • There's a youth hostel fairly close to Brecon—Ty'n-y-Caeau (*see below*)—though it requires a bit of walking for those without wheels. There's also an ample selection of B&Bs in the Llan Faes area, along Orchard, Church, and St. David's streets. During the Jazz Festival in mid-August, vacancies are scarce—definitely book ahead. **Tir Bach Guest House** (13 Alexandra Rd., tel. 01874/624551) is better than average, with antiques-decorated rooms and mountain views. The same goes for the peaceful **Cambridge House** (11 St. David's St., tel. 01874/624699), happily sequestered from the row of busier B&Bs on Orchard Street. At these guest houses, singles run £16–£17, doubles £32–£34. Neither accept credit cards.

Supermarkets dominate the center of Brecon, which is good news if you're sick of chippies, Chinese takeout, and kebab shops. **Top Drawer** (30 High St., tel. 01874/622601) sells goodies such as Welsh cheeses and breads, as well as health food and sundry snack items. **Bentley's** (The Bulwark, tel. 01874/624456) is a good late-night option, serving a wide range of inexpensive dishes. The **Salad Bowl** (The Bulwark, tel. 01874/625429) serves baked potatoes and sandwiches.

HAY-ON-WYE • The town's B&Bs fill up during the Festival of Literature in late May and on summer and holiday weekends, so book ahead. Happily, even during the high season most B&Bs don't charge more than £16 per person. In fact, rooms at the 16th-century **Brookfield House** (Brook St., tel. 01497/820518) cost £16–£18.50, no credit cards. If you want to stay in a first-rate farmhouse 3 mi outside town, **Castleton Barn** (Clifford, tel. 01497/831690) has large, picturesque rooms overlooking green fields for £18 per person, no credit cards. If you call in advance, they may pick you up in Hay or arrange for a taxi to collect you.

As long as **The Granary** (Broad St., tel. 01497/820790) remains open, eating in Hay will never be a problem; this is a place you'll want to come back to. Daily specials include soup with a roll, and goulash with a baked potato. **Old Stables Tea Rooms** (Bear St., tel. 01497/820563) is about as cozy as you can get. Come for morning coffee, light snacks, and homemade soup and rolls. The proprietor, Mrs. Price, closes the Old Stables on Monday and Friday to cook. **Old Black Lion** (Lion St., tel. 01497/820841) is a 13th-century inn with sandwiches and splurges like spiced chicken.

HOSTELS

Capel-y-Ffin YHA. This hostel on 40 acres of hilly farmland near Hay-on-Wye is within spitting distance of the Offa's Dyke Path and a great place to crash after a hard day's walk. Most guests either walk here, take a taxi from Hay-on-Wye (about £10), or fall right off the trail. Be sure to call ahead, because the hostel is closed December–January, on numerous Wednesdays throughout the year, and Friday and Saturday at the beginning and end of the year. Beds are £6.80. *Capel-y-Ffin, Llanthony, Near. Abergavenny, NP7 7NP, tel. 01873/890650. 40 beds. Curfew 11 PM, lockout 10–5. Kitchen.*

Ty'n-y-Caeau YHA. A large country house near the Monmouthshire and Brecon Canal holds this hostel. From Brecon it's an easy 2-mi walk along a bridle path; join the path near the hospital at the east end of Brecon. You can also take Bus 21 toward Abergavenny (ask driver for Ty'n-y-Caeau), which stops about a mile south of the hostel. Beds are £8.35. *Groesffordd, Brecon LD3 7SW, tel. 01874/665270, fax 01874/665278. 54 beds. Curfew 11 PM, lockout 10–5. Kitchen. Closed Dec.–mid-Feb. and some days early and late in season.*

Ystradfellte YHA. If you're set on exploring the park's waterfalls, this hostel makes a great base. The rooms are extremely basic, but a cozy pub down the road in the village takes care of food and drink. The hostel is virtually inaccessible without a car; once you've reached Ystradfellte, follow the YHA signs ½ mi south. Your only public transportation option is to take the bus that stops at Glyn Neath about 5 mi south on its way between Merthyr Tydfil and Swansea. Beds are £7.50. *Tai'r Heol, Ystradfellte, Aberdare, CF44 9JF, tel. 01639/720301. 28 beds. Curfew 11 PM. Kitchen. Closed weekdays Dec.–Mar. and some Thurs. year-round; call ahead. No credit cards.*

CAMPING

While there are plenty of campgrounds, many farmers set up private sites of their own, which you'll happen upon while traveling down quiet country roads. Partial listings are available at tourist offices, and rates run £2.50–£5 per person. It's against the rules to camp randomly in the park, but some people do it anyway. While most campgrounds near Brecon are accessible only by car, two sites are within reach of the Brecon–Hereford bus: **Lakeside Caravan and Camping Park** (tel. 01874/658226) and **Llynfi Holiday Park** (tel. 01874/658283). Both have shower and toilet facilities, charge from £3 per person, and are closed November–mid-March.

EXPLORING BRECON BEACONS

If you've only got a few days, base yourself in one of the towns listed below and spend your days hiking, cycling, pony trekking, or fishing. Otherwise, take a week to hike through a section of the park, crashing in hostels as you go. Most hostels and hikes within the park are inaccessible by bus, so if you really want to see the park, plan on plenty of long hikes.

In the south of Fforest Fawr, the **Waterfall Region** (or "Ystradfellte") has spectacular falls on the rivers Hepste, Mellte, and Nedd Fechan; 90-ft **Nant Lech,** the park's highest waterfall, is just east of the "official" waterfall region at Henhryd Falls. The Ystradfellte YHA (*see above*) makes a good base for exploring the area, if you can get there.

ABERGAVENNY

Abergavenny, a pleasant, bustling market town, makes a great base for exploring the Black Mountains and the Monmouthshire and Brecon Canal. Indeed, you may *have* to make it your base, because it's the easiest place to access by bus. Ask at the tourist office for the booklet on local walks, priced at about £2, which describes a variety of routes starting from or near Abergavenny, including the **Offa's Dyke Path** (*see* Hiking, *below*). From the bus station, walk past the tourist office and up Cross Street to reach the pedestrian-only town center, which is filled with standard British mall stores. Tuesday is the town's big market day (less frenzied markets also run on Friday and Saturday).

The biggest sight is no doubt **Abergavenny Castle** (Castle St., tel. 01873/854282), the foundations of which date from 1090. Wander the grounds for free or visit the attached **museum,** with exhibits on local customs and folklore, for £1. Abergavenny's annual **festival** takes place in late July/early August. For a Welsh version of a hoedown (involving plenty of livestock), check out the **Abergavenny and Border Counties Agricultural Society Show** at the end of July.

BRECON

The town of Brecon sits within the borders of Brecon Beacons National Park, so it's governed and protected by rules of the park—which means it's pleasantly devoid of tourist traps. It's also great for campers who want to stock up on groceries, rent equipment, and clue in to the area's best walks. All buses stop in **The Bulwark,** the center of Brecon; head uphill from here and turn right (look for the CAR PARK sign) to reach the tourist office. To reach **Llan Faes** (Brecon's medieval core) from The Bulwark, walk up High Street to Ship Street and cross the bridge over the River Usk.

You can easily cover the town's main attractions—the cathedral, the riverside promenade, the lazy canal, and all those darn hills—on foot. Housed in the former Shire Hall, a white stone classical structure, is the **Brecknock Museum** (The Bulwark, tel. 01874/624121), admission £1, with its collection of love spoons, displays of bygone rural life, and an old assize court preserved in all its glory. Those hankering for something less tranquil will enjoy the **South Wales Borderers' Museum** (The Watton, off The Bulwark, tel. 01874/613310), admission £2. Its Zulu War Room is filled with guns, uniforms, paintings, and other war paraphernalia from the past 300 years. Brecon's annual **Jazz Festival** (tel. 01874/625557), held in mid-August, brings 20,000 hipsters to this otherwise quiet town. The festival is excellent, drawing the likes of Pat Metheny and bassist Dave Holland to local venues. Individual concerts cost £6–£20, a daily stroller ticket £20, the all-festival stroller around £35. If you're in Brecon during the 51 weeks of the year when jazz doesn't fill the streets, you can visit the **Jazz Gallery,** a free museum on The Watton (tel. 01874/625557).

HAY-ON-WYE

In 1961, local resident Richard Booth opened a bookstore and began making outrageous predictions about Hay's future international reputation in the book world. Thirty-seven years later, this Welsh border town is a bookworm's dream and has actually become synonymous with secondhand and antiquarian bookstores. Witness the 10-day **Hay Festival of Literature** (tel. 01497/821217) in late May, which attracts major literary figures every year—among them Carlos Fuentes, Vikram Seth, Joseph Heller, and Naomi Wolf—to this tiny town (population 1,300). The rest of the year, Hay-on-Wye somehow maintains its 25 bookstores. The tourist office carries a pamphlet detailing each store's specialty.

OUTDOOR ACTIVITIES

In Brecon, you can obtain most supplies from **Crickhowell Adventure Gear** (21 Ship St., tel. 01874/ 611586), which rents caving lamps, rain gear, boots, day packs, and other equipment for climbing and backpacking. There are smaller branches of the same shop in Crickhowell (1 High St., tel. 01873/ 810020) and Abergavenny (14 High St., tel. 01873/856581). The aptly named **Paddles and Pedals** (15 Castle St., tel. 01497/820604) in Hay-on-Wye has mountain bikes, kayaks, and open-top canoes for hire (round-trip transport available from anywhere on the River Wye). **Mountain & Water** (2 Upper Cwm Nant Gam, Llanelli Hill, Abergavenny, tel. 01495/831825) and **Beacons Experience** (2 Forest Lodge Cottages, Libanus, Brecon, tel. 01874/636799) offer a range of outdoor activities including canoeing, climbing, gorge-walking, abseiling (rapelling), and caving.

CAVING

In the south of the park there are bands of young, carboniferous limestone where, over the centuries, slightly acidic water has managed to carve out huge caves—including the deepest and longest in Britain. While caving is a dangerous, muddy, and wet business, **Dan-yr-Ogof Showcaves** (tel. 01639/ 730284) in the Upper Swansea Valley allow an up-close view for £6.75 without the hassle of renting equipment and buying detailed maps. The caves are part of Britain's largest known cave system and contain displays on the history of caving. If you'd rather go it alone, tourist offices have pamphlets on caving that list caving clubs and professional guides—essential if you want to tackle the **Llangattock Escarpment** or **Clydach Gorge,** recommended for "experts only" by park staff.

CYCLING

Mountain biking is becoming increasingly popular in the Brecon Beacons. It is a wonderful upland terrain with a wide choice of trails through forests and up into open mountains, though the summit of the Beacons is only accessible to walkers. Several bridleways and RUPPs (Roads Used as Public Paths) crisscross the park. One good ride begins by following the **Gap Road** from Brecon up the steep slope past the Cribyn and down the other side by the picturesque Neuadd Reservoir. Continue on through the Talybont Forest and reservoir to meet the **Taff Trail** in Tal-y-bont, which will take you back to Brecon. The full loop is about 20 mi. For road cyclists, there are many country lanes which are relatively free from traffic and afford great views. In addition to the above outdoors shops that rent bikes, try **Bi-Ped Cycles** (4 Free St., Brecon, tel. 01874/622296), **Brecon Cycle Centre** (9 Ship St., Brecon, tel. 01874/ 622651), and **Garwnant Forest Centre** (*see* Basics, *above*), all of which rent mountain bikes for £14– £15 per day, with reduced rates for longer rentals.

HIKING

All tourist offices sell pamphlets listing walks in their particular region. The paths tend to be decently marked and well traveled, except during winter, when the weather is really terrible. Even if you're only stepping out for a 2-mi jaunt, bring water and some munchies; if you're really smart, you'll bring a compass, map, and first-aid kit.

If you leave the park without having traversed some of the 177-mi **Offa's Dyke Path,** you'll have to answer for it to annoying hostelers everywhere else you go in Britain. The path, the original line of demarcation between Wales and England, is well marked and runs all the way from Prestatyn (on the northeastern coast) to Chepstow (east of Cardiff). One of the best sections winds its way along the summit ridges of the Black Mountains between **Hay-on-Wye** and **Pandy** (7½ mi), 4 mi north of Abergavenny. From many points along the way you'll get a great view of both the Wye Valley to the east and the Brecon Beacons to the west, and on a clear day you can see to Black Mountain in the far west of the park.

The **Monmouthshire and Brecon Canal** starts at Pontypool, south of Abergavenny, and travels north-west to Brecon. You can join it at any point and wander along the flat, shaded trail. The Abergavenny–Brecon leg is an easy 20 mi. The **Usk Valley Walk** is equally popular, and tourist offices have a series of maps explaining every leg of it. Many people stretch the above two walks out over two or three days, staying in a B&B near **Llangynidir,** the halfway mark, or camping along the way.

From Brecon, you can hike your pick of the many peaks literally staring you in the face. Most of your hikes will start from **Cwm Llwch** or **Cwm Gwdi,** about an hour or so by foot south of Brecon. From here, you can hike up well-beaten trails to the summit of **Pen-y-Fan,** then traverse along the massive ridge to **Cribyn,** and loop back down to your starting point. The whole circuit takes about four–six hours. Keep in mind that you are climbing more than 2,500 ft and that the weather can change rapidly. An easier three-hour loop of Pen-y-Fan starts at Storey Arms, easily reached by the Silverline bus from Brecon.

To hike through some of the spectacular waterfall region, a good starting point is **Glyn-Neath** in the Neath Valley between Merthyr Tydfil and Neath. Start at the gate behind the Angel Inn pub in Pontneddfechan just east of Glyn-Neath, which you can get to by catching the bus between Merthyr Tydfil and Swansea (the pub also has maps of the trails). This is not a loop trail, so you should allow at least 1½ hours each way for the shortest hike. The path is moderate to strenuous and muddy year-round, so wear sturdy shoes with traction. Along the way you can see dozens of falls of varying sizes, such as the high **White Lady Falls** or the wide, U-shape **Horseshoe Falls.** The only drawback is that Glyn-Neath is still over 3 mi downhill from Ystradfellte and its hostel, so you should plan to start this hike early and allow up to two hours afterward to reach Ystradfellte by foot. Hikers are not supposed to camp along the trails, though some do.

PONY TREKKING

Wales is famous for its ponies, and here's your big chance to ride one. The itsy-bitsyest is the Welsh Mountain Pony, under 12 hands high, bred from ponies once used in the coal mines—though you'll probably be riding one of the larger varieties. Nearly two dozen pony-trekking centers operate through-out the park, most of which are in or near the Black Mountains and charge about £12.50 per half day. The tourist office's "Pony Trekking" booklet (25p) lists 20 places in the park to rent and (if necessary) get trained. One such place is **Grange Pony Trekking,** Capel-y- Ffin (tel. 01873/890215), which also organizes trips for riders with disabilities.

PEMBROKESHIRE COAST

Humans were not the first to discover the windswept, southwest corner of Wales. Seabirds and gray seals have been visiting this craggy coastline for hundreds of years. It's only recently that British tourists have come bustling through, packing previously quiet villages and tromping through what they've named the **Pembrokeshire Coast National Park.** It's the smallest and only seashore-based national park in the country, a unique coastal preserve that covers offshore islands, coves, and cliff-lined headlands. The focal point of the park is the 168-mi **Pembrokeshire Coast Path,** which runs from Amroth in Car-marthen Bay to Cardigan. To traverse the entire path you'll need plenty of outdoor gear and nothing on your travel calendar for at least a week. The truly intrepid can go "coasteering" (a combination of swim-ming, climbing, and guided jumping from cliffs into the sea below). Everyone else can tackle the path in daylong installments.

St. David's in the west makes the best base for a hike along the coast. In south Pembrokeshire, **Tenby, Saundersfoot,** and **Pembroke** draw the lion's share of tourists (mostly retired British couples in their Ford Fiestas) but are still unpretentious and lively. Seabirds frequent four famous colonies just off the west coast on Skomer, Skokholm, Grassholm, and Ramsey islands. Those traveling to Ireland will have to pass through either **Pembroke Dock,** a very unexciting port town, or **Fishguard,** which has an old attractive quayside area set below a steep gorse-covered headland.

VISITOR INFORMATION

There are six National Park Information Centres in or near the Pembrokeshire Coast National Park. The central office in **Haverfordwest** (Wynch La., tel. 01437/764636) organizes some 250 guided walks each

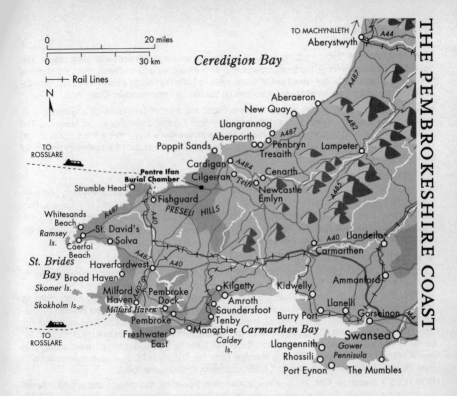

Map labels:

0 — 20 miles
0 — 30 km
⊢—⊣ Rail Lines
N

Ceredigion Bay

TO MACHYNLLETH
Aberystwyth
A44
A487

TO ROSSLARE

Aberaeron
New Quay
Llangrannog
Aberporth
Poppit Sands
A487
Penbryn
Tresaith
Lampeter
A482
Cardigan
A484
Cilgerran
Teifi
Cenarth
Newcastle
Emlyn
A485
Pentre Ifan
Burial Chamber
Strumble Head
Fishguard
PRESELI HILLS
A40
Whitesands
Beach
A487
Ramsey
Is.
St. David's
Solva
A487
Caerfai
Beach
St. Brides
Bay
Haverfordwest
A40
Llandeilo
A40
Carmarthen
A485
Broad Haven
Skomer Is.
Milford
Haven
Pembroke
Dock
Milford Haven
Kilgetty
Amroth
Saundersfoot
Kidwelly
Ammanford
Skokholm Is.
Pembroke
Tenby
Burry Port
Llanelli
Gorseinon
A44
TO ROSSLARE
Freshwater
East
Manorbier
Caldey
Is.
Carmarthen Bay
Llangennith
Rhossili
Port Eynon
Swansea
Gower
Pennisula
The Mumbles

---

year and publishes a host of publications. The free *Coast to Coast* newspaper, available at most hostels and tourist offices, is crammed with bus schedules, museum and events listings, and articles on park issues.

COMING AND GOING

Trains leave from Swansea for **Tenby** (7 per day, 1½ hrs, £12.80 return) and its unstaffed station on Lower Park Road, and for **Haverfordwest** (8 per day, 1 hr, 35 mins, £13.10 return). For schedules and train info, call 0345/484950. Though there's no direct train between Haverfordwest and Tenby, **First Cymru** Buses 358 and 359 run between the two towns every hour. If you're heading to northern Pembrokeshire or up the coast to Aberystwyth, **Richards Brothers** (tel. 01239/613756) offers the most frequent bus connections. From Haverfordwest or Fishguard, you can take Bus 411 to **St. David's** (hourly from Haverfordwest, once every two hours from Fishguard). If you plan on doing a lot of traveling in the area, consider the **West Wales Rover** good for one day (£4) or one week (£18) of unlimited travel on most services in southwest Wales—including the Pembrokeshire Coast and Ceredigion Bay.

From the Pembrokeshire coast, two ferry companies operate services to Rosslare in Ireland. **Irish Ferries** (tel. 0990/171717) depart from Pembroke Dock two times per day at 3:15 AM and 3 PM year-round. The four-hour trip costs £20 single and £35 return. The ferry jetty is about a mile out of town and ferry departure times are not coordinated with train and bus times. If you arrive by train, you'll definitely have to wait around for a few hours. Taxis to the jetty from town should cost about £3. **Stena Line** (tel. 0990/707070) operates two services from Fishguard. The fast Stena Lynx catamaran makes the 99-minute trip four to five times per day in summer, two to three times a day the rest of the year. Fares are £30–41. Stena's Superferry takes three hours and leaves at 3:15 AM and 3 PM throughout the year, except December 25th and 26th. Fares are £20–£25. Stena's ferry port is served by two trains per day, which are coordinated with Superferry departures. If you're taking the Lynx or arrive at other times, Richards Brothers runs buses from Fishguard to the port every half hour or take a cab for about £2.50.

TENBY

In the affable town of Tenby, a relaxed breed of holiday makers wander its narrow, twisting streets. Fortunately, it's easy to overlook the small crowds with all the beaches and sheltered coves surrounding Tenby, not to mention **Caldey Island** just offshore, site of a Cistercian abbey where monks still farm the land. Tenby is also a popular stopover for walkers on the nearby **Pembrokeshire Coast Path.**

High Street, which runs roughly parallel to the seafront, has most of Tenby's shops and restaurants. Nearby **Upper Frog** and **Lower Frog** streets have an indoor market, crafts shops, and tearooms. The most dazzling place to wander is **Castle Hill,** a tiny peninsula that's home to the town museum and numerous sandy benches neatly arranged to face the sea. Buses stop outside the multistory parking lot on **Upper Park Road.**

BASICS

With so many visitors, Tenby's **tourist office** (The Croft, tel. 01834/842402) is extremely busy and stays open quite late by British standards (until 9 PM July–August, until 5:30 PM the rest of the year). They book lodgings daily until about 5 PM, and post a useful list of taxis, banks, and emergency facilities outside. For £2.50 you can also buy Discover the Pembrokeshire Coast, which gives information on the Pembrokeshire Coast Path, which passes right by Tenby.

WHERE TO SLEEP

It's not difficult to find a B&B for around £15 per person in Tenby, but book ahead—especially during July and August. The best streets to try are Warren and Harding streets, and Deer Park, which are all near the train station. **Boulston Cottage** (29 Trafalgar Rd., tel. 01834/843289), run by a very matronly Mrs. Duran, offers rooms for £15–£18 per person, no credit cards. **Weybourne Guest House** (14 Warren St., tel. 01834/843641) is an informal, family-run establishment with well-equipped rooms costing £13–£15 per person. Just off a pleasant terrace overlooking South Beach is **Hereford House** (Sutton St., tel. 01834/843223), which has basic rooms (most with bath) for £14–£15; rates go down about £2 in the off season; no credit cards. The tiny **Meadow Farm** (tel. 01834/844829), a 15-minute walk uphill from the tourist office, has tent sites for £3–£5 per person, showers, and toilets.

HOSTELS • Manorbier YHA. Housed in a former military building, this modern and spacious hostel overlooks the Skrinkle Haven coastline—beaches are less than 200 yards away. Beds cost £10.15. *Manorbier, Pembrokeshire, SA70 7TT, tel. 01834/871803, fax 01834/871101. From Tenby, take Bus 358 or 359 toward Haverfordwest to Manorbier or walk 3½ mi west. 68 beds. Curfew 11 PM, lockout 10–5. Kitchen, laundry. Closed Nov.–mid-Feb.*

Pentlepoir YHA. Less than a mile inland from the Saundersfoot train station, what was once the village school has now been converted into a wee hostel. If you're traveling by bus from Tenby, ask the driver and he might just bring you straight here. Beds cost £6.80. *The Old School, Pentlepoir, Saundersfoot, Pembrokeshire, SA69 9BJ, tel. 01834/812333. 34 beds. Curfew 11 PM, lockout 10–5. Kitchen, laundry. Closed Nov.–Mar. and Wed.–Thurs. out of the main summer season.*

FOOD

The small **Tenby Market Hall,** just off High Street, has stalls with fresh fruit and meats. **Bay Tree** (Tudor Sq., tel. 01834/843516) serves substantial meals such as vegetable pasta bake and light lunches such as soup; on Saturday nights eat to the sounds of live jazz guitar. **Celtic Fare** (St. Julian's St., tel. 01834/845258) serves light lunches and has great homemade desserts. **La Cave** (Upper Frog St., tel. 01834/843038) is indeed a dark cavelike restaurant that serves an extensive menu including dishes prepared from fresh, locally caught fish. It usually stays open until midnight.

WORTH SEEING

Tudor Merchant's House (Quay Hill, tel. 01834/842279) is a medieval town house now owned by the National Trust; admission £1.80. Visit the **Tenby Museum and Picture Gallery** (Castle Hill, tel. 01834/842809) for fairly dull if sincere displays on the natural history and maritime traditions of the area, but with an excellent picture gallery with works by Augustus John; admission £1.80. About 20 minutes to the south via Bus 358, **Manorbier Castle** (tel. 01834/871394) is an unusually intact Norman baronial residence in a pretty spot overlooking the sea; admission £2.

Women aren't allowed inside the Cistercian monastery on nearby **Caldey Island,** but anyone can view the monks' daily service at 2:30 PM in the Abbot's Chapel. Otherwise, the island makes a great place to kick back with its clean, uncrowded beaches. From late May through September, ferries (around £6 return) leave Tenby's harbor, just off St. Julian's Street, about once an hour. The cliffs, sandy beaches, and a stone bearing Latin and Ogham script at the old priory church make for excellent photo ops.

ST. DAVID'S

The cathedral city of St. David's, which takes its name from the patron saint of Wales, has a magical charm. Set at the foot of a small rugged peninsula, the sea never far away, it is Britain's most minute, most peaceful city; an ancient settlement just oozing history. It is also undoubtedly the best place from which to explore the coast—especially the beautiful **St. David's Head,** which is somewhat of a Welsh Land's End without the crowds. Otherwise, most of the best coastal hikes are not more than a day's walk away. From the top of craggy **Carn Llidi** you can survey the coast as far as Strumble Head in the north and St. Brides Bay in the south. The two best nearby beaches are **Whitesands Beach,** near the hostel, and **Caerfai Beach,** about 2 mi south of town.

St. David's Cathedral (tel. 01437/720328) has the oldest foundation of any cathedral in Wales (it dates back to the 6th century). Tucked away in a peaceful, grassy hollow, it is an incredibly beautiful purple-stone building with an amazing, ornately carved roof of Irish oak. Behind the cathedral are the impressive and extensive 14th-century ruins of **Bishop's Palace** (tel. 01437/720517), though the inside isn't quite worth the £2 admission fee. **St. Non's Well,** where St. David was born in AD 500, makes an excellent 1-mi walk from town. You'll know you've found it when you reach a tremendous cliff overlooking the raging sea. Two competing aquariums, the **Oceanarium** (tel. 01437/720453) and **St. David's Marine Life Centre** (tel. 01437/721665), essentially offer the same fish in different environments: The Oceanarium uses large tanks, whereas the Life Centre houses its creatures within a system of caves and rocks. Both charge about £3 and are closed in the off-season. The **tourist office** (City Hall, tel. 01437/720392) is also a national park center, with a knowledgeable staff and reams of publications.

COMING AND GOING

Richards Brothers (tel. 01239/613756) Bus 411 leaves Haverfordwest's train station hourly for St. David's and Solva; the trip to either costs roughly £2.80 return. If you're coming from Cardigan, change at Fishguard. From Tenby, change to Bus 411 in Haverfordwest. Once in St. David's, you'll want to walk—or take to the water. **TYF No Limits** (High St., tel. 01437/721611) offers surfing, kayaking, and coasteering (an adrenaline–rush sport involving scrambling on cliffs and jumping into the sea).

WHERE TO SLEEP

Most B&Bs in St. David's offer decent rates—**Y Glenydd Restaurant & Guest House** (51 Nun St., tel. 01437/720576) is a comfortable Victorian town house with good in-room facilities and the benefit of an on-site bar and restaurant. Rooms cost from £16.50, single. Pick up the "St. David's Peninsula" guide from the tourist office for a list of more than a dozen nearby campsites.

HOSTELS • Penycwm (Solva) YHA. This hostel is near some beautiful beaches and somewhat hard to reach, unless you're hiking the Pembrokeshire Coastal Path, which passes by within 1½ mi. Otherwise, the bus from Haverfordwest to the village of Solva (4 mi away) drops you within a 40-minute walk of the hostel. Ask any local for directions, and prepare to be drawn into a long, friendly conversation. Beds are £9.15. *Hafod Lodge, Whitehouse, Penycwm, near Solva, Pembrokeshire, SA62 6LA, tel. 01437/721940, fax 01437/720959. 26 beds. Kitchen. No credit cards.*

St. David's YHA. This very quiet hostel occupies a rustic, stone farmhouse and sits almost alone in the ominous shadow of Carn Llidi—the highest point in the area. To get there, you'll have to hike or hitch-hike the 2½ mi from town. From St. David's, head north out of town following the signs for Whitesands, after 2 mi look for signs to the hostel. Beds are £7.50. *Llaethdy, St. David's, Haverfordwest, Pembrokeshire, SA62 6PR, tel. 01437/720345, fax 01437/721831. 30 beds. Curfew 11 PM, lockout 10–5. Kitchen. Closed Oct.–Mar. and Thurs. in summer.*

FOOD

Food is a major problem in St. David's after the sun goes down, when a couple of overpriced "bistros" charge £8–£10 for boring English food. Instead, do what the locals do: Head for the lively **Farmer's Arms** pub (Goat St., tel. 01437/720328), which serves tasty, sizable dishes of pub grub. During the day, fill up at the **Iron Kettle Tea Room** (High St., tel. 01437/720399), with sandwiches, home-cooked snacks, and Welsh cream teas (served with two Welsh cakes).

CARDIGAN BAY

The Ceredigion (pronounced care-e-DIG-ion) District, which runs from **Cardigan** up to **Aberystwyth,** is not as heavily trammeled as other Welsh coastal regions. Aberystwyth is the biggest town in the area, and it's positively sleepy outside the university community. But the beaches—especially at Tresaith, Llangrannog, Penryn, Mwnt, and Borth—are gorgeous. The water is so impossibly bright that it sparkles, and you can sometimes spot dolphins, porpoises, and sea otters off the **Heritage Coast,** some 22 mi of ancient settlements and scenic footpaths. Stop and breathe in the salty sea mist, then turn around to gaze back at the smooth green hills of west Wales.

BASICS

COMING AND GOING

The Ceredigion stretch of Cardigan Bay is not that long. It takes less than three hours to drive up the coast from Cardigan to Aberystwyth, past coastal valleys and tiny fishing villages. Trains go only as far as Fishguard in the south and Aberystwyth in the north, so you'll be relying on buses. **Richards Brothers** (tel. 01239/613756) runs routes from Haverfordwest to Aberystwyth and a service on Tuesday, Wednesday, and Friday on Bus 552 between Cardigan and Llangrannog. Richards Brothers's **Day Explorer Pass** (£3) is a good idea for beach-hoppers or for any trip with more than two stops. The **West Wales Rover** (see Coming and Going in Pembrokeshire Coast, above) is also valid on most services in this area.

Arriva Cymru Buses (tel. 01970/617951) run up and down the Welsh coast to the Llŷn Peninsula and the Isle of Anglesey. From Aberystwyth, Arriva buses stop in Aberporth, Aberaeron, Cardigan, New Quay, and Synod Inn; they also cross east toward Shrewsbury, Wrexham, and Chester. Arriva issues its own **Explorer** pass (£5)—useful for castle-hoppers who don't mind waiting for Godot. Their **3-day and 5-day Wanderers** cost £10 and £15. Note that buses from Bangor to Cardiff are not covered by the above passes, even though the buses are run by Arriva. If you want to rent a car, **Budget** (Unit 2, Somerfield, Park Ave., tel. 01970/626200) in Aberystwyth charges £32 per day, £160 per week.

CARDIGAN

Compared with St. David's to the south, Cardigan isn't much to write home about. It is, however, the largest coastal town before Aberystwyth, which makes it a strategic base for day trips to the Heritage Coast. In Cardigan itself, there's little to occupy more than an hour of your time—except the friendly people. The town's crumbling **castle** is owned by an eccentric octogenarian who won't let anyone on the premises. Within a few miles, though, there are several interesting sights. **St. Dogmael's Abbey,** a half mile to the west (take Richards Brothers Bus 407), is still a destination for pilgrims in spring. Near the abbey, inside the local parish church, is the **Sagranus Stone,** inscribed in both Latin and Goidelic, an ancient form of Welsh. (The stone provided the key to translating Goidelic, one of the oldest languages in Europe.)

BASICS

The **Cardigan Tourist Information Centre** (Theatre Mwldan, tel. 01239/613230) has plenty of maps and abundant info on things to do in the area. **High Street,** which turns into Pendre Road past the Guildhall, has everything: a post office, pharmacies, banks, even a launderette. Change money at **Barclays Bank** (32 High St., tel. 01239/612708) or **Midland Bank** (13 High St., tel. 01239/612452).

WHERE TO SLEEP

The tourist office will book you a B&B for free, but you're limited to the places that pay to be listed in the "Ceredigion Accommodation Guide." Book ahead for the popular **Brynhyfryd** (Gwbert Rd., tel. 01239/612861), one of the oldest houses in Cardigan, with single rooms for £17 and doubles for £19 per person, including breakfast; no credit cards. **Berwyn** (St. Dogmael's Rd., tel. 01239/613555) is situated in 2 acres of delightful grounds overlooking the River Teifi. Double rooms cost £19.50 per person (breakfast included) and are well-equipped with TV, clock-radio, and tea/coffee facilities; no credit cards. The nearest campsite is 3 mi north on A487 at **Brongwyn Mawr Farm** (tel. 01239/613644), with sites for £5–£8.

FOOD

At the covered **market** in the Guildhall, you can pick up cheeses, breads, and produce while browsing the craft stalls for bargains. There is also a decent selection of cafés lining High Street. **Cardigan Arms** (3 College Row, off High St., tel. 01239/614969) has the best fish-and- chips in town. **The Mariners** (Quay St., tel. 01239/614136), is a traditional Welsh restaurant in a charming 17th-century building overlooking the harbor. **Sylvia's Restaurant** (25–26 Quay St., tel. 01239/621882) is well loved by Cardigans for the brewed coffees and teas, friendly staff, and fairly priced snacks—sandwiches cost less than £1.70. Another option is the all-day breakfast, available until Sylvia's closes at 5 PM.

ABERYSTWYTH

Home to one of the first universities in Wales, the town is too small to be urban but too congested with traffic to be a peaceful harbor town. For an overview, climb the well-worn path up to **Constitution Hill.** It's steep, but the views of the bay are an ample reward. The salty ambiance of a Victorian beach town mixes surprisingly well with the rarefied air of higher learning, and students and townsfolk get along well. Aberystwyth's students are drawn to social issues such as AIDS awareness, the environment, and (in muted form) gay and lesbian rights—issues you're unlikely to find so openly expressed elsewhere in rural Wales. Despite the student life, you can still hear a pin drop in the streets after the shops close at 5:30 PM. Only the seafront shows any signs of nightlife, when rowdy scholars fill the pubs.

BASICS

Aberystwyth's **tourist office** (Terrace Rd., tel. 01970/612125) is a five-minute walk from the train station (head toward the water). Upstairs, the free **Ceredigion Museum** (tel. 01970/633088) highlights the folk history and culture of the Ceredigion people. The main **post office** (8 Great Darkgate St., SY23 1AA, tel. 01970/632600) is open Saturday 9–12:30 PM in addition to its weekday hours. A number of **banks** line Great Darkgate Street, Aberystwyth's main drag. If they're closed, **Thomas Cook Travel Agency** (4 Great Darkgate St., tel. 01970/617652) exchanges money for a variable rate of commission.

COMING AND GOING

There is no direct train service to Aberystwyth from London. If you're coming from London's Euston Station, take one of five daily trains to Shrewsbury and transfer there for Aberystwyth; the total trip takes five hours and costs £35 return. National Express runs one bus per day from London to Aberystwyth (£22 return) and a number of daily buses from Birmingham. **Traws- Cambria** (tel. 01970/617951) Bus 701 makes two runs per day from Cardiff (4 hrs, £18 return) and Bangor (3½ hrs, £22 return). From Cardigan, Bus 550 travels to Aberystwyth along Cardigan Bay (10 per day, 2 hrs, £4.60 West Wales Rover).

GETTING AROUND

Arriva (tel. 01970/617951) serves the town and surrounding area, but it's very easy to get around on foot and would take an effort to get lost here—especially with the sea serving as a marker. Within a half hour you can easily walk the promenade from the harbor and castle to Constitution Hill. If you don't want to hike uphill to the university, catch Bus 504, 512, or 514 from the stop just north of the train station (45p single).

WHERE TO SLEEP

It takes a little sleuthing, but reasonable B&Bs do exist. Walk down South Road to New Promenade and its side streets behind the castle, which are dotted with unobtrusive B&B signs. The nearest hostel (*see below*) is in Borth, one train stop away. During Easter break and from June to mid-September, the **University of Wales** (Penbryn, Penglais, tel. 01970/621960) provides on- campus B&B service for £15.50 per person in singles with bath as well as self-catering flats accommodating 1–11 people; cash only. Reservations are recommended. From the train station, it's a quick 5-minute trip via Bus 512 or 514. There are also many nearby campgrounds from which to choose.

Bryn Y Don. You'll get a nice welcome and well-equipped rooms for £16–£18 per person here. The central B&B is close to the train station, car park, and sea front. *36 Bridge St., tel. 01970/612011. 6 rooms, none with bath. No credit cards.*

Yr Hafod. This popular guest house is on the South promenade between the harbor and the castle. Most of the well-furnished rooms have panoramic views of Cardigan Bay and cost around £18 per person. *1 South Marine Terrace, tel. 01970/617579. 7 rooms, 2 with bath.*

Sunnymead Guest House. Look for the bright yellow doors outside and friendly Mrs. Morgan inside—all 10 minutes by foot from the train station. Large, airy rooms go for £16 per person. *34 Bridge St., te* *01970/617273. From train station, turn left on Gray's Inn Rd., right on Bridge St. 6 rooms, none with bath. No credit cards.*

HOSTELS • Borth YHA. The village of Borth is sleepy and somewhat run-down, but this cozy hostel sits right across the road from a beautiful sandy beach. From Aberystwyth, take Arriva Cymru Bus 511/ 512, 520/4 to Borth's train station; from here, turn right on the main road and walk for about 15 minutes. Beds are £9.15. *Morlais, Borth, SY24 5JS, tel. 01970/871498, fax 01970/871827. 60 beds. Curfew 11 PM, lockout 10–5. Kitchen. Closed Nov.–Feb. and some Sun. and Mon. in summer.*

CAMPING • The nearest campground is **Aberystwyth Holiday Village** (Penparcau Rd., tel. 01970/ 624211), ¼ mi outside of town, where tent sites cost £7.50–£9 per twosome, depending on the season. **Midfield Caravan Park** (Devil's Bridge Rd., tel. 01970/612542) is 2 mi from Aberystwyth and charges £9 for two people. Reservations are recommended in summer.

FOOD

Try Pier Street for restaurants and chippies, or shop for produce and baked goods on Chalybeate Street, east of Great Darkgate Street. **Spartacus** (Northgate St., tel. 01970/625885) makes huge sandwiches for less than £2. **Seafront Palace Chinese Takeaway** (5 Marine Terr., tel. 01970/626463) has an extensive menu and is open late (closed Wednesday).

Agra. This popular restaurant cooks up spicy Indian food. *North Parade, tel. 01970/636999.*

Tiffin's. Students come here for daily specials such as lentil crumble, cottage pie, or moussaka, though little old ladies also love this clean, well-lighted place for cream teas. Don't leave without trying a homemade cake. *28 Pier St., off Eastgate St., no phone.*

Y Graig. Anyone hungry for healthy, wholesome, and tasty food will find Y Graig a blessed haven. Relax while you wait and read the green newsletters posted on the walls. Feast on prawns, cockles, mussels, and local mackerel with organic brown rice, or pasta with zucchini. *34 Pier St., tel. 01970/611606.*

WORTH SEEING

Built by Edward I in the 13th century to instill fear among the Welsh, the ruins of **Aberystwyth Castle** are an idyllic place to view the town and sea. Pay £2 for a return on the **Electric Cliff Railway** (tel. 01970/617642), which since 1896 has been carrying passengers to the top of 430-ft **Constitution Hill.** Make the most of the panoramic views from the summit by visiting the **Camera Obscura,** a device of mirror and lens that magnifies your view of the surrounding coastline from Pembrokeshire to the Llyn Peninsula.

One of the extensive displays in the free **National Library of Wales** (Penglais Hill, tel. 01970/632800) shows the significance of the Eistedfodd—a distinctly Welsh musical and ceremonial event—and its connections to the Druidic and bardic verse traditions. The library has a great view of the town and houses most of Wales's important documents and rare books, including the 14th-century *White Book of Rhydderch,* one of the earliest written forms of the *Mabinogion,* ancient Wales's great epic.

Never mind that it's pricey and somewhat touristy—between April and October go to the train station and pay £10.50 to climb aboard the steam-operated **Vale of Rheidol Railway** (tel. 01970/625819). Originally used to haul lead ore, the Rheidol chugs through 12 mi of lovely countryside and farmland at a speed so slow you can identify trackside flowers. The train can drop you at the small **Devil's Bridge** (Pont-ar-Fynach), renowned for its spectacular waterfalls and gorge. Definitely get off at Devil's Bridge and make the short walk to the **Three Bridges** (50p), which span **Devil's Cauldron**: One bridge dates back to the 11th century, the others to the early 18th and 20th.

AFTER DARK

The huge student population makes for a lively after-dark scene, although pubs are synonymous with nightlife in this seaside town. The student's favorite watering hole is the lively **Glengower** on Marine Terrace, with jostling crowds and loud music. The **Coopers Arms** (Northgate, tel. 01970/624050) has a distinctly Welsh atmosphere. **Rummers Wine Bar** (tel. 01970/625177), the last building before Trefechan Bridge, is usually packed with students and locals chatting over pints. On summer weekends, come here for free live music.

Stop by **Andy's Records** (16 Northgate St., tel. 01970/624581) for advice on what's happening in Aberystwyth and a superb collection of CDs and LPs. The **Arts Centre** (Penglais Rd., tel. 01970/ 632800) on campus has galleries, a theater, and a concert hall. Across town, **Castle Theatre** (St.

Michael's Pl., tel. 01970/624606), run by the university drama department, presents works in both Welsh and English throughout the year.

OUTDOOR ACTIVITIES

With sweeping coastal views and good roads, the area surrounding Aberystwyth is great for biking—despite the brawny hills. **Summit Cycles** (65 North Parade, tel. 01970/626061) rents bikes from £12 per day or special weekly rates.

SNOWDONIA NATIONAL PARK

Towering mountains and misty moorland draw people to Snowdonia National Park, which stretches from Machynlleth all the way to the north coast. Lapped in scenic luxury, it contains spectacular highland and coastal landscapes. All in all, it's the biggest of Wales's three national parks and certainly the most breathtaking. Craggy **Mt. Snowdon** (Yr Wyddfa) itself rises to 3,560 ft in the northwest, establishing its rule over a troop of 2,000–3,000-ft peaks, among them glowering **Cader Idris** in the south near Dolgellau, the **Rhinogs** east of Harlech, and the **Aran** and **Arennigs** around Bala in the east. Sail-flecked Bala Lake (Llyn Tegid) is a great place to hang out and do nothing much but wander over hill and heather. In the center of the park, there are derelict slate mines around Blaenau Ffestiniog and castles and seascapes along the coast, south of Porthmadog. If you've come to Wales in search of outdoor pursuits, welcome to Snowdonia.

Snowdonia's beauty, however, is also its curse. The area around Mt. Snowdon itself is something of a Welsh Yellowstone, and the huge amount of wear and tear from visitors has upset the area's delicate ecological balance. Attempts have been made to minimize the deterioration by way of a voluntary ban on bicycles in certain parts of the park, a train that transports people up Mt. Snowdon, and the "Sherpa" buses that run around the entire park, obviating the need for cars. Unfortunately, these solutions are only partially successful as many people still prefer to take their cars rather than to rely on buses.

Llanberis is everybody's favorite Snowdonia base. Whether you're here for a few days or several weeks, be sure to talk up your fellow travelers, because they've often already discovered the best secrets about Snowdonia's trails and activities.

BASICS

VISITOR INFORMATION

There are five National Park Visitor Centres in Snowdonia. The main administrative office is the **Snowdonia National Park Office** near Porthmadog (Penrhyndeudraeth, LL48 6LS, tel. 01766/770274). Branches that specifically cater to visitors are in **Aberdyfi** (The Wharf, tel. 01654/767321), **Betws-y-Coed** (Royal Oak Stables, tel. 01690/710426), **Blaenau Ffestiniog** (High St., tel. 01766/830360), **Dolgellau** (Ty Meirion, Eldon Sq., tel. 01341/422888), and **Harlech** (High St., tel. 01766/780658). All park centers provide lodging reservations, weather forecasts, and dozens of books and maps.

Call the warden office at **Pen-y-Pass** (tel. 01286/872555) for info on hiking and how to avoid day- tripping tourists. While this isn't really a "visitor center," the staff is friendly and extremely knowledgeable.

PUBLICATIONS

The park is covered by four Ordnance Survey "Outdoor Leisure Series" maps: Bala and Cader Idris/Dyfi Forest, Conwy Valley, Harlech, and Snowdon. These are for the hard-core hiker. Tourist office pamphlets—notably the free "Snowdonia" newspaper and the leaflets for each of the six main paths up Mt. Snowdon—are generally good enough for the casual visitor.

WHEN TO GO

In winter, almost everything goes into hibernation. Many tourist offices close and most of the Great Little Trains stop running until April. However, winter is when experienced climbers come to Snowdonia, equipped with ice axes and crampons. As a result, B&Bs remain open throughout the year, and reservations are advised even in January. Almost all the hostels close down, with the exception of Llanberis which remains open until a week before Christmas.

COMING AND GOING

Buses give you more flexibility than trains: They're cheaper and they go where trains don't. Pick up the essential **"Gwynedd Public Transport Guide,"** which outlines all routes and provides timetables for all buses and trains in the area; it's free at most tourist offices. The **North and Mid Wales Rover** is a combined bus and train pass good for one day (£16), three days in seven (£24.50), or seven days (£38). It's valid on most bus routes in northwest Wales, all Arriva Cymru buses in the area, and all Regional Railway lines bound by Aberystwyth to Shrewsbury, Shrewsbury to Crewe, and Crewe to Holyhead. It's also valid for the Ffestiniog Railway.

BY BUS

A **Red Rover Day Pass** (£4.40) will enable you to ride most companies' buses in northwest Wales. Don't be discouraged by the dozens of bus companies that cover these routes. The drivers are friendly, helpful folk, and most of them will stop anywhere along a route. Companies that serve the Snowdonia area include **Arriva Cymru** (Bangor, tel. 01248/750444; Dolgellau, tel. 01341/422614); **K.M.P.** (Llanberis, tel. 01286/870880); **Williams Bala** (Bala, tel. 01678/520777); and **Williams Deiniolen** (Llanberis, tel. 01286/870484).

BY TRAIN

Two rail lines run into the park. The scenic coastal route goes from Porthmadog through Harlech to Aberdyfi (£8.80 return) and then inland to Machynlleth. The other line, the Conwy Valley train, chugs south from Llandudno to Betws-y-Coed (£3.60 return), near the park's eastern boundary, and then crosses west to the park's midpoint at Blaenau Ffestiniog (£5.10 return). From here, the Ffestiniog Railway (*see* Getting Around, *below*), one of Wales's Great Little Trains, connects to Porthmadog March–November. Sunday service is limited at best, and often nonexistent. It's important to have a current timetable, as many of the stops are by request only.

GETTING AROUND

BY BIKE

In an attempt to reduce erosion and to promote safety for walkers, bikers are asked not to use Mt. Snowdon's bridleways between 10AM and 5PM daily. The roads are always fair game, though. Snowdonia has no actual cycling map, but Ordnance Survey maps should serve you just as well. The best cycling route is the very difficult 22-mi haul up **Llanberis Pass** to **Pen-y-Gwrd.** The North Wales Mountain Bike Association puts out a leaflet, available at tourist offices and some outdoors stores, which outlines some less strenuous circular routes. **Beics Betws** (tel. 01690/710766), in Betws-y-Coed behind the post office off A5, and **Bikes Coed-y-Brenin** (tel. 01341/440666 or 01766/540569), inside the Forest Visitor Centre (8 mi north of Dolgellau in Ganllwyd), both rent bikes for around £4 per hour or £16 per day.

BY GREAT LITTLE TRAIN

Snowdonia is famous for the many narrow-gauge railways that putter through the park, providing a scenic and convenient way of getting around. Any tourist office or railway station in Wales should have comprehensive timetables and information leaflets on the Great Little Trains. Most trains cost £4–£12; if you want to hike at any point in between, you can request a stop and pay less for the partial journey. **Wanderer** tickets, good for unlimited travel on the eight so-called Great Little Trains, are available for four out of eight days (£32) and eight days out of 15 days (£42). Disabled travelers should call ahead.

The **Ffestiniog Railway** (tel. 01766/512340) is a 13½-mi track linking Blaenau Ffestiniog with Porthmadog (where you can catch a southbound BritRail train along the coast). The trains wind their way for an hour through some of Snowdonia's most spectacular scenery. The full trip costs £12.40.

Other GLTs include: **Bala Lake Railway** (tel. 01678/540666), which chugs along the southeast side of narrow Bala Lake; **Llanberis Lake Railway** (tel. 01286/870549), covering part of Llyn Padarn's northwest perimeter; and **Talyllyn Railway** (tel. 01654/710472), which connects the coastal town of Tywyn with the mountain halt of Nant Gwernol just beyond Abergynolwyn, at the southern end of the park.

BY SHERPA

Sherpas are inexpensive buses that run regularly around Mt. Snowdon, June–late October, schlepping walkers to the trailheads of all six paths to the summit and stopping on request at any point in the park. Easy pickup points are at Bangor, Betws-y-Coed, Caernarfon, Llandudno Junction, Llanrwst, and Porthmadog. For more info, contact the National Park Office (tel. 01766/770274), pick up a Snowdon Sherpa leaflet at a tourist information center, or check the free "Snowdonia" newspaper.

HIKING

There are trails everywhere, but most people head straight to Mt. Snowdon. There are six main paths to the summit (*see* Outdoor Activities, *in* Llanberis and Mt. Snowdon, *below*), and the tourist offices have leaflets (40p) describing each in detail. The park authority runs guided day hikes Easter–September; check "Snowdonia" for current schedules; the Garth Falls Walk at the west end of Betws-y-Coed features descriptive signs in Braille.

When hiking in Snowdonia, don't play games with the fickle Welsh weather, especially if you have your heart set on hiking up a mountain. The essentials from the feet on up: two layers of socks (a surefire way to prevent blisters), a sturdy pair of hiking boots with good thick treads, several layers of water- and wind-proof clothing (jeans are bad, but wool and Polartex or Gore-Tex are an unbeatable combo), wool-lined gloves, and a waterproof hat. In any season other than summer, seriously consider thermal underwear—it's windy up there, and once you stop moving it's darn cold. As for packing, bring maps, a compass, flashlight, whistle, spare clothes, and high energy food. The truly cautious will also bring a first-aid kit, ice ax, crampons, goggles, and a plastic sheet to lay over snow or ice—essentials in winter. Don't venture out alone in winter, especially if you're inexperienced.

You should also let someone know your destination and approximate route so rescuers don't have to thaw you out when the snow melts. Most accidents happen in the afternoon when hikers are tired but still determined to make it back down. The international rescue signal is six long shouts, blasts of a whistle, or flashes from a flashlight. Stop for one minute and repeat until help comes. Mountain Rescue squads are spread throughout the park should you need to be airlifted by helicopter. Last but not least, *always* contact Mountaincall Snowdonia (tel. 0891/500449) for weather forecasts and ground conditions before setting out.

DOLGELLAU

One of the best bus rides for your money is the wonderful, winding trip between Machynlleth and Dolgellau, an ancient market town with crooked streets and stoic, dark-granite buildings. On the bus you traverse huge hills, including 3,000-ft Cader Idris ("The Chair of Idris"). From Aberystwyth or Machynlleth's clock tower, take Arriva Cymru Bus 32 (six per day) or opt for the Red Rover ticket (£4.40).

Dolgellau is a great base for a few "leisure walks" (for which you don't have to be an advanced trekker to get awesome views). The **Precipice Walk** (3 mi one-way) passes through meadows and sheep fields, over stone fences, and along rocky foothills, affording great views of the Mawddach Estuary and the mountain ranges of Snowdonia. The walk begins from a car park off the Llanfachreth road, 3 mi from Dolgellau. Climbing **Cader Idris,** second in popularity only to Mt. Snowdon, takes about five hours round-trip on any of the three main routes. The 3-mi **Minffordd Path** is the shortest and steepest (up to 2,850 ft); it starts at the Minffordd parking lot (accessible by Bus 2) just after the junction of A487 and B4405. The easier and more trafficked **Pony Track** follows a gradual climb from Ty Nant, which is 3 mi southwest of Dolgellau on Cader Road. The third route is the longest of all, starting at the remote castle of **Castell y Bere,** in the hills north of the village of Abergynolwyn (you'll definitely need a car for this one).

If you hate hills, walk the 10 mi of abandoned level railroad bed from Dolgellau to **Barmouth** along the edge of the River Mawddach. Barmouth is a pleasant seaside resort with a lovely beach and a stunning mountain backdrop. There are a number of inexpensive restaurants and cafés in town, and, if you choose to spend the night, the seafront **Sandpiper** (7 Marine Parade, tel. 01341/280318), owned by the Palmers, who are keen walkers and can offer local advice, is an excellent choice at £14.50–£15.50 per person. A trail for the disabled has been incorporated into the walk at the Morfa Mawddach end of the path. For details, call the **National Park Headquarters** (tel. 01766/770274) in Penrhyndeudraeth.

BASICS

The **Tourist Information Centre** (Station Rd., Eldon Sq., tel. 01341/422888), also a National Park Centre, is near the bus stop. The **banks,** located around the square, are open weekdays only. The **post office** on Meyrick Street has Saturday morning hours. **Cader Idris Outdoor Gear** (Eldon Sq., tel. 01341/422195) sells clothing and equipment for hiking and backpacking.

COMING AND GOING

If you're headed to Dolgellau, you'll probably arrive via Machynlleth. This small village is a significant rail hub, serving as a junction for Shrewsbury (£14.50 return) in the east, Aberystwyth (£4.60 return) in the west, and Pwllheli (£12.30 return) in the north. (Pwllheli is the northern end of the line, and from there you must catch a bus to reach the train line that services Bangor and Holyhead.) Machynlleth's **train station** (Heol Penrallt) is a 10-minute walk from the town center.

Buses in Machynlleth all stop at the clock tower, including Traws-Cambria Bus 701, which joins Machynlleth with Cardiff (£27 return) and Bangor (£18 return). If you're planning on lots of connections, ask the driver for an **Explorer** pass (£5), not valid on Bus 701.

WHERE TO SLEEP

The B&Bs scattered through town charge £15–£18 per person. Not surprisingly, if you book a room at **Aber Café and B&B** (Smithfield St., tel. 01341/422460), the aromas and sounds of a café waft up to the rooms (£16 per person), no credit cards. Across the bridge (turn left on Barmouth Rd. and right past the police station), **Bryn Derw** (tel. 01341/422505) has two doubles (£32 each) and a single for £17, no credit cards. **Dwy Olwyn** (Coed-y Fronallt, tel. 01341/422822) is a 10 minute walk from town, has magnificent views of Cader Idris, and charges from £14.50 per person, no credit cards.

HOSTELS • King's YHA. King's sits in a beautiful wooded valley 4 mi west of Dolgellau across from the Abergwynant horse–trekking center. Reserve a bed (£8.10) ahead—there are 6 beds per room. *King's, Penmaenpool, Dolgellau, LL40 ITB, tel. 01341/422392, fax 01341/422477. Take Arriva Cymru Bus 28 (Dolgellau–Tywyn line) and ask driver to drop you off 1 mi west of Penmaenpool, then walk 1 mi down narrow lane. 42 beds. Variable curfew, lockout 10–5. Kitchen. Closed end Oct.–Jan.; Sun.–Thurs., Feb. and Nov.; and Mon.–Tues., Mar.–Apr. and Sept.–Oct.*

FOOD

There are a number of fairly priced restaurants and Spar markets to choose from in town. **Y Sospan** (Queens Sq., tel. 01341/423174) serves lunches such as pizzas, jacket potatoes, and toasties, including several vegetarian options and offers a bistro-type evening menu. **Cosy Takeaway Fish and Chips** (Meyrick St., off Eldon Sq.) does indeed look cozy in its white stone building—proving that a chippie doesn't have to look like a greasy dump—but, sadly, it's only open for lunch. **Dylanwad Da** (2 Ffos-y-Felin, tel. 01341/422870) means "good intentions," and this restaurant certainly lives up to its name, regaling you with superbly cooked dishes using fresh local produce such as Welsh sirloin with a mushroom-and-amontillado gravy, or hot smoked salmon fillet with a cream-chive sauce.

LLANBERIS AND MT. SNOWDON

Llanberis, at the foot of Mt. Snowdon, has a lively mix of locals and international travelers who come for the location, convenience, and atmosphere. Climbers, hikers, and backpackers converge in Llanberis to stock up on outdoor gear and food, and, at night, to relax in the friendly pubs. Of all Snowdonia's wee towns, Llanberis is the most popular. The town's position as the lower terminus of the Snowdon Mountain Railway means serious hiking trails are just a short train ride away. You don't have to be a hard-core climber to enjoy Llanberis, however; its two nearby lakes (Padarn and Peris) make pleasant short hikes. Thankfully, the railway is on the eastern edge of town, and most casual tourists hop on and off the trains without actually discovering that Llanberis is more than just a train depot.

BASICS

Llanberis's **Tourist Information Centre** (41A High St., tel. 01286/870765) offers comprehensive info about all of Snowdonia. Be sure to skim through the binders full of descriptions of each trail up to Snowdon. Llanberis's one bank, **Midland Bank** (High St.), is open weekdays 9:30–3. If it's closed, the **bureau de change** at the Snowdon Railway shop charges a £1.50 commission for every £30 exchanged. The

ost office (High St., tel. 01286/870201) has Saturday hours until noon. **Joe Brown's** (High St., tel. 1286/870327), a shop that sells everything from Power Bars to clothing to Ordnance Survey Maps, serves as an informal tourist office when the official one is closed.

COMING AND GOING

Llanberis is 7½ mi from Caernarfon and 8½ mi from Bangor, making it easily accessible by bus or car. Sherpa Buses 19 and 95 pass through hourly 9–6 in summer. Bws Gwynedd Bus 77 and Bus 88 run to Bangor about every hour and to Caernarfon about every half hour.

WHERE TO SLEEP

Llanberis is chock-full of good hostels. If you can't find a room in one, call **Maesteg** (High St., tel. 01286/870187), a comfortable friendly B&B, costing £16–£18 per person. Vegetarians are welcome and the owners can arrange climbing, guided walks, and aromatherapy. The **Heights Hotel** (74 High St., tel. 01286/871179) is a conveniently located place that has an excellent on-site pub and restaurant, with more than a few good veggie options. Hikers should try the practice climbing wall (£1). Choose between a double room with shower (£20 per person) or an alpine-style bunk bed (£12.50).

HOSTELS • Bryn Du. Though Bryn Du principally hosts groups taking canoeing and rock-climbing courses, they will happily accommodate backpackers if space permits. Beds cost £7. *Mountain Venture Ltd., Ty Du Rd., tel. 01286/870454. Walk north on High St., turn left on Ty Du Rd. 45 beds. Kitchen, laundry. No credit cards.*

Llanberis YHA. At the top of a hill overlooking Lake Padarn and the mountains, this large house serves backpackers with sprawling rooms loaded with bunk beds (£9.15 each). The Llanberis Path to Mt. Snowdon is only a half mile away. *Llwyn Celyn, Llanberis, LL55 4SR, tel. 01286/870280, fax 01286/870936. From High St., walk south on Capel Coch Rd., turn right at fork, and continue uphill. 60 beds. Curfew 11 PM, lockout 10–5. Kitchen. Closed Sun.–Thur., Nov.–Feb.; Sun.–Mon., Mar.; and Sun.–Mon., Sept.–Oct.*

Pen-y-Pass YHA. This hostel was once a favorite of Victorian climbers attempting the Miners and Pyg tracks to Snowdon's summit, and it's still the best place for that first climb up Snowdon. Two paths start across the road, where there's also a park office. The staff schedules rock-climbing trips throughout the area. Beds cost £9.15. *Pen-y-Pass, Nant Gwynant, Caernarfon, LL55 4NY, tel. 01286/870428, fax 01286/872434. From Llandudno, Llanberis, or Caernarfon, take the Snowdon Sherpa and ask for Pen-y-Pass. 84 beds. Curfew 11 PM, lockout 10–1. Kitchen.*

Snowdon Ranger YHA. This old inn on the north side of Llyn Cwellyn is one of the best hostels in all of Wales because of its scenic location, good food, and ambiance. The Ranger Path to Mt. Snowdon is at the hostel's doorstep, as is Lake Cwellyn. Caernarfon and its castle are a 25-minute bus ride away. Beds cost £9.15. *Rhyd Ddu, Caernarfon, LL54 7YS, tel. 01286/650391, fax 01286/650093. From Caernarfon or Llanberis, take the Snowdon Sherpa. 67 beds. Curfew 11 PM, lockout 10–5. Kitchen. Check days open in winter.*

FOOD

Becws Eryri Tea Room (High St., tel. 01286/870491) has sandwiches for around £2 and delicious scones for 80p. **The Heights** (High St., inside the Heights Hotel, tel. 01286/871179) is the place for decent, home-cooked meals. Try the cheese pizza or a potato slathered with hummus and garlic butter. **Pete's Eats** (40 High St., tel. 01286/870358) is a funky sort of place filled with bikers sporting leather and hikers sporting Gore-Tex. Pore over newspapers, weather forecasts, and climbing and hiking maps while downing homemade soup or the daily vegan special.

WORTH SEEING

A 30-minute walk east of town, **Dolbadarn Castle** features enough of a tower to offer a good view of Lake Peris beyond the slate quarries; admission is free. There's a small waterfall up the road past Dolbadarn Hotel (look for the sign). Llanberis is home to a mammoth hydroelectricity facility, buried inside the mountain that rises steeply from the shores of the lake. The appropriately named **Electric Mountain** (tel. 01286/870636) has a free hands-on visitor center and a wonderful underground tour (£5) of the gigantic tunnels and caverns created for the scheme. Going back a century or so, find out the gritty truth about the industrial era in north Wales by visiting the **Welsh Slate Museum** (tel. 01286/870630) for £3.50, open April–October. The **Llanberis Lake Railway** is a narrow-gauge line which costs £4.50 for a 2-mi trip along the scenic shores of Lake Padarn.

OUTDOOR ACTIVITIES

Outside (Old Baptist Chapel, High St., tel. 01286/871534) sells outdoor gear and climbing equipmen. **Padarn Water Sports Centre** (tel. 01286/870556), next to the Welsh Slate Museum, rents kayaks and canoes (from £5 per hr) and offers instruction throughout the summer. **Dolbadarn Pony Trekking Centre** (High St., tel. 01286/870277) leads daily treks (£10 per hr) from the Dolbadarn Hotel. If you're out of shape but keen to "conquer" Snowdon, do it the easy way by riding the **Snowdon Mountain Railway** (tel. 01286/870223) up the mountain, then walking down. During summer, trains are scheduled to run every half hour 8:30–5, though weather and demand dictate when they actually run. Tickets cost £10.80 single, £15 return, and £7 for standby trips down from the top.

HIKING • The longest but gentlest climb to the Snowdon summit is the **Llanberis Path,** which gets crowded with families and tourists during summer. The route starts in Llanberis and parallels the railway. Budget at least five hours for the 9-mi round-trip. The **Snowdon Ranger Path,** departing from the YHA hostel of the same name (*see* Where to Sleep, *above*), is another relatively easy path, with a few steep spots. Plan on 5½ hours to hike the 8-mi round-trip. **Rhyd Ddu**, perhaps the gentlest and least-used trail, affords impressive mountain scenery and stunning sunset views upon descent. Start from either Rhyd Ddu village or Pitt's Head (near Beddgelert) and allow at least five hours to complete the entire walk.

Miners' Track is the easiest of the trails beginning at Pen-y-Pass. The trail is 7½ mi round- trip and crosses the northeast section of Llyn Llydaw Lake—where King Arthur supposedly threw his sword, Excalibur, after slaying the giant Rhita Fawr at the summit of Mt. Snowdon. Plan on five hours of medium-paced walking; the last leg requires some serious climbing. The **Pyg Track** is a more challenging route to the summit from Pen-y-Pass that begins with a steep ascent. After about ½ mi, you reach a horseshoe of mountaintops overlooking a valley dotted with lakes. Be careful on this trail, as several places have suffered from erosion. Wardens suggest at least five hours to hike the 3½ mi each way. Couch potatoes should definitely stay away from **Watkin Path,** a difficult 4-mi climb up Mt. Snowdon along Lliwedd Ridge. The views are beautiful, though—waterfalls and rock pools. Plan on at least nine hours. *Only* experienced hikers armed with the right gear and weather info should think of hiking **Horseshoe Path,** which starts and finishes at Pen-y-Pass, with its 2,000-ft drops. Make sure you talk to a park ranger before attempting this trail to get briefed on—and maybe dissuaded from—this 14-mi endeavor.

NORTHWEST WALES

Snowdonia National Park subsumes roughly half of northern Wales, but there are regions to explore beyond the park—namely the town of **Caernarfon,** the **Isle of Anglesey,** and the **Llyn Peninsula.** Wales's northwest corner is where you'll find the highest concentration of Welsh speakers, and the quiet pride of a people never completely conquered.

Many travelers come to northwestern Wales to follow Edward I's **Ring of Castles.** It's worth taking some time to visit these atmospheric, weather-beaten ruins. The castles are the result of a major 13th-century building campaign by Edward I, who subjugated the south of Wales without much trouble but got bogged down fighting the pesky Princes of Gwynedd in 1282. To make a long story short, Edward eventually conquered north Wales, only to face yet another sticky problem: The Welsh princes' base of support was still strong in the mountains and moorlands of Snowdonia. Wary of a protracted guerrilla war, Edward I decided to build a ring of castles along the coast, each only a day's march from the next, to strangle the princes' hold on north Wales. Edward sent for a talented French engineer and conscripted thousands of men from around England to construct a series of magnificent concentric fortifications at key points: Beaumaris, Caernarfon, Conwy, Flint, and Harlech. If you plan to visit several castles, pick up an **Explorer Pass** at any tourist office. The pass allows a special-rate admittance to all five castles (and many other historic sites throughout Wales) for three days (£9, £15 for two) or seven days (£15, £20 for two). The **North and Mid Wales Rover** and the **Red Rover Day Pass** are both valid in this area (*see* Coming and Going *in* Snowdonia National Park, *above*).

LLYN PENINSULA

The peaceful and untrammeled Llyn Peninsula juts out toward the Irish Sea, separating the bays of Caernarfon and Cardigan. From various high points on the small peninsula, you can take in the surrounding sea and Snowdonia's mountains to the east. Fringed with sandy beaches, Llyn is a picturesque spot with fewer tourists than neighboring regions. The powers that be obviously appreciate the scenery, as do the residents, because some 55 mi of the peninsula's coastline have been designated "Heritage Coast," which means efforts are in progress to preserve its natural beauty. In addition to their terrific stretches of beach, **Pwllheli** and **Abersoch** today are important yachting and sailing areas, evidenced by the selection of Pwllheli as the yachting venue in Manchester's unsuccessful bid for the 2000 Olympics. Inland, fields and farms dominate the landscape, filled with the stuff of ancient legends: hill forts and prehistoric artifacts. **Porthmadog,** however, at the crossroads of Snowdonia and Llyn is a modern town that mostly serves as a transport hub for points north and south. **Caernarfon,** on the coast where the bay funnels into the Menai Strait, is not technically part of the Llyn Peninsula—though it is an important hub for peninsula-bound buses.

COMING AND GOING

The **Cambrian Coaster** line (tel. 0345/484950) travels a slow but scenic route between Aberystwyth and Pwllheli, with stops in Harlech, Porthmadog, Criccieth, and Penychain. The rest of the peninsula is covered by **Arriva Cymru Buses** (tel. 01248/750444). As it is part of the Bys Gwynedd network, the **Red Rover Pass** (£4.40) can be used on any of their buses. For info, phone 01248/750444.

Heading northeast, take the scenic, hour-long **Ffestiniog Railway** (tel. 01766/512340) from Porthmadog to Blaenau Ffestiniog; from there, you can make connections to north coast towns such as Bangor, Holyhead, and Conwy.

PORTHMADOG

Porthmadog was once a vital link in the north Wales slate trade, serving as a major port in the 19th century (when its population quadrupled over the space of 40 years) until the Cambrian Railway arrived in 1867, taking over slate transport and Porthmadog's raison d'être. Today it booms with tourism. In the high season, the town's main street is clogged with tour buses and hikers stocking up on food and gear for treks into the nearby wilderness. The sea is within walking distance, and the views are incredible, especially around the Borth-y-Gest area. Also nearby is **Black Rock Sands,** considered one of the finest beaches in Wales. To reach the beach from High Street, turn left on Bank Place and continue until you see reach the sea (3 mi), or the local bus will take you there during the summer.

BASICS

Porthmadog's **Tourist Information Centre** (High St., tel. 01766/512981), the largest and most comprehensive in the area, is open year-round. From the train station, it's an easy 10-minute walk across town and only two minutes by foot from the Ffestiniog Mountain Railway. The **post office** (High St., tel. 01766/512010) is located inside a pharmacy and open weekdays 9–5:30 and Saturday mornings. **K. K. Cycles** (141 High St., tel. 01766/512310), near the train station, rents bikes for £2 per hour or £8 per day.

WHERE TO SLEEP

B&B prices start at £13, but you should book ahead in summer to get the best deals. **Mrs. Jones** (57 East Ave., off Cambria Terr., tel. 01766/513087) runs a clean and friendly B&B, just minutes away from the train station with rooms for £15 per person, cash only. Above the restaurant of the same name, **Yr Hen Fecws** (16 Lombard Pl., off Bank Pl., tel. 01766/514625) provides spacious, airy rooms and a delicious breakfast. The agonizing 15-minute climb it takes to reach **Trefforis** (Garth Rd., tel. 01766/512853), a beautiful Victorian house, is rewarded with a breathtaking view of the harbor and Snowdonia. Mrs. Dickinson mothers you with a full English breakfast. She'll also store your backpack and let you hang your washing out to dry. £17 per person; no credit cards. From High Street, turn left on Bank Place, and left on Terrace Road. If you don't have any luck in Porthmadog proper, try **Borth-y-Gest,** a seafront area only a 15-minute walk away. The closest campground is the attractive **Tyddyn Llwyn Farm & Caravan Park** (Morfa Bychan Rd., tel. 01766/512205), 2 mi from Porthmadog near Black Rock Golden Sands. Tent sites cost £7–£8 for two people.

FOOD

Bakeries and small fruit and vegetable shops line **High Street,** satisfying every picnic need. The **Spar** is on High Street and open until late. If you're tired of limp lettuce and cardboard sandwiches then you'll find **Jessies** (High St.) a refreshing change. They serve an appetizing array of salads and sandwiches to eat in or take away. If it's fish-and-chips you fancy, **Allports Fish & Chips** is the locals' favorite (Snowdon St., at Madoc St., tel. 01766/512589); it's open daily in summer. You see a lot of dual-purpose establishments in towns this small—like **Yr Hen Fecws** restaurant and B&B (*see above*). Helen cooks up the best meals in town in this bistro.

NEAR PORTHMADOG

CAMBRIAN COASTER RAILWAY • The Welsh speak fondly of the Cambrian Coaster Railway (which runs from Pwllheli, through Porthmadog and Barmouth, and down to Machynlleth and Aberystwyth about eight times per day Monday–Saturday), claiming it's one of the most beautiful train trips in Britain. And they're right, even though this route isn't one of those "little" ones Wales is so famous for. At points along the route you can even walk right into Snowdonia National Park (*see above*). It makes sense to purchase a **Day Ranger Pass** (£5.70), which allows you a day's worth of unlimited travel for one day, since the day return fare from Porthmadog to Pwllheli is £3.60.

One of the first stops on the Cambrian Coaster Railway is the flower-bedecked village of Llanbedr. While it is not a particularly noteworthy place, the **Llanbedr YHA** (Plas Newydd, Llanbedr LL45 2LE, tel. 01341/241287, fax 01341/241389), closed November–March and some days out of the main summer season, makes a useful base for visiting Harlech (3 mi north) and Portmeirion. Beds at the hostel cost £8.35.

Even if you're just day-tripping along the coast, it's well worth alighting at the town of **Harlech.** From Harlech's train station, it's a ¼-mi walk into town. Stop by the **tourist office** (High St., tel. 01766/780658) for a comprehensive map of the town and all the public walkways in the region. **Harlech Castle** (admission £3), built by Edward I in the 13th century, is a masterpiece of medieval castle construction. Climb the battlements on a clear day to view the blue-tinged peaks of Snowdonia and the glistening waters of Tremadog Bay.

A few stops north is the town of **Criccieth,** with its beach and the majestic **Criccieth Castle.** The castle was built in 1243 by native Welsh princes, conquered by Edward I in 1283, recaptured during a Welsh rebellion by Madog of Llewelyñ in 1294, and sacked and burned by Owain Glyndwr in 1404. Although only a portion of the twin towers remains standing, it's worth the admission price. A charming place to sleep on the outskirts of Criccieth is **Stone Barn** (Tyddyn Morthwyl, tel. 01766/522115), a bunkhouse with a wood-burning stove and alpine-style sleeping platforms for a mere £4.50–£5. To get here take B4411 (Caernarfon Rd.) and turn right at the sign for Tyddyn Morthwyl Farm. In town, **Kairon Hotel** (23 Marine Terr., tel. 01766/522453) charges £14 per person (£18 with bath), cash only.

The terminus of the Cambrian Coaster Railway, **Pwllheli** (pronounced puth-LELL-ee) is an old seaside resort that won its charter in the early 14th century. The beautiful seaside promenade is reason enough to visit, though Pwllheli is an obvious beginning or ending point for a day's exploration. Get provisions at the large **market** held on Wednesday, or at one of the many grocery stores near the train station. Try **Village Coffee House and Bistro** (Y Maes, tel. 01758/613198) above Spar market for a "Village Club Sandwich"; and Mexican food is available in the evening. **Tapas** (Lower Ala Rd., tel. 01758/614069) serves up tasty morsels in a cosmopolitan atmosphere. The helpful staff at the tiny **Tourist Information Centre** (Station Sq., tel. 01758/613000) can help you find a room, or try **Llys Gwyrfai** (14, West End Parade, tel. 001758/614877) located opposite the sea and offering a warm welcome, comfortable rooms, and good food from £16.50–£18 per night for a single, no credit cards.

ABERSOCH • With a prime location on the southeast side of the Llyñ peninsula, Abersoch is a mecca for water-sports enthusiasts and competitive sailors. Owing to the influx of wealthy English boat owners, this place no longer feels very Welsh. However, the thriving social scene and lively but relaxed holiday feel of the place make it a great place to visit. To get here, take Bus 18 from Pwllheli (£1.80 return). **Manana Café** (High St.) is *the* place to eat or hang out and has a largely Mexican menu. Sink down a pint or two at **St. Tudwalls Inn** and then head to the beach for a midnight swim or impromptu beach party. The **tourist office** (Lon Pen Cei, tel. 01758/712929) has a listing of local B&Bs, along with a free town guide and sailing information. The **Belmont Private Hotel** (Lôn Sarn Bach, tel. 01758/712121) offers excellent B&B service for £18.50 per person, and the proprietor, Peter Masters, is a veritable fount of information on local history.

In case you want to see the world.

At American Express, we're here to make your journey a smooth one. So we have over 1,700 travel service locations in over 130 countries ready to help. What else would you expect from the world's largest travel agency?

do more **Travel**

**Call 1 800 AXP-3429 or visit
www.americanexpress.com/travel**

In case you want to be welcomed there.

We're here to see that you're always welcomed at establishments everywhere. That's why millions of people carry the American Express® Card – for peace of mind, confidence, and security, around the world or just around the corner.

do more

Cards

In case you're running low.

We're here to help with more than 190,000 Express Cash locations around the world. In order to enroll, just call American Express at 1 800 CASH-NOW before you start your vacation.

do more AMERICAN EXPRESS

Express Cash

And in case you'd rather be safe than sorry.

We're here with American Express® Travelers Cheques. They're the safe way to carry money on your vacation, because if they're ever lost or stolen you can get a refund, practically anywhere or anytime. To find the nearest place to buy Travelers Cheques, call 1 800 495-1153. Another way we help you do more.

do more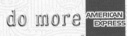

Travelers Cheques

PORTMEIRION • This delightful Italianate village is the jewel in the Cambrian coast's crown. Devised by architect Sir Clough Willams-Ellis with the aim of developing a naturally beautiful site without defiling it, the village inspires an enthusiasm for architecture even in the most unlikely visitors. There's a hotel and several lodgings which are beautifully furnished, but few can afford the price. There are plenty willing to pay the £4 admission charge to the village, especially fans of the '60s cult TV series *The Prisoner,* which was filmed here (the annual Prisoner convention is held in August), and devotees of Portmeirion Pottery. This place is curious but charming, and has a few gift shops. A local bus runs from Porthmadog, otherwise it's a 25-minute walk from Portmeirion's train station.

CAERNARFON

Since 1283, when Edward I recruited over 300 Englishmen to construct one of the mightiest castles in Britain, Caernarfon has been a center of Welsh nationalism and the most obvious symbol of English dominance. The castle stands as a "majestic badge of subjection," connecting the Llyñ Peninsula and the Isle of Anglesey with the rest of northwest Wales. The town walls were originally built to keep the Welsh out (except to pay taxes and to buy from the Anglo-Norman merchants living inside); these days, the eight-block-long walls simply keep tourists in one concentrated area. Even so, the town maintains a good balance, catering to the needs of tourists near the castle without allowing the consequences to take root elsewhere.

In an effort to win Welsh loyalty, Edward I is said to have presented his newborn son in 1284 as the "first native born Prince of Wales who speaks no English." The tradition of the monarch's firstborn son becoming the Prince of Wales continues to this day.

BASICS

The **Tourist Information Centre** (Castle St., tel. 01286/672232), off Castle Square, books rooms and sells guides to Snowdonia. The **post office** (Y Maes, tel. 01286/672116) is on the main square.

COMING AND GOING

To get here, take Traws-Cambria Bus 701 from Porthmadog (£2.55 return) or one of a dozen buses from Bangor (£1.70 return) or Llanberis (£1.30 return). **Castle Square** acts as Caernarfon's central bus stop. The **K.M.P.** bus company (tel. 01286/870880) also has routes in the area.

WHERE TO SLEEP

Most B&Bs are clustered on Church Street and, farther away, along North Road and St. David's Road. **Menai View Hotel** (North Rd., tel. 01286/673367) is a Victorian town house that overlooks the Menai straits and is close to the castle and town center with rooms from £14. Sleep close to the beach at **Snowdonia Guest House** (Dinas Dinlle, tel. 01286/831198), where doubles go for £28, no credit cards. Two minutes from the castle and the harbor, **Tegfan** (4 Church St., tel. 01286/673703) has thick carpets and British bric-a-brac. It's a good deal at £13–£16 for a single, £28 for a double; cash only. The nearest campground is **Llanberis Road Caravan Park** (tel. 01286/673196), a 20-minute walk from town. It's closed November–February. Sites cost £5.50–£9 for a small tent.

HOSTELS • **Bryn Gwynant YHA.** This stone mansion is set on 40 acres of parkland 50 minutes south of Llyn Gwynant. There's a game room and snack shop, not to mention great views of the lake. The Cambrian Way and Watkins Path to Mt. Snowdon are also nearby. Beds are £9.15. *Nant Gwynant, LL55 4NP, tel. 01766/890251, fax 01766/890479. From Caernarfon, take the Snowdon Sherpa and ask for Bryn Gwynant. 67 beds. Curfew 10:30 PM, lockout 10–5. Kitchen. Closed early Sept. and Nov.–Jan.; also Sun.–Wed., Jan.–Mar.*

Totters. If you were to make a list of all the things you wanted from a hostel, this place would pretty much fit the bill—bikes are even offered gratis to guests to help them tour the countryside. Close to Caernarfon Castle, Totters can be an ideal base from which to explore Snowdonia, Anglesey, and neighboring Welsh towns. The atmosphere is friendly and relaxed, the owners are fab, and the basement has genuine 14th-century walls. Beds cost £9.50, including bedding and breakfast. *Plas Porth yr Aur, 2 High St., tel. 01286/672963. 30 beds. No credit cards.*

FOOD

Pub grub around the castle will give you the biggest bang for your buck, but there are several decent restaurants, cafés, bakeries, and chippies along Hole-in-the-Wall Street. If you are willing to spend a bit more, sample the food at **Pigs and Stones Bistro** (Hole-in-the-Wall St., tel. 01286/671152), open Tuesday–Saturday evenings. The helpings are generous and their specialty, Welsh lamb, won't disappoint. **Just Pancakes** (34 High St., at Palace St., tel. 01286/672552) serves up scrumptious savory and dessert pancakes such as tuna and sweet corn in spicy mushroom sauce, and the chocolate delight.

WORTH SEEING

Caernarfon Castle (tel. 01286/677617), admission £4.20, is the crown jewel of Edward's ring of castles. After the defeat of the Welsh in 1282, Edward I decided to build his palace fortress here to take advantage of the surrounding natural resources. The Menai Strait and River Seiout act as the castle moat, and the Snowdonian mountains provide a massive wall of defense. Arrow slots, murder holds, and portcullises are everywhere, and winding, narrow staircases lead up dark towers that overlook the harbor. **Eagle Tower** houses a slide show that tells the castle's story with lots of sound effects and flashing lights.

Head down Pool Street and you'll find the **Segontium Roman Fort** (Beddgelert Rd., tel. 01286/675625), where Roman emperor Magnus Maximus lodged garrisons of soldiers in AD 383. The small museum, admission £1.25, contains artifacts from the large settlement, including some intimidating weapons.

ISLE OF ANGLESEY

The people of Anglesey (*Ynys Môn* in Welsh) farmed in peaceful isolation until 1826, when a suspension bridge over the Menai Strait smoothed the way for the London–Holyhead Road. Now tourists come to the Isle of Anglesey to catch ferries at Holyhead en route to Ireland and, if they're on a package tour, to visit **Llanfairpwllgwyngyllgogerychwyrndrobwllantysiliogogogoch** (a.k.a. "Llanfair P.G."), the longest town name in the world—a 19th-century publicity stunt (and the Rebels' password in the film *Barbarella*).

In contrast to Snowdonia, Anglesey's less dramatic terrain, with its dunes and flat coastal paths, makes for good bicycling and walking. You'll find some particularly good cliff walks west of **Amlwch**, from Dinas Gynfor to Cemaes. The stunning 125-mi coastline is largely classed as an "Area of Outstanding Natural Beauty" and its beautiful beaches attract many vacationers. The nearest hostel is in Bangor, so if you want to stay overnight, it's B&Bs all the way—or camping on farmland (with the owners' permission, of course).

BASICS

The tourist office in **Llanfair P.G.** (Station Site, tel. 01248/713177), open daily, has brochures and books rooms. Same goes for the one at **Holyhead** (Penrhos Beach Rd., tel. 01407/762622). At either you can buy "Anglesey Outdoors" (65p), which includes a tide table and activity guide.

COMING AND GOING

The railway line cuts right through Anglesey on its way to Holyhead, the end of the line for backpackers bound for Dún Laoghaire in Ireland. Prior to Holyhead the train also stops in Bodorgan, Llanfair P.G., Rhosneigr, Tŷ Croes, and Valley. **Arriva Cymru** (tel. 01248/750444) has bus routes all over Anglesey. If you're headed over to Ireland, **Irish Ferries** (tel. 0990/171171) runs two ferries per day to Dublin, and **Stena Line** (tel. 0990/707070) runs a number of different ferry services to Dún Laoghaire. Fares on Irish Ferries range £20–£25 single, on Stena's high-speed (99 mins) crossing, £26–£35.

WHERE TO SLEEP

If you miss your ferry to Ireland or your bus back to Bangor, the Holyhead tourist office (*see above*) will help you book a bed anywhere on the island. Otherwise, treat yourself to a night in **Swn-y-Don** (7, Bulkeley Terrace, Beaumaris, tel. 01248/8113620), a charming antiques-filled Grade 2 listed building, 200 yards from the castle, with magnificent views across the water to the mountains of Snowdonia. Rooms begin at £17 per person, no credit cards.

EXPLORING THE ISLE OF ANGLESEY

From Bangor, it's a 20-minute trip on Bus 53 or 57 over the famous Thomas Telford Bridge to **Beaumaris,** near the eastern tip of the island. With its compact main street, pubs, and bakeries, Beaumaris seems friendly even on the dourest of rainy days. Attractions include the **Victorian Gaol** (tel. 01248/811691), considered an innovative and humane prison when built in 1829 (admission £2.75). **Beaumaris Castle** (tel. 01248/810361) was the last of Edward I's defenses against the Welsh and remains the best example of concentric fort design. It was never finished, which explains why the towers and turrets seem a bit puny. All in all, it's worth the £2.20 admission. Not far from Beaumaris is **Penmon,** where you'll find a number of ruins, including those of Penmon Priory (founded around 549). The priory's remains actually date back to the 13th century, the original wooden buildings having fallen victim to a Viking attack in 971.

Of the many small beachside villages, **Rhosneigr** in the south is best known for great windsurfing and other water sports. Rhosneigr, a 35-minute walk from the nearest train station, became a holiday resort for English tourists over 100 years ago. Today, Edwardian summer homes sit alongside 20th-century counterparts. **Town Beach** and **Traeth Llydan,** which is opposite Maelog Lake along the main road, are both excellent beaches.

All along the southern edge of the island, the tidal streams of the Irish Sea make for excellent sea canoeing. Contact the **Anglesey Sea and Surf Centre** (Porthdafarch Rd., tel. 01407/762525 or 01407/760–495) for details on lessons and expeditions. Walk past curved glass walls with fishies swimming beyond at the very cool **Anglesey Sea Zoo** (Brynsiencyn, tel. 01248/430411). The Sea Zoo (admission £4.95) also displays artifacts from the *Lusitania,* a British ocean liner sunk by a German U-boat in 1915.

Anglesey has a lot of appeal if you're interested in (a) camping and surfing, (b) old Celtic and Christian ruins, or (c) birds.

The less energetic can always go bird-watching; much of the coastal area is managed by various organizations safeguarding the habitats of guillemots, razorbills, terns, puffins, and gulls. For a complete rundown on the bird scene, including free guided walks, call the **Royal Society for the Protection of Birds** (RSPB) at 01407/764973.

SCOTLAND

UPDATED BY STEPHEN FRASER AND STEWART HENNESSEY

You'd better get used to water if you want to visit Scotland. It's a country of rugged hills and over 130 islands carved, indeed sculpted, by the stuff. Water is a dramatic, shaping force throughout Scotland—and when water isn't immediately underfoot, expect it to come at you from the sky. The melting snows of late spring and early summer cover the Highlands with white-water streams, bringing life to the fertile glens below. From the sea comes life in other forms, maybe in the guise of North Sea oil, or maybe a newspaper cone of fish-and-chips. Meanwhile, the rich and peaty waters of the inland springs produce what Scotland is best known for internationally, whisky.

The ebb and flow in the lives of the Scottish people mirrors the racing rivers and surging tides. With a deep and convoluted history, the Scots are proud of their heritage. If Scotland has a singular identity, it is one, however, made up of many facets. Scotland, indeed, is a collection of regions, each with its own distinct character, each with its own past, all of them bound together by history and geographic convenience. Look at the map. The Shetland Isles feel closer to Norway than Scotland, which is no surprise considering they were a prime site for the Vikings to go and do their rape-and-pillage thing a thousand years ago. All that rampaging must have given the horned-helmeted horde an impressive image because each year Shetlanders dress up as Vikings and burn longships in celebration of their Norse forefathers. Farther south you find the huge land mass of the Highlands, both the Northern counties of Caithness and Sutherland and the Eastern and Western Highlands. Panning across the Great Glen—the massive geological fault line that runs left to right across the country diagonally, marking the borderline between Highland and Lowland—you find the Lowlands, rich agricultural land as fertile as much of the Highlands is barren. This disparity tended to annoy Highlanders, who would launch livestock-raiding parties on their more prosperous neighbors.

The one thing all Scots can agree on, however, is that Scotland is nothing like England. They were two separate countries, often waging bitter and bloody wars against one another, until 1603. In that year James VI of Scotland, son of Mary, Queen of Scots, succeeded the childless Elizabeth I of England and became King James I of both England and Scotland, a single king ruling two nations with two parliaments. The tenuous bonds between the two countries broke down (again) during the English Civil War, and after the execution of Charles I in 1649, Scotland was ruthlessly ravaged by Oliver Cromwell. When the monarchy was restored, the two countries were once again ruled by the same king but remained separate kingdoms. During England's Glorious Revolution of 1688, William of Orange took the crown with the understanding that he would allow the Scottish parliament to take more control of affairs than id his predecessor. Nevertheless, friction increased between the two countries, each of which maintained its own parliament, until the controversial Act of Union in 1707, in which the two parliaments were merged into one and the United Kingdom of Great Britain was born. Many believe this union still works to the advantage of England at the expense of Scottish interests: Close to 80% of Scotland's population favored the reestablishment of the Edinburgh Parliament, giving Scots more control of affairs close to home. In 1999 a Scottish parliament became a reality, following the landslide victory of the Labour Party in the 1997 general elections, which promised a referendum for an Edinburgh Parliament to have control over most Scottish affairs. Scotland now has significantly more home-based control over its government than at any time since 1707.

While tourist boards may try to exploit the image of the tartan-clad bagpiper for every pence it's worth, to the Scots the image is a reminder of a once-outlawed and viciously suppressed way of life. Many of the things considered typically Scottish—tartan dress, misty glens, bagpipes, shady lochs, tightly knit clans—are remnants of a northern Highlands way of life, which suffered a devastating blow after the British troops defeated the Bonnie Prince Charlie's armies at Culloden in 1746. The English government outlawed tartans, bagpipes, and clan armies, stripping rebellious clan chieftains of their power and, in many cases, land, which they passed on to more loyal members of the Scottish aristocracy.

Ironically, these symbols fashionably resurfaced in the 19th century—long after the threat of Scottish rebellion was dead—when several royals, notably George IV and Queen Victoria, fell in love with the country. They have proliferated and charmed tourists ever since, in the form of woolen shops, kilted bagpipers busking alongside touristed lochs, and tartan-covered shortbread tins.

COMMON PLACE NAMES:
Alba (Scotland), Ben (peak),
Burn (stream), Craig (rock), Firth
(estuary), Glen (valley), Kyle
(narrow strait), Loch (lake), Mon
(hill), Muir (moor), Mull (point),
Rannoch (bracken), Ross
(peninsula)

In fact, tartan is enjoying a new wave of popularity, with many Scots donning the highland dress for weddings and ceilidhs (music and dance performances). Still, many Scots feel that today's kilt is an emasculated version of the original Highland plaid, and purists regard its appropriation a form of continuing colonization by the English. However, Scots are nothing if not astute businessmen, and they've helped turned tartan into a massive money-maker. There remains a sense of unease. Despite the claims of modern hucksters, most of the tartans seen today were designed within the last century, with new patterns still being created. Only a handful of clan tartans are truly authentic, dating back to the early days of the country's history. Yet the beauty of symbols is that they mean different things to different people, and the loaded political implications of the kilt have been forgotten by some who want to wear it as an expression of their identity as modern Scots. Of course, others choose to wear kilts for much sillier reasons. It's a truth passed down from generation to generation of Scottish men that if they wear a kilt, some women will want to know exactly what a true Scotsman wears underneath. A sexist outlook, to be sure. Who says national fervor is the only motivation to wear a kilt?

In the end, modern Scotland can live up to any of the images writers and thinkers want to impose on it. It is not a land preserved in aspic, like a Brigadoon appearing out the mist. Far from it. It is a vibrant, advanced society. A third of all computers sold in Europe flash off assembly lines in central Scotland, while the skills learned from harnessing the North Sea's oil reserves—the latest machinery and emergent technology—are being applied all over the world. While the new industries are replacing the old and obsolete—the shipbuilding and the coal mining that once defined the culture of the central belt—the country is learning how to safeguard its advantages and, increasingly, to look after and preserve the beauty of its environment. Edinburgh and Glasgow are seen as the embodiments of a forward-looking, cosmopolitan society with enlightened ideals and a wealth of talent in all spheres of life. For some critics, modern Scotland is gaining on England in terms of new writing and contemporary art. The extraordinary success of Irvine Welsh's gritty novel, *Trainspotting*, and the film that followed, marks a new buoyancy in British culture that is hard to escape in Scotland's cities. Although Welsh led the charge, a wealth of local talent has made its influence known across the UK and beyond, from writers like Andrew 'O Hagan, Ian Rankin, and Al Kennedy to pop groups like The Stereophonics, Garbage, and Texas. Many claim the talent was always there, but it took a parliament to get it taken seriously. From trendsetting nightclubs to the rise of a new literature and cinema, you will find much more than tartan and shortcake in Scotland today. The harshness of the weather can be overstated—usually by native Scots—but all the facets of a complex country are there to be explored, whether you plan to stick to the tourists' golden triangle—people squeezing Scotland into their British trip often touch down in Edinburgh, then

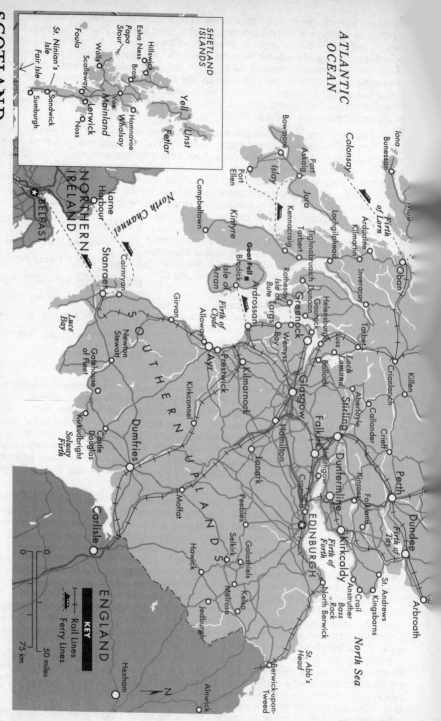

SCOTLAND

ATLANTIC OCEAN

Iona
Bunessan
Colonsay
Firth of Lorn
Mull
Oban
Killin
Crianlarich
Inveraray
Tarbet
Crieff
Perth
Dundee
Firth of Tay
Arbroath

Port Askaig
Port Ellen
Islay
Jura
Kennacraig
Tarbert
Tighnabruaich
Lochgilphead
Ardrishaig
Kilmartin
Arduaine
Loch Lomond
Aberfoyle
Callander
Falkland
Kingsbarns
Crail
St. Andrews
Anstruther
North Sea

Bowmore
Kintyre
Campbeltown
Claonaig
Rothesay
Dunoon
Gourock
Greenock
Helensburgh
Loch Lomond
Balloch
Stirling
Dunfermline
Kinross
Bass Rock
North Berwick

Goat Fell
Brodick
Isle of Arran
Ardrossan
Largs
Wemyss Bay
Bute Isle
Firth of Clyde
Glasgow
Hamilton
Falkirk
Linlithgow
Cramond
EDINBURGH
Firth of Forth
Kirkcaldy
St. Abb's Head
Berwick-upon-Tweed

Lorne Harbour
Stranraer
Cairnryan
Girvan
Ayr
Prestwick
Kilmarnock
Kirkconnel
Lanark
Peebles
Selkirk
Galashiels
Melrose
Kelso
Jedburgh
Hawick
Alnwick

Luce Bay
Newton Stewart
SOUTHERN UPLANDS
Dumfries
Moffat

Gatehouse of Fleet
Castle Douglas
Kirkcudbright
Solway Firth

BELFAST
NORTHERN IRELAND
North Channel
Carlisle

ENGLAND

N

KEY
— Rail Lines
--- Ferry Lines

0   50 miles
0   75 km

SHETLAND ISLANDS

Hillswick
Esha Ness
Papa Stour
Brae
Voe
Whalsay
Walls
Scalloway
Lerwick
Hannavoe
Foula
Mainland
Noss
St. Ninian's Isle
Fair Isle
Sandwick
Sumburgh

Yell
Unst
Fetlar

346

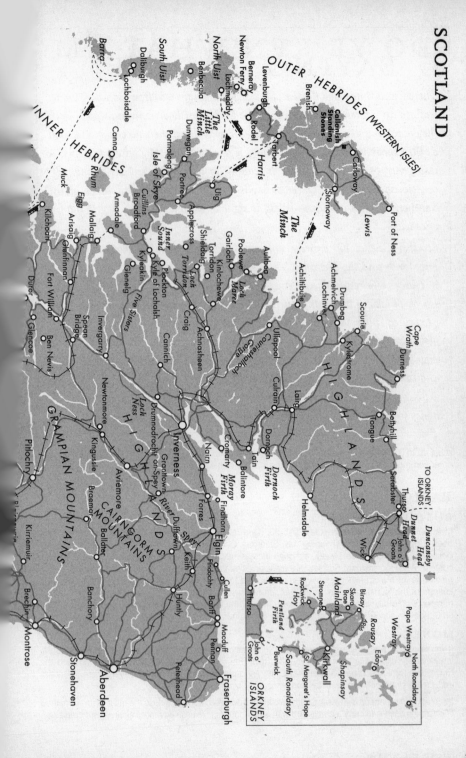

SCOTLAND

OUTER HEBRIDES (WESTERN ISLES)

Barra
South Uist
Daliburgh
Lochboisdale
North Uist
Benbecula
Berneray
Newton Ferry
Lochmaddy
The Little Minch
Levenburgh
Rodel
Harris
Tarbert
Brenish
Callanish Standing Stones
Carloway
Lewis
Stornoway
Port of Ness

INNER HEBRIDES

Canna
Rhum
Muck
Eigg
Kilchoan
Arisaig
Glenfinnan
Mallaig
Armadale
Dunvegan
Parinaleng
Isle of Skye
Portree
Cuillins
Broadford
Kyleakin
Kyle of Lochalsh
Plockton
Applecross
Shieldaig
Torridon
Loch Torridon
Gairloch
Craig
Achnasheen
Poolewe
Loch Maree
Aultbea
Kinlochewe
Gruinard
Uig
The Minch

Cape Wrath
Durness
Kylesku
Scourie
Drumbeg
Achmelvich
Lochinver
Achiltibuie
Ullapool
Culrain
Corrieshalloch Gorge

Duror
Glencoe
Ben Nevis
Fort William
Spean Bridge
Invergarry
Newtonmore
Kingussie
Aviemore
Braemar
Ballater
Banchory

Glenelg
Five Sisters
Cannich
Drumnadrochit-on-Spey
Loch Ness
HIGHLANDS
Inverness
Nairn
Cromarty Firth
Balintore
Tain
Dornoch
Dornoch Firth
Laing
Bettyhill
Tongue
Helmsdale

GRAMPIAN MOUNTAINS
Pitlochry
Kirriemuir
CAIRNGORM MOUNTAINS
Grantown
River Spey
Dufftown
Keith
Findochty
Cullen
Banff
Macduff
Pennan
Elgin
Forres
Findhorn

Brechin
Montrose
Stonehaven
Aberdeen
Fraserburgh
Peterhead
Huntly

Thurso
John o' Groats
Scrabster
Dunnet Head
Duncansby Head
Wick

TO ORKNEY ISLANDS

ORKNEY ISLANDS

Thurso
Stromness
Skara Brae
Mainland
Birsay
Rackwick
Hoy
Pentland Firth
St. Margaret's Hope
Burwick
South Ronaldsay
Kirkwall
Shapinsay
St. Mary's
Rousay
Eday
Westray
Papa Westray
North Ronaldsay

347

DO YE KEN WHAT I'M SAYING, LADDIE?

There was a time when the use of the Scots language was frowned upon, which leads to an interesting dichotomy in the ways most Scots communicate. When they're talking to an outsider, they tend to play down their accent, but as soon as they speak to friends, the formality is dropped and they return to Scots. A resurgence of interest in Scots is leading to a gradual erosion of this self-consciousness, so that Queen's English—the fine, modulated tones of the Southern English counties—is less de rigueur in polite Scottish society than it once was.

Scottish Gaelic, an entirely different language, is still spoken across the Highlands and the Hebrides. There's also a large Gaelic-speaking population in Glasgow (a result of the Celtic diaspora, islanders migrating to Glasgow in search of jobs in the 19th century). Speakers of Gaelic in Scotland were once persecuted, after the failure of the 18th-century Jacobite rebellions. Official persecution has now turned to guilt-tinged support, as the promoters of Gaelic now lobby for substantial public funds to underwrite television programming and language classes for new learners. One of the joys of Scottish television is watching the Gaelic news programs to see how the ancient language copes with topics such as nuclear reprocessing and the latest band to go number one.

scoot up to Inverness and over to Glasgow—or whether you plan to stay for months exploring life in the outer communities of the wild west coast, the islands, or the pastoral east coast.

BASICS

BUSINESS HOURS

Most businesses are open weekdays 9–5:30. It's a rare shop, probably heading for bankruptcy, that doesn't open on the main shopping day, Saturday. Occasionally you'll find some small town stores closed for a half day once a week, although increasingly, a fear of losing business is snuffing out this custom. Also, increasingly, Sunday in the major cities is becoming just another shopping day. What holds true for major cities does not necessarily hold for small towns, unless it's a place that earns its keep from the tourist trade, and even then, do not assume that shops and cafés will be open, though things are gradually changing in this regard. In the rural highlands, however, many shops do not open on Sunday, in accordance with strict Protestant doctrines.

MONEY

If you're coming from England, the first thing you'll notice is that there are three different banks in Scotland that are allowed to print currency: the Royal Bank of Scotland, the Bank of Scotland, and the Clydesdale Bank. Each bank's notes have different designs, but they're all valid everywhere in Britain, and it's the same with English notes and coins.

Internationally connected ATMs are fairly reliable but are often hard to find, so the most assured method of obtaining cash is to carry a credit card with a PIN and receive cash advances against your credit line.

MasterCard and Visa will work in most ATMs regardless of whether the international lines are function-ing. The major banks all have brochures listing their ATM locations available on request.

Every town has at least one branch of a major Scottish bank. Only some Hebridean islands and very small remote communities are served by a "bank van" that parks for a while in some central spot a cou-ple of times a week. Banks are usually open until 4 or 5 PM on weekdays only. Tourist information offices will generally change money whenever they're open, which often includes evenings and Sunday in sum-mer. You won't find late-night bureaux de change, except possibly in hotels and rare specialized kiosks in big towns (where the exchange rates invariably are terrible).

NATIONAL TRUST AND HISTORIC SCOTLAND PASSES

If you are touring the country you will undoubtedly want to visit some of the major historical and cultural sites. Scotland boasts one of the finest collections of castles and old buildings in the world. The lion's share of these are maintained under the auspices of two agencies: the **National Trust for Scotland** (NTS) (5 Charlotte Sq., Edinburgh EH2 4DU, tel. 0131/226–5922) and **Historic Scotland** (HS) (Salis-bury Pl., Edinburgh, EH9 1SF, tel. 0131/668–8600). The former is a charity and manages about 100 sites in Scotland (generally furnished properties), while the latter is a government body that administers over 300 castles, ruins, and monuments. If you're planning to visit lots of castles and stately homes, you can go a long way toward defraying the overall cost by investing in a membership in either organization, which is £26 per year per adult or £42 per family. Both agencies offer passes for seven or 14 days of unlimited access, perfectly tailored to tourists on whistle stop tours. A seven-day pass to National Trust properties costs £16 and £26 for single adults and families, respectively. Their 14-day pass is £24 and £42 respectively. Historic Scotland's seven-day pass is £13 for a single adult and £28 for families. Their fourteen-day pass is £18 and £36, respectively. (Admission to Edinburgh Castle alone costs £6.50).

You can write ahead for membership or instantly sign up at castles, museums, and attractions through-out Scotland. Unfortunately, being a member in one organization does not entitle you to the benefits of the other. However, if you belong to any international hosteling association (e.g., HI, SYHA, YHA), you are eligible for half-price admission at all sites administered by NTS. NTS membership will also get you free access to sites run by affiliated National Trust groups in England, Wales, and Northern Ireland. HS membership will get you half off the entry fees at English Heritage sites.

PHONES

British Telecom once maintained a monopoly on service in Scotland, but there is much more to choose from since the Conservatives deregulated the system. In case of an **emergency,** dial 999 from any phone in the country. This will put you in contact with an emergency operator, who can dispatch ambulance, fire, or police aid.

COMING AND GOING

BY FERRY

Ferries run all around Scotland and its islands, and a few companies offer international routes. **SeaCat** (tel. 0345/523523) and **Stena Sealink** (Stranraer Harbour, tel. 0990/707070) run regular ferries between Stranraer (*see* Dumfries and Galloway *in* Southern Scotland, *below*) and Belfast. Prices start around £46 return, £80 if you bring a car. **P&O** (tel. 0990/980660) serves Larne Harbour, 20 mi north of Belfast. In the northeast, **P&O** (tel. 01224/572615) runs myriad routes, often in conjunction with Smyril Lines. From their base in Aberdeen, **P&O** runs to Stromness in the Orkneys (£38 single in low season, £41 during high season), and Lerwick (£50.50 single in low season, £56.50 during high sea-son) in the Shetlands. Incidentally, there is no price reduction on return fares—they're double the sin-gle fare.

BY PLANE

Due to a marketing blitz on behalf of the Scottish government, it has recently become extremely inex-pensive to fly to **Glasgow Airport** (tel. 0141/887–1111) from the United States and the Continent, so before buying that ticket to London and catching a train to Edinburgh, shop around. Air Canada, British Airways, and many major U.S. airlines offer nonstop flights to Glasgow (*see* Air Travel *in* Chapter 1). **Prestwick Airport** (tel. 0541/569569), 30 mi south of Glasgow, has some international flights, most notably to Dublin. The prices on this service can vary from the absolutely dirt cheap—which you will only get if you book three months ahead—to the reasonably cheap, at around £65 return. **Ryanair** (tel. 0171/435– 7101) has the best bargains, but their low prices are reflected in the quality of the service. Thanks to the multi-faceted tourism ploys of late, if you travel from Prestwick, you can get a train ticket from anywhere in Scotland to the airport for just £5, and you can break your journey anywhere along the line if you want—a superb deal. If you are flying to Scotland from London, try **EasyJet** (tel. 01582/702900), a no-frills airline with flights for £29 one-way to Edinburgh and Glasgow.

GETTING AROUND

If you plan on doing a lot of traveling in Scotland, consider getting the **Freedom of Scotland Travelpass.** It's a combination pass that offers unlimited free train travel on ScotRail lines, free ferry services on almost all Caledonian MacBrayne routes, and 20%–30% discounts on P&O ferries to Orkney and Shetland. You can buy the pass at most ScotRail stations and in some BritRail Travel Centres. (tel. 0345/484950). It's valid for either eight days, during which you can travel four days, (£69), or 15 days, during which you can travel on 8 days (£99), or for the extreme rover, there is a 15-day pass during which you can travel on 12 days (£119). You can buy your ticket in the United States before departure from **BritRail Travel International** in North America (tel. 800/677–8585).

If you're traveling along smaller routes in the more remote regions like the Highlands, make sure you fill up with petrol (gasoline) when you can, as finding a rural petrol station open after 6 PM can be close to impossible. Caution: Don't demur if the petrol is priced higher in outlying areas, especially in the Highlands, than you would find in town. Most roads there are single-carriageway and twisty, so what on the map looks like a short drive can take much longer, especially if you encounter slow-moving farm equipment, or a tourist towing a caravan who refuses to pull over and let you pass in safety. Public transportation on a Sunday—outside the big towns—tends to be scarce, especially in the Highlands. Even in the major towns, services might be limited, so it's advisable to check in advance. Travel by train if you can—and for sure if you're heading up the east coast from Edinburgh to Aberdeen—and try to time your trip so that the sun sets while you're whizzing through the Angus countryside, because this route is seriously picturesque, and can be easily missed if you opt to join the commuters thronging the motorways.

BY BIKE

Cycling along Scotland's desolate roads or mountain trails is a great way to experience the landscape. Bike rental averages about £10 per day and is available in most towns. Bikes generally ride for free on the ferries, so by all means take yours along to the islands.

BY BUS

Buses are one of the cheapest ways to get around Scotland; bus fares are often ⅓ the cost of the train. There are hundreds of bus companies in Scotland, each serving their own (usually regional) routes and offering their own exclusive passes and fares. All-you-can-ride rover passes are often a good deal. Always ask about available discounts.

Caledonian Express (tel. 0990/808080), known as National Express south of the border, and **Citylink** (tel. 0141/332–2326) have merged to form one big company serving all major InterCity routes (including Edinburgh–Glasgow and Glasgow–Fort William). You can access their schedules over the Internet at www.citylink.co.uk. If you are under 25, you can buy a **Discount Coachcard** (£8 for one year), which gives you up to 30% discount on all their routes. The Discount Coachcard is honored by some regional bus lines affiliated with Citylink (among them, Stagecoach), so be sure to ask before paying full price on any bus line. There are also various **Tourist Trail Passes**, which work out at about half the price of the above train offers. Bus links also penetrate more remote parts of the country than the train, but on Scotland's long and winding roads even the comfiest bus can be a trial.

Within and around big cities bus service is cheap and frequent. It's when you get into the country that service becomes sparse to nonexistent. Even if you find routes in rural areas, most run July–August only, and even then only once daily. **Postbuses** fill part of the void. The Royal Mail takes passengers, along with the mail, to farms, castles, and villages beyond the reach of other transport. These red minibuses and cars travel more than 130 routes—often through much of Scotland's most beautiful countryside—for just a few pounds. Ask at tourist and post offices for local timetables, or contact the **Royal Mail** (102 West Port, Edinburgh, tel. 0131/228- -7407). Unfortunately, the schedules seem to change constantly, even mid-season.

BY CAR

Considering the high prices and limited routes of trains and buses, renting a car may be a good idea if you're traveling in a group. **Arnold Clark** (Tollcross, Edinburgh, tel. 0131/228–4747) has offices

nroughout Scotland with very competitive prices starting at £19 a day, and special weekend rates of
£45. You can also try **Hertz** (tel. 0131/557–5272) or **Avis** (tel. 0990/900500). Keep in mind the steep
price of gas (about £2–£2.50 per U.S. gallon) before renting that big gas guzzler. Driving in rural Scot-
and also demands nerves of steel. Not only must you drive on the left, but many roads are "single-
track," meaning that the road is only one lane wide. When you encounter someone coming in the
opposite direction, the first one to arrive at a "passing place" pulls over. Trucks and buses always have
the right-of-way, no matter what type of harrowing Bond-like maneuver you must make to get out of
the way.

BY FERRY
If you're headed north to any of the islands, ferry rides will account for a major portion of your travel budget. BritRail's **Freedom of Scotland Travelpass** (*see above*) gets you free travel on Caledonian
MacBrayne ferries. "CalMac" also offers passes of its own, notably the **Island Rover,** which allows
unlimited travel on nearly all routes; an eight-day pass costs £41, a 15-day pass £59. **Island Hopscotch**
tickets come in 23 different versions and are a good deal only if you can plan your itinerary in advance.
Prices vary wildly depending on how much ground you want to cover. No matter what pass you buy, your
bike travels for free. For more info, contact: Caledonian MacBrayne Ltd., The Ferry Terminal, Gourock,
PA19 1QP, tel. 01475/650100.

BY MINIBUS
An excellent alternative to public buses are either of Scotland's two backpackers' minibus services. **Haggis Backpackers** (11 Blackfriars St., Edinburgh, EH1 1NB, tel. 0131/557–9393) will keep you laughing
all around Scotland, as Donald, Alasdair, Peter, and Neill try to sucker you with wild Scottish tales while
onboard their jump-on, jump-off minibus service. A three-month ticket with unlimited stops costs £65
as long as you follow a circular path from Edinburgh, through Inverness and the Highlands, over to Skye,
and back through Glencoe and Loch Lomond to Glasgow or Edinburgh. If you are short on time and cannot be bothered with too much organizing yourself, they put together a three-day package that includes
accommodation for £75, six days for £139. They have recently added their first UK-wide tour, which
works on a jump-on/jump-off basis and lets you see some of England for £120. These guys will pack as
much fun and as many history lessons into your skull as is humanly possible. The only danger is the bottomless cooler of chocolate bars stowed under the seat.

Macbackpackers (28 North Bridge, Suite 8, Edinburgh, EH1 1NE, tel. 0131/558–900) also offers a
jump-on/jump-off service with roughly the same itinerary and similar packages. If you don't have time
to dawdle in Scotland properly they do snappy tours from Edinburgh through the Grampians, to Inverness and the most beautiful parts of the western Highlands, then back to Edinburgh through Loch Ness,
Glen Nevis, Glencoe, the Trossachs, and Stirling. There are lots of stops for walks, so you won't go men-
tal sitting in a van all day. In addition to these two, several new companies have started offering similar
tour services. For a complete list, check with a tourist office.

BY TRAIN
ScotRail (tel. 0345/484950), Scotland's national rail service, has been privatized in line with the rest of
Britain's rail network, a controversial and complex process. Consequently, the system has been
embroiled in administrative chaos, which can make life very difficult for the rail traveler. Although Scotland remains under the regulation of one company, getting there from England can be confusing, with
several operators traveling along different routes. Try **Virgin Trains** (tel. 0345/222333), whose cheapest
fair is the Virgin Value Return (£29), London to Glasgow. You can also use **Great North Eastern Railway**
(tel. 0345/484950), which travels up the attractive east coast, with prices starting at £36 return, super-
APEX. Be warned: If you don't book several weeks in advance and can't commit to dates for travel, you
will end up having to pay much more.

Rail routes are few and far between compared to other areas in Britain, so if you're considering buying
a rail pass, check carefully to ensure it won't cramp your itinerary or wallet. ScotRail accepts BritRail
passes and also offers a number of travel passes similar to those listed at the start of this section. There
are also two regional rail passes. **The Highland Rover** covers the area from Glasgow to Oban to Fort
William to Mallaig to Kyle of Lochalsh and across to Inverness, Thurso, Aberdeen and all areas in
between. It costs £39 for four out of eight days. The **Festival Cities Rover** (£29) allows travel between
Edinburgh, Glasgow, North Berwick, Stirling, the Fife Circle, Falkirk, all stations in between, and on the
Glasgow Underground, for three out of seven days.

THE BOTTOM LINE ON BOTHIES

A bothy is an old stone farmhouse, sometimes abandoned, sometimes refurbished, that provides basic shelter. Many unattended bothies are always open and are free to anyone who stops by; others are run as simple hostels for a small fee. Either way, bring everything you're going to need for the night and follow the code of bothy conduct: Leave the bothy in a better state than you found it, leave rat-safe food if you've any to spare, replace any kindling you use, and sign the guest book. For more info and helpful advice on bothy accommodations in the region you'll be traveling through, contact Ted Butcher, 26 Rycroft Ave., Peterborough, PE6 8NT, tel. 01778/345062.

WHERE TO SLEEP

B&Bs are ubiquitous and often the only place to crash in remote areas if you haven't brought your camping gear. Penny-pinchers should stick with hostels, campgrounds, and bothies (*see box*). "Wild" or "rough camping" is okay as long as you get permission from the landowner(s). Be warned, though, that in most situations you can't just crash out al fresco. It can be cold, even in midsummer, and it does rain a fair bit. But bring the right gear, and insect repellent, and you'll enjoy a closeness to nature you'd never find in a hotel room.

HOSTELS

The **Scottish Youth Hostel Association** (SYHA), which is affiliated with Hostelling International (HI) and the **Youth Hostel Association of England and Wales** (YHA), has 79 hostels throughout Scotland. International membership will cost you £6. The SYHA Handbook (£2 including post and package), available at any SYHA hostel and many tourist offices, is an indispensable guide to locations and facilities. There's also a free, less complete Scotland SYHA guide available at tourist offices. You can write ahead for reservations, make a phone reservation within a week of arrival, or have SYHA make a fax reservation for you via the Book-a-Bed-Ahead service (tel. 0541/553255, free). SYHA hostels do not generally accept credit cards. The only exceptions are for fax bookings made from SYHA hostels in Glasgow, Edinburgh, and Stirling, and from SYHA's main and district offices. For more info, contact SHYA directly. Main office: 7 Glebe Crescent, Stirling, FK8 2JA, tel. 01786/451181, fax 01786/891333.

SYHA hostels are graded Higher Standard, Standard, Standard-L, and Simple based on facilities, price, curfew, and daily lockout period. Except for Higher Standard hostels, found in larger cities, the other hostels strictly enforce an 11 PM curfew. SYHA hostels require that you make your bed by 9:30 AM, check out by 10:30 AM, and use a sleep sheet—if you don't have one, many hostels rent them for around 60p per night. For SYHA hostels throughout the chapter, we list the hostel's grade rather than repeat the same facilities and prices over and over.

Higher Standard hostels have the best facilities, are open all day (i.e., there's no lockout), have a 2 AM curfew, and allow you to check in until 11 PM. Most have a simple store selling canned and dry goods, and all have laundry facilities. Beds cost £6.50–13.00 depending on your age, the season, and the location of the hostel. The more expensive hostels are in Stirling, Glasgow, and Edinburgh, and those in Carbisdale (£10.05, plus a summer surcharge) and New Lanark (£9.25). These hostels also serve a free mystery-meat and cheese breakfast.

Standard hostels also have good facilities and are open during the day. They differ only in that the curfew is 11 PM, you can check in until 10:30 PM, and the rate for beds is roughly £2 less.

Standard-L hostels have lockouts during the day, usually between 11 AM and 2 PM. Some have stores, and it's hit or miss whether your shower will be hot or cold. You must also do a simple cleaning chore (like vacuuming) before checking out. Beds cost around £2 less than Standard hostels.

Simple hostels are the most basic, with no hot water and usually no showers. The lockout is 10:30 AM–5 PM. And don't forget about your chore. Beds cost around £5.

A nice alternative to SYHA hostels is independent hostels, which have no membership fees, curfews, lockouts, or chore or sleep-sheet requirements. New independent hostels seem to be popping up left, right, and center and now outnumber the official hostels. Many have banded together as the **Independent Backpackers Hostels Association** (contact Gavin Hogg, tel. 01397/712315.) Their brochure (20p) lists addresses and phone numbers for all member hostels and can be obtained by writing to IHO Information Office, Dooey Hostel, Glencolumcille, County Donegal, Ireland. Facilities and charges vary widely, but in general you can be assured that independent hostels are more laid-back than their SYHA counterparts. A second company—marketing the hostels in the Highlands only—has also been formed. Details of **Highland Bunkhouses, Barns and Bothies** can be found on the web at www.lochaber.co.uk/hbb, or through Gavin Hogg again. With the independent bunkhouses, you tend to get the tour information, entertainment, and transport all thrown together in the person of the bunkhouse owner.

Although we do note if hostels are closed for limited spans of time, it's always best to call in advance to confirm opening hours and off-seasons.

EDINBURGH

In contrast to much of the rest of Scotland, Edinburgh is often thought of as a white-collar city of well-to-do citizens with lilting accents and a stunning history of intellectual and artistic enlightenment—which is all true. Other cities may come and go, but Edinburgh will always command a place among the beautiful tourist meccas of the world. The city's foremost feature is **Edinburgh Castle,** looming authoritatively from the crags of an ancient volcano. Medieval Old Town tumbles down this steep hill toward Holyrood Castle, offering the best exploring and the most palpable sense of the city's past. Wynds (winding, narrow streets and walkways), and closes (medieval alleyways that connect the twisting streets) spill from the ramparts of Edinburgh Castle, much as they did in earlier centuries, and getting lost among them is one of the best ways to explore Edinburgh.

On the far side of the Princes Street Gardens is the beguiling **New Town,** a collective masterpiece conceived entirely by Robert Adam when he was only 26, but created with the assistance of a few other Enlightenment architects. New Town's meticulously planned squares and Georgian streets are the legacy of Edinburgh's unrivaled reign during the Age of Reason, when both David Hume, empiricist extraordinaire, and Adam Smith, father of laissez-faire economics, sprang from the city's fertile intellectual soil. Despite the relocation of the Scottish Parliament to London in 1707, New Town still maintains a most perceptible influence over the pulse of Scottish politics and commerce. The financial strength of this district is the backbone of its identity—these are the dearest flats in Scotland—and the reason most large Scottish companies are headquartered here.

Edinburgh is also the "Festival City," home of the world-renowned **International Festival,** the biggest arts festival in the world, held every year from mid-August through the first week of September. Other festivals have joined the party, most successful among them the **Fringe Festival,** a showcase for more experimental performing arts and a host of stand-up comics. In late summer, tourists and performers from all over the world converge here to celebrate music, dance, and theater—which is great if you love the arts and a real bummer if you despise thick crowds. In fact, excluding London, Edinburgh is Britain's most visited city, and if you can imagine what that might mean in a narrow and congested wynd in the middle of August, you'll probably want to avoid Edinburgh in late summer. But the atmosphere—feverish, cosmopolitan, and incredibly good humored—is unrivaled, and if it gets to be too much, you can always escape to the seashore suburbs of Leith and Portobello.

BASICS

AMERICAN EXPRESS
This office across from St. John's Church provides the usual cardholder services. The lines are always long, so come early. *139 Princes St., EH2 4BR, tel. 0131/225–7881 or 0131/225–9179. Open weekdays 9–5:30 (Thurs. from 9:30), Sat. 9–4.*

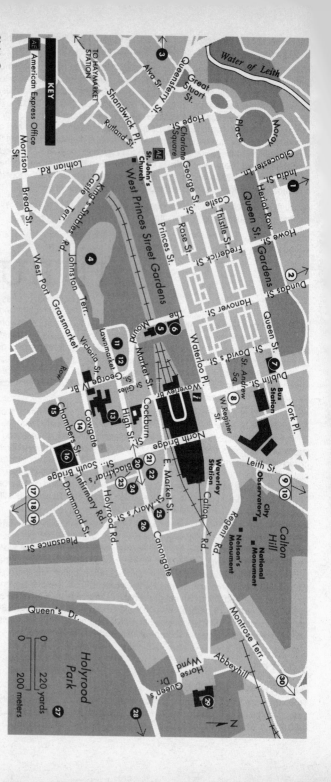

EDINBURGH

KEY

AE American Express Office

Sights ●
Arthur's Seat, **27**
Edinburgh Castle, **4**
Gladstone's Land, **11**
Holyrood Palace, **29**
Huntly House, **26**
John Knox House, **22**
Lady Stair's House, **12**
Museum of Childhood, **24**
National Gallery of Scotland, **5**
Old University, **16**
People's Story, **25**
Royal Botanic Gardens, **1**
Royal Mile, **20**
Royal Museum of Scotland, **15**
Royal Scottish Academy, **6**
St. Anthony's Chapel, **28**
St. Giles' Cathedral, **13**
Scottish National Gallery of Modern Art, **3**
Scottish National Portrait Gallery, **7**

Lodging ○
29 Oxford St., **17**
Ardenlee Guest House, **2**
Balmoral Guest House, **9**
Cowgate Tourist Hostel, **14**
Crion Guest House, **18**
High St. Hostel, **23**
Iolaire, **19**
Joppa Rocks Guest House, **30**
Malmaison, **10**
Royal Mile Backpackers, **2:**

DISCOUNT TRAVEL AGENCIES

With three locations, the STA-affiliated **Edinburgh Travel Center** has more info on budget travel than you could possibly want. *3 Bristo Sq., Edinburgh University, tel. 0131/668–2221; 196 Rose St., tel. 0131/226–2019; 92 South Clerk St., tel. 0131/667–9488. All open weekdays 9–5:30, Sat. 10–1:30.*

The **Backpackers Centre** is the perfect resource for the outgoing, fun-loving, budget-minded set. They can help arrange everything from bus and ferry (but no train) passes, to minivan tours and lodging. *7–9 Blackfriars St., tel. 0131/557–9393, fax 0131/558– 1177. Open weekdays 9–6, Sat. 10–6 (longer hrs during summer and festival).*

GAY AND LESBIAN RESOURCES

Despite the austere conservatism of Edinburgh, and the dour Presbyterianism that is said to lurk in its corners, Edinburgh has always been one of the most relaxed cities in Europe when it comes to sexual orientation. Many organizations are located at the **Lesbian, Gay, and Bisexual Community Centre** (58A Broughton St., tel. 0131/558–1279 or 0131/557–3620). You can also pick up the informative magazines *Gay Scotland* and *Scots Gay* at the nearby **Blue Moon Café** (36 Broughton St., tel. 0131/557–0911). For counseling, call the **Lesbian & Gay Switchboard** (tel. 0131/556– 4049) daily 7:30 PM–10 PM, the **Lesbian Line** (tel. 0131/557– 0751) on Monday or Thursday 7:30 PM–10 PM, or the **Bisexual Line** (tel. 0131/557–3620) Thursday 7:30 PM–9:30 PM.

LUGGAGE STORAGE

A left luggage service and luggage lockers are available at **Waverley Station.** Luggage lockers (£1–£3) are also available at **St. Andrew Square bus station** (*see* Coming and Going, *below*) Monday- -Saturday 6:15 AM–10:15 PM, Sunday 8:15 AM–9:30 PM.

The Lothian Coalition of Disabled People (8 Lothian Rd., near Easter, tel. 0131/555–2151) provides access info for sights, museums, hotels, cafés, restaurants, and pubs in and around Edinburgh.

MAIL

At Edinburgh's **main post office**—now relocated from its grand Waterloo Place edifice to the more pedestrian **St. James shopping center** (at the far east end of Princes Street), you can receive poste restante, buy stationery, and take glamorous photos of yourself at the coin-operated photo booth. *8/10 St. James Shopping Centre, EH1 3SR, tel. 0131/536–0478. Open weekdays 9–5:30, Sat. 9–7.*

MEDICAL AID

You won't be charged for consultation or treatment of minor medical problems at the **Royal Infirmary of Edinburgh** (1 Lauriston Pl., off Forest Rd., tel. 0131/536–1000), open 24 hours daily. Every pharmacy posts a list of nearby late-night pharmacies. **Boots** (Princes St., tel. 0131/225–6757, and 5-9 St. James Centre, tel. 0131/556–1062) is a good place to pick up aspirin and the like. Not a bad bet either if you're looking for somewhere to develop your holiday snaps.

VISITOR INFORMATION

The always crowded **Edinburgh Information Centre,** above the Waverley train station and shopping complex, has a bureau de change and loads of info on transportation and sights. For a £3 fee they will book beds in person or over the phone (tel. 0131/557–9655). The center also has a small tourist desk (tel. 0131/333–2167) in the main concourse of Edinburgh International Airport, across from Gate 5. *3 Princes St., tel. 0131/557–1700. Open Mon.–Sat. 9–6 (Apr.– Oct., also Sun. 11–6).*

COMING AND GOING

BY BUS

Buses are by far the cheapest way to reach Edinburgh from London, especially since privatization has made competition fierce. The only drawback is that the trip takes about nine hours—four hours longer than by train. **National Express** (tel. 0990/808080) has the cheapest fare (£25 return if you book seven days in advance and £29 otherwise), though the ride can be cramped. For only slightly more, **Silver Choice** (tel. 01355/230403) offers slightly less crowded conditions. Most companies have two departures per day—one in the early morning and one in the late evening. Buses also head north as far as Aberdeen (£18.50 return) and Thurso (£48.50 return); heavy sleepers should consider taking an overnight coach. Most long-distance buses arrive and depart from smoggy **St. Andrew Square** bus station (tel. 0990/505050), two blocks north of Princes Street. The main carriers are **Scottish Citylink** and **Caledonian Express** (tel. 0131/452–8777), both of which offer various discounts and passes (*see* Getting Around *in* Basics, *above*).

BY PLANE

Edinburgh International Airport (tel. 0131/333–1000), 7 mi from the city center, has benefited from a recent flurry of competition between airlines—major operators are busy cutting their fares. Flights to and from London can be as cheap as £29 single with **Easyjet** (tel. 01582/702900) if you don't mind flying from Luton airport (30 mi north of London, near Cambridge) and **AIR UK** (tel. 0345/666777), which offers return fares from London's Stansted airport for as little as £59. (Remember to add £5 airport tax to all prices.) You will pay more to fly from Heathrow and Gatwick airports with either of Britain's main air operators, **British Airways** (tel. 01345/222111) and **British Midland** (tel. 01345/554554), but you can still book reasonable deals—from around £75 return—if you are including a Saturday night in your visit. Luggage lockers at the airport go for £1.50 per day. Bus 100 (30 mins, £3) runs between the airport and Princes Street about every 15 minutes. Every half hour from 8:30 to 8:30, **Airbuses** (tel. 0131/556–2244) travel between the airport and St. Andrew Square bus station (£3.50 single). A taxi to or from the city center should cost around £12.

BY TRAIN

Edinburgh's main rail hub, **Waverley Station,** lies at the east end of Princes Street. From here you can catch a train to cities throughout Scotland and England, including London (15 per day, 5–6 hrs, £69 return) and Inverness (12 per day, 3 hrs, £31 return). Try **Virgin Trains** (tel. 0345/222333) and **Great North East Railways** (tel. 0345/484950) for cheap fares, bookable only in advance. For train info call 01345/484950 24 hours a day.

Trains from the smaller **Haymarket Station** (tel. 0345/484950), in the West End of Edinburgh in Haymarket Square, travel to points west. Twice-hourly departures to Glasgow (originating at Waverley) take 50 minutes and cost £7.30 single, £8.50 off-peak return and £13.90 return during rush hour.

GETTING AROUND

Edinburgh is a compact, walkable city, although a thorough tour will require you to negotiate (and invariably get lost in) the steep streets and tiny wynds and closes. Streets tend to change names after one or two blocks. If you're looking for a particular shop on, say, Grassmarket, you only need to worry about a section of street two blocks long.

Princes Street Gardens roughly divide Edinburgh into two areas: the winding, narrow streets of **Old Town** to the south, and the orderly, Georgian **New Town** to the north. **Princes Street** runs east–west along the northern edge of the gardens and is a magnet for tourists, but still worth taking a stroll along, particularly in the summer when the gardens are in full bloom and you have the spectacular facade of the Castle and Old Town skyline to wallow in. While one side is open to the gardens, the other is crowded with the usual mix of high-street stores, but it's worth dropping into Jenners, the closest Scotland gets to a Harrods. Other useful stores include Virgin Megastore and two well-stocked branches of the Waterstones bookstore (one of which includes a superbly positioned café with views of the Castle). Buses to every part of the city run along Princes Street, so always ask whether you need to catch the bus on the "garden" or "shop" side. The city is relatively safe and you can walk freely almost anywhere, although caution should be exercised in the Cowgate and Meadows areas after dark. Black **taxis** abound in Edinburgh and are easily hailed from the curb. It costs £1.50 to put your toe in and £1.10 every mile, plus a 10% tip.

BY BIKE

Rent your 21-speed mountain bike from **Cycle Safaris** (29 Blackfriars St., tel. 0131/556–5560) for £15 per day or £70 per week, or an 18-speed bike for just £10 a day or £50 a week. The **Bike Bus** (4 Barclay Terr., tel. 0131/229–6274) rents bikes starting at £8 per day. They'll also give you and your bike a lift to Perthshire for a day of riding (£10 return).

BY BUS

You'll see two types of buses in Edinburgh: maroon and white double-deckers operated by **Lothian Regional Transport** (LRT) (27 Hanover St. and 31 Waverley Bridge, tel. 0131/555–6363), with routes throughout the city and suburbs; and green double-deckers operated by **Scottish Metropolitan Transport** (SMT) (St. Andrew Square bus station, tel. 0131/558–1616), with local routes as well as service to ther cities and towns. Making sense of all the routes and fares isn't easy, so pick up the free "Edinburgh Travelmap" at a tourist or bus office.

Bus fares within the city range from 50p to £1.60 and LRT drivers do not give change—so arm yourself with a pocket full of coin. Both LRT and SMT offer **one-day passes** for £2.40 and **Ridecards**, good for a week of unlimited travel, for £10.50. Passes are a good idea if you're staying in the suburbs, but note that LRT and SMT passes are not interchangeable. For general route info, call the helpful Traveline (tel. 0131/225–3858).

WHERE TO SLEEP

Edinburgh B&Bs and hostels are busy year-round—always book ahead. The **accommodations desk** in Waverley Station stocks the free Edinburgh magazine and the comprehensive "Where to Stay" brochure and can book you into a B&B for a £3 fee. In a pinch turn to the friendly folks at the **Backpackers Centre** (*see* Discount Travel Agencies, *above*), who will help find you a bunk bed or room for a £3 fee. If you don't have a reservation for a B&B, take a stroll down **Minto Street,** southeast of Princes Street; from the shop side of the street, take Bus 3, 7, 8, 18, 31, 69, or 80. You can also try **Pilrig Street,** northeast of the city center; from the shop side of Princes Street, take Bus 7, 10, 11, 14, 16, 17, 22, 25, or 87. Edinburgh's SYHA hostel accepts faxed booking from other SYHA hostels; for details, *see* Where to Sleep *in* Basics, *above*.

During August and September, you're crazy to think you can find a cheap bed in Edinburgh. BOOK AHEAD, preferably months in advance.

UNDER £25 • Iolaire. On a residential street near a large park, Iolaire fills the gap between hostel and B&B, providing comfort, quiet, privacy, and rooms with TVs. Doubles cost £22, triples and quads £10 per person. *14 Argyle Pl., off Melville Dr., EH9 1JL, tel. 0131/667–9991. From Princes St. (garden side), take Bus 40, 41, or 41A. 52 beds. Kitchen. Cash only.*

Joppa Rocks Guest House. This friendly old guest house on a residential street is a well-kept secret, only 10 minutes by bus from the town center and 60 yards from Portobello Beach. Rooms in this homey establishment have TVs, tea and coffee-making facilities (with lovely crunchy biscuits), and bathrooms that come complete with bathrobes and slippers. Singles are £15, twins £17.50, and doubles £20. *99 Joppa Rd, EH15 2HB, tel. 0131/669–8695. From Princes St. take any Portobello bus. 5 rooms, all with bath.*

UNDER £60 • Balmoral Guest House. Marianne Wheelaghan has recently taken over this pleasant guest house. Only double rooms (£18–£20 per person, and depending on the season) are available, but all have a TV and the fixings for tea and coffee. Vegetarians won't go hungry for breakfast. Book ahead if possible, up to three months ahead during the Festival. *32 Pilrig St., EH6 5AL, tel. 0131/554–1857. 5 rooms, none with bath. Cash only.*

Crion Guest House. This family-run B&B about 1 mi from the train station features light, cheery rooms for around £25 per person, but prices vary depending on the season. Reserve at least two weeks in advance. *33 Minto St., EH9 2BG, tel. 0131/667–2708, fax 0131/662– 1946. 9 rooms, 5 with shower. Cash only.*

Ardenlee Guest House. Run by David and Judy Dinse, this is a cozy, well-situated home, just off Dundas Street. Breakfasts are good, and there are four family cats to keep you company. Expect to pay £29 per person. *9 Eyre Pl., EH3 5ES., tel. 0131/556–2838. 9 rooms, 6 with bath. Cash only.*

UNDER £100 • Malmaison. For those wishing to splurge, few places offer the quality of service and striking decor of Malmaison, situated in the newly renovated dockside community of Leith. All rooms are tastefully furnished and include a music system and TV, as well as tea- and coffeemaking facilities. In addition there is a vegetarian brasserie and a highly rated restaurant attached. As the name might suggest, prices are per room (French style), rather than per guest. A double room will set you back £99; if you want a four-poster bed you can add an extra £31 to the bill. The only drawback is that one person pays the same as two. *1 Tower Pl., Leith, EH6 7DB, tel. 0131/555–6868. Follow A900 to Leith Walk or take Bus 1 on Royal Mile (going downhill). 25 rooms with bath.*

HOSTELS

Belford Hostel. This beautiful independent hostel, housed in a former church, is close to Haymarket Station. There's no ceiling above the partitioned rooms, and though gazing up at the stained glass is nice, it can sound like an echo chamber. Dorm beds cost £10.50, double rooms £33 (£5 more mid July–August). *6–8 Douglas Gardens, EH4 3DA, tel. 0131/225–6209, fax 0131/539–8695. From Princes St. (garden side) take Bus 3, 4, 12, 13, 31, 33, or 44 to Palmerston Pl. (which becomes Douglas Gardens). 90 beds, 5 rooms. Kitchen, laundry. Cash only.*

Cowgate Tourist Hostel. Associated with the nearby Edinburgh College of Art, this Old Town hostel is open July–September for "American travelers who never bring towels with them." That's right, free linen and towels. Dorm beds, singles, doubles, and triples range from £11 to £13 per person (£12–£15 during the Festival). *112 Cowgate, EH1 1JN, tel. 0131/226–2153. 80 beds. Laundry. Closed Oct.–June.*

High Street Hostel. Always packed, High Street's supersocial common rooms are so entertaining that some people stay forever, or so it seems. Located just off the Royal Mile, it's a perfect base for exploring pubs and clubs in the Old Town and university areas. Beds start at £9.50, including linen. As an added bonus, for £2.50 the staff will take your laundry and return it to you the next morning, spanking clean and folded. *8 Blackfriars, EH1 1ME, tel. 0131/557–3984, fax 0131/556–2981. From Waverley Station, walk south on North Bridge Rd., turn left on High St., right on Blackfriars St. 158 beds.*

Royal Mile Backpackers. The supercasual Royal Mile hostel has a friendly community of semipermanent residents and a great location. Watch the queen ride down the Royal Mile to Holyrood when she's in town in July. Dorm beds cost £9.50, and there is free tea and coffee in the common room. *105 High St., tel. 0131/557–6162. 36 beds. Laundry.*

STUDENT HOUSING

29 Oxford Street. During July and August, several university-owned buildings are rented out as self-catering apartments. You come and go as you like (it's basically like subletting a shared room for the night). Beds are £10–£12. Call to inquire if there's any minimum length of stay. *29 Oxford St., EH8 9PQ, tel. 0131/668–3327 (ask for Neil Brown); 0131/445–3917 off-season. From North Bridge, take Bus 3, 5, 7, 8, 31, or 33 to Newington post office.*

CAMPING

Silverknowes Caravan Park. The lack of trees or sheltered areas at this park in the seaside town of Cramond means that the brutal wind may take your tent on a sudden, unwanted trip to the North Sea. Tent sites cost £11, or £12.50 with a car, and Caravans cost £16, assuming two people in each. There's a store on site. *Marine Dr., tel. 0131/312–6874. From North Bridge, take Bus 8A or 14A. 100 sites. Toilets, showers. Closed Oct.–Mar.*

FOOD

Dinner is always the most expensive meal, so sample Edinburgh's restaurants at lunch when prices are almost half the price of the evening menu. An inexpensive lunch at a pub or café usually runs £4–£6. Supermarkets and street grocers are an inexpensive alternative to eating out, and several delis provide good sandwich counters. Try **Di Placido** (36 High St., tel. 0131/667–2286) for well-proportioned rolls filled with everything from pastrami and mustard to Highland pheasant. The centrally located **Marks & Spencer** (54 Princes St., tel. 0131/225–2301) has a good food hall downstairs with an extensive range of sandwiches, soft drinks, and handy picnic bottles of wine.

UNDER £5 • Café Byzantium. Billed as the largest café in Edinburgh, Café Byzantium serves fresh, cheap, and delicious food in comfortable surroundings. Order the vegetarian buffet and get a plate piled high with rice and your choice of dishes like curry, spinach with cheese, and lentils. *9 Victoria St., between George IV Bridge Rd. and Grassmarket, tel. 0131/220–2241. Cash only.*

Café Florentin. At practically any hour you can order a cappuccino and a pastry (best in the city) at this Soho-style café, grab a rickety chair, and lose yourself in a book. There's an even better branch in Stockbridge (5 North Circus Pl., tel. 0131/220–0225). During the Festival, it's open 24 hours. *8 Giles St., tel. 0131/225–6267. Cash only.*

Cornerstone Café. Dine among the dead at one of the outdoor tables or in the stony interior of what once served as the catacombs for St. John's Church. For about £3 you can fill yourself with a wholesome sandwich, soup, or salad. Highly recommended, this is one of the few places that serves beer with breakfast. *Under St. John's Church, corner Lothian Rd. and Princes St., tel. 0131/229–0212. Cash only.*

Henderson's. Edinburgh's original vegetarian restaurant, Henderson's is always packed to the gills during the Festival, but is sadly sagging around the edges these days. Henderson's serves at least six hot ishes daily, along with an excellent selection of cheap salads and desserts. Try lentil stew with potatoes or a deliciously sweet trifle (bread pudding with grapes and apples). There is also live folk or jazz every evening. *94 Hanover St., tel. 0131/225–2131. Closed Sun.*

Queen Street Café. Located on the ground floor of the Scottish National Portrait Gallery, the Queen Street Café has a small but delicious selection—ahhh, that sumptuous lemon cake! It's also one of the few places that upholds the dying tradition of serving loose tea rather than tea bags. Before you leave, make sure you visit the portrait gallery for Avigdor Arikha's striking portrait of Queen Elizabeth the Queen Mother. It's definitely the sort of place to take your mother. *Scottish National Portrait Gallery, 1 Queen St., tel. 0131/556–8921.*

Susie's Diner. This place is legendary for its freshly baked brown bread. Diners flock here for cheap and filling vegetarian and vegan meals. During the Festival, it's open daily until midnight. *53 W. Nicolson St., tel. 0131/667–8729. Cash only.*

Valvona & Crolla. One of the best reasons for venturing east beyond Princes Street, Valvona & Crolla is an Edinburgh institution—an award-winning Italian deli with an airy café serving pasta and polenta dishes to the truly discerning. Take a stroll along the shelves crammed with olive oils, sun-dried tomatoes, Italian cakes, and salamis. *19 Elm Row, tel. 0131/556–6066. Closed Sun.*

UNDER £10 • Chez Jules. This small and homey restaurant is like a French country kitchen. You can bring your own wine, which makes it an exceptionally good value. *1 Craig's Close, tel. 0131/225–7007. Cash only.*

Indigo Yard. One of Edinburgh's more recent, and hippest, ventures with a good menu and an even better interior. An upstairs gallery provides good views of the action below while you tuck into your Thai fish cakes in spicy cucumber sauce, or just enjoy one of the fresh salads on offer. Brunch on Sunday is a particular joy. *7 Charlotte La., tel. 0131/220–5603.*

For truly gourmet haggis (tidbits of sheep's lungs, liver, and heart seasoned with spices and onions and tucked into a sheep's stomach), head to Charles MacSween & Son (130 Bruntsfield Place)—the organ-shy can order a veg version.

Kalpna. This Gujarati Indian restaurant has won national awards for its vegetarian cooking. The best deal is the £4.50 lunch buffet, served weekdays noon–2. There's also a dinner buffet, with higher prices. *2–3 St. Patrick Sq., south of Nicolson St. (which becomes South Bridge), tel. 0131/667–9890. Closed Sun. Cash only.*

Maison Hector. This hip spot is often crowded with media types during the Edinburgh Festival. Maison Hector's is best worth visiting for Sunday brunch. The unusual decor of the men's rest rooms is worth a detour alone. *47 Deanhaugh St., tel. 0131/332–5328.*

UNDER £25 • (Fitz)Henry. Arty without being intimidating, (Fitz)Henry has garnered several awards, a tribute to a wonderfully eclectic menu that can include specialties such as poached goose stuffed with chestnuts and mushrooms, game stew in a sauce enriched with bitter chocolate, and chocolate mousse with a saffron sauce. Dinner is around £22 for three courses, but worth every pound. *19 Shore Pl., tel. 0131/555–6625. Closed Sun.*

WORTH SEEING

It's not easy to get lost in Edinburgh with the castle perched at the top of **Old Town,** but simply walking around and popping down a darkened close or two will make you feel a little like Alice in a cobblestone Wonderland. Bisecting Princes Street Gardens is **The Mound,** a walkway between the Old Town and New Town, which began as a pile of earth gathered from construction sites around New Town in the 18th century. Venture north of Princes Street and you'll see the imposing stone houses and antiquarian bookshops that characterize **New Town;** contact the **New Town Conservation Centre** (13A Dundas St., tel. 0131/557–5222) for suggestions on scenic walks. Venture south for the **Royal Mile** and the University of Edinburgh. On misty, gloomy days, Edinburgh's museums and galleries, most of which are free, will keep you warm.

EDINBURGH CASTLE

Not only does the castle have symbolic value as the historic center of Scotland, but the views from its battlements are stunning: The whole of Edinburgh and the Firth of Forth can be seen from the towering ramparts (although the view from Arthur's Seat is even better—and free). It's not surprising that this site has been home to some sort of strategic stronghold since roughly 1000 BC, as recent excavations suggest. Most of the ramparts and buildings date back to the 14th and 16th centuries, but the oldest building, **St. Margaret's Chapel,** dates back as far as the 11th century, the only building to survive a Scottish attack in 1314 when it was won back from the English. The Scottish Regalia—the jeweled crown, scepter, and sword of Scotland—sparkle in the castle's **Crown Room,** along with the famous Stone of Destiny, recently returned by the queen as a goodwill gesture, but the wait just isn't worth it. Other sights within the castle include the **Scottish National War Memorial,** honoring 150,000 Scots who died in World War I. *Top of Royal Mile, tel. 0131/244–3101. Admission £6.50. Open daily 9:30–5 (Apr.–Sept. until 6).*

THE ROYAL MILE

The Royal Mile, a mile-long street that stretches from Edinburgh Castle to Holyrood Palace, is divided into four sections— Castlehill, Lawnmarket, High Street, and Canongate, the main street of Old Town. Pubs, shops, pubs, historic attractions, and pubs line its cobblestone length, which, if you're in the right mood, will transport you back to Edinburgh's medieval past. Because so many 16th- to 18th-century city dwellers wanted to live as close to the castle's walls as possible, many five- and six-story buildings went up in this prime real estate area. **Gladstone's Land** (477B Lawnmarket, tel. 0131/226–5856), admission £3.20, is one such six-story building, reflecting the typical architecture and decor of a 17th-century merchant's house. Around the corner, **Lady Stair's House** (off Lawnmarket, tel. 0131/529–4901) is another 17th-century building, which features exhibits on Scotland's literary greats—including Sir Walter Scott, Robert Louis Stevenson, and Robert Burns; admission is free.

Saint Giles' Cathedral (High St., tel. 0131/225–9442) dates from 1120, though a church has stood on this site since 854. **John Knox House** (43 High St., tel. 0131/556–9579) has a display on the complicated life of one of Scotland's most controversial figures: You can read about the good (universal education) and bad (religious intolerance and murder) attributed to his influence. Today, however, the primary attraction is not Mr. Knox, but the building itself, with its projecting upper story, built as early as 1490. The house is open daily April–October, and admission is £1.75. Across the street, lose yourself for a few hours in the **Museum of Childhood** (42 High St., tel. 0131/529–4142), which has free exhibits on the history of toys and other childhood issues. On Canongate you'll find two free museums: **People's Story** (163 Canongate, tel. 0131/529–4057), which traces the lives of everyday Edinburgh folk from the 1700s to the present, and across the street, **Huntly House** (tel. 0131/529–4143), which places more emphasis on the well-to-do.

HOLYROOD PALACE

This palace was founded in 1128, though most of the structure dates from the 16th and 17th centuries when it underwent extensive renovations during the reign of Charles II (1660–1685). As it's the official Scottish residence of Her Royal Highness, you're limited to the guided tour. Guides love to play up the murder of David Rizzio, secretary to Mary, Queen of Scots, by her jealous husband, Lord Darnley (who was murdered himself soon afterward). Before Rizzio's demise, he used to visit with the Queen in the midnight hour via the hidden stairs behind her bed (his room was beneath hers). After visiting the palace, wander around the ruins of **Holyrood Abbey,** originally a Norman church. As you leave, look for the brass letters "SSS" set in the road at the beginning of Abbey Strand (by the front gates). The letters stand for "sanctuary," recalling the years 1530–1880 when debtors and assorted criminals enjoyed protection as long as they stayed on the Abbey grounds or in the nearby forest. *East end of Royal Mile, tel. 0131/556–1096. Admission £5.50. Open Apr.–Oct., Mon.–Sat. 9:30–5:15, Sun. 9:30–4:30; Nov.–Mar., Mon.–Sat. 9:30–3:15.*

ARTHUR'S SEAT

This large volcanic hill, and its surrounding park, at the east end of Edinburgh are favorite hiking spots for both locals and tourists. At 823 ft, the summit is accessible to people of all fitness levels (plan on a 45-minute trek from Holyrood Palace) and offers incredible views of Edinburgh and the Firth of Forth. Several small paths along the way lead to further diversions. Turn left on Queen's Drive (the main road encircling the park) from Holyrood Palace to reach the ruins of **St. Anthony's Chapel,** overlooking the swans on St. Margaret's Loch. A path to the right as you cross Queen's Drive takes you under the sheer rock faces of **Salisbury Crags,** a spectacular line of cliffs.

CALTON HILL

You face yet another climb to get to the peculiar monuments atop this East End hill. The cylindrical tower, **Nelson's Monument,** was built to remind the sons of Edinburgh that they are to die for their counry when duty requires it (so says the grim inscription over the entrance). You can climb to the top for £1. Nearby, the wonderfully incongruous, half-completed, Greco-Roman **National Monument** was dubbed Edinburgh's Disgrace when funding ran out before it was completed in the 18th century. Now the center for an annual pagan festival to mark the arrival of spring each May, it gives Edinburgh's skyline an exotic touch at odds with its otherwise prim demeanor. Worth climbing for the views alone—even Robert Louis Stevenson came up here from time to time for inspiration—the hill is probably best avoided at night unless you are heading for the City Observatory, which also sits among this motley collection of monuments.

NATIONAL GALLERY OF SCOTLAND

This gallery along The Mound is a must-see. Pay your respects to the collection of Scottish art and then move on to the vast selection of Continental greats: Velázquez, Raphael, Titian, Rodin, Rembrandt, Degas, Monet, and van Gogh, to name a few. *Foot of the Mound, tel. 0131/556–8921. Admission free. Open Mon.–Sat. 10–5, Sun. 2–5.*

ROYAL BOTANICAL GARDENS

North of New Town, the Royal Botanical Gardens (Inverleith Row, tel. 0131/552–7171) are a must-see treat for the senses. Some of nature's finest offspring are cultivated in the 70 acres of immaculately manicured gardens, including the largest azalea and rhododendron collections in Britain. Meander through the rock garden, where rough terrain and delicate plants combine to form a fairy-tale-like setting, or duck into the greenhouses, which make an especially nice stop if it's raining. A newly opened Chinese garden is the latest draw. The gardens are open daily 10 until sunset, and admission is free. A walk along the nearby **Water of Leith** is also a beautiful stroll. Cross Inverleith Terrace to the Rocheid Path, which winds beside the river as it flows down to the Port of Leith, about 1½ mi away.

THE NATIONAL AND ROYAL MUSEUMS OF SCOTLAND

The splendid new National Museum, with a striking sandstone facade and a large, airy interior, displays artifacts—including many of the country's most treasured pieces—which chronicle the story of Scotland from the first settlers to the 20th century. The adjoining Royal Museum of Scotland, a grand Victorian-style structure, is crammed full of everything from stuffed animals to Chinese art and a fantastic collection of telescopes. In addition to the permanent displays on science, clothing, evolution, and art, the museum also features intriguing special exhibits in the main hall. Though technically separate entities, these two museums are under one roof, so they have the same hours and one admission gets you access to both. *Chambers St., tel. 0131/225–7534. Admission £3 for single entry or £5 for unlimited access for 1 year. Open Mon.–Sat. 10–5, Sun. noon–5.*

ROYAL SCOTTISH ACADEMY

Individual pieces here aren't labeled, so borrow a guide from the front desk if you want to identify the works or their painters. Exhibits vary, but there's generally an annual show of established and amateur Scottish painters, architects, sculptors, and printmakers. *Foot of the Mound, tel. 0131/225–6671. Admission £1.50. Open Mon.–Sat. 10–5, Sun. 2–5.*

SCOTTISH NATIONAL GALLERY OF MODERN ART

One of the truly splendid buildings in Edinburgh, housing an excellent collection of works by modern British, Continental, and Russian artists. Some of the best works are sculptures by Henry Moore and Eduardo Paolozzi, who is the focus of a new extension called the Dean Gallery, situated across the road. Also check out the woodcuts along the hallways. *Belford Rd., tel. 0131/556–8921. From George St., take Bus 13. Admission free. Open Mon.–Sat. 10–5, Sun. 2–5.*

SCOTTISH NATIONAL PORTRAIT GALLERY

In a nutshell, lots of portraits of famous Scots, all housed in a red-sandstone creation modeled on Venice's Doge's Palace. In the same building you'll also find interesting temporary exhibitions (oh, and a great café on the ground floor). *1 Queen St., tel. 0131/556–8921. Admission free. Open Mon.–Sat. 10–5, Sun. 2–5.*

FESTIVALS

Hardly a week goes by without some type of festivity in Edinburgh, though the main event is unquestionably the annual **Edinburgh International Festival** held in the last three weeks of August. Edinburgh lights up for the occasion, and everything stays open into the wee hours. Tickets are on the expensive side for the main venues. For ticket and event info, send a SASE to Edinburgh Festival, 21 Market Street, Edinburgh, EH1 1BW. Starting April 13, you can book tickets by mail. To reserve seats by phone, call 0131/473–2000 after April 22.

The **Fringe Festival** is held during the same three weeks as the International Festival, and has a reputation for being more experimental and alternative than the official festival could hope to achieve. Literally the entire city gives itself over, with performance venues squeezed into every available space. With more than 1,000 different events, the Fringe Festival is becoming almost as well known as the International Festival. For tickets and program information, contact Fringe Festival, 180 High Street, Edinburgh, EH1 1QS, tel. 0131/226–5257, fax 0131/220–4205, admin@edfringe.org.uk.

These festivals only begin to describe Edinburgh in August. **The Edinburgh International Jazz Festival** (116 Canongate, tel. 0131/557–1642), held around the second week, is billed as "one of the great events in the international jazz calendar" by the *Daily Telegraph*. During the last two weeks, filmmakers and screen stars converge on the city for the **Edinburgh International Film Festival** (The Filmhouse, 88 Lothian Rd., tel. 0131/228–2688, filmhouse@cityscape.co.uk). The annual **Edinburgh Book Festival** calls out the town's ecstatic readership; contact the Scottish Book Centre (137 Dundee St., tel. 0131/228–5444, fax 0131/228–4333) or James Thin Booksellers (james.thin.ltd@almac.co.uk) for details.

All this is not to say you're out of luck if you visit Edinburgh earlier in the year. Spring brings the **Peace Festival** (tel. 0131/229–0993), generally held in early March and organized by Amnesty International and the Peace and Justice Resource Center. There's a large-scale community festival in **The Meadows** during the first weekend in June, followed a few weeks later by Scotland's **Lesbian and Gay Pride festival** held alternately in Glasgow and Edinburgh. A reliable source of info for this and other lesbian and gay events is the **West and Wilde Bookshop** (25A Dundas St., tel. 0131/556–0079), or the Blue Moon Café (36 Broughton St., tel. 0131/557–0911). The **Royal Highland Show** (tel. 0131/333–2444), held at the end of June near the airport in Ingliston, showcases Scotland's strong agrarian heritage in a country-fair atmosphere. The **Edinburgh Folk Festival** runs at the end of March, bringing the best in traditional everything from throughout Scotland. For info, contact the Fringe Festival office (*see above*) or **Blackfriars Music** (49 Blackfriars St., tel. 0131/557–3090).

Although all of these festivals actually have some purpose, there is one that exists simply as a good excuse to party! **Hogmanay,** the last day of the year, is celebrated from December 27 to January 1 each year and is one continuous free-form bash. Over a quarter million people flock to the city to sing, dance, and ring in the new year with a little authentic auld lang syne, replete with fireworks on Calton Hill, and large outdoor rock concerts on the Castle esplanade. As you might imagine, you should book accommodations well in advance.

SHOPPING

You will find the standard issue High Street chains in Princes Street, invariably heaving with tourists, unless you walk on the park side, where the landscaped gardens provide a stunning vista of the castle. Leading stores here are Scotland's answer to Harrods, **Jenners** (4 Princes St., tel. 0131/225–2442), the vast **Virgin Megastore** (125 Princes St., tel. 0131/220–2230), and **Waterstones book stores** (14 Princes St., tel. 0131/556–3034; 128 Princes St., tel. 0131/226–2666). Otherwise, take yourself to Victoria Street where the truly sophisticated shop for their provisions: wonderful bread and pastries from the **Auld Alliance** (31 Victoria St., tel. 0131/622–7080), the best in Scottish cheese **from Iain Mellis Cheesemonger** (30 Victoria St., tel. 0131/226–6215), and the antique collector's paradise, **Byzantium** (9 Victoria St., tel. 0131/220–2241), a converted church crowded with antiques shops.

AFTER DARK

Edinburgh's nightlife runs the gamut from well-known pub crawls to the pas de deux of Europe's finest ballet companies. Old Town, especially **Cowgate** and the **Grassmarket** area, features the best selection of alternative-music venues and theaters as well as pubs. *The List* (£1.80), available at any local newsstand, is the bible for everything relating to the arts and music and is indispensable for finding out what's happening in Edinburgh and Glasgow.

PUBS

Pints or drams, Edinburgh is a city of pubs, pubs, and more pubs. Some pubs are licensed until midnight, others until 3 AM; though if you want to drink until 3, you must enter one of these late-night pubs by 12:30

м. Almost all of Edinburgh is patrolled by police officers on foot, making the city relatively safe until the ars close, though be careful in the Cowgate and the Meadows areas, which have rough reputations.

Café Royal Bistro Bar. This popular New Town pub is decorated with rugby memorabilia. Stand at the marble bar and appreciate the classy atmosphere minus the pomp and attitude. *17 West Register St., el. 0131/557–4792.*

Finnegan's Wake. One of the best of the many Irish bars with quite phenomenal nightly live music which often inspires traditional dancing. This place jams. *9B Victoria St., tel. 0131/226–3816.*

Last Drop. This cozy pub is named after its location: the exact spot where public executions were held for centuries. Fall in for a tall one or two. *74/78 Grassmarket, tel. 0131/225–4851.*

Malt Shovel. The selection of brews will make your head spin: 100 malts, eight cask ales, and a dozen local beers on tap. Then you can start on the whiskeys. They host live music Tuesday and Thursday and a quiz show on Monday nights. *11–15 Cockburn St., tel. 0131/235–6843.*

Po-Na-Na. A souk bar, apparently. Flamboyant decor featuring a tented ceiling has attracted a regular crowd on weekends, when queuing is usually necessary. A £3 charge for admission after 11 PM may seem off-putting but obviously not off-putting enough. *43B Frederick St., tel. 0131/226–2224.*

Rose St. Brewery. As you stumble along your Rose Street pub crawl, stop in for a home brew at the only spot in Edinburgh that makes its own beer. *57 Rose St., tel. 0131/220–1227.*

Tron Tavern & Ceilidh House. Its three levels are always mobbed. Pay a small cover to see jazz and folk on the bottom floor (no cover Tuesday and Friday) or listen to the fiddlers who occasionally play on the middle level. *9 Hunter Sq., tel. 0131/667- -2491.*

Whistle Binkies. Who knows what goes on in the dark back rooms, but in the front you can experience live R&B, rock, or comedy. Whistle Binkies is conveniently located one street over from the High Street Hostel, and it stays open until 3 AM. *4 South Bridge, tel. 0131/557–5114.*

MUSIC AND CLUBS

Kitchen (235 Cowgate, tel. 0131/225–5473) is a small and crowded, loud and smoky disco. If you feel like dancing, the grooves last until 3 AM, and there's no cover. **The Venue** (Calton Rd., tel. 0131/557–3073) is probably the loudest and most lively joint in town. Its three floors feature big-name bands and a variety of one nighters. A harder-edged crowd gathers at dark-and-smoky **Sneeky Pete's** (73 Lower Cowgate, Old Town, tel. 0131/225–1757) to listen to loud live rock. The unassuming, down-to-earth **Preservation Hall** (9B Victoria St., Old Town, tel. 0131/226–3816) hosts different music every night, but leans toward jazz, blues, and R&B.

GAY VENUES

The Broughton neighborhood, on the northeast side of New Town, is widely recognized as a gay community with a vibrant café culture that has developed rapidly in the last few years. Choose between a frothy café latte in **Cafe Kudos** (Greenside Pl., tel. 0131/558–1270), with it's warm, friendly crowd, or something stronger next door at **C C Blooms,** which has free disco most evenings and plenty of dark corners. Other venues in the vicinity include **Route 66** (6 Baxter's Pl., tel. 0131/556–5991), the **New Town Club,** with a slightly older crowd, and Edinburgh's most popular gay watering hole, the **Blue Moon** (36 Broughton St., tel. 0131/557–0911), which has excellent all-day breakfasts among other things, and tends to get crowded on weekends. For clubbing, try **Bent 100%** (369 Gallery, Cowgate).

THEATER

It's long been an inaccurate complaint that Edinburgh discovers culture for only three weeks in the year, meaning the numerous visiting troupes during the Festival. In fact, the sheer vitality of the city's home-grown talent provides many theater events worth catching during the year. Many theaters either don't have their own ensembles or only produce a few shows per season. The rest of the time they act as venues for touring companies like Communicado, Fifth Estate, and Benchtours—all very innovative and all badly funded.

Major theater venues include the classically minded **Royal Lyceum Theatre** (30 Grindlay St., tel. 0131/229–9697). **Theatre Workshop** (34 Hamilton Pl., tel. 0131/226–5425), a 10-minute walk north of Princes Street, produces more contemporary works. **Traverse** (Cambridge St., tel. 0131/228–1404) is similar in content but a bit more upscale; tickets are £8. **Netherbow Arts Centre** (43 High St., tel. 0131/556–9579) is a small contemporary forum in the John Knox House complex. Tickets range £2–£6. For comedy and musicals, try the **Gilded Balloon** (233 Cowgate, tel. 0131/226–6550).

FILM

The Filmhouse (88 Lothian Rd., tel. 0131/228–2688), south of Princes Street's west end, screens alter native international films, both current and older. Tickets run £2.80–£5.20, but can go as high as £7.00 during the Film Festival in August. For late-night cult classics, as well as independent films, try **Cameo Cinema** (Home St., Tollcross, tel. 0131/228–4141).

NEAR EDINBURGH

LINLITHGOW PALACE

The small village of Linlithgow, 30 minutes west of Edinburgh by train, is home to **Linlithgow Palace,** birthplace of Mary, Queen of Scots, in 1542. Although the original timber roof and wooden floors are gone (they were torched by the English in 1746), the castle's weathered walls and turrets remain. All in all, it's the dreamy setting of the castle's well-tended park and loch—rather than the castle itself—that'll stick in your brain. InterCity trains run between Edinburgh and Linlithgow until midnight (£3.10 single). Bluebird Coaches also stop near the castle. *Tel. 01324–623985. From train station, walk down embankment, turn left on High St., left at tourist office, and go uphill. Admission £2.50. Open Mon.–Sun., 9:30–4:30, (Apr.–Sept., until 6:30).*

NORTH BERWICK

This pleasant seaside village with spectacular views makes a great day trip, and it's easily accessed by train from Edinburgh (15 per day, 30 mins, £4 return). Stroll through the town's narrow streets to the sandy beaches or across the park and up to **The Law,** a 612-ft conical hill with ruins of a lookout from the Napoleonic wars; it's about a 40-minute walk from town, and the impressive views are well worth the effort. The spectacular **Bass Rock,** 3 mi from the coast, has been used as both a successful fortress and an unsuccessful prison: A group of Jacobite prisoners seized control of the prison in 1694, holding it for three years before finally surrendering. Bass Rock is now home to many and various seabirds. Another popular breeding ground for seabirds is **Fidra,** the horseshoe-shape island west of North Berwick. Stop by the helpful **tourist office** (Quality St., at East Rd., tel. 01620/892197) for more information on the area's sights, boat trips to watch the birds or seals, and lodging options. While you're here, don't miss the deep-fried bliss at **North Berwick Fry,** next to the tourist office, for a large portion of scrumptious fish-and-chips. The popular sandstone **Tantallon Castle** (tel. 01620/892727) sits on a spectacular cliff overlooking the entrance to the Firth of Forth, about 2½ mi to the east. A group of the "Red" Douglasses successfully held the castle against attacks by two Scottish kings, which didn't stop Cromwell's General Monk from blasting the site in 1651. Admission to the castle is £2.50.

DUNFERMLINE

Dunfermline, just over the Firth of Forth from Edinburgh, was the capital of Scotland for 500 years. If you're into the bloody complexities of aristocratic power-brokering, you couldn't choose a better day trip. Visit the **Dunfermline Palace and Abbey** (£1.80), where Robert the Bruce is buried—except for his heart, which is at Melrose Abbey (*see* The Borders *in* Southern Scotland, *below*). See some of the underwater wonders of Scotland's seas at **Deep Sea World** national aquarium (North Queensferry, tel. 01383/411880), where local and tropical creatures are on display. Admission is £6.15 for adults, and £4.25 for concessions. Andrew Carnegie, the American railroad and metal magnate, was born in town, and you can visit his **birthplace** on St. Margaret Street for free.

GLASGOW

Glasgow was founded in the Middle Ages and slowly coalesced from the sprawl of several neighboring villages. It wasn't until the Union of Parliaments between England and Scotland in 1707, however, that Glasgow had its first taste of wealth via the tobacco trade with the American colonies. Things really got going during the Industrial Revolution, when Glasgow's rapidly expanding shipbuilding and coal mining industries caused the city's population to grow from 80,000 in 1801 to more than 700,000 in 1901, confirming Glasgow's place as "Second City of the Empire." Today the legacy of Victorian optimism is apparent in the opulent architecture along Glasgow's well-planned squares and crescents. Remnants of the

GLASGOW

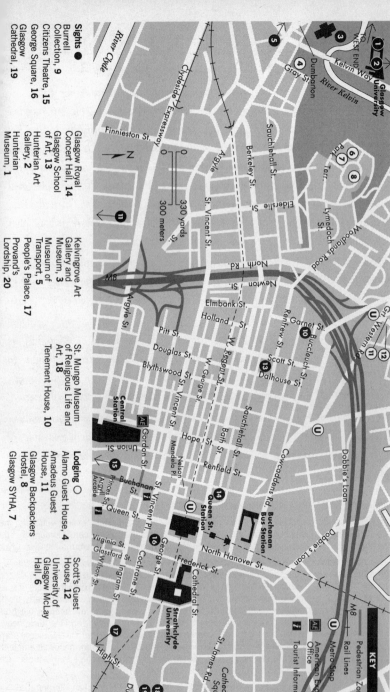

Sights ●
Burrell
Collection, **9**
Citizens Theatre, **15**
George Square, **16**
Glasgow
Cathedral, **19**

Glasgow Royal
Concert Hall, **14**
Glasgow School
of Art, **13**
Hunterian Art
Gallery, **2**
Hunterian
Museum, **1**

Kelvingrove Art
Gallery and
Museum, **3**
Museum of
Transport, **5**
People's Palace, **17**
Provand's
Lordship, **20**

St. Mungo Museum
of Religious Life and
Art, **18**
Tenement House, **10**

Lodging ○
Alamo Guest House, **4**
Amadeus Guest
House, **11**
Glasgow Backpackers
Hostel, **8**
Glasgow SYHA, **7**

Scott's Guest
House, **12**
University of
Glasgow McLay
Hall, **6**

River Clyde

TO
WEST END
Kelvin Way

Glasgow
University

River Kelvin

Dumbarton
Gray St.

Finnieston St.

N

330 yards
300 meters

Clydeside Expressway

Sauchiehall St.
Berkeley St.
Elderslie St.
Lynedoch St.
Woodlands Road
Park Terr.

Argyle

St. Vincent St.

M8

Argyle St.

North St.
Newton St.

Garnet St.
Buccleuch St.
Renfrew St.
Scott St.
Dalhouse St.

Elmbank St.
Holland St.
W. Regent St.
W. George St.

Pitt St.
Douglas St.
Blythswood St.
Sauchiehall St.
Bath St.
Hope St.
Renfield St.

Central
Station

Gordon St.
Union St.

St. Vincent St.
Nelson Mandela Pl.

Cowcaddens Rd.

Dobbie's Loan

Buchanan
Bus Station

Queen St.
Station

Buchanan St.
St. Vincent Pl.
Argyll Arcade
Princes Sq.
Queen St.

Virginia St.
Glassford St.
G. Wilson St.
Ingram St.
Cochrane St.
George St.

Frederick St.
North Hanover St.
Cathedral St.

Strathclyde
University

High St.

Duke St.

Cathedral Square
St. James Rd.

M8

KEY
Pedestrian Zone
Rail Lines
Metro Stop
American Express
Tourist Information

365

CHARLES RENNIE MACKINTOSH

Charles Rennie Mackintosh was a turn-of-the-century renaissance man, an accomplished architect, painter, and master of interior arts. He surrounded himself with the most talented of Glasgow's artistic community, including his wife, Margaret MacDonald, a painter, sculptor, and designer. Underappreciated in his own day, Mackintosh is now revered by Glaswegians, who view his works as Glasgow's principal attractions. Join one of the many different bus and walking tours run by the Charles Rennie Mackintosh Society (870 Garscube Rd., tel. 0141/946–6600) or pick up one of their brochures and explore at your own pace; either way, be sure to see these stunning buildings:

Glasgow School of Art. See students mill about and paint, keeping the spirit of Mackintosh alive in a building without equal. Call ahead for times and to reserve a space since tours fill up fast. 167 Renfrew St., tel. 0141/353–4526. Admission by guided tour only, £5.

The Hill House (located in Helensburgh, 23 mi northwest of Glasgow), is Mackintosh's masterpiece. Take a train from Queen Street Station to Helensburgh Central, from where the House is all up hill. Upper Colquhoun St., Helensburgh, tel. 01436/673900. Admission £6. Open Apr.–Oct., daily 1:30–5.

The Mackintosh House, within the Hunterian Art Gallery at the University of Glasgow, is a reconstruction of Mackintosh's home, with excellent examples of his furnishings. Hillhead St., tel. 0141/330–5431. Admission free. Open Mon.– Sat. 9:30–5.

early medieval villages persist as well; for though Glaswegians stand together against outsiders, they swiftly align themselves along burgh and precinct lines when left to themselves, demonstrating that this huge metropolis is really a collection of smaller settlements all mashed together around the River Clyde.

Glasgow's history is intertwined with its blue-collar industries, and the resulting working-class heritage is felt everywhere: from its long leadership in Socialist, Marxist, and Labor politics to its innovative Citizens Theatre and shop signs that proclaim themselves workers' cooperatives. It also bears the scars of failed social programs and the typical urban pressures of a large industrialized nation: rampant poverty, blocks of massive postwar concrete tenements, and a serious problem with violent crime in some neighborhoods (most in the form of gang conflicts). Fortunately, behind the tough attitude and the thick, heavily accented slang, Glaswegians are among the friendliest folks in the land. You'll find a lively student scene and a greater diversity of ethnicities here than anywhere else in Scotland. This cosmopolitan ambience along with the bustle of pedestrian traffic gives an excited anticipatory atmosphere to the streets. One can't avoid the feeling that things are happenin' here . . . and rapidly.

The Lighthouse. Mackintosh's first public commission, now restored and housing an Interpretation Centre on his life and achievements. 11 Mitchell Lane, tel. 0141/221–6362. Admission £2.50. Open Mon.– Sat. 10:30–6, Sun. noon–5.

here's a distinct sense that Glasgow is a city undergoing a modern renaissance, a metamorphosis predicted by the 90-year-old Scottish poet William Montgomerie: "Out of this ugliness may come/Some day, so beautiful a flower/That men will wonder at the hour/Remembering smoke and flowerless scum." Glasgow is indeed on the cusp of being reborn from the ashes of its former industrialism in true phoenix-like fashion as a technological giant of the electronic age. To match this new image of a modern metropolis, the city is undergoing dozens of massive construction projects, and scaffolding decorates the city almost as much as the ubiquitous banners and flags. The city's commitment to its architectural heritage and contemporary chic was reinforced by its reign as British City of Architecture and Design 1999. This current burst of optimism, combined with the presence of three large universities, makes for Scotland's best and wildest nightlife. You'll also find celebrations of the "Glasgow Style" and of turn-of-the-century art nouveau architect Charles Rennie Mackintosh. Moreover, Glasgow is a convenient transportation hub for the Isle of Arran and Kintyre Peninsula and is the perfect base for day trips to Ayrshire.

BASICS

AMERICAN EXPRESS

This central office provides the usual services for cardholders. *115 Hope St., G2 6LX, tel. 0141/221–4366. Open weekdays 8:30– 5:30, Sat. 9–noon.*

DISCOUNT TRAVEL AGENCIES

Usit Campus Travel. This should be your first stop for rail and bus passes and for cheap flights. *Two locations: 122 George St., tel. 0141/553–1818. Open weekdays 9–5:30 (Tues. from 10), Sat. 10–5; Glasgow University, The Hub, Hillhead St., tel. 0141/357–0608. Open weekdays 9:30–5 (Wed. from 10).*

The Lothians is the collective name given to the swath of countryside surrounding Edinburgh. Here the River Forth snakes across a floodplain on its descent from the Highlands.

Other local discount travel agencies include the ever-friendly **STA Travel** (90 John St., tel. 0141/552–8808) on the third floor of the Strathclyde University student union, **Trailfinders** (254–270 Sauchiehall St., tel. 0141/353–2224), and **Lunn Poly** (270–284 Sauchiehall St., tel. 0141/353–3532).

GAY AND LESBIAN RESOURCES

Strathclyde Gay and Lesbian Switchboard (tel. 0141/221–8372) offers counseling nightly from 7 to 10. **Glasgow Gay & Lesbian Centre** (tel. 0141/221–7203) is a good first point of contact through the day (10 AM–2 PM). Try the **Polo Lounge** (84 Wilson St., tel. 0141/553–1221) if you're just looking for new friends. The **Women's Library** (109 Trongate), open weekday afternoons, carries all sorts of regional and international women's publications. Pick up a copy of *Scotgay* magazine at gay cafés and bars for the latest on what's going on.

MAIL

Buy stamps and such at the **General Post Office,** which also handles poste restante. *47 St Vincent St., G2, tel. 0345/223344. Open weekdays 8:30–5:45, Sat. 9–5:30.*

MEDICAL AID

The Royal Infirmary (82 Castle St., tel. 0141/211–4000) provides 24-hour medical care. **Vantage Pharmacy,** in Queen Street Station, is open Monday–Saturday 8:30–5. Also look out for **Boots** at 200 Sauchiehall Street, tel. 0141/332–0774.

VISITOR INFORMATION

A 10-minute walk from Central Station, the superfriendly **Tourist Information Centre** offers free bookings for local B&Bs, hotels, and some hostels. Make the "Guide to Getting Around Glasgow" the first thing you pick up. It's a free map of the city and gives information on Strathclyde public transport. The office also has coach and ferry schedules and sells bus and train tickets. **Glasgow Airport** has a branch office, open daily 7:30–6. 11 George Square, tel. 0141/204–4400. From Central Station, walk north on Union St. (which becomes Renfield St.), turn right on St. Vincent St. and follow this to George Square. *Open July–Sept., Mon.–Sat. 9–8, Sun. 10–6;. May, Mon.–Sat. 9–6, Sun. 10–6; June, Mon.–Sat. 9–7, Sun. 10–6; Oct.–Apr., Mon.–Sat. 9–6.*

COMING AND GOING

BY BUS

The large, refurbished **Buchanan Station** (North Hanover and Killermont Sts., tel. 0141/332–7133), two blocks north of Queen Street Station, serves destinations throughout Scotland and England, as well as local routes. Buchanan's tourist desk is open daily 8–6. From Buchanan, **Citylink** (tel. 0990/505050), runs frequent buses to Edinburgh (70 mins, £4:50 single, £7 return), while **National Express** (0990/808080) offers £25 return fares to London to those with a Discount Coachcard (*see* Getting Around *in* Basics, *above*). **Silver Choice** (tel. 01355/249249) offers good deals to London for £24 return; there is one departure a day at 10 PM. **Stagecoach Western** (tel. 01387/253469) runs buses to Ayrshire, Dumfries, and Galloway for about £8–£10, and **Skye-Ways** (tel. 01599/534328) offers buses to Skye (£26 return).

BY PLANE

Glasgow Airport (tel. 0141/887–1111), 10 mi west of the city, handles the bulk of flights to and from London, Ireland, the Continent, and the United States. **British Airways** (tel. 0345/222111) flies many domestic routes, such as the daily Glasgow–Kirkwall hop (£135 return). Bus 501 connects the airport with Buchanan Station (25 mins, £2.50) and Edinburgh. The airport has a tourist center and an accommodations-booking service. **Prestwick Airport** (tel. 01292/479822) has a few domestic and international flights but is less convenient—it's 30 mi south of the city in Ayrshire, just over a mile north of Ayr. You can reach Prestwick by train from Central Station or by bus from Buchanan Station.

BY TRAIN

Central and Queen Street stations are about ½ mi apart from one another in the center of town. A shuttle bus (50p) connects the two stations every 15 minutes between 8 AM and 7 PM (there's no Sunday service), but it's as quick to walk.

Between Hope Street and Union Street, **Central Station** handles train travel to southwest Scotland and England, with many Virgin Rail connections to London (5 hrs, £69 return, £29 with 7-day advance purchase) via Birmingham and Carlisle. Destinations within Scotland include Wemyss Bay for the Isle of Bute, Androssan for the Isle of Arran, Stranraer (£23 return) for Northern Ireland, and towns throughout Dumfries and Galloway. **Queen Street Station** (corner West George and Queen Sts.) serves Edinburgh (20 per day, 45 mins, £6.95 single) and the north, including Oban (£22 return), Fort William (£36 return), and Mallaig. Fares will vary depending on the time of day, but keep an eye out for occasional special offers.

GETTING AROUND

The majority of Glasgow's sights and nightlife are in the city center and the West End, both north of the River Clyde. Each is easily walkable in and of itself, and the Underground conveniently links the two. **George Square** is the heart of the city center, with nearby **Sauchiehall** (pronounced SOCK-ee-hall) **Street** branching out west all the way to the West End. If you're willing to walk a bit, you can avoid the terror of trying to comprehend Glasgow's public transport network (there are 17 different bus companies). Like any major city, Glasgow has its tough and dangerous neighborhoods: Glasgow Green should be avoided after dark, and the south bank of the Clyde, a light-industrial area, can be troublesome.

Day Tripper tickets (£7.50) allow one adult and up to two children virtually unlimited travel on rail and bus lines as far south as Ayr and as far east as Lanark. For an additional £5.50 you can increase that to two adults and up to four children. The same thing goes for **Zonecards,** which allow unlimited travel on rail and bus in however many zones you buy the ticket for. The minimum ticket issued is for one week, is good for two zones, and costs £11. **Roundabout Glasgow** (£3.50) tickets get you one day's unlimited Underground service and free travel on some ScotRail lines. **Strathclyde Transport Travel Centre** (St. Enoch Sq., tel. 0141/332– 7133) can help you with routes, passes, and schedules throughout the Strathclyde region and accepts phone queries Monday–Saturday 7 AM–9:30 PM, Sunday 9–9:30.

BY BIKE

Rent bikes from **Dales** (150 Dobbies Loan, tel. 0141/332 2705) for a minimum of £25 for a two-day hire or **West End Cycles** (16 Chancellor St., tel. 0141/357–1344) for £12 per day.

Y BUS

...ere are 17 bus companies in the city, but most people rely on **First Bus**'s (tel. 0141/636–3195) ...ange, red, or white buses that cover almost every corner of the city. Most trips around the city cost ...out 65p. Strathclyde runs a night bus service on selected routes until about 3 AM. Each bus line offers ...s own passes; check with the Strathclyde Transport Travel Centre to see if any will suit your purposes.

Y TAXI

...lack cabs are plentiful but not cheap. Expect to pay £1.60 for the first half-mile and £1 for each mile ...hereafter. Private taxis, which you must order by phone (tel. 0141/357–2222), are slightly cheaper. ...otherwise, **Black Cabs** (tel. 0141/332–7070 or 0141/332– 6666) is a good bet.

BY UNDERGROUND

The **Underground's** (tel. 0141/332–7133) bright orange cars follow a circular route, earning the subway system the nickname Clockwork Orange. Fifteen stations, each marked by a giant orange U ring the city center, linking it with the West End and the South Side (south of the River Clyde). The Underground runs Monday–Saturday 6:30 AM–10:45 PM, Sunday 11–6. A single fare is 65p, but you can get day passes for unlimited travel for £2.50 at the Strathclyde Transport Travel Centre (*see above*).

WHERE TO SLEEP

Cheap, conveniently located beds can be hard to find in Glasgow (especially in summer) if you don't book ahead. The best hunting grounds for B&Bs are in the West End area, particularly Hillhead Street and just north of Kelvinbridge University.

Despite Glasgow's 1,400-year history, there are surprisingly few physical traces of the years before 1700. Two great fires in the 1600s devastated whole areas of the city.

Otherwise, book a B&B through a tourist office or at the kiosk in the bus station. In a pinch, try **Alamo Guest House** (46 Gray St., tel. 0141/339– 2395), which has a great location by Kelvingrove Park and the art gallery. Singles are £24, doubles £22 per person.

Amadeus Guest House (411 N. Woodside Rd., tel. 0141/339–8257), across the street from the university, is very friendly and homey. You get your own key and pay £18 for a single, £40 for a double, £51 for a triple. Next door, **Scott's Guest House** (417 N. Woodside Rd., tel. 0141/339–3750) has singles for £25, doubles for £35, or £37 for en suite rooms.

HOSTELS

Glasgow Backpackers Hostel. This excellent independent hostel is in the University of Glasgow's Kelvin Lodge residence hall. The spacious rooms have proper beds with real mattresses, and there are two lounges for hanging out. Beds are £9.50 in dorms, rising to £11.50 in twin rooms. *Kelvin Lodge, 8 Park Circus, G3 6AX, tel. 0141/332–5412. Take underground to St. George's Cross, walk south on St. George's Cross, turn right on Woodlands Rd., left on Lynedoch St., and continue to Park Circus Pl. (which becomes Park Circus). 50 beds. Kitchen, laundry. Closed late-Sept.–June. Cash only.*

Glasgow SYHA. This well-located hostel is in a gorgeous West End building (formerly a luxury hotel) near Kelvingrove Park. It's a super-busy place and way too popular with school groups, so book ahead. They also run an **SYHA Annex** (11 Woodlands Terr., tel. 0141/332–3004 or 0141/332–5007) mid-July–September in one of the university dorms. It's cheaper to stay in the annex, but they won't book anyone there until the main hostel is full. Higher Standard. *7 Park Terr., G3 6BY, tel. 0141/332–3004 or 0141/ 332–5007. Follow directions to Glasgow Backpackers Hostel (see above). 158 beds. Cash only.*

STUDENT HOUSING

University of Glasgow McLay Hall. It's just around the corner from the SYHA and Glasgow Backpackers hostels, so if they're full you can try here. Self-catering rooms are £13. Call to inquire if there is any minimum length of stay. *18 Park Terr., tel. 0141/330–5385. 2,500 rooms. Closed Oct.–May (except open at Easter).*

FOOD

Glasgow has the best variety of restaurants in Scotland, with everything from exceptional Indian and Caribbean joints to 1950s American diners. Glasgow also has an especially rich tearoom tradition. The best pubs, cafés, and cheap ethnic eats can be found on **Byres Road** in the West End, the **Hillhead** area

by Glasgow University, and on **Sauchiehall Street.** If you're cooking your own food, there's a Safeway
Byres Road at Grosvenor Lane, as well as many groceries, bakeries, and markets on Great Weste
Road and Sauchiehall Street. **Grassroots** (20 Woodlands Rd., tel. 0141/353– 3278) is a workers' coc
erative and whole-food store that specializes in macrobiotic food and stocks everything from sushi
vegan haggis (which, incidentally, is a great name for a Scottish alt-rock band).

UNDER £5 • Bay Tree Café. Nowhere else is quite like the Bay Tree, where a calm ambience ai
Middle Eastern dishes make it an ideal daytime venue for long afternoons. *403 Great Western Rd., te*
0141/334–5898. Cash only.

Insomnia. One of the few places in Scotland that never closes, this haven for night owls is located nea
Kelvingrove Park and some hostels. Try the daily specials, like the broccoli and almond quiche, or yo
can just get soup and a sandwich. There's also an adjacent deli with provisions and alcohol. *38–4*
Woodland Rd., tel. 0141/564–1700. Open 24 hrs. Cash only.

Tinderbox. A very, very cool place to hang out, with Vespa scooters parked outside and CD booths fo
those who like getting wired to sound as well as various styles of designer caffeine. Trendy food like mas
carpone and pepper bagels as well as a dizzying variety of Italian breads and sandwiches attracts a cul
following until 10 PM. *189 Byres Rd., near the university, tel. 0141/339–3108. Cash only.*

Toast. In the heart of the stylish Merchant City they couldn't get away without foccacia and ciabatta on
the menu, too. But toast is what they do and they do it best here, notably in the £3.95 all-day breakfast—bacon and eggs and lots of you know what. *84–86 Albion St., tel. 0141/552–3044. Cash only.*

Willow Tea Rooms. It's slightly pricier than most tearooms, but you're paying for the amazing art nouveau atmosphere in this striking Charles Rennie Mackintosh–designed space. If you want to splurge, try
the afternoon tea (£7.25). *Two locations: 217 Sauchiehall St., tel. 0141/332–6521; 97 Buchanan St.,*
tel. 0141/204 5242. Cash only.

UNDER £10 • Ashoka. Some of Glasgow's great Indian food can be found at this popular late-night
spot. The menu is replete with favorites like lamb curry and mixed vegetable biryani. *19 Ashton La., off*
Byres Rd., tel. 0141/357–1115. Cash only.

Café Antipasti. Bohemian, wonderfully atmospheric city eatery on two levels. Everyone from couples to
families comes here to enjoy the heart-melting tiramisu, and so should you. *337 Byres Rd., tel. 0141/*
337–2737. Cash only.

Café Gandolfi@CCA (Center for Contemporary Arts). It's the hip, avant-garde place to be on
Sauchiehall Street. It's also a bookstore, late-night wine bar, and first-rate restaurant. Current favorites
include avocado fritters, and baked brie with a raspberry coulis. *350 Sauchiehall St., tel. 0141/332–*
7864. Cash only.

Firebird. Not far from the youth hostels on Park Terrace, this place serves spectacularly tasty crispy
crust pizzas cooked in a wood-burning oven. The popular bar rocks on weekends with guest DJs spinning 'til midnight. *1321 Argyle St., tel. 0141/334–0594.*

Havana. This spot is close as you can get to Cuba without choking on Fidel's cigar smoke. Before you
hit the dance floor, fuel up on three tapas for £8.50 or tasty tortilla wraps for £6, served to the rhythms
of obligatory salsa and rumba numbers. *50 Hope St., tel. 0141/248–4466. Cash only.*

Kama Sutra. Part of the Akosha group of Indian restaurants, the groovy decor is based around,
well . . . love—the menu even includes cocktails with names such as Lingam and Yoni (ask the bar-
tender). Chicken Tikka Nawabi, and Lamb Pardesi are two menu favorites in this very cool joint. *331*
Sauchiehall St., tel. 0141/332–0055.

WORTH SEEING

Glasgow is extremely committed to high art and low prices, something that's immediately apparent from
the array of excellent and, largely, free museums. One of Glasgow's finest sights is the exquisitely preserved architecture of the **Victorian West End.** Walk about the crescents of the Kelvinbridge area (near
the SYHA and Backpackers hostels) for the best examples. Some spectacular architecture can also be
seen down in the **Merchant City** area between the Queen Street Station and the River Clyde. John Carrick, Glasgow's city architect from 1862 to 1890, had a huge influence on this area. Robert Adam and
David Hamilton also contributed to the city's grandeur, which is most evident along its rooftops. Pick up
some of the five architectural walking-tour brochures covering different sights such as "Hidden Glas-

w" and "Eat, Drink, and Design" at the tourist office. These tours were designed in 1999 to celebrate
asgow's year as Britain's City of Architecture.

URRELL COLLECTION

his is Scotland's best art collection, located about 3 mi southwest of the city in **Pollock Country Park.**
he treasure chest of a single collector, Sir William Burrell (a shipping magnate who died in the 1950s),
consists of a hodgepodge of art from the ancient Near East, Asia, and Europe. Medieval tapestries and
ained-glass windows win raves, as do the French impressionist paintings. *2060 Pollokshaws Rd., tel.*
141/649–7151. From Central Station, take train to Pollokshaws West. Or take Bus 45, 48, or 57 to the
ark entrance and catch the free shuttle bus. Admission free. Open Mon.–Sat. 10–5, Sun. 11–5.

GEORGE SQUARE

he official center of town has statues of just about everyone—including exceptional equestrian bronzes
of Victoria and Albert—except for its namesake, King George III. (The pillar originally intended for King
George was inexplicably topped by a statue of Sir Walter Scott instead.) The statues are set off by large,
colorful flower beds, and plenty of benches make this a great place to sit and gawk at other tourists.

GLASGOW CATHEDRAL

Dark and medieval, Glasgow Cathedral was nearly destroyed
during the Reformation, when opulent cathedrals were on the
outs. The townspeople rioted, however, sparing the cathedral
from being plundered for material to build houses. The cathedral dates from the 12th century, while the site is said to have
been consecrated by St. Ninian in the 4th century—the vol-
unteer guides have all the details. Step out behind the cathedral to the **Necropolis,** an eerie and ostentatious hilltop
cemetery that was the place to be buried in Victorian Glasgow.
Though it's in slight disrepair, it still has the best view of the
city. Cathedral guides advise against coming here alone at
night as heavy drinkers and drug takers are known to kick off

Glasgow is certainly the only city anywhere with minibuses boldly marked YOUR WEE HAPPY BUS. *University students, for one, know the phrase all to well: A full 75 percent of them live at home and commute to school.*

their evening at this spot getting stoned among the tombstones. *Castle St., tel. 0141/552–6891. Admis-*
sion free. Open Apr.–Sept., Mon.–Sat. 9:30–6, Sun. 2–5; Oct.–Mar., Mon.–Sat. 9:30–4, Sun. 2–4.

GLASGOW SCHOOL OF ART

Architects and designers come from all over the world to admire this, Charles Rennie Mackintosh's architectural masterpiece. Mackintosh designed the entire building, inside and out, for a £15,000 commission
when he was only 28 years old. Because it's a working school of art, access is limited unless you take one
of the excellent tours (£5) offered weekdays at 11 and 2 and on Saturday at 10:30 and 11:30; call ahead
to reserve a space. On the tour you'll see the fabulous **Furniture Gallery** and **Library,** each outfitted with
prime examples of Mackintosh's interior-design work. *167 Renfrew St., tel. 0141/353–4526.*

GLASGOW UNIVERSITY

The main building on campus, designed by Sir George Gilbert Scott, is an enormous Gothic-style structure with a 300-ft-tall tower that dominates the skyline above Kelvingrove Park. The university has a long
tradition of producing some of Scotland's leading thinkers, including famed economist Adam Smith and
the inventor James Watt, who made substantial improvements on the steam engine and coined the term
"horsepower." May–September, tours (£2) leave from the visitor center located in the main building
Wednesday, Friday, and Saturday at 11 and 2 (October–April, Wednesday only at 2). *Tel. 0141/330–*
5511. Open Mon.–Sat. 9:30–5 (May–Sept., also Sun. 2–5).

Afterward, wander over to the **Hunterian Museum** and **the Hunterian Art Gallery,** across the street from
each other on University Avenue in the center of campus. They both house the collections of William
Hunter, an acquisitive 18th-century Glasgow doctor who studied here. The museum, the oldest public
museum in Scotland, displays Hunter's hoards of coins, manuscripts, scientific instruments, and
archaeological artifacts—even a dinosaur. The gallery, distinctly more engaging, houses the doctor's art
collection, which includes prints and drawings by Reynolds, Rodin, Rembrandt, and Tintoretto, one of
the largest collections of James McNeill Whistler's work, and a strong selection of 19th- and 20th-cen-
tury Scottish painters. The highlight by far is **Mackintosh House** (*see box, above*), a reconstruction of
the architect's home. *Tel. 0141/330–4221 for museum or 0141/330–5431 for gallery. Admission free.*
Both open Mon.–Sat. 9:30–5.

KELVINGROVE ART GALLERY AND MUSEUM

The architectural plans of this huge, red-sandstone, turn-of-the-century building were mistake. turned around, and the error wasn't discovered until its massive foundation had already been laid. T museum had to be built back to front, and the architect became so distraught over this folly that he tc his own life. The collection inside is superb, including a natural history exhibit, an exhibit dedicated the main forces behind the Glasgow Style, an impressive armor collection, and some Dutch master among other things. *West end of Sauchiehall St., Kelvingrove Park, tel. 0141/287–2699. Admissie free. Open Mon.–Sat. 10–5, Sun. 11–5.*

MUSEUM OF TRANSPORT

If the broughams and boxcars on the ground floor of this immense brick building don't get you excited try the Nortons, Triumphs, "Easter Egg on Roller Skates," and other British rarities upstairs. You'll als. find a large exhibit on British shipbuilding with scale models and great quotes from the letters of me. who worked in the shipyards. *Kelvin Hall, 1 Bunhouse Rd., across from Kelvingrove Art Gallery an Museum, tel. 0141/287–2720. Admission free. Open Mon.–Sat. 10–5, Sun. 11–5.*

PEOPLE'S PALACE

This excellent museum in Glasgow Green tells the city's history, with an emphasis on Glasgow's industrial heritage and political controversies. Each floor chronicles a different era, from the Middle Ages to the 20th century. *Glasgow Green, tel. 0141/554– 0223. Admission free. Open Mon.–Sat. 10–5, Sun. 11–5.*

PROVAND'S LORDSHIP

Glasgow's oldest surviving house (circa 1471) is thought to have been built for a priest and 12 men who ran a nearby hospice. It was later abandoned and used by some of Glasgow's indigents. Nineteenth-century newspaper articles hanging in one of the rooms commemorate some of these well-known "street people." All in all, it's interesting if you have time to kill around Cathedral Square. *3 Castle St., tel. 0141/552–8819. Admission free. Open Mon.–Sat. 10–5, Sun. 11–5.*

ST. MUNGO MUSEUM OF RELIGIOUS LIFE AND ART

St. Mungo's has a heavy focus on religion through icons, artwork, artifacts, and interviews. Atheists may come away feeling vindicated or enraged, but it's worth a visit for the Salvador Dalí artwork. *2 Castle St., tel. 0141/553–2557. Admission free. Open Mon.–Sat. 10–5, Sun. 11–5.*

THE TENEMENT HOUSE

This Victorian flat was built in 1892, and Miss Agnes Toward lived here from 1911 to 1965, changing very little beyond the light fixtures. Now it's an impressive window on life in Glasgow's tenements during the early 20th century. The gas lamps are a modern addition, but most everything else—from the kitchenware to the ration books—are genuine relics of a bygone era. *145 Buccleuch St., tel. 0141/333–0183. Admission £3.20. Open Mar.–Oct., daily 2–5.*

FESTIVALS

Glasgow, like Edinburgh, seems to have both "official" and impromptu festivals nearly every day during summer, although the city's big arts jamboree, **Mayfest,** came a cropper (read: died) a couple of years back. Nothing on its scale is set to replace it, but events such as the **West End Festival** (tel. 0141/341–0844), which takes place over two weeks in June in the city's trendy university quarter, mix homespun charm with acts of genuine quality.

Glasgow also hosts a series of excellent music festivals throughout the year. In January **Celtic Connections** (tel. 0141/332–6633) is a celebration of Celtic music from around the world. The **Big Big Country** festival (tel. 0141/287–4000) doesn't just feature country music, but all sorts of Americana, including Cuban rhumba and blues. The first week of July draws noted jazz and blues greats, like Al Green, B. B. King, and Max Roach, to the banks of the Clyde for the Glasgow International Jazz Festival (tel. 0141/552–3552). Don't ask what the World Pipe Band Championships (tel. 0141/221–5414) are like—just make every effort to catch a few performances during the mid-August pipe fest. **Glasgay!** (held early November) is a popular lesbian and gay arts festival. For details, access the Festival's Web site at www.glasgay.com.uk or call/fax 0141/204–0741.

SHOPPING

Glasgow is a shopper's mecca, but the serious browsers can be found sipping their cappuccino in Princes Square (Buchanan St., tel. 0141/221–0324), a designer shopping mall. Find clothes by Katharine Hammett, Reiss, Ted Baker, cosmetics by Lush, and designer jewelry by Sheila Miller. Buchanan Street is the main shopping drag, headlined by the huge new Buchanan Galleries beside Buchanan Street Underground station, which includes the largest Habitat store in Europe. Farther down the street you'll find Laura Ashley, Burberry's, Liberty, Jaeger, and such, as well as **Frasers** (21 Buchanan St., tel. 0141/221–3880), Glasgow's largest department store. A leading Highland outfitter is **R. G. Lawrie Ltd.** (111 Buchanan St., tel. 0141/221–0217), the place for Scottish gifts and woolens. Alternatively, you can spend your afternoons watching others watching you at the chic **Italian Centre,** off Glassford Street. Café culture—and couture—was never better.

AFTER DARK

With more than three dozen clubs, two dozen theaters, and countless pubs, Glasgow is the acknowledged cultural heart of Scotland. In the high-cultural vein, **Glasgow Royal Concert Hall** (Sauchiehall St., tel. 0141/332–6633) hosts all sorts of music concerts and drama year-round. Tickets tend to be expensive (around £15–£20). **Royal Scottish Academy of Music and Drama** (RSAMD) (100 Renfrew St., tel. 0141/332–5057) offers standard classics of music and theater, as well as art exhibits, at very affordable prices. *The List* (£2.50), available at all newsagents, and the free "City Live!," found in pubs, all have comprehensive entertainment listings.

Java (152 Park Rd., tel. 0141/336–6727, www.linkcafe.co.uk.) joins Scotland's growing ranks of Internet cafés. Stop by to E-mail your friends over a cappuccino.

PUBS

Aragon. Near the elegant and very long wooden bar is a picture that says, "Welcome to the inn—beer is best." Have truer words ever been spoken? *131 Byres Rd., no phone.*

Brewery Tap. It's quite a large pub, with several cozy rooms, heaps of dark wooden tables, and a gazillion beers—including many small Scottish brewery ales—and live music, from jazz to techno depending on the night. *1055 Sauchiehall St., tel. 0141/339– 0643.*

Café Delmonica's. This is Glasgow's premier gay and lesbian café/bar, with lively karaoke nights on Sunday and Wednesday and a daily happy hour 5–7 when spirits and draft beers are £1.50. *68 Virginia St., tel. 0141/552–4803.*

Drum and Monkey. This pub has a classic Victorian look: dark polished wood, shiny brass, and scattered couches. Make sure you try the famous bangers and mash. *93 St. Vincent St., tel. 0141/221–6636.*

Horseshoe Bar. The enormous horseshoe-shape bar inside is allegedly the longest bar anywhere in the United Kingdom. The crowd is generally mellow, but special drink promotions during the summer often attract a livelier bunch. *17–21 Drury St., tel. 0141/229–5711.*

Nico's. Part of a string of trendy pubs on Sauchiehall Street, it's so crowded you need a shoehorn to squeeze your way up to the long marble bar. *375 Sauchiehall St., tel. 0141/332–5736.*

Old College Bar. It's Glasgow's oldest pub (estab. 1515), located in the Merchant City. On weekends there's live music at 9 PM. *219 High St., tel. 0141/552–0940.*

Uisge Beatha. The name is Gaelic for "water of life," which isn't a bad way to describe Scottish whisky. The pub is filled with an odd assortment of choir chairs, Victorian settees, and medieval-looking tables. The bartenders wear their kilts well. *232–246 Woodlands Rd., tel. 0141/332–0473.*

LIVE MUSIC

Big-name acts, like The Charlatans and the Breeders, play at **Barrowland** (224 Gallowgate, tel. 0141/552–4601), where tickets run £8–£15. Glasgow's best indie rock venue is probably **King Tut's Wah Wah House** (272 St. Vincent St., tel. 0141/221–5279), where the cover starts at £3.50. Lots of excellent indie and jazz acts also play at the **13th Note** (50–60 King St., tel. 0141/553–1638), often for free. **Nice 'n' Sleazy** (421 Sauchiehall St., tel. 0141/333– 9637) is a dive joint where you can hear indie and hardcore rockers jam for free. For traditional music, try **Renfrew Ferry** (Clyde Pl., tel. 0141/227–5511) for their weekly ceilidhs and other folk music events. **Jinty McGintys** (21 Ashton La., 0141/339– 0747) has Irish folk, free-flowing Guinness, and no cover.

CLUBS

Keep an eye out for flyers announcing the latest impromptu dance club. Covers are usually £5–£10. **Archaos** (25 Queen St., tel. 0141/204–3189) is a hot joint that's swiftly growing very popular. The crowd is thin early on, but it gets packed around midnight. Always a good bet is the **Velvet Rooms** (520 Sauchiehall St., tel. 0141/332–0775), the unofficial rendezvous point of the swank and pouty. This place gets packed early and stays that way. **Fury Murry's** (96 Maxwell St., tel. 0141/221–6511) is another particularly hot spot, with various DJs pumping out dance music and soul. **The Sub Club** (22 Jamaica St., tel. 0141/248–4600) is currently the hottest club in town—and some say Britain. It doesn't close until 3 AM—plenty of time to sample one of the heady drink specials.

GAY AND LESBIAN CLUBS

Everyone comes to shake it at **Bennet's** (80 Glassford St., tel. 0141/552–5761), a popular gay and lesbian dance club. **Caffé Latte** (58 Virginia St., tel. 0141/553 2553) is a popular and trendy gay bar in the Merchant City. **Sadie Frost's** (8–10 West George St. tel. 0141/332–8005) tends to fill up with a younger crowd. Unwind at **Delmonica's** (68 Virginia St., tel. 0141/552–4803), a café- bar packed to the gills with Glasgow's urban young trendies.

THEATER

The well-established **Citizens Theatre** (119 Gorbals St., tel. 0141/429–0022) has performances ranging from classical to modern on its three stages. Tickets start around £6, though there are a limited number of student tickets for £2 for many shows. **Tron Theatre** (63 Trongate, tel. 0141/552–4267) is in a beautiful old building and hosts an engaging variety of shows. **The Tramway** (25 Albert Dr., tel. 0141/287–5511), on the south side of the River Clyde, is only a few years old but already one of Glasgow's major venues for art exhibitions, modern music, and theater. Tickets cost £7. **Mitchell Theatre** (Granville St., tel. 0141/287–4855) is a small auditorium with up-close-and-personal performances ranging from Shakespeare to jazz and stand-up comedians. Ticket prices begin at £8.50 and vary widely. **Theatre Royal** (282 Hope St., tel. 0141/332–9000) is the home of the Scottish Opera and a popular stage for ballet and plays. Tickets run £4.50–£16.50.

FILM

Caledonian Grosvenor (Ashton La., Hillhead Univ., tel. 0141/339– 4298) is a cozy theater with a good selection of offbeat films. The **Glasgow Film Theatre** (12 Rose St., tel. 0141/332–8128), right off Sauchiehall Street, features alternative first-run films as well as cult classics.

SOUTHERN SCOTLAND

Southern Scotland is a joy for travelers who prefer their scenery unpackaged. Perhaps because of its proximity to the English Lake District, the gentle, rolling panoramas are largely unspoiled by tourist trails and kitsch, and the place never feels crowded. As in the far north of Scotland, it's quite possible to travel entire stretches of road without meeting company along the way. Homeland of Robert Burns and Sir Walter Scott, the towns and castles nestled in the hills throughout **the Ayrshire, Dumfries and Galloway,** and **Borders** regions can be covered on short trips from Glasgow and Edinburgh, though the area really deserves more time. While the region is hard to explore without a car (train service is minimal, and buses are both infrequent and expensive), it's laid out well for hikers and cyclists in search of peaceful country landscape. The most notable trail is the 212-mi **Southern Upland Way,** which traverses the south from one coast to the other. Ask any tourist office for brochures detailing the route.

AYRSHIRE

This coastal area southwest of Glasgow is full of seaside resorts and Robert Burns memorabilia. "The Bard" (the *other* bard, actually) is unavoidable in this region: Every town claims some sort of association th him, from locks of hair to houses where he allegedly slept. **Ayr** (pronounced "air"), the biggest town the shire, is also the region's main transport hub. Awash with the faded elegance of a 19th-century astal resort, the town has more recently made headlines in Scotland with lurid tales of high-profile stasy-related deaths on its club scene. But you can still enjoy yourself on the beachfront esplanade, kind of Scottish Coney Island, complete with swing sets, ice cream stands, and a mini "crazy" golf ourse. The superposh **Abbotsford Hotel** (14 Corsehill Rd., tel. 01292/261506) features frequent meet-gs of the Folk Music Club, often with notable guest musicians. Cover charges range from free to £4. September, the **Burns Festival** runs concurrently with the **Ayrshire Arts Festival** (tel. 01292/885777 or info on either). When you get tired of fighting the crowded High Street–merchant gauntlet, head own to the river with some bread and feed the swans and gulls, or stroll through the Low Green, the nassive lawn at the waterfront.

Alloway, really a southern suburb of Ayr (only 2 mi south), is the actual birthplace of Robert Burns, and they won't let you forget it. Its **Burns Cottage and Museum** (tel. 01292/441215) is basically a thatched cottage filled with Burnsiana; tickets cost £1.70 and include admission to the monument and 75p off the Tam o' Shanter Experience (*see below*). Most visitors use the cottage as the starting point for the **Burns Heritage Trail,** which encompasses the next five spots on its well-marked route. Down the road are the **Land o' Burns Visitor Centre** (tel. 01292/443700), with its free audiovisual presentation, and the **Brig o' Doon,** the bridge from the poem "Tam o' Shanter," which spans the River Doon. On the other side of the road, near the river is **Kirk Alloway,** the auld Kirk where the devil danced and where Burns's parents are buried. In the **Tam o' Shanter Experience** (£2.80) the famous poem is brought to life in a state-of-the-art multimedia presentation. Close by is the **Burns Monument,** a memorial containing the life-size carved figures portrayed in "Tam o' Shanter." Ascend the monument for views of the surrounding garden and the Brig o' Doon.

One of the best destinations is the popular seaside resort of **Largs,** where you can take a 10-minute ferry ride (£2.95 return) to the small island of Great Cumbrae, 25 mi up the coast from Ayr. **Waverley Steam Boat** (Waverley Terminal, Anderston Quay, tel. 0141/221–8152), Europe's last operating paddle steamer, runs daily in July and August from Ayr Harbour to the Isle of Arran and on to Campbeltown and the Mull of Kintyre. A short trip costs £11.95 and the whole circuit is about £21.

While in Ayrshire, follow Eisenhower's example and **visit Culzean Castle and Country Park.** On a warm summer evening, with the ebbing sun throwing long shadows on the lawns, you might think you had stepped into Paradise. Eisenhower had his own apartments in the elegant Robert Adam–designed castle (you can overnight in them if you really want to splurge). The castle dates from the 1770s and was built around an ancient tower on a bluff from which the clan Kennedy kept a wary eye on the coast until 1945, when they gave Culzean to the National Trust for Scotland. The armory room alone is worth the effort to visit. From the Sandgate bus station in Ayr, take Western Scottish Bus 60 (7 per day, £4.05 day return), then follow the signs on the path for 1 mi. Culzean, tel. 01655/760661. Admission to park and castle £7; to park £5. Castle open daily Apr.–Oct. Grounds open year-round.

BASICS

Ayr's year-round **tourist office** (Burns House, Burns Statue Square, tel. 01292/288688) has excellent brochures detailing hiking and cycling routes nearby. Other year-round tourist offices in Ayrshire include **Kilmarnock** (62 Bank St., tel. 01563/539090) and **Largs** (Promenade, tel. 01475/673765). There are seasonal offices, open Easter–October, in **Girvan** (Bridge St., tel. 01465/714950), **Millport** (Stuart St., tel. 01475/530753), and **Troon** (Municipal Bldg., tel. 01292/317696).

COMING AND GOING

Ayrshire is by far the easiest part of southern Scotland to get around in without a car. Ayr's **train station** (Station Rd., tel. 0345/484950) sits midway along the Glasgow–Stranraer line, which provides regular rail service six times a day (three on Sunday) up and down the coast, including a stop in Ardrossan Harbour for the ferry to Arran. If you want to go anywhere else, you'll have to connect through Glasgow.

As for buses, **Citylink** (tel. 0141/332–2326) joins Glasgow with Ayrshire. Ayrshire itself, however, is best served by **Western Scottish** (tel. 01292/613500), which doesn't honor Discount Coachcards. Still, their fares to Glasgow (£3.20 single) and Stranraer (£5.85 single) are as cheap as they come. From Ayr's bus terminal, **Sandgate Station** (Sandgate, at Boswell Pk., tel. 01292/264643), you can zip up to Alloway on the Glasgow–Stranraer bus (every 20–30 mins) for 95p. If you plan on traveling in southern Ayrshire, the **Strathclyde Transport Rural Day Card** allows unlimited travel on buses, and postbuses for £3.50 per zone per day. Contact the Strathclyde Transport Travel Centre in Glasgow (tel. 0141/226–4826) for more information. Rent a bike for about £10 per twenty-four hour period, or £15 all weekend (Friday–Mon day), from **AMG Cycles** (55 Dalblair Rd., tel. 01292/287580).

WHERE TO SLEEP

You'll find the best lodging options are in Ayr. Most of the bargain B&Bs are just south of the river around Queens Terrace, Eglinton Terrace, and Montgomery Terrace. **Mr. and Mrs. Anton** (Clyde Cottage, Arran Terr., tel. 01292/267368) offer three rooms for £16–£21 per person, with a £5 optional dinner charge. Near the train station, **Armadale Guest House** (33 Bellevue Crescent, GA7 2DP, tel. 0129: 264320) charges from £18 to £26 per person sharing in a double room. **Ayr SYHA** (5 Craigweil Rd., tel 01292/262322), Standard, in a miniature castle right on the beach, is by far your best option in Ayr. has fantastic views of Arran and is a 20-minute walk south of the train station; walk south on Alloway Place, turn right on Blackburn Road, right on Craigwell Road. Scott, the manager, is insanely knowledgeable about the area and can arrange bike rentals. He may even wake you up with his bagpipes.

FOOD

A number of cute cafés and takeouts line Ayr's River Street (just north of the river) and High Street. The teddy-bear-themed **Hunny Pot** (37 Beresford Terr., tel. 01292/263239) is all about home-style cooking. If what you want isn't on the menu, ask and they'll try to make it. Try **Pierre Victoire** (4 River Terr., tel. 01292/268087), part of the popular Edinburgh chain, for affordable, tasty French food. Self-caterers should visit the mammoth **Safeway** across from the tourist office.

DUMFRIES AND GALLOWAY

This large region of undulating hills in southwest Scotland has plenty of castles and stately homes—more than in any other Scottish region, except perhaps the Grampians. **Galloway,** the area west of Dumfries, has the advantage of a south-facing coastline. The North Atlantic Drift bathes the coast with warm(er) water, and as a result, Galloway has a number of resplendent gardens. With its woodlands, high moors, and craggy hills, Galloway offers a taste of the Highlands for those lacking the time for an adventure farther north. The 250-square-mile Galloway Forest Park (tel. 01671/402420 in Newton Stewart) has a network of trails winding through the glens and up the park's seven peaks, abundant wildlife, several bothies, and quite a few friendly rangers to point the way. The last week in May and into June, the **Dumfries and Galloway Arts Festival** generates lots of events throughout the region. For information, contact Gracefield Arts Centre (28 Edinburgh Rd., tel. 01387/262084), which has its own cool gallery and crafts shop. The towns of **Dumfries, Newton Stewart,** and **Stranraer** make good bases to explore the region.

Though the region is hard to explore without a car, the rolling terrain is dotted with campgrounds every few miles, which makes it easy to tackle by bike. The pamphlet "Cycling in Dumfries and Galloway," available at tourist offices, lists bike-rental agents and places to stay along the way. The first bike was actually invented in the region; the **Cycle Museum** at Dumlanrig Castle in the Dumlanrig Country Park has more details (*see* Dumfries, *below*). "Explore Dumfries and Galloway" is a detailed guide to all the events and attractions in the region, while "The Gardens of South West Scotland" tells you about just that, and is worth checking out—scenery is what the area's known for. If you want to explore more, "Ranger Led Walks and Events in Dumfries and Galloway" lists free and cheap walks taking place April–November. If you need a place to stay, pick up "Dumfries and Galloway 1998 Holiday Guide" for a list of campgrounds and B&Bs. All the above guides are free and available at any tourist office.

If you're headed to Northern Ireland, ferries leave from the port of **Stranraer.** Here you'll find St. John's Castle with an exhibit on law and order (admission £1.20), the nearby Ardwell Gardens, and a city museum. (For more info on ferry service from Stranraer, *see* Coming and Going, *below*.) Stranraer's **tourist center** (Harbour St., tel. 01776/702595) is now open year-round. Check London Road, near the train station, for B&Bs.

BASICS

There are tourist offices, open Easter–October, in **Castle Douglas** (Markethill parking lot, tel. 01556/502611), **Gatehouse-of-Fleet** (carpark, tel. 01557/814212), **Kirkcudbright** (Harbour Sq., tel. 01557/330494), **Moffat** (Churchgate, 01683/220620), and **Newton Stewart** (Dashwood Sq., tel. 01671/402431).

OMING AND GOING

you're traveling with two or three companions, consider renting a car. In Dumfries, you can rent one
m **Klic** (tel. 01387/268777) or **Arnold Clark** (New Abbey Rd., tel. 01387/263000). The going rate is
?0 per day or £115 per week, with unlimited mileage. You must be over 23, and there is an extra insur-
ice charge if you're under 25.

Y BUS • Local bus lines are run by **McEwan's** (tel. 01387/710357), **Scottish Citylink** (tel. 0141/332–
644), and **Western Scottish** (tel. 01387/253496); the latter serves the Dumfries– Glasgow route
£6.30 single). McEwan's will take you from Dumfries to Stranraer for £6 single. A **Day Discoverer** bus
ass gets you on virtually all bus services in the region for only £5. In a pinch there are always post-
uses; for current routes inquire at any tourist office or call the **Travel Information Line** (tel. 01345/
)90510) weekdays 9–5. In Dumfries there's no bus station per se, just a row of stands on **Whitesands,**
ight next to the tourist office. **National Express** also travels from Dumfries to Carlisle (£5.50 single),
Manchester (£19.50 single), and London (£25.50 single) and offers a bus and ferry service to Belfast
through Stranraer (£36 return).

BY FERRY • Three ferry companies serve Northern Ireland from Stranraer. **SeaCat** (tel. 0870/552–
3523) sails to Belfast Harbour (90 mins, £30 single) five times per day from West Pier, a 10-minute walk
from Stranraer's train station. Special three-day return tickets cost about £40 and six-day return tickets
are £50. Stena Line (tel. 011766/702262) sends about 10 ferries per day to Belfast Harbour (£22 single). **Stena Line** ferries leave from the ferry terminal outside Stranraer's train station and offer a 25%
discount to those with a hostel card. Although **P&O Ferries** (tel. 0990 980980) also serves Larne Harbour, 20 mi north of Belfast, its port is in Cairnryan, 5 mi north of Stranraer and a pain to reach. Standard return ticket costs are £42–£48 and five-day return tickets are £29–£36.

BY TRAIN • From Glasgow's Central Station there are several daily trains to **Dumfries** (1¾ hrs, £17.70
return). From Glasgow there are six trains per day (three on Sunday) to **Stranraer** (1½ hrs, £14.90 single) that deposit you next to the Stena Line ferry terminal at East Pier. Traveling into England from Dumfries is possible via Carlisle (£9.50 return). To reach Edinburgh, or anywhere else, you have to transfer
at either Carlisle or Glasgow. Call 0345 484950 for further information.

DUMFRIES

Easily the most English in appearance of Scotland's towns, Dumfries, along the River Nith, is another
Burns-fest. Robert Burns lived east of the river at what is now **Burns House** (Burns St., tel. 01387/
255297) for his last three years, and the town certainly makes the most of it. Lots of his personal belongings are found within; admission is free. Just to the east on St. Michael's Street is **St. Michael's Church,**
which houses his remains. Admission to this, Dumfries's original parish church, is also gratis.

Across the river to the west on Mill Road is the **Robert Burns Centre** (Mills Rd., tel. 01387/264808),
admission £1.20, which describes Burns's connections to Dumfries, focusing on the history of both the
poet and his town. Just north is **Old Bridge House,** (Mill Rd., tel. 01387/256904), the oldest dwelling in
the city, built in 1660. It now shows examples of quotidian life in the 1800s and 1900s for free. A couple of blocks south is the **Dumfries Museum** (tel. 01387/253374), housed in a cylindrical, white, windmill tower, which has exhibits on the area from prehistory to more recent times. Admission is free, but
there is a £1.20 fee to visit the camera obscura, the oldest in Scotland. Located on the top floor, it uses
reflected light to project pictures of the surrounding area.

If castles are your bag, head 8 mi south of Dumfries on B725 to **Caerlaverock Castle** (tel. 0131/668–
8600); admission is £2.30. Western Scottish Bus 371 (£1.80 day return) goes there several times a day.
This castle was fought over by England and Scotland and features a moat and high towers; it's très
medieval and set among 13,594 acres of salt marsh in the Caerlaverock National Nature Reserve. Western Scottish Bus 246 (£2.70) takes you from Dumfries to **Drumlanrig Castle** (tel. 01848/330248), 18
mi north. Get off on the main road and walk a mile to the 17th-century castle. They have a well-known
art collection, a bicycle museum, and a park where you can hire bikes. Admission to the castle is £4.

BASICS

Dumfries's **Tourist Information Centre** (Whitesands, tel. 01387/253862) books National Express tickets
and accommodations. They're open Monday–Saturday 10–4:30, with longer hours in summer. Another
useful place is **Dumfries Station** on Lovers Walk, at the northern end of town and open daily 6:30 AM–
7:30 PM. They store luggage for £1–£2 and sell train tickets. Pick up a bike at **Nithsdale Cycle Centre**

(Rosefield Mills, Troqueer Rd., tel. 01387/254870) starting at £9 per day or at **Grierson & Graham L'** (Academy St., tel. 01387/259483), where bikes cost £10 for 24 hours.

WHERE TO SLEEP

Plenty of B&Bs right outside Dumfries's train station await the weary traveler. Across the street, in fac Mrs. Maureen Lowe runs the homey **Fulwood Private Hotel** (30 Lovers Walk, tel. 01387/252262), wit singles for £18–£20, doubles for £32. **Shambellie View** (Glencaple Rd., tel. 01387/269331), 1½ m from the city center, has doubles for £31. The nearest SYHA hostels are **Minnigaff** (tel. 01671/402211 Standard-L, near Newton Stewart, closed October–March; **Kendoon** (no phone), Simple, near Cast| Douglas, closed November–April; and **Wanlockhead** (tel. 01659/742252), Standard-L, closed Novem ber–March. **Beeswing Caravan Park** (Drumjohn Mar, Kirkcudbrightshire, tel. 01387/760242), 7 mi wes of Dumfries on A711, closed November–February, charges £6.10–£7.20 per tent site.

FOOD

Hole i' the Wa' (156 High St., tel. 01387/252770), one of Burns's old haunts, was established in 1620. **The Old Bank** (94 Irish St., tel. 01387/253499), yes, in an old bank, serves vegetarian food. Another place for vegetarian food is **Raggazzis Café Bar** (19–21 English St., tel. 01387/255157). The **Jewel in the Crown** (50 St. Michael St., tel. 01387/264183) serves Asian and Indian meals. **Dumfries Health and Whole Foods** (29–31 English St., tel. 01387/261065) has local produce, organic cheese, and whole-grain breads. Burns called the **Globe Inn** (56 High St., at English St., tel. 01387/252335) "my favorite Howff," and hung out here with his pals. Sit in the courtyard and eat mealed herring, a favorite snack in his day.

THE BORDERS

Covering more territory than the name suggests, the Borders stretches from the Cheviot Hills at the English border, north to the Moorfoot and Pentland foothill ranges south of Edinburgh and east to the coast near St. Abbs Head. Once the site of many brutal battles with England, the only remaining evidence of warfare is the region's ruined abbeys. The Borders' endless tranquil hills and dells, soothing rivers, and expanses of forest and grassland have softened even the harshest of memories of its past.

The Borders region is known for its historic towns, most notably Peebles, Melrose, Jedburgh, and Kelso, and for their impressive Gothic abbeys. From just about any town in the region, it's only 3–5 mi to the next, so, like the rest of Southern Scotland, the Borders are a biker's and hiker's dream. Serious hikers may want to tackle the **Southern Upland Way,** which runs right through the middle of the Borders, and bikers can discover the 90-mi **Tweed Cycleway.** For info on tours and routes, contact the **Countryside Ranger Service** (Scottish Borders Council, Ancrum, Jedburgh, TD8 6UQ, tel. 01835/830281). They offer an impressive array of ranger-led walks, many of them free, throughout the region. Pick up their free brochure at any of the area's tourist info offices (*see* Visitor Information, *below*).

The quiet town of **Peebles** on the River Tweed makes a good base for forays into the nearby Glentress Forest. Along High Street, you'll find **Cross Kirk,** the ruins of a 13th- century church, as well as the interesting **Tweeddale Museum and Gallery** (tel. 01721/724820), which features contemporary art exhibits and all sorts of historical items. You can also visit the 14th-century **Neidpath Castle** (Old Town Rd., tel. 01712/720333), perfectly situated by the River Tweed, 1 mi from town. Admission to the castle, which also houses a small museum, is £2.50 **Traquair House** (Innerleithen, tel. 01896/830323) makes a good day trip from Peebles, especially for cyclists. It's trumpeted as the longest continuously inhabited house in Scotland and is packed with fascinating family heirlooms. They've even got their own brewery, where you can taste their ales daily April–September and weekends in October. You can also camp on the extensive grounds, which contain a hedge maze. If you're on foot, take Bus 62 and ask the driver to drop you near Traquair, from which it's a 2-mi walk. The house is open April 15–September, daily 12:30–5:30, and in October Friday–Sunday 2–5; admission is £5. If you need to hire a bike (£8–£16 per day), talk to the folks at **Scottish Border Trails** (3 South Park, tel. 01721/722935) in Peebles.

The tiny town of **Melrose** is in the shadow of the **Eildon Hills.** These relics of a volcanic past have some rich relics of their own to reveal: the remnants of both Celtic and Roman settlements. The **Trimontium** exhibition (Melrose Sq., tel. 01896/822463), admission £1.40, details excavations in the hills that are along the Southern Upland Way. **Melrose Abbey** (tel. 01896/822562), admission £2.80, built in 1136, has a subtle splendor. Though much of the ruins can be seen from the outside, the interior is richly detailed. This is the final resting place of Robert the Bruce's heart (brought back minus the body from he Crusade battlefields of Palestine). Sir Walter Scott once lived at the nearby **Abbotsford House** (tel. 01896/752043), and his great-great-great-granddaughters can still be found ambling about the house or gardens. The house is a Victorian extravaganza and one of the most beautiful in Scotland. Mounted stag heads, tartan throws, cozy library inglenooks, historic weapons (including some used by Rob Roy and Montrose), an eerie portrait of the beheaded Mary, Queen of Scots, painted the day after her execution—with decor like this, it's little wonder John Ruskin once called the house "the most incongruous pile that gentlemanly modernism ever devised." Located about 3 mi southwest of Melrose, the house is open daily March 20–October and is well worth the £3.50 admission. The **River Tweed,** one of the world's most famous salmon rivers, flows beside the town. A footpath along the river will lead you about 2 mi downriver to **Leaderfoot Viaduct,** a 123-ft-high red-sandstone colossus.

About 13 mi south of Melrose is the town of **Jedburgh** and the **Jedburgh Abbey** (tel. 01835/863925), noteworthy for its red- sandstone construction—the material of choice throughout this region for many centuries. Admission is £2.80, but you can see nearly all of the abbey from the perimeter. Afterward, cool down with a pint at the nearby **Jedburgh Arms** (Abbey Pl., tel. 01835/862540).

The little town of **Kelso,** at the junction of the rivers Teviot and Tweed, is filled with cobblestone streets and practically screams "picture postcard." **Kelso Abbey** was razed by the English during the "Rough Wooing," when the English attacked Scotland in an attempt to force a marriage between Henry VIII's son and the infant Mary, Queen of Scots. Just outside Kelso, **Floors Castle** (tel. 01573/223333) is the largest inhabited house in Scotland with grounds to match. Locals claim that Randy Andy brought the ladies here before marrying Fergie. Admission to the castle is £5 (£3 for the grounds only), but few rooms are open to the public.

VISITOR INFORMATION

The largest Borders Tourist Information Centre, and the only one open year-round, is in **Jedburgh** (Murrays Green, tel. 01835/863435 or 01835/863688). They book accommodations for free and hold luggage (as do most of the centers, except for Kelso). Each office has tons of free brochures on the region, or you can pick up the excellent (and free) "Visitors Guide to the Scottish Borders" for comprehensive listings. Tourist offices in **Kelso** (Town House, The Square, tel. 01573/223464), **Melrose** (Abbey House, Abbey St., tel. 01896/822555), **Galashiels** (3 St. John's St., tel. 01896/755551), and **Peebles** (High St., tel. 01721/720138) are open Easter– October.

COMING AND GOING

Getting to the Borders can be a bit of a challenge. From Dumfries and Galloway, in the west, you can't simply cut over east. Instead, you must take the train south to Carlisle in England and then transfer to a McEwen's (tel. 01387/710357) bus bound for the Borders—a £9 to £11 proposition. From the east, it's a bit easier: you can take the Edinburgh-London train to Berwick-upon-Tweed, just over the border in England. From here there are good (Lowland) bus connections to several Scottish border towns. If you are coming from Edinburgh, there are hourly buses that pass through Peebles and Galashiels. To reach some towns, such as Melrose and Kelso, you must transfer to a local route at the Galashiels station. Call **Lowland Omnibus** (Galashiels, tel. 01896/752237) for fares and schedules. They offer the **Waverley Rover Pass** (£11.20), good for a day's unlimited travel in the Borders region, plus a single trip to or from Edinburgh. The **Regional Rover Pass** (£8.20) is valid for a day's unlimited travel in the Borders region only. Buy either pass onboard any Lowland bus.

WHERE TO SLEEP AND EAT

JEDBURGH • Jedburgh is home to the **Spread Eagle Hotel** (20 High St., tel. 01835/862870), once frequented by such notables as Sir Walter Scott, Robert Burns, and Mary, Queen of Scots. In fact, Mary even lived here during her stay in Jedburgh, and you can stay in her room (and supposedly her bed) for only £16.50; double rooms cost £19.50. **Mrs. Bathgate** (30 High St., tel. 01835/862604) rents rooms from £16 per person. There's a long selection of sandwiches, pastas, and vegetarian entrées, as well as an ice cream counter, at **Mercat Café** (Canongate, tel. 01835/862255). **Simply Scottish** (High St., Jedburgh, tel. 01835/864696), a modern bistro- style restaurant and coffee shop, relies on fresh, local produce for such dishes as grilled Border lamb and heather-honey ice cream.

KELSO • If it's something with style that you're looking for, try the **Ednam House Hotel** (Bridge St., TD5 7HT, tel. 01573/224168), a very traditional, grand sporting hotel on the banks of the Tweed. There are 32 rooms, but none of them are particularly cheap. Prices for two sharing a double room start at £76 including breakfast; a single room will set you back £55. For a cheaper option, the centrally located **Inglestone Guest House** (Abbey Row, tel. 01573/225800), run by Eileen and Roth McArthur, is personable and cozy. Their three rooms start at £19, including breakfast. **Yetholm SYHA** (tel. 017573/ 420631), Standard-L, open mid-March through September, makes a good base for exploring the Borders sights and for those walking the Pennine Way, which ends 7 mi east of Kelso. If you have a craving for southwestern food, try the **Horse and Wagon** (Coal Market, tel. 01573/224568), which has generous daily specials like salmon steak. **Gandhi** (Inch Rd., off Bowmont St., tel. 01573/225159) serves good Indian food and also has takeout. For amazing (indeed, award-winning) baked goods visit **B. I. Hossack** (50 Horsemarket, tel. 01573/224139).

MELROSE • Mrs. M. Graham (Braidwood, Buccleuch St., tel. 01896/822488) offers rooms starting at £18 per person. **Melrose SYHA** (Priorwood, tel. 01896/822521), Standard, overlooking Melrose Abbey, is near walking paths galore; turn left on the pedestrian path behind the fishmonger shop on Market Square. If you've got money to spend, book yourself into **Burts Hotel** (Market Sq., TD6 9PN, tel. 01896/ 822285), a delightful 18th-century inn with an excellent restaurant attached and double rooms starting at £42 per person. Eat breakfast or lunch at **Pyemont & Company Tea & Coffee House** (28 Market Sq., tel. 01896/822223), a cute café right on Melrose Square. It's probably the only place in the Borders where they roast their own coffee, offer divine baked goods, and have a deli counter.

PEEBLES • The word immaculate best describes **Minniebank Guest House** (Greenside, tel. 01721/ 722093), run by courteous hosts Ken and Brenda Bowie. The house overlooks the River Tweed, and rooms cost £23–£25 per person, including breakfast. **Mrs. Mitchell's** (1 Rosetta Rd., tel. 01721/ 721232) is the cheapest B&B in town, with singles for £17, doubles for £33. But if you want to escape into the country you should head for **Cringletie House Hotel** (near Peebles, EH45 8PL, tel. 01721/ 730233; off the A703 Edinburgh–Peebles, 2 mi north of Peebles). Expect to shell out £60 a night per person sharing a double room. **Nanking Chinese Restaurant** (Port Brae, at the old Church, tel. 01721/ 723666) has a huge menu featuring delectable curried mixed vegetables. **Summerfield Supermarket** is open daily for all your grocery needs.

CENTRAL SCOTLAND AND FIFE

The easily accessible towns of Stirling and Perth are major gateways to the central Highlands, a scenic and spectacular land that stretches north of Glasgow. This isn't the great Highlands of the north, but it is beautiful in its own right—lush, green, and even warm (well, at times), especially **the Trossachs,** "Rob Roy Country," where deep lochs shimmer at the foot of gently sloping hills covered in shaggy birch, oak, and pine—a pristine landscape. Unfortunately, ever since Sir Walter Scott wrote up the area in his poems, Brits have been flocking to the lochs. It doesn't help, of course, that Edinburgh and Glasgow are barely a couple of hours away by train and bus. Even so, there's still much wild, high country to be had in the central Highlands. The Kingdom of Fife, from rolling farmland to rugged coast, is beautiful throughout. The many fishing villages that line the sea retain their nautical heritage while the inland pastures are the fertile heart of the region. Hardly wild but still very much worth a visit is the university and golf town of **St. Andrews,** a quintessentially Scottish town with romantic, stone houses and seaside ruins. With a golf course around every corner, Fife is said to have "more links than people."

STIRLING

Stirling's stunning and strategic position, on the lowest crossing point of the River Forth and central to all of Scotland's principal routes, made it an important city for aristocratic hopefuls, right up through the 18th century. **Stirling Castle,** like the one at Edinburgh, is built on a defunct volcano, dominating the local landscape. The Stuarts, including Mary, Queen of Scots, lived here until 1603, when James VI ran off to London to be crowned king of England. Two of Scotland's most critical battles during the Wars of Independence were also fought in the area: William Wallace's grassroots revolution led to his greatest victory over the English at Stirling Bridge in 1297, and Robert the Bruce defeated Edward II in the pivotal battle at Bannockburn in 1314. Today, Stirling is an important shopping center for locals and the main watering hole for students of the nearby **Stirling University.** The various military sights are fairly spread out, but within a day you can definitely manage to visit the castle, walk the streets, see the Wal-

e Monument, and enjoy the pub scene. Stirling's strategic location also makes it a good base for for-
s to the Trossachs and Loch Lomond—or even a cheap lodging alternative to Glasgow and Edinburgh
ring the summer festival season.

ASICS

ne main regional office of the **Loch Lomond, Stirling, and Trossachs Tourist Board** will sell you a town
ap, change money, and book B&Bs. **The Royal Burgh of Stirling Visitor Centre** (tel. 01786/479901),
astle Esplanade, has similar open hours and a slightly smaller selection of info, but they do have a fact-
led (and free) audiovisual presentation on the area's history in their small auditorium. *41 Dumbarton
Rd., tel. 01786/462517. Open July– Aug., daily 9–6:30; Sept.–Oct., daily 9:30–6; Nov.–Dec., 9:30–5;
an.–June, daily 9:30–5.*

COMING AND GOING

There is frequent rail service from centrally located **Stirling Station** (Burghmuir Rd., just east of Murray
Pl., tel. 0345/484950) to Edinburgh (1 hr, £4.80 single, £8.80 day return), Perth (45 mins, £7.30 single), and Glasgow (45 mins, £4.10 single). Stow your luggage in lockers for £1–£3. Between May and
September, the **Castle Shuttle** does a circuit from the railway station to Stirling Castle, via the SYHA,
every 20 minutes for 50p.

Buses aren't that much cheaper than the train for short trips, like the one to Edinburgh (£7.10 day
return) and the one to Glasgow (£6.15 return). **Midland Bluebird** runs almost all the services in and
around Stirling. Call 01324/613777 for route info daily 6 AM–10 PM. To reach town from the **bus station**
(Gooscroft Rd., tel. 01786/473763), just south of the train station, cut through the Thistle Centre, which
is connected by an overpass to the bus terminal.

WHERE TO SLEEP

Because of inexpensive and frequent transportation connections, Stirling is a good place to stay if Edinburgh is too crowded during the International Festival. The city attracts quite a few visitors in summer,
though, so book ahead to ensure you'll have a bed. Queen Street, in the town center, has several reasonable B&Bs, including **Mrs. Cosgrove** (32 Queen St., tel. 01786/463716) for £15–£17. **Mrs. Mac-
Gregor** (27 King St., FK8 1DN, tel. 01786/471082), located right in the thick of things, charges £16–
£19 per person. More expensive, at around £40 per person per night, the Royal Hotel (Henderson St.,
Bridge of Allan, FK9 4HG, tel. 01786/832284) has an excellent restaurant which makes good use of
local produce. The Stirling–St. Andrews bus drives right by **Witches Craig Caravan Park** (Blairlogie, tel.
01786/474947), a well-equipped campground 3 mi east of Stirling on the St. Andrews Road (A91). Tent
sites are £8 in low season, £12 in high season.

HOSTELS • Stirling SYHA. It has a prime location in the middle of Old Town (albeit up a killer hill).
Thankfully, the beds have wooden frames instead of the evil, screechy springs found in most SYHA hostels. Should your neighbor take a 6 AM shower, you get to wake up early, because there are no doors to
the in-room showers, just curtains. Higher Standard. *St. John St., tel. and fax 01786/473442. 126 beds.*

FOOD

There are plenty of places to eat in the town center around Murray Place, Dumbarton Road, and Barnton Road. If you want to see where Lord Darnley, the second husband of Mary, Queen of Scots, lived,
visit **Darnley Coffee House** (18 Bow St., tel. 01786/474468), a low- key café. **Paco's Restaurant** (21
Dunbarton Rd., tel. 01786/446414), a cool spot decorated with antique advertisements, old skis, and
climbing axes, has savory smoked salmon and a large vegetarian menu. Paco's is open daily from noon
"until the last table leaves." Stirling pubs also serve good grub; try **Behind the Wall Too** (61 King St., tel.
01786/461041) or **Stirling Café and Brasserie** (Baker St., no phone).

WORTH SEEING

STIRLING CASTLE • Stirling Castle is set on a volcanic crag and is every bit as impressive as Edinburgh's. But instead of the hip-to-bum crowds that plague Edinburgh Castle, here you get well-groomed
lawns, explorable nooks and crannies, and terrific views of the Forth Valley—all minus the maddening
tourist hordes. Just below the southwestern ramparts lies the curious, geometrically shaped **King's
Knot,** known locally as the Cup 'n' Saucer, originally a terraced garden built by William III. Jousting tour-
naments were held on the adjacent lawns, below the outcropping known as **Ladies Rock,** where the
women of the castle would assemble to watch the contests. These days it's a grassy park for children
and a great spot for a picnic. *Tel. 01786/450000. Admission £4.50. Open Apr.– Sept., daily 9:30–6:30;
Oct.–Mar., daily 9:30–5.*

BANNOCKBURN • This is the site of Robert the Bruce's victory over Edward II of England in 131? which firmly established his reign and effectively ended all challenges to Scotland's throne. The visit center has a great audiovisual account of the battle. The site itself is open daily dawn to dusk and is mi south of Stirling. *Tel. 01786/812664. Admission £2.30. Visitor center open Apr.–Oct., daily 10–5:3? Mar. and Nov.–Dec., daily 11–3. Closed Jan.–Feb.*

OLD TOWN • The unfinished, cannon-damaged **Mar's Wark** (Mar's Building), at the bottom of Cast Hill Wynd, was commissioned in the 16th century for the earl of Mar, keeper of Stirling Castle. Ju? behind it is the **Church of the Holy Rude,** the site of the coronation of King James VI (later James I England) in 1567. It was also Mary, Queen of Scots's favorite place of worship. The cemetery's large st? pyramid, not usually associated with the Church of Scotland, commemorates those martyred for seek ing religious freedom. **Argyll's Ludging** (Castle Hill Wynd) is a 16th- century Renaissance mansion that'? currently being converted into a museum. Follow Castle Hill Wynd and you'll stumble onto **Broad Street** once the center of trade for old Stirling. The 18th- century **Tolbooth,** formerly the town hall, features a traditional Scottish steeple and gilded weathercock. For centuries, the Burgh court handed down sentences here (the jail was next door). Today it's a fine café and theater, conveniently across from the SYHA hostel.

THE TOWN WALL • The **Back Walk** is a circular, somewhat steep walkway constructed in the 1700s along the Town Wall. The wall was built around 1547 to protect the town from attacks by Henry VIII, who wanted to force a marriage between the infant Mary, Queen of Scots and his son, Edward—the infamous "Rough Wooing." The walk winds from **Dumbarton Road,** near Stirling's commercial center, to the castle and around Castle Rock before heading back toward the Old Town. This path isn't heavily traveled, and the views of the valley under the towering western escarpment are particularly good.

WALLACE MONUMENT • This 220-ft monument towers above Abbey Craig, celebrating Wallace's victory over the English in the Battle of Stirling Bridge (1297), which took place over this stretch of the Forth Valley. An audiovisual display tells the story, though the real reason to make the 1½-mi trek from town is to climb the tower's spiral staircase for a good view. It is more popular than ever since the success of the movie *Braveheart,* scenes of which were filmed in the surrounding countryside. Grab a map from the tourist office and decide whether to cross the River Forth over the Old Bridge to the north of town or by the footbridge to **Cambuskenneth,** a 12th-century ruined abbey with only a bell tower remaining, but where James III and his wife, Margaret of Denmark, are buried. *Tel. 01786/472140. Admission £3. Open Apr.–Oct., daily 10–5* (slightly longer hrs in summer).

AFTER DARK

The **MacRobert Art Centre** (Stirling University, tel. 01786/461081) is the cultural backbone of the university and Stirling alike. You can get tickets to events at the "MacBob," as it is affectionately known, from £3.50 for adults, £1 for children. **All That Jazz** (9 Upper Craigs, tel. 01786/451130) is a lively bar with a great mix of music and excellent food, both traditional (haggis) and Cajun (jambalaya). **Barnton Bar/Bistro** (3 Barnton St., tel. 01786/461698) has art nouveau decor and marble tables. Some nights the crowd is heterosexual, some nights it's mixed, and some nights it's just plain ol' drunk. On Monday nights there's a ceilidh at the **Guildhall** in the Old Town. They'll teach you to dance and sing for £3.50 Listen to the tales told by a "son of the rock," as old men born 'n' raised in Stirling are called.

THE TROSSACHS

Technically speaking, the name Trossachs refers to a short gorge linking lovely **Loch Katrine** with the much smaller **Loch Achray** to the east. Sir Walter Scott put this area on the map by setting "The Lady of the Lake" here. Victorians predictably flocked to the region to see what inspired him, and visitors continue to flock today, especially during the summer. Despite the crowds, the Trossachs remain pristine and lush in a rugged sort of way. Loch Achray, for instance, should fulfill your expectations of a Scottish loch: sparkling waters surrounded by meadows, rhododendron thickets, and richly wooded hills. Aberfoyle in the south and Callander in the northeast are the gateway towns, but as soon as you arrive, you'll see that time is best spent in the hills, the old stomping ground of the famous MacGregor clan, rather than in these towns.

Unabashedly commercial, **Aberfoyle** is a blur of woolens shops with the occasional sheep show. Luckily, Aberfoyle is in the heart of the **Queen Elizabeth Forest Park,** just south of Loch Katrine and wedged between the Trossachs and Loch Lomond. The park is as royally scenic as its name implies, with a little more emphasis on "forest" than "park." Many hiking and mountain-bike trails cross the 75,000 acres of pine forest. Both **Trossachs Cycle Hire** (Trossachs Holiday Park, tel. 01877/387614) and **Forest Cycle Hire** (Main St., tel. 01877/382802) rent bikes for £10–£12 per day and offer route suggestions. Stop by Aberfoyle's **tourist office** (Main St., tel. 01877/382352) or **Forestry Commission Visitor Centre** (tel. 01877/382383), 1 mi north of town, for info on hiking, biking, and camping within the park.

Callander sits at the east end of the Trossachs, a few miles from Loch Vencachar. It is easily accessible from Stirling and the other Lowlands towns, making it a popular step-off point with many tourist services. From here, you can hike out to two different waterfalls. **Bracklinn Falls** can be reached via the short, 25-minute trail at the top of Golf Course Road at the east end of town. The **Falls of Leny,** by the Pass of Leny, are just north of Callander on A84. Rent a bike from the **Wheels Cycling Centre** (Invertrossachs Rd. Callander, tel. 01877/331100) and hit the road. The Centre also provides clean, modern, and inexpensive accommodations: dorms for £10 with bed and breakfast, £50 for a family room for four, with breakfast. If the weather is bad, your only real choice is "Rob Roy: Hero or Villain," a decent audiovisual display (£2), screened at the **Rob Roy and Trossachs Visitor Centre** (Main St., tel. 01877/330342), which describes the life of Scotland's cattle-stealing outlaw-cum-hero immortalized by Daniel Defoe, Sir Walter Scott, and, most recently, that Mel Gibson guy.

COMING AND GOING

The nearest major rail hub is Stirling, where buses to towns and villages throughout the Trossachs converge. The easiest way to get around is by car, but buses can get you into most areas from either Glasgow (1 hr) or Edinburgh (1½ hrs). To make sense of the local bus routes, grab a copy of the free "Aberfoyle, Callander, Killin, and Tyndrum Area Public Transport Guide" from any tourist office. **Midland Bluebird** (tel. 01360/440224 or 01786/473763) runs frequently between Stirling and Callander and between Glasgow and Aberfoyle.

Despite what Shakespeare would have you believe, Macbeth had an unusually prosperous and peaceful 17-year reign and is considered one of Scotland's finest kings.

Postbuses (tel. 01463/256228) cover most of the interior routes. Another good way to scoot around the area May–September is on the Trossachs Trundler (tel. 01786/442707), which loops through Stirling, Callander, Trossachs Pier, Aberfoyle, and back to Stirling for £6.20 every day but Saturday. Haggis Backpackers and Go Blue Banana also provide local service on their way to Glasgow and Edinburgh.

WHERE TO SLEEP

In Aberfoyle, stay at **Mayfield** (Main St., tel. 01877/382845) for £15 per person or at **Old Coach House Inn** (Main St., FK8 3UG, tel. 01877/382822), also £15 per person. **Cobleland Campsite** (01877 382392) run by the Forest Commission Visitors Centre, has 100 tent sites that cost £7.50–£8.60 each. It's 2 mi south of town on an unclassified road off A81; ask someone at the tourist office (*see above*) to draw you a map.

The Callander tourist office can provide a full list of available B&Bs. **Mrs. Collier** (Inver-enys, Ancaster Rd., tel. 01877/330908) is open all year with beds for £16–£17 in a relatively modern home. You'll pay a lot more (£40) for a more historic setting, such as **Leny House** (Callander, tel. 01877/331078), a 19th-century baronial mansion with lovely views to the mountains and glens.

ST. ANDREWS

According to legend, St. Andrews was founded in the 4th century by St. Regulus, who was shipwrecked here while carrying the relics (a few bones and whatnot) of St. Andrew. Another version of the legend has these relics arriving during the 8th century when the Culdees, a strict Christian sect, founded a settlement here. All accounts, however, agree that by the 12th century, St. Andrews had become the religious center of Scotland. When Bishop Henry Wardlaw founded **St. Andrews University** in 1412, he ensured the town's leadership in matters of both religion and education. Today the university is ranked as one of the top five in all of Britain. On the northeastern coast of Fife, the town is also framed by bountiful beaches and scenic seascapes, making it a popular retreat for tourists and Scots alike.

And then there's golf. Golfers come from all over the world to tee off at the sport's holiest of shrines, the **Old Course.** You must be a bona fide golfer and be in possession of a handicap card from your hometown golf course before you'll be allowed to set a cleated foot on the venerable turf. These people are serious.

Despite the wealth of sights, St. Andrews is a small town, easily seen in a day. St. Andrews Cathedral, the ruined castle, the stately buildings of St. Salvator's College (now part of the university) all lie within easy walking distance of the town center. **West Sands** beach, near the sacred golf course, may look familiar, and well it should: The famous scene of runners training for the Olympics from the movie Chariots of Fire was filmed there. If you want to cycle around, a great idea in good weather, rent a bike for £10.50 per day or £6 per half day from **Spokes** (77 South St., tel. 01334/477835). This is a great spot to try a little deep-sea angling, too, or watch the seabirds nesting on the cliffs.

VISITOR INFORMATION

The nice folks at the tourist office book rooms for free. Ask for free town map and load up on activity brochures. *70 Market St., tel. 01334/472021. Open Oct.–Apr., weekdays 9:30–5, weekends 2–5; May, Mon.–Sat. 9:30–5, Sun. 11–5; June and Sept., Mon.–Sat. 9:30–6, Sun. 11–5; July and Aug., Mon.–Sat. 9:30–7, Sun. 11–5.*

COMING AND GOING

There's no direct rail line to St. Andrews. From Edinburgh, ScotRail goes to **Leuchars** (£7.90 single), about 8 mi north of town. From here, catch Bus 94, 95, or 96 (£1), which run several times each hour to St. Andrews's bus station.

The cheapest way to reach St. Andrews from Edinburgh is on Fife Scottish (tel. 01592/261461) Bus X59 (12 per day, 2 hrs, £8.50 day return, £11 standard return). From Glasgow, Fife Scottish Bus X24 leaves hourly and connects with Bus X59 in Glenrothes (2¼ hrs, about £12 standard return), which will take you to St. Andrews. From the north (Perth, Inverness, or Aberdeen), **Scottish Citylink** will take you to Dundee, where you can catch Fife Scottish Bus 96 or **Moffat & Williamson** Bus X95 to St. Andrews for less than £4. **Bluebird** runs from Stirling (1½ hrs, £4.95 single) every hour. The **bus station** (Station Rd., tel. 01334/474–0238), which has a **left-luggage desk,** closes at 5 PM during the week and at noon on weekends. For info outside these hours, call the bus station in Kirkcaldy (tel. 01592/642394).

WHERE TO SLEEP

Most students live in residence halls and golfers can usually afford to pay high prices, so bargain accommodations are hard to come by—not the least because St. Andrews does not have a hostel. B&Bs in town cost £14–£18 per person, or for a few pounds less you can usually book yourself into something not-so-charming outside the city center (ask at the tourist office). Even **university housing** is expensive here, with rooms starting at £22.50. Three halls are available June–September; book by calling 01334/462000 or faxing 01334/462500.

Local buses loop around the south side of town, where the cheaper B&Bs are. If you arrive too late to find a reasonable B&B, try the guest houses on **Murray Place** and **Murray Park,** both jam-packed with B&Bs. They average £18–£28 for a single, but they're just off The Scores (the street that runs along the sea cliffs) and near the sights. **Mrs. Haston's B&B** (8 Nelson St., tel. 01334/473227), in a quiet neighborhood a 10-minute walk from town, is one of the least expensive places to stay in St. Andrews. She has three rooms (£13 per person) and is closed November–March.

CAMPING • One of the nicer caravan parks in Scotland, **Craigtoun Meadows Holiday Park** (Mount Melville Rd., tel. 01334/475959) has 98 tent sites (£12.50–£14.50) available on 31 partially wooded acres; closed November–February. It's also a mere 2 mi from the town center and next door to Craigtown County Park, which is filled with old trees, sumptuous gardens, and ponds. From the bus station, take Bus 64. Only 1 mi from town off A915, **Cairnsmill Caravan Park** (Largo Rd., tel. 01334/473604), closed November–March, has more agreeable prices: Tent sites start at £6.50.

FOOD

The lodging scene may not be ideal, but the food is at least reasonably priced. Eat at **Joe's** (170 Market St., tel. 01334/473035). Well, actually, you'll have to take it away. The staff has about as much personality as the dead fish they serve, but the prices are excellent and so is the grub. In the wee hours, you can get tasty grub at **All-Night Bakery** (4 Abbey St., tel. 01334/476016). **Victoria Café** (1 St. Mary's Pl., tel. 01334/476964), affectionately known as the Vic, gets thumbs up for serving breakfasts (bacon, sausage, egg, hash browns, tomato, and tea or coffee) all day. At night it's a popular student bar with pool and darts and a happy hour from 8 to 9. One of the nicest coffeehouses in town is **Brambles** (5 College St., tel. 01334/475380), a cozy stone- and brick-walled nook with a wall of recommendations by Egon Ronay and several corny pictures of the proprietor, Paul Rowe, and his family. The burgers and chips are homemade, and there's a good selection of salads and excellent sweets. The café has recently started opening as a pricier restaurant several evenings a week if you fancy a splurge (three courses for about £17). The very popular **Kinness Fry Bar** (79 Bridge St., tel. 01334/473802) serves fish-and-chips, some of the best pizza in town, and excellent kebabs. Except for the clueless staff and weak tea, the food at **Chesterhills** (104 South St., tel. 01334/473199) is reasonable enough. Expect steak and mushroom pie and unreconstructed Scottish stodge such as Clootie dumpling. If you want to brown bag it, stock up at **Tesco Supermarket** (144 Market Street).

WORTH SEEING

ST. ANDREWS CATHEDRAL • Standing above the drama of the North Sea, St. Andrew's magnificent 13th-century cathedral collapsed twice in the face of the wicked weather that plagues this unprotected peninsula. When intact, the cathedral was 355 ft long and 160 ft wide, the largest in Scotland. Today only the twin spires of the east and west ends remain, but nonetheless, the site is very impressive and makes for a supremely romantic silhouette on the cliff top. The grounds also contain a massive cemetery, a stunning place to visit. Nearby is **St. Rule's Tower,** built between 1127 and 1244 to honor St. Regulus, the legendary saint whose shipwreck brought St. Andrews's relics here. The 108-ft climb to the top affords wonderful views of the town. The on-site museum is only so-so. *East end of town, tel. 01334/472563. Admission to tower and museum £1.80; free admission to grounds. Joint ticket for cathedral and castle £3.50. Open Apr.–Sept., Mon.–Sat. 9:30–6:30, Sun. 2–6:30; Oct.–Mar., Mon.–Sat. 9:30–4, Sun. 2–4.*

After the Reformation, when St. Andrews Cathedral was in ruins, local townspeople used the stones to build their houses. They're tough to notice, since people put the sculpted side inward, so as not to get caught.

SEA LIFE CENTRE • Next to the ocean and just behind the British Golf Museum, this huge aquarium has a series of great displays on local sea creatures. Several gray seals frolic in their pool, while a massive open-topped tank allows you to pet friendly skates and flatfish. *The Scores, tel. 01334/474786. Admission £4.35. Open daily 10–6 (July–Aug. until 7).*

ST. ANDREWS CASTLE • Directly north of the cathedral stand the ruins of a castle strategically situated upon a rocky cliff, now home to hundreds of gulls and other birds. What a pious 13th-century bishop needed the castle for is open to speculation, but it certainly wasn't for "turning the other cheek"—just take a peek into the pit where they held Reformers in the 16th century before burning them. Journey down beneath the castle to the mine, dug by the earl of Arran to rescue his imprisoned son, and the countermine, dug by the castle guards to thwart his attempt. *The Scores, tel. 01334/477196. Admission £2.50.*

ST. SALVATOR'S COLLEGE AND UNITED COLLEGE • Across from the castle, between The Scores and North Street, are some of the university's venerable buildings. The university chapel, with its lofty tower, dates back to the time of Bishop Kennedy, who founded St. Salvator's in 1450. The grassy square within the walls of United College has a few benches placed where you can relax and breathe in the wisdom of the ages. During July and August, students lead free tours of the university; ask at the tourist office for times.

AFTER DARK

The considerable student population in St. Andrews is evidenced by a thriving pub scene. **The Central** (corner of Market and College Sts., tel. 01334/478296) is an antiquated pub popular with an upscale crowd, whereas **Burt's Bar** (South St., at Church St., no phone) and **Victoria** (1A St. Mary's Pl., tel. 01334/476964) are more casual student pubs. If you're interested in socializing with the silver-spoon toting Yas, Britain's answer to the American Greek system, they hang out at **Ma Belle's.** The pub is attached to, and shares a phone with, **St. Andrews Golf Hotel** (40 The Scores, tel. 01334/472611), where each Wednesday night from July to September it's "Scots Night." It costs £4.95 to attend this ceilidh, reportedly one of the best around, complete with haggis, neeps, and tatties (or turnips and potatoes, ultra-traditional Scots fare) for an extra charge. The **Byre Theatre** (Abbey St., at South St., tel. 01334/346288) produces top-notch professional plays from classical to contemporary; tickets cost £3–£8.50. **Crawford Arts Centre** (93 North St., tel. 01334/474610) is a free student gallery, open Monday–Saturday 10–5, Sunday 2–5, that occasionally puts on amateur theater productions. Call for a schedule of upcoming events.

THE NORTHEAST

The Northeast is a geographically diverse area, stretching north from the Angus Glens to the oil-rich waters of the North Sea. **Aberdeen,** the main port for North Sea oil operations, is the region's largest city, but elsewhere the area is predominantly rural. The **Grampians** and the **Cairngorms**—beautiful, mountainous regions of heather and forest, granite peaks and deep glens—are popular for hill walking in warm weather and skiing in cold weather. Always bring a compass and an Ordnance Survey map on hill walks, and always tell someone your itinerary, even in summertime. Mountain rescue teams still shake their head in bemusement at the tourist from Colorado who tried to climb one peak in tennis shoes, only to find herself slithering down a snowfield and breaking her leg. The guides only laugh about her because the story ended well and the helicopter got to her before hypothermia did. These mountains may look pretty in postcards but they are not places to mess around with.

This area is on the cusp of the Highlands and has a rich lode of storytelling and history, now being mined by tourist attractions capitalizing on Aberdeenshire's pagan past and proliferation of Pictish standing stones. **Archaeolink** (tel. 01464/851554) in the hamlet of Oyne, Aberdeenshire, is the latest and best evocation of this pungent and mystical past.

Deeside, the valley running west from Aberdeen along which the river Dee flows, earned its "Royal" appellation when Queen Victoria and her consort, Albert, built their exquisite Scottish fantasy house, Balmoral, here. To this day, where royalty goes, lesser aristocracy and fastbuck millionaires from around the globe follow. Their yearning to possess an estate here is understandable, since piney hill slope, purple moor, and blue river intermingle most sublimely, as you will see from the main road.

The main travel routes north of Aberdeen, both by rail and motorway, run through Elgin to Inverness. The big towns are well served by ScotRail and their competitor on the road, Citylink. But you might find it hard going without a car if you want to explore the peripheral towns, which jag away from this central spine like vertebrae.

ABERDEEN

Sprawled between the Rivers Dee and Don, this seaside city is the center of Britain's North Sea oil industry. During the oil boom in the 1970s, people came from all over to work here. There was a bust period in the 1980s when oil prices dropped, but Aberdeen survived it and came out stronger than ever. Oil businesspeople share this city with 25,000 students, and its current prosperity means it can be an expensive place to spend time. It has some interesting sights, unique architecture, and a relaxed atmosphere. It has a hopping nightlife, too: Every weekend thousands of people flock into bars and clubs on streets radiating off Union Street, the main drag.

BASICS

The all-knowing **Aberdeen Tourist Board** changes money, books accommodations for free, and publishes the helpful brochure "What's On." They also have lots of info on the Highlands. *St. Nicholas House, Broad St., tel. 01224/632727. Open July and Aug., weekdays 9–7, Sat. 9–5, Sun. 10–5; June and Sept., Mon.–Sat. 9–5, Sun. 10–2; Oct.–May, weekdays 9–5, Sat. 10–2.*

The **main post office** is at St. Nicholas Centre (tel. 01224/633065), but some packages are dealt with by the **Royal Mail Collection Centre** (Wellington Rd., Altens Industrial Estate, tel. 0345/740740). **Aberdeen Royal Infirmary** (Foresterhill Rd., tel. 01224/681818) is open 24 hours for emergencies.

COMING AND GOING

BY BUS • The **bus station** (Guild St., tel. 01224/212266) is right next to the railway station. **Scottish Citylink** connects Aberdeen to most major southern towns via Dundee, including Edinburgh (4 hrs, £13 single) and Glasgow (4 hrs, £13.30 single). **Bluebird Northern** can get you into the Highlands and has regular service to Inverness (3 hrs 30 mins, £10). Call the bus station for fare and route info for both companies.

BY FERRY • **P&O Ferries** (Jamieson's Quay, tel. 01224/572615) operates direct ferries to Orkney (8 hrs, £41 single) and to Shetland (14 hrs, £56.50 single). From June through August you can reach Norway, via the Shetlands, once weekly (30 hrs, £108).

PLANE • The airport is 6 mi northwest of the city center; take Grampian Transport Bus 27 (£1), ●ch also stops directly in front of the SYHA hostel. **British Airways** (tel. 01345/222111) offers flights ▪London as well as Orkney (from £87 return) and Shetland (from £110 return). BA will also allow a tri-▪gular course—Aberdeen to Orkney to Shetland to Aberdeen—which is horrendously expensive at ▪57 including taxes, but if you want to island-hop at least you know it's going to be faster than the ferry. ▪**syJet** (tel. 01582/702900), a leading budget option, offers extremely cheap deals on flights to Lon-▪n from Aberdeen, starting at £29 single.

▪Y TRAIN • Connections to Scotland's third-largest city are easy and frequent. **ScotRail** (tel. 0345/ ▪4950) offers direct service to Aberdeen from Inverness (2½ hrs, £17.60 single) and Edinburgh (2½ ▪s, £32.80 single). The centrally located **rail station** (Guild Street), south of Union Street via Bridge or ▪arket streets, has a **Travel Centre,** open daily 6:20 AM–9 PM, and lockers (£1.50–£4).

▪ETTING AROUND

▪berdeen is a fairly large and sprawling city, but busy **Union Street** and its side streets, especially from ▪ridge Street and Union Terrace northeast toward the harbor, are where you'll find most of the action. **Old Aberdeen,** the center of the city in times gone by, is about 1½ mi north of Union Street. At the cen-▪er of modern-day Aberdeen are three huge granite malls. **Alpine Bikes** (66–70 Holburn St., off Union ▪t., tel. 01224/211455) rents bicycles for £12 per day. If you want to do the whisky and castle thing, ▪renting a car is by far the easiest way to go. Try **Arnold Clark** (Girdleness Rd., tel. 01224/248842), which ▪charges £16 per day (£31 with unlimited mileage).

WHERE TO SLEEP

Bon Accord Street, Springbank Terrace, and Crown Street are good streets to try if you're looking for a B&B. **Mrs. Templeton** (263 Great Western Rd., tel. 01224/588195) has the least expensive beds in town at £14 single and £22 double. Bus 17, 18, or 24 will take you right past the door. Close to the city center is the **Stewart Lodge Guest House** (89 Bon Accord Street, tel. 01224 573823), with singles and doubles from £19 a night. If you stay at **Greyholme Guest House** (Springbank Terrace, tel. 01224/ 587081), you'll have several dodgy bars in the neighborhood from which to choose. It's not the quietest location, but it's near the bus and rail stations, the ferry terminal, and the city center. Singles and doubles are in the same range, from £19 up.

HOSTELS • King George VI Memorial SYHA. This large, granite house is a 15-minute walk southwest of Union Street. Beds cost £11.75 in July and August. The front door locks promptly at 2 AM and from 11 to 2 during the day. Bluebird Bus 201 stops directly across the street. Higher Standard. *8 Queen's Rd., AB1 6YT, tel. 01224/646988. From Union St., take Bus 14, 15, or 27 to Queen's Rd. 104 beds. Kitchen, laundry. Closed Jan.*

FOOD

The numerous pubs just off Union Street around the art gallery offer good, filling, and reasonably priced meals, and the university area is filled with inexpensive chip and baked-potato shops. Don't expect much from the restaurants lining the Beach Esplanade; they cater to tourists and families.

Canadian Muffin Co. There's more than muffins at this clean and cheery café. Bagels, sandwiches, and baked potatoes fill out the healthy menu. A good deal is the Souper Special: your choice of muffin (blueberry raisin gets our vote) and the soup du jour for £3. *15 Back Wynd, tel. 01224/624545.*

Owlies Brasserie. This peaceful restaurant serves French-inspired dishes, including vegetarian and vegan options, amid an interesting, eclectic decor. Try the Moroccan couscous for a taste of something different. *Littlejohn St., at West North St., tel. 01224/649267. Closed Sun.*

Wild Boar Gallery Restaurant. This casual place has comfortable velvet sofas and contemporary paintings. Try the spicy bean and vegetable casserole. The pastries are wonderful. It's open daily until midnight. *19 Belmont St., between Union St. and art gallery, tel. 01224/621533.*

WORTH SEEING

Okay, so you might have to go looking for the spark of humor and vibrancy that makes Aberdeen tick, as outwardly it can seem like a pretty quiet place. But you need look no further the student quarter, around Belmont Street, to find definite signs of life. The city's gray, granite architecture is quite picturesque glinting in the sun, nearly all the attractions are free, the old Footdee (pronounced Fittie) fishing village is interesting. The city also makes a great base for exploring Royal Deeside and Castle Country.

ABERDEEN ART GALLERY • The gallery houses a wide-ranging collection—from 18th-century to contemporary—including a good selection of 20th-century British paintings and sculptures. It has a

particularly strong Scottish section and a fairly adventurous approach to modern art and commu
projects. *Schoolhill, 1 block north of Union St., tel. 01224/632133. Admission free. Open Mon.–*
10–5 (Thurs. until 8), Sun. 2–5.

DUNNOTTAR CASTLE • This 12th-century fortress on the coast, just outside Stonehaven about
mi south of the city, is reason enough to come to Aberdeen. You may have seen this spectacular ruir
medieval castle on its cliff-top perch in the Mel Gibson/Glenn Close film version of *Hamlet.* Bluebird B
101 goes right to the castle Monday–Saturday. Or simply jump on a bus for Montrose and ask the d
ver to let you off at Dunnottar. On Sunday, take Bus 101 or 107 to Stonehaven and walk or hitch 1½
south. *A92, tel. 01569/762173. Admission £3. Open Apr.–Oct., Mon.- -Sat. 9–6, Sun. 2–5; Nov.–Ma*
weekdays 9–dusk.

MARISCHAL COLLEGE • The most imposing structure in Aberdeen, Marischal College was founde
in 1593 as a Protestant alternative to the Catholic King's College in Old Aberdeen (*see below*), thoug
the two merged in 1860 to form Aberdeen University. It's the second-largest granite building in the worl
(only the Escorial outside Madrid is larger), and on sunny days the delicate-looking gray facade sparkle
beautifully. There is also a museum with rotating exhibits. *Broad St., tel. 01224/273131. Admissio*
free.

MARITIME MUSEUM • Aberdeen is a port city, and this museum is the best way to learn about the
city's watery history, including info on the North Sea oil rigs. Now remodeled, the place has imported the
latest technology to tell the history and the current state of the Aberdonian affair with the sea. It's worth
coming in just for a glance or two at the massive oil rig dominating the central area of the four-story
museum. *Provost Ross's House, Shiprow, at Market and Castle Sts., tel. 01224/337700. Admission*
£3.50. Open Mon.–Sat. 10–5, Sun. noon–3.

OLD ABERDEEN • Formerly an independent burgh near the River Don, Old Aberdeen was swallowed
up by the main city before the end of the 19th century. Today it's the most picturesque area in
Aberdeen, with cobblestone streets that weave among homes dating back as far as 1500. Stroll along
High Street and check out the medieval **King's College Chapel,** now part of Aberdeen University; the
visitor center (tel. 01224/273702) is open daily. On the other end of High Street, to the north, lies **St.
Machar's Cathedral.** The foundation was laid in AD 1130 on the site of a 6th-century kirk, though most
of what is visible today was erected in the 14th and 15th centuries. The gravestones lining the walkway
to the cathedral stare at you as you approach. To get here, take Bus 20 from John Street or Bus 1, 2, 3,
4, 7, or 15 from King Street.

SHOPPING

The main shopping area radiates off the city's central artery, Union Street. There are three shopping
malls, offering the usual chain stores, while the Italian-flavored **Belmont** development, on Belmont
Street, offers a cornucopia of unusual, character-saturated retailers. **John Lewis** is a favored department
store (George St., reached via Bon Accord Centre, tel. 01224/625000). **Nova** (20 Chapel St., 01224/
641270) is popular for gifts. The family-owned **Esslemont and McIntosh** department store (Union
Street) is holding its own against the chain stores. Round the corner on Queen Street is **Mackays,** a
dusty, cluttered wonderful place that preserves—like a museum—the 1970s, the decade that taste forgot. At the **Aberdeen Family History Shop** (164 King St., tel. 01224/646323), browse through a huge
range of publications related to local history.

AFTER DARK

Grab a free copy of "What's On" or the council listings brochure from the tourist office or most pubs and
clubs for a comprehensive diary of events. The most popular (read: cheapest) plan of attack for a night
out is to have a few low-priced brews at a pub then head to the nightclubs, where the drinks are much
more expensive. **Ma Cameron's** (6 Little Belmont St., tel. 01224/644487) is the oldest pub in Aberdeen
and draws a crowd ranging from younger students to old-time drinkers. It vies with the **Prince of Wales**
(St. Nicholas La., tel. 01224/640597), which has a truly gargantuan bar, for the title of Aberdeen's most
authentically Scottish bar (the less studenty Prince wins the contest, just by the length of a pint of perfectly pulled heavy). Raucous company can be found in **O'Donoghue's** (16 Justice Mill La., tel. 01224/
575040), a three-bar complex on what has been dubbed Aberdeen's Sunset Strip, a row of brightly colored bars and clubs running parallel to Union Street. Far from being a pastiche of Irishness,
O'Donoghues concentrates more on atmosphere than authenticity and is all the better for it. If you're
looking for something a bit more refined, try **Under the Hammer** (11 N. Silver St., tel. 01224/640253),
a tiny and extremely popular basement wine bar. For late-night bootie-shaking, head to **Ministry of Sin**
(Dee St., tel. 01224/211661), **Oh Henry's** (20 Adelphi St., tel. 01224/586949), or **Zúú** (Windmill Brae,

Finally, a travel companion that doesn't snore on the plane or eat all your peanuts.

MCI *WORLDCOM*   *WorldPhone®*

123 456 7891 2345
J.D. SMITH

When traveling, your MCI WorldCom Card is the best way to keep in touch. Our operators speak your language, so they'll be able to connect you back home—no matter where your travels take you. Plus, your MCI WorldCom Card is easy to use, and even earns you frequent flyer miles every time you use it. When you add in our great rates, you get something even more valuable: peace-of-mind. So go ahead. Travel the world. MCI WorldCom just brought it a whole lot closer.

You can even sign up today at www.mci.com/worldphone or ask your operator to make a collect call to 1-410-314-2938.

EASY TO CALL WORLDWIDE

1 **Just dial the WorldPhone access number of the country you're calling from.**
2 **Dial or give the operator your MCI WorldCom Card number.**
3 **Dial or give the number you're calling.**

France ◆	0-800-99-0019
Germany	0800-888-8000
Ireland	1-800-55-1001
Italy ◆	172-1022
Spain	900-99-0014
Sweden ◆	020-795-922
Switzerland ◆	0800-89-0222
United Kingdom To call using BT To call using CWC	0800-89-0222 0500-89-0222

For your complete WorldPhone calling guide, dial the WorldPhone access number for the country you're in and ask the operator for Customer Service. In the U.S. call 1-800-431-5402.

◆ Public phones may require deposit of coin or phone card for dial tone.

EARN FREQUENT FLYER MILES

American Airlines®
A′Advantage®

Continental Airlines
OnePass®

▲ Delta Air Lines
SkyMiles®

■ MILEAGE PLUS®
United Airlines

US AIRWAYS
DIVIDEND MILES

MCI WorldCom, its logo and the names of the products referred to herein are proprietary marks of MCI WorldCom, Inc. All airline names and logos are proprietary marks of the respective airlines. All airline program rules and conditions apply.

MCI *WORLDCOM*

Fodor's

Distinctive guides packed with up-to-date expert advice and smart choices for every type of traveler.

Fodor's. For the world of ways you travel.

01224/572876). **Club Caberfeidh** (38 Exchange St., tel. 01224/212181) is the best choice for a gay ght out about town. For a more refined evening, visit **Aberdeen Arts Centre** (King St., at West North ., tel. 01224/635208), which presents classical and contemporary plays (£3.50–£7) and a variety of ns (£2–£3). Or walk a few yards down the street to the **Lemon Tree** (tel. 01224/642230), Scotland's ost credible multi-arts venue, where you'll find performance poets rubbing shoulders with jazz musi- ans and bands either too young to play the bigger halls or too discerning. Director Shona Powell can e seen here most nights, closely overseeing a remarkable and vibrant place.

ROYAL DEESIDE

he area along the River Dee, which runs from the Cairngorm and Grampian mountain ranges east to Aberdeen, has been called "Royal Deeside" ever since Queen Victoria visited it and liked it so much she bought the Balmoral Estate in 1848. Its charms are obvious, extending from the drama of the landscape to the quality of the fishing. The A93 winds its way through the wee towns of **Banchory** and **Ballater** to **Braemar.** Each of these towns is well served by public transportation, and it only takes a bit over an hour to reach Braemar from Banchory by bus. Getting to the castles around them can be another matter. Most are near A944, otherwise known as the **Castle Trail,** which runs along the River Don north of Dee- side. Unless you're a die-hard castle fanatic, don't kill yourself to hit every one. Just pick a few that seem interesting and enjoy the journey.

Banchory is a small town set between two popular castles. **Drum Castle and Garden** (tel. 01330/ 811204), admission £4.40, open daily May–September, dates from the 13th century and features rounded towers (built to make battering-ram attacks more difficult) and a tranquil rose garden. Bus 201 will drop you off a half mile from the castle. Three miles east of Banchory, **Crathes Castle and Garden** (tel. 01330/844525) is a 16th-century castle that has wackily painted ceilings covered with heroes and muses. Admission is £4.50, but you can always just opt for a ticket (£1.80) to see the beautifully man- icured gardens. Bus 201 drops you off right at the gate.

Ballater is the town closest to **Balmoral Castle,** which is 8 mi to the west. This one's the big draw, being castle of choice for the royals each August, but some think it's a bust for £3.50. The only part of the cas- tle you can visit is the ballroom, with its cheesy exhibit on the royal history at Balmoral. If you want to join the crowds, Bluebird Bus 201 stops right at the front gate. If you want to ditch the crowds queuing up for tours, take a walk (or a bike) around the grounds instead. The Royals are fairly relaxed about the public's right to roam the estate, which has paved paths and picturesque lakes and the perfect English country estate atmosphere, but police and security will warn you off if the family are around. They've been a tad more nervy ever since a Royal party came upon a group of naked mountain bikers at a lodge on the estate. The pink **Craigievar Castle** (tel. 01339/883635), open May– September, daily 1:30–5:30, still intact from 1626, is possibly the finest castle in the region, with storybook turrets and towers spring- ing out all over. Admission is £5.50, and it's also tough to get to. Take Bluebird Bus 201 from Aberdeen to the Crossroads Hotel, a few miles north of Lumphanan (where Macbeth lost his head); from here fol- low the signs 2½ mi north to Craigievar.

At the end of the line, **Braemar** is Scotland's version of an alpine village, surrounded by hills and bor- dered by the rushing River Clunie. The town is most famous for the **Braemar Gathering** (tel. 01339/ 755377), the mother of all Highland Games, sometimes attended by the Queen herself. Burly men with calves bulging between the hems of their kilts and the tops of their Nikes compete in events like tug-of- war, Throwing the Hammer, Putting the Stone, and the ubiquitous Tossing the Caber, and Highland dancing. About 20,000 people pack the town for this one-day fest, so if you're around on the first Saturday in Sep- tember, get your ticket (starting at £4 for standing room) early, and definitely book a room in advance with the tourist office (*see below*). For complete information, contact William Meston, Secretary, Brae- mar Gathering, Collarlech, Ballater, AB35 5UH (tel. 01339/55377). Another attraction is **Braemar Cas- tle** (tel. 01339/741219), a five-minute walk from town on A93, with extensive rooms and towers and an underground prison. Admission is £2 and the castle is closed Friday.

Braemar's real virtue is its breathtaking setting near the **Grampian Mountains,** making it a perfect hill- walking base. The **Linn of Dee,** where the otherwise peaceful river forces its way through a tight gorge, is only 6 mi from Braemar. A postbus runs up there Monday–Saturday. An intense hiking route in the area is the **Lairig Ghru,** which starts at Derry Gate and continues through 28 mi of the highest areas of the Cairngorms. There are several trails near the beginning, but all eventually converge at the bothy near the base of **Devil's Point,** a rocky pinnacle. If you follow the **River Dee** you won't go astray. On the other

side of the summit you'll find some remnants of the once great Caledonian Forest, before winding do
the pass to A9, roughly 5 mi southwest of Aviemore. A shorter (1½ hrs), yet extremely scenic and enj
able hike, begins just past the Chapel Brae duck pond and climbs 2,500 ft up the Morrone Hill. T
tourist offices have pamphlets like "Walking in the Grampians" (£1) and Ordnance Survey Maps for h
ing in the Deeside area.

BASICS

There are tourist offices in **Banchory** (Bridge St., tel. 01330/822000), **Braemar** (Mar Rd., tel. 0133
741600), and **Ballater** (Station Sq., tel. 01339/755306). Braemar is the best stocked, but Banchory
the friendliest and most informative. They're all open from March through October, and Braemar is als
open in the winter. Banchory offers an extremely good advanced reservation service, specially geare
for the U.S. market (tel. 01330/825917).

COMING AND GOING

Bluebird (tel. 01224/212266) Bus 201 is the lifeline of Deeside, running between Aberdeen and Brae
mar every 30–60 minutes, though less frequently on Sunday and in winter. Fares are expensive (£5), so
if you're moving around, invest in a **Day Rover Pass** (£8) that allows unlimited travel. Dedicated buses
also run along the so-called Malt Whisky Trail, a network of roads which take you past several of the
area's distilleries. This runs from Deeside to Tomintoul and is traversed by the Heather Hopper and the
Speyside Rambler. Bluebird are the people to call for timetable details. If you're only travelling short distances, check with local post offices over the availability of postbuses: you get to ride with the mail. It's
not quite Pony Express but they can sometimes be the best option—or the only one in remote areas.

WHERE TO SLEEP AND EAT

Royal Deeside is not cheap. The best guest houses tend to be in Braemar. **Cranford Guest House** (15
Glenshee Rd., tel. 01339/741675) has rooms for £20 per person, and the nearby **Schiehallion House**
(Glenshee Rd., tel. 01339/741679) charges £17–£19.50 per person. **Braemar SYHA** (Corrie Feragie,
21 Glenshee Rd., tel. 01339/741659), Standard, a five-minute walk uphill from the square, is closed
November–late December. The manager Alistair Hubbard is very friendly and his staff is extremely
knowledgeable about hiking in Deeside and the Cairngorms. Probably the best option if you have transport is the **Wolf's Hearth** (Tornaveen, tel. 01339/883460) near Torphins, halfway between Banchory
and Ballater. They have 14 big beds (from £9.50) and a huge stone fireplace, where you just want to circle three times and lie down on the rug.

Braemar also has the best dining scene around. For breakfast, try **Gordon's Tea Room and Restaurant**
(Mar Rd., tel. 01339/741247), which serves a good fry-up, a mountain of bacon and sausages that
might be described as a heart attack on a plate. Open only for dinner, the **Wishing Well** (15 Glenshee
Rd., tel. 01339/741675) offers affordable fine food, along with great atmosphere and quick service; veg-
etrarians will enjoy the veggie dish of the day. Stop in the popular **Fife Hotel** (Mar Road) and **Invercauld
Arms** (Invercauld Road) pubs for standard pub grub and pints.

HIGHLANDS AND NORTHERN ISLANDS

The most romantic images of Scotland are all drawn from the Highlands. Times have been hard for the
Highlands, however, ever since the Battle of Culloden in 1746, when the Jacobites (supporters of the
Stuarts and "Bonnie Prince Charlie") were ruthlessly crushed. After Culloden, the Highland clans that
had warmly embraced Prince Charles suffered the wrath of a vengeful government. Tartan was banned
and many of the Jacobites who escaped the massacre at Culloden and subsequent executions were
chased from their land in the chain of events leading to the Highland Clearances, where old and new
lairds alike forcibly evicted tenant farmers so they could use the land more profitably by raising sheep.

Still today, parts of the Highlands—without question Scotland's most breathtaking scenery—remain as
remote and wild as ever. The southern region, stretching south from Inverness and the Kyle of Lochalsh

t William, is the most accessible. Most visitors stick fairly close to easily reached areas like Loch
because it's tough going to reach many of the northern spots (but absolutely worth the effort). The
ern Highlands is the most sparsely populated area of Scotland but also the most topographically
d and dramatic, with high mountains on the west coast, moors in the desolate interior, and green
ands in the east.

of archaeological interest abound. Prehistoric burial cairns, Pict settlements and carved stones,
standing stones can all be viewed here. This expanse of bleak but beautiful country may hold more
of prehistoric significance than any other in the United Kingdom. That's not to say that the culture
is mired in the past—there is an annual **Highlands Festival** that boasts a fortnight of performances
ughout the far-flung corners of this vast region. For more information contact The Highland Festival,
Huntly St., Inverness, IV3 5HR, tel. 01463/711112. You can also check out this spirited affair on the
rnet at www.highlandfestival.demon.co.uk.

NVERNESS

e of Scotland's major shipping ports, Inverness, on the Moray Firth, is best known as the town from
ich visitors launch their search for Scotland's beloved Nessie, the Loch Ness Monster (*see* Loch
ss, *below*). The town itself is growing rapidly, and as the "Capital of the Highlands," it is the last sub-
antial outpost reached as you head north. In other words, if you do any traveling to the north or north-
st, you must pass through Inverness. The River Ness winds its way through the center of town, where
ou'll find the **Inverness Museum and Gallery** (Bridge Street), with exhibits on local art, history, and
ldlife. But Inverness's real beauty lies in the miles of trails that run alongside the dark waters of the
aledonian Canal leading to Loch Ness and into the Highlands. The waters of the Moray Firth hold
nother attraction: the most northerly pod of resident bottle-nosed dolphins. **Moray Firth Cruises** (Shore
t. Quay, tel. 01463/717900) offers rides to see the dolphins, which come right up alongside the ves-
el. They sail several times daily March–October. The 1¼-hour tours cost £7–£10.

BASICS

The **Inverness Tourist Information Centre** (Castle Wynd, tel. 01463/234353) books B&Bs for a fee,
changes money, and arranges Loch Ness tours. They also have information on ferries to the Orkney and
Shetland islands and the Hebrides. The main **post office** is on Queensgate, but to receive poste restante
you must visit the **Royal Mail Centre** (7 Strothers La., IVI 1AA, tel. 01463/256240) 7– 5:30 Monday
through Saturday. **Bikes of Inverness** (Grant St., tel. 01463/225965) rents bikes for £12-£14 per day.

COMING AND GOING

To visit the sights near Inverness, a **Highland Day Rover Pass** (available May 15–September 24) for
Buses 11 and 12 is your best bet. Buses leave from the Inverness bus station and make stops at Culloden, Cawdor, Fort George, the seaside town of Nairn, and 17th-century Castle Stuart. You can get on
and off all day for £8. Go Blue Banana and Haggis Backpackers both stop here regularly on their cir-
cuits. **Rabbie's Trail Burners** (tel. 0131/226–3133) offers day tours of Skye and other areas, departing
from Inverness hostels. **Europcar Interrent**'s (tel. 01463/235337) autos start at £29.25 per day.

BY BUS • Farraline Park Bus Station (Margaret St., tel. 01463/233371) is just a few blocks from the
train station. The major operator in Inverness is **Citylink** (tel. 0990/505050) for destinations like Edinburgh (£12.20 single), Thurso (£9 single), or Skye (£10.50 single); **Bluebird** for Aberdeen (£8.60 single) and Elgin (£4.50 single). There are other independent companies but this is a fast-moving sector
and you'd best call the station for updates on who survived the winter and Citylink's aggressive pricing.
You can leave luggage at the station for £1.

BY TRAIN • The train station (Academy St., tel. 0345/484950), in the heart of the town, has several
daily trains to Edinburgh (£29.60 single), Glasgow (£29.60 single), Aberdeen (£17.60 single), Kyle of
Lochalsh for the Isle of Skye (£14.60 single), and Thurso (£12.20 single). You can also stow luggage
here for £1–£3.

WHERE TO SLEEP

Inverness gets crowded during the summer, so book ahead. Head across the river to Fairfield Road or
Kenneth Street, both hotbeds of cheapish B&Bs. Or try the Crown District at the top of Castle Street
behind the hostels. The lovely and welcoming **Mary Ann Villa** (Mary Ann Ct., at Ardross Pl., tel. 01463/
230187), next to St. Andrews Cathedral, has £16 singles and £28 doubles.

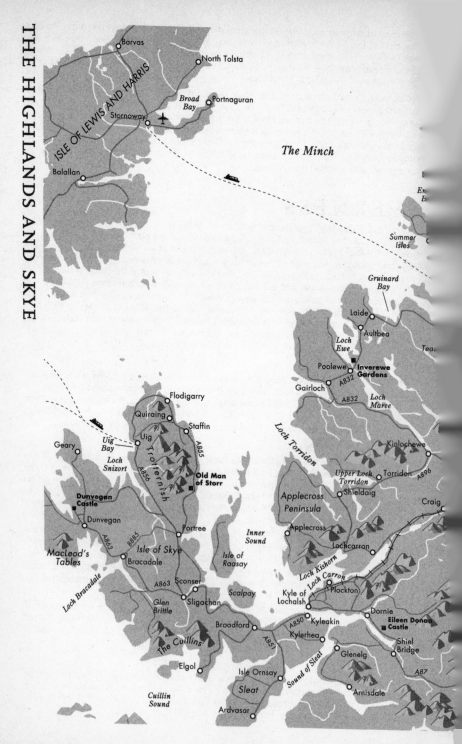

Barvas

North Tolsta

ISLE OF LEWIS AND HARRIS

Broad Bay

Portnaguran

Stornoway

Balallan

The Minch

Summer Isles

En B

Gruinard Bay

Laide

Aultbea

Loch Ewe

Poolewe **Inverewe Gardens**

Gairloch A832

A832 *Loch Maree*

Tea

Flodigarry

Quiraing

Staffin

Uig Bay Uig A855

Geary

Loch Snizort

Trotternish

A856

Old Man of Storr

Loch Torridon

Kinlochewe

Torridon A896

Upper Loch Torridon

Shieldaig

Dunvegan Castle

Dunvegan

Portree

Inner Sound

Isle of Raasay

Applecross Peninsula

Applecross

Lochcarron

Craig

Macleod's Tables

A863 B885

Isle of Skye

Bracadale

Sconser

A863 Sligachan

Scalpay

Loch Kishorn

Loch Carron

Kyle of Lochalsh

Plockton

Loch Bracadale

Glen Brittle

Broadford A850 Kyleakin

Kylerhea

Dornie

Eileen Donan Castle

The Cuillins

Elgol

A851

Isle Ornsay

Sleat

Sound of Sleat

Glenelg

Shiel Bridge

A87

Cuillin Sound

Ardvasar

Arnisdale

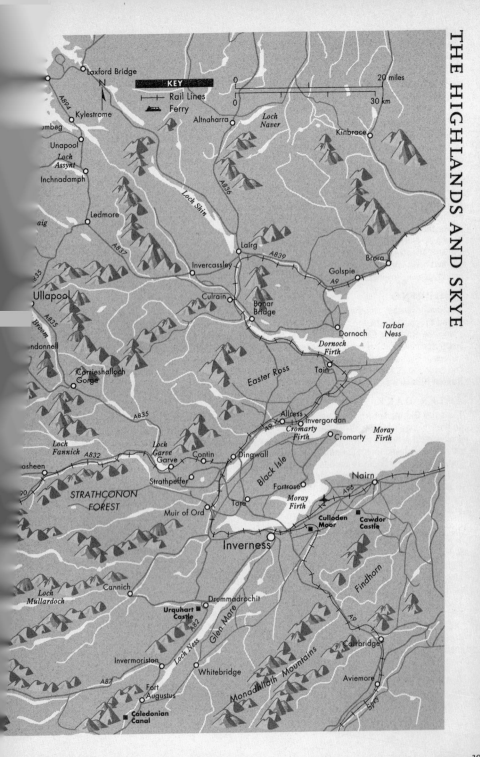

Loxford Bridge
N
Kylestrome
A894
ombeg
Unapool
Loch Assynt
Inchnadamph
aig
Ledmore
A835
Ullapool
A835
Broom
ndonnell
Corrieshalloch Gorge
Loch Fannich
A832
asheen
A832
Loch Garve
Garve
Contin
Strathpeffer
STRATHCONON FOREST
Muir of Ord
Cannich
Loch Mullardoch
Urquhart Castle
A82
Invermoriston
A87
Fort Augustus
Caledonian Canal

Altnaharra
Loch Naver
Kinbrace
Loch Shin
A836
Lairg
A839
Brora
Invercassley
Golspie
A9
Culrain
Bonar Bridge
Dornoch
Tarbat Ness
Dornoch Firth
Tain
Easter Ross
Alness
A9
Invergordan
Cromarty Firth
Cromarty
Moray Firth
Dingwall
Black Isle
Fortrose
Moray Firth
Tore
Nairn
A96
Culloden Moor
Cawdor Castle
Inverness
Findhorn
Drummadrochit
Glen Mare
Loch Ness
Whitebridge
Monadhliath Mountains
Cairbridge
Aviemore
Spey

KEY
Rail Lines
Ferry

0   20 miles
0   30 km

UNDER £60 • Daviot Mains Farms. A cozy, 19th-century farmhouse 5 mi south of town on A9 provides all the comforts of home and traditional Scottish cooking, but you'll pay for it. *Daviot Mains, Inverness, IV2 5ER, tel. 01463/772215, fax 01463/772099. 3 rooms, 1 with bath.*

HOSTELS • Bazpackers Hostel. The great spirit of Scottish hospitality has been revived by Baz, the congenial host. Perfectly located above the River Ness, this cozy hostel provides immediate access to shops and pubs. Dorm beds cost £8.50, doubles go for £24. *4 Culduthel Rd., tel. 01463/717663. From bus or rail station, walk left on Academy St., turn right on High St., left on Castle St. 40 beds. Reception open 7 AM–midnight. Kitchen, laundry. Cash only.*

Inverness Student Hotel. The relaxed, fun-loving atmosphere and the view overlooking the River Ness (ask for a room with a view) are reason enough to come. Beds cost £8.90. There's a small fee for credit-card use. *8 Culduthel Rd., tel. 01463/236556. Follow directions to Bazpackers (see above). 57 beds. Reception open 6:30 AM–2:30 AM. Kitchen, laundry.*

FOOD

The **Safeway** across from the bus station is the size of a small planet. Pub lunches around town are another budget option: Try **Phoenix Bar** (Academy St., tel. 01463/233685) with meals for £3–£5. **Castle Restaurant** (41 Castle St., tel. 01463/230925) is short on atmosphere but high on cheap grub, like the £5.20 patty melt with fixin's. It's the quintessential Scots-Italian café, run by the Boni and Lipton families. The **Royal Tandoori Restaurant** (99 Castle St., tel. 01463/712224) is just down from the hostels and open late. Eat beside the aquariums, or take out curry dishes. In addition to the above-mentioned eateries, Inverness has all the fast-food places you could possibly want.

SHOPPING

Although Inverness has the usual High Street stores and department stores—including Arnott's and Marks & Spencer—the most interesting goods are to be found in the specialty outlets in and around town. The **Riverside Gallery** (11 Bank St., tel. 01463/224781) sells paintings and prints of Scottish landscapes and natural history. **Duncan Chisholm and Sons** (49 Castle St., tel. 01463/234599) specializes in Highland dress, tartans, and Scottish crafts. Other gifts to please that lad or lassie back home can be found at **James Pringle Ltd.** (Holm Woollen Mills, Dores Rd., tel. 01463/223311) and **Hector Russell Kiltmakers** (4–9 Huntley St., tel. 01463/222781).

AFTER DARK

The small **Old Market Inn** (32 Church St., tel. 01463/220203) often has excellent fiddlers performing on the tiny stage. **Mr. G's** (9–21 Castle St., tel. 01463/233322), no longer the town's only nightclub, is a bit schlocky, but it's a fine place to dance after you've had a few drams. Otherwise, check out the exhibit on Highland music at **Balnain House** (40 Huntly St., tel. 01463/715757), where you can have a go on bagpipes, a fiddle, or harp for £2. The downstairs café is free and frequently has performances and workshops. **Lafferty's** (96 Academy St., tel. 01463/712270) is a traditional Irish bar, while next door is **Jock Tamson's** (108 Academy St., tel. 01463/233685), a rustic Scottish bar staffed by kilt-clad barmen and packed with sociable types from all over the globe.

NEAR INVERNESS

CULLODEN BATTLEFIELD

Eight miles east of Inverness, this broad open moor was the scene of the battle that signaled the beginning of the end for the Highland way of life. After a string of successes brought them as far south as Derby in England, the Jacobites retreated to fight on Scottish soil. They met the British troops on April 16, and were mercilessly crushed by the better trained and better equipped government army in less than an hour. The rout was total—1,500 Jacobites lost their lives compared to 50 government casualties, a near-total annihilation that ranks as one of the most horrifying battles ever fought (if you were a Jacobite, that is). An excellent **visitor centre** features an impressive permanent exhibition and commemorative videos. *Tel. 01463/790607, fax 01463/794294. Take Highland Bus 12 toward Nairn. Admission to visitor center £2.80. Open daily 10–4 (Apr.–Oct. until 6). Closed Jan.*

CAWDOR CASTLE

Lord and Lady Cawdor still live in this medieval stone castle, ornamented by fine gardens and pictures of the current family. Come to see the dwelling of Macbeth, whose noble deeds and fine reputation were kewered by the pen of an oft-times unscrupulous English bard (but we won't name names). *Tel. ●1667/404615. Take Highland Bus 12 toward Nairn. Admission £5. Open May–Oct., daily 10–5.*

.OCH NESS

"his most famous of Scottish lochs—23 mi long, 1 mi wide, and over 700 ft deep—is supposedly inhab- "ted by the Loch Ness Monster (bestia aquatilis), a shy beast that makes occasional appearances only when people—odd ones at that—least expect it. Whether or not Nessie lurks in the depths—highly in doubt following the 1994 deathbed confession of a man who took one of the most convincing photos of Nessie (it was a fake)—plenty of camera-toting, sonar-wielding, and submarine-traveling scientists and curiosity seekers haunt the loch looking for a glimpse of the elusive monster. If you've got £4.50 to burn, head to the **Official Loch Ness Monster Exhibition** (A831, tel. 01456/450573) in Drumnadrochit, where you'll see photographs, evidence of the unexplained sonar contacts, and the earnest testimony of eyewitnesses during the hour-long tour. In July and August it stays open till 7:30 PM to cater to the cred- ulous. On the west shore of the loch is **Urquhart Castle** (2 mi SE of Drumnadrochit, tel. 0131/244– 3101), destroyed before the end of the 17th century to prevent Jacobites from using it; admission £3. Highland buses make the 20-minute trip between Inverness and Drumnadrochit daily.

All sorts of boat and coach tours of Loch Ness and Urquhart Castle originate in Inverness. One of the best is **Jacobite Cruises** (tel. 01463/233999), which includes a boat ride down the Caledonian Canal to the loch and castle, and a bus ride back to Inverness, including a stop at the monster exhibition. The £12.50 tour also includes admission prices and lasts about 3½ hours.

WHERE TO SLEEP • Loch Ness Backpackers Lodge (tel. 01456/450807) is a cheery little hostel with friendly proprietors, a great courtyard, and tons of info on local hikes. It's in a small farmhouse in East Lewiston, 1 mi south of Drumnadrochit. Dorm beds cost £8.50–£9, doubles £22–£24. **Loch Ness SYHA** (Glenmoriston, tel. 01320/351274), Standard-L, closed November–February, is farther south off A82, a good 9 mi from the Nessie exhibition. You can camp at **Highland Riding Centre** (tel. 01456/ 450358), just beyond Drumnadrochit and only a ½ mi shy of Urquhart Castle. It costs £4.40 for a tent and two people. Take a car and it'll cost you a pound more.

THE WESTERN HIGHLANDS

The area west of the Great Glen, stretching from Fort William and Mallaig in the south to Ullapool and beyond in the north, is considered by many to be the most dramatic and captivating landscape in Scot- land. Large areas, like the coast and the interior between Glen Shiel and Mallaig, are almost completely inaccessible; this is truly a hiker's haven, where wandering around the glowing lochs and rocky out- croppings is the course of choice. The southern part of the region is the easiest to get to, with multiple links from Glasgow and Edinburgh. Coastal areas north of the Great Glen can be extremely difficult to reach. However, don't skip Wester Ross—the land of lochs and pencil-thin peninsulas spreading north from A87. Loch Torridon and Loch Maree are two of Scotland's scenic jewels.

One of the transportation gateways to the region is Fort William. The bustling township has frequent trains to Glasgow (£22.70 single), Crianlarich (£12.20 single), and Oban (£18.80 single). It's also the place to catch a train to Mallaig (£7.20 single), which ranks with the Orient Express as one of the most hyped train journeys around. The scenery is great, but not *that* great. For schedules and fares, call **Fort William Station** (tel. 0345/484950).

The major bus operators for Fort William are **Citylink** (tel. 0990/505050) to Glasgow, Edinburgh, Oban, and Skye; **Highland Countrybus** (tel. 01397/702373) to Inverness; and **Oban & District Buses Ltd.** (tel. 01631/562856) for service to Oban (runs in summertime). Go Blue Banana and Haggis Backpackers both stop in Fort William.

ROSS AND CROMARTY

Heading north from Maillag, interesting stops along the coast to Ullapool include that quintessentially romantic Scottish sight, **Eilean Donan** castle, at the head of Loch Duich. This was the setting for the film *Highlander* and is on nine out of 10 Scottish postcards. The castle was first built in the 1300s, destroyed in the 1710s following a Jacobite uprising, rebuilt in the 1930s, and sits on a small peninsula on Loch Alsh. The military is still present today: RAF fighters get a thrill out of swooping at nerve-wrenching speeds around the castle. About 10 mi east of Eilean Donan sits another postcard favorite, the **Five Sis-**

OBAN AND ON

The world-famous Oban Distillery (tel. 01631/564262), just off the waterfront in the Gateway of the Isles, has been in continuous production since 1794. Some 35,000 guests drop by the visitor center annually to tour the centuries-old distillery and learn the intricacies of single-malt production. The coveted liquid takes 14 years to mature, but you won't have to wait that long to get yours: After being shown how it is produced, you'll leave clutching a complimentary sample of the smooth, peaty, classic single-malt. Call ahead for information and tour schedules. Cheers!

ters, five giant grassy hills that dominate Glen Sheil right off A87. If you're headed to Skye (*see below*), it's likely that you'll pass over the new Skye Bridge from **Kyle of Lochalsh** to Kyleakin. Ferries also depart from **Glenelg** to Kylerhea on the Sleat Peninsula.

You may leave a mark on the ground at the spot where your jaw drops when visiting the beautiful **Loch Maree** or the nearby **Loch Torridon** beside the sea. Both are spectacular spots for viewing wildlife. Loch Maree is green and forested, with lots of deer, while Loch Torridon is encircled by the gigantic mountains of Beinn Eighe and Liathach, both topped with snow but still popular climbing areas. **Gairloch** makes a good base for exploring. It's a resort town on A832, but a quiet place with great scenery all around, including views to the Isle of Skye (when it's clear). Gairloch's **tourist office** (Auchtercairn, tel. 01445/712130) has info on hiking in the region. The A832, the main route toward Ullapool, curves north to hug the coastline. The entire route is nonstop beautiful. You could easily spend weeks tooling around between villages, hiking and boating all the while.

North of Gairloch, the road skirts around Loch Ewe, at whose southern tip, by **Poolwee,** are the exceptional (even if you're not a fan of plants) **Inverewe Gardens** (tel. 01445/781229). The warm Gulf Stream encourages an astonishing variety of plant life, which in turn attracts a multitude of birds. The garden's main trails can be heavy with tourists, so wander off and get lost in the wild rhododendrons, all the while getting views of Loch Ewe. The gardens are open April–October, daily 9:30–sunset. Admission is £4.50. If you're heading north to Ullapool, you'll have the joy of following the road around **Loch Broom.** South of Loch Broom, at the junction of A832 and A835, which leads to Inverness, you can walk the tiny, swaying suspension bridge over **Corrieshalloch Gorge,** an intensely narrow, shockingly deep slice between the hills; walk onto the suspension bridge and look down at the River Droma, which drops 150 ft over the Falls of Measach.

COMING AND GOING

Getting around without your own car can be a serious challenge. Hitchhiking should be avoided in these parts, especially since you'd be running the serious risk of being stranded on cold, single-track roads for days on end. If you chance it anyway, stick to the major routes, like the A835 south out of Ullapool, or the A890 to Kyle of Lochalsh. Trains from Inverness either go to Thurso or Kyle of Lochalsh. There are no direct routes between Thurso and Kyle of Lochalsh or between Fort William and Kyle of Lochalsh—you always need to go back through Inverness. Call the 24-hour train info line at 0345/484950.

Skye-Ways (tel. 01599/534328) will bring you from Inverness to Kyle of Lochalsh (£8 single) twice daily on the 917 bus, passing by the Five Sisters and Eilean Donan along the way. **Postbuses** are your best friend in this territory, though be alert to their ever-changing schedules. Some of the handiest routes include: Aultbea–Gairloch–Achnasheen; Kyle–Glenelg–Arnisdale; Kyle–Shielbridge–Dornie; Diabaig–Torridon–Kinlochewe; and Kyle–Plockton–Ardnarff. Always check with local post offices for the latest schedules and routes. Remember that a postbus will often take you somewhere that has no other transport out, so be prepared to stay until the next day's postbus comes along.

WHERE TO SLEEP

Pick up the free copy of the "Guide to Hostels & Bunkhouses in the Highlands" brochure, which lists a multitude of options. On the shores of Loch Broom, about 30 mi from Ullapool, stay at the strictly vegetarian **Tigh na Mara** (Ardindrean, tel. 01854/655282) with dinner, bed, and breakfast coming in at £34; they'll let you use their bikes, canoes, and windsurfing equipment. In Gairloch's square, the fancy-free **Mountain Lodge and Restaurant** (tel. 01445/712316) is a bit pricey with the cheapest bed coming in at £24, but they've got mountaineering and trekking paraphernalia everywhere, including a library for guest use and pictures of hikes they've taken their teddy bears on (a goofy tradition in these parts, to show that mountaineers can pit themselves against the worst of nature with a sense of humor). The restaurant serves excellent home-cooked meals. Across the street are a number of cheaper B&Bs including **Wayside** (Strath Sq., tel. 01445/712008), with rooms starting at £15.

HOSTELS • Gerry's Achnashellach Hostel. The train runs right by here, making it convenient to stay 2 mi out of town. This is the oldest private hostel in Scotland, but it doesn't look it. You can choose your own music on the hostel stereo, just as long as Gerry likes it. Dorm beds cost £7. Nonsmokers only. *Tel. 01520/766232. 30 beds.*

Sail Mhor Croft Independent Hostel. This hostel is at the base of An Teallach. Owners Dave and Lynda are happy to give advice on routes and gear. Beds cost £8. Breakfast is included for £11.50. *Camusnagaul, tel. 01854/633224. A few mi north of Dundonnell on A832. 16 beds.*

CAMPING • Seven miles off A832, on a tiny road in Badrallach beside Little Loch Broom, you can stay in **Badrallach Bothy for £3 per night. There's also a cheaper campsite. Book ahead for both by calling **Mr. and Mrs. Stott** (Croft 9, Badrallach, tel. 01854/633281). **Gairloch Holiday Park** (tel. 01445/712373), 3 mi out of Gairloch toward Melvaig, charges £4.50–£11 a site. It's near great sea cliffs and tidepools. All of the above are closed November–March.

SKYE

Like Bonnie Prince Charlie (and the other 600,000 people who visited here last year), you could easily slip "over the sea to Skye," never to return to the mainland. The sea and mist have bred ancient tales of heroes and giants, still passed on by the Gaelic-speaking natives. Many of the most famous legends have taken on a uniquely local character, tied inextricably to the surrounding landscape as is always the way with Celtic stories. Every hill, rock, and grassy tussock has a name and a history behind it, if you can find someone who knows the story (or the song).

Prior to the Celts, both Goths and Picts left their mark on the island. The Vikings were here for centuries, sent by the kings of Norway, asserting their claims to dominion over the Hebrides. Though there was some initial fighting, many Vikings soon settled into the local society and intermarried with the Celts. So successful was this conversion that within a single generation, longships full of Skylanders were raiding the coastal villages of Norway. New dispatches of troops were sent by King Magnus and his successors, but they usually opted to join the idyllic life rather than to try to conquer it. Norse attempts to control the Hebrides ended in 1263 with King Haakon being beaten by the Scots in the Battle of Largs. Still, their lasting influence can be seen in the abundance of Norse place-names, such as Uig (meaning "port"), while more than a few tall, fair-haired natives obviously sport Viking genes.

Skye's population at its prosperous peak reached 25,000, who were ruled by the powerful MacLeod and MacDonald clans. The Clearances hit the island hard, paring the population down to just a few thousand. Today only 9,000 live here, mostly in villages around the coast. They make their living from crofting, fishing, catering to tourists, or the new telecottaging businesses working in information technology and Internet services. Many still follow traditional customs, and each summer you can see the old pensioners out in the muirs cutting and stacking the peat for next winter's fires.

The interior is as varied as the best of the Highlands, with forested glens, hills of purple heather, and rocky waterfalls. The domed granite of the **Red Cuillins** and the spiky, jagged **Black Cuillins,** the island's highest peaks, stare at one another across the wide expanse of Glen Sligachan in the center of Skye. To the northwest, on the Duirinish Peninsula, the flat-topped plateaus of **MacLeod's Tables** are unmistakable; to the northeast, the **Trotternish Ridge** runs for 20 mi up the center of the Trotternish Peninsula, crowned at its northern end by the **Quiraing,** a marvelous collection of granite spires and bowls. Be warned: Skye's mountains, though seemingly small next to more famous and higher European peaks, are harsh adversaries of the ill-prepared. Every year a half a dozen or so hikers underestimating the severity of the terrain lose their lives, most of them from hypothermia. Always remember that Scottish weather can change at the drop of a hat. Don't underestimate the potential hazards of these peaks simply because of their low elevations. The high latitude adds a lot to the alpine conditions in an area mountaineers describe as one of the most challenging in Europe.

Portree is the capital of Skye and has the most services, including banks and restaurants, while **Broadford** and **Uig** offer more limited services. **Kyleakin,** the first town reached by most visitors, has a couple of small restaurants and a couple of huge hostels. Throughout the rest of the island, tourist services are expanding rapidly to accommodate the phenomenal increase of visitors. Tourism is booming, in no small part to the new Skye Bridge. So, too, however, is controversy. It turns out the bridge has a toll system that has the Skye residents in an uproar and, in fact, a campaign of nonpayment and civil disobedience has been waged by Skye natives against the government. Visitors should realize the bridge's "convenience" has both aided the tourist industry on the island and created a major political situation for Skye locals. To greet the swelling ranks of visitors, B&Bs in Skye are now omnipresent and each village has at least one general store where travelers can stock up on provisions. Next to Edinburgh, Skye has become the most popular tourist destination in Scotland.

BASICS

Portree's tourist office (Meall House, tel. 01478/612137) is open year-round while the smaller branch in **Broadford** (tel. 01471/822361) is open April–October. Both have hiking maps and info on outdoor activities and will book B&Bs for a small fee. Rent a bike from **Island Cycles** (The Green, Portree, tel. 01478/613121) for £12.50 a day, sports bikes for £7.50 a day, or from **SkyeBikes** (Kyleakin, tel. 01599/534795). There's also **Fairwinds Bicycle Hire** (Broadford, tel. 01471/822270) for £6 a day.

COMING AND GOING

With the completion of the **Skye Bridge,** for which there is a £5.40 toll in each direction, the ferries connecting Kyleakin with Kyle of Lochalsh were discontinued by government decree, a move met with furious opposition by locals, who feel the stiff tolls (which go into the pockets of the bridge's American financiers and German builders) are unfair. The toll is included in your bus ticket from Fort William or Glasgow. **Highland Omnibus** (tel. 01478/612622) runs to and from Fort William, and **Skye-Ways** (tel. 01599/534328) travels between the island and Glasgow (£16 single) stopping in Oban along the way. A private six-car ferry (tel. 01599/511302) runs Easter–October from the Glenelg to Kylerhea (£1 foot passengers), Skye's otter country.

If you're heading from Fort William to Mallaig, where the trains are timed to meet the ferries, catch the CalMac ferry to Armadale (30 mins, £2.30 single) on the Sleat Peninsula. Skye's ferry connections also make a good jumping-off point for exploring other parts of the Hebrides. From Uig, catch CalMac ferries to Tarbert (on Harris) or Lochmaddy (on North Uist). From Mallaig on the mainland, there are also connections to the tiny crofting communities on Rum, Muck, Eigg, and Canna. Off the eastern shore of Skye is the small island of Raasay, an excellent day-trip out of Broadford. Both Haggis Backpackers and Go Blue Banana stop in Kyleakin.

GETTING AROUND

Both **Highland** and **Skye-Ways** run buses from Kyleakin through Broadford (£3) to Portree (£5.60), sometimes all the way to Uig (£6.50). There is regular service to Armadale from Portree (£5.30) or Broadford. The fares around Skye are extraordinarily high, but Skye-Ways offers a **Student Day-Rover** pass for £7.50. Postbuses cover less traveled territory. Rent cars in Broadford from **Skye Car Rental** (tel. 01471/822225) at a daily rate of £30 or in Kyleakin from **Kyleakin Car Hire** (tel. 01599/534472), which charges only £3 per hour, making it a good deal when split between friends.

The best introduction to Skye is the daylong tour run by Nick at Skye Tours. (tel 01599/534087). For £15, Nick totes you in his minibus from Kyleakin in the southwest all over the island. He chooses a different route each day but always hits the highlights. Call ahead to reserve your seat as his tours are often booked. **Skyetrak Safari** (tel. 01470/582224) caters to smaller groups of just three to seven people, using a Land Rover. It tends to be more expensive but you get "wilderness experience" as well as incomparable historical insight and expertise from the operator, Rosie Somerville. The emphasis is more on using the wheels to get to inaccessible places, and then leaving the vehicle behind on a wilderness trek.

SOUTHERN SKYE

Most backpackers and cyclists visiting Skye arrive in **Kyleakin,** just across the water from Kyle of Lochalsh via the Skye Bridge. There's not a lot in town except the ruins of **Castle Moil,** a five- minute walk from the pier, and **King Haakon,** the more happening of the two pubs here. **Castle Moil Restaurant** (tel. 01599/534164), attached to King Haakon, serves veggie curry. Kyleakin makes a great base from which to explore southern Skye, but you're really missing out if you don't head farther afield.

The **Sleat Peninsula** makes up the southern wing of the Isle of Skye; it is called "An t-Eilean Sgitheanach" in Gaelic, meaning the winged island. In the southeast is **Armadale,** where the ferry from Mallaig docks. At nearby **Armadale Castle** is the **Clan Donald Visitor Centre** (tel. 01471/844305). The extensive center is set amid 40 acres of formal gardens and covers the 1,300 year history of the "Clan's Lordship of the Isles." Halfway up the Sleat Peninsula east from Armadale is **Teangue.** This tiny community, beside the waters of Cnoc Bay, is a great place to try some fishing or gentle field-walking. Lush vegetation along this southern side of the island keeps the climate mild.

Broadford, 8 mi west of Kyleakin, is the second-largest settlement on Skye and has plenty for visitors to do. **Skye Serpentarium** (Old Mill, tel. 01471/822209) has an awesome collection of reptiles and amphibians from around the world. The **Environmental Centre** (Harrapool, tel. 01471/822487) offers special nature-oriented holidays and day trips, but you must book a couple of days in advance. The town makes an excellent base for climbing **Beinn Na Cailleach** (2,403 ft), one of the Red Cuillins. The best hike is a horseshoe-shape traverse of ridges that connect it with **Beinn Dearg Mhor** (2,326 ft) and **Beinn Dearg Bheag** (1,916 ft), a five- to six- hour return journey that starts from the power station 1½ mi north of Broadford. Near the foot of the ascent path are the ruins of **Coire-Chat-Achan,** the house where Johnson and Boswell stayed during their Hebridean tour.

Broadford is also the best base for a trip to the island of **Raasay.** Ferries leave from **Sconser,** a few miles north of Broadford, to **Inverarish** (£3.15 return). In Inverarish you can stock up on supplies before you head into the backcountry. Towering above the island is **Dun Caan,** an extinct volcano. The 59-million-year-old dome is topped by a flat plateau where Boswell danced a jig after completing the 1,456-ft climb. At the north end of the island by **Brochel Castle** is ancient volcanic landscape believed by geologists to be almost half a billion years old. If you decide to stay overnight, **Raasay SYHA** (Creachan Cottage, tel. 01478/660240), Simple, closed October–mid-March, is 3 mi north of the ferry port.

Sligachan (pronounced Slee-ga-han) is the junction point between northern and southern Skye. This is the place, at the head of **Glen Sligachan,** to start your attack on the **Cuillins.** The first, right beside the highway, is the cone of **Glamaig** (2,542 ft). An annual race is run up the mountain during the first week of June to commemorate the feat of a member of the Queen's retinue who made the round-trip journey in an hour—without shoes! Today the runners wear substantially more elaborate gear and the record for the return time is a mere 46 minutes. The next Cuillin you'll see down the glen is **Beinn Dearg Mhor** (2,138 ft) and beyond that the massive **Marsco** (2,414 ft). To the west rises the black, triple peak of **Sgurr nan Gillean** (3,167 ft), Lord of the Black Cuillins, and a challenge to even the most experienced climbers. Its highest summit is sheathed in ice and snow year-round. To enjoy both Cuillin ranges from the lower elevations, you can follow the path that runs through the glen all the way to the sea at **Loch Corvisk.** It takes a good five hours of stiff hiking to reach the loch and from there a couple more hours to **Elgol,** where you'll find a small shop, a couple of B&Bs, and Blaven Bunkhouse. West of the Cuillins is **Portnalong,** with several good hostels and excellent hiking opportunities. A favorite local outing is a tour (£3) of **Talisker Distillery** (tel. 01478/640203). An even better choice is to head into the fields and make your way to **Glen Brittle,** where there are many excellent climbs and walks.

WHERE TO SLEEP

There are six or seven hostels around Kyleakin. On the waterfront, the white stucco **Kyleakin SYHA** (tel. 01599/534585), Standard, looks like a Miami hotel. The ultrafriendly manager, Pat, looks after a wild staff of fun-loving screwballs. A few doors down, **Skye Backpackers** (tel. 01599/534510) is another member of the High Street/Royal Mile hostel cartel, bringing you the same outstanding service and fun-filled atmosphere. Dorm beds cost £8.50–£9.50. A few miles from town on the road toward Broadford, the **Fossil Bothy** (13 Lower Breakish, tel. 01471/822644) is a small, simple hostel, closed November–Easter. It has only eight beds (£7), so you must book ahead.

On the Sleat Peninsula, sleep at **Armadale SYHA** (01471/844–260), Standard-L access during the day, closed October–mid-March, set amid the trees overlooking Armadale Bay. Right up the road from

Teangue is the **Hairy Coo Backpackers Hotel** (Toravaig House, tel. 01471/833231), with its own private trout brook running through the forested property. A bunk costs £7.50, a double £25, or you can camp on the grounds for a few pounds.

In Portnalong are **Skyewalker Independent Hostel** (Fiskavaig Rd., tel. 01478/640250) and Pete Thomas's **Croft Bunkhouse and Bothy** (tel. 01478/640254). Both offer beds for £7–£8.50 and plenty of advice on local activities. Twelve miles away, **Glenbrittle SYHA** (tel. 01478/640278), Standard-L, at the foot of the Cuillins, is popular with mountaineers.

NORTHERN SKYE

Skye's main hub and capital, **Portree** has brightly painted houses, a beautiful setting on a small and sheltered bay, frequent buses to the rest of the island, and myriad festivals during the summer. It caters to tourists with a number of B&Bs, hostels, restaurants, and pubs. Though it's a good place to stay overnight, you'll want to head out of town during the day and explore the Trotternish Peninsula.

Northwest from Portree, the road forks left toward **Dunvegan,** where you'll find **Dunvegan Castle**—pretty from the outside but not worth the £5 admission—and right toward the **Trotternish Peninsula.** This entire peninsula is experiencing a huge amount of land slippage—the largest ongoing movement in the United Kingdom. This constant shifting has formed the famous **Old Man of Storr,** a 160-ft pinnacle 6 mi northeast of Portree. Continuing north, you'll reach **Quiraing** with its breathtaking natural amphitheater called "the prison" and towering pinnacles left over from the ridge's volcanic origins. From the dirt carpark on A856, a well-defined path traverses its slope. On the west side of the peninsula, 14 mi north of Portree, are the impressive **Lealt Falls.** From the lookout point beyond the falls, you can see **Kilt Rock,** a huge cliff of basalt vertical columns, which lend it a pleated appearance. This stretch of coast has produced some top-notch Jurassic fossils, including icthyosaurs and tetrapods. You can see some of the locally found fossils on display at the **Staffin Heritage Museum** in a restored croft near Lealt Falls. The northwestern town of **Uig** provides several services, including ferries to the Hebrides.

WHERE TO SLEEP

If you're looking for a bed and breakfast with character, you should try **Mary McIntosh's** (tel. 01471/886294) croft house at Cnoc Ban, on the island. She provides a traditional Scottish breakfast, complete with kippers, as well as a good night's rest in this house set in woods. Single and double rooms (doubles are £16 per person) are available May to October.

The **Portree Backpackers Hostel** (Woodpark, tel. 01478/613641) is housed in a comfortable and accommodating building, with large beds for £8.50. From the bus stop walk on the road to Dunvegan and turn right at the Shell station. There is also the **Portree Independent Backpackers Hostel** (tel. 01478/613737). The prices, like the name, are virtually identical to the previously mentioned hostel.

INDEX

NOTES

NOTES

NOTES

Fodor's

Looking for a different kind of vacation?

Fodor's makes it easy with a full line of specialty guidebooks to suit a variety of interests—from adventure to romance to language help.

Fodor's. For the world of ways you travel.

IT'S YOUR TURN TO TALK BACK!

FILL OUT THIS QUICK SURVEY AND RECEIVE A FREE COPY OF FODOR'S *HOW TO PACK.**

Which Fodor's upCLOSE guide did you buy?

_____

What was the duration of your trip?

_____

How much did you spend per day, not including airfare?

❑ $100   ❑ $300

❑ $150   ❑ Other_____

❑ $200

Why did you choose Fodor's upCLOSE?

❑ Budget focus

❑ Fodor's reputation

❑ Opinionated writing & comprehensive content

❑ Other_____

Would you use Fodor's upCLOSE again?

❑ Yes   ❑ No

Which guides have you used in the past two years?

❑ Frommer's $-A-Day   ❑ Let's Go

❑ Rough Guides   ❑ Rick Steves'

❑ Lonely Planet   ❑ None

❑ Other_____

Did you like Fodor's upCLOSE better?

❑ Yes   ❑ No

Please rank the following features (1 = needs improvement / 2 = adequate / 3 = excellent).

Accommodations listings	1	2	3
Dining listings	1	2	3
Major sights	1	2	3
Off-the-beaten-path sights	1	2	3
Shopping listings	1	2	3
Nightlife listings	1	2	3
Public transportation	1	2	3

Please feel free to elaborate. _____

_____

_____

_____

Which of the following destinations would you like to see Fodor's upCLOSE cover?

❑ Alaska   ❑ Pacific Northwest

❑ Australia   ❑ South America

❑ Austria   ❑ Southeast Asia

❑ Eastern Europe   ❑ Switzerland

❑ Greece   ❑ Turkey

❑ Israel   ❑ More European cities

❑ New Zealand   ❑ More U.S. cities

❑ Other_____

You are ❑ Male ❑ Female

Your age is
❑ 18-24   ❑ 45-54
❑ 25-34   ❑ 55-64
❑ 35-44   ❑ 65+

You are ❑ Single ❑ Married

Your occupation is
❑ Student (undergraduate)
❑ Student (graduate)
❑ Professional
❑ Executive/managerial/administrative
❑ Military
❑ Retired
❑ Other_____

Which choice best describes your household income?
❑ Under $10,000
❑ $10,000-$19,999
❑ $20,000-$29,999
❑ $30,000-$49,999
❑ $50,000-$74,999
❑ $75,000+

Your name and address are

_____
_____
_____

Your E-mail address is

_____

Would you like to receive informational E-mails from Fodor's?
❑ Yes   ❑ No

Please return this survey to Fodor's Travel Publications, Attn: Fodor's upCLOSE Survey, 1540 Broadway, New York, NY 10036, for a free copy of Fodor's *How to Pack* (while supplies last). You can also fill out this survey on the Web at www.fodors.com/upclose/upclosesurvey.html.

The information herein will be treated in confidence. Names and addresses will not be released to mailing-list houses or other organizations.

While supplies last